本书属于华侨大学研究生院精品课程建设项目成果

文明以止

中国文化专题十讲（汉英双语版）

汤忠钢　袁张帆 | 编著

九州出版社

JIUZHOUPRESS

图书在版编目（CIP）数据

文明以止：中国文化专题十讲：汉英双语版／汤
忠钢，袁张帆编著 . -- 北京：九州出版社，2023.2
　　ISBN 978-7-5225-1561-8

　　Ⅰ.①文… Ⅱ.①汤…②袁… Ⅲ.①中华文化—汉
、英 Ⅳ.①K203

中国版本图书馆 CIP 数据核字（2022）第 231119 号

文明以止：中国文化专题十讲（汉英双语版）

作　　者　汤忠钢　袁张帆　编著
责任编辑　张万兴　周红斌　张里夫
出版发行　九州出版社
地　　址　北京市西城区阜外大街甲 35 号（100037）
发行电话　（010）68992190/3/5/6
网　　址　www.jiuzhoupress.com
印　　刷　唐山才智印刷有限公司
开　　本　710 毫米×1000 毫米　16 开
印　　张　26.5
字　　数　476 千字
版　　次　2023 年 8 月第 1 版
印　　次　2023 年 8 月第 1 次印刷
书　　号　ISBN 978-7-5225-1561-8
定　　价　99.00 元

前　言

著者在华侨大学为境外（研究）生讲授《中国文化概论》课程多年。该课程创设之目的，乃与华侨大学"面向海外，面向港澳台"的办学方针和"为侨服务，传播中华文化"的办学宗旨相一致。作为全国境外学生最多的高校之一，华侨大学高度重视本课程的独特价值。主管单位研究生院亦历来大力支持本课程教师团队搞好课程建设，以更好地助力于中外人民之间的文化交流与文明互鉴。

我们深知，要在全球化背景下让境外生朋友真正读懂传统中国、了解当代中国，必须借助好中国传统文化这个宝贵资源。但如何才能讲好中国故事、发好中国声音，让博大精深的传统文化能为青春活泼、思想多元的境外生们所乐于接受、深入认同，绝非一件容易之事。这也要求从事中国文化传播的教育工作者提高使命意识和自身素养，改革创新中国文化的传播方式与手段。

经过若干年的探索和实验，我们逐步摸索并践行了如下教学新模式，即：以中华文明精神作价值引领，知识目标、能力目标和情感目标三结合为教学架构，专题教学、田野考察、讨论深化、案例建设相融合为教学方法论，数字化、网络化平台建设为技术驱动的"道—法—术—器"四维教学法，并在课程教学实践中获得了良好的效果。

首先，我们的教师团队坚定文化自信，以中华文明的优秀精神作为课程的价值引领之"道"。此"道"，既指中华文化的优秀精神，又指习近平新时代中国特色社会主义思想，此两者是一脉相承内在一致的。我们认为中华民族是伟大的民族，中华文明是伟大的文明，蕴含着诸如天人合一、中庸之道、自强不息、厚德载物、爱国主义等优秀的精神要素，一以贯之地涌动在中华民族的文化生命之中，为之魂，为之魄。正是这个文化之道，历史地塑造了中华民族，也正时代性地为中华民族的伟大复兴发挥积极作用，无疑也持续贡献于人类文明。在中外文化交流工作中，中国文化的传播者应该以高度的自信与自觉，做中华文化代言人，发中华文明之光，耀中华人文之美。只有寓道于教，才能寓德于教、寓乐于教，真正在教学活动中实现知识目标、能力目标和情感目标的有机融合。

其次，我们重视教学体系创新，优化专题教学内容，努力做到精益求精。文化即生活，广义的文化几乎无所不包。但在教学学时有限和境外生中文水平参差不齐的实际情况下，大而全的中国文化教学几乎不可能实现。有鉴于此，我们删繁就简，不求大务全。在教学设计上以文化精神为经，以文化特征为纬，提纲挈领地设置了十个专题，从"文明以止""泱泱中华""千年道统""多元一体""大哉孔子""仁者爱人""尊祖重族""和而不同""崇文重教""美美与共"这些角度展开中华文明在文化特性、民族问题、思想人物、伦理道德、宗族制度、宗教信仰、教育传统、中外交流等多领域的基本风貌与精神特质。至于一般常见的衣食住行、冠婚丧祭、歌舞艺术、科技工艺等领域的文化内容，虽然同样精彩，但我们的课程暂未涉及、悬而不论。我们不求面面俱到，但却可以集中时间和力量，帮助境外（研究）生深入中国文化的精神殿堂以正解要义、领悟特质、明心见性。

同时，我们还积极借助项目经费支持，精心组织相关的田野调查和社会考察活动来开展实践教学。比较于课堂纯理论讲授，田野调查是实地化、情境化、也更为生动有趣的中国文化学习方法论。我们的经验是要注意处理好这么几层关系：（1）要紧密配合课堂相关知识点的教学；（2）要照顾中华文化和闽文化相结合的视野、突出华侨大学的侨校特色；（3）要对小组考察预案提供有质量的学术指导；（4）要在考察结束后帮学生及时梳理、深入总结、汇报交流，成果则用以建设课程案例库。实践证明，这种以社会考察配合课堂专题教学的实践教学法，非常有利于调动和增进个性张扬的境外生们学习中国文化的兴趣与热情，有利于他们在身临其境、知行合一中加深对中华文化的理解和认同，有利于综合地锻炼和发展其团队协作、调查研究、写作表达的能力与素质，从而也得到了他们的喜爱与好评，并深化了他们对华的友好感情。

另外，我们也认识到，积极学习和采用为达到教学目的服务的现代信息化手段和新媒体技术，建设网络教学平台和数字资源库非常必要。比如去年我们在华大研究生院的支持下，与智慧树平台合作录制了中英双语字幕的中国文化概论慕课。该项目经过精心打造，已上线运行。一学期来已经为多所高校、五千余人提供了网络教学服务，并入选教育部"国家高等教育智慧教育平台"（Smart Education of China Higher Education）。信息网络化，是我们都无可避免的时代大势。构建并不断提升中国文化教学的数字化程度，既适应了境外（研究）生的学习习惯，丰富了他们可兹利用的学习媒介与资源，也拓展了本课程的社会辐射面，可望发挥更广泛的社会服务功能。

呈现在您面前的这本小册子，就是我们在录制课程慕课时使用的中英双语讲稿的基础上整理而成的。叫它小册子，是因为严格地说它还不能算真正的学术作品——无论就论述的深度和写作的容量而言，它似乎都偏于通俗、流于浅显，因为它本身就是为录制慕课而临时编写的稿子，因而具有概要性而未及充分展开和详加论证。

我们之所以还是愿意将它出版出来，是因为它是我们探索课程建设之路上的阶段成果和小小总结。而且，它还是汉英双语的表述格式。福州大学翻译实践中心的林继红、钟晓文翻译团队历时数月，精心将本慕课讲稿编译为英文。翻译过程中，双方反复沟通、商榷措辞和句式，以使译文尽量符合我们的本义。他们一丝不苟的责任意识令我们感动，也使我们信赖他们的译文所具有的品质。需要说明的是，因限于篇幅，其中有一部分译文我们做了必要的删改以符合出版的要求。

文化的传播离不开语言，对外文化传播离不开英语。至少对于华大境外生朋友而言，无论是当作简明讲义或参考教纲，这本汉英双语小册子都是他们拿到成熟适用的课程教材之前可以使用的教辅读物。而华大研究生院也鼓励我们及时总结经验，把这门课推广给更多的境外生朋友去学习使用，并愿意支持出版经费，这对我们当然是一种莫大的鞭策和鼓舞。所以，我们不揣谫陋，先行付梓印行出来，且作为我们后期更扎实的专著或教材撰述的准备。

在此，要感谢华侨大学研究生院一直以来对本课程建设的重视和关怀。侯志强副院长多次开会指导慕课的录制工作，并为我们多方收集相关资料以助完善课件，这份辛苦我们不敢忘记，感念于心。

华侨大学马克思主义学院也给予了我们部分出版经费资助，谨向王丽霞副校长（兼马院院长）表示谢忱！

选修我们课程的华大新闻与传播学院研究生缪熙先生热情为我们翻译了部分文稿；我的朋友、马院的同事乔楚博士有求必应、鼎力相助，也帮忙做了很多稿件编辑和材料支持工作。也要向他们表示感谢。

全书中文讲稿由著者设计大纲，其中第四讲、第八讲和第九讲由袁张帆博士承担编写，其余则由著者完成，并负责全书统稿和最后改定。

因我们水平有限、编结仓促，书中粗陋失当之处定有不少，欢迎各位读者和专家对我们提出批评和教正，以帮助我们有所进益。

华侨大学　汤忠钢
2022 年 8 月 10 日于厦门

Preface

I have taught "Introduction to Chinese Culture" for overseas graduate students at Huaqiao University (HQU) for many years. The purpose of creating this course is consistent with Huaqiao University's school-running policy of "serving overseas Chinese and spreading Chinese culture" by facing overseas, facing Hong Kong, Macao and Taiwan. As a university with the largest number of overseas students or international students in China, HQU attaches a great importance to the unique value of this course. The graduate school of Huaqiao University—the supervisor of the course—has always been supportive of the course faculty in building the course so that it can better contribute to the cultural exchange and mutual appreciation between Chinese and foreign people.

For foreign students to truly understand traditional China and contemporary China in the context of globalization, we must utilize the valuable resources of traditional Chinese culture. However, it is not easy to tell Chinese stories, allow Chinese voices to be heard, and to encourage the young foreign students to accept and recognize the profound traditional culture. This mission requires educators to engage in Chinese cultural communication to improve their awareness of their role and their own quality, and to innovate the ways and means of Chinese cultural communication.

After several years of explorations and experiments, we have gradually incorporated the following new teaching model, coined: the spirit of Chinese civilization as the value leader, the triple combination of knowledge, ability and emotional objectives as the teaching structure, the integration of thematic teaching, fieldwork, discussion and case building as the teaching methodology, and the construction of digital and network platform as the technology-driven "Tao (laws or principles of nature), Fa (laws or methods of dealing with problems), Shu (abilities or skills) and Qi (utensils)" the four-dimensional teaching method has achieved good results in the teaching practice of the course.

First, our faculty team firmly believes in cultural confidence and takes the excellent spirit of Chinese civilization as the main line of value leadership of the course. (This main line is the Tao which contains the meaning of the road). The Tao refers explicitly to the excellent spirit of Chinese culture and implicitly to Xi Jinping's thought of socialism with Chinese characteristics in the new era. These two are one and the same. We believe that the Chinese nation is a great nation, and the Chinese civilization is a great civilization, containing such excellent spiritual elements as the unity of heaven and man, the middle way, self-improvement, virtue, and patriotism, etc. , which are consistently surging in the cultural life of the Chinese nation, as its soul and spirit. It is this cultural way that has historically shaped the Chinese nation and is playing an active role in the great rejuvenation of the Chinese nation, and undoubtedly has the universal value of continuing to contribute to human civilization. In the work of cultural exchange between China and foreign countries, we should be highly confident and self-aware to send the light of civilization and become the beauty of humanity. The only way we can teach morality and joy is by teaching the way, and in turn, we can truly achieve the organic integration of knowledge goals, ability goals and emotional goals in our teaching activities.

Culture is life, and culture in a broad sense is almost all-inclusive. However, under the actual situation of limited teaching hours and different Chinese proficiency of international students, it is almost impossible to teach them rich and in-depth Chinese culture in a relatively short period of time. With this in mind, we changed the complex content to be easily understood. We aim for a rich and simple introduction to the knowledge points (if any students are interested in which points, they can study them in depth separately) .

In the course design, we set up ten topics in an outline, from "Aiming at Civilization", "The Magnificent China", "Centuries-long Orthodoxy", "Diversity in Unity", "Confucius the Grand Master", "The Benevolent Loves All", "Respecting Ancestors and Valuing Relatives", "Unity in Diversity", "Advocating Literacy and Emphasizing Education" and "Shared Prosperity of Different Cultures" are the basic features and spiritual characteristics of Chinese civilization in the areas of cultural identity, ethnic issues, ideological figures, ethics and morality, clan system, religious beliefs, educational traditions, and Sino-foreign exchanges. As for the common cultural contents in the fields of clothing, food, housing, transportation, marriage, funeral, song, dance, art, technology, and crafts, although they are also wonderful, they are not covered in our courses and are left unattended. We do not aim to cover everything, but we can focus our time and efforts on helping foreign students to delve into the spiritual halls of Chinese culture to understand its essence, appreciate its qualities, and understood the truth of things completely.

At the same time, we also actively organize fieldwork and social research activities with the support of project funding to carry out practical teaching. In contrast to purely theoretical classroom teaching, this course also uses fieldwork to give students more realistic exposure to Chinese culture in their lives. The experience we need covers several relationships: (1) to match the teaching of relevant knowledge points in the classroom; (2) to focus on the vision of combining Chinese culture and Fujian culture and highlighting the characteristics of HQU as an overseas Chinese school; (3) to provide quality academic guidance to the group study tour pre-program; (4) students will be asked to compile, summarize and report in depth after the study tour. The results are then used to build the course case base. It is proved that this kind of practical teaching method of using social study tour to match with classroom topic teaching is very helpful to mobilize and promote the interest and enthusiasm of international students who have individuality to learn Chinese culture, to deepen their understanding and identification with Chinese culture through immersion, knowledge and practice, and to exercise and develop their ability and quality of teamwork, investigation and research, and writing and expression in a comprehensive way, which is also liked and praised by them. The program has been well received and we also recognize that the active participation in the program has helps deepen their understanding of Chinese culture.

In addition, we also recognize that it is necessary to actively learn and adopt modern technology and new media technology to serve teaching purposes and build online teaching platforms and digital resource libraries. For instance, we produced the Introduction to Chinese Culture with Bilingual online course in cooperation with the Wisdom Tree platform with the support of the Graduate School of HQU in 2021. The course has been carefully built and run online. Over the past semester, we have provided online teaching services for more than 5000 students in many colleges and universities, and have been selected as one of the "Smart Education of China Higher

Education" by the Ministry of Education of the People's Republic of China. Information networking is an inevitable trend of our time. The digitalization of the teaching of Chinese culture has been constructed and continuously upgraded to accommodate the learning habits of graduate students outside of China, enrich the learning media available to them, and expand the social reach of this course, which is expected to serve a wider social service function.

The booklet that in front of you is based on the bilingual lecture notes used in the producing of the course. It is called a pamphlet because it is not strictly speaking a true academic work—it seems to be on the general and superficial side in terms of depth of exposition and volume of writing, because it is itself a manuscript prepared to produce an online course, and thus is summary in nature and not fully developed and substantiated.

However, we are willing to publish it because it is the result of the stage and summary of our exploration on the road of curriculum construction. Moreover, it is also in bilingual format. The translation team of Lin Jihong and Zhong Xiaowen that from the Translation Practice Center of Fuzhou University worked for several months to carefully compile this catechism lecture into English. During the translation process, we repeatedly communicated and negotiated the wording and syntax to make the translation conform to the true meaning of the course as much as possible. We are impressed by their meticulous work ethic, so we trust the high quality of their translations. It should be noted that due to limited space, we have made necessary deletions and modifications to some of the English translations to meet the publishing requirements.

Culture cannot be spread without language, and English is essential for foreigners to understand Chinese culture. At least for international students at HQU, this Chinese-English booklet is also some kind of teaching aid they can use before they get a mature and applicable course textbook, whether as a concise lecture or reference syllabus.

The Graduate School of HQU encouraged us to summarize our experience in a timely manner and to provide publication costs. It gives us the opportunity to make it available to more international students. So, we decided to publish it first and prepare the subsequent complete textbook or academic monograph. I would like to thank the Graduate School of HQU for their guidance and care in the construction of this course. the Vice Dean of the Graduate School of HQU Mr. Hou Zhiqiang has met many times to guide the producing of this course and collected relevant materials for us to help improve the courseware.

The Marxism academy of Huaqiao University has also provided a part of the publishing funds to us, hereby we grab the opportunity to express our gratitude to the Vice President of the university Professor Wang Lixia (concurrently Dean of the Academy) for her strong support!

Mr. Miao Xi, a graduate student of our course, from the Journalism and Communication academy of Huaqiao University, very enthusiastically gave us a hand on the translations of some of the manuscripts; Dr. Qiao Chu, my friend and colleague at Marxism academy, who was very responsive and helpful also helped us a lot by editing lots os manuscripts and material support. Therefore, I'd like to grab this opportunity to express my gratitude.

The outline of the Chinese lectures was designed by me. The fourth, eighth and ninth lectures were prepared by Dr. Yuan Zhangfan, while the rest were completed by the author, who was also responsible for the final approval of the book.

Due to the limited level and hasty compilation, there may be translation errors or misunderstandings. We welcome readers and experts to criticize and correct our booklet to help us make progress.

Tang Zhonggang
Huaqiao University in Xiamen, China
August 10, 2022

目 录
CONTENTS

The Eighth Chapter：Unity in Diversity

第九讲　崇文重教

The Ninth Chapter：Advocating Literacy and Emphasizing Education

第十讲　美美与共

The Tenth Chapter：Shared Prosperity of Different Cultures

第一讲

文明以止
—— 中国文化·绪论

首先欢迎各位境外生朋友选修我们的中国文化概论课程。中国是一个伟大的国家，中国有灿烂的文明。在这片神奇的土地上，有我们奔腾的母亲河：长江和黄河，也有雄伟巍峨的三山五岳。在这壮美山川和辽阔疆域中，生活着中华民族勤劳、勇敢、智慧的儿女们，他们用自己的双手共同创造了历经五千年至今绵延不衰的中华文化。

要了解中国，饱览中国的名山大川和充满魅力的自然风光当然是重要的方式。但是，要想真正了解中国，更应该做的是走进她那源远流长、博大精深的传统文化，去领略和感悟她绚丽多彩的文明之光。因为，只有读懂中国文化，才能真正读懂中国和中国人！而这里首先涉及的，是这样三个问题：何谓"文化"？何谓"中国"？学习研究中国文化采用什么样的方法论？

1.1 "文化"概念的界说

我们知道，"文化"一词在我们的日常生活中的使用频率是非常高的，到处都在用它。但究竟什么是"文化"，它的定义到底是什么，则往往莫衷一是，可谓仁者见仁、智者见智。据美国文化学者 A. L. 克罗伯和克莱德·克拉克洪合著的《文化：关于概念和定义的综述》（1952）一书中统计的各种类型的文化定义，就多达 164 种。当然，我这里并不打算把大家带进入这个令人困惑的概念森林，而是径直地给出本课程对"文化"的定义方式和核心理解。

简单来说，我们认为"文化"概念有两层含义：（1）文化即生活；（2）文化即人化。

1.1.1 从广义上看：文化即生活——其内容无所不包

文化即生活，是人类生活的一切内容无所不包的整体。我们这个定义思路，取自中国近代思想家梁漱溟先生在《中国文化要义》一书中的看法，梁先生指出："文化，就是吾人生活所依靠之一切。……文化之本义，应在经济、政治，乃至一切无所不包。"① 与此相似的是，另外一位思想家钱穆先生也提到："文化就是人生。人生是多方面的，一个社会乃至一个民族一个成群的大团体所包有的多方面的生活，综合起来称人生，也就是文化。"② 其实，更早的时候，英国人类学家泰勒在《原始文化》（1871）一书中也写道："文化是一个复杂的整体，它包括知识、信仰、艺术、道德、法律、风俗以及作为社会成员获得的任何其他的能力和习惯。"③

这几位大师都强调了"文化"作为人的社会生活的综合整体的基本含义。在他们的理解中，文化学的基本任务就是研究人们如何生活。

按照"文化即生活"这一定义方式，则我们可以说，要了解"文化"，就得走进人们的生活世界（或曾经的生活世界），走进城市、走进乡村、走进遗址。去观察各地域、各民族、各阶层的人们的日常生活。去观察他们所依靠、所创造的一切。如他们的服饰和食物，他们的房屋和建筑的类型，他们的家庭模式和社会政治结构，去考察他们使用的工具，他们发明的科技工艺；去参与他们的节庆活动；去聆听他们语言；去阅读他们用文字书写的典籍；学会去欣赏他们的歌舞、绘画和戏剧作品，品味其间的美感形式和韵律；当然，还要去了解他们遵循怎样的伦理教条和制度规范；他们有何种哲学的信念和宗教的崇拜……

尽管不同时空背景下的人们的社会生活可能很不一样，但从某些角度看，我们又都一样。

图1-1　文化即是生活

① 梁漱溟. 中国文化要义 [M]. 上海：学林出版社，1987：2.
② 钱穆. 中华文化十二讲 [M]. 北京：九州出版社，2012：3.
③ ［英］爱德华·伯内特·泰勒. 原始文化 [M]. 上海：上海文艺出版社，1992：1.

　　可以说，有一样生活就有一样文化，甚至任何一种生活的元素都可以被归入一种类型的文化。如人要吃饭即有饮食文化，人要穿衣即有服饰文化，人要居所即有建筑文化，人要出行即有交通文化。人要生产和生育才能生生不息，这就有经济文化和婚恋文化。其他诸如歌舞艺术、节日庆祝、语言文字、科技工艺、政治组织、社会交往、民族民系，以及宗教崇拜等，都是生活的内涵，都属于特定的文化。

　　这一切经纬纵横、丰富多样的生活元素构成了人们的文化世界。人们需要凭借和依靠这一切（特定的）文化元素生存和生活。而人们也正是在这些文化元素的浸染和塑造下，形成了自己独特的生活性格、生活情趣与生活方式，才成为了他们自己而区别于彼此。

　　当然，鉴于生活内容的多样性，为了便于研究，文化学研究者往往会将各种生活元素或现象处理为不同范畴，区别为不同的层次。如：将文化对象区分为客观实体属性的"物质文化"和主观虚体属性的"精神文化"；或按自然科学和社会科学为标准，区分为第一类文化和第二类文化；这叫"两分法"。张岱年、方克立主编的《中国文化概论》教科书中则提出了将文化现象区分为：物态文化—制度文化—行为文化—心态文化的"四分法"①。另外还有所谓五层说、六层说等。一般地看，物质文化是文化的表层，精神文化是文化的内核。从物态文化逐步深入，则能穿越制度文化、行为文化而直达心态文化的彼岸。虽然这些分层并非绝对独立而是互相渗透、互相显见的。毋庸置疑的是，直观可触的物态文化生动活泼，而透过这种生动活泼，解释或揭示其内在而抽象的精神文化或心态文化，则需要下更大的功夫，这也是文化研究的重要目的与基本任务。即我们常说的由表及里，透过现象看本质，掌握其特性，领悟其精神。

　　这里需要指出的是，我们的课程是以"两分法"中的精神文化，或"四分法"中的心态文化为主要论述范畴的。也就是说，我们的讨论主要涉及精神领域的文化现象。

　　文化即生活，舍生活，则无文化。不走进生活，亦无所谓文化的研究。

　　这就是我们讲的"文化"概念的第一层含义。

　　依此层定义，则中国文化的研究者应当做的，就是走进中国人民真实而生动的日常生活，在中国各地、各民族丰富多彩的文化生活中做一名热诚的参与者与聪明的理解者。既要去到北上广深这样的一线城市，也要去到新疆的喀什、青海的玉树、西藏的阿里，以及黔东南的千户苗寨，或桂北的三江侗寨……这

---

① 张岱年，方克立. 中国文化概论［M］. 北京：北京师范大学出版社，2004：4.

样的中西部的山乡村落。既要去体验中国的高铁、5G网络和扫码支付等日新月异的科技进步带来的便捷和效率，也要去实地感受一下闽西客家人虔诚传续的"敬天法祖"的儒家伦理，去看看土家族少女在阿妈的指导下编织"西兰卡普"的古朴技艺。这些都是中国人民真实生活的镜像。正是这片土地上所有人共同参与创造、传续而成的生生不息的生活，构成了丰富多彩、多元一体的中华文化长河。学会聆听、详细记录并用心感悟，才能懂得其中蕴含的深沉的爱恨、善良与勇敢、坚持与牺牲、承担与追求，才能懂得中华文明的特征和中华民族的精神。

1.1.2　从本质上看：文化即人化——其目的在追求文明

"文化即人化"，这又是什么意思呢？"文化即人化"的提法，既指文化是人之所化，人是创造文化的主体，没有人，也就没有文化。但同时更强调：人是被自己创造的文化所影响、所改造的客体，通过文化，人才成为人。

我们知道，人类最初不过是一种"直立之兽"（王夫之语），就是靠着文化实践活动，不断地创造各种类型的物质生活和精神生活，发展出各有特色的物质文化和精神文化。在这个过程中，文化改造自然、改造社会，也改造了人自身，"将动物的人变为创造的人、组织的人、思想的人、说话的人以及计划的人"①。而马克思在《1844年经济学—哲学手稿》中把人类因文化而实现的对本能自我的超越的过程叫作"自然的人化"。文化是让人成之为人的主要力量或工具。有一种怎样的文化生活就有一种怎样的人之自我，各种文化生活和文化关系综合地起作用，推进了人类内在的本质性力量（即人性）②的逐步发展，不断展示出人区别于动物的理性形象与文明特性。

应该说，人类从很早就意识到并一再强调了经由文化、在自我塑造中自我超越的重要性。据《牛津词典》，拉丁文的"Cultura"，其本义是"耕种""培育"植物（Agriculture），或"陶冶"器物，进而引申为：要像培育植物一样，精心地陶冶人的性情、教化人的品德。这层引申，让我想起袁隆平先生为沈阳建筑大学作过的一个题词："稻香飘校园，育米如育人"。水稻要精心栽培才有收获。人也是如此，非用心栽培教化，不能成人。又如中文经典《周易·贲

---

① 庄锡昌，顾晓鸣，顾云深. 多维视野中的文化理论［M］. 杭州：浙江人民出版社，1987：107.

② 人类的本质性力量，按哲学人学的理解，即基于人类知、情、意的族类天赋，而在社会生活中历史地发展起来的求真、为善、向美为特征的人格修养及其所具有的文化实践力量。

卦·象传》中也明确宣告过：文明以止，人文也……观乎人文，以化成天下。而所谓"文明"，中国古人（孔颖达）的注解是："经天纬地曰文，照临四方曰明"。就是：智慧足以知晓天地万物的规律与秩序，如太阳一般普照天下。用今天的语言来说，文明就是道德理性之光，人文的使命就是启蒙天下的人民，驱散蒙昧和黑暗，同臻于至善。比较地看，这与西方语境下"文明"（Civilization）定义（脱离野蛮原始状态）确有异曲同工之妙。

在著者看来，人文（人类文化）的本质：就是要到达文明之境，让人成为文明人类。

纵观人类各民族的文化，虽然类型丰富，内涵万千、路向多样，影响力各异，有些文化圈也早已经消亡，但我们肯定：每个民族都可以有他们特色的文明，因为他们同为万物之灵长的人类，他们的文化生活差别背后无差别的，是它们都流露出人们对生命的肯定、对生活的热爱、对人性创造力的发挥、对自由和幸福的热望。这些伟大的文化情怀，塑造着人类的心灵，推动着人类在这个文化星球的各个角落，筚路蓝缕、行稳致远，走出原始和蒙昧，告别野蛮，高扬科学、民主之旗，辉耀正义、自由之光。正如俄国诗人廖里赫热烈讴歌的那样：

文化是对世界的景仰，文化是对人类的挚爱，文化是生命和美的融合，文化是高尚和文雅的集萃，文化是世人的工具……救星……动力……心脏①。

但我们必须承认，人类创造文化、脱离兽界、追求文明，但并不是说，他所创造的一切生活都必然是文明而阳光的。事实上，人类的生活千姿百态，也千奇百怪。有些文化能成人，有些文化则可能"吃人"。

文化学里有一个专有名词叫"亚文化"。它研究的，就是那些特殊的社会人群的特殊生活，如：乞丐、江湖等。亚文化当然是特定的人群创造和维持的生活，虽诡谲可恶，但却真实存在，所以它是一种文化。但它本质上又不是文明的生活，不是人的本质性力量的健康生长，反而是扭曲与毁灭，所以叫它亚文化。如奴隶制度下没有成人之美的阳光，纳粹的奥斯威辛集中营里没有"文明以止"的价值温度，"三寸金莲"（包小脚）和"三从四德"既不美，也不美好。形形色色的亚文化的存在，只证明了人性的复杂性、文化的杂糅性和文明的脆弱性。历史地看，任何民族的文化都是精华与糟粕的集合体，也是连续与变革中发展的生命体。至善至美的生活、理想型的文化，从来也不曾存在过。"文明只有一层皮那么薄，抓破了就流出野蛮的血"。这应当被看作是一种无奈

① ［俄］尼古拉耶芙娜. 文化学［M］. 王亚民，等译. 兰州：敦煌文艺出版社，2003：1.

的人类学领悟。

虽然如此，我们仍然选择信任人类自身，坚信人类是一种能对自己的生活和后人的前途作严肃思考，并愿意积极承担历史责任的文化种族。正如英国历史学家菲利普·费尔南多-阿梅斯托在他的名著《文明》一书中指出的：

文明史上纵然败绩累累——野蛮的胜利、愚昧的杀戮、进步力量的倒退、自然的反扑、人类寻求改善的失败——我们除了继续努力维持文明传统的生命，别无他策。即便是在海滩的沙砾地上，仍然"要耕耘自己的园圃"。①

因此，文化学研究者的使命，就是要在深入人类的生活世界，追寻种种之后，即使再失望，也仍能找到事实或理由，让自己或者让读者保留一点热情，并发展这样一种信心：人总归是渴望生存、热爱生活的。而任何一个民族的文化生活中，也总会有人性之美和文明之光的。只要相信，就能遇到。只要寻找，就能找见。这似乎又是另外一种顽强或乐观的人类学自信。没有这点信心，生活便会黑暗，人文便会毁灭。

总之，我们的文化观认为：文化即是生活，它是广义的包含了一切物质和精神的生活内容在内的复杂总体。文化更是人化，它在精神价值上追求成人之美，让人过文明而有价值的生活。综合起来即：文化是人化、走向文明的生活。文化学研究就是透过生活、找见文明的工作。

1.2　理解"中国"的三个维度

人类创造文化，不同的民族创造各自的民族文化。我们这里讨论的，当然是中华民族在东亚大陆这片广袤的土地上创造的中国的文化，所以也必须对"中国"这个概念略说一说。

"中国"之名是古已有之的，在如《诗经》《尚书》等古籍中早有所见。而"华夏""神州""九州""赤县""海内""震旦"等名词，也是为人所熟知的代指中国的称谓。

有两件涉及"中国"之名的出土文物，也是人们常常拿来说的例子。一件是1963年在陕西省宝鸡市鸡贾村出土的西周时代（公元前一千年左右）的青铜礼器——何尊（He Zun, ritual wine vessel）。在何尊的内壁上就赫然刻写有周武

① ［英］菲利普·费尔南多-阿梅斯托．文明——文化、野心以及人与自然的伟大博弈［M］．薛绚，译．北京：中信出版集团，2020：639.

王的训诰："余其宅兹中国，自兹乂民。"另外一件就是"五星出东方利中国"织锦。这是一件为了纪念西汉王室征讨南羌军事胜利而织造的护臂织锦，1995年出土于新疆和田地区民丰县尼雅遗址。据说中日联合考古队的队员看到上边的"五星"和"中国"字样的时候，都被这貌似不可思议的图文惊讶到瞠目结舌。

我们认为，对"中国"概念的理解中，需要注意"地理中国""文明中国"和"政治中国"这样三个维度。

1.2.1　天下之中——"地理中国"的内涵

"中国"的本义，指方位居四方之中的城市。"中"即天地之中；"国"，如图所示🀄，即有人口、有持戈卫士和城郭的城邑。上古时期的华夏族（即汉族前身），主要活动于黄河中下游流域，他们自认为其所居之地上应天中，乃天下之中央，故称此地区为"中原"和"中国"。并把居中原（国）以外和远方的非我族类称为：四夷（东夷、西戎、北狄、南蛮）。上文所提到的青铜礼器"何尊"的铭文中的"宅兹中国，自兹乂民"就是周天子定鼎洛邑（今洛阳）、开启治理天下的宏伟蓝图之意。又如《诗经》有云"惠此中国，以绥四方"。《庄子》里提到"中国之君子，明乎礼仪而陋于知人心"。《三国演义》中周瑜所言："（曹操）驱中国士众远涉江湖之间，不习水土，必生疾病"，都是指中原地区。所谓"逐鹿中原"，"得中原者得天下"，都说明在当时人民的心目中，中原作为"天下之中"，具有统御四方的政治象征意义。

当然，在随后的历史中，"中国"所依托的地理空间随着历代王朝政治版图的扩展而逐步扩大。正如梁启超先生指出的：中国人的"中国"视野，经历了"中国之中国""亚洲之中国"和"世界之中国"的变迁。大概到利玛窦（Matteo Ricci，1552—1610）把经过航海大发现的最新地理学成果勘校后确定的《坤舆万国全图》提供给中国人的时候起，我们就放弃了这样一种并不存在的"天下之中"的地理幻觉。也就是说，中原或者中国，从来就不是世界的中心。但这并不妨碍我们对脚下这片土地的热爱。

这片地处东亚大陆、疆域辽阔、纵横万里、负陆面海的"地理中国"，自古以来就是中华民族热爱的故土家园。她东临浩瀚的海洋，西有世界屋脊，北有广袤的草原、南有河网交织的水乡。"东西差落如此显著的三级梯阶，南北跨度又达三十个纬度，温度和湿度的差距自然形成了不同的生态环境，给人文发展以严峻的桎梏和丰润的机会。"① 勤劳智慧、勇敢温和的各族人民就是在这片土地上繁衍生息，创造出了既有多元个性，又有一体共性的，丰富多彩的中华地域文化。所谓"一方水土养一方人"，中国广大而多样的山河大地给中国文化提供了一个独特的生存场。各地域之间差别迥异的地理环境、历史沿革、人口与民族构成、方言、饮食、民间信仰、民居、民俗、交通等，构成了锦绣中华的历史画卷。有学者把它们划分为：十大自然生态文化区②。《中国地域文化丛书》则划分了二十四个地域人文区：

八桂文化、八闽文化、巴蜀文化、草原文化、陈楚文化、滇云文化、关东文化、徽州文化、江西文化、荆楚文化、两淮文化、岭南文化、陇右文化、齐鲁文化、黔贵文化、青藏文化、琼州文化、三晋文化、三秦文化、台湾文化、吴越文化、西域文化、燕赵文化、中州文化③。

读者可以通过这套丛书，更全面地了解到中华民族各族人民在这块古老的土地上，在悠久的历史过程中，是怎样在不同的自然环境和不同的社会历史条件下，用自己的劳动和智慧创造了自己的文化，形成了至今犹存的各具特色和地域性格的社会文化生活风貌。

当然，这些地域人文区的划分也是相对的，而且，在其区域内仍然可以继续细分。如我们身在福建，"八闽文化"就被细分为五个文化区：以闽都文化和船政文化为特色的闽东文化区；以客家文化和红色文化为特色的闽西文化区；以中原文化和海洋文化为特色的闽南文化区；以山林文化和朱子文化为特色的闽北文化区；以科举文化和妈祖文化为特色的莆仙文化区。

另外，如"航拍中国""美丽中国""百山百川行""跟着唐诗去旅行"以及"记住乡愁"等许多优秀纪录片，也是了解"地理中国"的极好素材。

1.2.2　儒教文化圈——"文明中国"的概念

英国学者、复旦大学中国研究院特邀研究员马丁·雅克先生（Martin Jacques）是一位知华友华的汉学家，也是 2004 年我在日本爱知大学学习期间的任课老师。在他广受好评的《当中国统治世界》一书中，他首次使用"文明国家"（Civilization-state）的概念来称谓中国，他指出：中国，并不仅是一个民族

---

① 费孝通 . 中华民族多元一体格局［M］. 北京 . 中央民族大学出版社 .2018；18.
② 十大自然生态文化区为：新疆沙漠绿洲文化、内蒙古草原文化、青藏高原高山文化、东北黑土地文化、华北平原文化、黄土高原文化、四川盆地文化、云贵高原区、华南妈祖海洋文化、江南水乡文化。
③ 该丛书全套 24 册，辽宁教育出版社 1998 年 6 月出版。

国家，还是一种文明。事实上，中国成为一个民族国家只是近代以来的事……①
马丁还有一个在网上流传甚广的比喻：中国其实是一个文明，但是它却"伪装"
成了一个国家的存在。我想到另外一个坊间流传的提法："美国其实是一个公
司，但是它却'伪装'成了一个国家的存在"。这当然是一个笑话，而马丁的描
述却在某个意义上提示了我们一个确实存在过的、关于"中国"作为一个文化
类型或文明体系，而非一般的以民族为基础形成的政治主权国家（National-
state）的理解方式。

回溯历史，我们确实发现，在"地理中国"概念产生的同时，也形成了
"文明中国"的概念。如《尚书》中说："华夏，谓中国也。"什么叫"华"，什
么叫"夏"？《左传》中解读说：中国有礼仪之大，故称夏；有服章之美，谓之
华。这就是说中国之为中国是因为在这片土地上或社会中，人民遵守和实行独
特的礼仪和服章制度而被界定。对这个独特性，《战国策·赵策》则说得更详细
一些：

中国者，聪明睿智之所居也，万物财用之所聚也，圣贤之所教也，仁义
之所施也，诗书礼乐之所用也，异敏技艺之所试也，远方之所观赴也，蛮夷之所
义行也。

这里的"中国"，被描述为一个居民有高度素养、经济发达、圣贤教化、仁
义流行、诗书礼乐流行、工艺繁荣、四方羡慕、值得效仿的地方。这些内容，
显然是华夏族从夏商周三代以降、特别是西周以来，以儒教文化为认同核心所
形成的社会文化图景与生活方式。《战国策》的作者认为，正是这种生活内容整
体地构成了中国成为中国的根本规定性。

北宋初年思想家石介在《中国论》中也以确定无疑的口吻说道："中国能礼
仪则中国之，中国不能礼仪则夷狄之，夷狄能礼仪则中国之。"石介看来，华夷
之辩、中外之别的标准，既不看地域，也不看种族，而是看是否遵循儒教文化
而界定。它严格强调了"中国"的文化规定性，能实行（儒教）"礼仪"则夷
狄即中国；中国不能实行（儒教）"礼仪"则中国即夷狄。近代学者章太炎先
生也用几乎同样的语言，重申了这一点。比较于《战国策》的提法，石介的
"中国标准"更定向、更强调于儒教礼仪，而前者则把居民、经济、技艺、教
育、伦理、区域影响力等因素综合起来讨论。其实，两者并不矛盾。文化本来
就是全套的社会生活，但又以化成人心、文明以止为直接任务的道德礼仪为文

---

① ［英］马丁·雅克. 大国雄心［M］. 张豫宁，张莉，刘曲，译. 北京：中信出版社，
2016：175.

化的核心。在中国，这个文化核心，无疑还是悠久的儒家礼教——这套理性早启、伦理本位的道德理性主义学说为主体内容的。

于是，"中国"遂成了一个既开放又狭隘的文明类型，或文化标签的概念——任何种族（及任何国家任何人），只要在文化心理与生活方式上能够认同并奉行儒教文明，他（它）才能（或就能）被称为中国人（中国）。而事实上，作为文化类型标签的"中国"一词，它是超越地域、种族和国别的。比如历史上的"中国"概念，从来不是中原汉族王朝所"独有"的概念，很多入主中原的少数民族政权（或非中原的地区少数民族政权）的统治者们，经常以"中国正统"自居①。甚至包括东亚儒学文化圈的国家如日本、朝鲜、越南，因长期受到中华文化洗礼，在文化心态上多少都表现过传承华夏、中华一脉的意识。今天很多海外第三代、四代华人移民后裔，虽然已经不懂汉语、国籍非我，但其在文化心理上，仍然自认是"中国人"（I'm ethically, culturally, linguistically Chinese.）即道德上、文化上、语言上的中国人（而非政治上的）。

当然，这种从文明类型的角度来使用"中国"概念，确实会引起许多交流上的紊乱。至少在今天的读者看来是陌生而感觉奇怪的。他们或许会反驳说，信奉儒家文明即为中国或中国人，这个方式岂不是太泛滥了吗？历史上那些不那么遵守儒教文化的中国政权如秦朝、元朝和清朝，是否还算是中国呢？更不用说中华人民共和国成立以后，儒学早已经权威不再，那中国还叫中国吗？毫无疑问，中国就是中国，这对"文明中国"的概念当然是一个有力的质疑。

总之，"文明中国"（或"文化中国"），是特指儒学认同为核心的文化类型的代名词。它可以简略成这么一个公式：中国，即行儒教之国；不行儒教，即非中国。

1.2.3 主权国家——"政治中国"的意涵

其实，今天的人们疑问于"中国"到底是政治概念还是文明类型不是没有道理的。据中华文明探源工程的研究，在距今 5000 年前，我国已进入文明阶段，出现了国家，进入"古国时代"。从那时以降，长久的中国封建时代所兴起的历代王朝，作为政治实体，它们都各有其王朝的国号，有曰夏商周，有曰秦

---

① 许多早期著名少数民族政权的统治者都自认是炎黄后裔，并以"中国"自居。如匈奴自认是"夏桀后裔"，建立后秦的氏族被认为是"有扈"（大禹之子）之苗裔，他们宣称其政权是中华的传续。可参看网文《从多民族视角考察古代"中国"观》[EB/OL].https：//www. 163. com/dy/article/GM1OIMHD051495OJ. html. 2021-10-11

汉隋唐，有曰宋元明清。故彼时只有秦国、大汉国、大唐国、大宋国，而未尝有以"中国"为国号的王朝。而作为文明类型的"中国"固然同时为它们所经常自我标志，但也只是宣示它们继承传统，服从于儒教文化体系来治国理政，并致力于以实现儒家的文明目标如大同之治仁政爱民。儒教文化是它们的御用意识形态，也是它们用以奠定其统治合法性与正统性的文化工具。正如中世纪基督教国家不尊重《圣经》，即是丧失其政权的文化合法性一样，是一件非常严重的事件。

当然，这种情况在近代悄然发生了变化。"文明中国"逐步向"政治中国"过渡，直接成为政权实体的代称。据史料，明末清初之际的西方传教士们已经开始在他们的私人著述与信件中称明朝，或清朝为"中华帝国"，简称"中国"。这已不是传统的"文化中国"的指称，而具有了近代政治主权国家的意义，但这仍然是民间的个人行为。而到 1689 年 9 月 7 日大清康熙皇帝派索额图与俄罗斯签订的国家间外交条约——《中俄尼布楚条约》(*Sino-Russian Treaty of Nibuchu*) 中，就第一次非常官方的、正式地使用"中国"(Sino-) 这个词来指称大清王朝。也就是说，直到 17 世纪末年，"中国"这个词，才被清朝官方作为政治主权国家的代名词，并一直沿袭至今。如在清朝末年使用的《满蒙汉合璧教科书》（第四册）就写到这样的文字："我中国居亚洲之东，……世世相传，以及吾身。吾既为中国之人，安可不爱中国也。"

至此，本义指黄河流域的"地理中国"、后来长期作为儒教文化类型代名词的"文明中国"，才实现了向政治主权国家的"政治中国"的变迁，即从 Country 到 Civilization 到 State 的变化过程。"中国"概念真正实现了整体的地理中国、文明中国和政治中国的统一。

今天，"中国"，就是作为政治主权国家"中华人民共和国"简称。

总结一下：第一，"中国"最初只是一个"天地之中"的地理幻觉，指洛阳和中原地区。第二，"中国"长期特指遵循儒家礼教为核心的社会生活方式或文明类型。第三，"中国"直到清康熙年间才成为一个作为政治实体的主权国家的代名词。

还有两点我想要补充说明的是：

1. 当代中国确实是一个"文明型国家"。

当代的政治中国，即作为主权国家的中华人民共和国，确如复旦大学张维为教授所说，是一个"文明型国家"(Civilizational state)。"文明型国家"的提法不同于狭隘的儒家认同为核心的"文明中国"(Civilization-state) 的概念。当代的政治中国站在新的时代，融合"地理中国""文明中国"为一体，"是一个延绵不断长达数千年的古老文明与一个超大型现代国家几乎完全重合的国家，即中国。"① 当代中国，以习近平新时代中国特色社会主义思想为指导，优秀传统文化（包括儒学）都得到了创造性转化、创新性发展。中国有超大型的人口规模、超广阔的疆域国土、超悠久的历史传统、超深厚的文化积淀、独特的语言、独特的社会、独特的经济和独特的政治，都标志着中国作为一个"文明型国家"，继往开来、古风新貌，正迎来民族复兴的无量前途。我们的《中国文化概论》课程所讨论的"中国文化"，正是基于作为"文明型国家"（而非"文明中国"）的中华人民共和国的版图空间的基础上，来探讨和研究其历史上所发生的文化生活现象。

2. 应该避免"汉族文化中心论"。

因为不仅中原（中国）从来都不是天下的中心，而且汉民族的文化，也不能完全代表整个中国的文化生态或整个中华文明的长河。我们不仅要看中原和汉族的文化，还要放眼全国，放眼各个地域、各个少数民族的文化。他们是多元一体的、完整的中华文明的多维的内涵。我们讲的"中国文化"，必须紧扣作为多元一体的中华民族在中国的土地上，认识与改造自然、社会与民族自身的历史过程中所创造与积累的全部文明成果。它反映了中国人特有的思维方式、生活个性和价值追求。必须明确，中华人民共和国疆域内所囊括的所有民族的历史和文化，均应该视为"中国史"和"中国文化史"的内容。只有在中国文化课程中凸显 56 个民族对多元一体的中华文化的宝贵贡献，才能完整从而准确地理解中华文化的深刻特征和独特品质，才能建设好我国各族人民共有的精神家园，筑牢中华儿女团结奋进、一往无前的思想基础。虽然我们的课程不能详细展开少数民族的丰富多彩的文化内涵，但这显然是中国文化研究不可或缺、必须更加重视的一大领域。

1.3 学习中国文化的方法论

中国文化源远流长博大精深，若从彩陶文化算起至今已有 6000 多年的历史，形成了世界上最丰富的文化积累。本课程所探讨的中国文化，主要是指近代鸦片战争（1840）以前的中国传统文化。

学习中国文化知识，是对当代大学生和境外生实施人文素质教育的基本环

---

① 张维为. 文明型国家［M］. 上海：上海人民出版社，2017：2.

节。我们开设本课程的主要目的，即在于（1）传播中华文化基础知识、分享中华文明精神价值。（2）读懂传统中国，了解当代中国。（3）增进对中华文明的理性了解和情感认同，并促进中外文明的交流互鉴。

作为一门知识性、理论性、实践性很强的课程，要求我们在学习过程中注意如下方法论：

一是真诚的敬意与谨严的理性相结合。

为何研究中国文化需要敬意意识呢？因为文化即是生活，文化中见生命。历史留存的物质（与非物质）文化遗产和精神文化产品，都是一代代先辈生命心血的结晶，很多是不可再生和复制的，非常宝贵而脆弱[①]，最容易被战争、水火灾害和生物蛀蚀、毁坏。如北京圆明园毁于战争抢劫；敦煌文物资料被盗取、塑像壁画被盗挖；世界文化遗产、有 1500 年历史的巴米扬大佛被轰然炸毁，等等。帕斯卡说："今天，即使是神也不能再创造一个雅典的柱式了。只有正宗和原初的才令人尊重。"所以我们主张，要把传统文化当成长者和弱者，去敬爱和仰望，凝视与呵护。任何妄自尊大的文化沙文主义，或妄自菲薄、对民族文化缺少文化自信心的历史虚无主义态度，都是不可取的。

当然，除了敬意意识，更需要谨严的理性，即以实事求是的态度去研究博大精深的中国文化，把握好历史梳理与逻辑分析相结合的方法。历史梳理就是以历时性为线索，作纵向梳理，搞清中国文化的来龙去脉；逻辑分析则是以问题为线索，作横向梳理，搞清中国文化的逻辑因果。在本课程中，我们删繁就简，以文化精神为经，以文化特征为纬，提纲挈领地设置了十个专题如下：1. 文明以止——中国文化·绪论；2. 泱泱中华——中国文化的基本特征；3. 千年道统——中国文化的基本精神；4. 多元一体——中华文化与中华民族；5. 大哉孔子——中国文化的至圣先师；6. 仁者爱人——中国传统伦理思想概说；7. 尊祖重族——中国村落宗族文化的要素；8. 和而不同——中国的多元宗教及其特质；9. 崇文重教——中国传统教育风貌掠影；10. 美美与共——中外文明的交流与互鉴。

我们不求面面俱到，集中时间、次序解读，希望能做到历史和逻辑的相统一。

二是典籍研习和社会考察相结合。

在学习这门课程的过程中，我们应当把阅读和研习优秀中国典籍作为必不

---

① 截至 2017 年 9 月，我国现有不可移动文物 76.7 万处，非物质文化遗产资源 87 万项。目前，有 56 项遗产列入《世界遗产名录》，位居世界第一。40 项遗产列入人类非物质文化遗产代表作名录，也位居世界第一。我国许多文物是以遗址状态存在的，它们是文化遗产的重要组成部分，是构成我国古代文明史史迹的主体。

可少的学习方法。中国悠久的历史积淀了丰富的浩如烟海的典藏，记录了中国人民创造中华文明的宏伟进程，也是了解中国文化必不可少的径路。我们当然不可能奢望每本书都看到，但有些基本的读本是学习中国文化所应该有所涉猎的。如著名学者钱穆先生推荐的"中国人所人人必读的书"是这样七部书：《论语》《孟子》《老子》《庄子》《六祖坛经》《近思录》《传习录》。这些书，也是有志于深入掌握中国文化知识的境外生朋友应该要阅读的书目。当然，我们也可以给学习本课程的朋友推荐一些必要的课程参考书目（见参考目录），如：梁漱溟著《中国文化要义》，张岱年、方克立主编《中国文化概论》，冯天瑜、何晓明、周积明著《中华文化史》，许倬云著《万古江河》，胡兆量著《中国文化地理概述》，费孝通主编《中华民族多元一体格局》等。

　　除了阅读书籍以外，学习中国文化必不可少的方法是进行社会考察，即走进各地的文化现场如各种博物馆、历史名胜地和遗址公园等。这就能直观地受到中国古代文化生动的熏陶，获得许多在课堂上纯粹理论讲授所不能给予的情境体验和灵感启发。

　　以在我们华侨大学境外研究生的《中国文化概论》课程为例。我们一学期的课程，至少安排三分之一的课时走出去做田野调查和实践教学。留学生们分专题小组各做考察准备，教师带队指导，带领他们走进闽南、闽西、闽北的古村落、古祠堂、古寺庙、古书院等文化现场，去直接接触传统的村落社会，去观察客家人和畲族、回族等少数民族的日常生活，去探访当地保存完好的传统的文化习俗、宗教崇拜，去感受八闽大地上传统的伦理生活和教育实践的历史遗迹，感触海上丝绸之路所联结的中外文明交流互鉴的历史物证。

图1-2　华侨大学境外研究生的田野考察

　　实践也证明，这种以社会调查配合课堂专题教学的教学法，非常有利于调动和增进青春活泼、个性张扬的境外留学生的兴趣与热情，有利于综合地锻炼和发展其整体的观察思考、写作和研究的能力与素质，有利于他们在知行合一中加深对中华文化的理解和认同，从而也得到了他们的好评，并拉近了他们对华的友好感情。当然，你若暂时没有机会和能力出门进行社会考察，也应当注意各种大众传播媒介如电视、杂志、微博和视频网站所介绍的中国文化的有关内容。

　　三是批判思维和创新性思维相结合。

　　中国传统文化包罗万象，有非常丰富和庞杂的内涵，是统一性与多样性、连续性与变革性、独立性与融合性、精华性与糟粕性的对立统一。这就要求学习者掌握辩证法和历史分析法，动态地、比较地、发展地去观察和研究中国文化的复杂内涵。尤其是对传统文化中那些糟粕与精华并存的成分，要以时代发展的要求为内在依据，有批判地继承、有创新地发展。对传统文化中明显具有落后性的封建糟粕（即所谓"亚文化"），则应持有彻底批判与摒弃的态度。而传统文化中的优秀遗产，则我们必须着意继承并大力弘扬，积极分享给当代世界。面向未来，发展生生不息、日新又新的中国文化，这应该是"文化中国"的题中之意。

　　四是交融互鉴的比较思维和人类命运共同体思维相结合。

　　正如习近平主席指出的：文明因多样而交流，因交流而互鉴，因互鉴而发展。

　　人类是个命运共同体，历史上中外文明之间早已有许多生动的交融互鉴的故事流传。今天更要秉承这种交融互鉴的思维和人类命运共同体意识，开放包容、和而不同，发扬各美其美、美人之美和美美与共的精神。在文化交流中，既有鉴别、有批评，但更多的是温情和友好的交融取益，从而扬长避短，互相促进，为创造各国各民族乃至整个人类的更灿烂的文化前景而一起工作。

The First Chapter:

Aiming at Civilization
—An Introduction to Chinese Culture

Hello, everyone. Thank you for attending the lecture of *"Aiming at Civilization—Ten Lectures on Chinese Traditional Culture"* .

As one of the oldest civilized nation with 5000-years culture, China is a great nation given with two spectacular mother rivers—the Yangtze River and the Yellow River. It's also a magical land pregnant with amazing tourist attractions like the Great Wall and Huangshan Mountain. And in these magnificent mountains and rivers and vast territory, the hardworking, brave and wise sons and daughters of the Chinese nation live. With their own hands, they have jointly created the splendid Chinese culture. To understand China, feasting your eyes on beautiful sceneries of great mountains and grand rivers is necessary and important. However, if you want to have best knowledge about China, you should step into the gorgeous palace of Chinese culture and explore her rich and time-honored history, because you can't expect an acute insight into China and Chinese before you have a good understanding of Chinese civilization.

In this first chapter *An Introduction to Chinese Culture*, we will focus on three topics: What is "Culture"? What do you know about "China"? And what is the methodology behind this course?

1. 1 The Definition of "Culture"

To begin with, let's have a look at the definition of "culture". Speaking of "culture", it is a word popular in our daily lives.

Yet what exactly defines culture? There is no decision reached yet. Various ideas have been echoing. For Alfred L. Kroeber and Clyde Cluckhohn from the United States, co-authors of *Culture: A Critical Review of Concepts and Redefinition*, nearly all types of answers were calculated in their book. And it turned out to be the amazing164 ones. Of course, I'm not going to take you into this dizzying conceptual forest, I just want to directly give the definition and core understanding of culture in this course. Then, in our course, how do we define culture? To put it in a simple way, two connotations deserve our discussion. That is, culture means life. And culture represents humanization.

1.1.1 Culture Equals to Life

To begin with, culture means life in a broad sense. It embraces all things happening around us. This idea comes from a book written by Liang Shuming, a great philosopher in modern China, *Fundamentals of Chinese Culture*. According to Mr. Liang, "Culture is all what we live on. Substantially, culture is all-encompassing for anything including economics and politics." Similarly, another ideologist Qian Mu noted the same idea. "Culture equals to life. Life itself is inclusive. A society, a nation, or even a large community, and their multiple aspects of daily activities, all of them together can be called life, or culture as well." As Edward B. Tylor, a British anthropologist, came to the same idea in his Primitive Culture. "Culture is a complex whole. It includes knowledge, belief, art, morals, laws, customs, and any other capabilities and habits required as a member of the society."

These masters all emphasized on its basic connotation. Culture, in their minds, is integral to our social lives.

According to this understanding, it can be inferred that to understand what culture is, one should know about his or her current life world, or passed stories. One should step into cities, or countryside, to observe daily activities of people from all walks of life, such as their ornaments, clothes, and food, their families and community structures, their architecture and structure for houses and buildings, their usage of tools, and their inventions of science and technology. One should also feel their festivals and customs, listen to their languages, read classical works written by their words, learn to appreciate their poetries. paintings and dramas, and to taste the sense of beauty and rhythm in them. Indeed, there is more than that. One should know about the ethics and rules obeyed by people, the philosophy and religion they believe, and so on.

It can be said that there is a kind of life, there is a kind of culture, or even any kind of life elements, can be classified into a type of culture. People need to eat, there is food culture; people need to dress, there is clothing culture; people need to live, there is architecture culture; people need to travel, there is transportation culture; People need to produce and give birth to live forever, which is economic culture and marriage culture. Others, such as music and dance, festival celebration, language, writing, science and technology, political organization, social communication, ethnic groups and religious worship, are the connotation of life and belong to a specific culture. All these colorful elements of life constitute the cultural world of humans. It is by these splendid cultural elements that humans survive and thrive. Furthermore, exposed to and forged by rich cultural elements, people gradually shape their own life interests and lifestyles.

It is to say, culturology is a comprehensive discipline studying how people live.

For sure, since life is complex and all-encompassing, from the perspective of culturology, they can be typically classified into different cultural types, or distinguished by different levels. For instance, various cultural elements or phenomena can be distinguished as material culture featured by objective entity, and spiritual culture featured by subjective entity. Or, according to the standards of natural and social science, culture can be distinguished as Culture Type I and Culture Type II. This is a dichotomous method. Or, according to the surface or deep level, culture can be classified into materials culture, institutional culture, behavior culture, and mentality culture. This is a quarter method. There are also quintile method and sextant method, etc. Generally speaking, material culture is the surface of culture, while spiritual culture is the core of culture. From the gradual deepening of material culture, it can go through the institutional culture, behavior culture and direct to the other side of mentality culture. Although these layers are not independent, but permeate each other. However, there is no doubt that intuitive and tangible material culture is vivid and active, and through them, it needs great efforts to explain or reveal some inner and abstract mentality culture, which is also the most important purpose and task of cultural research. That is, we often say from the outside to the inside, through the phenomenon to see the essence, grasp its characteristics, understand its spirit. Here, it should be noted that our course *An Introduction to Chinese Culture* focuses on the expositions mainly on spiritual culture of "Dichotomy" or mentality culture of "Quarter Method". In other words, our lecture mainly involves cultural phenomenon in the spiritual aspect.

So, culture means life. One cannot live without culture. Or culture cannot be studied without experiencing various kinds of lives. This is the first connotation of culture what we are lecturing.

1.1.2   Culture Represents Humanization

Then, let us move on to the second connotation of culture. Essentially, culture represents humanization. It aims to pursue civilization. Yet how to explain it? Why does culture represent humanization? Culture is humanization, which means that man is not only the subject and source of creating culture, but also the object that is influenced and transformed by the culture he creates. As a matter of fact, culture has its pursuit of value. It aims to make humans what they are.

As is well-known, human beings evolved first from animals walking upright. Through experiencing cultural practices and activities, then, their internal and natural power was gradually developed. And constantly, they created colorful material and spiritual lives. Humans changed the nature, the society, as well as themselves. "Culture distinguished men from animals. Creativity, organization, thoughts and language were developed. And planning was followed." This process was explained by Karl Marx as the "humanization of nature" in his book, *Economic and Philosophical Manuscripts of 1844.*

In other words, Human beings have long kept culture in mind. And it is culture that helps us self-cultivating. In Oxford English Dictionary, "Cultura" in Latin, and "Culture" in both English and French, their original meaning is "growing or cultivating" plants. Henceforth, like growing plants, culture means developing people's characters and qualities. This extended meaning is like what Mr. Yuan Longping have mentioned. He once inscribed a writing in Shenyang Jianzhu University. "Rice thrives as campus prospers. Growing rice is like cultivating talents."

Chinese classic *The Book of Changes* clarified the same connotation. "Elegance and intelligence regulated by the arrest suggest the observances that adorn human. ⋯ We look at the ornamental observances of society, and understand how the processes of transformation are accomplished under heaven." It helps describe the essence of culture. Culture aims to achieve civilization. It also educates all its people. The so-called "Wen Ming" (civilization) was explained by ancient Chinese as follows. "Wen" refers to mastering a wide range of knowledge about the universe. And

"Ming" refers to the strong light shed to every corner under heaven. It means that wisdom can help people learn. Rules and orders of everything are available for wise men. It is like the sun shining. And the sunlight drives ignorance and darkness away. As we all know, "Civilization" in western culture is defined as "the state out of savage". And the two definitions seem to share the same connotation.

History has witnessed numerous cultures of different nations. They feature abundant types, enriched content and various directions. Their influence varies in degrees. Some cultural circles have vanished. Yet there is something common behind those differences. It reflects people's aspirations for truth, kindness and beauty. The splendid cultures convey truths. They also nourish their people and adorn the society. Great cultural passion has mushroomed up. It not only shapes human spirit, but also keeps humans growing, developing and striving forward. Roerich, a Russian poet, once praised culture wholeheartedly. In his eyes, culture shows respect for the world. Culture reflects love towards humans. Culture combines life and beauty. Culture embodies nobility and elegance. Culture can be used as people's tools, helpers, and engine. The poet aims to eulogize the great spirit of culture. The spirit that emphasizes on developing civilization and cultivating humans.

Sure, we must admit a possibility of development. Humanity follows different paths. It can become either good or evil. All humans create culture and pursue civilization. But it does not necessarily follow that all lives created are good, become civilized and progressive. Some cultures may cultivate people. While some may destroy people.

In culturology, there is a term "subculture". Its subject focuses on special communities. And studies special lives of these communities. Take for example, the special groups of beggars, gangs, etc. Subculture is surely a type of life created and maintained by humans. Therefore, it symbolizes a culture. But in essence, it cannot be defined as civilized lifestyle. Thus, it is called subculture. In subculture, no sunshine can be found to cultivate humans. No warmth can be felt to value humanities. Various types of subcultures do exist. They indicate merely the complexity of humanity, the abusability of culture, as well as the vulnerability of civilization.

Civilization is skin-thin—scratch it and savagery bleeds out.

Even so, we still choose to believe human beings. We trust our capability to think seriously of our lives as well as the future of later generations. We also honor the sense of responsibility of humans. As for the nature of culture, it fundamentally looks for the shared sunlight so that everyone can enjoy truth, kindness and beauty. Its goal is to achieve valuable culture. And it reflects upon and eliminates subculture, which is anti-value and anti-civilization. Hence, it can be learned as culturology. It aims to study how people make themselves growing, developing and perfect, and how they make themselves advance or progress.

Thus, we conclude culture as follows: Culture means life. In a broader sense, it can be a whole complex. It contains all material and spiritual lives. More importantly, culture equals to humanization. It seeks for cultivating humans in spirit. Culture teaches people how to live a decent life and how to shape their qualities.

To sum up, Culture leads people toward humanization and civilization. Cultural research is such a kind of work: to find civilization through life.

1.2 The Notion of "China"

Human beings create cultures, and different nations create their own national cultures. What we are discussing here, of course, is the Chinese culture created by the Chinese nation in the vast land of East Asia, so we must also talk about the notion of "China".

The name of "China" firstly appeared in some ancient classics such as *Classic of Poetry* and *Book of History*. In addition, the name of "China" is found in two excavated artifacts, which are typical cases to talk about. One was unearthed in Jijia Village, Baoji City, Shaanxi Province in 1963. It's called He Zun, a ritual bronze vessel in the era of Western Zhou. Words of King Wu of Zhou Dynasty were inscribed inside the container: "I live in China, or Middle Kingdom, and rule the people here." Another one is the brocade "Five stars rise in the East", for the celebration of the Western Han's subjugation on South Qiang. It is a brocade armband. The artifact was unearthed at the Niya ruins in Xinjiang in 1995. It was found by Sino-Japanese joint archaeological team. When they saw the characters "five stars" and "China", they were said to be dumbfounded at the incredible graphics and characters.

We believe if we want to really understand the notion of "China", we should understand it from the following three perspectives: a geographic space, a kind of civilization, and a political entity.

1.2.1　China as a Geographic Space

First of all, let's look at China as a geographic space. "China" originally refers to a city in the middle. Etymologically, the character "（国 guo）" referred to the city with people, guardians armed with daggers and city walls.

The Huaxia tribes in ancient China, the ancestors of Han people mainly lived in the middle and lower reaches of Yellow River. They believed their dwellings were located in the center of the world, and in the middle of the earth. Therefore, they called this area as the Central Plains and the Middle Kingdom. Therefore, they called people living outside or far from their areas as barbarians. We mentioned the inscription inside the ritual bronze vessel He Zun: "live in the Middle Kingdom and rule its people". That means the Emperor of Zhou lives in Luoyi (now the City of Luoyang) and begins to govern the world. As it is mentioned in *Zhuangzi*, "The gentlemen of Central Plains pursue courtesy but do not know how to understand people." Zhou Yu, a famous general in *The Romance of the Three Kingdoms*, once said, "(Cao Cao) led soldiers from Central Plains to fight in the river basin. The climate didn't suit them and it would cause diseases." All these cases refer to the Central Plains. The so-called "chasing the deer on the Central Plains" and "he who wins the Central Plains will win the whole China." All these reflect the importance of the Central Plains in people's mind. The Central Plains, as the center of the world, had the symbolic political significance of governing over the World.

As the time goes, the geospatial significance of the "China" changes, and the political landscape expanded in the following dynasties. As Mr. Liang Qichao once said, Chinese people's understanding of the notion of "China" has changed from China as itself, China in Asia, and China in the world. Probably when Matteo Ricci showed *A Map of the Myriad Countries of the World* to Chinese intellectuals, Chinese people gave up the geographic illusion of China as the center of the world. Put it another way, nor the Central Plains or China is in the center of the world. However, we ardently love this country forever.

This country is located in the eastern Asia. It covers an area of 9.6 million square kilometers, and it faces the ocean. China, as a geographic space, was the home of Chinese since ancient times. Its east is the vast sea. There is the roof of the world

Himalaya in its west. In the north, there are vast grasslands. There is region of rivers and lakes in the south. Such a remarkable three-step difference between the east and the west, and a span of 30 latitudes between the north and the south, as well as the difference in temperature and humidity, have naturally formed different ecological environments, posing severe constraints and rich opportunities for human development. All diligent, brave, gentle and intelligent Chinese people lived and thrived here. The regional cultures they created are diverse but united. These regional cultures are colorful. Some scholars make a division for them: ten natural ecological and cultural zones or 24 regional cultural districts as follows.

Bagui culture, Bamin culture, Bashu culture, Grassland culture, Chenchu culture, Cloud Yunnan culture, Kanto culture, Huizhou culture, Jiangxi culture, Jingchu culture, Lianghuai culture, Lingnan culture, Longyou culture, Qilu culture, Qiangui culture, Tibetan culture, Qiongzhou culture, Sanjin culture, Taiwanese culture, Wuyue culture, Western Region culture, Yanzhao culture, Zhongzhou culture.

All kinds of different geographical environment, social reforms, population, dialects, diets, folk faith, folk houses, customs and transportation and so on, these elements constitute a great history of China. Of course, these regional cultural areas are also relative, and can still be further subdivided within their regions. For example, our Bamin culture (Fujian culture) can be subdivided into five cultural districts:

Eastern Fujian cultural area featuring Fujian capital culture and ship administration culture. Western Fujian cultural area featuring Hakka culture and revolutionary culture. Southern Fujian cultural area featuring central Plains culture and Marine culture. Northern Fujian cultural area characterized by forest culture and Zhuzi culture; Puxian (莆田仙游) Cultural area featuring by imperial examination culture and Mazu culture.

In addition, there are many great documentaries as "Aerial China" "Wild China" "Travel through mountains and rivers". "Nostalgia" They are good materials to know about China as a geographic space.

1. 2. 2 China as a Type of Civilization

Well, in the second part, let's look at China as a kind of civilization.

Mr. Martin Jacques, the Senior Researcher of Cambridge University, is a

Sinologist who knows China a lot. He is also my teacher during my study at Aichi University in Japan. In his well-received book *When China Rules the World*, he put forward the "civilization state", and he used this notion to call China. He said that: China is not only a nation state, but also a civilization. In fact, it is only since modern times that China has become a nation state. He argued that China was actually a civilization. But it disguises to be a nation state. His metaphor is very influential on the internet and is welcomed by Chinese netizens. Actually, before Martin Jacques' book, many international scholars like Russell have point it out, China is a cultural entity, or a civilization that surpasses the notion of nation state.

Look back the history, indeed we have found, with the advent of China as a geographic space, China as a kind of civilization was also formed. As the *Book of Documents* says, Huaxia means China. What is Hua? And what is Xia? The book *Zuo Tradition* gives a concrete definition. Xia signifies the grandness in the ceremonial etiquette of China. Hua means the beauty of dress and personal adornment. Therefore, China got its name Huaxia. It has uniqueness in ceremonial etiquette and dress.

About this kind of uniqueness, the book *Strategies of the Warring States* contains more details. It says that Chinese people are highly literate. China is a country of booming economy, holy education, ethics, prosperous techniques and followers. These were formed since Xia, Shang and Zhou Dynasties, especially in West Zhou Dynasty. Confucian culture became the core of their social lifestyle. The author of *Strategies of the Warring States* believed that, it was this life content that made China become itself, and made Chinese people become themselves.

Shi Jie was a thinker in the early Northern Song Dynasty. He said in a certain tone in the book *On China*, "China knows etiquette so it becomes China. If China doesn't know etiquette, it cannot call itself China. If barbarian kingdoms know etiquette, they can join to be China". This sentence is important. It distinguished Middle Kingdom and barbarians, China and foreign countries. It doesn't matter what regions and what races people belong to. It depends on whether Confucian culture is followed. Shi Jie's opinion is representative. It represents pinions of the whole Confucian class.

Of course, what "China" means to Shi Jie is different from the content in *Strategies of the Warring States*. Shi's opinion targets at or stresses the Confucian etiquette, while *Strategies of the Warring States* mentions citizens, economy, techniques, education, ethnics and regional influence and so on. It combines all these elements to discussion. In fact, these two types of opinions are not contradictory. Any culture is an inclusive and complete set of social life, but it also takes the moral etiquette as the core. In China, the core of this culture is undoubtedly the time-honored Confucian ethics.

Therefore, "China" then became an both open and narrow type of civilization, or the concept of cultural label. In other words, no matter what kind of people (and whatever country), as long as in their cultural psychology and lifestyle, they can follow the Confucian culture, they can be called as China (or Chinese). For example, the concept of "China" in history was never "unique" to the Central Plains dynasties established by the Han nationality. Many rulers of the ethnic minority regimes in the Central Plains (or regional minority regimes outside the central Plains) often regarded themselves as "Chinese orthodoxy". Even countries in the so-called East Asian Confucian cultural circle, such as Japan, Korea and Vietnam, have been baptized by Chinese culture for a long time, and have shown the consciousness of inheriting China in cultural mentality. Today a lot of overseas Chinese, although cannot speak Chinese, but its cultural psychology, still consider themselves "Chinese", they say "I'm ethically and culturally and linguistically Chinese." (Not politically)

Of course, this use of the concept of "China" in terms of civilization types does cause a lot of communication confusion. Strange, at least, to today's readers. They might retort that anyone who identifies with Confucian civilization can be considered Chinese, isn't this definition too boundless and rampant? Are those ancient Chinese regimes that do not adhere to Confucian culture such as Qin, Yuan and Qing Dynasties still China? Not to mention after the Republican era, Confucianism has lost its official guiding position. Is China still called China? This is certainly a valid question.

All in all, China as a civilization is a dedicated name, which represents social entities taking Confucian culture as their core. It can be abbreviated to a formula: China is a nation of Confucian culture. Without Confucian culture, China cannot be called China.

1.2.3 China as a Political Entity

In fact, it is not unreasonable for people today to question whether "China" is a political concept or a type of civilization. Feudal dynasties served as political entities. They had their own dynasty name respectively. Some was called Xia, Shang and Zhou.

Some was called Qin, Han, Sui and Tang. Some was called Song, Yuan, Ming and Qing. Therefore, there were Qin State and the Great Han State, and the Great Tang State and the Great Song State. However, there was no dynasty called China at that time. Although they often refer to themselves as "China", they only declare that they inherit the tradition, rule the country in obedience to the Confucian cultural system, and commit themselves to the civilized goals of Confucian culture such as the rule of Great harmony. Confucianism culture is their imperial ideology and the cultural tool they use to establish the legitimacy of their rule. just as in medieval Christian countries that did not respect the Bible and thus lost cultural legitimacy. It was a very serious matter.

Of course, this situation gradually changed in the seventeenth century. It was not until Ming and Qing Dynasties, missionaries from the west began to call the dynasty another name in their private writings and letters. They call this dynasty as "the Chinese Empire" or "China". This was no more Confucian China. It was no more China as a civilization. Instead, it refers to modern sovereign state. But it only limited to ordinary people.

On September 7th, 1689, Emperor Kangxi dispatched Suo Etu to sign a diplomatic treaty with Russia. In this treaty named *Sino-Russian Treaty of Nibuchu*, "China" was used to represent Qing Dynasty for the first time. That is to say, until in the late 17th century, the word "China" was officially accepted to be synonymous with sovereign state and has been followed so far. As we can see in the *Man Han Meng Textbooks* used in late Qing Dynasty. The book says "China is located in the east of Asia; Chinese culture is passed from generations to generations. I am a Chinese, so how can I not love China?"

So far, It originally means China as a geographic space in the Yellow River basin. Later it became China as a civilization representing Confucian culture type. Finally, it developed into China as a political entity representing sovereign state. China realizes the changes from Country to Civilization, and then to State. The concept of "China" truly realizes the unity of the whole geographical China, civilized China and political China. Today, China is the abbreviation of a sovereign state. Its full name is the People's Republic of China.

There are still two points that I want to call your attention.

Firstly, Contemporary China is indeed a "civilizational state" （文明型国家）

carrying forward the past and opening up the future.

Contemporary political China, namely the People's Republic of China as a sovereign state, is indeed a "civilizational state", as Professor Zhang Weiwei of Fudan University put it. The notion of "civilizational state" is different from the concept of "civilization-state" (文明国家), which has a narrow Confucian identity at its core. Contemporary political China is standing in a new era, integrating "geographical China" and "civilization-China". "It's a country where an ancient civilization that stretches for thousands of years almost coincides with a super large modern state, namely China." In contemporary China, under the guidance of the Thought on Socialism with Chinese Characteristics for a New Era, fine traditional culture (including Confucianism) has been innovatively transformed and developed. China has a super large population, a super vast territory, a super long historical tradition, a super deep cultural accumulation, a unique language, a unique society, a unique economy and a unique politics, which all mark that China, as a civilizational state, is ushering in the boundless future of national rejuvenation. The "Chinese culture" discussed in the course is based on the territory space of the People's Republic of China as a "civilizational state" (rather than "civilization-state") to explore and study the cultural life phenomenon in its history. It doesn't matter whether it belongs to Confucius culture in narrow sense.

Secondly, we should avoid the "Centrism of Han nationality's Civilization".

Because the Central Plains was never the center of the world. And the Confucian culture of Han people cannot completely represent the whole cultural landscape of China, or the long history of the whole Chinese civilization. We shouldn't limit to culture of the Han nationality, but also look at the culture of the whole country and all ethnic minorities in all regions. They are the multidimensional source of the pluralistic, integrated Chinese civilization. When we talk about "Chinese culture", we must make it clear that it refers to all the achievements of civilization created and accumulated by the pluralistic and integrated Chinese nation in the historical process of understanding and transforming nature, society and the nation itself on the land of China. It reflects the unique ways of thinking of Chinese people. as well as our lifestyles, and value pursuits. Only by highlighting the valuable contributions of the 56 ethnic groups to Chinese culture can we fully and accurately understand the profound characteristics and unique qualities of Chinese culture, build a good spiritual home for all ethnic groups in

China, and build a solid ideological foundation for the Chinese people to forge ahead in unity. It must be made clear that the history and culture of all ethnic groups included in the current Chinese territory should be regarded as the content of "Chinese history" and "Chinese cultural history".

1.3　The Ways of Learning Chinese Culture

Chinese culture goes back to ancient times. It has a history of more than 6000 years since the Painted Pottery Culture, forming the most abundant culture accumulation in the world. We can't cover everything, so we will focus on the traditional Chinese culture before the Opium War (1840).

For Chinese college students and overseas ones, learning Chinese culture is a basic process of humanistic quality education. Our course has a great aim. That is, to spread the basic knowledge of Chinese culture, to share the spiritual values of Chinese civilization, and to help people better understand the traditional and contemporary Chinese culture. By doing so, people's feelings and recognition of Chinese civilization can be enhanced. Exchanges and mutual learning among civilizations can be promoted.

As a practice-based course with rich knowledge and theories, it requires students to pay attention to the following methodologies when studying.

(1) Students should Combine Sincere Respect with Scrupulous Reason

Why studying Chinese culture needs a sense of respect? Because culture is life, and life can be seen in culture. All the tangible and intangible cultural heritage remained is valuable. So are those spiritual cultural products. They are the fruits of painstaking efforts of generations. Most of them are not renewable or replicable. They are very precious, fragile, and vulnerable to wars, fires, water disasters and biological moths. For example, the Summer Palace in Beijing was destroyed by war and looting. Many cultural relics, statues and murals in the Mogao Grottoes in Dunhuang were stolen. The 1500-year-old Bamiyan Buddhas is a world cultural heritage site. And it was bombed and destroyed. And so on. Blaise Pascal once made a remark. "Today, even God cannot create another form of the Athenian Pillar. Only the authentic and original deserves our respect. " Therefore, we advocate that the traditional culture should be treated as the elderly and the weak. We need to love and admire them. And we need to gaze at and care for them. Any overbearing cultural chauvinism is not acceptable. Nor the nihilistic attitude of self-delusion and lack of cultural confidence in national culture. We cannot hold these kinds of attitudes.

Of course, having the sense of respect is not enough. It is more important to hold a practical and realistic attitude. This kind of attitude is needed when studying the extensive and profound Chinese culture. We should adopt the method of both historical and logical analysis. The method of historical analysis takes time as its clue. It aims to carry out a longitudinal study of Chinese culture, so, as to find out the ins and outs of Chinese culture. The method of logical analysis takes questions as its clue. It aims to conduct cross-sectional research of Chinese culture, in order to make clear the internal logical cause and effect of Chinese culture. This course is not intended to be exhaustive, underlain by cultural spirit and characteristics of the Chinese nation, we cut the complexity and simplify it, and select ten topics. We will introduce them in order, and hope to achieve the unity of history and logic.

(2) We should Combine the Study of Ancient Literature with Social Investigation

When learning this course, we should adopt the method of reading and studying excellent Chinese classics, and regard it as an essential one. China has a vast collection of classics, which records the magnificent process of the Chinese people in creating Chinese civilization. Reading these classics is also an indispensable way to understand Chinese culture. Of course, we can't expect to understand every book we read, but some basic books should be covered in learning. The famous Chinese scholar Qian Mu once recommended seven books that all Chinese people should read. They are *the Analects of Confucius*, *The Mencius*, *Tao Te Ching*, *the Chuang Tzu*, *The Platform Scripture*, *Reflections on Things at Hand*, and *Chuan Hsi Lu* (or *Record of Instructions*). Of course, it is also a bibliography that overseas students who are interested in mastering Chinese cultural knowledge should read. Here is the bibliography of our course. We believe that they are helpful for better understanding this course. Two of them are most noteworthy: *The Essence of Chinese Culture* by Liang Shuming, and *Eternal Rivers* by Xu Zhuoyun.

In addition to reading books, there is an essential way to learn Chinese culture. That is, to conduct social investigation. Students should visit various cultural sites such as museums, historical spots and parks of ancient ruins and so on. In this way, they can be directly edified by the ancient Chinese culture. Our course, primarily for overseas graduate students of Huaqiao University, *An Introduction to Chinese Culture*, is a good example. During the whole semester, as least one third of classes will be spent going out and doing field works. Overseas students will be divided into project teams to make preparations respectively. They will visit the ancient villages, ancestral halls, ancient temples, and academies as well as other cultural sites in southwest Fujian, to come into close contact with the traditional village society, to feel the traditional patriarchal clan system and religious thoughts, to experience the traditional ethical life and educational practice, to perceive the historical process of exchanges and mutual learning between Chinese and foreign civilizations. This close-to-life observation method enables students to gain real experience. It breaks away from the conventional pattern of theory teaching. So, it is warmly and sincerely welcomed by students. Of course, if you don't have the opportunity and ability to go out for social investigation, you should also pay attention to various mass media such as TV, magazines, micro-blogs, and video websites. What they introduce about Chinese culture is worth your attention.

(3) We need to Combine Critical Thinking with Creative Thinking

Chinese traditional culture is all-encompassing. It has rich and complex connotations. And it is the unity of oppositeness between uniformity and diversity, continuity and revolution, independence and integration, essence and dross. In particular, in regard of those elements in the traditional culture that include dross and essence, we should be apt at sublating dialectically. Based on the requirements of the development of our times, we should inherit those cultural elements critically, and develop them innovatively. As for those backward feudal dross in the traditional culture, namely, "subculture", we should hold a thorough attitude of criticizing and discarding. While as for the excellent heritage of the traditional culture, namely, the excellent traditional Chinese culture, we must inherit and promote it earnestly, and actively share it with the contemporary world. We should face the future. and develop prosperous and fresh Chinese culture. This must be the significance of China as a civilization.

(4) We need to Blend with and Learn from Each Other

President Xi Jinping once pointed out a view: "Diversity spurs interaction among civilizations, which in turn promotes mutual learning and further development."

The world is a community with a shared destiny. In history, between Chinese and foreign civilizations, there have been many vivid stories of foreign exchanges and mutual learning. Today, it is of importance for us to uphold this vision of mutual learning, to be aware that the world is a community with a shared destiny. We need to stay open and inclusive and strive for harmony but not sameness. We need to respect the beauty of each civilization and the diversity of civilizations in the world. Both discrimination and criticism appear in cultural exchanges. But people are benefited from the warm and friendly exchanges. Thus, we can maximize favorable factors and minimize unfavorable ones. We can work together for nations and all mankind. And bring them a brighter future of culture.

第二讲

泱泱中华
——中国文化的基本特征

中国传统文化历久流传、气象万千。我们该从何处着手来研究它呢？我认为，由表及里、循序渐进是一个基础的方法。就如我们日常生活中看一个人，或观察一个事物，总是要先把握他（它）们表现出的特点或气质，然后渐进深入。也就是说，我们可以就中国文化外在的基本特征先作一把握，而后以此为基础，进一步去探求里面一以贯之的文化精神。

2.1 关于中国文化的特征研究

那么中国文化的基本特征是什么呢？所谓中国文化基本特征，即其历史地表现出来的与其他国家和民族的文化相区别的、独具特色的文化特性或气质。既然"文化是生活的一切内容无所不包的整体"，所谓文化的基本特征，则必定有很多不同的概括方式和结论。可以总体而宏观地看，也可以具体而微地看。完全取决于被考察的文化内容与对象而定。当然，也取决于研究者的知识构成与使用的学术方法①。

我们认为，一方面就总体特征上看，中国文化作为一个巨系统，当然会有一些比较明显的要点。比如梁漱溟先生在他的《中国文化要义》一书首章即提出了他对中国文化的总体个性的看法，其义有七：（1）原创性，即土生土长，非依他而有。（2）体系性：即独立成套、自成体系。（3）延续性，即历史延续、传承不绝。（4）同化性，即对内外诸种文化有融合同化的力量。（5）广大性，

---

① 有的学者选择从衣食住行婚丧节庆等各类生活内容做文化特征研究，有的学者则认为"物质文化、制度文化等方面的特质，固然也能甚而更能广泛地反映文化的民族性，但较之精神方面的特质，它就显得不那么集中、深刻"（李宗桂：中国文化概论［M］. 广州：中山大学出版社，1988：30.），因而他们更偏好从意识形态或精神文化的角度去概括中国文化的类型特征。

即它综罗万象而成其大。（6）早熟性，即理性早启、成熟不变。（7）辐射性，即有对外的文化传播与影响力①。

对梁先生上述判断，我们大概无以反对，国内学界似乎也大多持论如此。但这并不是说他的概括并非无可商榷。如对所谓中华文明的"原（独）创性""延续性"的判断上，西方汉学界就一直有质疑的声音。在这个质疑的声音里，1894 年英国伦敦大学教授、法国人拉克伯里（Lacouperie）发表的《中国上古文明的西方起源》（*Western Origin of the Early Chinese civilization*）是个代表。该书首倡"中国文明西来"之说。比如中国的人文始祖"黄帝"是来自巴比伦巴克族的 NaiHwangti、中国的八卦来自楔形文字等，通过中国文明与巴比伦文明有近百处相似点证明中国上古文明来自西亚。他这一观点经蒋智由的《中国人种考》介绍到国内引起轩然大波，并得到章太炎、刘师培等国学家的欣赏与支持。另外，"仰韶文化之父"、瑞典地质学家安特生（Johan Gunnar Andersson，1874—1960）也持有中国史前（前 21 世纪）彩陶文化与中亚、东欧史前彩陶相似之说。

"中华文明来源"的问题涉及中华文明是否具有独立性、原创性，事关中华民族的历史自信与文化自信，所以不纯粹是一件学术公案。但学术是科学事业，并非思想家在书斋里检阅文献典籍和上古传说可以完成，而全赖乎考古学用文物证据来说话。为了实证五千年中华文明的独立性和悠久性，二十世纪以来的中国考古界学人筚路蓝缕辛勤耕耘，一直在努力地以科学的精神推进这方面的实证研究。包括我们知道的山东济南城子崖文化遗址（龙山文化）和河南安阳殷墟的考古发掘（1928），就以中国本土文化史前时代的遗物证据，有力地反驳了当时流行的中国的"人和文化都是自西方输入的"错误观点。

这里必须提到于 2002 年立项启动的中华文明探源工程（全称"中华文明起源与早期发展综合研究"）②。这是一项由国家支持的，从多学科、多角度、多层次、全方位地研究中华文明的起源、形成与早期发展问题的国家级学术工程。该工程经过 20 年（分五阶段）的深入研究，在近 400 位学者的共同参与下，取得了大量以确凿的考古资料支撑的学术成果，宣告了中国有真实可信的百万年

---

① 梁漱溟.中国文化要义［M］.上海：上海人民出版社，2018：10–11.
② 见"中华文明起源与早期发展综合研究"（简称"中华文明探源工程"）成果发布会。［EB/OL］. http://www.scio.gov.cn/xwfbh/xwbfbh/wqfbh/37601/38374/index.htm；也可以参看韩建业著《中华文明的早期起源》（中国社会科学出版社 2021 年版。该书中华文明起源方面的考古学研究论文和普及性文章共 28 篇，从多个方面论述了中华文明起源、形成和早期发展的过程。

的人口史、一万年的文化史，五千年的文明史；证明了中华文明是一个土生土长的文明，既多元一体地融汇了中华大地诸多区域性史前文明的成果，又动态吸收了西亚等外来文明的元素。这个关于中华文明的起源和早期发展是一个多元一体的过程的论断，当然也可以看成是对梁漱溟先生早年观点的 21 世纪的论据支持。

又如梁漱溟先生主张"自来公认中国、印度、西洋并列为世界三大文化系统者，实以其差异特大而自成体系之故。"此处论及的是文明系统的划分问题。同时，他还认为中华文化辐射影响及于东亚，日本文化实无独立性和主体性。而反观国际学术界对文明类型的讨论，多有持"五大文明发源地"论者，费正清教授甚至提出"二十三个文明区域"说。在所谓"八大文明类型说"中，塞缪尔·亨廷顿则把日本文化作为"世界八大文明类型之一"。这种把日本文化当作一种文明类型并独立于东亚儒学文化圈（或中华文明圈）的观点显然与梁先生的提法大异其趣，是否妥当，兹不展开。

相对于对文化做总体性判断难免于"宏大叙事"的抽象空疏的流弊，选择从文化生活的具体领域入手并提炼其基本特征倒显得更切实际一点。梁漱溟先生在他的书里就讨论了中国文化所具有的十四个方面的特征。包括：中国有广土众民；偌大民族之同化融合；历史悠久并世中莫与之比；既有伟力以成之又不能确指其为何；历久不变的社会，停滞不进的文化；几乎没有宗教；家族制度在整个文化中根深蒂固；学术不向着科学前进；民主、自由、平等一类要求不见提出，法制不见形成；道德气氛特重；中国不属于普通国家类型；无兵的文化；孝的文化；隐士的文化。

我们注意到，梁先生选择说明的大概属于：疆域与人口、民族融合、历史传续、发展原因、社会状况、宗教信仰、家族制度、学术与科学、政法思想、道德氛围、国家类型、军事、孝道与隐士方面。应该说，这里的讨论当然都是局部而具体的，都是研究中国的社会文化所不能绕开的重要领域。有一类文化对象即可有一种文化的特征，细分起来，则可以有无数个。总体离不开局部，微观可以上达宏观。但实际上，任何学者都不可能无所不通。梁漱溟先生也说他只是就他有研究的领域发表他的看法。在《中国问题》（*The Problem Of China*）一书中，英国哲学家罗素（Bertrand Russell）就仅从汉字、行为准则和文官制度三个角度去概括中国文化的特征。他认为：（1）使用表意文字，不用字母；（2）受教育阶层修习儒家伦理，不信教；（3）科举取士，而非世袭贵族当政。罗素的这三点概括比较梁漱溟的十四个方面的讨论，是不是少了点呢？但这就是罗素观察和理解中国文化特征问题的视角及其得出的结论，也就是他所谓的"中国传统文化大致具有某些方面的特征，成就了特殊品格……最重要的三个特征"①。

文化生活丰富浩瀚，需要大批做具体而微研究的专家，这比较于疏空高蹈的谈中国文化的总体特性，似乎更应该被我们肯定。当然，今天这个时代"知识家凸显，思想家淡出"也成了一个问题。我们不能陷入文化的细节主义而失去从总体性高度洞察文化的深刻本质与根本精神的悟性与思想力。下面，我们试图综合学界的意见，同时结合自己的理解，谈谈中国文化在"多元融合""文明结构""经济类型""社群组织""政治理念""信仰状况"和"学术倾向"七个视野下所展示的重要特性与基本品格。中国文化的特征当然不止于这些，这里先提出来，当然是非论证的、纲要式的略说，具体的说明放在第四到第十章来展开。

2.2　满天星斗、众川归海的多元一体性

从文明的总体结构方式而言，中华文明最大最重要的特征，就是满天星斗、众川归海的多元一体性。正如习近平总书记指出的，"中华民族多元一体是先人们留给我们的丰厚遗产，也是我国发展的巨大优势"②。

"多元一体"的概念指的是中华文明不是单一的、孤立的文明，而是多元、多维的文化群在动态融合中构成的统一的文化生机体。它的特点不是强迫性的外在、暂时的结合，而是合规律的、自然形成从而可长可久的、内在的结合。这是整体与局部在水乳交融中生成的、有着强韧的生机性的一体。要理解多元一体的中华文明的特点，首先要通观中华大视野下的不同地域、不同民族、不同文化类型之间的交往、交流、交融。中华文明的演进过程实际上就是多种文明互补、逐渐相融并整合为一体的过程。

在上一讲中我们已经强调要避免中原（汉族）文明中心论或唯一论。中原华夏族的文化形态并不能完全代表整个中国（尤其是文明早期）的整个文化生态。要了解中华文明的早期起源，我们应该放眼黄河流域、长江流域和西辽河流域，放眼全国诸多的地区性文明遗址，如西北的齐家文化、东北的红山文化、北方的石峁遗址、东方的两城镇遗址、西南的金沙与三星堆遗址、中南的石家

---

① ［英］伯特兰·罗素. 中国问题［M］. 北京：中国画报出版社，2019：32.
② 习近平. 在全国民族团结进步表彰大会上的讲话［N］. 人民日报，2019-09-28（02）.

河遗址、东南的良渚遗址等。目前，我国已发现新石器时代文化遗址多达 7000
多处，已被命名为考古学文化的有几十种，并呈现出几个较大的系统和中心。
它们所包含的丰富灿烂的文明元素和文化信息，令人震惊和感动。区域性文明
彼起此伏、聚散存亡，历经长期的交流互动连锁形成一个更大的文化相互作用
圈（sphere of interaction）。其所孕育出的共同文化积淀、心理认同、礼制传统，
奠定了中华文明绵延发展的基础，并汇聚到了黄河流域和中原地区（河南洛阳
偃师的二里头遗址），这就是夏、商、周文明。

　　夏、商、周三代出现了青铜器、文字、大型城垣、礼仪中心等为代表的国
家文明要素，开启了中国王朝的文明时代。可以说，夏、商、周三代，本身就
是早期文明（甚至中外文明）多维信息的集大成者。它们一脉相承、损益相继，
是中华文明正式形成的标志和传续不绝的起点。以殷商文化来说，其本身的来
源也很复杂，有一部分显然受过西方的影响，一部分来自南亚，如水牛、稻米
及一些艺术。但文字、骨卜、龟卜、蚕丝业及一部分的农业和陶业及其雕刻技
术，又完全是在中国至少是东亚创始并发展的。"殷商文化只是把这些成分调和
起来，加了一个强有力的表现。"[①]

　　而三代以降，中国文化漫长的发展史上，这种一体多元的融构进程也与时
俱进，并在各方面得到了充分的表现。比如中华大地孕育了泱泱中华民族，这
是一体。而中华民族又是由各个民族经历五次大融合而形成的民族共同体。各
个民族当然各有其鲜明的文化个性与特色，但又都不是纯粹而单一的，而是彼
此之间在物态文化—制度文化—行为文化—心态文化的各个层次、各个领域中
兼收并蓄，就如石榴结实，籽籽相附。各民族兄弟共同开拓和保护了中华疆域、
创造了中华人文历史，共创了中华共有精神家园，熔铸了中华文明的璀璨光华。

　　而且我必须指出，这里所谓的"一体多元"，不仅是中华民族的总体结构，
也是中华民族内部各民族、各地域、各领域的文化生态普遍的构成规律。

　　以节日习俗为例而言。中华民族的各兄弟民族在节日习俗上，形成了许多
相同或相近的节俗现象。例如，年节不仅是汉族的传统隆重节日，同样也是其
他少数民族的传统隆重节日，并且在年节的时间计算上，汉族与蒙古族、满族、
朝鲜族、壮族、赫哲族、鄂伦春族、锡伯族、畲族、黎族、景颇族、拉祜族等
几乎完全相同。虽然其他许多少数民族在年节时间上也有差异，但是几乎所有
兄弟民族在年节活动内容中，大都包含着庆贺丰收、祈祷幸福、祭神祀祖、团

---

① 李济．殷墟铜器五种及其相关之问题：庆祝蔡元培先生六十五岁论文集［C］．广州：
　　"中央研究院"历史语言研究所，1933：73-104.

聚亲友、珍惜光阴、娱乐生活等这些共同性的意义。在年节活动方式上，如家人团聚、守岁、品尝美酒佳肴、举行拜年串亲活动等，也都大致相同。

如各民族共有的文化习俗中都有敬祖祭祖的文化传统。论根源，这都是从氏族时代的原始信仰中遗传下来的祖灵崇拜，这是共同的一点。但比较各民族祖先崇拜的具体内容和方式上，如祭祀的对象，少数民族崇拜的多是图腾始祖（兼有人文始祖），而汉族崇拜的多是人文始祖，尤其是历代血亲先辈祖宗。大部分少数民族没有汉族式规制严密、层级秩然的祠堂祭祀场所、无宗族族谱文献。另外，在祭祀时间、仪式与程序、主持人、有无相应的纪念性节日等方面，差别甚大。这是中国信仰文化中围绕祖灵崇拜表现的多元的一体。

又如由住房和城乡建设部牵头拍摄，已于 2022 年 1 月首播的大型 4K 纪录片《中国传统建筑的智慧》通过传统建筑居住者、使用者、改造者的故事，介绍了中国的传统建筑类型如庭院式建筑、干栏式建筑、厅井式建筑、围屋式建筑、窑洞民居、碉房民居、临时幕篷居所、祠堂和古村落、古镇。中华地域性建筑的多类型，既表现了内在形式的统一，体现着中华建筑文明的持久性和一致性；又体现了中华建筑文化的多样性和丰富的地区差异，体现着中华民族的生活智慧。

这方面的实例我们还可以举很多，兹不赘述。

多元一体是中华文明从起源、形成、发展至今的全过程一以贯之、令人印象深刻的根本特征，也是与世界各地的文化或文明类型最大的不同。从某些方面看，我们都一样，所以我们是一体。从某些方面看，我们又很不一样，所以我们是多元。"多元一体"的中华文化格局中，"多元"是前提和基础，"一体"是由"多元"长期碰撞、融合而来的，各文化因子和元素是中华文化大系统中的众多子系统。今日生机盎然的中华文化，是诸地域、诸民族的共同创造，是文化的"多"与"一"互动的结果。多元一体的中华文化"道并行而不相悖，万物并育而不相害"，所以我们生生不息传承不衰。

2.3　强同化力加持的文化生机性

对中国文化具有强大的生命力这一点，大概有争议的不多吧。

世界各大文明古国如潮起潮落，其早起而早衰者史不绝书。美国学者马修·梅尔科总结了人类 12 种古文明中已经消亡的 7 类文明：美索不达美亚文明、埃及文明、克里特文明、古典文明、拜占庭文明、中美洲文明、安第斯文明。唯有中华文明虽多经艰苦，屡遭危机，终能化险为夷，不废江河万古流。几千年来，中国人的文字、语法、思维逻辑和世界观，几乎就没有变化。某种意义上，今天的中国人还跟祖先们过着同一种生活，原因何在？这不能不说是一个令人深感疑惑的问题。

中国台湾学者韦政通先生在《论中国文化的十大特征》文中介绍并分析了几种可能的原因：重视现实生活的维持、保守、重视多子多孙、重视地理环境的保护、农业生活（恒久意识）的影响、国民性的世故圆滑而坚韧耐久，以及中国文化"重统绪"和"求久"的思想①。张岱年、方克立两先生主编的《中国文化概论》教科书则提出，中华文化强大的生命力来自：同化力（Assimilation）、融合力和凝聚力的三力合一。我们认为"同化融合说"是一个比较有深度的解释，它揭示了中华文明悠久的生机性的根源。

谈到中国文化强大的同化力，马丁·雅克先生开过一个玩笑，他说："如果我再多去几次中国，可能就变成一个英国籍的中国人，所以不要试图去同化中国人，因为首先你会被同化。"比如貌似现在中国的孩子们也喜欢看漫威系列电影，也联机玩手机游戏，也吃肯德基。但大家发现没有：肯德基从志在"改变中国人的饮食习惯"，到最后却不得不"迎合中国人的饮食习惯"——卖起了米粥、油条加豆浆。说不定以后会卖 KFC 豆腐脑、KFC 烧卖、KFC 饺子、KFC 火锅。这种西方餐饮的中国化蜕变，就是当代中国文化同化力的某种表现。又如西方的愚人节或圣诞节，在中国都变了味、走了样。宗教性的节日，成了"一个快乐的理由"或者，商家的营销手段。

中国文化的同化力何以如此之强，学者们早有深入探讨，如梁启超先生分析了中国历史上的"强迫同化"和"自然同化"之间的差别，并从多方面探讨了历史上汉族文化所表现出的强"同化力"的原因问题。梁先生的大意是：（1）主干文化的涵盖性影响使得栖息于此间者被其涵盖，难别成风气；（2）象形文字为诸族共用以传达思想，同文条件下渐化成一族；（3）华族以平天下为理想，以柔怀远，不排外而喜纳新；（4）地广人稀，能容纳各族迁徙安置而增其交感化合作用；（5）华族爱和平道中庸，对他族的习俗表示尊重，故渐柔以化；（6）华族坚信同姓不婚，故与他族通婚盛行，遂同化彼此；（7）华族经济发达外向进取，而新入分子于经济组织上被同化；（8）战争导致的主客异位，北族虽进而为熏染，汉族南迁亦播道于南。②

---

① 韦政通. 韦政通自选集［M］. 济南：山东教育出版社，2004：62-65.

② 梁启超. 饮冰室文集［M］. 北京：中华书局，1989：3230.

若以梁先生所言的八方面原因而论之，结果就很清楚了：一则外来的异域文明的元素被借鉴融合，二则内部各民族、各地域的文化又被融摄同构，逐渐形成多元一体的生机性的文化共同体，而生活在这个共同体中的各民族，对这个文化生命体有心理上的强烈的认同感、向心力和凝聚意识。借此，中国文化剪不断、打不散、海纳百川、历久弥新、生生不息。

正如习近平主席 2019 年 9 月 27 日在全国民族团结进步表彰大会上指出的："一部中国史，就是一部各民族交融汇聚成多元一体中华民族的历史，就是各民族共同缔造、发展、巩固统一的伟大祖国的历史。各民族之所以团结融合，多元之所以聚为一体，源自各民族文化上的兼收并蓄、经济上的相互依存、情感上的相互亲近，源自中华民族追求团结统一的内生动力。正因为如此，中华文明才具有无与伦比的包容性和吸纳力，才可久可大、根深叶茂"。习近平总书记这一重要论述，是对中国历史的高度浓缩，是对中华文明特征的高度凝练，具有重要的指导意义。

对中华文化何以能有强大的同化力的问题，还有一些有趣的解读方式。在第四讲《多元一体——中华民族与中华文化》中，我们再来详解之，这里先指出有此一特征即可。

2.4　情系田园的农业国民性

从经济类型的角度看，中国文化具有典型的农业文化特征。

早在七千年前，中国黄河流域和长江流域就孕育了早期的农耕文明。数千年来以农为主，又以工补耕、以商助农的自然经济生活，是中国传统社会主要的经济形态和物质基础，也从心态上、思想上和生活方式上铸就了中国文化农业型物态和心理特征。一代代中国农人为中华民族的文化基因里，融入了浓厚的农业国民性和农人精神、土地情怀。表现在：

（1）内敛敏感、务实勤俭的精神

中国的农民，北麦南稻，却共享了一种质朴、务实、勤俭以及内敛和平的农人精神。与逐水草而居的草原游牧民族的雄强豪迈、流动拓进的特点不同，农人们敬畏天命、热爱土地。他们日出而作、日落而息；他们勤于生业、崇尚节俭；他们老实、踏实、务实、朴实、实诚厚道。他们热衷于开垦土地，如广西龙胜梯田、湘西紫鹊界梯田、云南哈尼梯田、福建三明尤溪梯田，都是一代代各族人民自强不息以开创家园的见证。农人最渴望五谷丰登、六畜兴旺，他们是土地和劳动的信徒。"一分耕耘，一分收获"就是他们的第一信条，乃至他们今天的子孙后代都仍以种菜为乐事，人走到哪，菜就种到哪儿。有人开玩笑说：给英国人一块土地，英国人就能弄出一座花园来。给中国人一块土地，中国人就能给你整出一块菜园来。于是，当代中国人的菜，种到了泰国，种到了非洲，甚至，种到了北极。

图 2-1　农人是真正的大地之子

（2）安土重迁的田园情结与乡愁情趣

提到美食博主李子柒，大家一定不会陌生。这位美丽的四川姑娘以她自制美食为主要内容的视频节目征服了无数观众的心。李子柒的视频，画面宁静唯美、屋檐雨落、灶火炊烟，她肩背枯柴、手推碾磨，一种浓浓的农家烟火气，让人联想起孟浩然"开轩面场圃，把酒话桑麻"、陶渊明"种豆南山下，草盛豆苗稀"诗句中的田园情趣。人们喜欢李子柒的视频，说到底是它兴起了我们每个人骨子里沉淀的农人幽思和遥远的乡愁意识。

中华民族感恩天地、热爱家园。他们安土乐天、安土重迁，注重落叶归根，这种农业国民性，也可叫"田园情结"。田园情结，表现为中华民族挥之不去、萦绕心头的特别眷恋田园的乡愁情趣与自然情怀。中国的诗人们也把这份浓浓的乡愁写进他们的文字。比如李白的"举头望明月，低头思故乡"；杜甫的"露从今夜白，月是故乡明"；王维的"独在异乡为异客，每逢佳节倍思亲"，皆传唱后世，处处是知音。中国人无论走多远，心心所系的，还是自己梦里的家乡，即使自己从未踏足过那个祖先们生活过的土地。正如南洋华侨的坟茔区（如新加坡的咖啡园和马六甲的三宝园）的墓碑上，都写着墓主的中国祖籍地信息。而移民欧美的苗族同胞，他们仍然聚族而居，讲苗语、吹芦笙、穿苗族服饰。老人去世，还会请道公作法事、念"渡亡经"，超度亡灵回到中国西南部的老家与他们历代的祖先灵魂团聚一处。

（3）追求天长地久的恒久意识与和平稳定的观念

田园情结浓厚的中国农人是大地之子，他们崇尚自然敬畏天地，并感悟到青山不改、绿水长流，也渴望子孙不绝、万代恒昌，所谓"前人种树，后人乘凉""细水长流，细吃长有"。这种恒久意识其实是同信仰和追求"祖德流芳远，宗功世泽长"的中国宗族文化结合在一起的。宗族村落的民众奉行"不孝有三，无后为大"的孝道思想。他们上求光耀祖宗，下愿无愧于子孙，光前裕后是他们艰苦奋斗、追求事业成就的不竭动力。这种天长地久有时尽，人生代代无穷已的历史超越意识也被理解为中国传统文化得以悠久延续的重要原因之一。

与求长久的意识相应的，就是中国农民的求稳定的和平性格。农业文明的特点之一是定居生活，农业生产较稳定的收入使他们并不羡慕游牧和商业所产生的高额利润，因为它们同样存在着高风险。"三十亩地一头牛，老婆孩子热炕头"是一般农民的理想。他们满足于土地和自然的赐予，由于小生产的限制，对外部世界不感兴趣，缺乏探险的好奇和对外扩张的贪欲，修建长城便是证明，因为长城是防御的屏障而非扩张的利器。中国人崇尚和平主义，他们以耕读传家为本，视穷兵黩武为戒。和谐稳定的生活方式，生成了中国人乐天知命的性格。他们很少有大喜大悲的失态，崇尚克制和含蓄。

（4）悠久的农业文化传统留下了丰富的农业类物质与非物质文化遗产

在中国广袤的土地上，充满智慧的中国先民创造并留下了大量的、至今仍在造福子孙后代的农业类物质与非物质文化遗产，这是中华民族奉献给人类文明宝库的珍贵财富。截至目前，中国已有 19 项"世界灌溉工程遗产"，如被誉为灌溉文明"活化石"的浙江诸暨桔槔井；"山有多高，田有多高，水就有多高"的湖南新化县紫鹊界梯田；"无坝引水，水旱从人"的四川都江堰等；"多沙河流引水灌溉的典范"——内蒙古河套灌区等。中国入选"全球重要农业文化遗产"项目也多达 18 项，数量居世界首位。

而中国南北各地也保留了成百上千的古村、古镇，如世界文化遗产、徽州的宏村和西递，江西省吉安市钓源古村，福建省龙岩永定洪坑村，浙江省建德市大慈岩镇新叶村……这些村镇古色古香，存留了农耕时代的宝贵而丰富历史文化信息，可以让今天的我们仍有机会去近距离感受那个失落的梦里老家、心灵的故乡。

中华民族有大量的农业类节庆民俗文化，如汉族的春秋祭社；布依族的尝新节杀鸡焚香祭田神；藏族开耕节上举行"二牛抬杠"竞奔与洒青稞酒仪式；侗族牛王节时为耕牛们披红挂彩、喂糯米饭；彝族在作物收割后举办火把节；

西盟佤族则在新米节上开展叫谷魂、祭谷神的活动。这些祈福与庆丰收并融的节庆活动都热闹欢快，洋溢着大地之子跟自然母亲之间和谐一体的美好关系。

这是一片生机勃勃的土地。希望在田野上。希望在中国人民与时俱进日地保养和发展好这份深厚而珍贵的农业国民性上。

2.5　尊祖重族的文化宗族性

从社会结构方式看，中国文化有以家族为本位的村落宗族文化特征。中国社会上下几千年，宗族文化与家族制度是其中一以贯之的重要线索，是中国传统社会结构中最特殊的构成部分。

从原始社会氏族时代以来，人类最主要的居住方式是"聚族而居"，也就是以血亲家庭为基本单位组织去人和人的社会结构。同时，这种聚族而居的血亲群落，又传承和强调了对祖先的崇拜和对祖灵的祭祀这样一种文化价值观念。这两个特点，在人类许多国家和民族中是有共通性的传统生活方式和信仰类型。但是，与西方社会相比较，中国传统的家族文化又更加不同。它以儒家"尊祖重族"的宗法文化思想为指导，重人伦、孝父母、敬祖宗、建祠堂、编族谱、祭祖先、设义田，以及讲究家族伦理、注重家族教育和传承良好家风，从而达到维护家族的团结和人心凝聚，实现家族共同体生生不息的长远发展。

德国著名学者马克斯·韦伯曾从社会学的角度把 20 世纪 20 年代之前的中国社会特征概括为"家族结构式的社会"。如其所言，中国传统社会结构中最大的特色，是以家庭为社会活动的中心。某种意义上，传统村落中国人，日出而作日落而息，但知有家族和乡里，（几乎）不知有国家天下。除了家族生活外，没有公共政治生活。中国人最珍惜的还是家人之爱和宗族之情，这里寄托了他们几乎全部的人生意义和幸福感。

学者金耀基则分析指出：

中国传统社会的结构中最重要而特殊的是家族制度。中国的家是社会的核心。它是一"紧紧结合的团体"，并且是建构化了的，整个社会价值系统都经由家的"育化"与"社化"作用以传递给个人。[①]

直至今天，在中国各地尤其是南方许多省份，仍然较为完好地保持了村落宗族文化的传统和生活习惯。在我工作的福建，在闽南、闽西、闽北各处的山

---

① 金耀基. 从传统到现代［M］. 北京：中国人民大学出版社，1999：24.

区村镇，我们都能看到许多以姓氏宗族聚族而居的村落，那里有信仰着敬天法祖、亲亲尊尊传统伦理的朴实村民，有数百年传承的明清古祠堂，不绝于缕的祭祖的香火，连接着今人和祖先，似乎也融通了过去与未来。一套套族谱记录着完整的家族世系的线索，一页页翻动的不仅仅是历史，更是连绵无尽的生命精神。在我看来，传统的宗族文化算得上是一种通过家族生命的历史链接而帮助人们完成自我生命的超越与净化的特殊方式。所以它是伦理，是宗教，也是一种美学。

另外，必须注意的是，中国各地少数民族的信仰文化中普遍的有祖先崇拜和祭祖仪式，如苗族的盘瓠祭、土家族的舍巴日祭祀、蒙古族的敖包祭、彝族的"尼木措毕"送祖归灵活动等等。有些受汉族宗族文化影响较深的少数民族，如广西蒙山的壮族、福建泉州的回族、湖南永顺的土家族、浙江景宁的畲族等，他们也会建筑自己的宗祠、编撰自己的族谱，并以此为核心来建设自己的家族社区。

祠堂和族谱为核心的宗法文化，启示着我们生命的根本，也把儒家的传统价值追求鲜活地带进了 21 世纪。"礼失求诸野"，庆幸传统的儒家式生活方式通过民间宗族村落星布南北，温情未灭。可以说，只要宗族文化在，儒学的礼教就在，传统的"文化中国"就在。只有读懂宗族文化里的中国，才能读懂传统的中国人和他们的文化特性。关于这一部分，我们将在第七讲"尊祖重族——中国村落的宗族文化要素"中给大家做专门的讲解。我将围绕：家族和宗法、祠堂和祭祖、族谱和家风、族权和乡绅、义门和家园等传统宗族文化要素，给大家做具体的解读。

2.6　尊君重民相表里的王道政治理念

在张岱年、方克立主编的《中国文化概论》教科书中指出：从政治结构来看，中国文化有尊君重民、相辅相成的政治文化特征[①]。其大意是：由于农民的分散性需要集权君主来统合自保，所以发展出"尊君"（专制主义）。由于农业社会是农民的主体性故倡导民为邦本，所以发展出"重民"（民本主义）。

我们认为这一分析是对的，但对中国传统政治中的"专制主义"需要做历史的具体分析。

---

① 张岱年，方克立. 中国文化概论［M］. 北京：北京师范大学出版社，2004：276.

　　首先，自然经济时代的中国确实有一个以君王的专制权威为中心的政治结构。对这样一个权力中心和政治共同体化身，儒家是主张给予敬意和忠诚的，即孔子说的"臣事君以忠""礼乐征伐自天子出"。法家的韩非子则强调要"定于一尊"，历朝历代无不"收天下之权归一人"，努力加强君主的权威，从而形成了"东方专制主义"。君主专制主义当然意味着"普天之下莫非王土，率土之滨莫非王臣"，而"专制主义的唯一原则就是轻视人类，使人不称其为人，……哪里的君主制是天经地义的，哪里就根本没有人了。"① 长久的封建专制政治使得传统中国人养成了某种王权崇拜情结、官本位迷信、家长制权威的盲从，这种状态下自然是不可能有人的自由、平等与权利可言的。

　　但必须指出，"东方专制主义"在中国政治实践中不仅仅是凸显君王的专制权威，同时也凸显了"大一统"的政治价值观念。"大一统"和"君权至上"密切地联系在一起，形成"朕即国家"的统一格局。忠君与爱国被捆绑在一起，君主专制主义客观上起到了加强国家认同和民族社会一体化的积极意义。对培养中华民族的爱国主义和集体主义精神，对维护祖国的统一和民族的团结发挥了重要作用。其次，儒家政治文化所追求的深刻理念（王道政治），不能简单地说就是盲从和无条件地推崇王权专制。某种意义上，与其说儒家是推崇王权至上，毋宁说它是崇尚"道尊于势"而非"势尊于道"，其原教旨乃是追求天道流行、人道圆满的理想社会，即大同之治。

　　儒家的王道政治理念有三层要求：敬天—爱民—尊孔。（1）"天子受命于天"——法天而王：这是政治合法性的超越基础。（2）"得乎丘民而为天子"——生民往归：这是政治合法性的民意基础。（3）"罢黜百家，独尊儒术"——尊孔尊儒：这是政治合法性的文化基础。

　　王道政治观是儒家对王朝政治合法性的界定标准，更是对专制主义君主威权的教育、范导和约束的力量。是不是好的君王，即"圣王"，是不是合法的良善政治，即"仁政"，就看这三条你做得怎样。敬天（道）否？爱（生）民否？尊孔（儒）否？儒家希望"致君尧舜上，要使民风淳"，他们真诚地希望君王能成为遵守王道的理想主义的圣君，臣下们也应该自觉地辅助君王力行王道而共图天下大治。必须承认，儒家的王道政治观就像一个紧箍咒，曾受到古代明君的普遍重视和昏君的深深忌惮。

　　比较于具体的制度建构和改革实践层次，政治哲学是政治思想的出发点，

---

① ［德］马克思，恩格斯. 马克思恩格斯全集：第 1 卷［M］. 北京：人民出版社，1979：
　　411.

政治价值理念是政治活动的形而上的目标，儒家的"王道政治"融合天道—民意—儒学三层内涵为一体，是儒家政治哲学的核心。离开王道政治（也可以叫作"王道三纲"）的指导意义和约束要求，而单向度地强调所谓君主权威和专制权力，强调所谓"君为臣纲"，这是不符合儒家的本意的。尤其是这里提到的重民和民意合法性的标准，儒家强调得很严重。如孔子抨击苛政猛如虎，主张"节用而爱人，使民以时"。孟子更提出"民为贵，社稷次之，君为轻"。荀子则形象地比喻道"君者舟也，庶人者水也。水则载舟，水则覆舟"。一方面，"国以民为本"的民本主义抑制了专制主义的极端形态，王道政治的原意不允许绝对君权（暴政）的出现。对不符合王道标准的暴君，儒家主张顺天应民而"革命"之。儒家的"革命"思想的重要基础，就是民心和民意，这一点值得我们仔细思考。另一方面，民本主义毕竟不是民主主义，它的核心还是"民以君为主"，是"治于人者"对明主的呼吁与文化建言。至于统治者们听不听、理不理，儒家精英士大夫其实也毫无办法。

中国传统的民众，主要是安土重迁、尊祖重族的宗族村落的农人。他们平时忙于农事，依据习俗生活，乡绅族长们维持地方自治。鸡犬之声相闻，民至老死不相往来。乡村即天下。当然，既无必要、也无可能的制度途径让他们参加公共政治生活。如遇国事不堪、暴政扰攘，人民虽在乡里亦有倒悬之苦。他们或只能忍辱负重，或铤而走险起义革命，此外并无别路可走。

中国传统的王道政治，一贯对君王寄予道德理想主义的美好期待和深深期望，所谓"内圣开外王"。但君王们大多并不是圣王。事实上，靠封建君王和官僚们自觉的道德理性的修养，然后治国平天下这样一种"德性直贯"的伦理政治哲学，没有也不可能开显出现代的民主政治。哲学家牟宗三先生就指出：中国古代的儒墨道法等各家学派都有自己的治国之道（治道），但有治道而无政道，即无政权民主轮替之道。无政道，则政治始终无法上正轨。一部中华政治史，君道臣道，常不上道。始终找不到长治久安之法。王道之种，从没有开出大同之治的果实。根本问题还是儒家没有改变"势尊于道"的君主专制主义的封建政治权力结构。对不讲道德的、非理性的、腐败傲慢的专制权力系统，儒家（士阶层）跟它又有千丝万缕的利益交缠，剪不断理还乱，所以也找不出办法来。

总之，儒家王道政治视野下的民本主义讲的"民"，不是近代民主主义意义下的"民"，两者差了一个资本主义时代。我们不能奢望皓首穷经、生活在超稳固传统社会结构下、追求明心见性天人合一道德幻觉境界的儒家知识分子们提出任何有关民主、自由、平等、人权、法治的政治要求。这不是说那个时代已经有足够的自由和人权，而是说，这类思想不是民本主义时代的人民所能思考和提出的口号，更遑论具体的建制以实现其理念。

2.7　远神近人的人文生活信念

从宗教信仰状况看，中国文化有摆脱神学独断、过人本主义生活的特征。

关于中国古人的宗教信仰的生活状态，英国哲人罗素有一判断，即中国人"以孔子伦理为准则而无宗教"。其实这一说法并不准确，中国并不是没有宗教，而是有自己独特内涵、特殊类型的宗教。

一方面看，中国自古就有多元的宗教类型和丰富的民间信仰：中国的各个民族中从来不缺各种敬畏自然万物有灵、图腾崇拜和祖先祭祀等原始宗教类型。中国自古就有儒教、道教、佛教、伊斯兰教和基督教、摩尼教、印度教等本土与外来宗教的传播和广泛影响。中国民间至今流行如拜天公、祭河神，土地信仰、关公信仰、妈祖信仰、保生大帝信仰。而各种敬神、游神、走古事、赶庙会等带有宗教色彩和内容的节庆民俗活动也非常受群众欢迎。另外一方面，与世界各地的不同宗教之间常见的彼此对抗，甚至战争不同，中国的传统宗教多元并存、和而不同，具有儒家伦理本位和道家自然主义影响下的人文主义性格。儒家脱胎于上古的祭司阶层，专事主持敬天法祖的祭祀仪式。西周以后儒家逐步实现人文化，"由巫到礼，释礼归仁"（李泽厚语）。儒家总体上不否定鬼神，但又敬鬼神而远之。正宗的儒家士大夫注重德性修养，不语怪力乱神，而是关注伦理人间，认为"敬神不如敬祖"，因而更关心日常生活中遵守伦理教条、享受伦理之情、承担伦理责任、完成伦理人格。道家学派更是"尊道而贵德"，主张道法自然。而"道"作为天地之始万物之母，它不是创始主，不是神，而是宇宙的规律或根本的精神。道家最高尚的追求就是"道法自然"，是根据宇宙规律去过清净自然的美学式生活，实现天人合一的心境自由。

儒道两家的世界观和价值追求在中国文化中具有重大的影响力，这使得中国的本土宗教和外来宗教不得不遵循：伦理本位性、务实入世性、多元调和性、政教分离性等中国人文特色。像中国化的佛教大讲"报四恩"，突出孝道和王道，主张"农禅并重"，宣扬"佛法在世间，不离世间觉"，并在近代成为"人间佛教"或"人生佛教"。所谓"仰止唯佛陀，完成在人格。人成即佛成，是名真现实。"（太虚法师语）。外来宗教若不协调于中国文化的人文主义伦理本位的特色，则其注定无法在中国生存和发展。

正如梁漱溟先生指出的：中国宗教的特征是即宗教而超宗教的"人文教"或"伦理教"、而尊祖敬宗的宗族文化和信念，也在部分意义上代替了宗教的情感安慰的功能。中国人现实主义的生存态度使得他们倾心于实实在在的道德和政治，"内圣外王"成为最高的理想境界。他们追求的精神生活是"诚意、正心、修身"的道德自我满足，他们追求的现实生活是"齐家、治国、平天下"。他们对宗教采取了实用主义的态度，仅仅局限于祈福消灾，而没有沉迷在宗教世界被它绑架。儒家的道德理性和伦理情怀对宗教有一种替代作用，使得宗教思想始终作为一种附庸的存在。在中国历史上从来没有出现过西方中世纪那样的政教合一的时代。

总之，宗教和民间信仰的本质是"终极关怀"（生命怎样才有最终和最高的意义），中国宗教和民间信仰丰富多彩，是中国文化的重要组成部分，对中国古代哲学、政治、经济、文学、书法、绘画、雕塑、建筑以及名山大川的各个方面都有巨大而深刻影响。这一部分我们将在第八讲《和而不同——中国的多元宗教及其特质》中再详说。

2.8　伦理本位的学术倾向

从学术类型看，中国文化有重人伦道德、轻自然科学的学术倾向。

首先，中国学术历来以人为中心，关注人的现实生活，实行伦理本位。

中国文化对"人"这个概念的重视，可以说主要不是个人价值的自由主义的推崇，而是对"人伦"的重视。"伦理"就是社会中人与人之间的基本关系和应当遵守的行为准则。《孟子·滕文公上》中将"人伦"归纳为"父子有亲，君臣有义，夫妇有别，长幼有序，朋友有信"。其中三种是家族范围内的亲人关系，两种是超出家族范围的公共社会的人际关系。儒家强调等级名分，把人们纳入各自所属的社会位置与角色关系中去，并给予他们以相对应的伦理上的责任与义务。儒家还给这些伦理以形而上学即天理的威严性。伦理是天理的人间落实，是道德修养的主要领域，也是帮助人去完成社会化文明人格的主要手段。儒家推崇"仁义礼智信"五种道德。强烈的伦理道德氛围是中国人呼吸的空气，对上自天子，下至于庶民的整个社会各阶层、各个生活领域，都有其对人们的道德规范与指示。比如"以德治国"的政治文化、"德主刑辅"的法律意识、"诚信为本"的儒商精神、"美善和谐"的艺术美学、"希贤希圣"的君子人格、"天下归仁"的世界情怀、"修文柔远、协和万邦"的国际视野、"交融互鉴、互利合作"的丝路精神，等等。中国传统的德性文化注重伦理研究和修养，推崇仁德和良知，相信人性本善，又重视对治和克服私欲，追求高尚和伟大的境界。中华人文道德文化，塑造了无数善良、正直的"民族的脊梁"，养成了中国人民所珍视的仁爱孝悌、谦和好礼、诚信知报、精忠报国、克己奉公、修己慎独、勤俭廉正、见利思义、笃实宽厚、勇毅力行这十大中华传统美德，这些美德自古以来，奠定了中国社会的精神文化基石，铸就了民族的价值意识形态的坚实内核。

其次，以人为中心的人文学术在中国主要是表现为儒家的经学。

儒家的经学（十三经、四书五经）研究贯穿整个中国学术发展的历史并笼罩于一切文化领域。而这些经书又都是"人学"，都是探讨人跟生活世界的重要方面的关系，如：《易经》——人与自然的关系、《尚书》——人与政治的关系、《礼记》——人与伦理的关系、《春秋》——人与历史的关系、《诗经》《乐经》——人与艺术的关系。而《礼记·经解第二十六》中就记载了孔子对六经对人文教化和人格养成所具有的积极作用的看法。

孔子曰："入其国，其教可知也。其为人也：温柔敦厚，《诗》教也；疏通知远，《书》教也；广博易良，《乐》教也；洁静精微，《易》教也；恭俭庄敬，《礼》教也；属辞比事，《春秋》教也。"

应该说，在中国传统的学术史上，士人阶层最主要的研究，几乎都与经学有密切联系，这就形成了中国文化特有的经学思维和典籍诠释学传统：文有经、经有传、传有注、注有疏。冯友兰先生就形容中国古代学术史只有两个阶段：五百年的子学时代和两千年的经学时代。历代的经学研究者或者固守师说门户，坚持"我注六经"的传统；或者六经注我，假借经义、弘扬心学。但二者无论如何都没有离开儒家的根本典籍，这是一个深刻的注疏学大窠臼。此外，如佛经和道藏也可谓浩如烟海。中国经学诠释学的厚重传统的流弊就是在某种程度上导致了后代学人迷信圣贤经典，不敢越雷池一步。即使有新思想，也必须从经典中找依据，否则就是离经叛道。这对人的创造求新的精神是一种桎梏与限制，需要予以深刻反思与扬弃。

同时，经学学术的发达，映衬的是对于自然界本身的研究工作的轻视和科学文化的薄弱。

中国文化的人文主义传统注重道德反思和心灵直觉，追求天人合一，而中庸之道就是典型的辩证思维。而无论是辩证思维还是经学思维，虽然形式和层次不同，其性质都是一种直觉体验的思维方式。它们从日常生活经验出发，凭直觉行动，注重体验和顿悟，强调经验基础上的类比或类推，缺乏严密的逻辑推理和理论上的归纳演绎，具有情境化和模糊性的特点。这显然是会妨碍中国人抽象思维的发展和理论研究的深入的。虽说自古以来，中国就有不少杰出的科学家，各民族共同创造并留下了许多在天文、数学、医药学、建筑学方面的伟大成就，但科学（家）本身总体上是不受重视的，其研究范式深受心学和玄学的影响和束缚。而心学的所谓"心物一元、圆融无碍"，也始终没法解决"德"与"智"的关系问题，以至于在近代迅速拉开了同西方间科学的距离。这不是说中国人没有科学思维的能力，而是学术范式和思维方式的方向性差别造成了阻碍。一旦廓清障碍并更新范式，中国当代科学技术就能（并已经）获得长足的发展和进步。

　　总之，透过纷繁复杂的文化现象，分门别类地进行整理，我们就可以大致把握住中国传统文化的总体特性与重要领域的基本特征，并以此为基础，进一步去了解中国文化更内在的基本精神，这是我们在下一讲中的任务。

The Second Chapter:

The Magnificent China
—Essential Characters of Chinese Culture

2.1   On the Characters of Chinese Culture

China boasts profound and abundant cultures. Yet where to begin? Naturally, to start from outside to inside and step by step can be the most fundamental method for study. Just as we look at a person or observe a thing every day, we always must grasp the characteristics or temperament that they show, and then gradually deepen. In other words, we should grasp its basic external characters before further exploring its internal reasons or the fundamental spirit inside it. So, what are the basic characteristics of Chinese culture? The so-called basic characteristics of Chinese culture refer to the unique cultural characteristics or temperament shown in history that are different from the cultures of other nations.

Since culture includes all the contents of life in a broad sense, the so-called basic characteristics of culture must have many ways of generalization and conclusions. Can look overall and macroscopically, also can look concretely and micro. It all depends on the cultural content and objects being investigated, and of course, also depends on the knowledge composition and academic methods that researchers have.

From a general perspective, Chinese culture represents a whole with some conspicuous characters easy to distinguish. In his book *Fundamentals of Chinese Culture*, Mr. Liang Shuming summarized this kind of general characters respectively. According to Mr. Liang, Chinese culture bears seven main characters: originality, systematism, continuity, assimilation, broadness, premature, and radiation. We basically approve these comments.

However, it does not mean that they are undoubtable. One character mentioned by

Mr. Liang—originality or ingenuity of Chinese culture—remains controversial.

Generally, Chinese civilization is regarded as an original and independent civilization. But there are many doubts in western academic circles. For example, in 1894, the French, Terrien de Lacouperie, published the so-called *Western Origin of the Early Chinese Civilization*. In this book, "Western Origin of the Early Chinese Civilization" was firstly put forward. In his eyes, Chinese ancestor Huangdi was NaiHwangti, a Baak leader from Babylon. "The Eight Trigrams" originated from cuneiform characters. Both Chinese civilization and Babylon civilization shared hundreds of similarities. This viewpoint even received supports from masters of Chinese culture at that time, including Zhang Taiyan and Liu Shipei, etc. Swedish geologist Johan Gunnar Andersson (1874—1960), the father of Yangshao Culture, also said that the prehistoric pottery culture of China is similar to that of Central Asia and Eastern Europe.

The question of "the origin of Chinese civilization" concerns whether the Chinese civilization is independent and original, as well as the historical and cultural confidence of the Chinese nation. Therefore, it is not a purely academic case. But scholarship is a scientific enterprise, which cannot be accomplished only by thinkers reviewing literature and ancient legends in their study. It is all up to archaeology to speak for itself with cultural evidence. It can be said that in order to demonstrate the originality and longevity of Chinese civilization for 5000 years, Chinese scholars since the 20th century have been making great efforts to promote the research in this field in the spirit of science. The archaeological excavations, including Chengziya cultural site in Jinan, Shandong Province (Longshan Culture) and Yin Ruins in Anyang, Henan Province (1928), strongly refuted the popular view that "people and culture were imported from the West" with the evidence of the prehistoric period of Chinese local culture.

It must be mentioned here that the national research project on tracing the origins of Chinese civilization (full name is "Comprehensive Research on the Origin and Early Development of Chinese Civilization") was launched in 2002. It is a national academic project supported by the state to study the origin, formation, and early development process of Chinese civilization from multi-disciplines, multi-perspectives, multi-level and all-round. After 20 years of five stages of in-depth research, with the joint participation of nearly 400 scholars, the project has achieved a large number of academic achievements supported by solid archaeological data, declaring that China has a credible population history of one million years, a cultural history of 10000 years, and a civilization history of 5000 years. It proves that the Chinese civilization is a native civilization, which not only integrates the achievements of many regional prehistoric civilizations in China, but also dynamically absorbs the elements of western Asia and other foreign civilizations.

Other controversial ideas of cultural characters may also be referred. For instance, Mr. Liang Shuming's generalization of "systematism" and "radiation" of Chinese civilization. In his perspective, only China, India and the West have long been acknowledged as three civilization systems in the world. He noted that Chinese culture radiates the whole east Asia while Japanese culture fails to obtain unique character as a main part. Yet different from that of Mr. Liang, opinions as the so-called "5 Origins of Human Civilizations", "8 Human Civilizations", even "23 Civilization Areas", etc. are referred by various scholars. Samuel P. Huntington even put Japanese culture as one of the "8 human civilizations", together with Chinese civilization. For us who support the character of "radiation" as a popular idea, it is difficult to accept other contradictory views. This is the first main point.

Now let's come to the second point. In our view, culture represents life. The specific characters of culture can be categorized and judged according to the basic aspects or the main fields of cultural lives. Therefore, it's natural to see various ideas echoing. Take for example, in Liang Shuming's *the Essence of Chinese Culture*, he discussed specific characters of multiple areas of Chinese culture or its basic characters. In the book, fourteen general aspects are analyzed: territory and population, national integration, historical extension, cultural premature, social stagnation, religion, family system, academy and science, modernism, moral atmosphere, national type, military, filial piety, recluses.

In *The Problem of China* by British philosopher Russell, only three aspects are chosen—Chinese characters, codes of conduct, and guvnors' selecting system, to generalize the characters of Chinese culture. They are as follows: use of ideograms instead of alphabets in writing; substitution of the Confucian ethic for religion among the educated classes; governance by literati chosen by examination instead of by hereditary aristocracy. These are three general aspects of Chinese culture in his view.

Cultural life is rich and vast, and there is a need for many specialists to study specific issues. Compared with talking about the overall problems of Chinese culture in an abstract way, this seems to be more deserving of our affirmation. Of course, in today's era, "intellectuals highlight, thinkers fade out" has also become a problem. We should not fall into the cultural details and lose the understanding and thinking power of insight into the profound essence and fundamental spirit of culture.

Here, we would like to assemble opinions from different scholars. We will introduce specific traits of Chinese culture with an outline or the seven aspects of its basic characters. We hope it can help you roughly categorize and understand Chinese culture.

2. 2   The Cultural Diversity in Unity

In terms of the overall structure of civilization, the most important feature of Chinese civilization is its cultural diversity in unity.

The concept of diversity in unity means that the Chinese civilization is not a single and isolated civilization, but a unified cultural organism formed by the dynamic fusion of multiple cultural groups. It is not characterized by a forced external, temporary union, but by a regular, naturally formed, and thus long-lasting, internal union. This is the integration of the whole and the part, with a strong vitality of the unity. And I can show you some examples as follows.

To understand the early origins of Chinese civilization, we should avoid the "Centrism of Han nationality's Civilization". Because the Central Plains was never the center of the world. it cannot completely represent the whole cultural landscape of China. we should look at the Yellow River basin, the Yangtze River basin and the West Liao River basin, and look at the many regional prehistoric civilization sites nationwide, such as the Hongshan Culture in northeast China, the Qijia Culture in northwest China, the Shimao Site in the north China, the Liangchengzhen Site in the east China, the Jinsha Site and Sanxingdui Site in the southwest China, the Shijiahe Site in the south China, the Liangzhu Site in the southeast China and so on. At present, more than 7000 neolithic cultural sites have been discovered in China, and dozens of archaeological cultures have been named, and several larger systems and centers have emerged. They are the source of complete and diverse Chinese civilization. Regional civilizations rise and fall, gather and disperse, and form a larger sphere of interaction through long-term exchanges. The common cultural accumulation, psychological identity and tradition of ritual system laid the foundation for the continuous development of Chinese civilization, and gathered in the Yellow River basin and the Central Plains, which is the Xia, Shang and Zhou civilization.

Xia, Shang and Zhou Dynasties witnessed the emergence of the elements of national civilization represented by bronze wares, inscriptions on oracle bones, large city walls and ceremonial centers, marking the beginning of the age of civilization of Chinese dynasties. It can be said that the Xia, Shang and Zhou Dynasties themselves were the epitomes of the multidimensional information of the early civilization (even Chinese and foreign civilizations). They are a symbol of the formal formation of Chinese civilization and a new starting point for continuous transmission.

From three ancient dynasties—Xia Dynasty, Shang Dynasty, and Zhou Dynasty, in the long history of the development of Chinese culture, this process of diversity in unity of China has also kept pace with the times, and has been fully manifested in all aspects. For example, the Chinese land gave birth to the great Chinese nation, which is one unity. But the Chinese nation is a community formed by the integration of various ethnic groups through five times. Of course, each nation has its own distinct cultural personality and characteristics, but they are not pure and single. They are integrated in all levels and fields of material culture, institutional culture, behavior culture, and mentality culture, just like the seed of a pomegranate. Our compatriots of all ethnic groups have jointly explored and protected China's territory, created its history, enriched the Chinese cultural spirit, and created a common Chinese cultural homeland.

Moreover, I must point out that the so-called "unity and diversity" is not only the overall structure of the Chinese nation, but also the general constitution law of the cultural ecology of all ethnic groups, regions, and fields within the Chinese nation.

Among the 56 nationalities of the Chinese people have been formed many similar customs related to typical festivals of each nationality. For example, the important festivals of Han nationality are also observed by other minority nationalities. Moreover, Han nationality shares similar methods to fix festival dates with the Mongolians, the Manchus, the Koreans, the Zhuangs. Although the festival dates of these nationalities are different from those of the nationality, nearly all the festival activities of these nationalities either involve celebrating harvest, offering sacrifices to ancestors and gods, family reunion and amusements, or convey wishes for happiness and valuing time. As for ways of festival celebrations, such as the way family get together, the way they sit up through the lunar New Year's Eve, or pay visits on the lunar New Year's Day, they share more similarities than differences.

For example, all ethnic cultures share the tradition of ancestor worship. On the root, this is the ancestral spirit worship inherited from the original belief of the clan times, this is a common point. However, compared with the specific content of their worship, such as the object of sacrifice, the minority nationalities worship the totem ancestor and the human ancestor both, while the Han nationality mainly the human ancestor and the blood ancestor of all generations. Most ethnic minorities do not have the Han style of strict clan regulations, hierarchical ancestral worship places, no clan genealogy documents. In addition, there are great differences in sacrificial time, ritual procedure, host, and corresponding commemorative festivals.

The Wisdom of Traditional Chinese Architecture (10 episodes), a large-scale 4K documentary led by the Ministry of Housing and Urban-Rural Development, premiered in January 2022. Through the stories of the occupants, users and renovators of traditional buildings, this paper introduces the traditional architectural types of China, such as courtyard architecture, corral architecture, hall and well architecture, walled house architecture, cave dwellings, blockhouse dwellings, temporary canopy dwellings, ancestral halls, ancient villages and ancient towns, which not only show the unity of internal forms, but also embody the persistence and consistency of Chinese architectural civilization. It also reflects the diversity of Chinese architectural culture and rich regional differences. Embodies the wisdom of life of the Chinese nation.

2-2   Cultural Diversity in Unity of Chinese Civilization

In short, diversity and unity is the fundamental feature of the whole process of Chinese civilization from its origin, formation and development to the present. It is also the biggest difference from the types of civilizations around the world. In some ways, we're all the same, so we're the one unity. But in some ways, we're very different, so we're diverse. In the pattern of Chinese culture, "pluralism" is the premise, and "unity" is derived from the long-term collision and integration of "pluralism". Various cultural factors and elements are numerous subsystems in the grand system of Chinese culture.

Today's colorful and vibrant Chinese culture is the joint creation of all regions and nations. It is the historical product of the interaction between "many" and "one". In the Chinese culture of diversity in unity, "Tao goes hand in hand but does not contradict each other, and all things grow together but do not harm each other." That is why we live forever.

2.3 The Cultural Vitality with Strong Liveliness and Cohesion

The strong vitality of Chinese culture may hardly be doubted. History has witnessed waxes and wanes of various ancient civilizations. And many countries with early civilizations decayed at an early age. Matthew Melko, an American scholar, once concluded that humans have seen twelve ancient civilizations, of which seven had vanished, such as Mesopotamia Civilization, Egyptian Civilization, Minoan Civilization, Classical Civilization, Byzantine Civilization, Mesoamerican Civilization and Andean Civilization. Yet, only the Chinese civilization, through many hardships and repeated risks, had managed to survive and prosper. For thousands of years, Chinese writing, grammar, logic of thinking and worldview have hardly changed. In a sense, today's Chinese are still living the same life as their ancient ancestors. Then what accounts for this miracle?

Taiwan scholar, Professor Wei Zhengtong explained it with several possible reasons: Chinese people often value the maintenance of real life, obey conservative rules, and think highly of a thriving family. In addition, he also mentioned other reasons such as the protection afforded by the geographical environment, the concept of sustainable agriculture, the sophistication and resilience of people's characters, as well as the emphasis of unity and order and the desire for long-lasting generations. Zhang Dainian and Fang Keli, co-editors of *An Introduction to Chinese Culture* pointed out in their book: Why does Chinese culture bear such strong vitality and continuity? It comes from one unified power, the power of assimilation, integration, and cohesion. This is the very reason for it. We believe that "assimilation and fusion theory" is a more profound explanation, which reveals the root of the long vitality of Chinese civilization.

Speaking of the great assimilative power of Chinese culture, a joke was ever made by *Martin Jacques*— "If I visit China several more times, I may become a Chinese with British nationality. So, don't try to assimilate the Chinese people because you will be assimilated first." Just have a look at the Chinese kids today who seem to be addicted to KFC. Anyway, have you ever noticed that KFC "aimed at changing Chinese people's eating habits". Yet finally, it had to cater for Chinese diet. Now porridge, fried dough sticks, and soybean milk are available at KFC. As a result, KFC fails to change China. It is China that assimilates KFC. Who knows what KFC will sell in the coming days? Maybe bean curd jelly? KFC-made Siu Mai (shrimp and pork dumpling topped with crab roe)? Or KFC hot pot? The sinicizing western cuisine can be decoded as an indication of the strong assimilation power of contemporary Chinese culture.

The vigorous assimilation of Chinese culture had been deeply discussed by scholars ever before. Liang Qichao. For example, Mr. Liang Qichao analyzed the difference between "forced assimilation" and "natural assimilation" in Chinese history, and discusses the reasons for the strong "assimilation power" among the Chinese nationalities in history with the Han culture as the backbone as follows: to begin with, the covering influence of pillar culture. Second, the cultural function of "standardized Chinese characters". Third, Chinese people's ideals of pacifying the world and embracing new elements of culture. Fourth, a vast territory with a sparse population that suits immigrations and communications between nations. Fifth, the doctrine of mean and ardent love for peace as well as respect for different customs. Sixth, intermarriage between different ethnic groups and blood ties. Seventh, a booming economy and its extended influence. Eighth, wars that contribute to outward spread and expansion of culture.

If we adopt these eight aspects to discuss its assimilation power, the results are quite distinct. First, its strong assimilation helps integrate and accept foreign cultures. Second, the power enables cultures of internal ethnic groups or of different areas to embrace each other and form a shared community of culture in which beliefs and values etc. are not mutually exclusive and develop together without harm to each other. Thus, the community features diversity in unity and prosperity. All ethnic groups living in such a shared community, one with cultural lives, share strong sense of identification, unification and cohesion. In conclusion, Chinese culture boasts resilient, cohesive, inclusive, self-renewal, thriving and everlasting power of vitality and continuity.

As Chinese President Xi Jinping has pointed out at the national commendation conference for national unity and progress on September 29, 2019, a Chinese history is a history of the integration of all ethnic groups into a pluralistic Chinese nation, and a history of all ethnic groups working together to create, develop and consolidate a unified great motherland. The unity and integration of all ethnic groups and the unity of pluralism stem from the cultural inclusiveness, economic interdependence, emotional closeness of all ethnic groups, and the endogenous driving force of the Chinese nation in its pursuit of unity and unity. That's why Only in this way can the Chinese civilization have unparalleled inclusiveness and absorption, and can it be long-term, big, and deep-rooted.

This important exposition is a highly condensed version of Chinese history and a highly condensed version of the characteristics of Chinese civilization, which has important guiding significance. Why Chinese culture features such strong assimilation can also be explained by several other meaningful methods. In Chapter 4: Diversity in Unity— Chinese Nation and Chinese Culture, further explanations will be made to you. Here, we aim to put forward such a character ahead.

2.4　National Character Deeply Rooted in Agriculture

The third basic character of Chinese culture boasts its national character deeply rooted in agriculture.

In terms of economic type, Chinese culture indeed features typical agricultural characters. As far as six to seven thousand years ago, the river basins of the Yellow River and the Yangtze River had nurtured the early agricultural civilization. Thousands of years have seen agriculture developing as China's pillar industry assisted by manufacture and commercial activities. It is categorized as natural economy and represents traditional Chinese society's major economic formation and material basis. In terms of mentality, ideology, and lifestyle, it also helps forge the agricultural state of matter and psychological traits of Chinese culture. Therefore, generations of Chinese farmers have contributed to shaping in their genes strong national agricultural character as well as farmers' soul and ardent love for land. These spirits are manifested in several aspects:

(1) The Spirit of Being Introverted and Sensitive as well as Practical and Frugal

In Northern China, farmers grow wheat and, in the South, rice. Yet they manage to share the same spirit featuring simple, pragmatic, thrifty while introverted and calm. Compared with pastoralism by heroic and generous nomads with migrant and pioneering characters, farmers awe the nature and fate with enthusiasm for land. They work from dawn to dusk. They have kept committed to making a living, and leading a simple and frugal life. They are dependable, earnest, practical, easy-going, honest and kind. They are so keen on exploring the fields. The Longsheng terraces in Guangxi, Ziquejie terraces in western Hunan, Hani Terraces in Yunnan, and Youxi Terraces in Sanming, Fujian, are all testimony to generations of people of all ethnic groups' unremitting efforts to create their homes. farmers are so eager for bumper harvest and thriving living stocks that even their decedents today still enjoy growing vegetables. Chinese people keep their planting habits wherever they live.

(2) The Passion for Rural Life and Homeland, Unwillingness to Move or Migrant with Nostalgia

Chinese people are grateful to all given by nature and love their homes whole-heartedly. This kind of agricultural national character can be also called as "Pastoral Complex". This complex is reflected by the whole nation's special attachment to fields, and strong affection to homeland. In other words, it can be explained as their sense of nostalgia and nature.

Li Ziqi, a food blogger, who is well-known to all is a pretty girl from Sichuan Province in China. Her videos mainly record her home-made foods and strike the chord with countless audiences. In Li's videos, sceneries are peaceful, picturesque and aesthetic—rain flowing along the eaves of roofs, thin smoke curling up from the chimney of wood cook stove. Against that backdrop, Li carries withering firewood and does pan-milling by hand. Her activities express a natural rural life, which reminds people of the poem written by Meng Haoran, "Window opened, you immediately see threshing ground and vegetable garden. Wine cup in hand, we talk of harvest of grain and other crops." It also refreshes your memory of the poem by Tao Yuanming, "Beans planted under the southern hills. Yet the weed grows better than my bean seedlings." Both of poems reveal charms of rural life. Why Li's videos become so popular and successful, after all, is that they recall what is hidden deeply in our mind—meditation and nostalgia of farmers.

(3) The Trait of Stability and Peace Consciousness

Chinese farmers with strong passion for agricultural lifestyle can be called as "Children of the Earth". They understand that lucid waters and lush mountains are invaluable assets. For sure, they long for everlasting prosperity for their future generations. Just as the proverb says, "One generation plant a tree; the next sits in its shade." "Plan your consumption carefully on a long-term basis, and you need not worry when a famine occurs." This sense of permanence is combined with the belief and pursuit of the Chinese patriarchal culture of "The ancestral virtues are far away, and the ancestral achievements are long-lasting." This sense of permanence accounts for the continuity of the long-lasting traditional Chinese culture.

To strive for stability was one of Chinese people's major traits. Different from the mobile life of nomadic economy and commercial activities, the ordinary peasants' ideal was to possess "thirty mu of land and a wife, children, a warm bed and a cow". They were satisfied with what they got from land. Owing to the limitation of small-scaled production, they were not interested in the external world, with little curiosity for adventures and little greediness for expansion. The Great Wall, which was intended as a defense construction, not a sharp weapon for expansion, is a good example to show the Chinese people's love for peace. They were inclined to be satisfied with a simple and placid life with little aggressiveness. They had a kind of serene and sober dignity, and took an optimistic attitude to grievances and disasters. In their mild appearance surged high aspirations.

(4) Many Agricultural Tangible and Intangible Cultural Heritages of China

On the vast land of China, the wise Chinese predecessors have left many agricultural material and intangible cultural heritage for the benefit of future generations, which is the precious wealth that the Chinese nation has dedicated to the history of human civilization. So far, China has 19 "World Irrigation Engineering Heritage" and 18 "Global Important Agricultural Cultural Heritage" projects. The number ranks first in the world.

Hundreds of ancient villages and ancient towns have been preserved throughout the North and south of China, such as World Cultural Heritage sites, Hongcun and Xidi in Huizhou, Diaoyuan Village in Jiangxi Province, Yongding Hongkeng Village in Longyan Province... These ancient villages are very valuable to retain the historical and cultural information of the farming age.

In addition, the Chinese nation has many agriculture-related festivals and folk cultures. For example, the Han people offer sacrifices to the land god in the spring and autumn, the Buyi people offer sacrifices to the field god in the festival of tasting new millet. The Yi people hold the Torch Festival after the harvest... These festivals of blessing and harvest are lively and full of the harmonious and integrated relationship between the children of the earth and mother nature.

This is a land of life. The hope lies in the fields, and in the Chinese people forever maintaining this profound agricultural national character.

2.5   The Patriarchal Clan System Underlining Respect for Ancestors and Families

In terms of social structure, Chinese culture is featured by patriarchal clan system among villages with families as basic units. Chinese patriarchal culture and family system can be explained as a significant reason for its consistency. It's also the most special part that helps comprising traditional Chinese social structure.

Since the clan era of primitive society, the most important way of living for human beings is "living together", that is, taking the blood related family as the basic unit to organize the social structure. However, compared with the western society, family culture with Chinese characteristics is guided by patriarchal thoughts of Confucianism— respecting ancestors and families and worships the value of a community of kin. It emphasis on educating sense of responsibility, as well as the inheritance of family values. So that the solidarity of the family will be maintained, and the family members will be united. It contains strong inclination towards the characteristics of the transcendent belief in kin ethics.

Max Weber, a well-known German scholar, once studied China from a sociological viewpoint. In his eyes, before 1920s, Chinese society can be described as "a society with a family-style structure". This viewpoint is reasonable. The most distinctive feature of traditional Chinese society turns out to focus on family as the center of social activities. To some extent, when we look at Chinese people in traditional villages, they know all about families and local neighbors, yet nothing about their country. Besides their family lives, they rarely join in public social activities. What the Chinese people cherish most is the love of their families and the affection of their clans. Till today, in many parts of China, especially provinces in the south, traditions and lifestyles of village patriarchal culture are still well-preserved and followed earnestly. A typical example is that in Fujian Province, at various counties and villages in its southern, western, and northern regions, it is common to find that many villages are inhabited by lineages with the same surname. There, family members worship gods and ancestors. The simple villagers follow the rules of caring for relatives and respecting the elder. There, you can see century-old ancestral halls built in Ming and Qing Dynasties. And their descendants are burning incense for worshipping their forefathers. Connecting the souls of the present and the ancestors, decoded as a link between the past and the future. In every family tree, a complete family and its linage can be traced. Turning every page of the record, you are not only reviewing its history, but also appreciating the life spirit passed down from generation to generation. The patriarchal culture, with ancestral temples and family tree as its core, indicates the root of our lives. Therefore, I think patriarchal culture is a kind of transcendence and purification of personal life that helps us complete through the historical link of family life. It is ethics, religion and also art.

In addition, it must be noted that ancestor worship is a common tradition in the belief culture of ethnic minorities in China, such as Panhu sacrifice（盘瓠祭）of the Miao people, Shebari sacrifice（舍巴日）of the Tujia people, Aobao sacrifice（敖包祭）of the Mongolian people, Nimucuobi ancestor worship（尼木措毕）of the Yi people and so on. Some ethnic minorities deeply influenced by the patriarchal culture of the Han people, such as the Zhuang people in Guangxi and the Hui people in Quanzhou, will also build their own ancestral halls, compile their own genealogy, and build their own family communities based on this.

When one knows the patriarchal culture, you will find the core of Confucian culture, and understand China with its traditional culture. As to the patriarchal culture featured by family-orientation value it will be discussed in Chapter 7. During that lecture, more specific explanations will be made. I will talk about family and patriarchy, ancestral halls and worship, family tree and family rule, Clan authority and local gentry, "Yi Men" family and homestead, etc. These are all elements of traditional patriarchal culture. Further specific interpretations are available to you.

2. 6   The Principles of Country Ruling Featuring Mutual Respect between the Emperor and his People

The fifth basic character of Chinese culture lies in the concept of ruling the country with benevolence and righteousness (Kingly way), featuring the mutual respect between the emperor and his people.

To begin with, when China lived on the natural economy, there indeed existed a political structure featured by authoritative despotism with the emperor as its center. The emperor symbolizes the top power, the strategic hub as well as the social community. Facing such a powerful figure, Confucianism teaches people to show their respect and loyalty. This idea is described as " the courtiers serve the lord with loyalty"; and "the real power lies surely in the central authority". Han Fei Tzu, founder of the legalism, stresses the idea of " settle a given question on a single authority". Successive dynasties and authorities had seen constant promotion of collecting all power under heaven to one person. In this way, the authority of the ruler had been strengthened. Thus, the "Oriental Despotism" gradually took shape.

Despotism means that "all the land under the sky belongs to the king; all the people within this country are the king's subjects". Emperor claimed himself to be the Son of the Heaven, representing the Heaven to rule the whole country. And "the only principle of absolutism is to despise human beings and make people unlike human beings". The long feudal autocratic politics made the traditional Chinese people form the royal worship complex, the official standard superstition, the patriarchal system blindly. There can be no individual freedom, equality, or rights in such a state. But it must be pointed out, the notion of "unification" was associated with the notion of "reverence of emperor". The notion "a great national unity" in Chinese history played an important part in safeguarding the unification of the nation and the unity of all nationalities, and in promoting the development of the multi-national country. The values asserting collective interest also fostered the Chinese tradition of patriotism and collectivism.

Secondly, the philosophy pursued by Confucian political culture cannot simply be said to be the supremacy of royal power. In a sense, rather than advocating the supremacy of royal power, Confucian idealism has embraced a unique "benevolent governance (Kingly way)". This benevolent governance has three requirements: regard nature with awe; cherish people; worship Confucius.

The first point remains "The emperor is granted by the Heaven" —hence his rule is guided by nature and gods of the Heaven. This can be seen as a superior basis of political legitimacy. The second point, being described as "he who is accredited by people is then fit to be a king" means the importance of gaining people's trust. This represents the political legitimacy based on the public will. The third point is "paying supreme tribute to Confucianism while banning all other schools of thought", which means upholding the predominance of Confucius and Confucianism. This indicates the cultural basis of political legitimacy.

The political concept of ruling a country with righteousness (Kingly way) shows the criterion of the royal court's political legitimacy. Moreover, it can be defined as a model and restraining force that helps educate the emperor's authority under despotism. Therefore, this concept has received popular attention from open-minded rulers. Yet it remains a taboo among fatuous and incompetent emperors. Confucianists wish to "assist the emperor to become a wise ruler like Yao and Shun". They aim to help the emperor become a governor who follows the benevolent rules in an ideal way. Therefore, the lord will be praised as a sacred, intelligent, and virtuous ruler. Especially when it comes to the standard of the legitimacy of valuing people and their opinions, Confucianism stresses the benevolent governance seriously. For instance, Confucius criticized that "tyranny is fiercer than tigers". And advocated "cut down expenses and value talented people, and remind farmers not to miss the farming season". Mencius further promoted the idea of "The people are before the country, and the country is above the ruler." Xunzi uses a vivid metaphor to describe this concept. "The lord is the boat. The common people are the water. The water can support the boat. The water can also overturn the boat."

On the one hand, the idea of "to a country, people are all-important" serves as a people-oriented theory to curb the despotism from going to extreme and helps forbid the appearance of absolute tyranny of an emperor. To those tyrants failed to meet the standards of the kind rule, Confucianism would like to obey the public's opinion to "overthrow a dynasty under the order of Heaven". A significant foundation of the "overthrow" idea remains the willing and opinion of the public. And it is thought-provoking for us. On the other hand, the people-oriented concept does not equal to democratism for Westerners. It still gives priority to the monarch. But it symbolizes the appeal of the labor workers for a kind governor and their common value. For the emperor, he may choose to listen and follow the rule or not, and the Confucianists have no other choice.

Traditional Chinese people are mainly farmers in patriarchal villages who are unwilling to move or migrant to other regions and respecting their ancestors and families. They are committed to agricultural work from dawn to dusk and depend on local governors to maintain grass-root autocracy. "The voices of the fowls and dogs should be heard all the way from it to us, but I would make the people to old age, even to death, not have any intercourse with it." People living in the countryside regard the village as their whole world. Absolutely, there is no necessary or possible system or way for them to participate in public political activities. For tyrants and their tyranny, common people at the bottom of the heap have no other choice but to meet the violence with violence and fight for a new dynasty and a better ruler.

The philosopher, Mou Zongsan once pointed out that ancient China boasts the way of governance rather than the way of controlling political power, which can be understood as the lack of a regime for democratic shift of power. Without the way to control power, Chinese politics was never able to be on track. The history of Chinese politics shows that the ways of being a popular emperor and helpful courtiers often can't meet the needs of the country very often. And the ways of prolonged political stability are finally failed to be found. The seed of benevolent and righteous governance (Kingly way) was never able to grow the expected fruit of building the country into a commonwealth state shared by all. To explore the root cause of this result, it is the feudal political structure that failed to be changed by Confucianism. This kind of despotism "regards the authority higher than justice". But for those immoral, irrational, and arrogant power system of the corruptive despotism, the Confucianism is inextricably linked to and mixed with it, forming a complex and intertwined whole. Therefore, no solution can be made.

In all, "people" under the Chinese people-oriented concept are different from those living in modern western democratism. There stands a gap—a process of capitalism between two groups of people. Thus, it is inappropriate to question or accuse traditional Confucian intellectuals of never promoting any political demands on democracy, freedom, equality, human rights and the rule of law. They are ideas and slogans beyond the understanding of Chinese people with local people-oriented thoughts, let alone building a concrete system to achieve this dream.

2.7　Faith in Humanistic life—Staying away from Gods and Focusing on Humans

In terms of religious belief, Chinese culture features the release from theological dogmatism and the embrace of humanistic life.

On the one hand, history has seen diverse religions as well as abundant folk beliefs developing in China. China is never short of primitive religious beliefs such as animism, totem worship and ancestor worship, etc. Confucianism, Taoism, Buddhism, Islamism, Christianity, Manichaeism, Hinduism and even Judaism all enjoy a long history in China. Both the local and foreign religions were spread in China and influenced Chinese society. Among various ethnic groups in China, ceremonies such as worshiping the Jade Emperor, the God of River, the God of Earth, Guan Yu (the God of fortune), Matsu (the God of Sea), the God of Medicine, etc. are still celebrated now. And various folk activities, like worshipping ceremonies, the deity parades, the Running Ancient Numen of Yantou, temple affairs, etc. With religious meaning and contents remain popular among the general public. On the other hand, in many parts of the world, disputes or even wars may happen frequently between religions. Yet the situation is quite different in China. Here, traditional religions coexist well and remain harmony in diversity. Influenced by the ethics-oriented Confucianism and the naturalism of Taoism, Religions in China boast a humanistic character.

Confucianism grew out of the ancient priestly class, specializing in presiding over the worship ceremony. After the Western Zhou Dynasty, Confucianism gradually realized the transformation of humanism, "release sorcery to return courtesy, return courtesy to benevolence". The Confucianism respects gods and ancestors. They do not deny gods but aim at "respecting religion but keeping themselves away from it". Authentic Confucianists pay attention to moral cultivation, and never talk about monstrosities. Instead, they focus on ethics of humans under heaven, believing that "worshipping ancestors is more important than worshipping gods". Therefore, they care more about daily routines, such as observing ethical doctrines, enjoying happiness of family relationships, as well as burdening ethical responsibilities. For Taoism, it further "honor the Tao and exalt its outflowing operation" and promotes "the law of the Tao is its being what it is". Tao represents where the Heaven and Earth sprang and the mother that rears the ten thousand creatures. It is neither a creator nor a god, but the fundamental rule or spirit of the universe. The most noble pursuit of Taoism is to "follow nature", to live according to the laws of the universe, and to achieve the unity of nature and man. With world views and value of Confucianism and Taoism as pillar theories in Chinese culture, other Chinese local religions, together with foreign ones must consider their ethnic standards, practical worldliness, harmonization of multiple factors, and the separation of religion and state, and other Chinese humanistic characters.

For instance, the Sinicized Buddhism ardently promotes "gratitude for four kindnesses". It emphasizes filial piety and benevolent governance, the "equal attention to agriculture and Zen Buddhism", and advocates that "always practice the Dharma you have learned to your life, for life is the real path of self-cultivating". In addition, Buddhism in modern world has developed into the so-called "living Buddhism". "The Buddha represents the saint in virtue for people to look upon, And People must complete their own character to attain the Buddha's conduct. To become a sage or a saint as a human is the best reflection of reality. " (Master Taixu)

Professor Liang Shuming pointed out that Chinese religions feature representing both religions and beyond religions. It can be categorized as "doctrine of humanism" (伦理教) or "doctrine of ethics", in which patriarchal culture and faith of "respecting and worshiping ancestors" may in some ways substitute the function of condolence offered by religions. Atheism was the essential ideology of traditional Chinese culture. Under the influence of such a culture, the spiritual life for the Chinese people was sincerity, honesty, and cultivation of their moral characters, to fulfil their moral pursuit. While the realistic life they pursued was to run the royal government well and bring peace to the entire country, they took a practical attitude toward religion. In the traditional society of China, morality functioned as a substitution for religion. Consequently, this dominant position of morality in the traditional Chinese culture resulted in the subordinate position of religion. China boasts colorful religions and folk beliefs, which represent a component of Chinese culture as well as extended influence in philosophy, politics, economy, literature, calligraphy, painting, sculpture, architecture as well as famous mountains in ancient China in all respects. However, its whole background remains humanistic and people oriented. We will talk about this topic in Chapter 8—Multiple Religions and its characteristics. We look forward to further discussions with you.

2.8　The Academic Preference for Ethical Norms

In terms of ideology, Chinese culture features an academic incline to ethics and an underestimation of natural science.

In the Chinese traditional culture, priority was granted to man as the fundamental of the universe. Yet, this attention to man was not paid to man's personality and freedom, but to human relations which referred to the basic interpersonal relations and the behavioral norms for people to observe in the traditional society of China. In the first volume of *Teng Wengong*, *Mencius*, human relations are summed up as something that covers " affection between father and son, rites between the emperor and his subjects, a hierarchical order between husband and wife, the old and the young, and fidelities between friends". Confucianism emphasizes hierarchy, brings people into their relative social positions and roles, and gives them corresponding ethical responsibilities and obligations. It also provides some metaphysical basis for these ethics from philosophy, that is, ethics is the human implementation of heaven's principle or heaven's way. Confucianism advocates five kinds of morality: benevolence, righteousness, propriety, wisdom and fidelity. It has its moral norms and instructions for the whole social stratum and every field of life, from the emperor to the ordinary people. Morality is the light that is everywhere to be illuminated. Such as the "rule of virtue" political culture, the " morality given priority over penalty " legal consciousness, the "honesty is the best policy" Confucian spirit of merchants, the "harmony between beauty and kindness" aesthetics, the "pursuit of progress" for man of virtue, the "put the society on track of humanity" world view, the "treat foreigners friendly and keep good relationship with other countries" international prospective.

The strong moralistic culture helps lay a spiritual and cultural foundation for Chinese society. And it is also committed to the solid core of the nation's ideological value building. Traditional Chinese moral culture thinks highly of research on ethics and self-cultivation, promotes benevolence and conscience, believes in " Man on earth, Good at birth", and values resisting and overcoming selfish desire so as to pursue a noble and great state of mind. The Chinese humanistic moral culture also helps cultivate people of integrity and kindness, being praised as "backbone of the nation". The culture nurtures virtues of what Chinese people cherish, such as filial piety and benevolence, modesty and courtesy, honesty and gratitude, loyalty to one's country, wholehearted devotion to public rather than advantage to oneself, cultivation of one's personality without discovery, frugality and transparency, remembering justice when facing benefits, earnest and kindness, as well as bravery and diligence.

Secondly, the humanistic study with people as its center is mainly manifested in the tradition of exploring Confucian classics. The classics of Confucianism may equal to "humanism" as well, which explore the relationship between people and important aspects of the life world—the relation between man and nature in *The Book of Changes*, the relation between man and politics in *The Book of Documents*, that between man and ethics in *The Book of Rites*, man and history, *The Spring and Autumn Annals*, as well as man and art, *The Book of Songs* and *The Book of Music*. Therefore, nearly all studies in the educated classes share a close relationship with the study of Confucian classics. Altogether, the hermeneutics of Confucian classics gradually takes shape as a unique tradition in Chinese culture: a subject with Jing (classics), Zhuan (records), Zhu (explanations of Jing or Zhuan) as well as Shu (further addition to Zhu) . Researchers of classics may strictly follow the learning from their teachers, keeping the tradition of "I guided by the Six Classics", or to choose "the Six Classics guided by me" and to justify these theories in real life. Anyway, their studies never get rid of the basic classical works in Confucianism, such as *Thirteen Classics* of Chinese philosophy and literature or the well-known *Four Books and Five Classics*. Therefore, it is a large home to Chinese hermeneutics. In addition, there was an immense collection of Buddhist sutra and the Taoist canon. In the thinking mode of Confucian classics' study, can be found a blind worship of the classics by the sages and men of virtue: no step was encouraged to walk out of the threshold of these classics. This way of study seriously bound people's creative aspiration, thus becoming a kind of spiritual fetter.

In addition, the well-developed study of Confucian classics indicates the ignorance of studying the natural world itself as well as the weakness in Culture of Science. Chinese humanism focuses on reflection of moral rules and human instinct and the critical thinking of "man in one with nature". However, by comparison, it is short of formal logic and the strict training of technical rationality. Different as they are in forms, both the dialectical thinking and the thinking in the mode of Confucius classics' study are, by nature, an intuitive and empirical way of thinking. Both proceeded from experience of daily life, acting according to intuition, and learning through enlightenment. They also emphasized analogy based on experience without logical inference and theoretical deduction and induction. These cognitive methods hindered the development of abstraction and further theoretical study through classification. Therefore, they have some limitations. Although China boasts "the four great inventions" as representatives for its achievements in traditional science and technology, due to the underestimation of science, its research is still affected and restricted by School of Mind and Metaphysics.

Yet the idea promoted by School of Mind—the so-called "perfect penetration without obstruction" can never fetch out ways to handle the question of the relationship between "virtue" and "intelligence". Thus, in modern times, it turned out that the western science surpassed that of China with astonishing speed. This is not to say that the Chinese people do not have the ability of scientific thinking, but that the directional differences in academic paradigms and modes of thinking have caused obstacles. Once the obstacles are cleared and updated, China's modern science and technology can (and has) achieved considerable development and progress.

In conclusion, we look through the complicated cultural appearances to categorize them accordingly. We are then able to decode the overall and basic characters of Chinese traditional culture. And based on this analysis, we will further explore the internal spirit of Chinese culture. This is what we will further explain in the next chapter.

第三讲

千年道统
——中国文化的基本精神

上一讲，我们考察了中国文化在不同领域的基本特征，透过这些外在的文化特征，我们会发现，整个的中华文化及其各个领域、各个层次中，都流动着一些相通的、内在的文化精神。所谓中国文化的基本精神，是指为中华民族绝大多数人所接受和尊崇、成为他们生活行动的最高指导原则的一些思想观念或固有传统，这些思想观念或传统对维系中华民族的生存、推动中华文明进步，发挥过积极的历史作用。

那么，中国传统文化的基本精神主要表现在哪几方面呢？我们认为主要有四个方面：（1）天人合一；（2）中庸之道；（3）自强不息；（4）厚德载物。

3.1 天人合一的世界观

首先来看第一点：天人合一的世界观。通俗地说，天人合一即人和天地万物在本质上是同一的，所以人的一切生活均应顺乎本真之道，达到人与自然、人道与天道的和谐统一的美好境界。但这个提法在中国哲学史上却有其更微妙而复杂变的演变发展过程。删繁就简，我这里以孔子的见解为依据略作说明。

孔子和儒家认为：所谓"天"有三义：物质之天、神灵之天和义理之天。

物质之天就是自然。像孔子说的"天何言哉，四时行焉，百物生焉"。这里的"天"就是物质之天。老天爷不说话，四季轮替，万物生长。所以这是唯物论意义上讲的有内在的科学规律的自然。神灵之天即如孔子说的"获罪于天，无所祷也"。得罪了老天爷，你再怎么祈祷也是无济于事的啊。这个得罪不得的"天"，显然是宗教或神学意味的人格神。而义理之天则更为微妙。它不是自然，不是神，它是非人格的天理、天道（Tao），或者按西方哲学的讲法，叫它"宇宙精神"。像孔子说的"天生德于予""五十而知天命"。这里的"天命"和能赋予人类以德性的"天"，都是道（Tao）。学者们也叫它"义理之天"。

因此，对应这三层天，就有相应的三种与天合一的类型：像《周易·乾·文言》中讲的"与日月合其明，与四时合其序"，这当然是指与物质之天的规律或节奏的合一。而"与鬼神合其吉凶"，那自然是与神灵之天的合一以趋吉避凶。"大人者，与天地合其德"，这即是通过德性而达到与天道的合一。那么同时做到了这三种合一，无疑就是"大人"或圣人了。这三层"天"以及这三种天人合一类型，虽然各有其特点，但在孔子儒学中都是真实存在的。它们"三位一体"，各有其影响力和受众群，我们不能只见其一不见其余。

在我看来，中国文化中的"天人合一"，确实可以分为这样三个表现形式：第一种：通过科学和规律，与自然之天合而为一，以开创家园、繁衍生息。第二种：通过宗教和修持，与神灵之天合而为一，以求蒙福报、获得恩典。第三种：通过道德和伦理，与本体之天合而为一，以明心见性、实现真我。

3.1.1　与自然之天的合一

首先我们来看第一种：与自然之天的合一，也可叫生态意义的天人合一。这是当代人发挥得最多，最被重视的一种天人合一类型。

（1）从发现和利用自然规律以开创家园的方面看

中国人历来敬畏大自然，他们深深地懂得：人是大地之子，生活永远离不开自然母亲的怀抱。古人从很早的时候开始就提出要"道法自然"。表现在他们因地制宜，努力把他们的生产生活同所在自然环境相融合，这就要求积极认识和准确把握自然界的各种秘密和规律，"为自然立法"。进而利用这种真理的发现，为自己谋取生活的福利。天和人之间，交相胜、还相用，彼此相得益彰。在我看来，中国古人发明、创制和利用的天文、历法、水利、农耕、医药、养生、建筑等科学技术成果，都可以看成是古人"与日月合其明，与四时合其序"，即与物质之天相合一的杰出作品。

（2）从爱惜生灵和维护生态方面看

第一，儒家很注意生态保护和建设，反对破坏自然环境和滥杀生物。

如孔子任鲁国司空之职时，就广泛考察鲁国的自然地理环境，因地制宜大兴农林建设。今天的曲阜孔庙、泗水县安山寺、潍坊公冶长书院等处都还留有老夫子当年手植的千年老树。《礼记》中明确要求，春天"禁止伐木""毋杀孩虫"。什么叫"孩虫"？也就是幼兽，怀孕的母兽也是不可以杀的。孔子说"钓而不纲，弋不射宿"（《论语·述而》），孟子也说"数罟不入洿池，鱼鳖不可胜食也；斧斤以时入山林，材木不可胜用也"（《孟子·梁惠王上》）。佛道两家都提倡素食，珍惜生灵。中国历朝历代的各地官员也重视植树造林，如福州又叫"榕城"、泉州别称"刺桐城"都是因历史上大面积引种了来自异域的榕树和刺桐而得名的。

第二，民间村落的人民和有着自然崇拜的少数民族群众的生态保护意识尤其自觉。

古代的汉族民间村落历来非常重视生态保护，因为他们认为风水和自然环境的优劣事关家族福祉和子孙运气，所以他们把保护生态的思想写进他们的族谱和乡约，变成人人遵守、违者追责的家族行为规范。如在龙岩连城县培田村的《培田吴氏族谱·族规十则》中，我们就看到此类与维护生态（风水）相关的族规条文："后龙水口，蓄树木而卫风水。前朝屏山，拱祖堂而壮观瞻。路内水圳，护祖堂而便汲饮。田禾蔬菜，备饥荒而佐餐飨。松杉竹木，生财源而资利用。"而中国的少数民族大都崇拜自然，从而在生活中很注意保护生态环境。比如生活在鄂、湘、渝三地交界地区的湖北百福司镇土家人，他们"视水为母、拜山为父"，一草一木都悉心保护，决不乱砍滥伐，表达了对天地的敬畏和对山水的热爱。央视知名纪录片《记住乡愁》里大部分内容，就是介绍我国各民族各地区的人民，尤其是传统村落如何身体力行"青山绿水百福来、天人合一兴家园"的生态伦理思想和美好传统。

图 3-1　天人合一：静观万物皆自得

第三，传统中国文人更是普遍地表现出向往自然的生活情趣。

仁者乐山，智者乐水。有思想力的文人士大夫追慕"静观万物皆自得，四时佳兴与人同"的生活意境，欣赏"好鸟枝头亦朋友，落花水面皆文章"的美感情趣。如陶渊明世外桃花源的梦想，王维《山居秋暝》里"明月松间照，清泉石上流"的闲适静谧，以及雅士们各种传世的山水画、古琴曲，皆可见古人的生活美学大半在山水之间。有时，当我读陶渊明的诗时，我会想起美国哲人梭罗（Henry David Thoreau，1817—1862）和他的《瓦尔登湖》。他们都是大自然的儿子。在他们的心里，"鸟儿不在岩洞里歌唱，鸽子也不在鸽笼里保护自己的纯真"。人生最美好、最快乐的生活方式，就是天人合一、回归于自然。

今天，反思和吸取各种破坏自然、反噬人类的教训，中国人民正在努力建设"望得见山，看得见水，记得住乡愁"的生态文明和美丽中国，也取得了显著的成绩①。"绿水青山就是金山银山"已成为中国未来发展的座右铭。中国坚持环境优先，坚持走绿色发展道路。保护青山绿水，是我们的责任。这也正是中华民族对古人万物一体、天人合一传统的一脉相承。

关于与神灵之天的合一。儒家思想中并不否定神灵之天，还主张要敬之、畏之，虔诚肃穆地祭拜之，所谓敬天法祖、天地君亲师。敬神灵之天是儒教祭祀的第一位的内容，不可谓不重要。而且在祭祀的过程中要虔诚感格，洋洋乎如在上下。孔子也说"丘之祷也久矣""与鬼神合其吉凶""下学而上达，知我者其天乎"。这都透出孔子和儒家有和神灵之天合一的倾向和维度，不容否认。而佛、道等宗教信仰流行于民间社会，通过礼敬、祭拜、冥想等修持方式以感通和合于天地神灵，以免"天谴"获罪，以求趋吉避凶、平安幸福，以得修行境界的提升等，都可以看成中国古人与神灵之天人合一的重要表现。但比较而言，与神灵合一不是以人文主义为特质的中国文化的主要导向，所以这一部分我们这里不展开。

3.1.2 与义理之天的合一

对儒家而言，天人合一的主要形式和根本方法还是"与天地合其德"。

因为在儒家看来，德是天命所赋的道德理性（良知），是人生而有之的先天本性。借着德性的超越性特质，人就可以实现和天道的本质联系。而在孔子看来，这个得天所赋、与天道同一的德性，就是仁（也叫仁德、仁心）。孔子说"仁者爱人"，又说"仁者，己所不欲勿施于人"，他更指出"克己复礼，天下归仁"。曾子解为：推己及人、将心比心的忠恕之道。确实，仁德的重要特性就是能推，它以"感通为性，润物为用"（牟宗三语）。仁者一本于至诚，在感通

---

① 中华人民共和国成立以来，中国人民在党和政府领导下坚持以绿治黄，大规模推进国土绿化，持续实施三北防护林建设、退耕还林还草、京津风沙源治理、南水北调等重大生态工程，如大家知道的"塞上江南"塞罕坝林场、黄土高原重披绿装以及中国政府制定的各种绿色低碳发展目标，有序推进碳达峰、碳中和等，都是中华民族古今一脉相承的生态文明思维的表现。

之中"浑然与物同体",即与任何对象合而为一,并润泽和朗照它们。如见父自然知孝、见幼自然知爱、见君自然知忠、与朋友交自然知信,见鸟兽、草木、瓦石和天地山川,也无不能兼爱同怀。仁德之心就有这种克服外在对立而融合一体的超越之力。

正如王阳明在《大学问》里举的几个例子:

是故见孺子之入井,而必有怵惕恻隐之心焉。是其仁之与孺子而为一体也。孺子犹同类者也,见鸟兽之哀鸣觳觫而必有不忍之心焉,是其仁之与鸟兽而为一体也。鸟兽犹有知觉者也,见草木之摧折而必有悯恤之心焉,是其仁之与草木而为一体也。草木犹有生意者也,见瓦石之毁坏而必有顾惜之心焉,是其仁之与瓦石而为一体也。

王阳明说:当你看到一个小孩马上要掉进水井去了,你一定会产生惊恐和恻隐同情之心啊,你会不假思索地要去救他,这就是你的仁德跟小孩合为一体了;你听到被捕杀的鸟兽发出悲楚的哀鸣,如我们见到待宰的牛羊颤抖着向人屈膝下跪眼中流泪的样子,一定会油然而生不忍之心而不再想去餐食它的肉。这就是你的仁德和鸟兽合为一体了。如果说小孩是同类,鸟兽有知觉,我们会产生同情,但草木和瓦石呢?如我们看到草木菁华被无端砍伐摧折,或看到建筑杰作的圆明园和巴黎圣母院被烧毁成一地瓦砾,我们不也由衷地感到一种深沉的痛苦和悲哀,有一种悯恤和顾惜之情吗?这就是你的仁德和草木、瓦石合而为一了。

这感通万物并与其完全合一的仁德,以同情心(恻隐、不忍、悯恤、顾惜或慈悲)的方式,使人的生命发出光辉,融化人我内外的界限。仁德让人超越了自我的有限性和渺小性而显得无私、博大。这仁德之心的光辉,满心而发,层层通透,层层扩大,家国天下,乃至无一人、无一物不被其涵括和澄明为无分内外的一体——"一即一切,一切即一"。这个大爱无疆的境界,就是孔子说的"一日克己复礼,天下归仁"的境界。

在孔子和儒家的心性之学看来,仁爱天下、博爱无疆并不是道德浮夸,而是基于仁心内在本性的一种自然呈现。儒家信仰这一点,所以说人性本善,也说满街都是圣人。就如是鸟就能飞,是鱼儿就能游水,人只要"大其心",或"致良知",就一定能大爱无疆于天地人寰之中,而这也就是人生意义的最高表现。儒家基于仁德的本体论而发明的性善论,无疑能大大激发作为肉身凡夫的我们一种极大的欢喜和热情:每个人的内在竟然有如此的伟大的宝藏,我也可以大作一个我啊!

如阳明所说:"大人者,与天地万物为一体也。其视天下犹一家,中国犹一人焉。"当然阳明也指出：若偏执人我内外的形骸之别，那就是个自私纵欲的无知者，那就是麻木不仁了。麻木就不能感通，心性的光辉就被遮蔽而流露不出来，当然就不能知道何为感动，何谓无私的爱。试问：人从来不曾为别人的悲哀而流泪，从来不以能为他人谋福利而欢喜，又谈何能领略天人合一的境界呢？

对于有志于追求天人合一的学者们来说，儒家会教导他们，天人合一是如实和率真的伦理生活，而不是谈玄说妙、苦禅静坐、玩弄光景。你也不能离群索居、遁入深山，必须在日用百行中，在伦理—政治的社会生活之中，认真地修身为本、敦伦尽分——要去明心见性，即敞开你得天所赋的这颗光明的仁德的本心达到一个极致。总有一天呢，你会顿感心底无私天地宽，顿感与天地精神相往来，人和人的世界突然地恢复到天人合一的本真妙境。这个天人合一的本真妙境之中，仁心之光普照万有，让万物生出光辉。每一件哪怕是再微小的事物——鸢飞鱼跃、草木菁华、一缕浮云、一声蝉鸣，或者一颦一笑、一段时光，都能毫无亏损地、忠实地反映出它与世界的本真之奥、一体之美。天人合一者明心见性的眼睛能看透这世界的美好。

他们能看到"一花一世界，一叶一菩提"。他们能从"一滴水中看到整个太阳的光辉"。他们能从"万物之中看到上帝"。他们说"人皆可为尧舜""满街都是圣人""处处都是佛国"。他们甚至说："道在蝼蚁、在稊草、在瓦壁、在屎溺。"蝼蚁之中有道，稊草乃至屎溺之中都有道，这个境界，不是仁心大照、天人合一境界中的人，又哪里能体悟得了呢？

仁就是人与天地万物共通的最高同一性的保障和体现。克己复礼、明心见性、仁者爱人、天下归仁，就是孔子儒学的真正奥秘，也是儒家天人合一哲学最核心的智慧。是一种绝对平等、人人可到的真实境界。也是中国文化所追求的至善境界、自由境界、真乐境界。借用陶渊明的诗句就是"俯仰天地间，不乐复何如"，"纵浪大化中，不喜亦不惧"。

总之，中国古人追求：与自然和谐、天人合一兴家园；与众生和谐、天人合一享太平；与神灵和谐、天人合一得皈依；与宇宙和谐、天人合一证圆融。天人合一的思想和境界表现了人和自然的共生一体性，彰显了人的文化主体性，是中华民族仁爱无疆、美德懿行的根本源头，是中华民族的自强不息、乐观奋斗精神的内在动力，也是中华民族追求和谐天下、四海一家的本质原因。这种亦哲学亦宗教、亦美学亦伦理、亦理论亦生活的天人合一思维，造就了中国文化高远的价值境界与生存格调。中国古人追求并安心于这超然功利、顿忘物我、融合天人的精神境界，享受着他们圆融一体、静美有情的生活氛围。"乃不知有汉，无论魏晋。"

今天，世界人类正深陷于功利主义和技术主义的烦恼中，人天分裂、万物敌对、生态破坏，人心支离破碎，人情冷漠抑郁，国家地区之间冲突不断，正需要这种圆融一体、静美有情的天人合一思维与境界加以对治超拔。中西方文化各自长于天人合一和主客二分思维，二者又都是人类本质性力量的展开。如何综合地统筹妙用，全在智者一心起念之间。相信随着中西文化的更多良性对话与交融，未来的人类文化更能发挥主体性的智慧，以期达到二者兼备、两全其美的目的。

3.2 中庸之道的辩证方法论

尚中道、致和合，是中国文化一个极高明的精神，是中国人长期尊奉的理性方法论，也是儒家和道家文化中非常重要的思想，在中华民族和中国文化发展过程中起过十分重要的作用。中庸，也叫中庸之道或中道。

大家要了解中庸之道，可以先看看中国的太极图。太极图有一阴一阳，代表了所有属性对立的正反两方面事物。阴与阳：相反相成、动态转化，它们对立统一又本质同一。太极图的哲理其实就是东方的辩证法，它的方法论启示就是：凡事不可静止地偏执一面，而应具体考察事物的发展状况，采取恰如其分的适宜方法，以求得无过无不及的适中状态，从而促进事物的持续发展的目的。

首先，中道反对偏激，追求事物发展的适中程度（适度）。

"中"被看成事物发展状态上无过无不及的恰当的度，也称"中正"。就如亚里士多德《伦理学》讲的"中道"：过度与不及都是恶，只有适中是善。如奢侈和吝啬是过与不及的恶。慷慨呢，恰得适中，是善。鲁莽和懦弱是过与不及，是恶，唯有勇敢是适中的善。纵欲淫荡与麻木不仁是过与不及的恶，适中的节制，就是善。其实孔子也说过相似的话。他点评他的学生子张与子夏的为人性格：一者过，一者不及，而过跟不及是一样的。就如狂与狷，一者急躁冒进，一者畏缩不前。都不好，都不如"中行"。"中行"也就是根据实际情况而懂得有所为、有所不为的恰当状态，也就是适中与适度。孔子借此是提醒人们注意"度"的问题。他提倡要在对立面之间不走极端，而是适度适中。如为人太文雅就显得矫揉，太质朴则显得粗野，两方面适中，"文质彬彬，然后君子"。孔子自己的形象给人的印象就是：温而厉、威而不猛、泰而不骄；或"望之俨然，即之也温"。这就是一种对立气质之间的对冲，从而达到了某种平衡与适中。就像《登徒子好色赋》中的描写的那个"东家之子"：增之一分则太长，减之一分则太短。著粉则太白，施朱则太赤。

中国人特别注意适度的原则，认为月满则亏、水满则溢、物壮则老、乐极生悲。比如一般在农村祠堂或民居的前面会开掘一个半月形的池塘，而不会是圆形。这就是忌"圆满"。圆满不如半满之犹有发展空间，仍存在进步的生机性和生命力。一旦圆满了，就要开始走下坡路了。也是出于这个道理，老子在《道德经》里就教导人们要"知强用弱""知荣守辱"，"复归于婴儿"。理学家朱熹给自己取的号叫"晦翁"，曾国藩给自己的书斋取名"求阙斋"。为了求得最好的利益，凡事能保持适中适度（而不求圆满）的状态则可以永葆生机、一往无前、生生不息。中国人日常生活中也讨厌极端行事，遵循：话不可说满、福不可享尽、事不可做绝。这都是中庸之道关于度的哲理所塑造的民族性格。

其次，中道在实践上要求要务实决策，以恰如其分、行事有成。

这里，我先举几个儒家中庸之道的生活运用的例子来做说明吧。

（1）以孝道为例：儒家一般认为，孝就是顺从和无违，忤逆或违反父母之命就不是孝了。但根据中庸的原理，顺从和违逆，一阴一阳，顺从有时恰成不孝，而违逆有时却恰成其孝。比如"耘瓜受杖"的故事。有一次曾子不小心锄断了瓜秧，他父亲就拿棍子打他，打得痛死过去曾子也不逃走，他这是以顺从为孝啊。但孔子却说这不是孝，因为这迎合了情绪化和非理性的父亲，令他可能杀子犯法锒铛入狱，至少是会被乡党诟病或后来追悔自责，这难道是孝子当为的？相反的，大舜被他的父亲和后妈联合暗害，可大舜没有坐以待毙，设法逃避了，他的内心并没有仇恨，对父母的敬意未尝减少。后来他当了天子还善待那些伤害过自己的家人。大舜以违逆而保全了自己，更保全了亲道，恪尽了孝道。他的孝心是饱满的，也是理性的，他懂得在顺从和违逆之间作出正确的选择，所以被列为二十四孝第一位。

（2）比如礼：按儒家的看法"男女授受不亲，礼也"。但孟子就说假若嫂子掉进水里快淹死了，要不要救？救则难免肢体接触而破坏了男女授受不亲的礼法，不救则眼睁睁看着嫂子被淹死。怎么办呢？孟子认为此时特殊情况，权宜从事就该救，发生肢体接触也情有可原。若固守礼法而不救那就是禽兽了①。

（3）又比如诚信：人而无信不知其可，诚信是美德。但对恶棍呢？对毁我家园的强盗呢？也要一五一十讲诚信，知无不言言无不尽？当然不可以，孔子

---

① 如关于礼的变革与保守，孔子说："麻冕，礼也。今也纯，俭，吾从众。拜下，礼也。今拜乎上，泰也。虽违众，吾从下。"

就把死守诚信不知变通的人叫顽固的小人①。而孟子也说"言不必信，行不必果"，而看道义所在而定。这也叫小信与大信的区别，大信不拘泥，而以是否符合正义（目的和效果）为转移。

如上所述，则能看出孔子是一个非常务实的哲人，他强调"毋意，毋必，毋固，毋我"，他很懂得根据此一时、彼一时的具体情况做适当的判断和适宜的选择。孔子说：君子对于天下的事，没有规定一定要怎样做，也没有规定一定不要怎样做，而只考虑怎样做才合适恰当，就行了。这就是孔子所谓的"无可无不可"的行事方法论。就如太极图里的一阴一阳，你中有我，我中有你，本质同一，又何必偏执一定呢？凡事具体问题具体分析，手段为目的服务，策略为理念服务，只要符合道义，都可灵活权变地采用。孔子总是根据实际的情况而"两可"地、务实地做判断决策，总是谆谆教导学生多从两方面想想各自的利弊，而他的言语行为被认为都符合中庸之道，所以孔子被人们称为"庸言庸行"的"圣之时者"。

道家也认识到所谓世界的变化之道，"反者道之动""正复为奇，善复为妖"。既然万事万物随时变化，行事上也就不必过于保守。如《道德经》第八章中就教导人们："上善若水。水善利万物而不争。处众人之所恶，故几于道。居善地，心善渊，与善仁，言善信，政善治，事善能，动善时。"这里老子连用了七个"善"。此"善"之为善，全在一个随机应变中的妙智观察和灵活权变，迂腐的固执者自然是望尘莫及的。故君子不争环境，而善因地制宜、因时而异，这样就不会有怨咎。庄子的齐物论思想也是主张"以道观之，何贵何贱"，天下事物换个角度看，谁又没有一定的合理性和值得被肯定的一面呢？所以，你呼我以马则我应之马，呼我以牛则我应之牛。是牛是马无不可，何必贵彼贱此、互为高下呢？朝三暮四与朝四暮三，美女与夜叉，小草与楠木，有用与无用，生死寿夭，无非如此。本质同一，不必偏执，全在具体的当下作智慧的考察。

以上两层其实都可算在"用"上讨论的、作为实践方法论或生活技术的中庸之道。

中庸之道的方法论价值是明显的，也是人们最常注意和宣讲的部分。但中道的深刻处，其实还是一套本体论。辩证法不仅仅是对立统一的方法论，更是

---

① "言必信，行必果，硁硁然小人哉。"（《论语·子路》）如孔子过蒲城，当地人正在闹叛乱，就逼迫孔子签订盟约不去卫国，但孔子后来并未遵守，他不认为这是不守信，因为这是被逼迫签的约，是神也不听的"要盟"。小信与大信之别，一者死守形式而固执不变，一者谨遵正义，懂得权宜变通。

通向一定的本体论的。如黑格尔的辩证法就通向"绝对观念"，佛家的中观就通向"空性"。儒家的中庸之道的本体论就是"静态之中"和"动态之和"的统一与同一的"中和论"。这个话题太哲学，我们这里略提示几个关键词即可。

根据《中庸》所谓："喜怒哀乐之未发，谓之中，发而皆中节，谓之和；中也者，天下之大本也；和也者，天下之达道也。致中和，天地位焉，万物育焉。"这里有四个很重要的关键词："中"是天下万物的本体，它寂然不动、渊深静默，是万物的本性与本真。"和"是率性成道，"中"之本体感通天下，用"中"致"和"，行事权变得中。"致中和"静处涵养本心，事上磨炼本心，时时在"中"，时时得"和"，层层深入。"天地位、万物育"中和功夫到极致，与道为一，天地泰宁、万物顺遂祥和。这当然就是中国人特别追求的明心见性、天人合一的、宇宙万物的大和谐，即太和。正是因为中庸之道的深入处，其境界乃如此之高，以至于孔子认为中庸是至高的道德，鲜有人能做到啊，就算你能放弃国家和爵禄，能上刀山下火海，想做到中庸也是不可能的啊。

以上呢，我们解析了中庸之道的两层义理：第一，作为辩证方法论，它强调发展状态上过犹不及，适度最好。行为决策上务实抉择，适合最好。第二，作为本体论：中庸之道指示以天下大本之"中"致大化流行之"和"，时时在"中"，处处得"和"。最终呢，达到天地万物内在圆融、祥和清宁、生生不息的太和境界。

总之，尚中道、贵中和，是中华民族重要的国民性，而这皆得力于中庸之道这一文化精神的熏染塑造之功，让中华民族养成了不偏执、不极端，重实际、灵活而不教条、求是务实的理性头脑与温和性格。进而形成了中和圆融、天人合一的整体和谐观、太和生存观。中国人在政治上追求仁和礼、德治与法治相统一；伦理上追求"内圣外王"相统一，"合内外之道"；经济上追求义利兼顾、贫富相安；人格塑造上追求"德才兼备""刚柔并济""文质彬彬"；教育方法上追求"教学相长""学思并用""知行合一"。毛泽东主席提倡要形成"既有集中又有民主，既有纪律又有自由，既有统一意志，又有个人心情舒畅，生动活泼"这样一种良好的社会局面；习近平主席提出要把追求"中华民族伟大复兴"和构建"人类命运共同体"相统一。可以说，这都是儒家中道思想的历史运用和当代创新发展的表现。这里提到的范畴，本质上都是对立统一的。智者当在对立面之间做到无过无不及、不偏不倚的相对平衡和动态和谐。形象地说，就是"择其两端而用其中"。

当然，实际之中，中庸之道也常被人曲解成模棱两可与含混模糊之道，也就是和事佬式的折中之道。可和事佬的"中道"里面呢，内无本真理念为魂，外无正义底线可言，一味地讲"无可无不可"，把个好好的中庸之道，弄成和稀泥式的庸俗之道了。

3.3　自强不息的人格精神

自强不息，可以被看成是中国传统文化在中国人的生存态度上积极的价值反映，也是对中华民族整体人格状态的历史概括与现实写照。《易传》对自强不息的思想做过经典性的表述：天行健，君子以自强不息。意谓：天的运动刚强劲健，相应于此，君子也应刚毅坚卓，发愤图强。以天体运行无休无止，永远向上的规律，要求人们积极有为，勇于进取，这大概也是"顺乎天而应乎人"的天人合一思想的一种表现吧。

那么，中华民族是怎么养成了这样一种自强不息、刚健有为的文化精神的呢？

首先，自强不息是无数的天灾人祸的历练下养成的民族文化精神。

我们常说中国是一片美丽富饶的土地。但其实幅员辽阔的中国也是一个被叫作是"饥荒的国度"（The land of Famine）。邓云特先生的《中国救荒史》一书中曾经统计过：从秦汉至于明清，中国就发生过各种灾害和饥馑多达 5079 次。其中水灾 1013 次，旱灾 1022 次，雹灾、风灾、蝗灾、疫灾、霜雪灾、地震、饥馑，等等，数之不尽①。而《中国历代战争年表（上下）》统计了从公元前 26 世纪—公元 1911 年间，中国历代共发生各种战事合计 3791 次。可以说，自古以来，中华民族经历和承受了无数天灾人祸的苦难命运，但中国人民没有因此而屈服或沦亡，他们选择了奋斗和自强。从各种流传至今的成语故事中，我们也能窥见一斑，如：女娲补天、夸父逐日、后羿射日、大禹治水、精卫填海、愚公移山等。

以"夸父逐日"和"后羿射日"为例。每个国家都有太阳神的传说，在部落时代，太阳神有着绝对的权威。而纵览所有太阳神的神话你会发现，只有中国人的神话里有敢于挑战太阳神的故事：因为太阳太热，夸父就去追逐太阳，他想把它摘下来。神箭手后羿则把太阳射了下来。当然，最后夸父累死了。但是中国的神话里，人们把他当作英雄来传颂，因为他敢于和看起来难以战胜的力量作斗争。"任何神话都是借助想象以征服自然力，支配自然力，把自然力加

---

① 邓云特. 中国救荒史［M］. 北京：商务印书馆. 2011：21.

以形象化。"（马克思）中国人的祖先想用这样的故事教育后代：在天灾人祸面前，可以输，但不能屈服。上一节我们提到天人合一的概念。在天人合一的关系里，人和天"交相胜，还相用"。人在天地面前并不是一个无所作为的奴隶。《荀子·天论》里的这段话讲得很好啊：大天而思之，孰与物畜而制之！从天而颂之，孰与制天命而用之！望时而待之，孰与应时而使之！面对大自然的深沉难测和无限的洪荒之力，人类要想生存，就只有振作自强！当中华先民呐喊出"我命在我不在天"，甚至是"人定胜天"的口号的时候，他们充满了决绝与豪迈！没有这点决绝与豪迈，就没有我们这个民族生生不息的文明史！

其次，自强不息更是中国人特别推崇、历史传承的民族文化精神。

中华民族自古以来就是一个注重教育和文化传承的民族，而自强不息文化精神的生命教养和人格修行就是其中非常重要的内容。我们可以从如下几个方面略加以探讨：

第一，自强者首先要强于明强，即领悟"强之为强"的本质。

在我们看来，真正的强者，是拥有真理的人们。真理，在中国文化语境下，就是"道"，如孔子所说：志于道，据于德，依于仁，游于艺（《论语·述而》）。志道，就是追求真理。我们前面也介绍到了，儒家的天道就是天人合一的宇宙人生的真理。或者说，就是自然之道、历史之道、生命之道。"志于道"就是要追求宇宙人生的真理，进而让天下苍生都能按照真理去生活，这是一个目的性。正如《周易》中指出的："文明以止，人文也。……观乎人文以化成天下。"要获得真理、传播真理，就要发扬求道和弘道的主体性精神。孔子指出"人能弘道，非道弘人"，真理是需要人们自己去发现和弘扬的，道是不会自己来化成人类至于完美的。一切伟大的民族和强大的人民，都是立志追求真理、弘扬天道的民族和人民。我们应该用真理作我们的信仰和力量源泉，这样，我们才能真正地强大。人民有信仰，则国家有力量，民族才有希望。

强者不能没有热诚追求真理的高尚精神。没有获得天道和人道的真理，又如何能真正地自强？又如何能化成天下、实现社会的文明？没有真理的强，只会是霸道和强权之强，是毁灭性而非建设性的强。有一次，子路向老师孔子请教一个问题"什么叫强？"引出了孔子对"强之为强"的一番议论。

子路问强。子曰："南方之强与？北方之强与？抑而强与？宽柔以教，不报无道，南方之强也，君子居之。衽金革，死而不厌，北方之强也，而强者居之。故君子和而不流，强哉矫！中立而不倚，强哉矫！国有道，不变塞焉，强哉矫！国无道，至死不变，强哉矫！"（《礼记·中庸》）

孔子之言翻译过来大意就是：你问的是哪种地方的强呢？"南方之强与？北

方之强与？"这个要先搞清楚。和北方之强的金戈铁马、逞凶斗狠相比，南方之强很不错。因为他用宽容柔和的精神去教育人，人家对我蛮横无理也不报复。南方之强和顺温柔而不随波逐流，保持中立而不偏不倚，永远坚持原则、保持操守，也就是说南方之强文德宽柔、中庸理性。这也就是儒家推崇的中国文化的强之为强：理性与爱心。

被誉为"中国最美大学"的厦门大学的校歌唱道：

自强！自强！学海何洋洋！谁欤操钥发其藏？鹭江深且长，致吾知于无央。吁嗟乎！南方之强！吁嗟乎！南方之强！自强！自强！人生何茫茫！谁欤普渡驾慈航？鹭江深且长，充吾爱于无疆。吁嗟乎！南方之强！吁嗟乎！南方之强！

此歌有唱到两句很重要的词，"致吾知于无央"，"充吾爱于无疆"。致知和充爱，这就是理性和慈悲。中国人民就是用这样的文德和理性精神来教育自己的青年领悟"强之为强"的真精神。可以说，中华民族过去、现在和未来，都是一个热爱和平的理性、慈悲、有爱的民族。侵略和强暴的霸道，不是中国的文化传统和国民性所能允许的。中国将坚定地走和平发展的道路，即使再强大，也永远不当强权，永远不称霸。

第二，自强者必须把艰苦治学和发奋有为相结合。

志于道，不是空谈，而要求学以得道、研究以得真理。求学必须艰苦力学，勤学、好学、善学并终身学习。中国古人在这方面给我们留下了大量感人的榜样啊。如西汉的匡衡"凿壁借光"，朱买臣"负薪挂角"，东汉孙敬、战国苏秦"悬梁刺股"，东晋的车胤和孙康"囊萤映雪"，祖逖"闻鸡起舞"，北宋欧阳修"以荻画地"，杨时"程门立雪"等。这些中华教育史上矢志求道、艰苦力学的经典人物故事，永远鼓励我们要学以求道、学以强己、学习强国。自强的人就是要努力地学以致用、学以报国、学以济世，有所作为取得成就以利益天下。

中国古人提倡"三不朽"，哪三不朽？首先就是"立德"，即修养高尚完美的道德；其次是"立功"，就是为国为民建立功绩；第三就是"立言，即写出具有真知灼见的言论。这都是有所作为的表现，也足以使人流芳不朽。立德、立功、立言都不容易。如立言，写出你所发现的真理，这容易吗？不容易。正如司马迁在《史记·太史公自序》里头写道：

西伯拘而演《周易》；仲尼厄而作《春秋》；屈原放逐，乃赋《离骚》；左丘失明，厥有《国语》；孙子膑脚《兵法》修列；《诗》三百篇，皆圣贤发愤之所作为也。

这些中华圣贤所启示者发奋有为，不因艰难困苦而失志灰心。正义之事就是再难也要做，而且要做好，即使付出惨重的代价，也要尽自己的天命，去做出成绩以惠泽天下苍生，而这也是足以使人获得流芳百世的不朽。中国人认为立德、立功、立言，是每个人应该致力去承担的事业，而事实也证明，"我们自古以来，就有埋头苦干的人，有拼命硬干的人，有为民请命的人，有舍身求法的人……虽是等于为帝王将相作家谱的所谓'正史'，也往往掩饰不住他们的光耀，这就是中国的脊梁"。（鲁迅）

第三，自强者特别的表现为强于气节。

气节，也可以叫骨气，是因为信念而获得的坚韧不拔的生命品格与精神力量，孟子把它叫作"浩然之气"。有了浩然之气，就不会懦弱胆怯，就会有坚不可摧的气节。自强者的生命每个细胞都充满了浩然正气，他们坚守真理和正义，不为威逼利诱而放弃自己的原则，甚至宁死不屈、视死如归。中华民族自古就信仰"富贵不能淫，贫贱不能移，威武不能屈"的大丈夫精神，敢于面对一切的艰难困苦和威逼利诱。为了求道和弘道，为了保护家园和父母妻儿，他们哪怕死亡，也要矢志不移、视死如归地进行斗争。孔子说："志士仁人，无求生以害仁，有杀身以成仁。""三军可夺帅也，匹夫不可夺志也。"文天祥说："人生自古谁无死，留取丹心照汗青。"这都是一种威武不屈、藐视死亡的冲天的气节。

抗日战争爆发后，时任商务印书馆董事长的知名学者张元济先生编著了一本《中华民族的人格》，1937年5月出版后引起热议。这本书里头讲述了八位中华民族历史上视死如归的气节壮士的故事。这其中有臣子的忠义，有君子的孝悌，有大复仇的精神，有国士报恩的自觉。如开篇所述的就是著名的"赵氏孤儿"的故事。"公孙杵臼的死，是死于忠；程婴的死，是死于信。"第二个故事讲的是伍子胥兄弟的复仇故事。楚王抓了伍尚和伍子胥的父亲，告诉他们如果回国就放了他们的父亲。伍尚明知这是个必死无疑的圈套，但是依然选择亲自回去救父亲，而让他的弟弟活下来报仇。第三个故事讲的是孔子的弟子子路在卫国公室发生内乱之时，因"食人之禄不避其责"，明知事不可为而为之，遂结缨力战，从容赴死。另外还有如荆轲刺秦王、田横五百士之类，这些忠义之人其实都可以不死，但是他们最后都选择了死，这并不是有不得已的原因。这里的死，都有着更加重要的理由，那就是比个人生命更重要的道义，是道德的信念使得他们无惧于死亡。

他们的故事启示了：中华民族从不缺少顶天立地的豪杰，他们或重然诺、讲信义，或临危不苟、忠肝义胆，甚或杀身成仁、舍生取义。这才是中华民族的真人格、真精神。

第四，自强者还要强于达观，永葆初心、韧性前行。

中国人民的自强精神，还表现在他们的乐观主义和强大的恒心。中国人是乐天知命的达观的民族。他们一方面积极承担天命和道义，另外一方面又了知世俗的命运。这两者之间，该做的一定要做，责无旁贷舍我其谁。世俗命运的羁绊，他们安之若素。他们明白，成功不必在我而真理必胜，就像孔子说的，继往开来的天道再过百千年也仍然会起作用，这是可以预料得到的。"其或继周者，虽百世可知也"（《论语·为政》）。这就如我们今天所说的，风云过眼，真理和正义终将赢得历史和未来。蒲松龄曾撰写过一副自勉的对联流传后世，也成为青年人们在困境之时勉励自己的绝佳的对子。"有志者事竟成，破釜沉舟，百二秦关终属楚。苦心人天不负，卧薪尝胆，三千越甲可吞吴。"当我们念到这样的诗句的时候，一定会由衷地产生一种振作之气、奋进之心，光明在前，贵在自强，贵在坚忍地战斗与恒久地坚持自己的一份初心与信念。

这里就把乐观和恒心联系在了一起。中国古人论述恒心的语录很多，比如"子在川上曰：逝者如斯乎，不舍昼夜"。曾子说："任重道远。仁以为己任，不亦重乎？死而后已不亦远乎？"如曹操的诗所写到的："老骥伏枥，志在千里；烈士暮年，壮心不已。"就是刘禹锡的诗里写到的："莫道桑榆晚，为霞尚满天。"也是李商隐的诗中写到的："春蚕到死丝方尽，蜡炬成灰泪始干。"《周易》有云："不恒其德，或承之羞。"什么意思？人要是没有恒德，没有恒心，做事有始无终、虎头蛇尾，那就会遭到羞辱啊。所以要有始有终，不忘初心，永远砥砺奋进。这也是一个自强者强之于强的表现。

总之，刚健有为、自强不息的精神一直是中国传统文化的主导精神，如长江黄河，奔涌在中华民族的身上，就像黄山泰山、像万里长城，支撑在中华民族的精神天地之间，激励这个民族勇往直前、坚韧创业，永远屹立在世界民族之林。可以说，波澜壮阔的中华民族发展史，就是一部艰苦奋斗创造文明的历史。包括新中国成立七十多年来的历史，也是发扬传统，从站起来、富起来到强起来的光荣的历史。正如习近平总书记指出的："在一百年的非凡奋斗历程中，一代又一代中国共产党人顽强拼搏、不懈奋斗，涌现了一大批视死如归的革命烈士、一大批顽强奋斗的英雄人物、一大批忘我奉献的先进模范，形成了井冈山精神、长征精神、遵义会议精神、延安精神、西柏坡精神、红岩精神、抗美援朝精神、'两弹一星'精神、特区精神、抗洪精神、抗震救灾精神、抗疫精神等伟大精神，构筑起了中国共产党人的精神谱系。我们党之所以历经百年而风华正茂、饱经磨难而生生不息，就是凭着那么一股革命加拼命的强大精

神。"① 中国共产党人的精神谱系也就是中华民族自强不息精神在当代的生动
体现。

自强不息、刚健有为、天道酬勤，就是我们这个民族万古长青的成功秘诀。

3.4 厚德载物的仁爱情怀

中国文化富有厚德载物、太上立德的可贵品质和优秀精神。英国哲人罗素
曾这样评价说："中国人天然态度宽容友爱，以礼待人，亦望人以礼答之。……
道德上之品行，为中国人所特长。如此品行之中，余以具'心气平和'（Pacific
temper）最为可贵"②。

关于中国人的仁爱情怀，有一个最日常的例子。比如中国人平时见面的时
候会问"你吃了没？"这跟西方人打招呼问候天气不同。原因何在呢？这是因为
中国人认为"民以食为天"，挨饿是最不幸的，而衣食无忧是最大的幸福。当你
问候的人吃不上饭的时候，你的同情心是过意不去的，因此就要关心他，给他
饭食的帮助。人们之间彼此关心对方最根本的生命福祉这种言语和行为，相沿
成习，成了中国人日常打招呼的固定口语。这不能不说是一种朴素而高尚的美
德，表现了中国人为人处世以爱心为本位的道德生活方式。强烈的伦理道德氛
围是中国人呼吸的空气。自古以来，社会各阶层、各个生活领域，都有着鲜明
而严格的、人们必须遵守的各种道德规范与行为指示。而中华民族之所以"以
道德上之品行"为特长，这其实离不开其所深受的儒家价值观的教化影响。我
认为，儒家道德文化的特质有如下三个层次。

第一，"道德一体"的形而上学体系，而非有德无道的实用道德。

中国古人的道德观一贯把道与德联系一起，对道德的形而上学的本体论有
深入的发明。中国文化从先秦诸子时代就注重对天道的探讨，并明确地把人们
的德性修养同这个形而上学的天道本体密切地结合起来给予讨论。道家认为
"万物莫不尊道而贵德"。儒家明确说要"志于道，据于德"。这个道，不是宗
教性质的、人格化的神，而是义理性质的天道，它是万物的根本、宇宙的精神。
而"天生德于我"（孔子），"德者得也，得其道于心而不失之谓也"（朱熹），
这就为"人性本善"奠定了源自天道的先验的理论基础。有超越的天理而后有

---

① 见习近平在党史学习教育动员大会上的讲话（2021 年 2 月 20 日）.
② ［英］伯特兰·罗素. 中国问题［M］. 北京：中国画报出版社，2019：219.

内在心性的修养、人格的养成和伦理生活的社会实践，一以贯之。

第二，"依于仁"的主体性道德，而非外在服从的庸俗道德。

与先前儒哲讲道德的那种外在路向不同，孔子发明仁德这一内在的先天德性，弘扬生命的主体性，强调"我欲仁，斯仁至矣""克己复礼天下归仁"。道德是自己的事，是一颗善心不能不表现的事。没有这真诚为善的仁爱之心，又谈何礼乐之道呢？孔孟的道德观"从心讲起"，以仁德来实现道德，以主体性融会客体性，内圣开外王，尽心知性则知天。这就是孔子孟子开辟的心性儒学的新方向。心性儒学的道德观重视的不是外在的政刑法纪的约束制裁，而是人们基于自己的良知的自觉修养。所有的中华美德如忠孝廉节，都以仁心的真诚流露为第一原则，否则便是道德的形式主义。这是孔子道德观的伟大之处。

第三，伦理本位的实践道德，而非托之空言的口头道德。

道德一体、践仁知天不是玄谈而是真实的生活和日常的修养。儒家要求人们"安土敦乎仁"，仁心大爱要像大地一样广博无涯，承担天下的一切责任，尤其是扣住一个人和人的伦理义务和责任做功夫，并不离开人的生活世界而论所谓人生的境界。孔子就说"道不远人，人之为道而远人，不可以为道"（《中庸·第十三章》）。这就确定了儒家和中国文化的人本主义的倾向，关注人间、关心人生、关注人的伦理生命，成为根本趋向。儒家强调人伦的名分，即把人们纳入各自所属的"五伦"为主的社会人际关系中，并给他们以相对应的责任与义务。伦理是天理的人间落实，人伦世界是道德修养的主要领域，也是帮助人去完成社会化文明人格的主要手段。

这三点结合起来，我们可以把中国传统的道德观描述为以伦理为本位、天道人心相贯通的人生修养和生活风范。或者说是：上对得起天，内对得起良心，外对得起人。

我们认为，以儒家道德观念为主干而形成的传统道德文化系统是支撑中国伦理型社会的精神基石，筑就了中华民族的价值意识形态的坚实内核。中华民族确实以注重道德品行为特长，也以道德品行的修养为日常生活的重要使命。从天子至于庶民，敦伦尽分，一是以修身为本，整个社会各领域流动着浓厚的道德氛围，这种道德主义的普遍表现大概如此：（1）政治领域上中国文化提倡"为政以德、以孝治国"，推崇敬天、重民、尊孔的王道政治。君仁臣忠，正德立身、恪尽职责。以实现天下为公的大同社会为最高目标。（2）法律领域上中国文化提倡"德主刑辅"，反对政刑严苛。以道德立法，重尽家族的道德义务，而不重满足个人权利。（3）经济领域上中国文化推崇"诚信为本"的子贡遗风，讲究义利兼顾、义以为上。如晋商和徽商的文化内核，都是一种儒商情怀。

（4）宗族领域上宗族是乡土社会践行儒家礼法的主力军。特别重视祠堂祭祖、家谱编修、遵守族规和传承家风，家族内部有共财、通财、分财与施财之义，实际是利益互惠、风险共担的经济共同体。（5）文艺领域上儒家"兴于诗，立于礼，成于乐"。文以载道、以文化人。艺术家们外师造化、内法心源，追求文质彬彬，乐而不淫，哀而不伤，尽善尽美，思无邪。（6）外交领域上中国人向往"天下太平、协和万邦"，修文德以柔怀远人，没有侵略的基因。用罗素的话来说就是"世有不屑于战争（too proud to fight）之民族乎？中国人是已。"中国虽是大国，但从不以大欺小，而是"大国以下小国"。国家交往中尊重差异和多样性，讲究平等互利，文明交流互鉴。（7）宗教领域上中国文化提倡人间宗教，重孝道和王道，庄严国土利乐有情，主张佛法在世间，人成即佛成。强调诸善奉行、诸恶莫作，好人得福报，善心成正果。（8）社会领域上官方、宗族或社会的义士常乐于创办各类公益慈善性质的义学、义仓、义田，乐善好施者修路架桥、施粥舍药、赈济灾民等。

　　中国传统道德文化推崇仁德和良知，相信人性本善，注重伦理修养，讲究改过迁善、从善如流，追求高尚和伟大的人格境界。中华道德文化塑造了温柔敦厚、心气和平的民族道德心理和集体人格，使中国人民养成了所珍视的各种感人的中华传统美德。中国人民珍视自己民族的道德文化传统，敬慕和赞美历史上的各种美德人物如贤母慈父、孝子烈女、明君贤相、干臣清流、仁人志士、英雄侠客、高僧大德、儒商国医……并为他们树碑立传，将他们载之煌煌史册，供奉于松柏森森的祠庙，表彰于巍峨庄严的牌坊，对他们的美德懿行如数家珍、深切感怀，借以激励自己，也传承给后来的子孙。

　　当然，任何道德文化类型都有一定的时代和阶级的局限，儒家为主的传统德性文化的阴影面如礼教文化的封建化底蕴，道德体系形而上的抽象，对世俗生活合理性价值的忽视等，都曾对人的自由和全面发展造成了一定的桎梏。但是，经过正本清源和有扬弃的创新，传统道德观所追求的天人合一、中正仁和、仁者爱人、义利兼顾、四海一家等价值境界及其所具有的超越时代的历史魅力和恒久人文价值，一定会在新的历史起点继续发散光辉。当代中国人民继往开来，在民族复兴的新时代，也涌现了许许多多感动中国的美德人物。他们热爱祖国、服务人民、承担职责、恪尽义务，表现出了熠熠生辉的人格高度和生命风采，他们是共和国的脊梁和我们民族的骄傲，令人仰之弥高①。

---

　　①　可参看由新华社组织编撰的《100位新中国成立以来感动中国人物书系》（广东教育出版社2009年版）.

总之，中国传统文化源远流长，其内涵的基本精神是以天人合一、中庸之道、自强不息和厚德载物这四点为代表的。这些文化精神在中华文化的成长过程中，发挥了诸如民族凝聚功能、精神激励功能、整合创新功能等建设性作用，滋养了数千年来中华儿女的精神世界，是真正生生不息的传统优秀文化的内核亮点。在文化全球化和呼吁建设人类命运共同体的今天，中国传统文化的精华越来越有着世界性的价值和意义，是值得我们去好好珍视和承继弘扬的。

The Third Chapter:

Centuries-long Orthodoxy
—Spirit of Chinese Culture

In the last chapter, we talked about the basic characteristics of Chinese culture in different fields. Through these external cultural characteristics, we can find that they all flow with some same and internal cultural spirit. What is the basic spirit of Chinese culture? It is accepted and respected by the vast majority of the Chinese people, and become the highest guiding principles for their lives and actions. It refers to some ideas or inherent traditions of Chinese people. These ideas and traditions are significant. In regard of maintaining the survival of the Chinese nation, and promoting the progress of Chinese civilization, they have played an active historical role.

So, how can we get to know the basic spirit of traditional Chinese culture? And in what aspects is it mainly manifested? We believe that it is mainly manifested in the following four aspects: unity between man and nature; the doctrine of the mean; unremitting self-improvement; great virtue.

3. 1   Unity of Man and Nature

Let's start with the first aspect: unity of man and nature. What is the "unity of man and nature"?

Generally speaking, it refers to that man and all other things are the same in nature. So people's life should be in accordance with the human nature and the essence of life. So as to achieve the harmony between man and nature, as well as harmony between the Tao of Human and the Tao of Heaven. However, in the history of Chinese philosophy, this idea has a more subtle and complex evolution and development process. To put it simply, I will give a brief explanation based on the views of Confucius. According to Confucius and Confucianism, the so-called "Tian" (often translated "heaven") has three connotations: the Heaven of Matter, the Heaven of God, and the Heaven of principle.

The Heaven of Matter is Nature. As Confucius said, "What does Heaven say? Nothing. Yet the four seasons do function, and all the things do grow up." The "Heaven" here refers to Nature. The heaven does not need to say, but four seasons change and all things grow. So, this is a Nature with inherent law in the sense of materialism. As for the Heaven of God, as Confucius said: "He who offends the Heaven of God has none to pray to." That is to say, once you offend the Heaven of God, it's useless to pray. And this saying emphasizes the Heaven of God. This "Heaven" is obviously religious or theological. As for the Heaven of principle, it is not Nature or God. It refers to Tao or the Way of Heaven. Tao is the world spirit of the impersonal god, or spiritual principles of the world. Confucius said: "Heaven has endued me with virtues." "At fifty, I knew the decrees of Heaven." And "the decrees of Heaven" here refers to Tao. Tao, so does the "Heaven" in the saying: "Heaven has endued me with virtues." That is, the Way of Heaven (Tao).

Therefore, corresponding to these three types of heaven, there are three types of unity with heaven. As the saying in *Book of Changes*: "In his brightness, he is in harmony with the sun and moon; in his orderly procedure, he is in harmony with the four seasons." It refers to unity with the Heaven of Matter. Or we can say, it refers to unity with Nature. "In his relation to what is fortune and what is calamitous, he is in harmony with the spirit-like operations." It refers to unity with the Heaven of God. "He is great who is in harmony, in his attributes, with heaven and earth." So, what does the "harmony with heaven and earth" mean? It refers to unity with Tao (Way of Heaven or Tao). The man who achieves all these at the same time can be regarded as a great man, and he is almost a sage. Although these three aspects of heaven are different, so are the three types of the unity of man and nature, they have their own characteristics, they all exist in Confucianism. They are trinitarian. And each of them has its own influence and audience. We should attach importance to them all.

In my opinion, unity of man and nature in Chinese culture can be divided into three forms: first, to achieve unity with Nature through science and law, so as to establish homelands for multiplying and living. Second, to achieve unity with the Heaven of God through religion and practice, so as to be blessed and receive grace. Third, to achieve unity with the Heaven of Ontology through morality and ethics, so as to see the inner nature and find the true self.

3. 1. 1　Unity of Man and Nature

What is unity with Nature? It can also be called unity of man and nature in the ecological sense. Which is the most practiced type of contemporary people, and it is valued most by them.

Firstly, from the discovery and use of natural laws to create homes.

Man is the son of the earth, and can never live without the Mother Nature. Since ancient times Chinese people have known how to make use of the laws of nature. "Human Beings Making Law for Nature". They were well aware that unity of man and nature makes the homeland prosper. They adopted effective measures according to local conditions, and worked hard for production and life. They observed the natural conditions then they understood and grasped various secrets and laws of nature. And people made good use of the truth and scientific discovery for their own benefits. Man and nature complement each other. Ancient Chinese people invented many things, including astronomy and calendar system, water conservancy and terraced fields, traditional Chinese medicine. These achievements manifested the harmony with heaven and earth, mountains and rivers, representing as outstanding works of unity of man and nature.

Secondly, from the aspect of loving and protecting the ecological environment.

Confucianism pays great attention to ecological protection and construction, and opposes the destruction of the natural environment and the indiscriminate killing of lives. For example, when Confucius was the Minister of Public Works in the State of Lu, he studied the natural geographical environment there and took measures to develop agriculture and forestry in accordance with local conditions. Today, in Confucian Temple in Qufu and other places millenarian trees planted by Confucius still stand. In *the Book of Rites*, it is clearly required that we shouldn't cut down trees or kill unformed lives. Mencius also said: "There will be much more wood available if we cut down trees at the right time." Both Buddhism and Taoism advocate vegetarianism and cherish living things. And officials around the country in all dynasties also paid great attention to afforestation. For example, Fuzhou of Fujian Province is also called "City of Banyans". And Quanzhou is called "City of Zayton". Why did they get such names? Because banyan and zayton (Erythrina variegata) were planted massively in these two cities before.

The people of the ancestral village in ancient China and the ethnic minority people with natural worship were especially conscious of ecological protection. The ancestral villagers attached great importance to ecological protection, Feng Shui (geomantic theory) and sustainable development of families. These ideas were written into their pedigrees and family regulations, and became a code of conduct that everyone would consciously abide by. Anyone who violate it would be strictly penalized. Take *the Genealogy of Wu Family* of Peitian Village as an example. *Ten Rules of Clan Regulations* regulated the public affairs of the family. It also contains the regulations about the locations of mountains and rivers, water systems for irrigating the farmland, vegetables in the fields, all kinds of trees and plants and so on. Most of the ethnic minorities in China worship nature and pay special attention to protecting the ecological environment in their lives. For example, the Tujia people in Baifusi Town, Hubei Province, who live in the border area of Hubei, Hunan and Chongqing, "regard water as their mother and worship mountains as their father". They carefully protect every tree and grass and never cut them down too much. They express their awe of heaven and earth and their endless love for this landscape. There is a documentary called *Nostalgia* by CCTV, it introduces how Chinese people of all ethnic groups and regions in different areas practice traditions practice the faith of " green mountains and lucid waters bringing blessing, and unity of man and nature prospering the home".

Thirdly, as for the traditional literati, they generally showed their taste toward naturalism.

The wise find pleasure in waters while the virtuous take delight in mountains. The intellectual literati admired a kind of artistic conception of life, with which people can get infinite pleasure if they see everything calmly and quietly, and have the same interest in the beautiful scenery throughout the year. They believed that the beautiful birds on the branches are also their good friends, falling flowers floating on the water are all wonderful articles. And all these common scenes are worth our appreciation. Sometimes, when I read Tao Yuanming's poems, I think of the American naturalist poet Henry David Thoreau (1817—1862) and his *Walden*, they were probably both sons of nature. In their hearts, "birds don't sing in caves, and pigeons don't protect their innocence in pigeon cages". The best and happiest way of life is to return to nature and to get the unity with the nature. In addition, Wang Wei, a poet of the Tang Dynasty showed his carefreeness in his poem *Autumn Evening in the Mountains*. Refined scholars produced a variety of landscape paintings and Guqin music. All these show Chinese people's aesthetic attitude towards life, and their devotion to beautiful landscape.

Nowadays, drawing lessons from being punished for humanity's destruction of nature, Chinese people are working hard to make contributions to their common home, to make it a nostalgic home where people can see the mountains and the water, and a beautiful home of ecological civilization. Remarkable achievements have been made. Today, the concept of "lucid waters and lush mountains are invaluable assets" has become a motto for China's future development. Now that China has put the environment first, and is following a green development path. This is the continuation of the tradition of ancient Chinese nation.

According to the second aspect is about unity with the Heaven of God. Confucianism does not deny the existence of the Heaven of God. Instead, it advocates that we should respect it in awe, and worship it solemnly. That is what we call "worshiping nature and ancestors". Confucius once said: "I have long been praying." The saying like: "I learn earthly knowledge and understand the course of Heaven. Maybe it is only Heaven that knows about me!" Show a main point. That Confucius was disposed to the unity with the Heaven of God, which cannot be denied. Buddhism, Taoism and other religious beliefs are popular in the folk society. Through polite acts, worshiping, and meditation Chinese people can communicate with the heaven, the earth and the gods, so as to avoid the punishment of the heaven and pursue good fortune and avoid disaster, or to improve and complete their spiritual realm, which can be regarded as an important manifestation. However, comparatively speaking, the integration with gods is not the main orientation of Chinese culture characterized by humanism. Therefore, this part, I'm not going to expand it here.

3.1.2　Unity with the Way of Heaven, or with Tao

For Confucianism, what is the main form and the fundamental method of the unity of man and nature? The answer is "the harmony between man's attributes and heaven and earth". This is because, virtue is endowed by heaven in the view of Confucianism, it is the innate nature of human beings. So, with the transcendent nature of virtue, people can be connected to the divine order of things. This virtue, endowed by heaven and in harmony with order of things, refers to benevolence. Confucius said: "The benevolent have love for others. And they would never impose on others what they would not choose for themselves. "① Zeng Zi once made an explanation. Putting oneself in another one's place is the principle of benevolence and reciprocity. Indeed, the important characteristic of benevolence is to be considerate. To consider others in one's own place. To consider the extension of love to everything on earth in all sincerity. As the philosopher Mou Zongsan said: "benevolence takes empathy as its nature and compassion as its function. " Therefore, people's virtues can unite with anything into one when feeling empathy for them. At the same time, will embellish and illuminate them. So it is natural to be filial towards the father, to be loyal to the emperor, and to be honest with friends. When seeing birds and animals, grasses and stones, heaven and earth, mountains and rivers, and all other things in nature, we can also harbor love and respect. The heart of benevolence has the transcendental power to overcome external opposition and achieve internal unity with everything.

Wang Yangming, a great philosopher in the Ming Dynasty gave some examples in his work, *The Great Study*. Now we can have a look at these examples.

When you see a child who is about to fall into a well, you will immediately be frightened and have compassion for him, and you want to save him at once without thinking. That's because your benevolence and the child have become one. When you hear the doleful cries of birds and animals being killed, or see the cattle and sheep being slaughtered kneel to people, and their eyes are full of tears, pity and sympathy will stir in your hearts spontaneously, and you will no longer want to eat their meat. That's because your benevolence and these animals have become one. Some say that the child is a human and our fellow, birds and animals are living beings. So, it's natural for us to have compassion for them. Moreover, we have the same feeling towards lifeless things like grasses and stones. For example, when we saw the grasses and woods being cut down and destroyed, the world's architectural masterpieces, the Summer Palace in Beijing and Notre Dame Cathedral in Paris being burned down we were tortured by heartfelt pain and misery, and we had pity and sympathy for them. That's because your benevolence and these grasses and stones have become one.

―――――――――――

① And according to Mencius, What men can do without learning is a result of inborn ability (良能); what men know without contemplating is a result of intuition (良知).

This emotional connection and unity of one's benevolent and other things, do transcend the ego of the smallness and limits, The heart of benevolence can penetrate everything. It can be expanded to the ruling of the country and the governing of families. It can contain and clarify every person and everything. Or "One is All, All is One". This state of mind is in accordance to Confucius's word. He said: "Once everybody has become self-restrained and observed the rules of propriety, benevolence will prevail in the whole world."

This is not an external moral compulsion, but an inner nature of benevolence. Confucianism believes in this. Just as birds can fly, fish can swim, people's benevolence or conscience can be boundless, and bring true benefits to everything on earth. So, Wang Yangming said: "The great man is an all-pervading unity, which is one with heaven, earth, and all things. He considers the world as one family, and the Middle Kingdom as one man." Of course, if you want to be paranoid about the difference between the inner and the outer, others and self, and insist on being a selfish and unworldly ignorant person, then you will be numb, so numb that you cannot feel, your heart will be covered and your kindness can not be revealed. So, you cannot understand why people can be moved and what is selfless love. If you never shed tears for the sorrow of others, if you never feel happy for contributing to the benefits of others, how can you understand and appreciate unity of nature and man?

For scholars who aim at pursuing unity of nature and man, Confucianism will make them appreciate it more. Unity of man and nature is not about taking something mysterious or sitting quietly and in deep meditation. You cannot live in isolation and retreat into mountains. You must cultivate the moral character and regard self-accomplishment as basis, respect and abide by the social ethics and morality, and undertake your own responsibilities, and do your best to be a good person. You are endowed with a bright heart, you have to trust it, perfect it and expand it. Then one day, you will suddenly feel that something has changed. You can keep close to the spirit of heaven on your own. Your world will suddenly be restored to a state of perfection, where unity of man and nature can be achieved.

In this realm, the light of benevolence shines on everything, and make everything brighten. Every little thing can reflect their beauty and inner nature. A flying hawk, a leaping fish, a blade of grass, a drifting cloud, a singing cicada, or a period of time, can faithfully reflect its true beauty without loss, as well as its unity with the world.

The one who believes in unity of man and nature can see through the beauty of the world. They can understand the world in a wild flower, and the bodhi in a leaf. They can see the whole brightness of the sun in a drop of water. They can see God in all things. They say that all men can become sages like Yao and Shun, sages can crowd the streets, any place can be the land of Buddhism. They even say that the Tao can be seen in mole crickets, ants and weeds. It be seen in tiles and feces. People can learn the Tao from mole crickets and ants, weeds and feces. But only the benevolent can truly understand this. And it is beyond the understanding of common people.

So, I hold that "if you can overcome selfishness and keep to propriety, everyone in the world will return to humaneness" is a truth, which is the essence of Confucianism, and the its core wisdom of the unity of man and nature of Confucianism. It is a real realm of absolute equality that everybody can reach. Pursued endlessly by Chinese people, it is also the state of perfection, a state of freedom and true happiness. As described in Tao Yuanming's poem: "What could be more enjoyable than to look at the universe far and wide in the twinkling of an eye?" "Let nature take its course, and neither rejoice in the long life nor mourn the short one."

In short, what the ancient Chinese seek are: to achieve harmony with nature for the prosperity of homeland; to achieve harmony with all living beings for the lasting peace; to achieve harmony with the gods and spirits for converting to religion; to achieve harmony with the universe for the completeness and compatibility. The ideology and state of unity of man and nature is very profound. It reflects the symbiosis of man and nature. And highlights the cultural subjectivity of human. It is the fundamental source of the Chinese nation's boundless love, as well as their great virtue. It is the inner driving force of their unremitting self-improvement and their optimistic spirit of struggle. It is the essential reason for the Chinese nation to pursue a harmonious world and cosmopolitanism. This thinking of unity of nature and man is both aesthetic and ethical, both philosophical and religious, both theoretical and practically. It has resulted in lofty values and lifestyles in Chinese culture. Chinese people pursue and feel at ease in this spiritual realm of transcendent utility where they are unconscious about oneself and the external world, and become a part of nature. They enjoy their quiet and beautiful living atmosphere of compatibility. Time will wear on slowly. As if people have not even heard of the Han Dynasty. Not to mention the Wei and the Jin Dynasty.

Nowadays, people are deeply stuck in the trouble of utilitarianism and technologism, people violate the laws of nature. Everything is in a state of hostility or rivalry. Whole chains of the ecology is being destroyed. People are indifferent to each other with broken hearts. And there are constant conflicts between countries and regions. That's why we need this ideology and method of unity of man and nature. With the help of it, we can solve these problems and make contributions to our world. Both Chinese and Western cultures have their own strengths. Chinese culture emphasizes the unity of man and nature while Western culture stresses subject-object dichotomy, both of which are the expansion and development of the essential strength of human beings. How to make a comprehensive plan and make the most of their advantages? It is all in the mind of the wise. As Chinese culture and Western culture contact with each other more frequently, there will be more beneficial cultural dialogue and integration. Maybe people in the future will be able to exert the wisdom of subjectivity in cultural activities, so as to keep the good points of both culture.

3.2　The Doctrine of the Mean: a Methodology of Dialectics

People should abide by the Doctrine of the Mean for achieving moderation and harmony. This is a remarkable spirit of Chinese culture, and a rational methodology respected by the Chinese people for a long time. It is also a very important thought in Confucianism and Taoism. During the evolution of the Chinese nation and Chinese culture, it has played a very important role.

The Doctrine of the Mean is also called the Golden Mean or the Principle of Impartiality. What does it mean? Does it refer to compromise (doing things no more than halfway)? We believe that the Doctrine of the Mean, as a methodology, emphasizes moderation: moderation in nature (degree) and suitability in choice.

If you want to understand the Doctrine of the Mean, you can take a look at China's Diagram of the Supreme Ultimate. There are two concepts in the Diagram of the Supreme Ultimate: Yin and Yang, which represent everything opposite but coexist in harmony. Contrary yet complementary, Yin and Yang constantly transform into each other. They achieve unity in oppositeness with the same essence. Therefore, the philosophy of the Diagram of the Supreme Ultimate is a kind of dialectics of the East, It

3-2 Diagram of the Universe

provides a methodology for us: people shouldn't see only one aspect of things so stubbornly. They should see the development of things specifically, so as to take appropriate methods, and achieve the state of moderation. And finally promote the sustainable development of things.

First of all, the Doctrine of the Mean opposes going to extremes, and seeks the state of moderation in development. During the evolution of things, "moderation" is regarded as a proper degree, which is also called "impartiality".

Aristotle, a great thinker and philosopher in ancient Greece mentioned the Principle of Impartiality (golden mean) in his work, *Nicomachean Ethics*. He said that going beyond and falling short are both evils, and only the state of moderation can be regarded as a good. For example, being extravagant is going beyond while being miserly is falling short. So they are both evils. In contrast, being generous and magnanimous is a good. Being impertinent is going beyond while being coward is falling short. And they are both evils. Only being courageous is a good which achieves the state of moderation. Being intemperate is going beyond while being indifferent is falling short. In contrast, being temperate is a good.

In fact, Confucius held the same view. He once commented on the characters of his students Zizhang and Zixia. He said that Zizhang often goes beyond while Zixia still falls short. And going beyond is as wrong as falling short. Just like the radical and the over-cautious. The radical keep forging ahead while the over-cautious act with some reservation. None of them are as good as the people who stick to the Principle of Impartiality. The Principle of Impartiality refers to take actual situation into consideration. And do something more important by leaving the others undone. That is what we call "moderation". By doing so, Confucius tried to tell people to handle matters with discretion. He advocated that we should not go to the extremes, but to keep the state of moderation. Being too polite is a kind of affectation. While being too rustic is a kind of insolence. If we follow the principle of moderation, we can be gentlemen with refine manners. Confucius left such an impression on people that he is gentle but severe, august but not fierce, poised but not arrogant. When viewed from a distance, he appears stern; when approached, he looks mild. This is a collision between opposing temperaments. But these opposing temperaments coexist with one another in harmony.

In his work *Deng Tuzi Fond of Beauty*, Song Yu, a writer in the Warring States Period described a lady living next door. There was such a beautiful girl.

If she were one inch taller, she would be too tall. If she were one inch shorter, she would be too short. If she used powder, her face would be too white. If she used rouge, her face would be too red.

The description means that her figure and complexion were just right.

Chinese people pay special attention to the principle of moderation. They believe that the moon waxes only to wane, and water surges only to overflow. Things reach their prime and then decline. Joy surfeited turns to sorrow. For example, in rural areas, a half-moon pond will be dug in front of ancestral temples or residences, rather than a round one. This is the taboo of perfection. Perfection is not as good as half full still has room for development, there is still the vitality of progress. Once complete, will be going down in the dumps. It is also for this reason that Lao Tzu taught people to "know the strong and use the weak" and "know the honor and keep the disgrace". Zhu Xi called himself "Huiweng" （晦翁, a gloomy old man）, and Zeng Guofan named his study "Qiuque Study" (求阙斋, the study of longing for imperfections) .

In order to obtain the best interests, people try to keep themselves in a moderate state, so as to keep the vitality and move forward forever. Chinese people also hate extreme actions in their daily life. They insist that one shouldn't speak absolutes, leaving no room for compromise; one shouldn't enjoy all the benefits and blessings, otherwise he will be envied and isolated; and that one shouldn't get things into an impasse and leave himself no room for manoeuvre. These sayings show the national character of Chinese people shaped by the philosophy of moderation.

Second, the Doctrine of the Mean opposes adherence and bigotry.

It requires people to make pragmatic decisions by accommodating to the changing situation so as to achieve an appropriate result. Now, I will give you some examples of the Doctrine of the Mean applied to people's life so as to help you better understand it.

(1) Take Filial Piety for an Example

Confucianism generally believes that filial piety is obedience and no violation, so disobedience to parents is not filial piety. But according to the Doctrine of the Mean, obedience and disobedience are just like Yin and Yang. Sometimes obedience does not mean filial piety while disobedience can be regarded as filial piety. Take Zengzi as an example. Once, his father beat him with a stick because he accidentally hoed the melon seedlings, but he didn't run away and he was almost beaten to death. He believed that obedience is filial piety. But Confucius said that this is not filial piety, because you were catering to your irrational and emotional father. And you would make him offend the law and be imprisoned for murdering. To say the least, he would be criticized by fellow villagers or feel remorse for what he had done. Is that what a filial son should do? In contrast, Shun's father and stepmother conspired to murder Shun. He didn't listen to them but managed to escape. He didn't resign himself to death. And he didn't hate them. He still had respect for them. After he became the emperor, he was still kind to those who had hurt him. Therefore, Shun saved himself by disobedience. and preserved his filial piety and fulfilled his filial duties. So, he had enough filial respect to his families. He was rational rather than foolish. He knew how to make rational choices between obedience and disobedience. No wonder Shun was selected as the first one in China's twenty-four stories of filial piety.

(2) Take Propriety as an Example

Males and females should not give or receive things from hand to hand. It is a rule of propriety, right? Dallying with girls with no reason is an irreverence, and it is wrong. But Mencius asked, if your sister-in-law is drowning, should you give her your hand? If you give her your hand, you will break the rule of propriety. But if you don't, she will be drowned. What should you do? Mencius believed that people should act accordingly. So you should give her your hand when it is due. The occurrence of physical contact in such an emergency is also excusable. If you don't, you will be nothing but a ruthless jackal.

(3) Take Credibility as an Example

Man should not go without credibility. Being credible is a good and it is due. But if you come across villains, robbers, or aggressors who invade our home, will you be trustworthy to them? will you tell them everything you know without reserve? Of course not. In the eyes of Confucius, those who are always true to words and too stubborn to accommodate to circumstances are rigid fellows. "Those who are true to every word and seek result in every action are rigid petty fellows. " Mencius also said those in superior position may not be true to every word or seek result of every action. They base their choices only on justice. This is the difference between small credibility and big credibility. Big credibility does not stick to the form, but depends on whether it conforms to justice.

It can be seen that Confucius and Confucianism are very pragmatic. And Confucius is a pragmatic philosopher. He committed no subjective suspicion, no absolute assertion, no routinism, and no egoism. That is to say, people should abstain from prejudices or superstitious dogmas. He knew well that it's important to take specific condition into consideration. and make appropriate judgments and choices according to the specific situation at that time. Confucius said: For a superior man, there are no rules about how things must be done, or how they must not be done. He just needs to think about how to do it appropriately, so that it can accord with the due social and ethical norm. That is, what Confucius called the "do not care one way or another" method of doing things. It is like Yin and Yang in the Diagram of the Supreme Ultimate. Yin is in Yang and Yang is in Yin. They are same in essence. So we shouldn't look at them stubbornly. Therefore, we should analyze the specific conditions to make appropriate decisions. We should take purpose-based methods, and adopt idea-based strategies. As long as it conforms to morality and truth, it can be adopted flexibly and expediently. Confucius always paid attention to the facts, and made judgments and decisions pragmatically and equivocally. He always taught his students to think about the advantages and disadvantages of each side. His own words and actions were said to conform to the Doctrine of the Mean. So he was known as the "Sage of Flexibility" whose ordinary words and conducts are in accordance to the Doctrine of the Mean (among the sages, Confucius was the timely one).

Taoism also recognized the change of the world. "In Tao the only motion is returning. " "The normal would immediately revert to deceitful, and good revert to sinister. " Since everything changes at any moment, there is no need to be too rigid when handling matters. For example, people have learned a truth from *Tao Te Ching*. The highest good is like that of water. He should act like water and do not stick to one pattern. He should get along with others and get on in this world flexibly.

When choosing his dwelling, he should know how to select a suitable one. When cultivating the mind, he should know how to attune it to become profound. When dealing with others, he should know how to be gentle and kind. When speaking, he should know to grasp the difference between big credibility and small credibility. When governing, he should know how to maintain order by using hard and soft tactics in turn. When handling matters, he should know how to maximize favorable factors and minimize unfavorable ones. Lastly, he should know how to choose the right moment to make a move. So gentlemen do not contend against each other for favorable conditions. Instead, they are good at acting according to circumstances. So there will be no complains or blames.

So why the "know how" we mentioned above is a good? It is because of one's resourceful observations when adapting to circumstances. Zhuangzi also held the same opinion in *the Article of Qiwu Lun*. "If we look at everything from the viewpoint of Tao, There is no such distinction of high and low. " If we look at everything from a different perspective, everything can be reasonable, valuable and worthy of being affirmed. So, if you call me a horse then I'm a horse, and if you call me an ox then I'm an ox. It is fine to be called a horse or an ox. And there is no need to hold oneself high and hold others low. "Three in the morning and four in the evening" and "Four in the morning and three in the evening", are different in name but same in essence. As to beauty and yasha, grass and Nanmu tree, the useful and the useless, life and death, Long life and short death there is no essential difference between them. Everything should be based on the specific, current, sapiential, and integrated investigations and understandings.

The two aspects we mentioned above can be regarded as the Doctrine of the Mean applied in "use", which can be taken for a practical method or life skill. In its profoundness, the Doctrine of the Mean is an ontology. The ontology of moderation and consonance. The methodological value of the Doctrine of the Mean is obvious. And it is worth our attention and preaching. But in its profoundness, it does contain an ontology. Dialectics is not only the methodology of unity of opposites, but also leads to a certain ontology. For example, Hegel's dialectics leads to the ontology of "Absolute Idea". Buddhism's Madhyamika leads to the ontology of "Emptiness". Confucianism's the Doctrine of the Mean is the ontology, which harmonizes in "moderation of static state" and "consonance of dynamic state". This topic is too philosophical, here I will only point out some keywords for you.

It is mentioned in *the Doctrine of the Mean*. To have no emotions of pleasure or anger, sorrow or joy, welling up', this is to be described as the state of Chung. To have these emotions welling up but in due proportion, this is to be described as the state of ho (harmony) Chung is the chief foundation of the world. Ho is the great highway for the world. Once Chung and ho are established, Heaven and Earth maintain their proper position, and all creatures are nourished that everything will grow and multiply between them. "

There are four important keywords in this saying. (1) The first one is Chung (moderation), which is the essence of everything. Still and without movement, it is the nature and truth of everything. (2) The second one is ho, which means to follow the inner nature. Chung penetrates forthwith to all phenomena and events under the sky. People should achieve ho, by achieving Chung. And adopt a flexible method in handling matters for achieving Chung. (3) The third one is achieving Chung and ho. One should restrain oneself when staying alone, and cultivate conscience when handling matters. So as to maintain Chung and ho all the time. (4) The fourth one is that Heaven and Earth will both keep their places, and everything will grow and multiply between them. If Chung and ho are achieved to extremes and combined with the way of things, peace will prevail under the heaven and everything will go well. Then, of course, this is what Chinese people pursue. That is, to find one's true self, to achieve unity of man and nature, and to achieve great harmony of everything.

After analyzing the two aspects of the Doctrine of the Mean from the superficial to the deep, we can draw some conclusions. First of all, as a methodology of dialectics, it emphasizes that going beyond is as wrong as falling short in terms of the state of development. It is best to achieve the state of moderation. In terms of making decisions, it emphasizes that there is nothing ought to do or not to do, It is appropriate to make pragmatic decisions and choices. Second, as an ontology, it directs us to achieve ho "consonance" by achieving Chung. And maintain the state of Chung and ho all the time. Finally, the great harmony can be achieved. Where everything will enjoy repose and continue to grow.

It is by virtue of its profundity that the Doctrine of the Mean reaches so high. And Confucius even made a comment that it was difficult or even impossible to forsake country and nobility, to undergo the most severe trials for the Doctrine of the Mean. "

In short, abiding by the Doctrine of the Mean and advocating Chung and ho, are important national characters of Chinese nation, and it is because of the cultural edification of the Doctrine of the Mean, a great ethos, that Chinese people do not go to extremes, that they are practical, flexible yet not dogmatic, and that they are rational and realistic with gentle nature. They pursue Chung and ho and believe in unity of man and nature. Thus, they have gradually formed the view of great harmony between Heaven and Earth and everything. For instance, in politics, it signifies the unity of benevolence and rites, rule of virtue and rule of law; while in economy, the unity of righteousness and interests; in the molding of personality, the unity of virtues and abilities, magnificence and simplicity, strength and gentleness; in education, the unity of teaching and studying. Chairman Mao Zedong advocated to form a good social situation that "there is both concentration and democracy, discipline and freedom, unity of will, and personal ease of mind and liveliness"; president Xi Jinping proposed to unify the "rejuvenation of the Chinese nation" with the construction of a "community with a shared future for mankind". It can be said that they are all the historical application of the Confucian doctrine of the mean and the expression of contemporary innovation and development.

It must be pointed out: in our life the Doctrine of the Mean is often misinterpreted by some people. They think that it is very ambiguous and equivocal, And regard it as the halfway work of peacemakers. This kind of "the Doctrine of the Mean" does not contain any truth, or any bottom lines and justice. It keeps emphasizing the saying like "There is nothing ought to do or not to do". It is no longer the Doctrine of the Mean. but debased as common words with unrefined taste. Whether it is the Doctrine of the Mean or not, that's what we need to identify.

3.3 The Spirit of Seeking Unremitting Self-improvement

Seeking unremitting self-improvement can be regarded as a reflection of traditional Chinese culture. It is reflected in Chinese people's attitudes towards life and their personalities. What's more, it is a historical generalization and accurate portrayal of the overall personality of Chinese nation. In *Yi Zhuan*, the second part of *Book of Changes*, there is a classic expression about seeking self-improvement. Heaven, in its motion, gives the idea of strength. The superior man, in accordance with this, nerves himself to ceaseless activity. It means that as Heaven keeps vigorous through movement, a gentleman should unremittingly practice self-improvement. The law that Heaven keeps moving ceaselessly requires people to be active and work energetically. Which is probably a manifestation of following the mandate of Heaven, and the manifestation of complying with the wishes of people. And it is a manifestation of unity of man and nature. So how did Chinese nation develop such a cultural spirit? This spirit encourages them to strengthen themselves unremittingly.

Firstly, seeking unremitting self-improvement is a national spirit that is developed by them under countless natural and man-made calamities since ancient times.

We often say that China is a beautiful and rich land. But in fact, the vast territory of China is also known as "the land of famine". According to *The History of Famine Relief in China* by Deng Yunte, from the Qin Dynasty (221—206BCE) to the Qing Dynasty (1636—1912), there were as many as 5079 disasters and famines. Among which there were 1013 floods, 1022 droughts, and many countless hailstorms, windstorms, plagues of locust, epidemic diseases, frost and snow disasters, earthquakes, famines and so on. According to *Chronology of China's Ancient War*, we also notice a statistical data. That is, from the 26th century BCE to 1911 CE, China experienced as many as 3791 wars. So it's safe to say that since ancient times, Chinese people have experienced and suffered countless natural and man-made disasters. But they didn't yield to mishaps. Instead, they chose to fight and seek self-improvement. From the folk tales which have passed from generation to generation, we can get a glimpse of it.

We have the following folk tales. Kua Fu chased the sun and aspired to catch up with it; Houyi shot the sun for the purpose of saving mankind; Yu the Great tamed the Yellow River for stopping people from suffering torrential floods; Jing Wei filled the sea with pebbles relentlessly with firm determination; Yu Gong carried the stones and earth of the mountains to the sea with his families. As you known, every country has the legend of the sun god. In tribal times, the sun god had absolute authority. If you look at all the myths of the sun god, you will find that only the Chinese myth has a story that dares to challenge the sun god: because the sun is too hot, Kua Fu went to chase the sun to take it down. The archer Hou Yi shot down the sun. Of course, Kuafu died of exhaustion. But in Chinese mythology, he is celebrated as a hero who dared to fight against seemingly insurmountable forces.

By telling these folk tales, the Chinese ancestors were giving their instructions. In the face of natural and man-made disasters, one may lose, but one should not yield. Earlier, we mentioned the concept of unity between man and nature. The relationship between man and heaven is mutually victorious, but also mutually used. Man is not a slave to inaction before heaven and earth.

Just as the saying in *Xunzi*: rather than exalting Heaven and contemplating it, it would be better to tend its creatures and regulate it. Rather than obeying Heaven and singing hymns to it, it would be better to regulate its mandate and use it. Rather than watching for the season and awaiting what it brings, it would be better to respond to it and exploit it. They observed the natural conditions then they grasped various laws of nature. And people made good use of the truth for their own benefits. Man and nature complement each other. In the face of the unpredictable and boundless power of nature, the only way for human beings to survive is to cheer up and strengthen themselves! When the Chinese ancestors shouted out that "my destiny is controlled by myself and not by heaven", or even "man can conquer heaven", they were full of determination and heroism! Without this determination and boldness, there would be no endless civilization of our nation!

Secondly, seeking unremitting self-improvement is a national spirit that is highly respected by Chinese people. It is repeatedly educated to Chinese people and passed down from generation to generation.

In terms of the seeking unremitting self-improvement reflected in personality cultivation and life practice, I believe that it can be discussed from the following aspects:

(1) Those Who Seek Self-improvement Should Know What is Fortitude

That is to say, you should understand what does "fortitude" mean. And what is the real fortitude. In our view, the real strong are those who have the truth. Truth is "Tao" in the context of Chinese culture. Confucius said: "Be resolved to seek the truth, hold fast to moral principles, base your conducts on benevolence and relax in the study of the arts. " That is to say, people should pursue the Tao (the way of Heaven). As we mentioned above, the way of Heaven in Confucianism refers to the truth of unity of man and nature. So "seeking the truth" means to seek unity of man and nature. And seek the true nature of everything and let Tao follow what is natural.

This is a purpose. Just like Chinese classic *The Book of Changes* clarified the same connotation. "Elegance and intelligence regulated by the arrest suggest the observances that adorn human... We look at the ornamental observances of society, and understand how the processes of transformation are accomplished under heaven." Confucius also said: "The human being manifests the Tao. The Tao doesn't manifest the human being." That is to say, we should carry forward the subjective spirit of seeking and promoting Tao. If people have faith, the country will have strength. So the nation will have hope. Those who seek self-improvement cannot do without the noble spirit of sincere pursuit of truth. How can we strengthen ourselves without obtaining the truth of heaven and humanity? How can we nourish their people and adorn the society? Without the strength of truth, it will only be hegemonic and bandit, but destructive rather than constructive.

Zilu, one of Confucius's students, once asked his teacher what fortitude is. Confucius asked him what kind of fortitude he meant, the fortitude of the southerners, or that of the northerners? Then Confucius continued, the northerners lie upon sword and shield, ready to fight even at night and fear no death. Compared to the that of the northerners, the fortitude of the southerners is even better. Why? Because the southerners stress edification with lenience and gentleness, and do not take vengeance against those who do them wrong. They harmonize without following blindly. They keep to the middle course without partiality. And they hold to their ideas all the time. That is to say, the fortitude of the southerners is lenient, gentle, and in accordance to the Doctrine of the Mean. Confucianism advocates that the meaning of fortitude in Chinese culture, refers to rationality and benevolence.

There are two important phrases in Xiamen University anthem: "We have the fortitude of the southerners, the fortitude of the southerners; we pursue knowledge endlessly. We live with others harmoniously. Pursuing knowledge endlessly and loving others mean rationality and benevolence." It is with such moral and rational spirit that the Chinese people educate their young people about the true spirit of "strong is strong". Therefore, Chinese nation was, is and will always be a rational and compassionate one who loves peace and its people. The irrational behaviors like aggression and violence, are not allowed by Chinese people's cultural nature. Therefore, we will never try to exert power on other countries or seek hegemony.

(2) Those Who Seek Self-improvement Should Combine Diligent Study

and Endeavor

Those who seek self-improvement should devote themselves to study. Because seeking the Truth is not merely a talk. It requires us to study diligently, and to pursue truth endlessly. We should study with assiduity, diligence and inquisitiveness. We should be good at studying and pursue lifelong studying. Many ancient Chinese people have studied hard. They have set many good examples for us.

We have Kuang Heng who bored a hole in the wall to make use of the neighbor's light to study, Zhu Maichen who kept reading while walking with firewood on his back, Sun Jing who tied his hair to a beam to keep from dozing off when studying, Che Yin and Sun Kang who read by the light of bagged fireflies or the reflected light of snow, Zu Ti who rose up upon hearing the crow of a rooster to practice sword playing, Ouyang Xiu's mother who taught her son to read and write by painting the land with grass because of her poor family, and Yang Shi who stood in the snow in front of his teacher Cheng Yi's gate waiting for the teacher to wake up from his nap. All of them are good examples of studying with assiduity despite difficulties. They encourage us to study with diligence and assiduity, study to improving ourselves and make our country stronger.

Those who seek self-improvement should accomplish something. That means they should make achievements. They should make use of what they have learned. By doing so, they can serve the country and do good to society. And finally they can benefit all mankind. Chinese people emphasize three immortals.

To set one's virtue, which refers to cultivating a noble mind. To set one's meritorious, which refers to making contributions for the country and people. To expound one's ideas in writing, which refers to putting forward correct and profound insights.

These are all manifestations of accomplishing something. It must be admitted that these three immortals are difficult to achieve. Take "to expound one's ideas in writing" as an example, is it easy for you to write down the truth that you have discovered? Of course not. But will you give up just because it is not easy to do? No. You should stick to doing it and make it a success, so that your name can perpetually be remembered by posterity. Just as the saying in *the Records of the Grand Historian*.

When Emperor Wen of Zhou Dynasty was imprisoned at Youli, he expanded Book of Changes. When Confucius was in distress he made the Spring and Autumn Annals. When Qu Yuan was banished he composed his poem "Encountering Sorrow". After Zuo Qiu lost his sight he composed the Narratives of the States. When Sunzi had had his feet amputated he set forth the Art of War. Most of the three hundred poems of the Book of Songs were written when the sages poured forth their anger and dissatisfaction.

We may safely draw the conclusion that it's not easy to expound one's ideas in writing. The Chinese people believe that these three immortals all are big undertaking that everyone should be committed to. Of course, there also emerged a variety of outstanding figures in history, they are the backbone of China.

(3) Those Who Seek Self-improvement Should Have Moral Integrity

Integrity, also known as backbone, is to adhere to truth and justice, not to give up one's principles for coercion and inducement, or even to die rather than surrender and see death as home. Mencius called it "the natural greatness of a soul" (浩然之气). Those who seek for self-improvement are people with the natural greatness of a soul and moral integrity, so they will never be afraid of death. Since ancient times, Chinese people have held the following beliefs. That is, neither riches nor honors may induce great men to corrupt; no poverty or lowliness may cause them to waver; no might or force may compel them to submit. These great men dare to face all threats and entices. In order to pursue justice and truth, to protect their country and families, they will not shrink from dangers or even death, but adhere to their determination and fight dauntlessly. Confucius said: "A man of ideal and moral integrity will not seek to survive at the expense of morality, but would sacrifice his life for a just cause." "While a great army might do without its commander, a man cannot go without an ambition." Wen Tianxiang, a national hero in the Song Dynasty, said: "No death can be avoided for any living soul, but a loyal heart can live forever." They show a kind of formidable and unyielding spirit, and a moral integrity which defies death.

Since the outbreak of China's War of Resistance Against Japanese Aggression (1931—1945), Zhang Yuanji, an outstanding publisher and patriotic industrialist in modern China complied a book, which is called *the Personality of the Chinese Nation*, and was published in 1937. This book introduced eight national heroes in Chinese history who were all great men with moral integrity. Among them, there is the loyalty of the ministers, the filial piety of the gentleman, the spirit of great revenge, and the self-consciousness of the national scholar. For example, the opening is the story of the orphan Zhao. "The death of Gongsun Chukui was due to loyalty; Cheng Ying died by faith." Another story is about Revenge story of Wu Zixu brothers. The king of Chu arrested Wu Shang and Wu Zixu's father and told them that if they returned, he would set their father free. Wushang knew that this was a certain death of the snare, but still choose to save his father, let his brother live to revenge. When there was a civil unrest in the State of Wei, Zi Lu, a disciple of Confucius, knew that he would be killed if he went back, but he still resolutely returned to fight and died calmly. Why? Because it's a warrior's duty for him. There are other stories such as Jing Ke stabbing the emperor of Qin, Tian Heng and his 500 loyal soldiers. In fact, these loyal people can avoid death, but they finally choose to die, here is not a forced reason, the death here has more important reasons of morality and justice. As for them, morality and justice even more important than life. From those stories we learn that our nation has never been short of indomitable heroes who thought highly of keeping their words and remaining loyal to friends, or stayed calm in the face of danger and acted with loyalty and righteousness, or sacrificed their own lives for a just cause.

In a word, these are the true characters and spirits of Chinese nation.

(4) Those Who Seek Self-improvement Should be Optimistic Person with Perseverance

The spirit of self-improvement of the Chinese people is also reflected in their optimism and strong perseverance.

Chinese people are the optimistic person, they are content with their life, comply with the way of Heaven, and recognize the limitations set by the mandate of heaven. They will do what they should do, and bear hardship with equanimity. Therefore, we do not have to claim credit but always make contribution to the success of the cause. Truth and justice will prevail in the end. Just as Confucius said "in this way, what continues from the Chou, even if 100 generations hence, is knowable". When the wind and the wind pass, truth and justice will win history. And every mission that we have promised was accomplished eventually. Pu Songling, a fiction writer in the Qing Dynasty, wrote a couplet to encourage himself, which has been handed down to posterity. "Where there's a will there's a way, determination has its reward. Heaven won't disappoint hardworking people, perseverance ultimately leads to success. " This couplet also encourages many young people today, when facing difficulties, they may look at this couplet and then urge themselves on. So, I think, when we recite such inspiring poems, we will have a desire to work hard and make progress. Light is waiting for us not far away. All we need to do is to fight against difficulties and seek self-improvement.

Strong perseverance, that is to say, to carry something through to the end and never give up halfway. And this is in accordance to Confucius's word. "Time elapses just like the surging current, day and night without cease." And this means to spare no effort in the performance of one's duty till the end of one's days. Cao Cao, Emperor Wu of Wei at the end of Eastern Han Dynasty, wrote a poem: "An old steed in the stable still aspired to gallop a thousand li. An old hero still cherishes high aspirations." Li Shangyin, a great poet in the late Tang Dynasty, wrote: "Till the end of life a silk worm keeps spinning silk. Till burning itself out a candle goes on lighting us." There is a saying in *Book of Changes*: "One who does not continuously maintain his virtue may be subjected to humiliation." What does it mean? It means that if people do not maintain their morality or virtues, other people will regard it as a kind of disgrace and humiliate them. So people should remain true to their original aspirations. and forge ahead with determination forever.

In short, the spirit of being vigorous and seeking self-improvement has always prevailed in traditional Chinese culture. It is like the Yangtze River and the Yellow River, surging ceaselessly within the body of Chinese people. It is like the Huangshan Mountain, the Taishan Mountain and the Great Wall, supporting the spirit of Chinese nation unshakably. It inspires us to march forward bravely, begin great undertakings tenaciously, and achieve the great rejuvenation of Chinese nation and stand firm forever among other nations.

In other words, the development of Chinese nation is like a magnificent epic. It is a history of working hard and producing civilization. The history of People's Republic of China over the past 70 years is glorious. It is a history of passing down fine traditions and achieving tremendous transformation. During this process Chinese nation has stood up, grown rich and become strong. As president Xi Jinping pointed out: "In the extraordinary course of their 100-year struggle, generations of Chinese Communists have worked hard and tirelessly,... forming the Jinggangshan spirit, the long march spirit, the Zunyi Conference spirit, the Yan'an spirit, the Xibaipo Spirit, the Hongyan spirit, the spirit of resisting US aggression and aiding Korea, 'the two bombs and one satellite' spirit, the spirit of the special zone, the spirit of fighting floods, the spirit of earthquake relief, the spirit of fighting epidemics and other great spirits have built the spiritual pedigree of the Chinese Communists." In fact, these spirits are vivid expressions of the contemporary inheritance and development of the Chinese traditional spirit of Seeking self-improvement.

Seeking unremitting self-improvement, being vigorous and promising, and working hard, are the secrets of our nation's prosperity and everlasting.

3.4 The Strong Sense of Social Responsibility Built on Great Virtue

Chinese culture is indeed rich in valuable qualities and excellent spirit. And Chinese people do have great virtues and moral integrity. The strong ethical and moral atmosphere is the air that the Chinese people breathe. Bertrand Russell, a British philosopher once made a comment on Chinese people. "It is very natural for Chinese people to do so: getting along with others with benevolence and kindness, treating people with courtesy, and expecting them to respond with politeness. Morality is the light that is everywhere to be illuminated. China has its moral norms and instructions for the whole social stratum and every field of life. " This kind of moralism is mainly affected and decided by the doctrines of Confucianism. And the moral culture of Confucianism can be divided into three levels.

The first level is a metaphysical moral system of Tao and Virtue, instead of a practical one which only emphasizes Virtue. For ancient Chinese people, Tao and Virtue, or the Truth and the moral principles are always linked together. Chinese culture has been paying attention to the exploration of the Tao (Way of Heaven) since the time of the hundred Schools of Thought in the pre-Qin Dynasty, and has closely combined people's moral cultivation with this metaphysical ontology for discussion. There is a saying in Daoism: All things without exception worship Tao and exalt Virtue. There is also a saying in Confucianism: be resolved to seek the way of Heaven, and hold fast to moral principles. The "Tao or the way of Heaven" in these sayings do not refer to religious convictions, but the root of everything and the spirit of the universe. Also the conduct norm which is in accordance to ethics and morality. "The way of Heaven endows me with moral nature" (Confucius). "Virtue is to gain, virtue is obtained from the way of Heaven in the heart, and we can't lose it, which is called virtue" (Zhu Xi). This is the transcendental theoretical basis for the theory of the inherent goodness of human nature. Combining Tao and Virtue together is meaningful to the metaphysical ontology of morality. And it has realistic and practical significance for our life.

The second one refers to the morality of subjectivity, instead of those obedient morality of unrefined taste, just like the saying "base your conducts on benevolence". Different from the morality defined by previous Confucian philosophers such as Ji Dan, the Duke of Zhou, which emphasizes extrinsic actions, the morality defined by Confucius emphasizes people's inner nature, benevolence. And it aims at promoting and advancing people's subjectivity so as to help them to transcend themselves. Morality is your own business, is a matter of good heart. Without this sincere and good heart of love, what is morality? People should start with basing their conducts on benevolence, they should achieve morality by acting with benevolence. And they should integrate subjectivity with objectivity. This is Mind Confucianism, a new kind of Confucianism developed by Confucius and Mencius. All Chinese virtues are revealed with benevolence. This is the greatness of Confucius' moral view.

The third one refers to morality which has practical significance and conforms with ethics, instead of those oral morality without real contents. Confucianism requires us that our benevolence and love should be as broad and boundless as the earth. We should shoulder all the responsibilities in the world. Especially, we should attach importance to the ethical obligations between people. We can not talk about the so-called spirit realm by not mentioning the moral practice and cultivation in people's life. Just like Confucius said: "Tao is not far away from people. People can't be Tao if they are far away from people." Therefore, We can see that Confucianism and Chinese culture are inclined to humanism. They require that we should pay attention to our world, our life and our ethics, which has become a fundamental trend. Confucianism emphasizes hierarchy, brings people into their relative social positions and roles, and gives them corresponding ethical responsibilities and obligations. The main field of moral cultivation, and the main means to help people to complete the socialized civilized personality.

Combined with these three points, we can describe the traditional Chinese morality as: worthy of Heaven upside, worthy of conscience inside and worthy of man outside. In other words, it is a set of life style based on ethics and connected with Way of Heaven and Way of people.

We say that moral idealism, shaped by Confucian values, lays a solid foundation for China's ethical society. It supports the spiritual edifice of China's ethical society.

And help to form the solid core of Chinese nation's value ideology. Indeed, Chinese people are good at practicing moral conducts. And they regard the cultivation of morality as an important mission of life. Therefore, from the emperor down to populace, all respect and abide by the social ethics and morality, and undertake their own responsibilities, and they take self-cultivation as their essential task. Therefore, in every field of the whole society, there is a strong atmosphere of moralism.

(1) In terms of politics: to govern by means of morality and filial piety is advocated; to respect Heaven, protect people and honor the doctrines of Confucianism is advocated. Emperors should love their ministers with kindness and benevolence, so that ministers would be faithful and loyal to them. People should uphold morality, cultivate themselves, scrupulously fulfill their duties, and regard achieving great harmony that the whole world as one community as their highest goal. (2) In terms of law: it is advocated to follow the principle of "Morality Has Priority Over Penalty". Strict penalty is opposed, and moral legislation is preferred. It is advocated that people should pay attention to their moral obligations, instead of seeking only their rights as individuals. (3) In the field of economy: it is advocated to run a business with integrity, pay attention to both justice and benefit while justice should come first. There were many provincial business groups in ancient China such as Jin merchants, Hui merchants and so on. All of them believed in Confucianism, and regarded the doctrines of Confucianism as their core ideas. (4) In terms of patriarchal clan system: it is advocated to worship nature and ancestors; people should love relatives and respect worthy persons. People should make sacrifices to ancestors in the ancestral hall, compile genealogies, obey the family disciplines and regulations, and carry forward fine family traditions. Within a patriarchal family, there are the principles of money sharing, circulating, distributing and philanthropical giving, which shows that the family is an economic community of mutual benefits and shared risks. The rural communities, they are the main force in practicing rituals of Confucianism. (5) In terms of literature and art: Confucianism advocates to start self-cultivation with inspiration from *the Book of Songs*, gain a firm footing with the regulation of the rules of propriety and strive for perfection with the edification of music. It is believed that literature can convey Confucian ideas, the truth and moral values carried by literature can educate and cultivate people. During artistic creation, people should learn from nature. and appreciate its beauty by heart. They pursue being a true superior and

perfect man who has the proper combination of exterior brilliancy with plain nature. And they wish to achieve the state of mind of no evil thoughts. (6) In terms of diplomacy: Chinese people long for peace and harmony in the world, and would like to develop civilization and win others over by benevolence. Aggression is not in the genes of Chinese people. Is there, in Russell's words, "a nation too proud to fight? The Chinese are". China is a big country, and Chinese people will never bully the weak by being strong, but kindly treat a country smaller than ours own. They carry out economic activities based on equality and mutual benefits, and promote exchanges and mutual learning between Chinese civilization and other civilizations. (7) Then, in terms of religion: it is advocated that Buddhists should practice morality and ethics in everyday life; once you have achieved moral integrity, you will become a Buddha. It is stressed that people should do all the things that are good and should not do anything that is evil. People with a good heart will conquer ill fortune. (8) In terms of society governments of all levels, families or the righteous men carry out a variety of charitable activities: they build free schools, set up charity granaries and reclaim land for the poor. The philanthropic people repair roads and build bridges. They give gruel or rice to the hungry and give medicines to the sick. And they also subscribe and give aid to calamity-stricken masses.

Traditional Chinese moral culture advocates people's benevolence and conscience, believing that people are born good. Chinese people pay attention to the cultivation of ethics and morality. It is advocated that people should correct evil doings and become good. The Chinese humanistic and moral culture plays an important role in shaping Chinese people's personalities. It helps to form the national moral psychology and collective personality of gentleness, sincerity and calmness. What's more, it helps to cultivate various traditional virtues cherished by Chinese people. Chinese people cherish their national moral and cultural traditions. They admire and praise all men of sublime virtue in history: like virtuous mothers and benevolent fathers, filial sons and chaste daughters, wise princes and famous prime ministers in ancient China, capable ministers and man of noble characters, the benevolent and people with lofty ideas, heroes and the chivalrous men with a strong sense of justice, eminent monks and man with great virtue, scholar-merchants and doctors of traditional Chinese medicine, and so on. Chinese people glorify them by erecting monuments for them and compiling their biographies, writing their deeds into the annals of history. They are very familiar with their great virtue and noble deeds, and often recollect them with sincerity. By doing so, Chinese people inspire themselves, and pass on great virtues reflected by these people to future generations.

Of course, any type of moral culture has limitations in history and class. Traditional Chinese culture dominated by Confucianism also has its limitations. For example, the feudal ethic code oppressed ancient Chinese people; the ethical metaphysics was too abstract to understand; the rationality of the value of secular life was often neglected. These limitations brought a shackle to the freedom of people's personality, and people's overall development. However, through radical reforms and innovations of sublation, such traditional moral values like achieving unity of man and nature, adhering to the Doctrine of the Mean and treating others with love and benevolence, achieving the great harmony that the whole world as one community, as well as their historical enchantment, and their everlasting humanistic significance, will continue to shine at the new starting point. Contemporary Chinese people carry forward the cause pioneered by their predecessors and forge ahead into the future. In the new era of the great rejuvenation of Chinese nation, there have emerged many virtuous figures, who love their motherland, serve people, assume their duties and fulfill their obligations. They fully show their noble personalities and fine qualities. They are the backbone of our country and the pride of our nation. The more we look up to them, the loftier they seem to us.

In short, the time-honored traditional Chinese culture has rich connotations. Its basic spirit is mainly embodied in the following four aspects: unity of man and nature, the Doctrine of the Mean, unremitting self-improvement and great virtue. During the development of Chinese culture, these cultural spirits have promoted the national unity; inspired people to move forward and make progress; promoted the integration and innovation of Chinese culture. They have nourished the spiritual world of Chinese people for thousands of years. These spirits will never die out. They are the true cores and shining points of excellent traditional Chinese culture. Nowadays, the world advocates the cultural globalization and calls for a community with a shared future for mankind. So, these great spirits has more and more global values and significance. and they are worth cherishing and carrying forward by us.

第四讲

多元一体
——中华文化与中华民族

4.1　中华民族的概念

　　我们知道，文化是人所创造的，而中国文化是中国人民创造的。我们把这里的中国人，叫作"中华民族"。中华民族是中国这片土地的主人，也是中华文化的共同创造者。中国自古以来就是一个统一的多民族国家。中华人民共和国成立后，通过民族识别并经中央政府确认的民族共有56个。由于汉族以外的55个民族人口较少，习惯上称为"少数民族"。

　　中国各民族分布的特点是大杂居、小聚居，相互交错居住。汉族地区有少数民族聚居，民族地区也有汉族居住。这种分布格局是长期历史发展过程中各民族间相互交往、流动而形成的。少数民族人口虽少，但分布很广。主要分布在内蒙古、新疆、宁夏等省、自治区。

　　中国学界在一段时间以来，都把中华民族当成一个从广义上来说的、由汉族和55个少数民族组成的总称，它是一个政治学范畴的称谓①。应该说，把中华民族广义地看作是包含56个民族的综合整体的提法是主流和基本的理解，也没错。但与此不同的是，费孝通先生在1988年独创地提出："中华民族"是一个民族学范畴，是以汉族为凝聚中心的、既多元又一体的、自觉的民族实体（而不是56个民族加在一起的总称）。费先生这里所谓"多元"是指多个起源，即五十六个民族。所谓"一体"是指五十六个民族融合形成了中华民族这个新的民族实体。费先生认为，作为统一的民族实体的"中华民族"的标志，就在

---

　　① 梁启超先生在《中国学术思想之变迁之大势》中最早使用"中华民族"概念。历史的考察，"中华"原初义，略同"中国"，主要是指遵守儒家文化的区域和民族，即华夏汉族的意思。如"中华者，中国也。亲被王教，自属中国，衣冠威仪，习俗孝悌，居身礼仪，故谓之中华。"（《唐律名例疏议释义》）

于这个民族实体具有四个方面的共同点：1. 共同语言——共用一种国家通用语言——普通话。2. 共同地域——共居于中国的版图。3. 共同经济生活——共同参与中国特色社会主义经济。4. 共同文化心理——认同并形成一种中华民族精神。

应该说，当代中国学界对此提法，虽然仍有许多争议，但总体上来说，已经大致接受了费先生这个看法。比如费先生所说的：第一，作为一个从历史上独立的多个民族发展形成的、新的自觉的民族实体，中华民族整体上已经是相互依存、相互统一而永远不可分割的生机体。第二，这个新的民族实体的形成是经过了漫长的历史生活的过程，经历了民族和民族之间的分分合合、合合分分的阶段性融合的成果，最终在近代尤其是以中华人民共和国的诞生为标志，形成的一个统一的民族实体。第三，多元一体不妨碍各民族在中华民族的新生机体中维持其个性的文化传统和生活特点，对原生民族的传统认同和中华民族的一体认同，兼容并包、并行不悖，前者是局部认同，后者是根本或高阶认同。各民族生动丰富的个性使得中华民族充满了多元色彩和全新活力。

当然，关于中华民族形成多元一体格局的历史过程，历史学和民族学研究界有各种观点，如三阶段论、四阶段论等①。我们这里按历时性维度，以民族互动融合的发展线索，略给大家梳理如下几点信息。

第一，中华民族的史前记忆：在多元起源中，首先是关于创世造人造物的传说（多见于少数民族的创世古歌或故事中），比如彝族的始祖是尼支呷洛，壮族的始祖是布罗陀，土家族始祖是"巴务相"，称为"廪君"，苗族、畲族信仰盘瓠始祖，等等。这些族群都经历了从穴居到屋居，从摘猎到稻作的过程。而知名的史前考古遗迹，如山顶洞人的起居生活复原、半坡文化、仰韶文化、河姆渡文化、大汶口文化、三星堆文化等都值得我们关注。

第二，中华民族形成的起点：夏、商、周的相继崛起。公元前2070年，炎黄、东夷、苗蛮、戎狄互动整合建立了夏朝，他们定九州、安雅言、序幕天下、以铜为兵、农率均田。这一阶段有了赫赫始祖即三皇五帝之说②，尤其是华夏文化集团的首领炎黄。几千年来，炎黄二帝作为中华民族始兴之祖和统一的象征，对于海内外中华儿女的民族认同和增强凝聚力、向心力，发挥了巨大的作用。夏之后是为文化基础扩延阶段的第一个阶段——青铜文化阶段。公元前1600

①　高翠莲. 试论中华民族多元一体格局发展的阶段划分 [J]. 中南民族大学学报（人文社科版），2004（04）：55-60.

②　按《尚书大传》"三皇"为：燧人、伏羲、神农；按《大戴礼记》"五帝"分别为：黄帝、颛顼、帝喾、尧、舜。

年，殷商王朝开启了六畜兴旺、市肆繁盛即"商人"之源的青铜文化。到公元前1046年的周朝，通过封邦建国、井田分封、六律八音、宗法制和礼乐制度，开启了和谐安邦，铸成中华文化内核的阶段。

第三，战国时期随着农业发展、铸币流通、交通发达、城市兴起，到秦汉阶段，中华民族的互动达到第一次高潮，通过郡县制、书同文、行同伦、车同轨、治驰道而促成的大互动、大认同、大融合，使中华民族格局逐步形成，民族融合的中心——汉族形成。

第四，到了魏晋南北朝时期，群雄闪烁、分裂混战，各民族大规模迁徙、融合，破坏了中原政权和经济架构，也使得北方游牧民族和中原汉族产生了充分的文化交往，各民族之间达到了第二次互动高潮。同时，也使得中华民族之间互动范式出现了转折点，即形成了大一统、胡汉融合以及璀璨恢宏的"唐文化"。

第五，中华民族的第三次互动高潮是五代十国、宋辽金夏。这一时期，战争与和平交织，民族互动与认同深入，少数民族进入中原，汉族南迁，整个民族之间的认同不断深入。元明时期，蒙古军队一步步降服畏兀儿、占哈喇鲁、吞西夏、征服金朝、招抚吐蕃、平定大理、灭南宋、统一中国，"以马上得天下"。

第六，中华民族融合在清代的大发展与民国阶段的新认同。清初时期清朝统治全国各民族，主要是汉族、蒙古族以及其他南方少数民族等"剃发易服"，可以说，这是一定程度的汉族的"满化"。当然，后来更多是满族的"汉化"。伴随着清军入关、定鼎燕京及语言文字、风俗习惯、生产方式等均因受汉族的影响而发生变化。发展到清中后期，除皇室以外，入关的八旗将士根本不会说满语，其姓氏也从原来的复姓变为单姓，有的甚至采用汉姓。辛亥革命后建立中华民国，第一次实现了从传统的"天下"国家向到近代民族国家的过渡。孙中山先生提出"天下为公""五族共和"，提倡建设"中华民族国家"之"国族"。而近代百年以来通过甲午战争、虎门销烟、扶清灭洋、义和团运动、抗日战争的磨砺，也使中华民族作为一个多元一体的民族整体这一概念逐渐进入到各民族国人的自觉意识之中。

第七，中华民族在中华人民共和国的国歌声中真正诞生，迈入与时俱进生机盎然的新阶段。中华人民共和国成立后，中国共产党和中国政府坚持贯彻执行民族平等政策，少数民族的语言文字、宗教信仰等都得到了应有的尊重和法律的保障。中国政府结合中国实际情况采取民族区域自治制度的基本政策，这也是中国的一项重要政治制度。1945年5月，中国建立了中国共产党领导下的第一个相当于省一级的民族自治地区——内蒙古自治区。中华人民共和国成立以后，又相继建立了新疆维吾尔自治区、广西壮族自治区、宁夏回族自治区和西藏自治区。截至目前，全国55个少数民族中，有44个民族建立了自治地方，自治面积占全国国土总面积的64%左右。中华民族大家庭一起走上了充满活力、前途光明的伟大的复兴之路。

4.2 中华民族在融合中形成

上面我们简单梳理了中华民族的概念及中华民族多元一体格局形成的历史轨迹，接下来，我们要讨论一下中华民族各民族之间的融合进程及其发生原因。英国历史学家阿诺尔德·汤因比在和日本宗教文化活动家池田大作的一次学术对话中如此说道："就中国人来说，几千年来，比世界任何民族都成功地把几亿民众从政治文化上团结起来。他们显示出这种在政治、文化上统一的本领，具有无与伦比的成功经验。"① 汤因比是对的。但几千年来中国人何以能如此成功地在政治文化上把各民族民众团结起来？这确实是一个值得探讨的有趣的题目。

4.2.1 民族融合的几个例子

应该说，中华民族之间的融合确实是人类文明史上的一个壮观奇迹。我们上面介绍了这片土地上曾发生过多次民族大融合，也在这一进程中历史地形成了以华夏—汉民族为核心的中华民族融合的共同体。各民族以各种途径走近彼此，形成"你来我去、我来你去、你中有我、我中有你"的格局，他们各具特点和特长又（在文化的各个层次和领域中）互相学习和吸收，少数民族一定程度的"汉化"与汉族一定程度的"胡化"双向推进未尝少歇，而各民族之间相互涵化是民族融合的推进因素。

少数民族的汉化相对而言更为明显。如匈奴——战国秦汉时代扰攘汉地不得安宁的知名游牧大族——部分外迁到欧洲后成为土耳其人和匈牙利人的一部分；内迁的部分则在南北朝时期演变为羯族和氐族，而后汉化消失。如东胡：与匈奴同时的东北族群，后演变为乌桓—鲜卑—柔然。而后，柔然之一部分演变为室韦—蒙古，另外一部分演化为契丹和女真，女真即今天的满族人。又如

---

① ［日］池田大作，［英］阿·汤因比．展望二十一世纪——汤因比与池田大作对话录［M］．荀春生，等译．北京：国际文化出版公司，1997：283.

藏族，也经历了羌—吐蕃—藏族（羌—党项—木雅藏族）的演变史。

我们多次提到的《中国文化要义》的作者、思想家梁漱溟先生祖上也是蒙古族。他自述道："我家祖先与元朝皇帝同宗室，姓'也先帖木耳'，蒙古族。元亡，末代皇帝顺帝携皇室亲属逃回北方，即现在的蒙古，而我们这一家未走，留在河南汝阳，改姓汉姓梁。……说到种族血统，自元亡以后经过明清两代，历时500余年，不但旁人早不晓得我们是蒙古族，即自家人如不是有家谱记载也无从知道了。但几百年来与汉族通婚，不断融合两种不同的血统，自然是具有中间的气质的。"①

我国的回族也是民族融合的产物。一般认为回族是在宋元时代的蕃客和回回军基础上大量和汉族通婚后而形成的包括所有在中区各省信仰伊斯兰教的人。如我们福建泉州就有好几个回民乡村：台商区百崎回族乡②、永春南美回族村。

犹太人散居在世界各地，都能保持其遗风故俗不同化于人，但唐宋时代即入中国，高鼻梁、蓝眼睛的犹太人在中国则大为同化，明清两代犹太人不乏应试做官者。昔日河南开封地区的所谓"青回回""挑筋教"，"一赐乐业人"（黄种犹太人）据说就是他们的后裔③。

在姓氏方面，很多在汉族文化区生活的少数民族改为汉姓，费孝通先生主编的《中华民族多元一体格局》中就介绍到了这方面的一些表现：如山东章丘市术姓，河南固始县的祝姓，河南地区孟津、新安、渑池等县的李姓，平顶山市的马姓、宣姓，镇平、内乡、淅川、新野、新召、南阳六县的王姓，福建惠安县的出姓，南安县丰州的黄姓等，晋江的丁姓、郭姓和蒲姓，他们的原籍非蒙古，即色目，后来逐渐汉化。④

至于各民族同胞在粮食作物、瓜果菜蔬、衣着服饰和日常起居器物与工艺制造等方面，也是大量的相互学习、融合使用，限于篇幅，在这里暂不多介绍。

而华夏汉族作为民族凝聚和融合的核心，也是在这个不断融入少数民族因

① 汪东林．梁漱溟问答录［M］．长沙：湖南人民出版社，1988：1-2．民族通婚混血使得各民族在基因上生物学地不断接近。这种通婚混血的结果就是南方北方的各个民族就血缘的基因指数分析而言都不单纯，没有不是多种族混血的后代。

② "八闽回族第一乡"——百崎回族乡是福建省18个少数民族乡中唯一的回族乡，也是泉州市唯一的少数民族乡。百崎回民的先人是由"海上丝绸之路"来华经商的阿拉伯穆斯林，百崎回民尊元朝末年郭德广为开基祖，百崎回民称他"宣慰公"。

③ 可参看报告文学作品《河南犹太人》，作者王春来，2006年由中国文联出版公司出版。

④ 当然，改用汉姓并不表示他们已完全成了汉人，只能表明他们已不再抗拒汉化了。请参看费孝通．中华民族多元一体格局［M］．北京：中央民族大学出版社，2018：163-164.

素的过程中形成的。费孝通先生就指出：

距今 3000 年前，在黄河中游出现了一个由若干民族集团汇集和逐步融合的核心，被称为华夏，像滚雪球一般地越滚越大，把周围的异族吸收进入这个核心。它在拥有黄河和长江中下游的东亚平原之后，被其他民族称为汉族。汉族继续不断吸收其他民族的成分而日益壮大，而且渗入其他民族的聚居区，构成起着凝聚和联系作用的网络，奠定了以这个疆域内许多民族联合成的不可分割的统一体的基础，成为一个自在的民族实体，经过民族自觉而称为中华民族。①

关于汉族的形成和发展，大家还可以参看徐杰舜先生著《汉民族发展史》的相关介绍。

4.2.2　民族融合的主要作用因素

首先，文化基因的凝聚力是底蕴，形成了民族共通的价值观。

文化基因是指各民族共享的核心文化元素，或内在相通的相似的价值观。汉族文化在农耕区的黄河长江流域当然是无争议的主干文化，而汉族文化的主干又是儒家文化。这使得大杂居小聚居、日渐融合中的各民族逐渐接触和接受了汉族儒家文化生活方式的覆盖性影响。

比如儒家礼教重视婚姻的社会意义，以"六礼"确定婚姻的合法性。六礼即纳彩、问名、纳吉、纳征、请期和亲迎。今天汉族送礼的时候要送糖、烟、酒、茶、肉等。而回族婚礼程序中也有如：请媒人提亲、说"色俩目"（也叫定茶）、插花（也叫定亲）、迎娶、阿訇念"尼卡哈"、撒喜、闹洞房、摆针线等环节。维吾尔族婚礼中也有类似共同点：也要提亲，请一位德高望重的长者见证，迎娶时送布料、盐、馕等礼物。

又如儒家倡导宗法文化、尊祖重族，按世系流传编族谱传家风，逢年过节祭祀先祖。许多少数民族在与汉族杂居共处中也受此感化和影响。比如广西壮族、湖南永顺土家族、浙江丽水畲族、泉州回族的民众也建有自己的家族祠堂（如泉州晋江陈埭丁氏宗祠和惠安百崎郭氏家庙就是融合汉族和回族特色、阿拉伯和中国传统风格的回族祠堂），他们也会编修自家的族谱并订立家规，新婚媳妇进门也要向祖宗禀告行礼。《畲族祖图》是畲族人祭祖时的重要祭拜物。畲族人对祖图非常重视，每年农历二月、七月和八月十五祭祖日的时候，畲族民众都要把该图拿出来供奉。这个跟汉族的拜祖先牌位和祖宗像如出一辙。这些都可以算作广义的中华宗族文化的不同形态。

---

① 费孝通．中华民族多元一体格局 [M]．北京：中央民族大学出版社，2018：17.

更重要的一点，就是在历史长河中，中华民族逐步形成了以爱国主义为核心的团结统一、爱好和平、勤劳勇敢、自强不息的伟大民族精神，这既是汉族也是各个少数民族共有的文化符号，是今天中华民族的核心价值认同。

关于民族地区受汉族儒家文化和价值观念影响的研究著作所在不少，如《宋明理学在广西的传播》《儒家的孝与云南少数民族》《从河西走廊看中国》《心向慈母——纳西族与中华民族共同体》等著作中，都可以窥见儒学与中国少数民族思想文化影响关系之一斑。

其次，边疆对中央的向心力是民族融合的关键。

向心力是指向往中心，是一种灿烂文化的魅力的吸引或者征服，进而要求归附或纳入版图，希望建立更密切与一体化的关系。在中国历史上，边疆对中央的向心力，主要表现在内附册封、入朝纳贡和请婚和亲三种。

一是内附册封：即地方民族政权派遣世子为质，表示臣属，以明确其首领的政治身份的形式。如公元653年，彝族首领细奴逻敬服唐朝的高度文明，派子逻盛炎赴长安朝见高宗，表示愿意归附唐朝。唐高宗封细奴逻为巍州刺史，从此南诏接受了唐朝中央政府的领导。细奴逻逝后获谥号司禾府印。如元朝封藏族宗教领袖八思巴为大元国师、帝师大宝法王；雍正皇帝则颁给达赖喇嘛以金印，以及土尔扈特（蒙古族部落）长途跋涉从俄国返归中华的动人故事都是这方面的实例。

二是入朝纳贡：即各少数民族入朝纳贡、进奉礼物表示服从中央政权。西域各地政权从丝绸之路长途跋涉入汉朝纳贡，如太和六年，西域诸国向西汉王朝朝贡"献汗血马、火浣布、犀牛、孔雀、巨象及诸珍异二百余品"。一些存世文物，如古滇国青铜器储贝器，就形象地反映了古滇国向唐王朝纳贡的队列场景。陕西咸阳市汉昭帝平陵中出土的和田玉奔马，唐代的玉飞天，李白诗句"兰陵美酒郁金香，玉碗盛来琥珀光"中所描述之物（葡萄酒和玉碗），皆是当时贡入的域外之物。

三是请婚和亲。知名的人物故事有汉朝的昭君出塞，细君公主与解忧公主远嫁西域；唐朝的文成公主进藏。这些都是民族联姻的历史佳话。

再者，草原与农业的亲和力是民族融合的内因。

一般而言，"南有大汉、北有强胡"的对抗格局确实相对地形成了两大文化区。正如费孝通先生所说的"这条战国秦汉时开始修成的长城是农业民族用来抵御牧畜民族入侵的防线"，但因此也推动草原文化和农业文化形成了某种互补性结合与结构性结合。

（1）互补性结合：农—牧贸易从来都是双方面和互通有无的。农区在耕种及运输上需要大量的畜力，军队里需要马匹，这些不能由农区自给，同时农民也需要牛羊肉食和皮毛原料。而在农区对牧区的供应中，丝织物和茶叶是重要项目，因而后来把农牧区之间的贸易简称为"马绢互市"和"茶马贸易"。如唐与回纥之间有"绢马互市"，彼此供给，形成了南北互市的枢纽——如安徽的寿春、湖北襄阳。

（2）结构性结合：说的是农业区和游牧区的区分是相对的，在南北各地都是综合性发展，要加以区分的是农牧业在各自经济中所占比重大小多少。牧区的结构性结合表现例如汉将李陵后人黠戛斯人"颇知田作"、乌孙墓葬里出土有彩陶流器、纺织织染器具；而农区的结构性结合的表现如广西德保地区的壮族以养殖矮马知名，此马与人齐高，适合山地拖运物资。广西瑶族聚居区放牧毛南菜牛作为他们的日用肉食品。汉族和非汉族地区的互相支持的结构性结合是有利于产生彼此的亲和力的。

总之，文化凝聚力就是凝结民族之魂的亲和力，草原文化和农业文化相互作用，从古至今谁也离不开谁。各个民族之间积聚、黏合、融合在一起，汇聚成推动社会进步的力量。这是中华民族走向多元一体的深层次内涵所在。这里的观点与材料多采自费孝通先生主编的《中华民族多元一体格局》一书，里面还有很多有趣的讨论，这里不能多做介绍了。

4.3　少数民族对中华文化的重要贡献

在中华文化琳琅满目的精彩内容中，少数民族文化所占的比例远远超出他们的人口比例，他们为中华民族丰富多彩的文化宝库奉献了自己可贵的珍宝。

（1）少数民族在政治文化上的贡献：在中国历史上，少数民族或者各据一方，开疆拓土，或交往迁徙杂居群处，或主政建国定鼎中原，或者保家卫国、反抗侵略，实际上为今日中国的政治版图的基本规模奠定了地理基础，也为维护国家和民族的历史共同体的生存和安全作出了各自的贡献。虽然在历史上，各民族的政权之间有分有合，有和谐的交往，也有战争的烟火，但国家统一和民族团结始终是历史发展的主流和基本趋势。而且，各民族政权下也从来都是多民族参与，互相支持。我们完全有理由认为中华民族共同创造中国这个家园，每个民族都是这个家园的家人，都曾经也必将为捍卫和繁荣这个家园而继续奋斗。

（2）少数民族在思想文化上的贡献：千百年来，少数民族群众将汉族文化或外国文化与本族文化融为一体，从而创造出更富意蕴的民族文化。如藏传佛教的"天圆地方""内圆外方"等思想，就是印度、尼泊尔的佛教与藏族的苯教、北方游牧民族的萨满教结合的产物。"万物有灵"的萨满文化是古往今来北方游牧文化的精神支柱，至今仍完整保存在东北鄂伦春等民族的文化生活中。回族尊崇敬主忠君，既信仰伊斯兰教，又效法儒家道德伦理的"二元道德律"，他们的和谐理念、协商民主以及"经商为了行道"的理念，就是伊斯兰文化和儒家文化融合的产物。而回族的这些思想也丰富了中华民族的伦理思想宝库，充实了与人为善、与邻为伴的和谐社会理念，增加了亦商亦农、农商互补的中华民族经济发展观。

（3）少数民族对中华民族语言文字的贡献：世界9大语系中，中国就有汉藏、阿尔泰、印欧、南岛、南亚5种和语系不明的朝鲜语等。少数民族语言不仅丰富了中华语苑，而且一些少数民族语言对国家通用标准语——汉语标准语的贡献也是相当大的。今天的汉语普通话是以北京语音为标准音，以南方话为基础方言，以典范的现代白话文著作为语法规范的。其中就有许多少数民族语言成分，较早的如元代的蒙古语，其后是清代的满语和满式汉语。中国有22个少数民族拥有自己的文字，大多数少数民族同胞除了使用汉字外，还能熟练使用本民族文字。而历史上，少数民族文字更是色彩斑斓，都在为中华的文字体系添光增彩。

（4）少数民族对人文科学的贡献：少数民族古文献也是浩如烟海，其中如汉族卓尼版3万多册的大藏经《甘珠尔》《丹珠尔》，彝族的十月太阳历及《西南彝志》等古文献，用纳西东巴文写成的500多卷700多万字的东巴经，维吾尔族前身"回纥"所使用的察合台文文献，中世纪后的蒙古文献，清代以来大多译自汉文经典的新老满文档案文献等珍本、善本，回族的《古兰经》珍本和经堂用语文献，还有占敦煌文献珍品1/3的少数民族文献，这些都是少数民族对中华文献宝库的卓越贡献，具有很高的学术价值和收藏价值。

（5）少数民族在自然科学上的贡献：许多少数民族的科学家为祖国的发展作出了卓越的贡献。如元代回族天文学家札马鲁丁编制的《万年历》曾颁行全国，他还制成了浑天仪、方位仪、斜纬仪等7种天文仪器。元代维吾尔族鲁明善编写的《农桑衣食撮要》是我国农业科学史上第一部系统完整的农事历书体裁的农学专著，为元代三大农书之一。16世纪伊希马拉珠尔著的《甘露之泉》，被誉为蒙医基础理论的经典之作；占布拉道尔吉著的《蒙医本草图鉴》，载药物879种，每味药都以汉蒙藏三种文字对照，成为学习和研究蒙药学的范本。17世纪初蒙古族外科专家墨尔本、卓尔济著有《医学大全》和《药剂学》，被世人称为当代华佗。著名的云南白药是彝族医生曲焕章根据祖传秘方研制而成的神奇外科止血良药。

（6）少数民族在文学和歌舞以及绘画编织艺术上的贡献：少数民族在对中华民族文化上的充实还表现在他们丰富的史诗文化和歌声文化上。如被搬上银幕成为经典的彝族民间叙事长诗《阿诗玛》；被称为少数民族三大史诗的藏族的《格萨尔王传》、蒙古族的《江格尔传》、柯尔克孜族的《玛纳斯》，伟大文学作品维吾尔族的《福乐智慧》、蒙古族的《蒙古秘史》；北朝的著名汉乐府民歌《敕勒歌》《木兰辞》等都是在匈奴、突厥的粗犷豪放的乐曲影响下形成的。少数民族表达人间真情、男女爱情等内容的民歌从古到今比比皆是，如蒙古族的长调民歌、广西的壮歌、西北各民族的"花儿"等。民歌的代表作如赫哲族的《伊玛堪》、朝鲜族的《阿里郎》、满族的《尼珊萨满》等。哈萨克族就是靠着一代代的"阿肯"弹唱，讲述、传承本民族的思想文化。壮族歌墟、侗族大歌、白族踏歌、京族歌堂等，都是这些民族用来结交朋友，交流思想，从而增强民族凝聚力的重要形式。少数民族不仅能歌，而且善舞。凡有聚会就会翩翩起舞，热情奔放，与汉族农耕民族的沉稳气全然不同，维吾尔族的赛乃姆、蒙古族的安代舞、藏族的囊马、朝鲜族的长鼓舞、傣族的孔雀舞、苗族的芦笙舞等，在我国都是负有盛名，他们可以说拥有在歌舞的海洋中度过群体联欢的一生。另外，像藏族的唐卡卷轴、西域的晕染画法、壮族妇女编织的壮锦，土家族妇女编织的西兰卡普，以及在布依、苗、水族等众多少数民族中流传的蜡染工艺，都与汉族的名绣相媲美并享誉中外。甘肃回族的砖雕艺术也是我国砖雕艺术的杰出代表之一，使来访的全国各族雕刻名家络绎不绝。

（7）少数民族对节日文化的贡献：少数民族的节日文化丰富多彩。如满族的颁金节是满族的"族庆"节；回族的开斋节是为了感谢封斋一个月后真主对信徒衣食住行的赐予；维吾尔族的古尔邦节是以宰牲庆祝一年来真主所给予的幸福生活；哈萨克族的那吾热孜节则是庆祝一年之春万木复苏，农业牧业的万象更新；藏族的藏历新年是为了庆祝一年周而复始所带来的丰收硕果；傣族的泼水节来源于佛教的浴佛节，如今则是以相互泼水来消除灾难、祝福新年；拉祜族的芦笙会是庆祝新年的舞会，这种用芦笙伴奏的腿脚舞跳得越欢快，越能预示来年的粮多、钱多、牲畜多；壮族的三月三则是源于祭祀的小年等。由于少数民族多居处深山老林、高原草原、山河源头、戈壁大漠，艰苦的生活环境锻造了他们的强壮体魄，因而也形成了一些独具特色的体育锻炼项目，并被纳入其民族节日中。

（8）像建筑方面，也有少数民族可圈可点的贡献：如世界闻名的敦煌石窟，云冈石窟等都是汉、鲜卑、吐蕃及西域人民共同创造的。闻名世界的布达拉宫和大昭寺是藏族建筑的艺术精华。元代回族建筑学家亦黑迭儿丁设计和领导修筑的大都工程，为以后北京城的发展奠定了基础。

总之，中国各个少数民族创造了丰富多彩的文化珍宝，并在彼此交往、相互融合的过程中，共同为气象恢宏的中华文化作出了历史的贡献。我们当代的民族文化研究的重要任务，就是深入民族大家庭的百花园，去分析和总结各个民族的文化底蕴、象征符号、故事人物、标志性事件、民族品格，进而发现这些丰富的内容如何相互紧密联系、相辅相成，组成一个有机整体，共同构成了中华民族共有精神家园。只有建设好中华民族共有精神家园，才能筑牢中华民族共同体意识的思想基础，为中华民族的生生不息、团结奋进提供不竭动力源泉。

4.4　海外赤子——华侨华人

提到中华民族，我们还必须提到华侨华人——我们身在海外的同胞兄弟。这里有三个概念。华侨：是指侨居国外仍持有中国国籍的人员。华人：是指归化所在国成为其在籍公民的人员。华裔：是指华人或者华侨在国外出生的后代。我想大家这个很清楚。

（1）中国海外移民及其分布

我们知道，中国文化是安土重迁、家园意识浓厚的农业型文化，但自古以来就有不少人民因为各种原因，迁徙远走，移民他乡。商末至汉初，战乱造成几次大规模向朝鲜和日本的移民。唐末的黄巢起义军残部定居印尼苏门答腊岛。宋代时越南北犯后掳走大批岭南的难民。到明代，东南沿海的广东、福建和海南等地有大量去往南海的移民。而清代"下南洋"的传统更盛，出现了契约华工。当然，现代社会，因商贸务工留学等需要而走出国门或迁居国外的，就更甚于昔日，可以说，凡是有水的地方，就有华侨华人的身影①。

据国务院 2007 年发布的《华侨华人分布状况和发展趋势》统计资料显示：当今生活在海外地区华侨华人人数在 6000 万以上。各大洲华侨华人人数以国家排名而论：泰国位居第一位共 939 万，马来西亚列居第二，有 665 万，位居第三

---

① 庄国土，李瑞晴. 华侨华人分布状况和发展趋势 [M]. 国务院侨务办公室政策法规司编，2011：10.

的是美国，有 379 万，位居第七位的加拿大有 148 万，第八位是拉美的秘鲁有 130 万。像印尼、新加坡、缅甸、澳大利亚、法国、英国、意大利等国的华侨华人亦不在少数。

中国人移民国外，人数多、规模大、分布广，形成了遍布世界的格局。其中福建人较多去往马来西亚、新加坡、文莱和菲律宾；广东潮州人则偏爱泰国；客家人和海南人更多移居印度尼西亚。因此闽南语、粤语和客家话在南洋非常流行。福建更是被网民誉为"中国移民海外最牛的省份"，现已出现过 7 位总统和 1 位总理。如菲律宾前总统科拉松·阿基诺夫人和阿基诺三世母子，分别是华人第四、第五代，祖籍福建漳州龙海鸿渐村；新加坡前总统王鼎昌，华人第三代，祖籍福建厦门；印尼前总统瓦西德，祖籍福建省石狮市；菲律宾前总统杜特尔特也是。另外，像新加坡开国总理李光耀、第三任总理李显龙父子，泰国前总理他信与英拉兄妹，都是客家人，他们的祖籍都是广东梅州市。美国华人船王赵锡成和他的女儿美国首位华人部长赵小兰祖籍是上海嘉定。世界著名实验物理学家、诺贝尔奖获得者丁肇中是山东日照人。雅虎（Yahoo!）的创始人与行政总裁杨致远是台湾台北人。

我们应该明确，扎根世界各地、在宽广领域中开创新生活、创造新业绩的广大华侨华人，他们勤劳勇敢智慧，是优秀的中华儿女，也理所当然地属于广义的中华民族共同体的一分子，并为人类文化的多元发展和文明进步作出了重要的贡献。

（2）华侨华人是促进中外文化交往的中坚力量

远离祖国的海外游子身在异乡为异客，日久他乡即故乡。他们把对故土家乡的思念之情化作了在新土地上努力拼搏开创新家园的热情和干劲，同时也承担起了沟通中外、传播中华文化的历史使命。

一方面，华侨先民在海外，面对新环境、新挑战，秉承中华民族敢于冒险、开拓务实的精神，克服种种艰难险阻，垦荒辟地，掘矿筑路，经商贸易，发展工业和服务业，建设城乡，为住在国的经济社会发展做出贡献，被各国载入史册。另外一方面，移民海外的华人先辈们筚路蓝缕、胼手胝足，他们或者移植中国的社会制度和礼仪文化，带去中国成熟的耕作和养殖技术，扩大中国传统民俗文化的海外传承。如今天的菲律宾华人风俗中仍保留了许多中华遗风，如婚姻父母安排、尊崇祖先、建立祠庙、尊敬长辈、孝敬父母等都源自中国。此外，东南亚等国，有些族群将中国的盘、碟、碗等瓷器，当作传家之宝，在特别的节日祭祀、婚丧嫁娶中才拿出来使用。同时，下南洋的华人移民还与当地土著民族通婚和繁衍人口，造就了包含中华文化基因的混血族群文化，独具特色。如马来西亚的"峇峇娘惹文化"（土生华人）就是这样一种独特文化的历史结晶①。

　　近现代以来的华人移民还建立各种华人社团组织（宗亲会或同乡会等社团），或创办演出团体、华文报纸杂志，设立华文学校和电台电视台等媒体，在丰富海外华侨华人娱乐生活的同时加强彼此的认同感与团结力，也向当地百姓展现中华民族绚丽多彩且的文化，并努力弘扬自强不息厚德载物的中华精神。而唐人街——海外华人赖以生存发展的家园，也是他们展示和传播中华文化，融会中外文化的基地。

　　华侨华人在推动中华文化向外传播的同时，也将西方社会的先进文明带入国内，让国人得以开眼看世界，了解西方文明，特别在近代史上，华侨华人在促进与推动国人对西方社会的认知上所起的作用不可忽视，为近代中国寻找国家出路的探索提供了帮助。华侨身居海外，心系祖国和家乡，他们或汇款赡家，买田建屋，修葺祖坟；或回国投资发展民族工业，振兴中华；或捐资兴办公益事业，促进侨乡经济社会发展，厥功至伟。在近代中国一系列重大事件如辛亥革命、航空救国、"飞虎队""南侨机工"等爱国和反法西斯正义运动中，都有大量的华侨华人毅然回国，英勇参战为国牺牲。如被毛泽东誉为"华侨旗帜、民族光辉"的陈嘉庚先生心怀大爱、倾资兴学，创建了厦门大学和集美学村，至今还在惠泽万千学子②。而当祖国发生各种严重自然灾害的时候，海外华侨华人都会发扬骨肉之情、同胞之爱，全力驰援各种急需物资。对此，祖国人民将永远感念不忘！

　　当然，随着代际的传承和深入融合于当地社区，华人后代可能也没有机会再接受华语教育，但我们仍然能感动地听到他们用当地语言诉说他们对祖国的一份思念和祝福之情，他们变的可能是语言，甚至是肤色，但内心不变的是一颗颗中华儿女的中国心。"别看我们完全不懂中文，我们的思想举止都是非常中国式的。"（巴拿马华侨如是说）就像张明敏《我的中国心》里歌唱到的：河山

---

①　"峇峇娘惹"是 Baba nyonya 的音译，即"土生华人"，是十五世纪初期中国移民和东南亚土著马来人通婚所生的后代。

②　著者工作生活在陈嘉庚先生的家乡厦门集美，对陈先生为家乡福建所作出的贡献有切身的感受，也每每为其伟大的人格所感动。正如习近平主席 2014 年 10 月 17 日给厦门市集美校友总会的回信中提到的那样，陈嘉庚先生"爱国兴学，投身救亡斗争，推动华侨团结，争取民族解放，是侨界的一代领袖和楷模。他艰苦创业、自强不息的精神，以国家为重、以民族为重的品格，关心祖国建设、倾心教育事业的诚心，永远值得学习。"陈嘉庚先生作为华侨爱国爱乡精神的典范，有德有功有言，如日月经天，将恒久闪耀在海内外华人的心中。

只在我梦萦，祖国已多年未亲近，可是不管怎样也改变不了，我的中国心。这份割不断的故园乡愁让这些海外游子无论身在何方都永远是中华儿女，是一个"文化意义的中国人"。

总之，6700多万华侨华人遍布世界160多个国家和地区，成为中华文化的传播者、中外交往的友好使者、"一带一路"建设的参与者、和平统一的促进者。我们要加强海外爱国力量建设，涵养壮大知华友华力量，促进中外文化文明交流互鉴，海外华侨华人是我们必须珍视、重视和团结的重要力量。

（3）为侨服务的华侨大学

华侨大学与暨南大学是统战部所属的两所以"为侨服务"为办学宗旨的国内高校。我们华侨大学创办于1960年。最初，她是中国政府为适应华侨青年学生回国接受高等教育的需要，在周恩来总理亲切关怀下创办的华侨高等学府。现在华侨大学在泉州厦门都有分校，学生总数超三万，也是中国拥有港澳台侨学生最多的大学之一。

华侨大学六十多年来的建设发展的历程，也是承蒙海外侨亲关爱而发展壮大的历史。陈嘉庚纪念堂、侨总图书馆、陈延奎大楼、菲华楼、吕振万楼等一座座矗立于华园的侨捐建筑，无言地述说着海外华侨华人关爱资助华侨大学的动人故事①。他们当中，许东亮、庄善春、陈永栽、杜祖贻、曾宪梓等一个个名字，在学校办学历程上熠熠生辉。

华侨大学非常重视对在校侨生的教育工作，不断改进提高对侨生教学服务的工作水平与质量。经过长期的实践与探索，我校确定了以培养"坚定爱国者"为国情教育目标，并行"从大类到分类演变"的课堂教学和"从理论向实践深化"的实践教学两条路径，统筹优化"教材、教师、教学"三个要素，围绕增强港澳台学生"国史知识、家国情怀、强国意志、报国行动"等四个方面，有针对性地推进实施"国史研习、国情调研、国防教育、国青培养"四个教育模块，逐步构建了求知、养情、锻意、笃行的"知情意行"融合发展的国情教育体系。

---

①　统计数据显示，自1963年收到第一笔华侨捐赠起，截至2018年，华侨大学共接受华侨捐赠数百项，捐资总额超5亿元人民币。1980年成立的华侨大学董事会，广泛凝聚、团结海内外董事及热心侨校教育人士，为学校建设发展献计献策、捐款捐物，在扩大学校海外影响、开拓海外生源、奖励或资助优秀学生、资助教师海外学术交流、开展海外华文教育以及改善教学生活硬件设施建设等方面作出了卓越贡献。

图 4-1　"知情意行"融合发展的华侨大学港澳台侨生国情教育体系

以实践教学为例。我校常年围绕"根在中国"主题，积极实施"中国文化之旅"实践、"侨乡文化研习"实践、"海外文化传播"实践等各种文化研修活动。其中，"中国文化之旅"夏（冬）令营是华侨大学在中央统战部、国务院侨办的大力支持下，从 20 世纪 80 年代以来即已组织实施的常设文化研修项目。学校以"弘扬中华文化，培育家国情怀"为出发点和落脚点，每年均会组织港澳台侨学生和部分内地学生前往祖国各地开展"学游结合，以学为主的"文化研习活动。旨在让营员们在文化研习活动中体验、内化和践行中华优秀传统文化，增进营员对中华文明的亲近感和认同感，培养新时代青年的家国情怀和使命担当。我们相信，他们将会作为新时代的新锐力量，为促进中外人民之间的友好关系作出应有贡献。

总之，中华民族是中华文明的共同创造者。在长期的发展过程中，中国各民族的文化相互交融，构成了生机勃勃、多元一体的中华民族共同体。而华侨华人是联通中国与世界的民间大使，是链接中华文化与世界文化的桥梁，是中华民族共同体的组成部分。正如习近平总书记指出的，我们要持续"加强海内外中华儿女大团结，团结一切可以团结的力量，齐心协力走向中华民族伟大复兴的光明前景"。

The Fourth Chapter :

Diversity in Unity
—Chinese Nation and Chinese Culture

4. 1　The Definition of the Nation of China

As we all know, culture is created by humans. And Chinese culture is created by Chinese people. We call Chinese people here as "the Chinese nation". They are the masters of China, and the co-creators of Chinese culture. It is true that China has been a united multi-ethnic country since ancient times. After the PRC was established, the central government confirmed altogether 56 ethnic groups within the country. Due to the overwhelming population of the Han nationality, the other 55 are considered to be ethnic minority groups. Each of China's ethnic groups are distributed throughout the country, mutually coinhabiting small as well as larger regions. The minorities live in regions of the Han, while the Han inhabit regions of ethnic minorities. Over the course of history, this pattern of diffusion has developed as each ethnic group associates with each other, making mutual exchanges.

But intellectuals have long regarded the Chinese nation in a broad sense as a general term composed of Han and other 55 ethnic groups. That's to say, it is still a political term. It should be said that it is the mainstream and basic understanding to regard the Chinese nation in a broad sense as a comprehensive whole including 56 ethnic groups. But, different from that, in 1988, the famous Chinese sociologist Mr. Fei Xiaotong firstly proposed that the Chinese nation was an ethnographic term, a self-conscious ethnic entity with the Han people as the cohesive center, both pluralistic and integrated. The so-called "pluralistic" here refers to the multiple origins, i. e. , the fifty-six ethnic groups. The so-called "integrated" refers to the integration of fifty-six ethnic groups to form Chinese nation—this new ethnic entity. According to Mr. Fei, the hallmark of the "Chinese nation" as a unified national entity lies in its commonality of following four aspects: (1) Common language. The Chinese nation shares a common national language—Mandarin. (2) Common territory. They co-live in the territory of China. (3) Common economic life. They jointly participate in building the socialist economy with Chinese characteristics. (4) Common cultural psychology. They identify with Chinese culture and have developed a Chinese national spirit.

It should be said that contemporary Chinese intellectuals on the whole have generally accepted Mr. Fei's view. We also believe that first, the Chinese nation developed from many historically independent nations. It is a new conscious national entity. The Chinese nation in its entirely is already interdependent, unified and forever inseparable as a living entity. Second, the formation of this new national entity has gone through a long history. It went through the division and merging of nationalities, and achieved the integration. Finally in modern times, especially after the birth of the People's Republic of China, a unified national entity was formed. Third, diversity in unity does not prevent each nationality in the new body of the Chinese nation from maintaining its individual cultural traditions and lifestyles. The traditional identity of the native nation and the unified identity of the Chinese nation are compatible and parallel. The former is a partial identity, while the later is a fundamental or high-level one. The vivid and rich individuality of each nationality makes the Chinese nation full of pluralism and new vitality.

Here, according to both diachronic clues and developmental clues of ethnic interaction and integration, we will give you a brief overview of the following noteworthy information.

(1) The prehistoric memory of the Chinese people: among the multiple origins, the first is the legend about the creation of man and things. For example, the ancestor of the Yi people is Nizhixialuo. And the ancestor of the Zhuang people is Buluotuo. These groups have gone through moving from cave dwelling to house dwelling and from hunting to rice farming. Among the multiple origins, the famous archaeological remains include the restoration of the living of the upper cavemen, the Banpo culture, the Yangshao culture, the Hemudu culture and the Dawenkou culture.

(2) The beginning of the formation of the Chinese nation: the successive rise of Xia, Shang and Zhou Dynasties. In 2070 BCE, Yanhuang, Dongyi, Miaoman and

Rongdi interacted and integrated to establish the Xia Dynasty. They pacified China and unified languages. They forged weapons in bronze and divided their fields. Then the original ancestors were said to be the Three Sovereigns and Five Emperors. Particularly, the creators of Chinese culture were said to be Emperor Yan and Huang. For thousands of years, these two emperors, as the ancestors of the Chinese nation and the symbol of unification, in strengthening the national identity and cohesive and centripetal force of Chinese people at home and abroad have played a great role. After Xia Dynasty, the first stage of the cultural foundation expansion began. It was the Bronze In 1600 BCE, with thriving domestic animals and flourished markets as the source of merchants, the Shang Dynasty developed the bronze culture. By 1046 BCE, through establishing feudal states, dividing the fields, promoting elegant music, implementing patriarchal system and the systems of rituals and music, the Zhou Dynasty began a period of harmony and peace and forged the core of Chinese culture.

(3) The Warring States period: in this year, there were the development of agriculture, the circulation of coins, the development of transportation and the rise of cities. By the Qin and Han Dynasties, the interaction of the Chinese nation reached its first climax. Through the system of counties, the same characters, the same behavioral standards and width of vehicle tracks and roads, and through such great interaction, identification and integration, the core of the Chinese nation was gradually formed. And it also brought the birth of the Han people.

(4) By the period of Wei, Jin and North and South Dynasties, the flickering of domestic groups, the splitting and mixing, the mass migration and integration of various ethnic groups destroyed the regime and economy of the Central Plains. It brought the northern nomads and the Han people in Central Plains a full cultural interaction. It brought the second climax of interaction between Chinese various ethnic groups. And at the same time, it brought a turning point to the ways of interaction among Chinese ethnic groups. Characterized by great unification, the fusion of Hu and Han cultures and brilliance, the Tang culture was formed.

(5) The third climax of the interaction of the Chinese nation was in the period of Five Dynasties and Ten Kingdoms, Song, Liao, Jin and Western Xia Dynasties. During that period, war and peace were intertwined, and ethnic interaction and identity were deepened. As ethnic minorities entered the Central Plains and the Han people moved southward, the identity of the entire Chinese nation deepened. During the Yuan and

Ming Dynasties, the Mongolian army subjugated the Uihur and Halalu tribes, conquered the Western Xia and Jin State, and Tibetan regime. They also pacified Dali, destroyed the Southern Song Dynasty, and unified China "on the back of horses".

(6) The great development of Han nationality as a core of Chinese nation in the Qing Dynasty and the new identity of the Republic of China. When the early Qing Dynasty ruled the whole Chinese nation, mainly the Han people, Mongolians and other southern ethnic minorities. People changed to shave the Manchu-style hair and dress. This policy was called changing hair style and dress style. We can say, this was a certain degree of Manchuization of the Han people. Of course, later there were more Hanization of Manchu people. As the Qing army entered the country and settled in Yanjing, the language and writing, customs and production methods of Manchu people changed due to the influence of the Han people. To the middle and late Qing Dynasty, except the imperial family, soldiers of the eight ethnic groups couldn't speak Manchu at all. Their surnames have also changed from original compound surnames to single surnames. Some even adopted Han surnames. For the first time, the Republic of China has realized the transition from a traditional "world" country to a modern nation-state. Sun Yat-sen proposed the "five nationalities Republic" and "the whole world is for the public", and advocated the construction of the "national race" of the "Chinese nation state". In modern times through destruction of Opium at Humen, the Boxer Movement and the War of Resistance against Japanese Aggression, the Sino-Japanese War, the Chinese nation, as a nation state of diversity in unity, was gradually known to people of all ethnic groups.

(7) Finally, the Chinese nation was truly born with the anthem of the People's Republic of China. After the founding of new China, the Communist Party of China and the Chinese government continues to implement policies of equality with regards to the ethnic groups' languages systems of writing, and religious beliefs. All are respected and protected by law. The regional autonomy of ethnic minority regions reflects the government policy that links them together. This was a major decision in politics. On May 5, 1945, under the leadership of the established Chinese Communist Party, the first provincial level autonomous region was designated—Inner Mongolia. Later, the People's Republic of China established in succession: the Xinjiang Uighur, Guangxi Zhuang, Ningxia Hui, and Tibetan anonymous regions. Currently, of the 55 ethnic minority groups, there has been established 44 autonomous regions, occupying an area

of about 64% of China's total land mass.

The big family of the Chinese nation is full of vitality and has a bright future.

4.2 The Formation of the Nation of China Through Integration

Now, I would like to briefly introduce the great integration among the various ethnic groups of the Chinese nation. Arnold Joseph Toynbee was a famous British historian. Daisaku Ikeda was a Japanese religious and cultural activist. Once in their academic dialogue, Toynbee said: "Chinese people for thousands of years, have united hundreds of millions of people more successfully than any other countries, culturally and politically. They have shown their ability to unitize people politically and culturally and their unparalleled success. " What Toynbee said is correct. How the Chinese have had such a successful ability for thousands of years to bring people together both politically and culturally? What is the story of their success? This is indeed an interesting topic worth exploring. This is a question that we mentioned in the second chapter "the features of Chinese culture".

4.2.1 Several Examples of the Integration·of Ethnic Minorities

It should be said that the integration of Chinese ethnic groups is indeed a miracle in the history of human civilization. As we summarized above, there occurred many times great ethnic integration in China. It is here that cohesive body of Chinese nation, with the Huaxia-Han people as its core, was historically formed. Ethnic groups have come closer to each other in various ways. Among Brethren Ethnic Groups, "I Am in You and You are in Me". Each has its own distinguishing features and specialties, and they from each other, then the " Sinicization " of ethnic minorities and the "Huization" of Han people have been developed in both directions without stopping. Assimilation between different ethnic groups was a promoting factor for ethnic integration.

For example, the Xiongnu were a well-known nomadic tribe during the Warring States, Qin and Han Dynasties that disturbed the Han China. The Huns who migrated westward to Europe became part of the Turks and Hungarians. While those who migrated eastward in the Northern and Southern Dynasties evolved into the tribes of Jie and Di tribes. And then integrated into the Han People. Donghu was a northern ethnic group which co-existed with Xiongnu. It evolved from Wuhuan, Xianbei to Rouran Khaganate. Some part of Rouran evolved from Shiwei of Mongolian, and another part evolved to Khitan and Nvzhen tribes. The Nvzhen tribe is Manchu people today. Another example is Tibetan who also went through the evolution from Tubo Kingdom, Qiang, Tangut tribe to Muya Tibetan.

Mr. Liang Shumin was a thinker and author of the Essence of Chinese Culture which we have mentioned many times. His ancestors were also of Mogolian origin. He described his ancestors as follows:

"My ancestors belonged to the same clan with the emperor of Yuan Dynasty, shared the same Tibetan surname as 'Esentemur'. After the collapse of the Yuan Dynasty, Emperor Shun, the last emperor of Yuan, with his family, fled back to the north. That is, the current Mongolia. But my ancestors didn't follow the departure. They stayed in the City of Luoyang in Henan Province, and changed to the Han-style surname, Liang. When it comes to racial lineage, since the collapse of Yuan Dynasty to the Ming and Qing Dynasties, more than 500 years have passed. Not only others fail to know that we are Mogolian, but even our own family members would not know it without genealogy. But hundreds of years of intermarriage with the Han Chinese brought constant integration of the two different lineage. Our family naturally enjoys the characteristics of both bloodlines."

Chinese Hui ethnic group is another example. After many intermarriages among Tibetans, Hui army and Han people occurred in Song and Yuan Dynasties, the Hui develops and includes all Muslims in the whole China. For example, we have several villages of Hui people in Quanzhou City, Fujian Province: Baiqi Hui Ethnic Township in Hui'an County and Nanmei Hui Ethnic Village in Yongchun County.

Jews are scattered all over the world. They keep their traditional customs different from those of other people. But the high-nosed, blue-eyed Jews that came to China in Tang and Song Dynasties were greatly assimilated. In the Ming and Qing dynasties, many people took the imperial examinations to become officials. In the past, they were the so-called "Qing Hui Hui" and "Tiao Jin Jiao" in Kaifeng City, Henan Province.

In terms of surnames, many ethnic minorities living in Han cultural areas have changed to Han-style surnames. According to the documentary records and social surveys: the surname Zhu （术）in Zhangqiu county of Shandong Province. Zhu （祝）in Gushi county in Henan Province. Li in Yujin, Xin'an and Mianchi and other counties in Henan Province. Ma and Xuan in the City of Pingdingshan. Wang in the 6 counties of Zhenping, Neixiang, Xichuan etc. Chu in Hui'an county of Fujian Province. Huang in Fengzhou township of Nan'an county and so on. The origin of these people is either Mongolian or Semu. They gradually transformed into Han Chinese.

As for the food crops, fruits and vegetables, costumes and daily utensils, peoples of different ethnic groups also learn from each other. Here we won't go any further.

In addition, as the core of national cohesion and integration, the Han nationality is also formed in the process of continuously integrating ethnic factors. Mr. Fei Xiaotong pointed out:

3000 years ago, there appeared a core in the middle reaches of the Yellow River, which was gathered and gradually integrated by several ethnic groups. It was called Huaxia. It was snowballing like a snowball, and the surrounding ethnic groups were absorbed into this core. After having the East Asian plain in the middle and lower reaches of the Yellow River and the Yangtze River, it was called the Han nationality by other ethnic groups. The Han nationality continues to absorb the elements of other ethnic groups and grows stronger day by day. It also infiltrates into the inhabited areas of other ethnic groups, forming a network that plays a role of cohesion and connection, laying the foundation for an inseparable unity formed by many ethnic groups in this territory. It has become a free national entity and is called the Chinese nation through national consciousness.

For the formation and development of the Han nationality, please refer to Mr. Xu Jieshun's book *Development history of Han nationality*.

4.2.2　The Main Factors of Ethnic Integration

First, the cohesion of cultural gene is culture, forming a common value.

Culture genes refer to the sharing of common cultural elements with each other, and inherent connection in some similar values. Han culture in the farming region of the Yellow River and Yangtze River valleys is of course the undisputed main culture. And the backbone of Han culture is Confucian culture. That has forced ethnic groups that increasingly integrated with each other to adapt to and gradually accept the great influence of Confucian lifestyle of Han people.

For example, Confucian ethics attaches importance to the social significance of marriage, and determines the legitimacy of marriage by "Six Rites": marriage proposal, finding bride's name and birth date, matching birth dates, exchanging wedding gifts, sending letter with the wedding date and greeting the bride. Today, the Han Chinese still need to give gifts of sugar, cigarettes, wine, tea, meat, etc. In the Hui wedding procedure, there are also such links as asking the matchmaker to propose a marriage, saying selianmu (also known as fixed tea), arranging flowers (also known as fixed marriage), getting married, the Imam reading "Nikaha" to the newly married couple, scattering happy candies, making a scene in the bridal chamber, and playing the needle and thread.

In addition, Confucian culture stresses the rule of clan law and respects to ancestors, they make up genealogies and pass on family customs according to lineage, and offer sacrifices to ancestors on festivals. Many ethnic minorities living together with the Han people are also affected by Confucian patriarchal culture. For example, The Zhuang people in Guangxi and the Hui people in Quanzhou also built their own ancestral halls (Ding's ancestral hall in Chendai, Jinjiang is a famous ancestral hall integrating Han and Hui characteristics, Arab and Chinese traditional styles), compile their own genealogies. She Ancestral Chart attach great importance to the chart. On the 15th day of the second, seventh and eighth lunar month, She people will take out the chart for worship. This is the same as the Han worship of ancestors, ancestral statue and "ancestral chart". All these can be considered as different forms of Chinese clan culture in a broad sense.

In the long history, the Chinese nation has formed a great national spirit with patriotism as the core, which is unity, peace loving, hardworking and courageous, and constantly striving for self-improvement, which are the common cultural symbols of the Han people and all ethnic minorities. It is the core value identification of the Chinese nation today.

There are many works about the influence of Confucian culture in the minority regions, such as the Spread of Song-Ming Neo-Confucianism in Guangxi, Filial Piety and Minority in Yunnan, Looking at China from the Hexi Corridor, and Heart to China. From these works we can see the influence of Confucian philosophy on the thought and culture of China's ethnic minorities.

Second, the cohesion that border areas showed to the central places is crucial.

The cohesion here refers to the yearn for the center, a kind of attraction and subjugation of the central places. A requirement for subordination or inclusion in the territory, and a desire to establish a relationship to be closer and more integrated. In Chinese history, the cohesion that border areas showed to the central places was mainly manifested in three ways: subjection, tribute and marriage alliances.

(1) The first way is subjection. King of local ethnic group send a prince as a hostage to express his subordination, and to define the political identity of their leader. In 653, Xi Nuluo, the leader of the Yi nationality, sent his son Luo Shengyan to Chang'an to meet Emperor Gaozong of the Tang Dynasty because of his admiration for the high civilization of the Tang Dynasty, and expressed his willingness to join the Tang Dynasty. Emperor Gaozong of the Tang Dynasty appointed Xi Nuluo as the governor of Weizhou. From then on, Nanzhao accepted the leadership of the central government of the Tang Dynasty. Ba Siba, a Tibetan religious leader, was be honored as the National Master Ba Siba of Yuan Dynasty, the Emperor Yongzheng in Qing Dynasty awarded the gold seal to Dalai Lama, and the moving story of Tuerhute (a Mongolian tribe) returning to China from Russia in Qing Dynasty. which all were the examples of the first way.

(2) The second way is to pay tribute. That is, the ethnic minorities pay tribute and offer gifts to show their obedience to the central government. For example, people of the western regions traveled from the Silk Road to the Han State to pay tributes. In the 6th year of Taihe period, the tributes of the western regions to the Western Han Dynasty included more than 200 items such as Ferghana horses, asbestos cloth, rhinoceroses, peacocks, elephants and other treasures. Some cultural relics such as bronze shell storage vessels, vividly reflect the scene of the ancient Dian state paying tribute to the Tang Dynasty. The galloping horse carved in Hetian Jade from the tomb of Emperor Zhao of the Han Dynasty in Xianyang City, Shaanxi Province, the things described in Li Bai's poems of "the wine of Lanling is full of fragrance of tulips, the wine in the jade bowl reflects the color of amber", were all tributes from outside the region.

(3) The third way is marriage alliance. The famous character stories are like Zhaojun's going out of the frontier in the Han Dynasty, Princess Xijun and Jieyou of Han Dynasty. The Princess Wencheng going out of the Frontier in Tang Dynasty. Which are good stories about the marriage of different nationalities.

In addition, the affinity between grassland and agriculture is the inner force.

Generally speaking, "the Han people in the south and the Hu people in the north", the confrontation brought two major cultural zones. But it also promotes the complementary combination and structural combination of grassland culture and agricultural culture.

(1) The complementary combination means that trade is two-direction and interchangeable. Much animal power is in need in agricultural areas for farming and transportation. But the army needs horses which must not be supplied by farmers themselves. At the same time, farmers also need raw beef and mutton, hides and furs. While in the supply of farming areas to the pasturing areas, silk products and tea are often important items. Therefore, the trade between farmers and herdsmen was later called as "horse-silk mutual market" and "tea-horse trade". For example, Tang Empire and Huihe people exchanged agriculture products and pasture products, and formed the hub of the north-south mutual market——the City of Shouchun in Anhui Province and Xiangyang in Hubei Province.

(2) The structural combination means that the distinction between agricultural and nomadic areas is relative, and it's developed integrally throughout the North and South. Farming and herding were combined with each other. What's important to distinguish is the percentage of agriculture and husbandry in the economy. The expressions of structural combination in pastoral areas are: Kiryiz people, descents of Li Ling who was a general in Han Dynasty, were quite familiar with how to plant. In the ancient tombs of Wusun Tribe, there are colored pottery flow vessels, textile and dyeing instruments. The expressions of structural combination in agricultural areas: the Zhuang people in the Debao area of Guangxi are famous for raising ponies, which are as high as people and are suitable for hauling materials in mountainous areas. Maonan beef cattle are herded in the Yao inhabited area of Guangxi, which is also their important meat food. In this structure, between Han and non-Han regions, we can see the structural feature of mutual support, which also tends to generate mutual affinity.

All in all, cultural cohesion is the affinity that condenses the soul of the nation which is accumulated, glued and integrated. Grassland culture and farming culture have interacted with each other, and neither can be separated from the other till now. This is the deep-seated concept of the Chinese nation's diversity in unity.

4.3   The Important Contributions of Ethnic
Minorities to Chinese Culture

Among the dazzling and vivid contents of Chinese culture, the proportion of minority cultures far exceeds the proportion of their population. They have contributed their treasures to the colorful cultural treasures of the Chinese nation.

(1) The contribution of ethnic minorities in political culture: In Chinese history, some ethnic minorities have occupied their territory or developed their borders. Some migrated and lived in mixed groups. Some established nations in the Central Plains. Some defended their country against foreign invasion and aggression. In fact, they have laid the foundation of the geographic space for the basic scale of political map of today's China. And they have made their own important contributions to the survival and security of the historic community of the nation. Although throughout the history, there have been divisions and unions among the various ethnic regimes, harmonious interactions and fierce wars. However, national unity and ethnic solidarity have always been the mainstream and basic trend of historical development. Moreover, under all ethnic regimes, there has always been multi-ethnic participation and mutual support. We have every reason to believe that with common efforts, the Chinese people have made China a common homeland. People of every ethnic group are members of this homeland. They will continue to struggle to prosper this homeland.

(2) The contribution of ethnic minorities in ideology and culture: For thousands of years, ethnic minorities have integrated Han culture or foreign cultures with their own, and have created a national culture richer in meaning. For example, Tibetan Buddhism's ideas like "round sky and square earth" and "a circle inside a square" are the product of the combination of Indian and Nepalese Buddhism, Tibetan Bonism, and Shamanism of the nomads in the north. Another example is Shaman culture where everything is believed to have spirit. Shaman culture has been the key content of the nomadic culture in the north. This spiritual culture is kept intact in the Oroqen and other ethnic groups in Northeast China. The Hui people respect and are loyal to their ruler. They believe in Islam, and follow the dual-ethical principles of Confucianism. Their notion of harmony, consultation and democracy, and the concept for " doing business for sermon" are the products of the integration of Islamic and Confucian cultures. The essence of these thoughts of Hui people has also enriched the ethical thoughts of the Chinese nation, enriched the concept of harmonious society where people are good to each other, and developed the economic development view where commerce and agriculture are important and complementary.

(3) The contribution of ethnic minorities to the Chinese language and characters: Among the nine major language families in the world, there are five in China, Sino-Tibetan, Altaic, Indo-European, Austronesian and Austro-Asiatic language family and Korean in undefined language family. Minority languages enrich the variety of Chinese languages. And some of them make a significant contribution to the national standard language—Mandarin. Today's Mandarin is based on Beijing phonetics as the standard sound, on Southern dialect as the basic dialect, and on Baihua (vernacular written Chinese) as the grammatical norm. Among them are many minority language components, such as Mongolian and Manchu-style Chinese. Twenty-two of China's ethnic minorities have their own characters, and most of these people are proficient in their own characters in addition to Chinese characters. Throughout the history, minority characters have been brilliant. Their addition expanded the Chinese writing system.

(4) The contribution of ethnic minorities to the humanities: There are also a great number of ancient documents of ethnic minorities, such as the tripitaka *Kangyur* and *Tengyur* which were issued over 30000 volumes in Zhuoni county, ten-month solar calendar of Yi people, ancient documents like *Perspectives on the Yi of Southwest China*, over 500 volumes and 7 million words of Dongba Scripture written in Dongba language, Cahetai literature used by Uighur ancestors, the Mongolian literature of the post-medieval period, the old and new Manchu archival literature most of which were translated from the Chinese classics since the Qing Dynastythe rare edition. The *Quran* of the Hui and literature of scripture hall languageas well as minority literature which accounts for 1/3 of the Dunhuang literature. Those are the remarkable contributions of minorities to Chinese literature. They are of great value in academics and collection.

(5) The contribution of ethnic minorities in natural sciences: Many scientists from ethnic minorities have made outstanding contributions to the development of their country. Jamal al-Din, a Hui astronomer, wrote *Perpetual Calendar* in the Yuan Dynasty which was issued to the whole country. He also invented seven astronomical instruments like the armillary sphere, azimuth instrument and inclinometer. The book

Summary of Agriculture, *Mulberry*, *Clothing and Food* written by Lu Mingshan, a Uyghur agriculturalist, is the first systemic and complete agricultural monograph in the genre of agricultural calendar in the history of agricultural science in China. It is one of the three major agricultural books in Yuan Dynasty. In the 16th century, *Ganluzhiquan* (The Spring) by Yiximalazhu, a famous Mongolian doctor, was regarded as a classic work of the basic theory of Mongolian medicine. The book *Mongolian Compendium of Herbs* by Zhanblaudolge records 879 kinds of herbs. And every herb is described in three kinds of characters: Chinese, Mongolian, Tibetan. This book has become a model for learning and studying Mongolian pharmacology. In the early 17th century, Melben and Jorge, Mongolian surgeons, co-wrote the *Complete Book of Chinese Medicine* and *Pharmacy* and were called as contemporary Hua Tuo by the world. The famous surgical hemostatic medicine Yunnan Baiyao was developed by Yi doctor Qu Huanzhang based on his ancestral secret recipe.

(6) The contribution of ethnic minorities in literature and arts: The enrichment of minorities towards Chinese national cultures also manifested in their rich epics and songs. For example, the long folk narrative poem *Ashima* has been put on the screen and become a classic. The three major epics of ethnic minorities are *King Gesar of the Tibetan*, *Jianggar of the Mongolians* and *Manas* of the Kirgiz. There are also *Qutadghu bilik* of the Uyghur, *Secret history of the Mongols*, and some famous folks songs in Han Dynasty like *Chilege Song* and the *Ballad of Mulan*. These were all formed under the influence of the rough and bold music of the Xiongnu and Turkic peoples. There are countless folk songs expressing the true feelings of human beings and love between men and women from ancient times to the present, such as the Mongolian folk songs in long tune, Zhuang songs of Guangxi and Hua'er folk songs in various ethnic groups in the north. The masterpieces of folk songs such as *Imakan* of the Hezhe, *Alilang* of the Korean, and *Nishansaman* of the Manchu, etc. The Kazakh rely on generations of Aken (story-tellers) to tell and pass on their ideas and culture. Gexu Singing Festival of the Zhuang, Dong-style songs, Bai-style music and dancing and the Gin music gala are all important forms used by these ethnic groups to make friends and exchange ideas and thus enhancing national integration. Ethnic minorities are not only able to sing, but also good at dancing. Where there is a party, there is a passionate dance. They are different from Han people who are dull farmers. Dances like Sanam of Uyghur people, Andai Dance of the Mongolian, Nangma of the Tibetan, Long-Drum Dance of the

Korean, Peacock Dance of the Dai and Lusheng Dance of the Miao, enjoy great popularity in China. They can be said to spend almost their whole life in a sea of songs and dances in groups. In addition, Tibetan Thangka Painting, Halo Painting in the west, the Zhuang brocade woven by Zhuang women, the Tujia brocade Xilankapu woven by Tujia women, and the batik art passed down among many ethnic minorities such as the Buyi, Miao, Shui, are all comparable to the embroidery of the Han and are well-known around the world. The art of brick carving of the Hui in Gansu Provinceis also one of the representatives of brick carving art in China. It has led to an endless stream of carvers around the country.

(7) The contribution of ethnic minorities in Festival culture: The festival culture of ethnic minorities is rich and colorful. For example, the Banjin festival is a Memorial Day for the birth of Manchu. The Festival of Fast-breaking is celebrated after the end of the one-month fast, and to thank God for blessing the livelihood to Muslim after the fast month. On Gurban festival of the Uyghur people will prepare delicious food to celebrate the happiness of the Muslim nation over the year. Nauryz Festival of the Kazakhis celebrated the renewal of nature, and the renewal of agriculture and husbandry. The Tibetan New Year is to celebrate the bountiful harvests in the past year. The Water-Splashing Festival of the Dai originates from Bathing Buddha Festival. People today splash water to each other to bring good luck for the coming year. The Lusheng Festival in Lahu is celebrated with a dance performance to celebrate the New Year. The more joyful the lap dance with the accompaniment of the Lusheng, there are said to be more food, money, pigs and cattle in the coming year. The lunar March 3 is originated from the rituals in the little new year. As most ethnic minorities live in the highland grassland, mountain and river sources and the Gobi desert, the hard living environment has forged their strong bodies. As a result, some unique physical exercise programs have also been developed over time and incorporated into national festivals.

(8) In architecture, there are also notable contributions from minorities. For example, the world-famous Mogo Grottoes in Dunhuang and Yungang Grottoesare the joint creation of people in the Han, Xianbei, Tubo and the west. The well-known Potala Palace and Dazhao Temple are the essence of Tibetan architecture. The design and construction of capital Dadu of Yuan by Ye Hei Die Er, an architect of the Hui, laid the foundation for the development of Beijing in the future.

In short, all ethnic minorities in China have created rich and colorful cultural treasures, and in the process of mutual exchanges and integration, they have made historical contributions to the magnificent Chinese culture. The important task of our contemporary national culture research is to go deep into the flower garden of the national family, analyze and summarize the cultural background, symbols, story characters, symbolic events, and national character of all ethnic groups, and then discover how these rich contents are closely linked and complement each other to form an organic whole, which together constitutes the common spiritual home of the Chinese nation. Only by building the common spiritual homeland of the Chinese nation can we cast a solid ideological foundation for the Chinese nation's community consciousness and provide an inexhaustible source of power for the Chinese nation's endless growth, unity and progress.

4.4 Our Compatriots Across the Sea: the Overseas Chinese

When we mention the Chinese nation, we must also mention the overseas Chinese, our overseas compatriots. Here we should grasp three concepts. Huaqiao (华侨) means a Chinese emigrant who still retains Chinese nationality. Huaren (华人) means ethnically Chinese people. Huayi (华裔). It refers to descendants of Huaren or Huaqiao. Huayi often are called ethnic Chinese, and are usually born in a country other than China.

(1) As for Overseas Migration and Distribution

As we know, Chinese culture is a farming culture with a strong sense of home. But since ancient times, there have been many people migrated far away and emigrated to other countries for various reasons. In the late Shang to early Han Dynasty: warfare caused several large-scale migrations to Korea and Japan. In the late Tang Dynasty: remnants of Huang Chao Uprising settled in Sumatra, Indonesia. In the Song Dynasty: large numbers of refugees from Lingnan were taken captive after the Vietnam invasion. In the Ming Dynasty: in cities on the southeast coast like Guangdong, Fujian and Hainan, there were a large number of immigrants going to the South China Sea. In the Qing Dynasty: "going to the South China Sea" (下南洋) became more prevalent and there were Chinese indentured laborers. In modern era: people move for trade, work and study. There is an old saying that where we can find the sea, we can find overseas

Chinese.

According to the *Distribution and Development Trend of Overseas Chinese* released in 2007, the statistics (and ranking) of the Chinese population: the number of overseas Chinese today is over 60 million. According to the country, Thailand ranked in the first place with 9. 39 million overseas Chinese, Malaysia ranked the second with 6. 65 million overseas Chinese, The United States ranked in the third place with 3. 79 million overseas Chinese. Canada ranked in the seventh place with 1. 48 million overseas Chinese. In addition, Peru in Latin America had 1. 3 million overseas Chinese. Countries like Australia, France, Britain and Italy, Indonesia, Singapore, Myanmar also had a large number of Chinese.

Overseas Chinese has a long emigration history, with the features of great amount, large scale, and wide distribution. More Fujianese went to Malaysia, Brunei, Singapore and the Philippines. People in the City of Chaozhou, Guangdong Province preferred Thailand. Hakka and Hainan people moved more often to Indonesia. Minnan dialect, Cantonese and Hakka languages were popular in the South Seas. Fujian was even the most powerful province in China in terms of emigration overseas (a total of 7 presidents and 1 prime minister have appeared). Mrs. Corazon Aquino, the former President of the Philippines and her son Aquino Ⅲ were the fourth and fifth generations of Chinese respectively with ancestral roots in Hongjian Village of Fujian Province. Ong Teng Cheong, former President of Singapore, was the third generation of Singapore Chinese, with ancestral roots in Xiamen, Fujian. Abdurrah man Wahid was the former President of Indonesia with ancestral home in Shishi prefecture of Quanzhou City in Fujian Province. Lee Kuan Yew, Singapore's founding prime minister and his son Lee Hsien Loong, the Former Prime Minister, Thaksin Shinawatra, Former Thai Prime Minister and his sister Yingluckare all Hakka people with ancestral home in City of Meizhou in Guangdong Province. The American Chinese ship king and his daughter Zhao Xiaolan, the first American Chinese minister, are of Shanghai ancestry. Ding Zhaozhong, a world-famous experimental physicist and Nobel laureate, is from Rizhao, Shandong Province. Yahoo Yang Zhiyuan, the founder and CEO of the company, is a native of Taiwan, China.

We should make it clear that the vast numbers of overseas Chinese, who have taken root in all parts of the world, also belong to a part of the Chinese nation community in a broad sense and have made important contributions to the diversified development of human culture and the progress of civilization.

(2) Overseas Chinese are the Backbone of Cultural Interaction between China and Foreign Countries

These people live in the foreign country, and after a long time, they treat the foreign land as their land, take foreign place as their hometown. On one hand, the overseas Chinese overcame new challenges and difficulties abroad. They are audacious and pragmatic to develop virgin land, mines, railways, and service industry, and construct cities and villages, contributing to the economic and social development of countries of residence. They have gradually won full recognition and high praise from the local people and the international community. On the other hand, the Chinese ancestors who emigrated overseas have helped to spread Chinese social system and ritual culture, they took with them the Chinese mature techniques of farming and breeding, expanded the overseas inheritance of traditional Chinese folk culture. Let's take the customs of Filipino Chinese as an example. Such as their customs of arranged marriage, honoring ancestors, respecting elders and filial piety to parents originate from China. In addition, in some countries of Southeast Asia, some ethnic groups treat Chinese porcelain plates, dishes and bowls as their heirlooms, and only take them out for use in special festivals or activities like rituals, weddings and funerals. Simultaneously, through the multi-ethnic marriages and population reproduction, they have also created a new indigenous culture with elements of Chinese culture. For example, "Baba Nyonya culture" in Malaysia is such a unique cultural historical heritage.

In modern times, Chinese immigrants have also established various Chinese Associations (such as clan associations or fellow townships), or established performance groups, Chinese newspapers and magazines, Chinese schools, radio and television stations and other mass media, so as to enrich the entertainment life of overseas Chinese and strengthen their sense of identity and unity. It also shows the colorful culture of the Chinese nation to the local people, and strives to carry forward the Chinese spirit of constant self-improvement and morality. Chinatown, which is essential to the daily life of overseas Chinese and performs the function of Chinese culture dissemination and business interchange.

While promoting the spread of Chinese culture abroad, overseas Chinese also brought western advanced civilization into China, allowing Chinese people to see the world with open eyes. Especially in modern history, the power of overseas Chinese in promoting Chinese people's understanding of Western society cannot be ignored, which provides the possibility for modern China to explore a national way out. Oversea Chinese sent money back every month to support his family's living, buy real estate in China, and renovate family grave. Meanwhile, they made enormous investment and donated much to the charity programs in China, promoting the economic and social development of their hometown. In modern times, they provided great support to the Xinhai revolution led by Mr. Sun Yat-sen, bravely joined in the second sino-Japanese war, contributed a lot to Chinese people's victory in wars against feudal governance, Japanese invaders, colonists, and Fascism. Overseas' leader, Mr. Tan Kah Kee who poured money into education and established Xiamen University and Jimei School Village, which still benefit thousands of students. When various natural disasters or public crises occurred in the motherland, we can still be moved to see that overseas Chinese carried forward the love of their compatriots and rushed to help all kinds of urgently needed materials. The people of the motherland will never forget this beautiful feeling.

Of course, as generations pass on and integrate deeply into the local community, the descendants of Chinese may not receive Chinese language education, but we can still be moved to see or hear them express in the local language their longing and blessing for China, their motherland. They may change their language, or even the color of their skin, but their heart as the children of Yan Huang will never change. Just like what Zhang Mingmin sings in the song *My Chinese Heart*: Country lingers in my dream, I've been away from motherland for years, However, nothing may change my Chinese heart. This constant homesickness makes these overseas travelers always Chinese descendants wherever they are.

Nowadays, over 67 million overseas Chinese live in more than 160 countries and areas, playing the role of Chinese culture disseminator, envoy of friendship between China and other countries, promoter of One Bell One Road, and supporter of peaceful reunification. Efforts should be made to strengthen the ranks of patriots overseas, and help more foreigners understand and become friendly to China, so as to boost exchanges and mutual learning between Chinese and foreign cultures. Overseas Chinese and ethnic Chinese are important forces that we must cherish, attach importance to and unite with.

150

(3) Huaqiao University Serving Overseas Chinese

Huaqiao University and Jinan University, both are domestic universities directly under the United Front Work Department targeting overseas Chinese. HQU was founded in 1960. At first, she was founded by the Chinese government under the kind care of Premier Zhou Enlai to meet the needs of overseas Chinese young students returning to China to receive higher education. It has branches in Quanzhou and Xiamen, with a total of over 30000 students and is one of the universities in China with the largest number of overseas Chinese students from Hong Kong, Macau and Taiwan. The more than 60 years of construction and development of HQU is also a history of development with the strong support of overseas Chinese. The Tan Kah Kee memorial hall, the overseas Chinese general library, the Chen Yankui building, the Filipino Chinese building and other overseas Chinese donation buildings standing on the campus of the University tell the story of overseas Chinese who care for and support Huaqiao University. Among them, Xu Dongliang, Zhuang Shanchun, Chen yongzai, Du Zuyi, Zeng Xianzi and other names are shining in the school running process.

HQU attaches great importance to the education of overseas Chinese students, and constantly improves the level and quality of teaching services for overseas Chinese students. After long-term practice and exploration, HQU takes the cultivation of "firm patriots" as the goal of the national education. With the classroom teaching of "evolution from large categories to detailed classification" and the practical teaching of "deepening from theory to practice", we optimizes the three elements of "teaching materials, teachers and teaching" in an overall way. Focusing on strengthening the four aspects of "national history knowledge, family and country feelings, strong will and action to serve the country" for Hong Kong, Macao and Taiwan students, we will promote the implementation of the four education modules of "national history study, national situation investigation, national defense education, and national youth training". We have gradually built a national education system that integrates "knowing, thinking and doing" to seek knowledge, cultivate temperament, forge ideas and practice perseveringly.

Take practical teaching as an example. Around the theme of "Roots in China", we actively implement various cultural training activities. With the strong support of the central United Front Work Department and the overseas Chinese Affairs Office of the State Council, since the 1980s, HQU has taken "promoting Chinese culture and cultivating family and country feelings" as the starting point and destination, every year, it organizes students from Hong Kong, Macao, Taiwan and overseas Chinese, as well as some mainland students to travel to various parts of the motherland, carry out cultural study activities with the characteristics of "learning first, combining learning with tourism". The purpose is to let campers experience, internalize and practice excellent traditional Chinese culture, enhance campers' sense of closeness and identity to Chinese civilization, and cultivate young people's family feelings and mission responsibilities in the new era. We believe that they will be the new force to promote the friendly relations between Chinese and foreign people.

In short, the Chinese nation is the co creator of Chinese civilization. In the long-term development process, the cultures of all Chinese nationalities have blended with each other, forming a vibrant and pluralistic Chinese nation community. Overseas Chinese are non-governmental ambassadors connecting China and the world, bridges linking Chinese culture and world culture, and components of the Chinese national community. As the president Xi Jinping pointed out that we should continue to "strengthen the great unity of the Chinese people at home and abroad, unite all forces that can be united, and make concerted efforts to move toward the bright prospect of the great rejuvenation of the Chinese nation".

第五讲

大哉孔子
——中国文化的至圣先师

在本讲中，我想给大家介绍一下中国文化的至圣先师——孔子。

图 5-1　孔子塑像（曲阜孔子博物馆）

　　孔子（Confucius），不仅在中国，甚至放到世界上都是一位伟大的人物。他不仅在中国文明中被尊为伟大的先师和圣人，深受尊敬和热爱，也被世界人士当作"世界十大哲人之一"、中国文化的代表性符号。对西方人而言，提到中国的文化符号，最先想到的无非是：万里长城、功夫、熊猫以及我们的孔子。那么，孔子这位中国的先知、耶稣式的圣人，他的生平有过怎样的心路历程？他的文化生命精神又有哪些闪光点？作为两千多年前的古人，他的思想在今天还有其价值吗？这是我们这里要给大家讨论的问题。首先，我们结合司马迁的《孔子世家》的线索来看看孔子的生平。

5.1　孔子的生平概说

（1）孔子的出生和少年

公元前551年9月28日（鲁襄公二十一年），一声婴儿的啼哭打破了尼山的寂静，颜征在回娘家的路上把我们伟大的孔子生产在这荒郊野外"夫子洞"里，那时，空中瑞彩祥云，似有飞龙腾跃、仙人庇佑。没错，同学们若是到山东曲阜去考察，会听到当地的导游这样给你介绍夫子的降生。这让人想到耶稣或者释迦牟尼的诞生故事，一样的光怪陆离。这位因父母祷于尼丘之山而得的孩子被取名为丘，因在兄弟中排行第二，而取字仲尼，他是"以勇力闻于诸侯"的鲁国陬邑大夫——叔梁纥的老来得子。但这个源自宋国而来的家族早已衰落，"风流总被雨打风吹去"，并没有给孔子留下任何值得凭靠的资源。而且在孔子三岁时，他的父亲就去世了，母亲无奈地带着他回到阙里与颜氏母族同住。

幼年的孔子文静颖悟，不爱玩寻常儿童的调皮玩意儿，倒是经常带小伙伴们进行陈列俎豆、演习礼仪的游戏，正如南宋理学家朱熹幼时也一个人静静地在沙滩上画八卦、少年陆象山仰望星空思考着"天之上还有更高的天吗"的问题。这大概是天赋异禀的孩子们一个值得注意的共通的特性呢。孔母非常重视儿子的品德教育，她在教孔子识字读书之隙常讲孔父叔梁纥的英雄故事。这些故事深深地刻在少年孔丘的心里。与母亲相依为命的孔子，早早地承受了生活的磨砺，这是一个从底层社会的种种贫寒交集、势利逼迫的命运泥涂中摸爬滚打、锻炼成长起来的孩子，一定有着少年老成的性格气质。他自己就说"吾少也贱，故多能鄙事"。

幸好孔子继承了父亲叔梁纥的健康基因，身高长到九尺六寸，即1.9米以上，人称"长人"，且臂力过人，身体素质是很好的。平日里他或者去给季氏当管牛马的杂役（乘田），料理库房的账目（委吏），或去给人家当丧事祭祀的相礼。生活虽然艰难，但他不怨天尤人，做事都能恪尽职责。到17岁的时候，孔子的母亲也去世了。孔子成了无父无母的飘零世间的孤独行者。孝心少年做了一件值得所有人刮目相看、肃然起敬的事情，就是多方寻访父亲叔梁纥的墓地，并破天荒地为父母合葬一处，树立坟堆和墓碑。这中间的慎思与孝亲的拳拳之心，不能不说是令人感动的。

（2）孔子的青年和中年

孔子虽然在逆境中成长，幸得了一份家庭的慰藉。十九岁那年，他娶了宋国书记官的女儿亓官氏为妻子，第二年生了个儿子，鲁昭公还派人送来一尾鲤鱼作为祝贺，所以取名为孔鲤，字伯鱼。孔子还有一个女儿叫孔娆，后来嫁给了他的学生公冶长。

青年时代是孔子的奋发期，他继续"十五有志于学"的初心，为了追求宇宙和人生的真理而勤学、好学、善学，这使得他"三十而立"，成为以"博学好礼"而知名的学者。据资料显示孔子二十三岁（或说三十岁）就"初设教席于阙里"，是与"学在官府"相对的民间私学的开先河者。孔子老师实行"有教无类"的原则，采取平民教育的态度，"自行束修以上，吾未尝无诲焉"（《论语·述而》）。他早期的弟子主要是子路、曾点和原宪等底层人士构成，即所谓"先进于礼乐者，野人也"。既有小他三十岁的颜回，也有小他六岁的颜回之父颜路。随着孔子学术声名的彰显，他获得国家的关注和认可，就连齐景公来访鲁国，都邀请孔子作为国家学者参与接待，并备咨询国政大事。而他的回答鞭辟入里，给齐景公留下了深刻的好印象。

鲁国还资助孔子在他三十四岁那年，前往东都洛邑访学，考察东周的文物典章制度。在那里，孔子还拜见了国家图书馆馆长、伟大的道家思想家——老聃，并向他学习了三个月有关礼教和哲学上的知识。当他离开的时候老子赠言给他说："去子之骄气与多欲，态色与淫志，是皆无益于子之身。"对这位神龙见首不见尾般的大师，孔子是非常推崇和感激的。

春秋时的天下形势"王纲解纽、礼崩乐坏"，鲁国的贵族季氏僭越于公室，各国情况也差不多，陪臣执掌国政，僭离于正道。所以孔子无意从政，退而修诗书礼乐，专心于教育事业，甚至有过退隐江海的想法①。其间虽然有一些机会，包括权臣阳虎向他摇动橄榄枝（包括一些叛乱者的邀请），孔子都没有接受，他说："不义而富且贵，于我如浮云""不患无位，患所以立。"可见他非常爱惜自己的羽毛，不愿无原则地与乱政者同流合污，而是默默地耕耘在自己思想文化的天地，学问和学生就是他的全部，传道、授业、解惑就是他的生活，《庄子·渔父篇》曾记载："孔子游乎缁帷之林，休坐乎杏坛之上，北子读书，孔子弦歌鼓琴。"这段时间一直持续到孔子五十岁之前。

（3）孔子的壮年

但到因缘俱足的鲁定公九年（公元前501年），五十一岁的孔子终于接受任命成为中都宰，即今天山东济宁的市长吧。他力行改革，各项社会建设事业都取得可观的成绩，深得民心，一年后就升任司空及大司寇，在鲁国的农林建设

---

① "子欲之九夷"（《论语·子罕》），"道不行，乘桴浮于海"（《论语·公冶长》）。

部部长和司法部部长的岗位上做了许多的工作。比如他在司空任上带领弟子和署衙工作人员跋山涉水，勘察土性，足迹几乎遍及全国各地。然后根据勘察所得和年轻时做委吏、乘田的实际经验，将全国土地划分成山林、川泽、丘陵、坟衍（高原）、原隰（湿地）五种类型，再根据这五种土性的特点，因地制宜，或植树造林，或发展鱼盐之利，或栽种果树，或种植各种不同的农作物。这都表现了孔子深谙"开物成务"的技术理性。又如在大司寇任上他打击犯法、不徇私情，但又鼓励"道之以德，齐之以礼"，刚柔相济、宽猛得中，使得鲁国的社会风气丕变一新。在主持鲁国同齐国的夹谷会盟中，他摄行相事，奉行"文事必有武备"的预案，以不卑不亢的态度，有力地维护了国家的尊严，完成了盟会，并收回了汶上三城。

孔子还试图实现削弱"三桓"（即季孙氏、孟孙氏和叔孙氏这三家专政大夫），加强鲁君的权威。但"隳三都"的工作功败垂成，没有彻底完成。三家权贵为维护自己的统治利益，打击和排挤孔子，沉溺于齐国不怀好意送来的"女乐文马"，不理朝政，还不按礼制给孔子分发祭祀后的"膰肉"，这其实就是排挤孔子，让他识相地自动离开。孔子当然会离开，道不同不相为谋嘛。但他迟迟其行，满怀对"父母之国"的忧患和眷恋不舍，远望着国都，唱了两首歌，其中一首是：予欲望鲁兮，龟山蔽之；手无斧柯兮，奈龟山何！是啊，手无权柄，无奈权臣，心怀鲁国，却有心无力。从此，孔子便踏上了长达十四年之久的周游列国的传道之路。

（4）孔子的暮年

公元前497—前484年这十四年，孔子在卫、陈、宋、叶、陈、蔡、楚等国家颠沛流离，带着他的"吾党小子"，他那批矢志追随的儒党成员，周旋于各国政坛，古道热肠、舌敝唇焦地试图能推广自己的伦理政治理念和以礼治国的方案，这里面也有许多的动人故事流传。我曾经写过一首《孔子歌》，其中关于孔子周游列国的几段如下：

怅然夫子挥袖去，周游列国十四秋。十四秋，出卫入郑滞陈蔡，此间辛酸堪泪流。

卫国奉粟六万石，虚情假意待孔丘。弃若敝屣走陈国，却遭匡人误截留。

此命在天不在尔，刀兵阵中意气遒。意气遒，斯文在，待人谋。

过蒲又发违心誓，强盟不碍我自由。不之小信求大信，唯义所在法中庸。

见南子，子路丑，妖姬艳冶能魅世，灵公昏聩成老朽。

岂见好德如好色，夫子深叹复出走。复出走兮东西走，郑人笑丘丧家狗。

惶惶然兮家何在，东望泰山参北斗。陈蔡绝粮无粒米，我自弦歌无忧愁。

富贵荣华皆过眼，道甚高，世难容。难容然后见君子，郁郁文哉吾从周。

吾从周兮吾从周，沧海横流志难酬。替天弘道年华老，老去正可写《春秋》。

（5）孔子的去世与孔子世家

68 岁那年，孔子得到鲁国的允许，返回了阔别多年的祖国。虽然被尊为"国老"和"尼父"，但仍是虚敬而不重用。而他似乎也不再热衷于政治，在最后的岁月里安静地从事着整理多年周游从列国收集来的文献资料，删订《诗》《书》，写作《易传》，编著《春秋》，培养人才。不幸的是，他心爱的弟子颜回、子路，和他的儿子孔鲤都先他亡故，所谓白发人送黑发人，哀哀之心，可以想象。也许，只有在深沉的梦里，这位老人才能看到象征着盛世的金凤凰展翅飞翔，清明仁政得以实施，"有教无类"惠及天下学子，"路不拾遗，夜不闭户"的和谐景象流行于乡里……

鲁哀公 16 年，孔子患病，日渐沉重。一天早上，他拄着拐杖，到了门前，临风而叹了人生最后的悲歌：太山坏乎！梁柱摧乎！哲人萎乎！歌后七日，也就是公元前 479 年的 4 月 11 日，一代圣哲、伟大的思想家、教育家和政治家，儒家思想的创立者——孔子，溘然长逝，离开了这个他深爱的世界，享年 73 岁。

孔子死后"葬鲁城北泗上，弟子皆服三年"。子贡筑庐于冢上，服丧六年而后去。

孔子的直系后裔至今仍然居住在阙里，守护着这位圣人的庙墓之地。从宋代起，孔子嫡系后裔就世袭衍圣公的爵位，到清代位更列文官一品，享受各种尊荣富贵，可谓叨沐祖德。迄今为止，孔氏后裔已经传至了 105 代，人数已多至 400 余万人，遍布全球，又以韩国为最。而且代有贤达，学者、文艺家层出不穷。如著《中庸》的孔伋，秦末"鲁壁藏书"的孔鲋，"四岁让梨"的孔融，"遍注群经"的孔颖达，《桃花扇》作者孔尚任，一生低调、研究古礼的末代衍圣公孔德成等。世代居住在曲阜的孔子后裔门第隆盛，声名显赫。他们继承先祖志向，主持祭祀、管理林庙、修身齐家，形成了堪为世范的家风。孔府的饮食器具、衣冠服饰、书画文玩品类丰富，特色鲜明，卷帙浩繁的孔府档案真实地记录了这一世家贵族近五个世纪的历史。庭院幽深，弦歌绕梁，开启孔府的大门，犹如打开一幅具体而微的中国传统文化画卷。

大家将来有机会，请记得到山东曲阜的"三孔"（孔庙、孔府、孔林）胜地去参访一下，相信一定能获得古意盎然的殊胜体验。

5.2　孔子的文化人格和生命精神

纵观孔子这一生，我们可以发现，他确实具有一种独特的情怀与高尚的境界，他表现了堪称中华民族典范的文化人格和生命的精神之光。以我肤浅所见，主要是这样五个方面。

（1）孔子是热爱生命、热爱人类的生命本位主义者

孔子特别重视人，他说"天地之性人为贵"。人是最高贵的，对待人不应轻慢和卑贱他，而要尊重和实现他的价值。所以他抨击"苛政猛于虎"，反对各种不拿人当人的暴虐政策，他甚至无法忍受制作人形陶俑拿来殉葬的做法，他愤怒地谴责道："始作俑者，其无后乎！"发明陶俑陪葬的人啊，你是会断子绝孙啊！（《孟子·梁惠王上》）夫子的愤怒于人俑殉葬，因为他认为那也是在侮辱人类自身。这也可以看成孔子对一切昏君酷吏和黑暴政治发出的人道主义的正义怒吼！

孔子认为国家要关注人间事，"务民之义，敬鬼神而远之"（《论语·雍也》）。每个人也应该热爱活着的可贵，首先关注自己的生命和现世的生活。他说："未知生，焉知死。未能事人，焉能事鬼？"（《论语·先进》）儒家并不主张因为敬畏鬼神和重视祭祀就忘记人生的这个根本位置。儒家之学根本上就是为人之学、生命之学，"仁者，人也"。孔子和儒家文化研究为人之学，追求人的自由与完美境界。儒家所教授的"礼乐射御书数"的"六艺"技能是为人的社会生活服务的；儒家研讨的"六经"之学也是研究人之为人的学问，都围绕人这个中心来做文章。离开人这个中心和本位，就没有了儒学。而这就根本奠定了中国文化热爱生存、生命本位的人文主义思想倾向和文化底质。

（2）孔子是克己复礼、仁爱天下的天人合一境界的化身

一方面，孔子是重视礼法制度的。周公创制了儒家的礼乐教化系统，即吉、嘉、宾、军、凶五礼。孔子对此五礼，用心研究、悉心教化和积极推广。他是希望借由礼的普遍遵守而达到"和"的目的，并为人的自我完善服务。美国哲学家赫伯特·芬格莱特在《孔子：即凡而圣》中就说"圣人境界就是人性在不离凡俗世界的礼仪实践中所透射出的神圣光辉"。但另外一面，孔子的新礼教又与世俗的外在学礼、形式守礼、呆板行礼的思维不同，他说"人而不仁，如礼何？人而不仁，如乐何？"（《论语·八佾》）他深知，礼并不是一堆钟鼓玉帛的简单堆砌与表演，若没有内心的仁德精神，就不能奢望礼制的真正落实，甚

至会陷入礼教的形式主义和强权主义。

孔子伟大于周公之处，在于他是一个哲学家，他为"礼"寻找到了仁德的内在根据（周公"摄巫归礼"，孔子"释礼归仁"）。孔子发明"仁"这一天赋的先验德性，以仁德奠定人性本善，以仁德修养作为人生的主要任务，从而在日用百行中，以不忍人之心，兴起感通和润泽的功夫，引导各阶层的人们自觉履行自己的伦理义务、承担自己的道德责任、完善自己的道德人格，最后实现"克己复礼、天下归仁"的天地境界。

我们说孔子是仁德天下的境界化身，通俗地说，就是孔子是一个特具爱心的仁者，爱心善行是孔子表现其天人合一境界的直接方式。在《论语》中就多处记载了孔子的美德懿行。如他孝亲、尊老、敬长，他同情别人的不幸遭遇，他照顾盲人乐师，他念旧惜缘，对老朋友原壤义气相助，他对学生患病和不幸去世的悲恸不已。而各种语录也透露孔子对自然生灵都有爱护之意，如"钓而不纲，弋不射宿"，就是不要去射杀夜宿的鸟，也不要用多钩网线去打鱼。孔子和儒家虽然不是素食主义，但绝对是反对嗜杀、重视素食的养生功能的，如孔子说"食肉者勇敢而悍，食谷者智慧而巧，食气者神明而寿"（《大戴礼记·易本命》）。他还要求留着破车盖以埋狗，留着破帷幕以埋马，以免这些家畜的尸首直接埋陷于泥土。可见孔子和圣王商汤一样，网开三面、仁及禽兽。这与后来孟子所谓"亲亲而仁民，仁民而爱物"、宋明理学家们的"民胞物与""好鸟枝头亦朋友"，可谓是一以贯之的线索，表现了中华民族万物一体、众生平等、同怀兼爱的至善境界。

也就是说，孔子教导后人的不是不要礼教和礼法，而是更要体悟礼法的内在精神，是基于仁德之心去过厚德载物、博爱无疆的礼乐精神生活。孔子对仁德这一先天本性的发明，是第一次敞开并弘扬了生命的主体性，开辟了内在超越的心性儒学的新方向，具有伟大的点亮人心的哲学意义。这就奠定了宋明儒学甚至整个中国文化的根本的人生—宇宙的智慧路径。

（3）孔子是乐天知命、自强不息的生命精神的典范

正如梁漱溟先生指出的：与认为"人生是苦"的古印度佛教不同，"全部《论语》都贯串着一种和乐的人生观———一种谨慎的乐观态度"。确实，孔子是个快乐的哲人，儒家是个乐观的学派，儒学有其乐天的精神。

生活中的孔子并不刻板愁苦、冷若冰霜。他平时"申申如也、夭夭如也"，显得很轻松愉悦。师门中讨论问题实行开放、平等和辩论的风格，有时说急了，师生之间也会彼此揶揄几句。比如子路嘲笑说夫子的"正名"思想真是迂腐啊，孔子也不以为忤，只是嘲讽子路真粗鲁。他喜欢笑，也喜欢开玩笑。颜回的观

点让他很开心，他就说等颜回有钱了给他当管家。学生孺悲恼了他，他就恶作剧般地发布托词说老师病了不见客，等孺悲一转身要离开，孔子却在屋里欢快地弹琴歌唱。孔子是要借此滑稽搞笑的一幕敲打傲慢的孺悲去自反自省。但实际上，我们知道以孔子这一生而言，他是个命途多舛的"苦命人"：他三岁丧父，母子依命，少年贱贫，管牛管马。后来从事政治又掣肘于权贵，被迫流浪于诸国，匡人围，蒲人堵，郑人笑，隐者讥，桓魋砍其树，陈蔡绝其粮。归国后虚尊而不用，一丧独子、再丧爱徒，周公梦远、西狩获麟，饭疏食饮水曲肱而枕，他这一辈子可谓经历了常人无法承受的艰难困苦！

各位可以试想一下，如果你们一无财而贫，二无位而贱，三无友而孤，四无居而窘，五见责而辱，六居险处困，七生死逼迫，八诸求不得，还能笑对人生吗？而我们的夫子安之若素、弦歌不辍，乐在其中，不改其乐。如面对经济的困窘，他会说，"不义而富且贵，于我如浮云"。面对卑微的政治地位，他会说，"不患无位，患所以立"。面对孤独无友，他会自信地说，"有德者，必有邻"。面对居住环境的糟糕，他会说，"君子居之，何陋之有"？面对被人羞辱讽刺，像被郑国人嘲笑为丧家之狗，他还说形容得恰当，一笑了之。面对权贵凶暴，他会自信地宣布："天不灭斯文，匡人其如予何？""三军可夺帅，匹夫不可夺其志也。""志士仁人，无生以害仁，有杀身以成仁。"这些乐观豁达、坚定豪迈的语言和背后卓越的生命激情是中华民族精神世界的滚滚长江，鼓舞了中华民族砥砺前进，克服一切困难和战胜一切敌人，永不屈服、永不言弃。

孔子的快乐和达观，来自很多方面：读书之乐、贤友之乐、乐山乐水、弦歌游艺之乐，得英才而教育之乐，可能美食、美服和体育运动都能给他以快乐。但孔子的快乐、"孔颜真乐"，更源自他敞开自我、明心见性，深入地发展了仁德和理性的天赋，从而发现并获得宇宙人生的真理所拥有的一种绝对自信与笃定。他一方面乐天知命，因而自觉地承担真理和道义的责任，知其不可而为之。另外一方面又了知世俗的命运，安之受之。他根据实际情况立身处世，发挥中庸智慧，有所为有所不为。暂时做不到的，则付诸阙如。但初心不忘、热衷不改，坚信"天不灭斯文"、真理必胜，所谓"其或继周者，虽百世可知也"。

对儒家的真君子而言，无论是富贵还是贫贱，是流落夷狄，还是患难之境，无论被命运的狂潮卷挟到任何的处境，都能安之若素，无不自得如意。如苏东坡天纵才华却半生流官各地，他却欣慰地吟诵道："莫听穿林打叶声，何妨吟啸且徐行。""问汝平生功业，黄州惠州儋州。"心学大师王阳明屡遭政治困厄，被贬到莽荒的边地贵州，他却能置之死地而后生、顿悟格物致知之旨。由此可见，儒家君子安贫乐道，怀抱"无入而不自得"的心境，越是艰苦，越是挫折，可能越是他们人生巅峰和生命的光辉时刻。

孔子教导了中华民族，君子有忧，即先天下之忧而忧天下之忧。但君子更有乐，却未必要后天下之乐而乐，可当下有乐、随时有乐，无一日不可乐。所以，请记住这个温和的、喜乐的、爱笑的可爱可敬的老头和老师。正如纪伯伦诗歌里形容耶稣的话：耶稣……愿和听众戏谑，乐意开玩笑，说说俏皮话；即使当他的眼光中有远虑，话音里有忧愁之时，他也会开怀大笑。他是快乐的人。在快乐之路上，他结交万众的忧愁，从他忧愁的顶峰上，他又俯视众生的欢乐（纪伯伦《人子耶稣》）。

我认为这段话也是对孔子和一切乐天知命的人们的生命风采的准确描述。

（4）孔子是中华民族艰苦力学、学以弘道的人格高峰

孔子十五有志于学，三十而立，四十而不惑，五十而知天命，六十而耳顺，七十而从心所欲，不逾矩。终达身与道一、心与理一的圣人境界。应该说，孔子乃是终身学习的典范。他自己也说，十户人家的小地方，可能有忠厚诚信如他这样的人，但绝找不到比他还更刻苦好学的人了。孔子主张诚实向学，知之为知之，不知为不知。"三人行必有我师"，他虚心地向各种师友求学，既向老师学，又学无常师。他学礼于老子，学乐于苌弘，学琴于师襄。好学的孔子甚至不耻下问，拜神童项橐为师；他跋涉于各种典籍，以古人为师；他行走于自然山川，以天地为师。他爱岗敬业从工作实践中学。而且，孔子的求学不是浅尝辄止，而是精益求精、不达到目的绝不轻言放弃的，这一点从孔子学"文王操"的故事中即可知。孔子珍惜光阴，常说"逝者如斯乎"，治学也当"不舍昼夜"。他学而不厌、废寝忘食，乃至忘记自己"老之将至"。因为用功太勤，以至于牛皮筋连缀的竹简都翻断了三次，这叫"韦编三绝"。学生子贡厌倦这样高压力的学习生活，就问孔子：难道我就不能休息一会儿吗？孔子的回答几乎是不近人情的。他说：赐啊，你看天边山脚下那些坟墓，又像锅子、又像盖子。只有到那里，才有我们休息的时候啊。这种生无所息、死后而已的精神，实在是让人闻之唏嘘欲泪。

有人质疑说孔子讲过"民可使由之，不可使知之"，乃是在提倡愚民主义。这其实不过是一种断句错误所造成的误解。正解应该是："民可，使由之；（民）不可，使知之。"也就是说强调的是民可与不可之间的策略区别性，突出的是民本的在先性，追求的恰恰是基于沟通和理解的政治理性，是"使知之"。孔子思想一方面主张仁德至上，另外一方面是中道理性至上。他主张所有人都应该发掘仁且智的天赋，敞开自己最本真的光明人性，达到最高尚的人格，他怎么可能主张愚民主义？这实在是没有道理的。中华民族一代代的伟大人物无不如此

重视学习和教育，提倡勤学好学，一辈子手不释卷，也以读书治学作为开启性灵、实现自我、发明真理、利济天下苍生的根本手段，留下了许许多多的动人传说。今天我们也要继续发扬这种求知若渴的生命精神。

当然，孔子的文化精神还可以有很多别的概括，我这里只是就我感受深刻之处，略说几点而已。比如我们还可认为，孔子是自古以来立心传道、重教爱生的教育精神的榜样。作为一个师者，孔子在教育过程中的主导作用和学生作为教育的主体地位结合得非常融洽，师生之间的关系可谓严肃认真，又和乐融融，令人如坐春风。孔子对学生赤诚无隐、襟怀坦白、因材施教，讲究方式方法。在学业上又要求严格，对学生的缺点直率批评，对他们取得的进步和成就也中肯表扬和热情鼓励。孔子像一位慈父，深切地关怀和爱护他的学生，对学生的不幸有着深切的慈悲。而学生们对老师也是矢志追随、由衷赞颂。这也堪为我们这些后世的教育工作者去用心追慕和学习的。

总之，孔子的文化人格与生命精神，虽然隔着悠悠千古，却总能让后人兴起"高山仰止，景行行止。虽不能至，心向往之"的崇敬之情，既指示了后人的前进方向，也代表了中华民族的人格的境界与精神的高度，是我们这个民族的光辉典范。

5.3　孔子儒学的永恒价值

孔子的儒学在他身后经历了漫长岁月的演变和发展。牟宗三先生把自孔子、孟子、荀子到董仲舒划为儒学发展的第一期，宋明理学为第二期①，近代"五四运动"以来称为新儒学复兴的第三期。第一期儒学（孔孟荀）的主要内容是关于"士"的修身的道德规范和从政方面的治国原则，是关于人们应该怎么去做的直接指示。第二期儒学（宋明理学）则吸收融合玄学、佛学和道教的理论构筑了一套"天理"和"心性"为核心的形而上学，以告诉人们为什么要这么做。两者主要是儒学道德修养方面的思想学说。第三期近现代新儒学则是近代中西文明碰撞下产生的新的儒家学派，主要是引用西方哲学方法重新解读儒学，以"返本开新"，实现传统儒学的现代化，并在当代人的道德修养和民族主体意

---

① 按牟宗三意见：第一期儒学以孔孟荀为主要代表，第二期儒学以北宋的程颐程颢，南宋的朱熹陆九渊和明代王阳明为主要代表。第三期以梁漱溟、熊十力为主要代表。而政治制度化、谶纬神学化的汉代儒学在牟宗三看来价值不大。

识的确立方面发挥积极作用。

儒家思想是中华文化传承两千多年的体现，具有丰富而深刻的思想内涵，在中国和东亚具有广泛的影响。同时，作为东方传统的主要代表之一，"儒学"也与西方文化对话交流中相互补充，随着时间的推移变得越来越重要。穿越历史的漫漫红尘，飞扬天地人寰的思想风云已经无可辩驳地证明：孔子的儒学是中华民族主干的文化体系，是曾经深刻影响和塑造了"文化中国"的芸芸众生的思维方式、价值态度和生活方式的核心意识形态。

怎样评价孔子和他的儒学？这在孔子生前就已经是个见仁见智的问题。历史地看主要有这样七种方式。第一种是"圣化"：把孔子当作仁且智的圣人，这是孔子弟子和后儒为之。第二种是"矮化"：庄子和战国道家为之。第三种是"正统化"：西汉武帝"罢黜百家、独尊儒术"，孔学被官方正统化。第四种是"神化"：东汉谶纬之学把孔子的形象神学化。第五种是"僵化"：宋明阶段，理学家吸收佛老之学把孔学形而上学化，科举考试更使得其思想逐步教条化和僵化。第六种是"维新化"：康梁变法中把孔子包装成"托古改制"的改革家。第七种是"丑化"：近代新文化运动和"文革"中，打倒孔家店，各种丑化孔子。

尽管众说纷纭，但总的来看，自古以来，孔子在中华民族的心目中地位还是非常崇高的，评价也主要是积极而褒奖的。历代帝王推崇儒学的治国理政、教化人心的价值功能，对孔子也多有封谥：如唐玄宗封孔子为"文宣王"，元武宗封孔子为"大成至圣文宣王"，嘉靖皇帝明世宗封孔子为"至圣先师"。汉高祖、唐玄宗、宋真宗、清康熙和乾隆等帝王，都曾亲临曲阜孔庙和孔林，隆重进行祭奠，以表达国家对儒学的尊崇。而饱受儒家文化熏陶教养的中国人民亲切地称孔子为"夫子"，将其礼敬为"万世师表"，而"三孔圣地"也被视作东方的圣城而悉心保护。改革开放以来，随着国家对传统文化的重视，孔子庙保护、修复工作在各地陆续开展。现在全国恢复比较完整的近200座。世界各地共有孔子庙2300余座，其中，海外有600多座。有的是政府的行为，也有民间自建、侨胞捐建的。孔庙已经成为追思孔子、传播儒家文化的重要文化场所。

我们认为：

第一，孔子是古代的，更是时代的，他永远在中华民族的文化发展史上熠熠生辉。

孔子的学说具有丰富的内涵、深刻的智慧，具有穿越时代的永恒价值。

他要求国家的领袖实行仁政德治、爱惜民力、为政以德、追求王道和大同之治；他要求从商者要见利思义，善于周济贫苦者，多做慈善之举；他要求知识分子坚守道义和中庸理性，持守士君子的节操；他要求人人都从日常伦理做起，克己复礼，成为善人和好人。他也相信仁者人也，"我欲仁斯仁至矣"，只要努力，人人都可希贤希圣。他还主张文以柔远、反对强权暴力，追求民族和国家之间共享天下太平。他令人感动的还有"有教无类""因材施教"的公平教育、平民教育的创举。孔子是中华民族道德理想主义的文化化身与人格典范，他阐发的各种道德范畴如仁、义、礼、智、信、恭、宽、信、敏、惠等，都是值得我们继承和发扬的中国式的"普世价值"。中国共产党人是历史的唯物主义者，在中国革命、建设和改革发展的每个时代，都非常注意扬弃地创新发展传统优秀文化，古为今用。这也是一个把马克思主义中国化和探寻中国特色的革命、建设道路的历程。比如毛泽东主席经常灵活运用孔子的各种思想，他指出："孔夫子是圣人，几千年只此一个。""从孔夫子到孙中山，我们应当给以总结，承继这一份珍贵的遗产。"习近平主席也非常重视传统国学的时代价值，他曾亲临山东曲阜孔府和孔庙视察，在孔子研究院听取汇报、关注《儒藏》的编辑出版。在纪念孔子诞辰 2565 周年的国际学术研讨会上，他这样高度评价孔子儒学：

"孔子创立的儒家学说以及在此基础上发展起来的儒家思想，对中华文明产生了深刻影响，是中国传统文化的重要组成部分。儒家思想……记载了中华民族自古以来在建设家园的奋斗中开展的精神活动、进行的理性思维、创造的文化成果，反映了中华民族的精神追求，是中华民族生生不息、发展壮大的重要滋养。……而且对人类文明进步做出了重大贡献。"

可以说，孔子儒学为代表的优秀传统文化至今仍是中国人不可或缺的宝贵的文化资源，将为中国人民走向新时代的民族复兴发挥重要的建设性作用。

第二，孔子是中国的，也是世界的，其思想将为世界文明价值继续积极奉献。

孔子儒学的影响力，在东亚文化圈自不必说。欧洲也很早就从文化交流中知道孔子之名。传教士们用各种语言翻译儒家经典到西方文化界，也由此掀起过研究儒学的汉学热潮，产生了"欧洲的孔子"伏尔泰、"美国的孔子"爱默生等学者。他们编办刊物、著书立说，传播孔子的思想和语录。德国哲学家雅思贝尔斯把孔子视为"轴心时代"诞生的，可与释迦牟尼、苏格拉底和耶稣齐名的世界"四大哲人"之一。尤其是两次世界大战后，西方思想界痛定思痛，反思到社会达尔文主义不行，绝对的个人自由主义也不好，而主张仁爱和德政的孔子的学说，可以拯救西方文化的没落和危机。1988 年十几位诺贝尔奖得主就在巴黎发布宣言：人类要在二十一世纪生存下去，必须回到二千五百年前中国的孔子那里，去寻找智慧。这可视作是西方知识界对东方的孔子的一次跨越时空的遥远敬礼吧。

今天，孔子学院遍布全球 154 个国家和地区，成为向全世界青年开放的传播汉语和中华传统文化的载体，正受到越来越多国家人民的了解和欢迎。我们相信，孔子的思想和文化价值，必将在 21 世纪为人类文明进步继续作出宝贵的贡献。

图 5-2　曲阜孔庙祭孔场景

有留心的同学会注意到，每到孔子诞辰日（9 月 28 日），海峡两岸和海内外的著名孔庙都会钟鼓四起，在袅袅香烟和雅乐声声中，人们肃立追思、缅怀先师，也感受到胸中跳动着的那颗四海一家的文化同理心，思古之情沛然而生。许多学者和社会贤达都提议，重新将孔子的生日作为国家教师节。对这个提议，我们在此也表示热忱的赞许和完全的支持。

这说明，随着时代的进步和文化的发展，孔子思想正本清源、慧日重光，已经成为大家重新欣赏和热爱的精神文化资源。

The Fifth Chapter:

Confucius the Grand Master
—Great Sage and the First Teacher of Chinese Culture

Confucius is a great figure not only in China, and even in the world. He is not only revered as a great teacher and sage and is highly respected and loved in China, but is also regarded in the world as "one of the ten philosophers of the world" and a representative symbol of Chinese culture. For Westerners, when talking about the symbols of Chinese culture, some names that come to their mind usually include the Great Wall, Kung Fu, Panda and Confucius, right? So, what about the great deeds and biography of Confucius, a Chinese prophet and Jesus-like saint? What about his adventures on the voyage of the mind? What are the shining spirits of his thoughts? As a great thinker more than 2000 years ago, are his thoughts still valuable today? This is the question we would like to discuss today.

5.1   The Life of Confucius

From *Hereditary House of Confucius* in the *Historical Records* written by Sima Qian, we could find the brief biography of Confucius.

(1) Confucius's Birth and Boyhood

On September 28, 551 BCE a baby's cry broke the silence of Nishan Hill. On her way back to her parental home, Yan Zhengzai gave birth to Confucius in a cave of the wild which was later on named Fuzi Cave. At that time, the sky was full of auspicious clouds. It seemed that there were flying dragons and fairy blessings. Yes, if you visit Qufu in Shandong Province, the local tour guide will tell you the story about the birth of Confucius in this way. It will make you think of the same amazing story of Jesus or Siddhartha Gautama. The child was named *Qiu* because his parents prayed on the Niqiu Hill and got him. And because he was the second boy in his family, he was given the courtesy name Zhongni. His father Kong He, an officer of Zou (near present-day Qufu), was quite old when Confucius was born. But his family which originated from the state of Song had long since declined. "All gallant deeds now sent away by driving wind and blinding rain. " Therefore, the family left almost no inheritance to Confucius.

Unfortunately, when Confucius was three years old, his father passed away. His mother had to take him back to live with her parents in Queli. As a young boy, Confucius was quiet and clever, and did not like to play with ordinary kids' toys and games, but often played special games with his young friends. such as displaying sacrificial beans and practicing etiquette. Just like Zhu Xi, the philosopher of Neo-Confucianism of Southern Song Dynasty, when he was young, he would draw the Bagua map on the beach alone quietly. Lu Xiangshan, another important Chinese philosopher, often observed the sky when he was young, and wondered that "anything higher than the sky". This is probably a noteworthy common characteristic of those gifted children. Mother attached great importance to the cultivation of virtues, and always told him some stories about his father who was full of valor and heroic spirit. These stories are deeply engraved in the heart of young Confucius.

Confucius lived with his mother in a state of poverty, and endured the hard life at an early age. This was a child who has grown up from poverty, and snobbery forces in the bottom of society. He had a wise head on young shoulders. He described himself as "poor and from a lowly station, thus skilled in many menial things". Fortunately, Confucius inherited the gene of health from his father Kong He. Confucius was more than 1. 9 meters tall. At that time, people called him "Changren" (tall man). He excelled in arm power and had good qualities of physical fitness. Confucius sometimes worked for Ji family (an aristocratic family of state Lu) as an odd-job man taking care of cattle and horses, sometimes worked as a "Weili" (bookkeeper) to manage the bills of the property, or worked to host the funerals and sacrificing ceremonies. Although his life was hard, he never complained anything but fulfilled his duties in everything. When he was 17, Confucius' mother also died. Since then, Confucius became an orphan in the world. The young Confucius of filial piety did something that deserved everyone's respect and admiration, that is, he endeavored to find his father's grave and took the unprecedented step of burying his parents together in one place, then erected a mound and a tombstone. The prudence and filial piety of Confucius towards his parents were very touching.

（2）Confucius's Youth and Middle Age

Although Confucius grew up in adversity, he was fortunate to find solace in his family. At the age of nineteen, he married his wife, Qiguan, the daughter of the official of State Song. A year later the couple had their first child. Duke Zhao of State Lu sent a carp (Chinese name Liyu) as a congratulation. Therefore, Confucius named his son as Kong Li, with a courtesy name as Boyu. Confucius also had a daughter named Kong Rao, who was later marry his disciple Gongye Chang.

In his youth, Confucius continued his original intention of "at fifteen my heart was set on learning". To pursue the truths of the universe, life and society, he studied diligently with curiousness, which made him "stand firm at thirty", and become a "knowledgeable and well-mannered" and famous intellectual. According to sources, at the age of 23, some say 30, Confucius "opened a private school in Queli". He was the founder of private school, which was over against the "official school". Confucius asserted that in teaching there should be no distinction of classes, and he promoted education for all. His early disciples mainly were from the lowly station such as Zi Lu, Zeng Dian and Yuan Xian. As Confucius says: "If one seeks to learn rituals before he is an official, he is a less sophisticated common person." The less sophisticated common person is those in the lowly station. Confucius had disciples as young as Yan Hui who was thirty years younger than Confucius, and as old as Yan Hui's father Yan Lu who was only six years younger than Confucius.

As Confucius attained some degree of fame for his philosophy, he gained the attention and recognition of his state. Even when Duke Jing of Qi State visited the Lu State, he would invite Confucius to participate in the reception as a state scholar, and would be ready to consult on state affairs with him. Confucius would often give some insightful answers, which left a deep and good impression on Duke Jing of Qi State. State Lu also sponsored Confucius, when he was thirty-four years old, to go to Luoyi, the capital of Eastern Zhou, to study the Zhou ritual system, where Confucius met the keeper of archival records (today's national head librarian) and the great thinker of Taoism—Lao Dan. Confucius learned from him for 3 months about rites and philosophy. When it's time to leave, Lao Zi told him: "Get rid of your arrogance and excessive desires; get rid of your immoderate expression and exorbitant ambition. All of these are not good for you." Toward this mysterious master, Confucius showed great respect and gratitude.

The situation in the Spring and Autumn period was called "voidance of the law and propriety-music disintegration". One of the three aristocratic families Ji family usurped power. The situation was similar in all countries. Dozens of small kingdoms vied with one another for imperial domination. Everything deviated from proper ritual form. Therefore, Confucius had no intention to engage in politics, but worked on poetry, music and rites, and focused on education. In the meantime, although there were some opportunities, such as olive branches from powerful officials and even invitations from rebels, Confucius did not accept them. He says: "Wealth and rank attained through immoral means nothing but drifting clouds." "I am not concerned that I am not in office. What I am concerned is how I may qualify for office." It's evident that Confucius cherished his fame and was unwilling to be associated with rebels and traitors without principles. Instead, he silently worked in the world of his own thoughts and culture. Preaching, imparting knowledge and resolving doubts are his all life. *Zhuangzi* once recorded that: "Confucius traveled in the forest of Ziwei, rested on the apricot altar, and the students read. Confucius sang string songs, played drums and played zither." This stage lasted until Confucius was fifty years old.

(3) Confucius' Prime of Life

But in the 9th year of Duke Ding of Lu, or 501 BCE, Confucius who was fifty-one years old finally accepted the appointment of the State Lu and became the steward of Zhongdu which is similar to today's mayor of City of Jining in Shandong Province. He made great achievements in his job by carrying out reforms. After a year, he was promoted to Director of Public Works and later Director of Crime. In the position like today's Minister of Agriculture and Forestry and Minister of Justice in the State Lu, he did a lot of work. For example, when he was Director of Public Works, he extensively explored the five kinds of geographic environment of State Lu including mountains and forests, rivers and ponds, hills, plateaus, plains. Then according to local conditions, he led people to plant trees, develop industry of fish and salt, and plant fruit trees or various crops. This shows Confucius' special technical rationality of "understanding the truth of things and handling affairs successfully". And when he was Director of Crime, he fought against lawbreaking and did not show favoritism, but he also encouraged "in practising the rules of propriety, a natural ease is prized". He was so rigid and gentle that he created a new social atmosphere of State Lu. At the conference between Lu and Qi at Jiagu, he played as a role of prime minister and followed plans of "civil affairs must be accompanied by military preparations". Without being humble or pert, he successfully defended the dignity of his state, completed the conference and took back the three cities of Wenshang.

Confucius tried to weaken the power of "the Three Huan" namely Jisun, Mengsun and Shusun clans, the power of these three dictatorship aristocratic clans. But he failed to demolish these three families. He didn't completely complete it. In order to maintain their own political interests, the three powerful clans suppressed and ostracized Confucius by deliberately indulging in the singing and dancing girls sent by State Qi, and staying away from affairs of state. In addition, they didn't follow rites to give Confucius the sacrificial meat. Their purpose was to let Confucius leave the imperial court. Of course, Confucius would leave, because there is little common ground for understanding between persons of differing principles. But he took a long time to depart, full of worries and longing for his mother country. At his departure, he looked far away from the capital and sang two songs. One of them was:

I wanted to see my State Lu, but the turtle mountain blocked my sight. Without an axe in my hand, what can I do with it!

Indeed, without any power in hand and any idea toward powerful officials, although he cared for State Lu, he could do nothing about it. From then on, Confucius embarked on his 14-year travel to courts of various princes.

(4) Confucius' Late Years

During the fourteen years from 497 BCE, to 484 BCE, Confucius was displaced in states such as Wei, Chen, Song, She, Chen, Cai and Chu, with his disciples and his Confucian followers. They moved around the political arena of various countries. Confucius was warm-hearted, passionate and talkative. He hoped to promote his ideas of ethical politics and his program of ruling the country by ritual. There are many moving stories in their travels.

I once wrote "Song of Confucius". I can show you some part about his experience of travels around various states.

Confucius was depressed, so he left his state to travel around other states for fourteen years. During the fourteen years, he came to the state of Wei, Zheng, and was struck in the state of Chen and Cai. He spent a very hard time. State Wei offered Confucius an official position and food of 3. 6 million kilograms. However, Wei treated Confucius with false affection. Confucius was not entrusted with the important task, so he went to State Chen. But he was misunderstood and intercepted by people of Kuang City on his way. "My life is in the hands of heaven rather than people of Kuang City." He was high-spirited and vigorous in face of turmoil of war. And believe that whether this culture can be preserved depends on people's efforts. When passing through Pu City, he was forced to take a vow against his heart. "The covenant made under compulsion is invalid and does not bind my freedom." He didn't care about small trustworthiness but sought the big one. That's where righteousness lies and consistent with the mean. Confucius went to meet Nanzi, the wife of Duke Ling of Wei. It made Zilu very unsatisfied. The beauty of women represented bad virtue and could be very harmful. Duke Ling of Wei gradually became a dotard, and appreciated the beauty of women more than rituals and noble men. Therefore, Confucius left State Wei again with a deep sigh. Confucius once again moved here and there, and people of State Zheng laughed at him as a homeless dog. He didn't know where his home was. And he just looked east at Mount Tai with reference to the Big Dipper. Trapped in the state of Chen and Cai, Confucius did not have half a grain of food. But he sang and played his string without any worries. Glory and wealth are all fleeting. Confucius' morality was so high that the world could hardly contain him. But this just proves the greatness of a gentleman "Culture of State Zhou flourished. I now follow the Zhou." "Following the Zhou, Following the Zhou," but his ambition was not fulfilled. Confucius wanted to spread the Tao but he was old. Old as he is, he can still use his last days to write the Spring and Autumn Annals.

(5) Confucius' Death and Descendants

At the age of 68, Confucius received permission from State Lu and returned to his homeland where he had been absent for many years. Although he was revered as the old head and "Nifu" (courtesy name), he was still vainly revered but not relied on by the rulers. It seemed that he was no longer keen on politics, but spent his last years quietly compiling the documents that he had collected during his travels around the world. He revised *Classic of Poetry* and *Book of History*, wrote the *Book of Changes*, compiled *the Spring and Autumn Annals* and cultivated talents. Unfortunately, his favorite disciples Yan Hui and Zilu And his only son Kong Li died before him. We can just imagine how sad Confucius was! Maybe, only in this old man' dream, he would see the pictures: a peaceful and prosperous era with phoenix flying above, people getting the education they want, fair and just governing of a state...

In the 16th year in the rein of Duke Ai of Lu, Confucius fell ill and became increasingly severe. One morning, with his crutches, he went to the door sighed at the wind, and sang the last lament of his life. Mountain Tai is about to fall! The pillars are about to break! The philosopher is about to die! On April 11, 479 BCE, seven days after the lament, Confucius, the great thinker, educator, statesman and the founder of Confucianism, passed away at 73, leaving the world he loved so much.

After his death, Confucius was buried in the northern part of the City of Lu, by the Sishui River or today's the cemetery of Confucius and his descendants in Qufu Prefecture, Shandong Province. The direct descendants of Confucius still live in Queli until now, and guard the cemetery of the sage. Since the Song Dynasty, the direct descendants of Confucius have inherited the position of Duke of Yansheng. And in the Qing Dynasty, they were ranked among the first class of civil officials, enjoying all kinds of honor and wealth, so they can be said to have benefited from the ancestral virtue. To date, the descendants of the Kong family have reached 105 generations and numbered more than 4 million people all over the world, with Korea being the largest. Moreover, there have always been many scholars, writers and artists in Kong family, such as Kong Ji, the author of the *Doctrine of the Mean*, Kong Fu, who protected Confucian books secretly, Kong Rong, who gave the bigger pear to his brother at four, Kong Yingda, who was well-read and knowledgeable, Kong Shangren, the author of *the Peach Blossom Fan*, and the last duke of Shengyan Kong Decheng, who studied ancient rites in a low profile all his life.

In the future, if you have the opportunity to come here, please remember to visit the three sacred sites in Qufu: the Temple of Confucius, the Cemetery of Confucius and the Kong Family Mansion.

5. 2　Confucius's Cultural Personalities and Spirits

Throughout the whole life of Confucius, we find he did have a unique sentiment and higher state of moral consciousness, and he demonstrated his cultural personalities and spirits which were exemplary of Chinese people. In my opinion, I believe that they are mainly manifested in the following four aspects.

Firstly, Confucius was a life-oriented person who loved life and humanity.

Confucius paid special attention to people. He said benevolence is humanity, and he believed that the human being is the heart of heaven and earth. Man is the most noble. We should respect every individual and help to achieve their values. Thus, he criticized that "tyrannical government is fiercer than a tiger". He opposed all kinds of tyrannical policies that did not treat people as human beings. He could not even stand the practice of making human figurines for burial, and he angrily condemned: "Was he not without posterity who first made earthen images to bury with the dead?" That's to say, the man made the semblances of men and used them for that purpose, should die childless. Confucius was angry to the martyrdom of human figurines, because he considered that also an insult to humanity itself. This can be seen as a kind of humane and righteous rage of Confucius against all tyrants and fierce officials. Confucius believed that the state should concern with the affairs of people. "To give oneself earnestly to the duties due to men, and, while respecting spiritual beings, to keep aloof from them." Everyone should also love the preciousness of life. We should first focus on our life and the present. He said: "While you don't yet understand life, how can you understand death? While you fail to serve the living well, how can you serve the ghosts?" Confucianism didn't forget "man lives and he must deal with the present" just because of the fear of ghosts and gods and the importance of rituals.

Confucianism is fundamentally the study of man and life. Confucius and Confucian culture study why man is a man, and pursue man's freedom and perfection the "Six Arts" of the Confucian, namely rites, music, archery, chariot racing, calligraphy and mathematics, are skills that serve life. The "Six Classics" of the Confucian also study why man is a man. The Six Arts and the Six Classics both revolve around the center of man. If we leave the center and the essence—man, there will be no Confucianism. This has fundamentally established the people-oriented Chinese culture, which stresses survival and life.

Secondly, I believe that Confucius stands for subduing self, observing proprieties, benevolence, morality and the nature-man unity.

Confucius, on one hand, valued the system of rites and laws. He attached importance to the ritual and music system of the Duke of Zhou, and the "five rites" — auspicious, inauspicious, military, hosting and congratulatory rites. Towards these five rites, Confucius studied them with great care, and taught them to his students and actively promoted them, hoping to achieve the goal of "harmony" through the universal observance of the rites. The American philosopher Herbert W. Fingerle, in his book *Confucius, the Secular as Sacred*, says: "The divine light of the sage sparks through human nature in the practice of daily rituals."

But Confucius differed from the worldly thinking of learning rituals externally, observing rituals formally, and performing rituals rigidly. He says: "What can a man do about the rites if he is not benevolent? What can he do about music if he is not benevolent?" Confucius knew that rituals are not tangible like bells, drums or silk fabrics. Without the spirit of benevolence in the heart, one cannot expect the real implementation of rituals and will even fall into the formalism and authoritarianism of rituals.

The reason why Confucius was greater than the Duke of Zhou lies in the fact that Confucius was a true philosopher who found the inner basis of benevolence and virtue in "rites". Or to say, Duke Zhou's credit is to promote witchcraft to etiquette, while Confucius found the foundation of benevolence for etiquette.

Confucius invented "Ren" (benevolence) which was a virtue endowed by heaven. With benevolence, the original goodness of human nature was laid down. He advocated to take benevolence cultivation as the fundamental task of life. Thus people in their daily life, with the benevolence, they can be sensible and improve the world. And then they would fulfill their own ethical obligations, assume their moral responsibilities, realize their moral personality and finally become a saint. That is, "if people control himself in conformity with the rules of propriety, benevolence will prevail in the whole world".

We say that Confucius stands for benevolence and virtue in the world, and *the Analects of Confucius* records his virtues and good deeds many times. For example, Confucius respected senior people, sympathized with the sufferings of others, took care of the blind musician, helped his friend Yuan Rang in a righteous manner, and was deeply distressed by the illness and misfortune of his students. The various quotations also reveal that Confucius had a loving heart for natural creatures. For example, he says "do not shoot birds at night, do not fish with multiple hooks and nets". Although Confucius and Confucianism were not vegetarians, they definitely opposed irregular killing and valued the health-supporting vegetarian diet. For example, Confucius said: "Carnivores are fierce and brutal, while those who just live on Yi (air) are divine and long-lived." Those who take in too much meat will be fierce and aggressive. Those who feed on cereals and vegetables can be divine and long-lived. In addition, Confucius asked to keep the broken carriage cover to bury the dead dogs, and the broken curtain to bury the dead horses, so that their corpses would not be buried directly in the mud. We can see that Confucius, like the virtuous King Tang, was benevolent even to animals. This was in accordance with what Mencius mentioned: "Men of virtue love and care for their loved ones, they are therefore kind to other people. When they are kind to people, they treasure everything on earth." and what Neo-Confucianists in Song Dynasty mentioned "people are my brothers and all things are my kind" and "good birds on branches are also my friends". These can be said to be a thread that expresses the supreme goodness of the Chinese culture in which all things are unity, all beings are equal, and all people love with each other. In other words, what Confucius taught us was not to dispense with rituals and ritual laws, but more to realize the inner spirit of them, and based on the heart of benevolence and virtue, to live a ritualistic spiritual life full of universal love. Confucius' invention of benevolence which was inborn helped to disclose and promote the subjectivity of lives for the first time and open up a new direction of Confucian for self-improving. It is of great philosophical-historical significance in illuminating people's hearts. This laid down the fundamental wisdom ways to Confucianism in Song and Ming Dynasties and even in Chinese culture as a whole.

Thirdly, I believe that Confucius is a model of spirits of happiness and unremitting self-improvement.

Just as Mr. Liang Shuming pointed out, unlike ancient Indian Buddhism which believed "life is suffering", all of *the Analects of Confucius* has a harmonious and happy outlook on life, a cautiously optimistic attitude. Indeed, Confucius was a happy philosopher, Confucianism is an optimistic school of thought, and Confucianism has its joyful spirit. The Confucius in his life was not stiff, sad and cold. When the Master was unoccupied with business, his manner was easy, and he looked pleased. When discussing academic issues, Confucius and his disciples carried out open and equal debates. And sometimes being absorbed in debates, they would mock each other. For example, Zi Lu once mocked Confucius, saying "my teacher, you are really pedantic", and Confucius was not displeased to hear that. Confucius liked to laugh and joke. When Yan Hui's reply amused him, he would say: "Yan Hui when you are rich, I will be your butler." When another disciple, Ru Bei, annoyed Confucius,

Confucius issued a prank-like pretext that he was ill and could not meet guests. But when Ru Bei was about to leave and was just outside the door, Confucius purposely played a music instrument and singed loudly, Confucius used this comical scene to request the arrogant Ru Bei to self-reflect.

But in fact, we know how many misfortunes did Confucius suffered in his life. He was a "miserable man": he lost his father at the age of three, leaving him and his mother dependent on each other. He was poor as a young man, and lived on looking after cattle and horses, just like Bimawen, the Keeper of the Heavenly Horses in *the Journey to the West*. Later on, he was engaged in politics but was constrained by the rich and powerful. He had to wander around various countries to achieve his ambition. During his travels, he was stranded by people of Kuangcheng and Pudi, and was laughed at by people of State Zheng and other states. Yuan Tui wanted to kill him, and State Chen and Cai cut off his food. After returning to his country, he was still not properly appointed. He lost his only son, and then his beloved pupil. He hadn't dream the Duke of Zhou for a long time. and was sad that auspicious unicorn was shot and hurt by Duke Ai of Lu. He ate only coarse grain, drank water and used bent elbow as a pillow. So, he experienced hardships that no ordinary man could bear in his life!

You can just imagine, if you suffered from the following difficulties: 1. Being poor being the lowly status being alone without friends. 2. Nowhere to go. 3. Being dishonored and disgraced. 4. Living in danger and being trapped. 5. Facing with being killed. 6. Failing to get whatever you want. Can you smile at life? And can you even smile? But Confucius was at peace with those miseries and continued his music. He was glad to be in them and never changed his minds. For example, when faced with financial difficulties, he would say: "Wealth and rank attained through immoral means nothing but drifting clouds". When faced with the humble political status, he would say: "I'm not concerned about not being in office, but how I may qualify for office." When faced with being alone without friends, Confucius would confidently say: "If you are virtuous, you will not be lonely. You will always have friends." When faced with the terrible living conditions, Confucius would say: "How could we call a place 'humble' when a man of complete virtue lives there?" When faced with being abused, like being laughed at as a homeless dog by people of State Zheng, he didn't care it and just smiled. He thought he was just like a homeless dog, and what those people said was not wrong. When faced with the powerful, rich and fierce, Confucius would confidently declare: "While Heaven does not let the cause of truth perish, what can the people of Kuang City do to me?" "An army may be deprived of its commanding officer, yet a man cannot be deprived of his will."

These optimistic words and the remarkable passion for life behind them have inspired Chinese people to forge ahead, overcome all difficulties, while never giving up. Confucius' happiness and optimism came from many sources: reading, studying, making friends, talking with virtuous friends, enjoying mountains and waters, singing, playing arts and getting talented students to educate. Perhaps delicious food, beautiful clothes and sports could also bring Confucius happiness. But Confucius' happiness and being positive in whatever conditions, originates from his absolute confidence and determination to open himself up, develop benevolence and reason and thus discover and obtain the truth. On one hand, he's happy to know his fate, so he consciously assumed the responsibility of spreading truth and morality, though he knew it was impossible to achieve that. On the other hand, he was pleased to accept the fate of the world. Confucius gave play to the wisdom of the golden mean. Thus he selected something to do. For something that cannot be done for the time being, cast it away. As it says, success does not have to be in me. However, Confucius never changed his passion and forgot his original intention. He believed that "heaven does not let the cause of truth perish" and truth will prevail. As it says, "what continues from the Zhou, even if 100 generations hence, is knowable".

For the true Junzi (exemplary person) of Confucianism, whether rich or poor, drifting in other countries or being in a state of distress, or in any situation wrapped up in fate, could be at ease and self-content.

For example, Su Dongpo was talented, but he was relegated to various places for most of his life, but he was pleased to announce: "Listen not to the rain beating against the trees. Why don't you slowly walk and chant at ease?" "If you ask me where have I achieved my greatest success? Just being relegated to Huangzhu, Huizhou and Danzhou."[1] Wang Yangming, a master of psychology, suffered political hardships repeatedly and was demoted to the wilderness border of Guizhou where he forgot about life and death, and suddenly realized the nature of things. Therefore, the more hardship and frustration people suffer, the more likely he can make some

---

[1]   These are the three places where Su Dongpo was exiled due to his political frustration.

breakthroughs.

Confucius taught the Chinese people Junzi has worries, that is, his first concern is affairs of state; but Junzi has more joy, and he isn't necessarily the last to enjoy comforts. He can enjoy himself at the moment and at any time. Therefore, between Confucius and Fan Zhongyan, I think there is still a big difference. We should learn from Confucius. So please remember this gentle, joyful, smiling, lovely and respectable old man and teacher. As Kahlil Gibran describes Jesus in his poem: Jesus was willing to banter with his audience, to joke and to make wisecracks. Even when there were worries in his eyes and sorrow in his words, he would laugh with joy. He was a happy man. In the way to joy, he met the sorrows of all. And from the summit of sorrows, he looked down on the joys of all. (Taken from *Jesus: the Son of Man* by Kahlil Gibran.)

Fourthly, I believed that Confucius stands for the spirits of working hard and studying to spread the truth of Chinese people.

Confucius set his heart on learning at fifteen, stood firm at thirty, no longer suffered from perplexities at forty, and knew what were the bidding of Heaven at fifty. We should say that Confucius is the typical lifelong learner. He himself also said in a small place with ten families, there might be people as loyal and honest as him, but there was no one who was more diligent and studious than him. Confucius learned from his teachers, but from no constant teacher. He learned rituals from Laozi, music from Chang Hong and Guqin from Shi Xiang. He learned from various teachers and friends. "When three people are traveling together, there must be a teacher for me. " He often sought answers even from his subordinates and took whiz kid Xiangtuo who was 7 years old as his teacher. He read various ancient and modern classics, taking the ancients as his teachers. He walked through mountains and rivers, taking all things in the nature as his teachers. He loves his post and works hard and learns from his work practice. Moreover, Confucius' pursuit of learning is not just a matter of taste, he strove for perfection and never gave up until he achieved his goal. Confucius' pursuit of learning can be seen from the story of Confucius learning "King Wen Cao".

Confucius cherished the time, and said "times passes by like this", so studies should be done "day and night". Confucius never felt boring to learn, and often forgot to sleep and eat properly, and even forgot that old age was fast upon him. Because he read bamboo books so frequently that bamboo slips connected by cowhide tendons were broken three times. This was called "bind of the book having been fractured three times". Zigong, one of Confucius' disciples was tired of such a high-stress and constant study, and asked Confucius: "Master, can't I just take a break?" Confucius' answer showed he was almost unsympathetic. He said: "At the foot of mountains, there are tombs which look like pots, pans and lids. When you get there, you are gonna have time to rest." The spirit of hard working to this degree really makes people surprised and moved.

Some people question that Confucius' saying "the people may be made to follow a path of action, but they may not be made to understand it" was a kind of advocating foolishness. But actually, this is a misunderstanding caused by a wrong sentence break. The correct interpretation should be: "About the policy, if people understand, followed; if do not understand, let known." That's to say, if the people agree, we all come together to abide by it; if the people disagree, we should do a good job of communication so that the people understand and comprehend what we mean and what this policy is meant to be. In other words, it pursues political rationality based on communication and understanding, which is "to let known". Confucius' thought, on one hand, is the supremacy of benevolence and virtue; on the other hand, it is the supremacy of the doctrine of mean and reason. He advocated that all people should explore their inborn benevolence and wisdom, open up their most genuine and brightest human nature, and attain the noblest personality. So how could he advocate to fool the people? It's really unreasonable.

Of course, Confucius' spirits in culture can be summarized in other ways. Here I'm just gonna mention a few points that I feel deeply about. For example, we can consider Confucius as an example who preaches virtues, values education and loves students. As a teacher, Confucius combined his leading role in the education process and the students' position as the main body of education very well. Their relationships can be described as serious, but also happy and harmonious, which makes people feel very comfortable. Just like a loving father, Confucius deeply cared for and loved his students, and had a deep compassion for their misfortunes. The students, of course, also praised and followed their teacher with all their hearts. It is also worthy for today's educators to follow and learn.

In short, Confucius' cultural personalities and spirits, although passed thousands of years, can always inspire us to think of the sentence. "We may gaze up to the mountain's brow; we may travel along the greater road. Although we cannot hope to reach the goal, still we may push on thitherwards in spirit." They represent the realm and height of the Chinese personalities and the brilliant example of Chinese culture.

5. 3   The Eternal Value of Confucianism

Confucianism has evolved and developed over a long period of time. Mr. Mou Zongsan classified Confucius, Mencius, Xunzi to Dong Zhongshu as the first stage of Confucianism; the Song and Ming Dynasties as the second stage and the modern times since the May Fourth Movement as the third stage, namely the revival stage of Confucianism. The founding concepts of primitive Confucian doctrine during the Pre-Qin era mainly refers to the moral standards for cultivating people of virtue and principles for governing a country. Confucianism was called the Neo-Confucianismin the song and Ming Dynasties, due to the fact that it greatly differed from the original Confucian theories. Generally speaking, the beginning stages of Confucian study only told us what and how in relation to conduct in daily life, but did not explain why. While an ideological system containing cosmic principles and conscience was established after the idealist philosophy, absorbing and amalgamating the theories of metaphysics, Buddhism, and Taoism. Modern New Confucianism emerged in the modern eras as a result of the influx of western culture into China, and the collision of the philosophical ideas of the East and the West. The modern school of thought aimed at promulgating the traditional cultural norms by means of modern interpretations so that it could play an active role in moral cultivation and the establishment of nationalized ideological principles.

As an embodiment of Chinese culture passed down for over 2000 years, the Confucianism is rich and profound in ideological connotations, with extensive influence in China and East Asia. Meanwhile, as one of the main representatives of oriental traditions, Confucianism is mutually complimentary among Western cultures, becoming increasingly significant with the passage of time.

Through the long history, among all kinds of thoughts, it has been proved without doubt that Confucianism is the main system of the Chinese culture, and the core ideology of Chinese's ways of thinking, value attitude and lifestyle which have profoundly influenced and shaped "Chinese as a civilization".

(1) How should we evaluate Confucius and Confucianism?

This was a matter of opinion even during Confucius' lifetime. Historically, there are mainly seven ways of evaluation. "Sanctification": Treat Confucius as a saint, which is called sanctification. It mainly happens among Confucius' disciples and later Confucians. "Defaming": Zhuangzi and the Taoists of the Warring States liked to dwarf Confucius. "Orthodoxization": After removing hundreds of schools of thought and respecting Confucianism exclusively in the Han Dynasty, Confucius and Confucianism entered the imperial court, and became the official ideology. "Deification": The divination in the Eastern Han Dynasty deify Confucius. "Rigidity": During the Song and Ming Dynasties, Confucianism was metaphysical, the imperial examination made his thoughts more dogmatic and rigid gradually. "Modernization": In Hundred Days of Reform, Confucius was packaged as a reformer who changed the old system. "Scandalization": During the New Culture Movement and the Cultural Revolution, Confucius was scandalized by all kinds of acts.

But on the whole, since ancient times, Confucius has held a very high status in the hearts of the Chinese people, and the evaluation has been mainly positive and commendatory. The emperors of dynasties respected the value of Confucianism in governing and educating people's hearts, and they have given Confucius many posthumous titles. For example, Emperor Xuanzong of Tang sealed Confucius as the "King of Culture". Emperor Wuzong of Yuan sealed him as "Great Completer, Ultimate Sage and Exalted King of Culture". Shizong of Ming sealed him as "the Greatest Sage and Teacher". Emperors like Gaozu of Han, Xuanzong of Tang, Zhenzong of Song, Kangxi and Qianlong of Qing, all visited Temple and Cemetery of Confucius in Qufu, and paid solemn tribute to Confucius to express their respect for Confucianism. The Chinese people, who have been nurtured by Confucian culture, affectionately call Confucius as "Kung Fu-tzu" and respect him as "the teacher of all teachers". "Three Holy Sites of Confucianism" was also regarded as the holy city of the East and was carefully protected. Since the reform and opening up, with the country's emphasis on traditional culture, the protection and restoration of Confucius temples have been carried out in various places. According to statistics, there are more than 2300 Confucius temples around the world, among which more than 600 are overseas. The Confucius Temple has become an important cultural place for the remembrance of Confucius and the dissemination of Confucian culture.

(2) We believe that Confucius is of the history, but even more of the age. And he will always spark in the history of Chinese cultural development.

Confucianism is rich in connotation, profound in wisdom, and has eternal value through the ages. He asked the leaders of the country to practice benevolent and virtuous rule, to cherish the people's power, to govern with virtue, and to pursue kingly way and the Great Harmony. He asked the businessmen to think of business ethnics, to help the poor and do some charity, and to be a "Confucian Entrepreneur". He asked intellectuals to stick to morality and rationality, and to uphold the moral integrity of a scholar and gentleman. Confucius asked everyone to start with daily ethics, to restrain themselves, follow rituals and become nice people. Confucius also believed that the virtuous are also human beings. "I need only desire to be benevolent and benevolence will arrive. " Therefore, as long as one works hard, everyone has the opportunity to be virtuous. Confucius advocated to used culture to attract remote people. If those people are not submissive, civil culture and virtue are to be cultivated to attract them. When they have been so attracted, they must be made contented and tranquil. Therefore, Confucius opposed power politics and violence, and pursued peace among peoples and nations. Confucius also put forward "teaching without discrimination", the fair education in which teaching is according to students' abilities and education for the common people. In short, Confucius stands for cultures and personalities of the Nation of China. He expounded the various moral standards such as benevolence, righteousness, propriety, wisdom, faith, respect, generosity, trust, tactfulness and virtue. These are all Chinese "universal values" worthy of our inheritance and development.

The Chinese Communists, being historical materials, in every era of China's revolution, construction and reform and development, have paid great attention to the innovative development of traditional outstanding culture and the inheritance of the ancient culture. It is also a journey of Sinicization of Marxism and of building the revolution and road with Chinese characteristics. Chinese Chairman Mao Zedong, for example, often flexibly used various thoughts of Confucius. Mao pointed out that: "Confucius is a sage, and the only one for thousands of years. " "From Confucius to Sun Yat-sen, we should learn from them and inherit their precious thoughts heritage. " At the International Conference in Commemoration of the 2565th Anniversary of

Confucius' Birth, President Xi spoke highly of Confucianism, and he said:

"The Confucian philosophy and the Confucian ideology established thereafter have exerted profound influences on the Chinese civilization. They are an important component of traditional Chinese culture. Confucianism recorded Chinese people's many achievements since ancient times in building their homeland including their spiritual activities rational thinking and cultural achievements. It reflected spiritual pursuits of the Chinese nation, and provided a key source of nutrition for the survival and continuous growth of our nation... it has also made significant contributions to the progress of human civilization as a whole."

Therefore, we could say the excellent traditional culture represented by Confucianism is still an indispensable and valuable cultural resource for the Chinese people. And it will play an important role in the national rejuvenation of the Chinese people towards a new era.

(3) At the same time, we also believe that Confucius belongs to both China and the whole world, and that Confucius' thoughts will continue to offer the world the positive impact of its values.

The influence of Confucianism in East Asian cultural circles goes without saying. In Europe, the name of Confucius was known from early cultural exchanges. Missionaries translated Confucian classics in various languages into Western culture, and this led to Confucianism studies boom in western countries, resulting in such famous scholars as Voltaire, the "Confucius of Europe," and Emerson, the "Confucius of America". They organized publications and wrote books to spread Confucius' thoughts and quotations. The German philosopher Karl Jaspers believed Confucius was born in the "Axial Age", and together with Buddha, Socrates and Jesus were the "Four Great Philosophers" in the world. Especially after the two world wars, the Western intellectual circles have learned a bitter lesson and reflected that social Darwinism was not that good, so was the absolute individual liberalism; while the doctrine of Confucius, which advocates benevolence and virtue, could save Western culture from decline and crisis. In 1988 a dozen Nobel laureates issued a collective declaration right here in Paris: if mankind is to survive in the twenty-first century, we must go back to Confucius in China twenty-five hundred years ago to find wisdom. This is probably a distant salute from the Western intellectual community to Confucius of the East across time and space.

Today, the Confucius Institutes under the name of Confucius have spread to 154 countries and regions around the world. They have become a carrier for spreading Chinese language and traditional Chinese culture to young people all over the world. They are being understood and welcomed by more and more countries and people. We believe that the ideas and cultural values of Confucius will make a great contribution to the construction of human civilization in the 21st century.

Those who are attentive will notice that on every Confucius' birthday, that is, September 28, the famous Confucian temples on both sides of the Taiwan Strait and at home and abroad will be filled with bells and drums, and amid the curling smoke and the sound of elegant music, people will stand in solemn remembrance and pay tribute to their patron saint, and they will also feel the universal cultural empathy of the family beating in their chests, and their feelings of pining for the past will arise. Many scholars and social leaders have proposed that Confucius' birthday be reintroduced as the national legal teachers' day. For this proposal we would also like to express our enthusiastic praise and full support. This shows that with the progress of the times and the development of culture, the thought of Confucius has become a spiritual and cultural resource that everyone appreciates and loves anew.

第六讲

仁者爱人
——中国传统伦理思想概说

我们知道，人文主义或人本主义是中国文化的一大特色。中国文化历来重视人这个中心，但这个所谓的"人"不是自由主义的个人，而首先是生活在人群之中的人，他一定具有他的各种人际关系。这种人们之间的相互关系，就是我们讲的"伦"。儒家在各种纷繁复杂的人伦关系之中，首先重视的是五伦，即父子、君臣、夫妇、兄弟、朋友。五伦，是人所不能免的最基本的人际身份和社会关系。五伦就像人人要去走的五条大道，而儒家也为人们走好这五条道路设定了相应的交通规则以安排和处理好这些人际关系，使其具有合理秩序，这套价值原则就是"伦理"。《孟子·滕文公上》有一个最为经典的概括：父子有亲、夫妇有别、长幼有序、君臣有义、朋友有信。在儒家看来，伦理是天理在人间生活的落实，是道德修养的主要领域，也是帮助人去完成社会化文明人格的主要手段。儒家的五伦之理各有要义。孔子就认为父要慈、子要孝、夫要义、妇要听、长要惠、幼要顺、君要仁、臣要忠、朋友要互信，从而编织起覆盖从家庭到社会，从宗族到政治，从男女到长幼的所有人际领域，以仁心为本、情感和合、互爱互重、整体平衡为特征的东方德性主义伦理体系（即儒家的礼教）。无论是官方或者民间宗族，对恪守伦理的优秀社会成员都会不吝褒奖，甚至树立祠庙和牌坊予以表彰。下面，我就对这五种在传统中最被重视、历史地规范和约束并深刻影响和塑造了中国人文化国民性格的五伦之理略做梳理。

6.1 夫妇有别——中国古人的夫妻之道

"五伦者，始夫妇"，先要有夫妇，而后有父母跟子女的关系。所以，我们先来谈夫妇有别：中国古人的夫妻之道。

谈到夫妇，其实得先说男女。中国传统社会中的男女观念很有意思，它很平衡，就如太极图所展示的那样，是"一阴一阳谓之道"的理解模式。阴阳之间相辅相成、相生相化、对立统一。男女性别的文化定位也因此得到了一种特别的描述：男子为乾，女子为坤；男子为天，女子为地；男子为日，女子为月；男子为阳，女子为阴；男子为外，女子为内；男子动，女子静；男子刚，女子柔；男子强，女子弱；男子攻，女子守……这个模式明显表现了基于男女之间的性别差异而形成的某种生机性互补，而这是维持人道的天然基础。男女是性别差异的一体，就如柏拉图《会饮篇》写道：以前人类是两性同体的，宙斯把他们分成了两半，从那时起，这两半就开始在世界上游荡，相互寻找，而爱情就是对我们失去的另一半的渴望。

可以说，中国古人一方面体认人道之常，认为男女是阴阳互补的一体，从而承认"食色性也""饮食男女，人之大欲存焉"（《礼记·礼运》）。但同时又严肃的认为，男女之间"发乎情，止乎于礼"（《诗经》毛诗序），应该安排礼仪制度，以遂其情。比如，你首先得成年啊，男子二十行加冠礼、女子十五行加笄礼①，而后可论婚姻。而婚姻之事，结两姓之好，关乎家族的发展、子孙的繁衍，不可不谨慎筹划，循"六礼"而后成。那么什么是"六礼"呢？"六礼"形成于周代，是缔结婚姻关系的六道礼仪程序，依次是"纳彩"：媒人提亲，男方求婚。"问名"：问询女方的姓名与生辰八字。"纳吉"：祖庙里去卜卦，或测八字属相，问佳配否。"纳征"：亦称纳币，就是男方向女方家提交聘礼。"请期"：男方家择定日期，征询女方家结婚的日子。"亲迎"：女方送嫁、男方迎家，举行所谓拜天地的仪式。当然，后代程序简约，六礼都浓缩进纳彩、纳征和亲迎这三个环节。古人认为，只有符合六礼的婚姻才具有合法性，否则，即是非礼，是不为人所耻的"野合"。

6.1.1　中国传统婚姻的几个特点

第一就是中国古代的婚姻，确实主要是包办婚姻而非自主婚姻。

包办婚姻即所谓"父母之命，媒妁之言"。男女双方基本上无接触和了解，也不会有多少个人的意见发表的权利，纯粹由父母、媒妁做安排。其实，汉族在《诗经》时代（先秦），自由恋爱似乎还是较为常见的。翻看孔子删订的《诗经》，里边就有上百首诗歌是关乎男女情爱和婚姻的，语言热情浪漫，情境

---

① 古代汉族民众成年就要举行特殊的成人仪式分别叫作"冠礼"和"笄礼"。不同民族的成人时间各不一样，如我国瑶族男子 10～20 岁之间由师公挑选吉日行"度介"仪式（翻云台、上刀山、走火海）而后有成人的社会权利。普米族少女十三岁即行成年礼，改发易服。土家族男女于婚前一二日举行成年礼，叫作"陪十姊妹"和"陪十兄弟"。

缠绵悱恻，读之令人心往神驰。如《郑风·溱洧》和《郑风·出其东门》就对三月三上巳日郑国青年男女在溱水和洧水岸边游春时的浪漫恋情作了生动描写。翻译过来就是：

出其东门，美女如云。虽然如云，非我所思。白衣绿巾女，才是我的心上人。

出其闉闍，美女如花，虽然如花，非我所念。白衣红巾女，才是我的开心果。

这与我国许多少数民族常见的以"摘葱节""山歌节""芦笙会""女儿会"等场合行男女恋爱之事的习俗，仿佛相似。可惜后来礼教严苛，渐失了上古自由活泼的风习。当然，即使是自由恋爱之后也仍然需要经过父母之命、媒妁之言，循六礼以缔结婚姻的。比如《卫风·氓》里的卖丝女和她在市场上认识的情郎，纵然是相爱，良媒—纳吉—纳征—亲迎之礼数也是一样都不能少的。尊重父母，尊重礼仪程序，是一种尊重生命的伦理自觉。

第二，古代的婚姻就对象而言，以外婚制为主，而不废内婚制。

中国古人提倡是同宗同姓不婚，即血亲禁婚，而以异姓婚姻为主，这叫外婚。"内婚"就是姑舅姨表亲婚姻，即兄妹的子女之间、"亲上加亲"结成的婚姻。这种情况，在古代和近代都非常的普遍（有些少数民族如土家族还特别规定婚姻以姑舅表亲优先，叫作"还骨种"。不然需要向舅家支付补偿金）。另外就是寄家的童养媳，这也是一种变相的内婚。另外，过去在一些民族地区还存在所谓"收继婚"，即兄亡弟收嫂，弟亡兄收弟妻，称为"转房"，这也算是一种特殊的内婚形式。当然这些内婚现象今天早已经消失不见了。

第三，古代的婚姻特别重视婚姻双方家庭背景的相匹配，遵循"门当户对"的原则。

门当、户对，本是汉族民居建筑中门厅的两个构件，后用来代指称婚嫁双方应该家世相称、实力等量、人品配合（类似彝族的"等级婚制"）。社会等级条件不合的坚决不能娶嫁。比如，女有"五不娶"的提法，即有造逆之家、淫乱之家、刑犯之家、有恶疾之家，以及母亲早逝的家里长大的女孩子是不太考虑的。当然也有例外，并不是所有家庭的家长，都固守"门当户对"的原则。有些家长慧眼识人，给女儿挑选潜力股"下嫁"。如孔子挑女婿就很奇特，他的学生公冶长，是"在缧绁之中"的戴罪之身。但孔子认为，公冶长是个好人，他入狱而非其罪也，所以，把自己的女儿嫁给了他。

第四，古代中国的婚姻特点，就是特重女德或妇道的修养。

以男子中心主义为传统的中国社会，特重妇德和妇道。用司马迁的话来说，

"乐得佳女以配君子"，因为好女生发家兴业啊——有好女生就会有好媳妇，有好媳妇就会有好妈妈，好妈妈就会培养出好的孩子。一个女生的品格可事关一个家族的兴衰与未来，如此的重要，所以古人特别的注意"好女生养成计划"，提倡"三从四德"为中心的女德修养。"三从四德"的观念源自儒家的《仪礼》和《周礼》，后来在汉代班昭的《女诫》为代表的《女四书》等古典闺房女训教本中被大肆提倡。所谓"三从"就是未嫁从父，既嫁从夫，夫死从子，总之都有一个"顺从、依从、依附"的关系。这是"三从"。"四德"，就是女德、女容、女言、女功。说做女子的，第一要紧是品德，能正身立本；然后要言辞恰当、而不能伶牙俐齿毒舌生事；"容"即相貌不求艳丽，而要端庄稳重，不要轻浮随便；"功"，即治家之道，包括相夫教子、料理衣食、持家生业等生活方面的细节。当然，各个时代妇道和女德规范会有差异，但主要的内涵还是"三从四德"。

第五，古代的离婚问题。

依照女德的线索，女子若失德或不守妇道，就可能受人诟病遗弃。这里就会发生古代的"休妻"即离婚的问题。古代对离婚的讲究是"七出"与"三不去"。"七出"就是七种可以离婚的状况，包括：不孝顺父母、无子绝嗣、淫乱、妒忌、有恶疾、口多言，还有盗窃。《红楼梦》里的王熙凤被休的原因主要是什么？一是无子，二是不孝顺父母，三就是窃财，可以说，她是七出皆犯。而所谓"三不去"就是三种绝不可以离婚的状况。首先是"有所娶无所归"。娘家没人了，你把她赶出去，让她去哪里是归宿？唐代有一首《弃妇诗》就写道："古人虽弃妇，弃妇有归处。今日妾辞君，辞君欲何去。本家零落尽，恸哭来时路。"无家可归的弃妇真可谓惨矣，所以"弃妇"要格外慎重。其次是"与更三年之丧"，就是侍奉双亲，守过三年之丧的媳妇，这个也不能再提离婚之事。最后就是所谓"前贫后富"，跟你一起走过了困难的岁月，所谓"糟糠之妻不下堂"。这三种不允许离婚的情况说明古人并不是完全不照顾女子的位置来考虑问题的。

按照儒家早期的态度，"夫妇，朋友也，可合可离"，里头有一种略为轻松随缘的关系。中古以前，离婚的社会现象也并不稀奇。按《礼记》的说法，孔子家庭就是"三世出妻"。孔子的妻子、儿媳妇和孙媳妇都离开了他们孔家，都叫作是被"出妻"吧。《礼记·曾子问》之中还有三个月的非正式婚姻期的提法，所谓"三月而庙见，称来妇也"。就是结婚三个月以后才去祖庙里拜见祖宗，婚姻才取得正式的宗族的合法性，叫作"来妇"。还有许多材料证明，在北宋的家族文化之中，苛责再婚妇女失节或不贞的另类歧视尚非主流，甚至还有关于女子再婚的经济资助的规定。这在范仲淹订立的范氏家族的《义庄规矩十三条》里就有明确的文字记载。这也算是对弱势女子的一个保护与支持的措施吧。

6.1.2　中国古人的婚姻质量、夫妻之情到底怎样

第一，传统的包办婚姻下中国的夫妻之间也有爱情，当然它也未必更美好。

爱情是没有理由的事情，即使是包办婚姻的重石之下，它也可以生根发芽。中国古代文学史话中有许多经典的爱情名言，可以为证。《诗经》中就有很多夫妻之间互诉情愫的诗篇。如"死生契阔，与子成说。执子之手，与子偕老"（《邶风·击鼓》），如辜鸿铭把《小雅·常棣》中描述的"妻子好合，如鼓瑟琴。兄弟既翕，和乐且耽。宜尔室家，乐尔妻孥"的家庭生活看成是天堂在地上的微缩版。唐代诗人朱庆馀的《近试上张籍水部》中这样写道：

洞房昨夜停红烛，待晓堂前拜舅姑。妆罢低声问夫婿，画眉深浅入时无？

我们可以在脑中勾画出这样的场景：一位含羞的新娘略忐忑地等待天明时去拜见公婆。她梳妆完毕后，轻声细语地询问她的丈夫，她的眉毛是否画得大方入时。这难道不是爱情的味道？尽管他们在婚前并未见过面，在婚礼后的第二天清晨，他们也已经产生了爱情。诸如此类的妻子写给丈夫，丈夫写给妻子的爱情诗在中国文学史话上俯拾皆是，都令人印象美好。如辛弃疾的诗里说："若教眼底无离恨，不信人间有白头。"李清照写道："花自飘零水自流，一种相思，两处闲愁，此情无计可消除，才下眉头，却上心头。"苏东坡则说："十年生死两茫茫，不思量，自难忘，千里孤坟，无处话凄凉。纵使相逢应不识，尘满面，鬓如霜。"这首《江城子》是苏东坡怀念自己的发妻王弗的哀歌，斯人已逝，只能梦中泪目相看……

试问，如果中国古典婚姻中没有真挚深切的夫妻之情，这样的文字能瞎编得出来吗？可见包办婚姻的时代，也有爱情，还爱得浓情蜜意共白头。我家族之中就有好几位长辈是旧式的包办婚姻，甚至有两位是童养媳婚姻。他们都走过了白头偕老、恩恩爱爱的一生。传统的婚姻态度中有某种"一人就是一生"的皈依感。"从一而终""相依为命"的信念反而让他们对彼此的接纳和认可达到这样一个水乳交融、不可分割的程度。若包办婚姻即等于无爱情，则中国文化史岂不成了无爱情的历史，我们都是无爱情者们的后代！我们还会懂得去爱吗？我表示怀疑！

当然我不是说包办婚姻比自主婚姻更好。可能实际的情况是包办婚姻虽未必没有爱情，但也未必就更好。按照费孝通先生在《生育制度·夫妻的配合》

中指出的：传统的夫妻关系往往会屈服于家庭的发展。妻子帮助丈夫，照顾老人和孩子。另一方面，丈夫常常努力向前，使家庭兴旺发达。因此，发展家庭往往比夫妻之间的个人情感更为重要。从这个角度来看，他们的家庭可能是稳固而幸福的，但丈夫和妻子不能享受完整的爱。他们都忙于家庭事务，而疏于或也没有时间和对方交流感情。用今天的话来说，可以这样描述：因为爱变成了亲情，所以老夫妻之间不交流彼此的爱。它就像一双手——左手和右手彼此依赖配合，但这种感觉真的意味着爱吗？这真的很难说。

第二，在我们批评中国传统的夫妻之道中存在着压抑女权的糟粕的同时，仍要对传统女性的坚强韧性和无我的牺牲精神表示敬意。

传统的女德和妇道教育涉及的是多方面的内涵，要看哪些是受到男子中心主义的封建观念污染的态度，哪些又是基本可取的有价值的美德。男子有男子之德，女子有女子之德。无德不成人，一个有很好的道德品格的女生总是更让人钦佩和喜欢。而寄望女子成为美德淑女或贤妻良母，正如要求男子成为有气节的君子和贤者，这本身是没有问题的。传统社会中，女子们被要求在家做好女儿，出嫁做好媳妇，生育后做好母亲。她们从小未得若何之教育，成人后别离父兄出嫁人家，善事姑翁、相夫教子，负责各种大小家务的统筹料理，承受方方面面的严苛看待和评价的氛围重压，经冬历春、无怨无悔。所以所谓"好女人"的这个"好"的核心标准，在传统社会，是一切以家庭和家人为中心，是勤持家务、温顺处世，甚至是无私和无我的。

辜鸿铭曾借用希伯来女性诗歌形象来比较中国女性，认为两者都是他心目中的理想女性（feminine ideal）：

谁能找到一个贤惠的女人？因为她的价值远胜红宝石。她的丈夫真心地信任她。天还没亮她就起床了，给家人准备食物，给未婚的女孩备嫁妆。她手放在纺锤上，手指握着拉线棒。为了家人都穿上漂亮暖和的衣服，她不惧冬雪。她轻声细语，温柔和善。她对家人照顾周全，从不游荡懒散。她的孩子们长大成人并感恩于她，她的丈夫也喜爱并日日赞美她。①

可以说，在一个民族中，女性是文明之花，是那个民族的生命品格和人文精神的最佳体现。一个理想的中国传统女性温良恭俭让，几乎是熠熠生辉的家中圣人。但这种高尚的光辉背后又有多少忍辱负重和慷慨牺牲？她们用如此的无私忘我换来一个个家庭的幸福、稳定与昌盛绵延。没有伟大的贤妻良母们，就没有伟大的中华民族和伟大的中国文化史。比如历来为人所诟病的"寡妇守

---

① 辜鸿铭. 中国人的精神［M］. 上海：上海三联书店，2012：47.

节"，且先莫急着谴责。在那些牌坊上镌刻的冷冰冰的"立节完孤""矢贞全孝"的褒美之辞后面，其实又有多少苦衷需要我们更多的同情和理解呢？对孀妇而言，丈夫亡故，她或许可以一走了之另外改嫁。但亡夫的家里上有老人、下有幼儿，又怎能忍心一走了之呢？她一走，这个家岂不是完蛋了呢？"寡妇守节"在某种意义上可谓是无可奈何的牺牲自我、成全家庭的美德行为。

在安徽歙县棠樾村有一处专为奉祀鲍氏家族中的贞孝节妇的女祠"清懿堂"，其后室楹联这样写道："清容肃仪，看历代名媛淑女，矢贞全孝，寡鹄悲鸣声在耳。懿德冰操，仰先宗贤妻良母，凤娴内则，鹿车共挽并肩归。"传统的女德，固已为今人所隔阂甚至厌弃，但细细感悟，古来女子那种清夜时垂泪、苦难中开花的坚毅品格，那种为家人而活的"忘我的信仰"，却不能不令人动容和仰望。

第三，男权中心的传统封建礼教是损害夫妻婚姻关系的毒药。

托尔斯泰说：所有幸福的家庭都是一样的，不幸的家庭则各有各的不幸。在中国传统婚姻下，如果有不幸婚姻的原因，那么大概有这样几条：

首先，包办婚姻下父母之命的不可违，结婚、离婚选择的不自由。夫妻是婚配结合在一个家庭的男女。按照今天的理解，自然是要鱼水相欢情投意合。可包办婚姻下，娶妻嫁郎都身不由己，彼此本不认识。爱情能否从婚后开始培养，性格是否合适，也未可知。就算幸运，夫妻竟能相互契合，父母高堂不中意也枉然。例如《孔雀东南飞》里焦仲卿与刘兰芝的哀歌，《钗头凤》里陆游和唐婉的劳燕分飞，《浮生六记》中沈复与陈芸的悲剧，都是有力的证明。婚姻在传统社会中从一开始就不是男女之间的私事，婚事是家事，是全族的事，决定权不在夫妻本人，而在父母或宗族。这在今天的婚姻观来看，完全是本末倒置了。

其次是"夫为妻纲"的观念污染和"一夫多妻"的制度扭曲。中国封建礼教中充满了男子对女子的优越感，如"男尊女卑"或"夫为妻纲"，这就为夫妻和家庭关系的不和谐埋下了祸根、制造了麻烦。中国古代长期实行的是名义上的一夫一妻制，而实则为多妻、多妾的制度。男人为什么需要这么多妻妾呢？冠冕堂皇的说法是"不孝有三，无后为大"，要纳姬妾以广后嗣。这是拿孝道当借口。还有男子为官为商在外，需要有人随身陪侍以料理起居，这是"工作—生活需要论"的解释。更有一种"性别天然论"的解读。如民国学者辜鸿铭曾经发表的一种所谓"茶壶茶杯论"。他把男子比成是茶壶，女子比成是茶杯。一个茶壶配多个茶杯，所以一夫多妻天经地义。他还把妻子允许（甚至主动给）丈夫安排纳妾（且不嫉妒），当作是中国传统女性"忘我的信仰"这样一种美德来赞许。这当然是非常可笑的。一夫多妻制是中国传统家庭伦理中的一个糟粕，是应该批判的亚文化。其根源说白了还是男性的一种本能泛滥。在《男人这种动物》中，日本作家渡边淳一就从生物医学的角度分析了男人本质上就是欲望的动物，其花心几乎是天性难改的。

当然，更应该被批判的，不是男性的天性，而是对人性的贪欲起到放大器作用的封建制度。是男子中心主义的礼教制度，使得男子能以各种貌似合理合法的方式占有和支配更多的女性，并且把一些在今天看来很变态的观念强加给女子，如男尊女卑的观念、处女观念、柔顺服从的观念、"饿死事小、失节事大"的贞节观念。另外，还有所谓的缠足文化、奴婢文化等，都是中国古代妇女不幸的社会生活的多面表现。陈东原先生在《中国妇女生活史》一书的绪论中甚至直接认为："我们有史以来的女性，只是被摧残的女性，我们妇女生活的历史，只是一部被摧残的女性底历史。"①

小结：我们必须公允地说：原始儒家的伦理文化以"一阴一阳谓之道"的哲理从根本上保障了男女之间差异而平等的文化地位的先验基础。而为后世封建礼法迭代沉淀的各种男尊女卑、戕害女性的糟粕，其实是违反儒学的原教旨和真精神的，是孔子、孟子和真正的儒者所必不能接受的一种对"男女之道"的扭曲和异化。孔子既尊重人类的人道情感和正常欲望，又重视礼法程序。他坚信人性的善良，但也对人们"德之不修，学之不讲，闻义不能徙，不善不能改"（《论语·述而》）充满了忧虑。他严厉抨击纵欲主义，认为"宫室有度，无禁则淫，无度则失，纵欲则败"（《孔子家语·六本》）。对婚姻中那种薄情寡义之人，孔子更是直言鄙薄。如古诗有云"唐棣之华，偏其反而。岂不尔思？室是远而"。翻译过来就是"唐棣树的花儿，翩翩地摇摆，难道是我不思念你吗？那是因为家住的太远了"。听这口吻肯定是一个不思念妻室的负心男子为自己的薄情找的理由。孔子对此直接点破说："未之思也，夫何远之有？"（《论语·子罕》）那是你没有真正的思念之情啊，如果真有思念之情，又怎么会觉得遥远呢？（不是越遥远，思念之情愈甚吗？）另外，上面提到过，孔子家族"三世出妻""三月而庙见"的"试婚期"之类，亦可为证。

儒家提倡的夫妻之道和婚姻伦理的观念早已随着现代社会的发展，慢慢失去了它的影响力。今天的人们早已获得了基于男女平等基础上自由恋爱、自由婚姻、自由结婚、自由离婚的机会与权利，但是自由恋爱和婚姻自主真的就带来了幸福吗？事实证明了并不尽然。人们忙着享受自由地追逐情欲，随意结婚、

---

① 陈东原. 中国妇女生活史 [M]. 北京：商务印书馆，2015：17.

随意离婚的快感。自由是自由了，但自由过后除了一声长叹之外，也并没有留下更多有价值的东西。诸如不婚主义、丁克生活、AA 制夫妻、各种婚外情等。未来还需要婚姻吗？未来还需要家庭结构之下的一夫一妻吗？很多人对此越来越失去了信心。

以我看来，真正的文明是有生机性和生命力的，当现代社会离婚率高企而生育率低下的时候，文明就不再是文明，这意味着我们对人和生活的未来，失去了信任和信心。但是，依中国传统的伦理概念来说，婚姻和家庭仍是值得拥有的。孔子说："君子之道，造端乎夫妇。"婚姻和家庭是所大学校，可以启发我们的爱心、灵感和责任感，能让我们学会承担和真正成长。家庭和家人的存在甚至能感动我们至于无我和无私，因此我们的生命得以避免浅薄，并体会到作为一个人真正完整的、有温暖、有内涵、回味无穷的幸福。在这方面，古人那种白首同心、相依为命、无私牺牲的家人之爱，还正有我们所不能及的人格境界呢。

无感于现代婚姻的一地鸡毛，遥想当年，别有一番滋味上心头。

诗人写道：

从前车马很慢，书信很远，一生只够爱一个人。（木心《从前慢》）

6.2 父子有亲——中国人浓厚的孝亲之思

"父子有亲"，讲的是父母与子女之间的伦理关系。中国伦理文化要求做父母的要慈祥，做子女的要孝顺。但实际中似乎更侧重在子女这边，要感恩图报，做孝子贤孙。

6.2.1 孝道是为人的根本

儒家认为"夫孝，德之本也！"（《孝经》）"孝悌也者，其为人之本欤？"（《论语·学而》）为何孝道是道德之本，也是为人的根本呢？在中国人看来这似乎不应是一个问题。因为父母，就是我们生命的根本。除了孙猴子是天生地养、石头里蹦出来的外，人总都是父母生养，而不是凭空来到这个世界的。为了子女，父母劬劳辛苦，用尽一生无限的爱心。中国人民对父母历来不吝感恩赞美之辞。如《诗经·小雅·蓼莪》篇中就动心地写道：

哀哀父母，生我劬劳……哀哀父母，生我劳瘁。……无父何怙？无母何恃？出则衔恤，入则靡至。父兮生我，母兮鞠我。拊我畜我，长我育我，顾我复我，出入腹我。欲报之德，昊天罔极！

《蓼莪》可谓字字泣血，算得上是中华民族咏颂父母恩德的最早悲歌！

中国化的佛教非常重视儒家的孝道思想，造了一部《佛说父母恩重难报经》。其中提到，父母的深恩大德有十个表现，这十大恩德是：怀胎守护恩；临产受苦恩；生子忘忧恩；咽苦吐甘恩；回干就湿恩；哺乳养育恩；洗濯不净恩；远行忆念恩；深加体恤恩；究竟怜悯恩。读此经文、感此十恩，为人子女的，谁不会为父母这伟大的慈爱而痛感亏欠？谁又不会暗暗发愿，一定要好好地回报父母、恪尽一份孝道呢？像陈百强的"念亲恩"歌里唱到的：父母亲爱心柔善像碧月，常在心里问何日报?！

父母之恩虽是无可报答的，但中国古人却非常真诚、非常努力地去作自己的回报！子路百里负米以奉双亲而自食藜藿。闵损芦衣顺母、甘受委屈而遭鞭责。可爱的吴猛，恣蚊饱血；天真的黄香，扇枕温衾。东晋时无锡人华宝，七十老矣却还梳着儿时的发髻，只为父亲离家时一句"等我回来，为你行成年礼"的叮嘱，就期望了这一生！不冠不婚，不悔年华老，但恨父不归。而清代徽州棠樾村人鲍逢昌则幸运得多，他十四岁时出门寻找失散多年的父亲，一路沿街乞讨终于在山西雁门关附近父子相聚。他还为重病的母亲攀岩寻药，甚至割肉疗疾，可谓精诚大孝，天人同赞。

如此类的中华孝亲故事，可谓史不绝书，读之常能催人泪下。孔子说"父母在，不远游"，在今天固已不现实，但对我们这样为生活而不得不漂泊异乡的游子而言，只能在夜深人静之时，遥望明月思念家园，那种时光荏苒有家难回、亲颜难见有儿若无的悲哀，实不足为外人道也。可以说，中华民族数千年的孝亲文化传统，在世界民族之林中也是卓越的一族。中华儿女的孝亲之心，就像棠樾村的慈孝里牌坊，穿越了历史的晨光暮照、风霜雪雨，虽已青苔斑斑，却依旧伟岸肃穆，恒久地矗立在苍天之下、大地之上，象征着中华民族思本报源、感戴亲恩、推崇孝道、表彰孝行的拳拳真心和集体意志。

6.2.2　儒家"孝道"的四个层次

我们这里简略地介绍一下儒家"孝道"思想的几个层次：

第一，孝是孝顺与孝敬的一体。

（1）孝的基本表现当然是要孝顺——"顺"就是子女和父母的相处之道上，凡事首先是要顺从、要听话，不能忤逆，别对抗着去。《论语》中记载："樊迟御，子告之曰：'孟孙问孝于我，我对曰无违。'"（《论语·为政》）子曰："事父母几谏，见志不从，又敬不违，劳而不怨。"（《论语·里仁》）《弟子规》① 中也如此写道："父母呼、应勿缓，父母命、行勿懒，父母教、须敬听，父母责、须顺承。"

这里其实涉及了一个孝的形式问题。

与今天很多年轻朋友的态度不同，在父母子女之间的互动方式上，儒家主张：一方面子女应该尊重父母的话语优先权，应该虚心地接受他们的教导和提出的建议。其实，父母的话语优先权并不难理解，这不是一个法律问题，而实是一个情感问题。毕竟父母总是最爱自己孩子的人，他们的人生经验和智慧，又恰恰是孩子们所缺少的。所以在孩子们的成长路上，多倾听父母的意见，接受父母的指导，这不是坏事，只会是好事。即使意见分歧很大，孝亲的人总能做到有话好好说，保持一份和颜悦色。依我们的生活经验，父母子女乃是生命的一体，只要耐心沟通，即使分歧再大，最后总能互谅互让。可惜现在的人心浮气躁，戾气重，就算家人之间都很难心平气和地讨论问题。就算命运真让你摊上了那么糟糕的家庭，父母真让你受了很大的委屈。但你毕竟是他们的子女，他们毕竟是你的父母，无论如何，这层关系就是你的天命，所谓"不知命无以为君子"。在儒家看来，逆境中尽孝更能体现出一个人的孝心。《弟子规》中说"亲爱我，孝何难。亲憎我，孝方贤"，既然遇到了，那就坦然接受，用坚韧和勇气去面对和承担这命运。其实人无完人，真不必奢望或苛责他人的不完美。况且亲人就是亲人，天然的血脉连接能创造包容和体谅的奇迹。不管你信不信，爱让你能做到。

谚语说：生活给你荆棘，你却笑对生活以花香。我也要说：乌云和暴风雨是天空最好的洗礼。孝亲路上的一切不如愿、不如意，也是对人性最好的考验和洗礼。

（2）孝的本质精神是子女内心对父母的一份敬爱。

儒家固然强调"无违"和顺从，但儒家对孝的本质理解是透过这个"顺"字看到一个"敬"字。顺的背后应该是敬，敬重和敬爱。"敬"是第一义，"顺"是第二义。孔子在回答子游问孝的时候特别的指出这个"敬"字，他说：今天的孝啊，常被理解为在物质生活上的奉养。其实，你们家的犬马，你还要给它一份给养，如果没有敬爱的心，又怎么来区别呢？

这就提出了一个孝的实质或本质精神的问题。

孝，不是盲听盲信的绝对服从，或好吃好喝、锦衣玉食的优渥奉养，孝之

---

① 《弟子规》，清代康熙时山西绛州人李毓秀（1647—1729）所作。

为孝关键是要有"敬"。那何为敬呢？在我看来，敬是因美好而感动，更是因高尚而仰望。正是有父母的生养抚育，慈心大爱，犹如三春之光辉，使我们足以为人在世。想起"哀哀父母"这一生的种种不易和无私付出，我们腆然愧受了这份美好的大爱情深，方寸之心中常涌起难言难状的感动。这份良知的感动，融融切切，让子女依恋父母永如儿童，自卑自弱；也让子女仰望父母永如苍天，愈尊愈贵。大地岂能与苍天齐高？子女岂敢与父母平等？这种发自内心对父母的无限感戴、仰望的热爱之情，就是敬！在儒家看来，孝亲，必先有敬亲之心。若有敬爱之心，则孝行自会满心而发，如有源头活水。如《弟子规》中所谓"冬则温，夏则清。晨则省，昏则定。出必告，反必面"以及"不独擅、不私藏"，为亲所好，去亲所恶，等等。由衷的敬爱让你不假强求、心甘情愿地去做好各种照料父母生活的孝行。

　　以我所知，真正的中国孝子女永远都是把父母放在心头，当作生活的第一位来优先对待的。吃到可口的美食，第一个念头就会是："要是父母也能品尝到该多好啊！"看到一处美丽的风景，第一个念头就会是："要是父母也能看到该多好啊！"孝子女时时刻刻都心系父母，愿意把最美好的奉献给父母。而千头万绪总归一个心思：取悦父母，愿亲安康！若父母身体有恙，则恨不能以身相代！这一念发动处的真情，如玉壶冰心，是最可珍贵的为人子女的天德与良知。有了这一念真心，孝亲才是我们的本分和天命，是人生莫大的喜乐和幸福。

　　第二，孝是有始与有终的一体。

　　（1）孝之有始，始于洁身自好。《孝经》中说："身体发肤，受之父母，不敢毁伤，孝之始也。"这是说，孝亲的人应当珍惜自己的身体，要自爱。我们的身体不仅仅是我们自己的，我们的身体一半是父亲的，一半是母亲的，是"父母之体"，岂敢亵渎和毁伤。曾子临终之前还命弟子"启予足！启予手！"知道自己的手脚都完好无损后，他才安然而逝。为保全这"父母之体"，他如临深渊如履薄冰一般谨慎小心了一辈子，现在毫发无损、全体而归，算是对得起父母了。孔子提出："一朝之忿，忘其身，以及其亲，非惑与？"（《论语·颜渊》）这就是教导人们（尤其是年轻人），行事切忌一时的鲁莽冲动而招致伤身害命，甚至连累父母家人陷入灾难。《弟子规》里说："身有伤，贻亲忧。德有伤，贻亲羞。"一个孝亲的人，对人不轻慢、不与人交恶、不争斗，也不做任何违法或败德的恶行，以免双亲之忧，以保家族的声誉。自珍自爱，这是孝之始。

　　（2）那孝之终是什么呢？孝之终就是"立身行道，扬名于后世，以显父母"（《孝经》）。古人看来，人生在世当发奋有为，立德、立功、立言，皆可以不朽于后世。而这不单单是个人的成就，也是父母和家族的成就，是大家共同的荣耀。比如古代科举考试金榜题名，或担任品官，政绩卓越，朝廷就会按例诰封官员及其父母先人，或敕建牌坊予以表彰，可谓美誉如潮。这无疑让父母因子而显贵，祖宗就是在天有灵，亦得其光荣。在龙岩永定的林氏家庙前有一片为获得功名成就的族人树立的石旗杆，上面镌刻着他们的姓名、世系和官职。这些都可算是显扬父母、为祖宗增光添彩之举。即使在今天，一个考上重点大学的中国孩子也仍能给父母和家庭带来巨大的荣耀。每年暑假，在江西吉安地区的农村家族祠堂里都会为准大学生们举办赠送贺喜对联的仪式，敲锣打鼓、燃放鞭炮、大摆宴席，全村的人都来祝贺围观，所见都是羡慕的眼神，所闻皆是祝福的暖言。毋庸置疑，这会是这个家庭的高光时刻，学子深感光荣，父母肯定更是志得意满，一种特别的幸福感和成就感在每个细胞里闪光。父母子女本就是休戚相关、与荣与辱的生命共同体。但是反过来说，你若无所成就，让父母家人跟着你贫寒交迫、甘居人下，那就是不孝了。《孝经》所谓："家贫亲老，不为禄仕，二不孝也。"你不能不做事，有机会发展，你不能消极懈怠、甘受贫寒。所以，孝道就变成了一种激励人们为父母和家人的荣耀而奋斗的精神动力。

第三点，孝是生前与身后的一体。

尽孝，当然主要是生前的。但对儒家而言，生命总有始有终，而灵魂是不灭的，人们的孝心也应该是无尽的。孔子就说："事死如事生，事亡如事存，孝之至也。"（《中庸》）父母活着的时候子女要孝亲，父母故去了也要以礼葬之，以礼祭之，并依制守孝，"三年无改于父之道"。违反这条制度的，就是不孝了。这里且不去讨论"三年之丧"有无必要的问题。我们要体会的，是这种慎终怀远的心理，它寄寓的是至亲至爱之间超越生死、永恒怀思这样一种动人的情怀。

二十四孝故事里的"子路负米"的故事讲到，子路为人淳朴非常的孝顺。年轻时因家穷，他常到百里以外去挑米回来奉养父母，而他自己呢，吃藜藿，也就是野菜。后来他当官发达了，锦衣玉食。但他经常感觉到一种忧思，为什么呢？因为父母已经不在人世了。他常常叹息道："即使我想吃野菜，为父母亲去负米，又哪里能够再得呢？"孔子听到后赞许说：子路侍奉父母，可谓"生事尽力，死事尽思"（《孔子家语·致思》），尽显了他的孝心，真不愧是一个孝子啊！又如王裒"闻雷泣墓"的故事说魏晋时人王裒的母亲生前非常害怕打雷，一到打雷的时候，她总是吓得瑟瑟发抖。母亲去世后，每到打雷闪电的风雨夜，这个孝子王裒就会跑到母亲的坟墓边上去安慰母亲的在天之灵，口中念道"裒儿在此，母亲勿惧"。这种行为，今天的人们是不会干的。逝者已远，"闻雷泣墓"岂不是一种愚昧？但对爱戴父母的孝子女而言，这就是一种视死如生的行为，是基于他们饱满的孝心和恒久的怀思使然。

中国古人这种孝思无尽的文化表现有很多方面啊——他们为父母先人依制守丧三年；他们为祖宗们修建祠堂、四时八节如礼隆重祭祀。族中凡有大事，如举行成人礼和婚礼，新修族谱，或族人金榜题名等，他们也会及时禀告祖先的在天之灵知道，请祖宗明鉴垂佑，此所谓"告庙"。另外，他们还自觉践行"不孝有三，无后为大"的原则，不让祖先遗留下来的血脉断绝于己手；他们把祖先的生平业绩、赫赫美德都写进族谱，把祖先的谆谆教诲变成家规家法，让后代都铭记于心，激励自己和后代子孙奋发上进，以求光宗耀祖。儒家学说就是这样给人以启示并激发人们内心的强烈情感，使人们遵守道德准则，并借此醇厚了一代代中国人的道德人格。曾子认为："恭谨地对待去世的父母，追念久远的祖先，百姓的道德就自然敦厚了。"（"慎终追远，民德归厚矣。"）我可以断言：一个怀思祖先、关心家族未来命运的民族，不能不说是一个道德醇厚、文明伟大的民族。

第四点，孝还是道德与理性的一体。

儒家首重孝道，认为这是人首先应该修养并践行的一种家庭美德。正如《孝经》中说的："不爱其亲，而爱他人者，谓之悖德；不敬其亲，而敬他人者，谓之悖理。"但儒家所要求的孝道，不是外在的强迫性的命令，而是人的内心的良知所要求的自觉的行为。孔子在回答宰我对"三年之丧"的质疑的时候就提出："汝安乎？"关键是看你内心，你是否安心。良知是天赋的道德理性，它天然的"知善知恶"，也天然地要求人们去做应该做的、正确的事情。也就是说，作为理性行为，儒家的孝道不仅要我们有真诚的爱，也要求人们有理性，要理性地去爱，中庸地行孝。

我们已经讲过，儒家的中庸之道是根据实际情况来处理问题、追求适度与适中的理性方法论。就孝道而言，也要贯彻这个方法论。孝亲不等于愚孝，它并没有一定不可以或者一定要怎样的形式主义规定。比如，我们提到孝要"顺"，要"无违"。但这个也要根据特定情况来分别讨论。一般情况下，孝首先是要顺从父母，我们也反对子女以粗暴的态度跟父母吵闹。但是在另外一些情况下，我们却会发现，不顺从，逆反甚至也可以是一种孝的形式。什么情况呢？比如大舜逃杀的故事所讲的那样。大舜的父母不喜欢舜，必欲置之死地而后快。但大舜他并没坐以待毙、乖乖受死，而是首先设法保全自己，保全了自己才能保全亲道，才有可能恪尽孝道。而孔子的弟子曾子呢，傻傻地守着孝是"不违"的教条，他父亲往死里打他，他还是顺从不逃，所以孔子说曾子这样是愚孝，不是真正的孝道。这也就是说，依据儒家的本义，孝是人人都有的一种道德理性，仁者爱人，但要以中庸的理性方法来爱人。爱敬父母的孝道也应该根据中庸的理性来审时度势、便宜行事。对那些野蛮而不慈祥的父母，人们可以选择权宜之计，灵活地对待。啥都盲听盲信，"父要子死，子不得不死"，那是最大的愚孝，荀子说，天下大概也没有这样的愚孝之人吧①。

又比如尽孝必有孝行，但无论论生前尽孝还是身后之孝，孝行又须因人而异、量力而行。古人说的好："百善孝为先，论心不论迹，论迹寒门无孝子。"每个人都想把最好的给父母，以报答父母的深恩。但每个的能力和财力又是不同的，如果一定要用富人的标准来定义尽孝的方式，那穷人家岂不是没法尽孝了呢？所以，何为孝行，这个没法生硬的规定。尽心则无愧，哪怕是些小微末，哪怕是默默的一念爱亲敬亲之心，也算是极好的孝道了。就如祭祖之礼，固然力求隆重，但更重要的是子孙的一份诚意。对普通人家而言，就是奉献刚刚采摘的菜蔬、洁净的瓜果、新出的稻米作为祭品，也是最好的奉献。孔子曰："虽疏食菜羹，瓜祭，必齐如也。"（《论语·乡党》）只要心诚如玉，祖宗必悦纳之！这也是一种实事求是的中庸行孝的表现。

我们今天讲孝道，不能不加分析的认为孝道是传统时代父母用来压制子女的一种过时的封建糟粕。相反，我们要看到，经过与时俱进的扬弃，中华传统孝亲文化里面仍有相当的价值可供我们去学习和继承。而今天很多时代的问题，恰恰是从家庭中缺少孝亲的温情这个根子上发展起来的。试问一个对父母都不爱敬的社会，哪里还有文明进步可言呢？

一言以蔽之，人人念亲恩，则社会大和谐。

6.3　长幼有序——中国人长者优先的伦理原则

长幼有序，指的是年长者和年幼者之间的先后尊卑的伦理关系，也叫"长幼有序"。这里讲的长幼，既指家中平辈兄弟姐妹之间，也指家族各辈分成员之间。根据"老吾老以及人之老，幼吾幼以及人之幼"的精神，长幼有序也应该是整个社会中的年长年幼的人们中普遍起指导作用的伦理原则。孟子就说："天下之达尊三，爵一，齿一，德一。"（《孟子·公孙丑下》）中国人尊长敬老，长幼有序，大一天也是长；长一辈，年龄再小也是长，也要实行长者优先的原

---

① 子从父，奚子孝？臣从君，奚臣贞？审其所以从之之谓孝、之谓贞也。（《荀子·子道》）

则。长幼有序的原则历久流传、蔚然成风，成为中国传统伦理的重要内容。

（1）《弟子规》中长幼有序、尊老敬长的具体要求

上一节我们也提到过了《弟子规》。它虽然是一本童蒙教本，但影响力非常大，可以帮助我们略窥中华传统伦理教育的一般要求。我们正在讨论的"长幼有序"的原则，在《弟子规》中也有很好的解读。

"兄道友，弟道恭。兄弟睦，孝在中。财物轻，怨何生。言语忍，忿自泯。或饮食，或坐走。长者先，幼者后。长呼人，即代叫。人不在，己即到。称尊长，勿呼名。对尊长，勿见能。路遇长，疾趋揖。长无言，退恭立。骑下马，乘下车。过犹待，百步余。长者立，幼勿坐。长者坐，命乃坐。尊长前，声要低。低不闻，却非宜。进必趋，退必迟。问起对，视勿移。事诸父，如事父。事诸兄，如事兄。"

这里首先提到了兄弟之间的相处之道。作兄长的要爱护弟弟，做弟弟的要尊敬兄长。兄弟和睦，这也是对父母的一种孝道。把财物看得轻淡些，兄弟之间就不会相互怨恨，处处忍让，和言爱语，如此便不会引起忿恨。其次就更广泛地谈到了一般的长者幼年之间的相处态度。比如其中提到：吃饭宴饮的场合，不管就座，还是离席，要礼让长者优先。如果长者叫人，你就要替他去叫。如果他叫的那个人不在，那么你就要替代那个人去应付长者的差事。对称尊长，你不能直呼其名。在尊长面前，你也不要表现自己的能耐。在路上遇到长者，你要赶快上前作揖行礼。长者不说话，你就安静地待在旁边，恭敬地伫立。你在骑马或者坐车，遇到长者，就要赶紧下马，赶紧下车。你走在长者的前面，看见长者在后面来了，那你就要静静地在原地等待。长者还站着，幼者就不可以坐，待长者坐下后，招呼幼者坐下，幼者才可以坐下。在尊长前讲话声音要轻柔，但低到让人家听不清，也是不合适的。要见尊长的时候，动作要敏捷。告退时，动作要缓慢。尊长问话，要站起来回答，不可左顾右盼。对叔伯舅舅要像对父亲一样恭敬，对诸表兄要像对亲兄长一样恭敬……

这些点滴细节，尽显中国人的尊长敬长的心意。

（2）长幼有序伦理原则的思想探源

其实，若论中国伦理文化中尊长敬老、长幼有序的原理的缘起，我觉得至少可以追溯到周公旦的"制礼作乐"时代。周公旦的"制礼作乐"形成了中华礼乐文教的基础，其中有好几方面是跟这里提到的长幼有序原则有关系的。

其中第一条就是宗庙祭祀制度的昭穆制度，就表现了所谓的长幼有序。宗庙里头的神主牌位摆放的原则是"左昭右穆"：父子相对，祖孙同列，显示家族成员不同辈分之间的尊卑、长幼、亲疏之别。这在后世宗族文化、祭祀文化和

墓葬文化中都是特别遵守的一条原则。比如入关后的清朝皇帝就依昭穆次序分别入葬位于河北遵化的清东陵和河北易县的清西陵两处皇陵。

周公旦的"制礼作乐"里奠定的第二条重要的原则，就是嫡长子继承制度，这也典型地凸显了长幼有序的要求。西周实行世袭王权与宗法相结合的制度，这是一种以嫡长子为继承人的分权制度。嫡子和庶子是主要血统和次要血统的差别。在"立嫡以长不以贤"的原则下，即使你更聪明，更贤能，如果不是嫡妻所生的嫡长子，你是没有继承尊爵显位的这种权利跟机会的。应该讲，中国古代王朝或贵族的继承人制度的主要原则还是嫡长子继承制。"废长立幼"从来都会引起政治的风波。而作为非嫡长子的那些兄弟，要非常自觉地做到不与兄争。比如季札"三让位"的故事，说的是春秋时期吴国的季札很贤明，但他却不觊觎大位，他的父兄几次让他继承王位，但他都屡屡推辞不受。这也是遵循长幼有序的伦理原则在政治上的表现。嫡长子继承制看起来挺美好，符合"兄道友，弟道恭。兄弟睦，孝在中"的精神。悌道也就是兄弟之道，做好悌道也就是尽孝道（让父母省心开心）。兄弟之间纷争不断，自然就是家庭的不幸。但实际上，中国政治史上真正以嫡长子当皇帝的例子也不多（像唐太宗李世民的"玄武门之变"，康熙王朝的"九子夺嫡"）。

第三条就是乡饮酒礼。乡饮酒礼属于古代之嘉礼之一，也是西周时代已经流行起来的一种敬贤尊老的礼仪活动。一般在孟春正月及孟冬十月举行，并伴有"读律令"和训诫致辞的内容，以此来劝导民众尊亲敬长、遵守国法。据《礼记·乡饮酒礼》记载得很清楚：六十岁以上的人可以坐着，五十岁的人就站着侍候，听候使唤，这表示对年长者的尊敬。六十岁的人只上三个菜，七十岁的人就有四个菜，八十岁的人可以有五个菜，而九十岁的人能有六个菜，上菜的多少，也表示出对老人的奉养标准随年龄而不同。《礼记》的作者认为只要百姓懂得尊敬年长者，懂得奉养老人，在家里就会孝顺父母、敬事兄长。到社会上就能尊敬年长的人和奉养老人，然后才能形成教化，国家才能安定。

孔子非常赞赏乡饮酒礼的创制，认为借此推行王道也并非难事。孔子当然也参加过这样的乡饮酒礼的仪式。在这种以尊老为主要内容的乡饮酒礼活动中，老人家们喝完酒，拄着拐杖出去，孔子就自觉地跟在老者的后面，不会跑到老者的前面去。可见孔子确实是一个很尊重老人、践行长幼有序伦理的模范。孔子和学生讨论人生志向的时候就说了，他的人生志向就是："老者安之，少者怀之，朋友信之。"这个就是他非常生活化的、非常朴素的一种人生志向。这里一个很重要的内容就是"尊老爱幼"。孔子曾经批评过一个阙党童子，就是孔子家阙里一个乡党的孩子，他大概是来孔子家传递主人的什么信息。这个小孩走了之后，学生就问孔子：夫子，您觉得这个小孩怎么样？将来会有出息吗？孔子说：没有出息！因为这小孩竟然不分大小，跟长辈们并列坐在一起，与长辈们并列齐肩地一起行走，这不是谦虚求取益处的样子。这种小孩太急于求成，太想把自己当成一个成年人了，而欲速则不达，不知礼是不会有成就的。

　　这里又转回到我们开头讲到的《弟子规》里也提到的就座礼仪了。我们知道，就餐礼仪方面，中国人也非常讲究。一般而言，老人应邀赴宴是主家的殊荣，主家会热情引导长辈老人先入座位，他们的座位往往也是客厅或餐桌上最尊贵的位置，而宾客们也会自觉谦让以待长者。宴席开始后，主人会主动为长者夹菜添酒，像藏族和蒙古族宴席中会割取羊头和背脊肉给长者，以表示对他的特别敬意。长辈不动筷，晚辈不夹菜；宴席结束时候，长辈不起身，晚辈不离席。这种礼仪与西方人宴会优待女士、以主人自为中心入座的习惯迥然有别。

　　其实不止就座礼仪可见长幼伦理，其他生活待遇方面，如居室的安排方面也可见一斑：潮汕地区非常有代表性的民间建筑格式叫"四点金"。在居室的分配使用方面，也是历来遵循长幼之序、长者优先的原则的。在"四点金"的这个房屋中间的大厅，那是祭祖的地方，大厅两边的"上房"是长辈们居住的卧室，而门厅两侧的"下房"是晚辈与仆人的居室。

　　在我国各民族不论是汉族还是少数民族中，大都有尊重长者和老人的传统。比如满族。传统中，满族晚辈每隔三天要给长辈打千请安，隔五天见长辈得叩头。水族同胞每逢年过节，都会争相邀请村社的寨老来家中赴宴。寨老们德高望重，被看作是幸福的使者，能邀请到他们来自己家里吃饭，对主家而言是个极有面子的事。藏族同胞非常讲究礼仪，在家里，父母长辈是最受尊敬的人；在社会上，年长者也是最受尊敬的人。感恩长辈，以碰头礼为最高，对嫌弃老人，虐待子女或弃婴现象是绝对不能容忍的。鄂伦春人的公社内部要事都要由"乌力楞"会议来商讨决定，而会议成员主要是由各户的老年男女所组成，男子当中以其胡须越长越有权威。而朝鲜族自古以来，就把尊重老人视为家庭乃至整个社会生活中的极为重要的礼节。朝鲜族人民还会为60岁的老人举行生日宴席，叫"花甲宴"。自1982年以来，延边朝鲜族自治州还将每年的8月15日定为老人节。汉族当然也有自己的老人节或敬老节，这就是九月初九重阳节。"重阳"意谓再度焕发青春，寓意健康长寿。

　　总之，长幼有序、尊老爱幼的美德，是中华民族大家庭一个共有的传统。老人们生活在中国，享受着人们的礼敬、爱戴和各种优待照顾。今天社会的发展进步更为老人的健康长寿创造了各种条件，这里真是老年人的幸福乐土。这和我们听到的另一种说法，说"美国是年轻人的天堂、老年人的坟墓"可谓是大异其趣了。还记得新冠疫情暴发之初，呼吸机资源紧张，在西方就出现过所谓的先救年轻人，后救甚至是不救老人的情况。有网友甚至讥称新冠肺炎是"老人清除剂"。而在中国，截至 2020 年 3 月，湖北省共治愈八十岁以上的肺炎患者三千六百多人，医生护士们都以"老人现在比任何时候都需要我"为一种情怀努力地投入自己的工作。这都是值得我们学习的尊老敬老美德精神的表现。

6.4　君臣有义——中国文化对君臣关系的理想图画

中国古代是君主专制时代，君主集权而群臣襄助，共治天下。儒家先哲对建立良好的君臣之道，作了许多的思考。孔子在《论语·为政》中就大量地讨论到了他的政治思想，对如何为君，如何为官，如何治国理政，如何治民等问题提供了他的看法。概论儒家的君臣之道，就两个字——正名。也就是君君、臣臣，各自克尽本分，彼此良好合作，则大同之治可期。若君不君、臣不臣，则必然走向政治的紊乱和失败。这也就是孔子说的："名不正则言不顺，言不顺则事不成，事不成则礼乐不兴，礼乐不兴则刑罚不中，刑罚不中，则民无所措手足。"（《论语·子路》）所以，我们先看一下君之为君、臣之为臣之政治伦理之道。

（1）王道政治视野下的"君君、臣臣"

据统计，中国的封建君主从秦始皇（公元前 221 年）到清宣统（1912）合计出过 493 位帝王。古代的中国人把君主看成"天子"，是臣民的"君父"，臣民自称"臣子""子民"。过去在中国人家庭的中堂一般都悬挂着"天地君亲师"的牌位，可见君主的地位在传统社会中，是很高尚而尊贵的。

按儒家的政治哲学，理想的君主应该努力成为一个明君，他要实行王道政治的"敬天—爱民—尊孔"的三条原则。所谓"敬天"即敬受天命、道尊于势。只有敬天，政权和君王才有超越的合法性；"爱民"即民为邦本、天下往归。只有爱民，政权和君王才有民意的合法性；"尊孔"即尊孔重儒、崇文重教。只有尊孔，政权和君王才有文化的合法性。符合这三条，就是儒家理想的王道政治。践行王道政治的君主，就是好君主，是明君、圣君。古代也确实有一些知名帝王，他们雄才大略、文治武功，在中国政治史上为人所称道，如炎黄二帝、秦始皇嬴政、汉武帝刘彻、唐太宗李世民、女皇武则天、宋太祖赵匡胤、元太祖孛儿只斤·铁木真、明太祖朱元璋、清圣祖爱新觉罗·玄烨、清高宗爱新觉罗·弘历等。

以唐太宗李世民（599—649）为例，这确是一位"马上争天下、马下治天下"的一代英主。毛泽东主席曾总结李世民值得称道的工作方法有四：用怀柔政策平定四方，不急功近利而劳民损兵；不贪图游乐，每早视朝，用心听取各种建议，出言周密；罢朝后和大臣们推心置腹讨论是非；晚上同人高谈经典文事。而在太宗统治时期，政治比较清明，社会相对统一安定，经济繁荣，国力强盛，史称"贞观之治"，使中国成为当时世界上最富强昌盛的封建国家。李世民曾亲撰过一部《帝范》，总结了他心中的人君之道，展现出对人生和世界的深刻体悟，也是他作为开国君主一生经验的总结。《帝范》里阐述的明君之道，包括自身修养的学问、运用权力的学问、使用人才的学问、选任官员的学问、听取意见的学问、杜绝小人的学问，以及如何防止骄傲产生过失、侈靡导致堕落、不公招致乱政等12个重要方面，可说是古代帝王成为明君的基本要求，在今天也仍然值得为国政者参悟借鉴①。综合来看，唐太宗确实符合儒家的王者之道，算得上是我国古代杰出的政治家。

而对何为臣道、何为臣德之类，历来也是学者们乐于讨论的问题。西汉刘向在《说苑》中就把人臣分为所谓的"六正六邪"。西汉刘向在他的《说苑》一书中也论述了为臣之道的"六正六邪"，这"六正"是：高瞻远瞩，防患未然，此为"圣"；虚心尽意，扶善锄恶，此为"良"；夙兴夜寐，进贤不懈，此为"忠"；明察成败，转祸为福，此为"智"；恪尽职守，廉洁奉公，此为"贞"；刚正不阿，敢争敢谏，此为"直"。那么，为臣的"六邪"呢，就是：安官贪禄，不务公事，此为"庸"；溜须拍马，曲意逢迎，此为"谀"；巧言令色，嫉贤妒能，此为"奸"；巧舌如簧，挑拨离间，此为"谗"；专权擅势，结党营私，此为"贼"；幕后指挥，兴风作浪，此为"险"。

在我看来，按儒家的根本思路，要把握"人臣之道"同样需要将其纳入王道政治的大框架来理解。即臣者的角色是在臣职的位置上，襄助君上力行王道，要上应天命、仁爱生民、弘扬儒道，所谓"致君尧舜上，要使民风淳"，实现"复三代"即大同之治的理想社会。正臣道、修臣德、尽臣职，是臣子本分和根本任务。能恪尽此道，则臣是贤良之臣，官是正直之官，是社稷栋梁，是天下干才，值得国家好好重视和爱惜。我国古代的名臣代不乏人，如周公旦、管仲、李斯、萧何、曹操、诸葛亮、房玄龄、王安石、岳飞、文天祥、耶律楚材、刘

---

① 在紫禁城中许多殿堂中都悬挂着各种匾额和楹联，如太和殿的"建极绥猷"匾、中和殿的"允执厥中"匾，保和殿的"皇建有极"匾，乾清宫的"正大光明"匾，养心殿的"中正仁和"匾，西暖阁的"勤政亲贤"等。它们都蕴含着供皇帝们参悟和践行的有关治国理政的"王道智慧"。

基、张居正等，不胜枚举。他们都在为臣之道（某些方面）上可圈可点。

以北宋的"包青天"包拯（999—1062）为例，我看他是在为臣之道的"六正"上做得比较全面的一位名臣。包拯，字希仁，北宋庐州合肥人。包拯历仕端州知州、知谏院、庐州知州、开封府尹、监察御史、龙图阁直学士等职，在宦海中沉浮 24 年。他之所以得到"包青天"的美誉，在于他不徇私情、大奸必摧的无畏精神和忧国忧民的高尚品质。如在庐州知州任上，包拯的舅舅触犯法律。包拯秉公执法，将舅舅处以鞭笞之刑。为此，包拯郑重其事地订立了包氏家训："后世子孙仕宦有贪赃枉法者，不得葬于包家坟茔，不从我志，非我子孙！"他一生曾向仁宗上奏章数百次，主要内容有：练兵选将，防止契丹和西夏的侵扰；救济饥民，反对横征暴敛；弹劾皇亲国戚、贪官污吏。这洋洋数百篇奏议，既洋溢着疾恶如仇的凛然正气，又充满了对国家、对黎民大海一样的深情。包公的故事虽经后人演绎而有所变形，但人民把他作为清官的化身，使他成为黎民百姓向往正义、鞭笞邪恶的精神寄托。

当然，中国文化也用自己特有的方式表达了对"清正廉洁"政治品格的欣赏和追求。如历朝历代都为忠廉正直之臣立各种牌坊和祠庙，尊为人臣的楷模与典范。如各地官署和衙门都会铭刻各类德政楹联和牌匾敦促官员们自省自警。河南省内乡县古县衙是我国目前保存较完整的封建时代县级官署衙门之一，在这个衙门大门上有一副远近闻名、睹之令人肃然的楹联："得一官不荣，失一官不辱，勿说一官无用，地方全靠一官。吃百姓之饭，穿百姓之衣，莫道百姓可欺，自己也是百姓。"如为纪念东汉清官羊续拒贿悬鱼，而将"悬鱼"化为民居建筑屋脊边缘的一个装饰性构件，以尊崇清廉的品德。在福建省福安市有一个唐肃宗敕封的山村，就叫"廉村"，提倡清正廉洁正是这个村落的传统特色。而明代曹瑞的《官箴》三十六字，言简而意深，流传至今，仍在国家反腐倡廉工作中为人所引用："吏不畏吾严而畏吾廉，民不服吾能而服吾公。廉则吏不敢慢，公则民不敢欺。公生明，廉生威。"

（2）君臣之道转向公民之道

按儒家的理想，君王和臣下是在王道政治的理念下同心同德、各司其职、相互合作的一群"替天行道"的执政人群。为了共同的理想和事业，"君使臣以礼，臣事君以忠"（《论语·八佾》）。如此的明君，臣子当忠敬其事，要尽心地辅佐，所谓"勿欺也，而犯之。"（《论语·宪问》）如诸葛亮事刘备，鞠躬尽瘁死而后已。君无大过，臣辄不守其道，渎职卸责，甚至僭越不轨，则为乱臣贼子不容于天下，此又如曹操篡汉例。对无德乱政的昏君暴君，儒家是反对滥行愚忠的。拥有中庸智慧的儒家的行事风格，从来都是实事求是的。孔子就认为君主"其身不正，虽令不行"（《论语·子路》）。孟子提出"民贵君轻"的看法，认为君臣以礼对等相待，你不拿臣下当人而轻践若犬马土芥，那君臣之间只能是寇仇关系了①。对原始儒家而言，"王道"最重要的是"道"，而不是"王"本身。他们认为对不守王道而失去合法性的暴君暴政，革命是必然而必需的。如"汤武革命，顺乎天而应乎民"，所谓"文王一怒而安天下之民"（《孟子·梁惠王下》）。

但革命纠偏论似乎也不能根本上解决问题。因为换过一个王朝，还是会出各种不守王道的昏君暴君和形形色色的乱臣贼子。他们沆瀣一气、荼毒天下，然后呢，又起而革命，治乱交替、清浊相激，往复循环，把儒家那套君君臣臣和仁政王道的梦想踩得粉碎。一部中华政治史，君道臣道，总不上道。王道之种，从没有开花结果，健康的政治伦理关系始终是虚空幻影。根本原因还是儒家没有可能改变"势尊于道"的专制主义的封建政治权力结构。

儒家这个由祭司阶层进化而来的士大夫集团，是知识分子和官僚阶层合二为一的封建统治阶级的主体。他既是传统的王道政治（及其指导下的君臣伦理关系）的设计者，同时也是封建专制主义权力结构体制的建构者。他一方面大讲特讲修身为本、内圣外王和君君臣臣之道，充满了道德理想主义的美好氛围。但另外一方面，他又建构和细密化了以神权、君权、夫权、族权为媒介，以控制人、轻视人、异化人为特征的东方专制主义政治体系。理想主义的人文梦想掩饰或装点着专制主义的权力傲慢，这两者都是儒家，表里相关、交织而生，剪不断理还乱。或者说，儒家的王道政治，它固然包含着部分的民本政治的理性诉求，但儒家的民本政治不是当代的民主政治。民本政治是君主做主的古典政治，不是人民民主的理性政治。两者隔着一个资本主义的时代差距。传统政治现代化的过程，就是走出专制独断的"权力的傲慢"的过程，就是建立开放的、可制衡的、可有效有序及时更新的民主的公共权力的过程。

当代中国当然早已经没有了君主制度，也再没有君臣伦理关系的问题，我们都是有独立人格和自由精神、遵守契约和依法行事的现代公民。但即便是作为公民，我们仍然需要践行一定的政治伦理。如我们仍然要忠于我们的国家，仍然需要加强爱国主义教育、弘扬爱国主义精神，为国家的复兴和强大而努力工作。现代的爱国主义者要有世界视野和人类命运共同体意识，这也是儒家讲的天下意识和宇宙情怀。

---

① 君之视臣如手足，则臣视君如腹心；君之视臣如犬马，则臣视君如国人；君之视臣如土芥，则臣视君如寇仇。（《孟子》）

现代公民政治中的从政者，当代的政治家们当然需要有大量古人没有的现代新知识与技能。但他们仍然需要谦虚地从儒家传统智慧中汲取治国理政的有益经验和反面教训，以锻炼和增强自己为国家服务、为人民服务的现代政治本领。孔子儒学中很多思想都涉及今天所谓的"领导力"修炼。从政者如何加强自我修养？主政者应有何种驭人之术？理政当如何循序渐进？以及今天追求的善治是什么？目的如何完成？诸如此类。古人仍可以给我们宝贵的教导和启迪。传统的中国士大夫所崇尚的青松之志、冰雪之操，他们那种向道崇德、清正廉洁、坚毅刚正和兼济天下的情怀和追求，都值得我们今天的政治家和公务员们去继续弘扬。

6.5 朋友有信——中国古人的处友之道

《诗经》有云："伐木丁丁，鸟鸣嘤嘤。出自幽谷，迁于乔木。嘤其鸣矣，求其友声。"

这诗写得好，就在于它说出了诗人渴望友情的真心诚愿。朋友是社会生活中非常普遍的人际关系。朋友的存在让我们不那么孤独寂寞冷。朋友也不在乎数量，所谓"人生得一知己足矣，斯世当以同怀视之"。那中国古人的处友之道又是怎样的呢？

首先，在儒家看来，"益者三友，损者三友"。益友还是损友，先要搞搞清楚。

所谓"益者三友"即友直、友谅、友多闻（《论语·季氏》）。"友直"就是直率无隐，互相给予忠告。孔子主张朋友间要坦诚相见，有意见要直说。如孔子的发小原壤"夷俟"，也就是叉开两条腿坐着迎接孔子，而孔子见他如此无礼，就不客气地数落他"幼而不逊悌，长而无述焉，老而不死，是为贼"（《论语·宪问》），意思是"你小时候就不谦恭敬长，长大了没有什么值得称道的成就，老了还不死掉，真是个害人的家伙"。这话听着虽然很刺耳，但孔子跟原壤本是发小关系，一辈子的友情，所以孔子对他有意见也不会藏着掖着。而那种心里头有意见，嘴巴上不说，表面上还装作跟他友好即"匿怨而友其人"，在孔子看来，是虚假而可耻的行为。当然，朋友之间，坦诚归坦诚，提意见也要讲究方式方法。子贡问友，子曰："忠告而善道之，不可则止，无自辱焉。"（《论语·颜渊》）实在不听也就算了，不然反而会自取其辱。"友谅"呢？友谅就是朋友应当彼此包容、互相体谅对方的难处。即便原壤被孔子骂得很不堪，但孔子仍然包容这位老兄弟，对他热忱关怀和帮助。原壤的妈妈死了，孔子就过去帮忙料理后事。而原壤不但不帮忙，还跳到棺材上载歌载舞。学生们都看不下去，劝孔子别搭理这样放浪的发小了。孔子却说："丘闻之，亲者毋失其为亲也，故者毋失其为故也。"（《礼记·檀弓下》）亲人终究是亲人，老朋友终究是老朋友，又怎么能忍心抛却？可见孔子是一个惜缘、念旧、重感情的人，因此他对朋友总能有最大的包容和体谅。那"友多闻"呢？就是朋友要博学多识。孔子自己是好学之人，他当然喜欢广见多闻之人，可以互相交流探讨感兴趣的学问。但他的朋友当然三教九流社会各界，未必都是知识分子。但有一点，"多闻"的指向就是好学，不断追求人生有所进益，而无论是求学上，还是人格修为上皆如是。如孔子所欣赏的好友、卫国贤人"蘧伯玉年五十而知四十九年非"（《淮南子·原道训》）。所以深得孔子的敬重和赞叹。贤友益友，互相丰富、彼此提高、滋养性灵。所以孔子说"乐多贤友"，又说有朋自远方来不亦乐乎，显然，这些都是生命之友的相会，故而令人有欢喜雀跃痛快淋漓之状。而"损者三友"呢，即"友便辟，友善柔，友便佞"，也就是口是心非、巧言令色，不真诚、无爱心之辈，当然很讨厌，生活中要尤其注意鉴别，敬而远之。

其次，儒家认为朋友之间要讲义气、愿帮忙。

所谓患难见真情，有人和我们能"出入相友，守望相助，疾病相扶持"（《孟子·滕文公上》），那真是人生的大幸事了。真正的朋友平时彼此不客气，有事讲义气，做人有豪气。须知：朋友意气相投，更该义薄云天，彼此有担当的义务。孔子平时对朋友就不客气，除非分享祭祀之肉，朋友送他再名贵的车马，孔子都不会说个谢字。但若遇到朋友不幸去世而无人收殓，孔子就会义不容辞地出来承担。在周游列国的路上，有一次在野外偶遇神交久矣的贤人程子，孔子非常欢喜得偿所愿。在得知程子生活困窘后，孔子就让子路从后车取来十匹鲁缟，赠送给程子改善生活，子路老大不情愿地抱怨老师不该在路上交朋友，出手还这么大方。孔子就借用《诗经》里的诗句来启发子路说：野有蔓草，零露溥兮。有美一人，清扬宛兮。邂逅相遇，适我愿兮。可见，孔子对自己认可的朋友，一见如故，对接济他们的困难也是责无旁贷而毫不计较的。

再次，朋友有信，也是儒家再三强调的处友之道的重要原则。

孔子人生三大愿就是："老者安之，朋友信之，少者怀之。"所谓"朋友有信""与朋友交，言而有信""人而无信不知其可"之类的语录都反映出孔子特别重视这个"信"字。"信"是信任，但更是诚信。也就是说你有真诚实在的德性，人品可靠，你说的话做的事，才是可信的，值得信托和依靠的。如孔门子路就是非常实诚守信的人，"千乘之国，不信其盟，而信子之一言"（《左传·哀公十四年》），可见信之为德的重要性。孔子所赞叹的吴国的贤人季札也是一个非常诚信的君子。《说苑》中记载了一段"季札挂剑"的故事："季札将使于晋，带宝剑而行，过徐君。徐君观剑，不言而色欲之。季子为有晋之使，未之献也，然其心许之矣。反，则徐君已死于楚。悔之，……乃至墓，以剑悬徐君墓树而去。"季札这种虽未明言承诺，仅仅因为一念"心许之"就一定要做到，实在算得上诚信的最高境界了。

另外，儒家还乐观地相信，有德者必有友。

我们每个人都可以得到别人的友情，但有个前提，就是你先是个好人。像孔子说的"德不孤，必有邻"，相信一个善良的好人是不会孤单的。德性如玉，就那么人见人爱。只要我们是谦谦君子，居心"敬而无失，与人恭而有礼，四海之内皆兄弟也"。孟子更指出要交"一乡之友""一国之友"乃至交"天下之友"而犹不足，就尚论古人，与古人做跨时空的精神之友。诗人和理学家们从天人合一、万物一体的哲学高度上拥抱天地万物，说："静观万物皆自得，四时佳兴与人同。""好鸟枝头亦朋友，落花水面亦文章。"这种视野中，心性明通、万物有灵，鸥鹭忘机、猿猴献果，真可谓是处处可得其友了。这让我想起我喜欢的美国作家梭罗《瓦尔登湖》里的一段话："就在这滴答滴答的雨声中，我屋子周围的每一个声音和景象都有着无穷尽无边际的友爱，……每一支小小松针都富于同情心地胀大起来，成了我的朋友。"

总之呢，中国传统的友道思想历久流传深入人心，在悠久的中华文化史上留下了许多可圈可点的友情故事。如俞伯牙与钟子期高山流水遇知音的幸运，真是可遇不可求。魏晋名士"竹林七贤"志趣相投，交情颇深。他们常为竹林之会，纵情美酒、畅谈人生。其中的嵇康曾和山巨源因事绝交，而他临死前却嘱咐儿子嵇绍说："巨源在，汝不孤矣。"这种人绝交而情至坚的友谊，也是让人唏嘘相看的。而唐诗三百首中很多诗篇，抒发的也是满满的朋友之情。这些友谊的诗歌，或写"故人具鸡黍，邀我至田家"的农庄相聚的惬意，或写"劝君更尽一杯酒，西出阳关无故人"的惜别依依；既有抒发"海内存知己，天涯若比邻"的欣慰，更有"莫见长安行乐处，空令岁月易蹉跎"的叮咛。如李白与杜甫、白居易和元稹这些名士，他们对挚友也是各种魂牵梦萦、精诚相推，让读者为他们在字里行间所流露出的尚友高风所深深触动、怀想连连。

最后，在儒学影响下形成的中国传统伦理思想体系博大精深气象万千，它注重人伦、人道的研究，首推五伦，讲究父慈子孝、夫义妇听、君仁臣忠、长惠幼顺、朋友有信，倡导"四维八德"等修己待人的美德范畴的涵养，更从根本上发明人性本善的原理，为教化人心，对治人欲，修炼品性，完成人格，为中华民族的文明成长作出了重要的贡献。在我看来，《朱子家训》中的这段话，可谓是中华民族传统伦理思想的精粹和集中概括，我们可以一起用心诵读一遍，共同体会一下古仁人之心的所珍所贵：

　　君之所贵者，仁也。臣之所贵者，忠也。父之所贵者，慈也。子之所贵者，孝也。兄之所贵者，友也。弟之所贵者，恭也。夫之所贵者，和也。妇之所贵者，柔也。事师长贵乎礼也，交朋友贵乎信也。见老者，敬之；见幼者，爱之。有德者，年虽下于我，我必尊之；不肖者，年虽高于我，我必远之。慎勿谈人之短，切莫矜己之长。仇者以义解之，怨者以直报之，随所遇而安之。人有小过，含容而忍之；人有大过，以理而谕之。勿以善小而不为，勿以恶小而为之。人有恶，则掩之；人有善，则扬之。处世无私仇，治家无私法。勿损人而利己，勿妒贤而嫉能。勿称忿而报横逆，勿非礼而害物命。见不义之财勿取，遇合理之事则从。诗书不可不读，礼义不可不知。子孙不可不教，童仆不可不恤。斯文不可不敬，患难不可不扶。守我之分者，礼也；听我之命者，天也。人能如是，天必相之。此乃日用常行之道，若衣服之于身体，饮食之于口腹，不可一日无也，可不慎哉！

　　中国人民将永远珍视自己民族的传统伦理，创新发展古典的美德精神，向世界展现中华民族在新时代的文明风范和美好形象。

The Sixth Chapter:

The Benevolent Loves All
—Traditional Chinese Ethics

You may have noticed that humanism boasts one of the characters of Chinese culture. Chinese culture has always valued the human being, but this man, but the man represents the one living in their groups. He then should belong to various kinds of relations that deal with people. This is what we call "ethics". In other words, values and principles that arrange and handle these relations and make them suitable for social order can be defined as ethics. Confucianism, among various kinds of relations between humans, puts "the five ethical relationships" which means relations between father and son, sovereign and subject, husband and wife, as well as brothers and friends. The five relationships are the unavoidable and fundamental human identity and social relations. They are like five paths that everyone needs to follow. In order to guide people to these five paths, Confucianism helps set the corresponding "traffic" rules. In the first volume of *Teng Wengong*, *Mencius*, human relations are summed up as something that covers "affection between father and son, rites between the emperor and his subjects, a hierarchical order between husband and wife, the old and the young, and fidelities between friends". The rule of five ethics contains meanings respectively. According to Confucianism, ethics is the human implementation of heaven's principle or heaven's way, the main field of moral cultivation, and the main means to help people to complete the socialized civilized personality. And it wishes to guide everyone to their place and act dutifully—father and mother to be kind; son and daughter to be filial; the husband to walk the right way and the wife to follow her husband; the elder to love the young; and the young to listen to the elder; the sovereign to be benevolent and courtiers loyal; as well as friends to trust each other. Thus, an Oriental ethical system of morality is woven, which covers all interpersonal fields from the families to the society, from clan to politics. From men and women to the young and old, and is characterized by benevolence-orientation, mutual love and mutual respect, emotional harmony and overall balance. Now, I will analyze more about the five cardinal relationships and in such a society of Chinese people, their real power and influence.

6.1　Different Emotion Expressions between Husband and Wife—How Couples Got Along in Ancient China

The five relationships begin with that between husband and wife. Husband and wife are the origin of the later relationship between parents and children. Therefore, we first talk about different emotion expressions between husband and wife.

When we talk about couples, we have to talk about men and women first. The concept of male and female in traditional Chinese society is very interesting. It is very balanced, as shown in the Taiji diagram, which is the understanding model of "the way of Yin and Yang". Yin and Yang are complementary, mutually growing and unified. In the traditional Chinese society, man and woman are positioned unequally. It can be explained like this: for man and woman, man is called "Khien", while woman is called "Khwan"; man represents heaven and woman, earth; man, the sun and woman, the moon; man, Yang and woman, Yin; man working outside the family, and woman doing housework; man, energetic and woman, calm; man, severity and woman, mercy; man, strength and woman, delicacy; man, ambitious and woman, conservative. The Yin-yang theory clearly shows a kind of dynamic complementarity based on the gender difference between men and women, which maintains the natural foundation of human society. Men and women are the integration of gender differences, just as Plato wrote in the *Symposium*: in the past, human beings were bisexual. Zeus divided them into two halves. Since then, the two halves have been wandering around the world looking for each other, and love is the longing for the other half we have lost.

It can be said that ancient Chinese, on the one hand, recognized the humanity, and that men and women were a complementary body of Yin and Yang, they acknowledged that love happens between men and women represents the rules and orderliness of heaven and earth. It is only right and proper to see men and women attracted by each other and enjoy a relationship. Yet ancient Chinese also noticed other aspects. To express temperament is people's nature restrained by the ritual. Families should therefore arrange etiquette to fulfill their wish. For example, you first must become an adult, such as the male 20 lines plus crown ceremony, the female 15 lines plus hairpin ceremony, and then can discuss marriage. The ceremony of marriage is to bind the love between two different surname's families, which concerns the growth and prosperity of their future generations. Therefore, the ceremony should be arranged with caution. Six ceremonies should be arranged before the marriage.

Specifically, six ceremonies of traditional Chinese marriage represent six procedures: 1. Proposing: the match maker proposes a marriage, and the bridegroom makes a proposal. 2. Birthday matching: asking the birthday of the bride. 3. The boy's family's divination: to make a divination at the ancestral temple to see if the couple match each other. 4. Wedding gifts: also known as "betrothal gifts", which means the male send betrothal gifts to the bride. 5. The fifth rite boasts "Picking auspicious wedding date", which means the boy's family fixing the date for wedding and ask for the girl's approval. 6. The six represents Wedding Ceremony, which means the female's family send their bride, while the male's family welcome her together, and hold the so-called heaven and earth worship ceremony. These six procedures are carried out in turns. In the ancient people's eyes, only the marriage that follows the six rites are legislative. Or else it can be regarded as indecency, the shameful "illicit affair".

6.1.1   There are several characteristics to understand about Chinese traditional marriage

Firstly, Chinese marriage in ancient times was indeed forced marriage, rather than self-determinate marriage—the match arranged by parents' order and matchmakers' word. Under that circumstance, the unmarried barely knew or got contact with each other and they seldom enjoyed any right to deliver their own opinions. Their marriage was totally arranged by parents and matchmakers. In fact, free love was common in the pre-Qin period. There are hundreds of poems in *The Book of Songs* that talks about love stories, being both sentimental and romantic and move readers deeply. For example, in *Riverside Rendezvous* and *My Love in White*, romantic affairs of young men and women in the State of Zheng were vividly described when they were having spring together on the banks of the Zhen river and Wei river on March 3rd. This seems to be similar to the customs of many ethnic minorities in China, which use " Onion Picking Festival"

"Folk Song Festival" "Long-Drum Meeting" "Daughter's Meeting" and other occasions to do love affairs between men and women. It is a pity that the feudal ethics became more and more restrictive and conservative, thus losing the ancient free and lively customs.

Secondly, ancient marriage mainly followed the exogamy system without forbiddance of endogamy. What does "exogamy" mean? Ancient Chinese advocated no marriage among the families with the same surname. Therefore, marrying people from other families is called "exogamy". Whereas "endogamy" represents the marriage cousins (the children of a brother and sister). Some ethnic minorities, such as the Tujia ethnic group, have a special rule that girls are given priority to marry their uncles' sons, which is called "returning bones". Otherwise, it is necessary to pay compensation to the uncle's family. Another example of endogamy features the child bride living in the future-husband's house. It is a disguised endogamy. Of course, these endogamies are long gone.

Thirdly, in the ancient times, when it came to marriage, people paid special attention to the background of both families. It followed the custom of couples from "houses of similar 'Men Dang' and 'Hu Dui'". "Men Dang" and "Hu Dui" are two components of the hall in Chinese traditional architecture. Later, they were used as metaphors to indicate that couples should come from families of equal social status. From similar family background, boy and girl may also share equal level quality. What's more, unqualified men and women for marriage are also noticeable. For instance, five kinds of women that men should never marry as follows—families with rebels, licentious members, criminals, incurable or contagious diseases, or that lose their mother at an early age. Girls growing in these families may not be the good choice for marriage. Surely, there exists exception as well. Not all families and parents strictly follow the principle of choosing men or women of equal social status. Some parents are visionary and far-sighted. Thus, they choose men with a promising future to marry. Take Confucius for an example. One of his students—Gongye Chang used to be in prison. Yet in Confucius' perspective, Gongye is both a good student and a dependable person. He was put into prison with an unwarranted charge. Hence, he agreed that Gongye Chang married his daughter.

Fourthly, in the ancient times, when it came to marriage, people paid especial attention to requirements of feminine virtue and ethics. In the traditional Chinese society, good qualities and moralities of women were widely requested, which, in Sima Qian's word, can be explained as "it is delightful for a man to meet with a right woman". It is because a good woman can prosper a family. Why? A good-natured girl will turn to be a virtuous wife, and a virtuous wife will turn to be a kindly mother, then a kindly mother will also cultivate an adorable child. The moral character of a girl can affect the rise and fall of a family, which is so important, therefore, ancient Chinese people highly emphasized "the value of educating a qualified girl", and promotes cultivating women with "Three Obediences and Four Virtues". The so-called "Three Obediences" represents obedience to father before marriage, obedience to husband after marriage and obedience to son after husband's death in all, these rules indicate the requirements of women to be obedient, submissive and compliant. The above are the "Three Obediences". When it comes to the "Four Virtues", They are: first womanly character; second, womanly conversation; third, womanly appearance; fourth, womanly work. Womanly character means not extraordinary talents or intelligence, but modesty, cheerfulness, chastity, constancy, orderliness, blameless conduct and perfect manners. Womanly conversation means not eloquence or brilliant talk, but refined choice of words, never to use coarse or violent language, to know when to speak and when to stop speaking. Womanly appearance means not beauty or prettiness of face, but personal cleanliness and faultlessness in dress and attire. Lastly, womanly work means not any special skill or ability, but assiduous attention to the spinning room, never to waste time in laughing and giggling and work in the kitchen to prepare clean and wholesome food, especially when there are guests in the house. The "Three Obedience" and "Four Virtues" originated from the Confucian *Rites of Rites* and *Rites of Zhou*, and were later advocated in classical women's education books such as *Four Books for Women* represented by Ban Zhao's *Lessons for Women* in the Han Dynasty.

Fifthly, the issue of divorce. According to the clues of female morality, if a woman loses morality or does not obey the feminine way, she may be criticized and abandoned. Which brings us to the issue of divorce. We also need to know about what divorce means in the ancient times. Rules have also been noted as "Seven Reasons for Abandoning a Wife" and "Three Forbiddances for Husband to Abandon a Wife". The "Seven Reasons" listed seven occasions that allow divorce: disobeying their parents, having no son, having an affair, envying other wives, suffering from incurable disease, stirring up trouble and stealing. I wonder if anyone has ever noticed why Wang Xifeng, a famous character in *The Story of the Stone*, was abandoned by her husband. What are the reasons for it? First of all, she has no son; second, she steals money; third, she is said to disobey parents of her husband, etc. She can be defined as one committing all the seven abandoning reasons. What are the three conditions? First, the wife who does not have parental home to return to, which means she has no one to depend on anymore, if she is driven by husband. Then, where can she go? Second, if she takes care of the husband's parents with him and observe the "three-year-funeral-period", then the husband should never mention the idea of divorce. Third, the woman has been through ups and downs with her husband should not be abandoned, either. It is said that "the wife one married when he was poor should not be discarded in his affluence". Therefore, divorce cannot happen in the above three circumstances. What does these rules tell us? Ancient Chinese were not totally unaware of women and put value only on the male's perspective.

According to the attitude of early Confucianism, "couple are like friends who can live together and separate as well", in which we can see a concept featuring rather relaxing and less serious relation. Before Middle Ages, divorce was also not a strange phenomenon. Confucius family can be regarded as another example. Three generations of Confucius' family had seen divorce. Confucius' wife, his daughter-in-law, as well as his granddaughter-in-law, all had to leave their husbands. In *the Book of Rites*, there are even the proposal of three months of trial marriage. That is, "three months later, the bride should go to the ancestral temple and report to these spirits that she has come here to be the housewife" (temple presentation 庙见). So, before entering the ancestral temple, the so-called "probation period", they are not qualified to be the "housewife". Much evidence proved that among family cultures during the Northern Song Dynasty, discrimination did not happen a lot to remarried women. Compared with men who married again, there were even more supporting conditions for those women. In *the Rule of Yizhuang* (land for charity) established by Fan Zhongyan, it was distinctly manifested in the 13th rule. It also showed protection and assistance towards women who were more vulnerable in the society.

6.1.2　How to Describe the Quality of Ancient Chinese Marriage?

Firstly, the traditional arranged marriages are not all without love, Of course, it may not be so good. Love is a thing without reason, even under the heavy stone of arranged marriage, it can also take root and sprout. So the arranged couple does not mean that they do not have passion for love. It is true that in China the bride and bridegroom as a rule never see each other until the marriage day, and yet that there is love between even bride and bridegroom, such as the vows of loving couples in *Book of Poetry*: "Loving union with wife is like the music of lutes." "We held their hands; we were to grow old together with them." "For life or for death, however separated, to our wives we pledged our words."

In addition, love also can be seen in these four lines of poetry from the Tang Dynasty below. "In the bridal chamber last night stood red candles, waiting for the morning to salute the father and mother in the hall. Toilet finished, in a low voice she asks her sweetheart husband, are the shades in my painted eyebrows quite à la mode?" We can picture such a scene in our minds: a shy bride is waiting for the morning to meet her husband's parents. After she finished dressing, she asked her dear husband softly whether her eyebrows were painted generously and in style. It can be seen from this that there is love between them, although they did not meet before marriage. Even then, they also had love on the second day of the wedding.

Another ancient Chinese female poet Li Qingzhao said: "The flowers were silently falling, into the river quietly flowing; there should be one love knot tight, that tied the two lovesick far apart. How could I dispel the emotion that just left from my knitted brows. Then entered into my stirred heart?" As an poet of the Southern Song Dynasty Xin Qiji said in his poem: "If I'm not suffering from the parting pain, I won't believe gray hair in the world to gain." Still Su Shi said: "For ten long years the living of the dead knows nought. Through to mind not brought, could the dead be forgot? Her lonely grave is for, a thousand miles away. To whom can I my grief convey?" This is the poem he made to memorize his wife, who died ten years ago. And the poem was passed down through generations for thousands of years.

It can be said that if there remained no sincere love between Su Shi and his wife, he would not make up stories with such touching words. If so, he could not wrote such a poem and opera that really strike a chord with us. Hence, it can be seen that even in times of arranged marriage, love, and even sweet and long-lasting romance still existed. There are several elders in my clan whose marriage had been arranged, and two of them even married their child-bride. But both have enjoyed their marriage and grew old together with their wife. If arranged marriage means no love, then is Chinese culture lack of the history without love? And are we descendants of people who never enjoyed love? Are we able to love others? I really doubt this judgement!

Of course, I'm not saying that arranged marriage is better than self-determinate marriage. Perhaps the truth is that arranged marriages are not necessarily loveless, but they are not necessarily better. According to professor Fei Xiaotong, in his book *Fertility System: Cooperation of Husband and Wife*. Traditional couple relationship often gives in to the development of a family. Therefore, developing family is often much more valued than personal emotion between the couple. They are both busy with family affairs and too tired to communicate with each other. In today's words, it can be described as follows—since love turns to kinship, old couples do not communicate mutual love with each other. It's like a pair of hands—the left hand and the right hand, yet is this feeling really means love? It is really hard to tell.

Secondly, while we criticize the dregs of suppressing women's rights in the traditional Chinese way of husband and wife, we should still pay tribute to the strong resilience and selfless sacrifice of traditional Chinese women.

The traditional female morality education involves various connotations. It is necessary to analyze which are the attitudes polluted by the feudal concept of male centrism and which are the basic desirable and valuable virtues. In traditional societies, women were expected to be good daughters at home, good daughters-in-law in marriage, and good mothers after giving birth. They didn't get any education since childhood. When they became adults, they separated their families and married others. They tried to be filial to their parents-in-law, take care of their husband and children, and take charge of the overall management of all kinds of household chores. After winter and spring, they had no regrets. And at the core of this "good women" is everything centered on home and family, and even total selflessness.

Ku Hung-Ming once used Hebrew poetry to compare Chinese women and believed that both were his feminine ideal: "Who can find a virtuous woman? For her price is far above rubies. The heart of her husband doth safely trust in her. She rises also while it is yet night and giveth meat to her household and a portion to her maidens. She loved her hands to the spindle and her fingers hold the distaff. She is not afraid of snow for her household; for all her household are clothed in scarlet. She opened her mouth with wisdom and in her tongue is the law of kindness. She looked well to the ways of her household and eaten not the bread of idleness. Her children rise up and call her blessed, her husband also and he praised her. " It can be said that in a nation, women are the flowers of civilization and the best embodiment of the life character and humanistic spirit of that nation. An ideal traditional Chinese woman who is gentle, courteous and frugal is almost a shining sage in her family. But behind this noble brilliance, how much humiliation and generous sacrifice, such selflessness, in exchange for the happiness, stability and prosperity of families. Without great good wives and mothers, there would be no great Chinese nation and Chinese history.

For example, the "widow's observance" has always been criticized. In fact, we need to give more sympathy and understanding to them. For a widow, she may be able to leave the family and remarry when her husband dies. But there are old people and young children in the home, how can she bear to walk away? In that case, "widow's chastity" is still a virtue behavior of sacrificing oneself and completing the family in a sense. I know that the traditional values of women's morality have been estranged and even rejected by modern people, but the noble character of ancient women that blooms in suffering and the "selfless belief" that lives for their families cannot help but make people look up and move.

Thirdly, the traditional feudal ethics of the male power center is the poison that damages the marital relationship between husband and wife.

Tolstoy once said: "Happy families are all alike; every unhappy family is unhappy in its own way. " Under traditional Chinese marriages, if the cause of unhappy marriage can be analyzed, then it should be listed as follows.

To begin with, orders from parents to marry someone can't be refused. The young have no freedom to choose the one for marriage or divorce. Since the wife he marries is not known by him, it's hard to meet a soul mate. Even if one finds his or her true love, the marriage won't happen without the approval from their parents. As the tragedy of Jiao Zhongqing and Liu Lanzhi in the poem—A Pair of Peacocks Southeast Fly; the story of Lu You and Tang Wan in the Phoenix Hairpin; as well as the story of Shen Fu and Chen Yun in Six Records of a Floating Life. In traditional society, marriage is not a private affair between men and women, but a clan family affair from the beginning. The decision to marry or divorce is not made by the husband and wife, but by the parents or clans.

Secondly, one significant reason goes to the male-chauvinism or the men-oriented concept. It is the conventional discrimination such as "the husband guides his wife" or "women are inferior to men" that lays up trouble for the disharmonious. We can take the popularity of polygamy as a example. Ancient people advocated polygamy, featuring three wives and four concubines. Why do men need so many concubines? The grand saying is "there are three unfilial, no children is the greatest", so to take more concubines to have more children. It is heard that Ku Hung-Ming, a scholar of the Republic of China, who advocated polygamy once delivered a concept of "teapot and teacups". He described man as teapot and woman as teacup. According to him, a teapot is born to be matched with several cups. He also praised wives' permission, even initiative, to arrange concubines for their husbands (without jealousy) as a virtue of "selfless altruism" in traditional Chinese women. This is, of course, very ridiculous. Then, why did a man need so many wives and concubines? In my eyes, it can be traced back to their innate evil nature. Master Watanabe Junichi, uses biomedical knowledge to analyze man's instinct. Man is essentially animal driven by desire and nearly impossible to avoid playing the field.

What should be criticized more, however, is the feudal system of male chauvinism that amplifies the greed of human nature. It was this system that enabled men to possess and dominate more women in a variety of plausible ways, and imposed on women some ideas that today seem perverse, such as the idea that men are superior to women, the idea of virginity, being loyal to one's husband and "keeping chastity is prior to starving to death". In addition, there are some other feudal subcultures that severely restrain women, such as maid culture and foot-binding culture, maid culture, chastity culture, and even some so-called "wife-renting" culture all represent the cruel restraints for ancient Chinese women that made their lives a misfortune. In the introduction to *the history of Chinese women's life*, Mr. Chen Dongyuan even directly declared:

"The women in our history are only the women who have been destroyed. The history of our women's life is only a history of women who have been destroyed."

Brief summary: the original Confucian ethical culture fundamentally guaranteed the completely equal cultural status of men and women with the philosophy of "one Yin and one Yang is the way of heaven". Therefore, all kinds of feudal dregs of male supremacy and female inferiority deposited in later generations violate the tenet and true spirit of Confucianism, which must not be accepted by Confucius, Mencius and true Confucianists. Confucius respected people's natural desire, and at the same time he attached importance to the procedure of etiquette and law. He firmly believed in the goodness of human nature, but he was also worried about people's failure to integrate knowledge with action and change their ways. Confucius severely criticized carnalism, believing that excessive carnation would lead to failure. Confucius criticized the indifferent playboy by saying: "O, Tang Di flowers! You're so beautifully swinging. How can it be said that I don't miss you, it's only because I live too far away. " Confucius made a judgement to this explanation: "Still, you don't really miss her. Otherwise, the distance is out of question. "

With the evolvement of the society, based on equality between men and women, free love, free marriage, as well as free divorce are all permitted for common people. However, do free love and free marriage really bring happiness to people nowadays? As it turns out, the answer is not always positive. As men and women are busy satisfying their emotion and feeling the delight of random marriage and divorce, the freedom they boast never brings them true love. Such as non-marriage, dink living, Dutch couples (financial independence), various extramarital affairs. Is marriage necessary in the future? Do couple that consist of a family remain necessary in the future society? Many people have lost faith in it.

It seems to me that when the young of mankind no longer believe in love, do not want to marry, have no enthusiasm for procreation, the society as a whole is old and lifeless, it is a warning. True civilization is alive and vitality, when the divorce rate is high and the fertility rate is low, civilization is no longer civilization. according to the traditional Chinese ethical concept, marriage and family are still worth having. Marriage and family can inspire our love and sense of responsibility, enable us to learn to bear and be willing to sacrifice. The existence of family can even move us to be selfless. Therefore, we can avoid superficiality and realize the complete meaning of life as a person. Actually, the ancients had a level of personality beyond our reach.

With no feelings for modern marriages, it is hard not to contemplate love stories in the past. As a poem wrote:

Once upon a time, horses and carriages were slow,
letters had a long distance to travel,
and he or she is your whole world.

6. 2   Affection between Father and Son—the Deep Filial Piety of Chinese People

The affection between father and son tells the ethical relationship between parents and children. From the principle of mutual respect and mutual benefit, parents should be benevolent while children are required to be filial.

6. 2. 1   Filial Piety Means the Foundation of Being a Human

According to Chinese people, filial piety means the foundation of being a human. It can be explained that it is parents that give us life. Except for the Monkey King-Sun Wukong who was created by the heaven and earth, and was given birth by a stone, humans are born and raised up by parents rather than coming to the world without reason. The growth of child consumes so many efforts of parents that they selflessly give every love and care. As is impressively said in the poem *Reed* (also translated as *The Parents' Death*) in the *Book of Songs*:

"*My father give me birth; by mother I was fed. They cherished me with mirth, and by them I was bred. They looked after me, and bore me out and in. Boundless as sky should be, the kindness of our kin.*"

The *Reed* can be said to contain gratitude in every character and the earliest sad melody made by Chinese people to praise the kindness of parents.

Sinicized Buddhism also pays highly attention to filial piety of Confucianism and wrote a *Buddha's Illustration on the Unrepayable Love of Parents*. In it, ten kindness of mother and father, which is heart-breaking enough, is praised as follows: "Taking care of children when pregnancy. Bearing the pain when giving birth. Loving the child even forgetting the pain she suffered. Feeding the child with delicacy. Warming the child when she is exposed to coldness. Feeding the child with breast milk. Washing the child with clean hands and making her hands chap. Longing for the child when the child is away. Willing to suffer instead of the child. Endless compassion for the child. " Keep the ten kindness in mind while reading the illustration, who won't feel guilty for receiving such great benevolence from parents? And isn't everyone vowing in mind that he or she will return filial piety to their beloved parents?

Although parents' love is never enough to repay, Chinese ancients are sincerely trying their best to express their gratitude! Zi lu carried sacks of rice for more than a hundred li only to raise his parents. While he himself took wild vegetables as food. Min Sun, wearing "reed catkins-padded cotton cloths" from stepmother in winter, did not explain for himself when being scolded and lashed by his father. The lovely Wu Meng, being only eight years old, took off the clothes for the mosquitos to bit himself instead of his parents. The naive Huang Xiang, cooled the mattress with a fan in hot summer and warmed the quilt with his body in cold winter for his father. Hua Bao of the Eastern Jin Dynasty (266—420) still wore the bun of his childhood until he was 70 years old, only for the reason that his father told him when leaving home to "wait for me to come back and celebrate for your adulthood". Therefore, he kept waiting for his father the whole life! He didn't celebrate the adulthood or get married. Nor did he regret waiting for so long. It was only a pity that he didn't see his father return as expected. Comparatively speaking, Bao Fengchang, a native of Tangyue Village in Huizhou, was more fortunate. When he was only 14 years old, he begged along the road, looking for father who left home because of battle, and eventually he met him at the ancient temple of Yanmen Pass in Shanxi. Later when his mother got seriously ill, he climbed cliffs to get medical plants for her, and he even cut flesh from his own leg to cure her. This sincere filial piety has won the praise of heaven and man.

Chinese history is full of such stories of filial piety, which can often move people to tears. "When parents are still alive, don't be away from home. " For us who have been away from hometown and cannot take care of parents by their side and show our filial piety, we can only miss them with tears in our eyes, and wish to see them in our dreams. It can be said that traditional filial culture lasting for thousands of years in China can be seen as unique in the world. Like the memorial archway at Cixiao Li of Tangyue Village in Huizhou City, it has been through twists and turns of the passing years and keeps mighty and solemn standing in awe despite various mossy spots. It means that the ideas of "little help brings much return", always feeling grateful to parents, advocating and praising filial piety, are deeply and sincerely approved by all Chinese people.

6.2.2　Filial Piety in Confucianism can Be Sorted into Four Levels

(1) Filial Piety Represents the Integration of Obedience and Respect

First, the basic appearance of filial piety comes to obedience—follow parents' idea and listening to their advice rather than resisting or arguing with them. As Confucius told his students, filial piety means not disobeying your parents, when giving advice to parents, the way of speaking is of great significance. If your opinions are not adopted by them, you can never bear a grudge in your mind. Instead, you should keep respecting them and be willing to whatever you can for them. It is said in *Disciple Gauge*:

When father and mother are calling, answer them right away. When they give you directions, obey them without hesitation. When your parents need to instruct you, respectfully do as you're told. Whenever your parents must scold you, acknowledge your errors and faults.

This actually involves a question of the form of filial piety. On the interaction mode and discourse right between parents and children, different from the attitude of many young friends today, Confucianism advocates "no violation" and obedience, and believes that children should respect their parents' discourse priority and should humbly accept their teachings and suggestions. In fact, there is nothing hard to understand. After all, parents always love their children most. Their life experience and wisdom are exactly what children lack. Therefore, it is not a bad thing for children to listen to their parents' opinions and accept their guidance during their growth. It will only be a good thing. Even if opinions differ greatly, you should be gentle, speak well, and listen respectfully to your parents' reproaches. Since parents and children are an integral part of life and the loved ones of each other, no matter how big the differences are, as long as we understand each other and communicate patiently, there can always be a good coordination method. Isn't that good? Relatives are always willing to make concessions for each other. Even if you are unlucky, let you meet so bad parents, they really let you suffer a lot. But after all, they are your parents and you are their children. This is your destiny which you can never deny. Now that you have met the destiny, you can only compromise and bear the burden of humiliation, and use wisdom and courage to face and bear the burden of this fate. In the view of Confucianism: "When parents have loving regard, obeying them is not hard. Parents who are hateful and cruel, test the worth of one filial heart. " Relatives are relatives after all. This natural blood connection can create a miracle of tolerance and understanding, and eliminate all previous estrangement and hatred. Believe it or not, love makes you do it. Grievances and blows that you suffered from are special tasks for self-cultivation of your mind. Just as the dark clouds and storms represent the best baptism of the sky, all dissatisfaction and failures are also the best ways to pure your life.

Second, the essence of filial piety lies not in giving parents material support, but in the emotion of love and respect sincerely.

Although Confucianism emphasizes "no violation" and obedience, it pays more attention to the respect and love behind obedience. Confucius then explained that filial piety would often equal to satisfying the material need of parents. But when it comes to meeting the material need, your horse and other pets also count on you for survival. Therefore, if you do not treat parents with respect and love, what is the difference between caring them and your pets? Then we may be asked, how to explain "respect"?

In my opinion, respect is moved by goodness and looked up to because of nobility. Filial piety is a natural love for our parents, we show respect to parents because we know them giving birth to and upbringing us. Their love and kindness are like gentle beams of spring sun that we are guilty to receive. Then the sense of esteem and devotion arises spontaneously, which is sincere and whole-heartedly. This sense of respect makes children cling to their parents, and always remain inferior and weak as kids before their parents. This sense of respect makes children look up on their parents, and always see them as Heaven, being more and more honorable and noble. As the earth trying to reach the sky, is it reasonable for children to seek equality between them and their parents? Or do children even able to speak out such word without shame? This heartfelt gratitude and love for parents is respect!

So, whether we have compassion and love for our parents are known clearly by ourselves. If we do respect and love them, we will put it into action. If we see something good to eat and drink, the first thing that comes to my mind is to bring it to my parents so that they can taste it. If there is something fun and enjoyable, It will become a pity that my parents are not around to enjoy it with me! If parents were ill, I would wish to suffer it for them! Filial children have only one thing in mind—to please their parents and wish them peaceful and healthy forever! According to me, the true love that comes out of this thought represents the most precious virtue and conscience of a child. With this love full of sincerity, filial piety is our duty, destiny, joy, and happiness. We can do all kinds of filial piety with an unshirkable heart.

(2) Filial Piety Boasts a Unity of a Beginning and an End

What is the beginning of filial piety? It begins with self-protection. "The body, hair, and skin, all have been received from the parents, so that one doesn't dare damage them-that is the beginning of xiao". The first requirement of being filial is to cherish one's own body, for it belongs not only to us. Our body is created by both our father and mother. It therefore also belongs to them and should not be easily hurt by oneself. Therefore, in order to protect our "body from parents". Before dying Zeng Zi let his disciples check whether his hands and feet were still intact. He had been careful all his life to preserve the body which his parents had given him, and now he was worthy of them. According to Confucius: "Some people cannot endure uncompellingly for a while and forget the dangers he himself and his beloved are faced with. Surely it doesn't mean that they are not bewildered." So, we don't slight others, avoid becoming enemy with others, and choose not to fight with others, or not to do illegal and immoral things. What is the reason for that? Misbehaviors may hurt our bodies and even get our parents involved.

Then what is the end of it? The end of filial piety is to win glory for parents. According to the ancients, people should work hard and make achievements, and their virtues, words and achievements can be immortal in future generations. This is not only an individual's achievement, but also the achievement of parents and families. For example, if a scholar succeeded in the imperial examination or became an official of a senior rank with outstanding political achievements, the imperial court would, according to the rules, bestow on him honor and reputation, or issue an imperial edict to erect a memorial archway to commend them. So that his parents would become famous and his ancestors would be blessed and honored. We can see that before the ancestral temple of the Lin family in Yongding county of Longyan City, there stands many stone flagpoles carved with dragon that recorded family members who had made contributions and brought honor to the family. Some dragon stone flagpoles were also erected outside the gate of the mansion. Even today, a Chinese child admitted to a key university can bring great glory to his parents and family. Every summer vacation, the ceremony of presenting congratulatory couplets to students who are admitted to the university is held in the family ancestral hall in Ji 'an, Jiangxi Province. The whole village people will come to congratulate the students by beating drums and setting off firecrackers, and banquets will be held. There is no doubt that this will be a highlight moment for the family.

However, as is said that if one's family is poor and one's parents are getting old, yet one does not become an official to provide for his parents, it is the second kind of unfilial performance. You are not allowed to try nothing. And once you get an opportunity to develop, you should never let it go and give in to poverty. If you lead a poor life so that your family and parents have to struggle for survival. Then, you should surely be criticized as unfilial.

(3) Filial Piety is the Combination of Both Life and Death

Filial piety, of course, is mainly before death. But people will leave the world one day. For Confucianism, although life has birth and death, the soul is immortal, and filial piety should be endless. Confucius said: "Though the former king was dead, serving him as if he were alive. Although the former king died, serving him seems to exist. It can be said that he is filial to the utmost. " We should be filial to our parents when they are alive, and continue to keep them in mind after their death. According to Confucius, parents should be buried with rituals and offered sacrifices, and the idea of "keep his father's good doctrine unchanged for three years after his father's death" should be obeyed. Those who violate this requirement are unfilial. Let's not discuss the necessity of the three-year mourning here. What we need to understand is this special psychology and emotion, which embodies the moving feelings of transcending life and death and eternal nostalgia between our close relatives.

For example, Zhong You, with the alias of Zilu, a disciple of Confucius, who loved his parents deeply and walked for more than a hundred li to buy rice for his parents. While he himself ate the cheap and unappetizing wild vegetables. He then became an official and didn't need to worry about food and clothes anymore. However, his parents had already died before his success. Therefore, he often felt sad that "Even if I am willing to go back to the times when I ate wild vegetables and carried rice for more than a hundred li to raise my parents, how could that be possible?" Confucius praised: "You took care of your parents, which can be commented as doing one's best during parents' life time and missing parents after they depart out of this world!" So, he deserved to be praised as a filial son. Another story is about Wang Pou, who would cry by the grave when thunder rolled. Wang's mother dreaded the sound of thunder-claps, and she would shake with fear every time she heard the thunderstorm. After her death, her filial son, Wang Pou, on every thundering night, would run to his mother's grave to accompany her spirit and keep her from fear by repeating: "Don't cry mother. Your son is here!"

This represents some behavior that common people would never do and see it as a foolish deed. Yet for filial children, it is an act of serving death as if he or she were alive, which is required by their filial piety. There are many cultural manifestations of Chinese people's endless filial piety. For example, people at all levels in the whole country pay special attention to the funeral and sacrifice of their parents and ancestors. They followed strict rules of etiquette and mourned for three years after their parents passed away. They built ancestral halls for their ancestors and offered sacrifices at four seasons and many festivals to show that they did not forget their ancestors. At the same time, whenever there is an important event in the family, such as holding adult rites and weddings, or revising a new genealogy, and clansman passing the imperial examination, they would always report to their ancestors' spirit in time and pray for their blessings. In addition, they also consciously practice the doctrine that "there are three unfilial acts, no descendants is the greatest", ancestors left blood cannot be cut off by their own hands. They have written their ancestors' lives, their virtues and teachings into the genealogy, and turned them into family rules to inspire themselves, educate their children, and let their children and grandchildren remember them. They must work hard to make achievements in order to glorify their ancestors.

The Chinese respect, miss and worship their ancestors. It seems that the souls of their ancestors have always continued to participate in the life of their descendants in this world in a special way. That is how Confucianism, awakens and kindles in men, the inspiration or living emotion necessary to enable and make them obey the rules of moral conduct. Thus, Confucianism also mellowed the people's moral personality. Zeng zi, further says: "By cultivating respect for the dead, and carrying the memory back to the distant past, the good in the people will grow deep."

(4) Filial Piety also Combines Morality with Rationality

Which means to repay relatives rationally and to perform filial piety in a mean way. Confucianism attaches great importance to filial piety, which is a family virtue that people should cultivate and practice first. As the book of filial piety says: "Those who do not love their relatives but love others are against morality; those who do not respect their relatives but respect others are against reason. " The filial piety required by Confucianism is not a compulsive order, but a conscious act of respecting everyone's moral rationality. In other words, as a rational behavior, Confucian filial piety not only requires us to have sincere love, but also requires people to be rational, to love rationally, and to be filial according the doctrine of the mean.

We have already said that the Confucian doctrine of the mean is a rational methodology that deals with problems according to the actual situation. As far as filial piety is concerned, this methodology should also be carried out.

We mentioned that filial piety should be "obedient" and "without violation". But this also has to be discussed on a case-by-case basis. Under normal circumstances, filial piety is first to obey their parents, and we also oppose children to quarrel with their parents in a rough manner. But, when confronted with barbaric parents who lose their mind, we have to be expedient and flexible with them. For example, when Shun found himself in danger of being murdered by his family, his father Gusou, stepmother and half-brother Xiang plotted to kill him for many times, but Shun didn't lay down and die. Instead, he chose to escape and protect himself first. Afterwards, Shun didn't resent and was still humble to his father and loved his younger brother. He protected himself firstly, that's also a protection for his families, only by preserving himself can he fulfill his filial piety. However, Zengzi was so stupid that even being exposed to his father's crazy beat, he chose not to escape and bore the attack. According to Confucius, it is the foolish behavior, which cannot be counted as filial piety. Filial piety is a kind of moral rationality that everyone has. It should also be based rationally on the doctrine of mean to judge the situation and act accordingly.

For indeed, "causes and conditions come before achievement". As the ancients said: "Of all virtues, filial piety is the most important. " Intention is more important than the achievements, for people from poor family are too poor to care their parents in all aspects. Since they are already striving for survival, how much on earth can they do to repay the kindness of their parents? Therefore, the key is to try one's best and keep the respect in mind. Even the filial piety is hidden in detail, it can be regarded as the excellent performance of obedience and respect. Just like the ancestor worship ceremony, although we strive to be solemn, what is more important is the sincerity of our descendants. For ordinary people, it is also very good to offer fresh vegetables, clean melons and fruits, or newly ripe grains as sacrifices. This is also a manifestation of rational filial piety according to the principle of the golden mean.

When we today talk about filial piety, we cannot simply deny the value of it or easily regard it as an outdated feudal dross that deprives human rights. Therefore, we should look with a dialectical and historical perspective into the filial culture and pay special attention to absorbing the beneficial and valuable components. The problems of today's times are precisely developed from the lack of filial piety at home. In conclusion, the world will be in great harmony if people all keep filial piety in mind.

6.3　Proper Priority between Young and Old
—the Principle of Putting the Elder First

The concept of proper priority between young and old is widely accepted by not only brothers in the family, but also members of various generations in the family, and even the whole society. According to *Mencius*: there are three most noble things in the world, one is rank, the other is age, the other is virtue. For Chinese people, the elder are respectable. Even if he or she is only one day elder than you, he or she will be seen as the elder and given priority. The principle of "respect for seniority" has been circulating for a long time and has become a significant component of traditional Chinese ethics.

(1) Specific Requirements of the Priority Given to the Elder

In the previous section, we also mentioned *Standards for Students*. Although it is a textbook for children, it has a great influence on Chinese people, and can help us to have a glimpse of the general requirements of Chinese traditional ethics education. The principle of respect for seniority that we are discussing is also well explained in this book. In *Standards for Students*, there are more specific requirements of the priority given to the elder and respect shown to them.

When all the brothers are friendly, and sisters show respect, the harmony blessing these children, is a sign of the Filial Way. If wealth is not viewed as essential, how could resentment arise when words are both gentle and patient, bad feeling will soon disappear. When people are eating and drinking, or when it is time to sit down. Let those who are older go first, the young ones should follow behind. If an elder is looking for someone, you run the errand instead. If the person you seek can't be found, return and offer to help in his place. In speaking to those who are older, use the right term of respect. When facing your teachers and elders, don't show off or try to look smart. When an older person is standing, children should not take a seat. But wait till the elder is seated, and then sit when you are told. Be swift when it's time to move forward, go last when it's time to return. Stand up to answer when questioned, your gaze held steady and calm. Before an elder, speak softly. But if our voice is too low and hard to hear, we are being improper. We should regard our aunts and uncles as if they were our parents, and our cousins as if they were our siblings.

Here, the author first mentioned the way to get along with brothers. Secondly, also broadly related to the general attitude of the elderly to get along with each other when they are young. For example, "when speaking to those who are older, use the right term of respect", which is an interesting expression. Different from westerners, if Chinese children call the elder's name directly, or call their parents by their names, what will happen? It's some behavior without fun at all. All these details fully show the Chinese people's respect for the elderly.

(2) The Origin of the Principle of "Respect for Seniority"

In fact, we cannot simply regard *Standards for Students* as basis to judge the traditional culture of Chinese people's respecting and giving priority to the old. As far as the Western Zhou Dynasty, and in the "system of rites and music", the principle of "proper priority between young and old" was set as the foundation of ethics.

Among the "system of rites and music", the first important principle boasts the Zhaomu System that regulates the sacrifice ceremony at the ancestral temple, which indicates the relation between the elder and the young. In the temple, the ancestral tablets would be placed according to the principle of "Zhao on the left and Mu on the right": tablets of father and son always standing opposite to each other while grandsons remaining in the same line with the grandfather, which tells the differences between the noble and the mean, the elder and the young, as well as the immediate and extended family. This is a principle especially observed in the patriarchal culture, sacrifice and burial culture of later generations in China.

There is another distinct regulation—the system of primogeniture, which representatively shows the proper priority between young and old. The Western Zhou practiced the system of hereditary kingship combined with a patriarchal clan system, which is a power division system with the essential feature of having the wife's eldest son a heir. Within the clan there was a distinction between major and minor lineages. "The successor of the family should be the eldest son of the formal wife rather than the smartest one. " Therefore, even if you are more intelligent and capable of leading the family, so long as you are not the first son of the formal wife, you never get the privilege and chance for succeeding the leader's role. It should be said that in ancient times, especially in the pre-Qin period, it was the system of primogeniture that stabilized the succession system of the dynasty or noble families. Therefore, as a brother of the legal successor, one should be quite conscious of not scrambling for the place. Such as Ji Zha from the State of Wu (during the Warring States Period) was an intelligent person. Yet he gave in three times the chance of succeeding the family to his elder brothers, which also follows the ethical rule of giving priority to the elder in political fields as well as in political life.

But there were few such cases in the ancient Chinese history.

The third regulation boasts the ceremony of village drinking, which became prevalent during the Western Zhou Dynasty as a ritual event to show respect to the intelligent and the elder, which often took place on the lunar January and October, accompanied by the "popularizing order" and speeches to educating the public to guide citizens to respect the elder and observe the national law. According to *the Book of Rites*: "The ceremony of village drinking, people over 60 years old sit, and people over 50 years old stand and wait on them. This shows respect for the elderly. People aged 60 serve three dishes, people aged 70 serve four dishes, people aged 80 serve five dishes, and people aged 90 serve six dishes. " This shows that the elderly have received good care. Confucius highly appreciated the creation of the village drinking ceremony and thought that it was not difficult to promote the Kingly Way by means of it. Of course, Confucius joined the ceremony of village drinking which was popular in his era. In the ceremony, when the old man was walking slowly with the stick, Confucius, with self-conscious, followed politely the old rather than walking passes him.

When Confucius talked with his disciples about his life ambition, he depicted his goal as seeing: "The aged can enjoy ease and comfort, the young can get every concern, and friends have trust in me. " This saying represents his life goal which is both lifelike and ethical. One time, a child from a family from Que Li to convey a massage to Confucius. After this child had left, one disciple asked: "Master, what do you think of this kid? Is this a boy who seeks to make progress?" Confucius answered: "No, this kid knew nothing about proper priority. I saw him sitting and walking together with elders. He shows no humility. He is impatient for success and wrongly takes himself as an adult already. Thus, this kid knows nothing about rites. "

Here we return to the seating etiquette also mentioned in *the Standards for Students* mentioned at the beginning about the table manners of "seating" the elders. The Chinese pay special attention to dining etiquette. The head of the table is also called "the seat of honor", which represents the most honorable position of the hall or the table. People tend to leave this best seat to the elder. After the banquet begins, the host will generally take the initiative to add food and wine for the elderly. The young won't start eating until the elder begin their dishes. The younger generation won't leave the table until the elder leave his seat. This habit of giving priority to the elderly is quite different from the Western habit of giving priority to ladies at banquets and taking the host as the center.

In addition, we can also have a look at the arrangement of the rooms. The typical "gabled chambers" architecture of buildings in Chaoshan area shows clearly the principle of giving priority to the elder. As you can see from this picture, in the building of "gabled chambers", the hall in the middle is the place for worshipping the ancestors, while the "large rooms" by its side represent bedrooms for the elder. Only the "inferior rooms" that flank the hall are rooms for the young and servants.

Actually, most of the nationalities in China, whether Han or minority, have a tradition of respecting the elders and the elderly. Such as Manchu. In the tradition, the Manchu younger generation would greet their elders every three days, and kowtow to their elders every five days. Every new year's festival, the Shui compatriots will vie to invite the elders of the village community to their homes for dinner. The elderly with a long life are highly respected and regarded as messengers of happiness. Tibetan compatriots pay great attention to etiquette. In daily life, when you see an elderly or respected person, you should take off your hat, bow and bend 45 degrees. It is the highest courtesy courtesy putting heads together of thanking the elders. Tibetans will never tolerate the phenomenon of abandoning the elderly. The younger generation of Oroqen should be respectful and behave appropriately in front of their elders. More than 60 years ago, all important matters within the commune had to be discussed and decided by the "wulileng" meeting. The members of the conference are mainly composed of elderly men and women from various households. Among men, the longer their beards, the more authoritative they are. The Korean people hold a birthday banquet for the 60 year old, called "Huajia banquet". Since 1982, Yanbian Korean Autonomous Prefecture has also designated August 15 as the old people's day. The Double Ninth Festival, is also known as the day of Han nationality for caring the elder. "When brothers carry dogwood up the mountain; each of them a branch—and my branch missing. " This is a poem describing the Double Ninth Festival.

It seems that the old living in traditional China could enjoy courtesy, love, respect and various kinds of care from the young. Today's social development and progress have created favorable conditions for the health and longevity of the elderly, which making China a paradise for the old. Another saying we hear is that America represents "paradise for the young while grave for the old", which is quite opposite to the situation in China.

When the pandemic initially broke out and ventilators were in urgent need, cases in the western world showed the so-called priority given to the young whereas the treatment for the old being delayed or even cancelled. Some netizens even ridiculed the coronavirus as the "remover of the old". As for China, by March 1st, 2020, the number of coronavirus patients over the age of eighty cured in Hubei Province had totaled over three thousand and six hundred. Doctors and nurses all kept the idea of "the elder are in need of my help more than ever" in mind and devote themselves to work as heroes in harm's way.

6.4　Righteousness between Sovereign and Subject—an Ideal Picture of the Relationship between the Lord and Courtiers

Ancient China witnesses the autocratic monarchy system in which the lord holds the absolute power while the courtiers assisting him. And together, they rule the country with joint efforts. Confucianism has provided with many thoughts on how to build a good relationship between the emperor and the officials.

Take Confucius for example, in *The Analects of Confucius-About the Governing of One's State*, he talks a lot about his political ideas of how to become a good emperor as well as a good official, how to govern the nation and manage political issues, and how to rule the people, etc. In conclusion, the way of the sovereign and his officials getting along with each other can be described as "The Rectification of Names", which means the lord should be like a lord and the courtier, a courtier so that all of them would fulfill their duties and interact with each other in order. Or else if the lord doesn't behave like a lord, nor does the courtier, the politics of a nation will become a mess and end up with failure.

(1) Emperors and Courtiers in the Perspective of Kingly Way

First, we will talk about "the lord being like a lord", which means that an emperor should behave himself as an emperor. The autocratic monarchy system of feudal China in ancient times sees a total of 493 emperors from the First Emperor of Qin Dynasty to Emperor Xuantong of Qing Dynasty. As we know, in the central hall of traditional Chinese family, there hangs the "Heaven, Earth, lords, forefathers and ancestors, teachers" tablet. Chinese people regard their sovereign "the son of Heaven", as well as the "father of courtiers". Thus, the officials and common people regard themselves as sons of the emperor.

It can be concluded that the emperor is noble and respectable and represents the combination of the supreme power, the strategic hub as well as the community of his people. Therefore, he is supposed to do his best to be a qualified ruler. According to Confucianism, a qualified ruler means to follow the rites, act with virtues and implement the three principles of "the Kingly Way". To begin with, the emperor should respect the Heaven, for he is appointed by the Heaven and regards the Tao higher than authority. Only then emperors and regimes derive their legitimacy from the transcendent way of heaven. Secondly, the emperor should always keep his people in mind. People are the foundation of a nation and would gather under the rule of a benevolent emperor. This represents the political legitimacy based on the public will. Thirdly, the emperor should show respect to Confucius. Only when he honors Confucianism and advocates educating people can his governance and throne be legitimate in the cultural field. A king who follows these three rules can be praised as following the way of a benevolent king. "When there is a great order across the land, the real power lies surely in the central authority."

China, as a community with the shared culture, gives high expectations of the emperor. And there were indeed some great emperors praised by their people, such as

Huangdi, the Common Ancestor of Chinese Nationality; First Emperor Ying Zheng of the Qin Dynasty; Emperor Li Shimin, the Second Emperor of the Tang Dynasty; Empress Wu Zetian, the Empress of the Wuzhou (Tang) Dynasty; Emperor Li Longji, the Fourth Emperor of the Tang Dynasty; Emperor Zhao Kuangyin, the First Emperor of the Northern Song Dynasty; Emperor Taizu of the Yuan Dynasty, Gengis Khan; Zhu Yuanzhang, Emperor Taizu of the Ming Dynasty; Aixinjueluo Xuanye, Emperor Shengzu of the Qing Dynasty; Aixinjueluo Hongli, Emperor Gaozong of the Qing Dynasty.

As we known, Li Shimin (600—649), Emperor Taizong of the Tang Dynasty, represents a great ruler featured by both excellent military power as well as the ability to rule the nation. Chairman Mao Zedong once summed up Li Shimin's commendable working methods as follows: "He calmed the world with the policy of control through conciliation, and did not rush for quick success and instant benefits to avoid laboring the people and damaging the army. He was not greedy for pleasure and went to the court every morning to discuss national affairs, listened attentively to various suggestions, and spoke carefully. After leaving the court, he would also discuss the right and wrong of state affairs with the ministers frankly. In the evening, he talked with people about classical literature. " In the years of Zhenguan reign, the country experienced a period called "Zhenguan's Prosperity", which means a period with a relatively clear politics, stable and unified society, booming economy and strong power. China then was considered as the most powerful and prosperous country in the world of that time. He once wrote a book named *The Requirements for an Emperor*, in which he talked about the way of being a qualified ruler in his perspective and expressed his feelings and thoughts of life and the world. It can be seen as the conclusion of a sovereign's life experience and the basic requirements of being a wise emperor as well. As stated in Emperor Taizong's *The Requirements for an Emperor*, 12 aspects are involved in the ways of being a great emperor. Including the way of self-cultivating, the way of using power, the way of arranging talents, the way of selecting the officials, the way of listening to other people's opinions, and the way of preventing from villains, the way to prevent mistakes caused by pride, the way to prevent corruption caused by extravagance, and the way to prevent disorder caused by injustice, etc. It is very worth learning and using for reference for Chinese politicians. Li Shimin was really one of the outstanding statesmen among all the emperors and kings in the Chinese history, esteemed as a model of reasonable and enlightened ruler.

Then, we come to the topic of "the courtiers being the courtiers", featuring the officials behaving themselves like the officials. This is also an issue that people have always been happy to discuss.

Liu Xiang of the Western Han Dynasty wrote in his *Shuo Yuan* his analysis of the "Six Goods and Six Evils" —Six fundamentally opposed political characters or political accomplishment. The "Six Goods" are as follows: being far-sighted and preventing from the risks can be seen as "saint"; being humble and endeavoring to help the good, "kind"; early to rise and late to retire while continuing to recruit talents, "loyal"; searching for the fact and turning the disaster into fortune, "intelligent"; observing one's duty strictly and being honest and public-spirited, "faithful"; being upright and ready to fight for justice and advice the ruler, "righteous". Then, when it comes to the "Six Evils", they are: being greedy for money and higher position without focusing on public affairs, "mediocre"; currying favor with people from higher rank and bowing down to everything said or done by them, "adulatory"; being filled with honey words and flattering looks while jealous to the intelligent, "treacherous"; having a glib tongue and sowing discords among others, "dishonest"; being autocratic and ganging up for selfish interests, "sneaky"; pulling the strings behind the scenes and act in a random way, "vicious". As is mentioned above: observing one's duty strictly and being honest and public-spirited is seen as "faithful".

For Confucianism, the way of being a helpful courtier, the virtues of the courtier, or the duties of the courtier should also be added into the big framework of "the benevolent and righteous governance" by officials with self-conscious. The role played by the subject means to stand right in the position of the subject and assist the emperor to practice the way of being a qualified king so as to achieve the goal of answering the call of Heaven, show benevolent to people advocate the thoughts of Confucianism, and build the nation into the great harmony. "To assist the king so that he will perform better than Yao and Shun, and to make the society enjoyable and simple." Their goal is to let more than three dynasties enjoy the ideal society with great harmony. Therefore, to follow the way of the courtier, to cultivate the virtue of the courtier and to fulfill his tasks represent the fundamental duties of the courtier.

It can be said that ancient China boasts a large number of great courtiers. As the pictures show, they are Zhou Gongdan, Guan Zhong, Li Si, Xiao He, Cao Cao, Zhuge

Liang, Fang Xuanling, Wang Anshi, Yue Fei, Wen Tianxiang, Yelv Chucai, Liu Ji, Zhang Juzheng etc. They may all did good job in certain aspects of implementing "the way of courtiers".

Take Bao Zheng, the "Bao Qingtian" in the Northern Song Dynasty as an example. I think he is a famous official who is more comprehensive in the "Six Goods". During the following 24 years, Bao Zheng was appointed to various important positions. He was honest and upright, and had amazing ability in settling lawsuits. He always put the interests of the country and people in the first place, never swayed by personal interests. That was why he won the reputation of Just Magistrate Bao. When Bao Zheng was the head of Luzhou, his uncle violated the law. Bao Zheng handled the matter strictly in accordance with the law and did not spare any unjust mercy on his uncle. In this connection, he told his family: "If any member of the Baos takes bribes and violates the law, he will not be allowed to be buried in the cemetery of the family. I won't take the one who is against my will as my offspring." Throughout his life, Bao Zheng submitted hundreds of memorials to the throne, covering: reinforcing defence to prevent the intrusion of Qidan and the Western Xia regime; aiding the poor and reducing extorting illegal taxes; impeaching guilty members of the royal family and corrupt officials. All these memorials showed his hatred for evils and love for his country and people. After Bao Zheng's death, many stories about him have been acted out on the stage. In this way, the Chinese people express their longing for justice and for just officials.

Of course, Chinese culture also reaffirms and emphasizes the appreciation and pursuit of "clean and honest" political character in its own unique way. For example, all dynasties have built memorial archways for honest and upright officials. Various kinds of couplets and plaques will be engraved in the official offices to make officials introspect and alert themselves. In Neixiang County of Henan Province, there still exists a well-preserved Guxian Yamen, one of the county-level government offices in feudal China. A well-known antithetical couplet is shown at its gate:

"*It is not a great honor or humiliation to gain or loss a government post. Don't regard the official as people of no use, for it is the official that people can rely on locally*" as its former verse. "*Provided by food and clothes from the people, the ruler should never see people easy to confuse, for he himself represents one of them*" as the proceeding verse.

The core quotations in *the official proverbs* of Caorui in the Ming Dynasty are still used for reference by today's politicians:

Subordinates are not afraid of my severity, but of my honesty. The people do not admire my talent but my justice. If you are honest and clean, the subordinates dare not neglect. If we do things fairly, the people dare not cheat. Only when officials are fair can politics be clear. Only when officials are honest can they have prestige.

(2) The Way of Monarch and Courtier Turns to the Way of Citizen

The sovereign and subjects, guided by the idea of benevolent governance make concerted efforts, perform their functions and cooperate with each other. "A lord gives orders to his courtiers according to the proprieties while the courtiers serve their lord with loyalty." When the lord and courtiers strive for the common ideal and business, they may become a much-told tale of wise emperor as well as loyal helpers. Faced with a great emperor like this, the courtiers should be faithful and fulfill their tasks. "I desire to do all I can, even to the last drop of my blood" comes from Zhuge Liang who wrote the article to express his mind. If the emperor makes no huge mistake, yet the subject does not fulfill his duty and tries to usurp the throne, then he can be criticized as a rebellious villain and be criticized and condemned by the whole country. An example is Cao Cao who tried to overthrow the Han Dynasty. If the emperor does not follow the right way of being the king and does harm to the nation and people without regarding himself an emperor, the subjects then have their rights not to obey their ruler's order. Confucianists oppose being foolish and loyal to those despots and tyrants who have no virtue. For the lord who doesn't behave like a lord and doesn't govern the nation with benevolence and righteousness. His courtiers do not need to obey without doubt, they should rather, according to Confucianism, protest, resist or even resort to revolution. If one does not lead by example and conduct himself with dignity, then how can you manage to be respected and followed? And who can you give command to? Therefore, the revolutions started by Shang Tang and King Wen and Wu of Zhou Dynasty are actions of justice that follow the guidance of the Heaven and people. As is said that "So long as the leaders behave well, the people will follow you even if no orders are issued." Otherwise, the people won't follow you even if orders are given. Mencius also mentions the idea of "people are more important than the monarch" and advocates equal respect and rites between the lord and courtiers. If you don't look down on courtiers as dogs and horses, then it should be the relationship between enemies. The revolution of Shang Tang and Emperor Wu of Zhou Dynasty are following the guidance of the Heaven and answering the call of people! The King Wen of the Zhou Dynas started military action to comfort people.

Historically, there revolution is of Confucianism can never solve this problem totally. "Once a new emperor sent hroned, a new group of officials will take office." Since various tyrants who never offered benevolent governance were unavoidable, countless rebellious courtiers and villains who didn't fulfill their duties and sought for personal interests. Then the revolution would take place. The benevolent governance may not last long, nor does the tyranny. And history is filled with twists and turns. The history of ancient Chinese politics shows that the way for how to be a good Emperor and helpful courtiers often can't meet the needs of the country. The seed of benevolent and righteous governance was never able to grow the expected fruit of building the country into a commonwealth state shared by all. What is the root cause? In my opinion, the reason remains that Confucianism failed to change the feudal political structure, the despotism that "regards the authority superior to justice (Tao)".

Confucianism, a scholar bureaucrat group evolved from the ancient wizard class, is a combination of intellectuals and bureaucrats. He is not only the designer of the traditional kingly politics (and the ethical relationship between monarchs and ministers under its guidance), but also the constructor of the feudal autocratic power structure system. Kingly politics is its dream, and absolutism is its masterpiece. On the one hand, he talked about self-cultivation as the foundation, the inner saint and the outer king as well as the way of kings and ministers, which was full of a good atmosphere of moral idealism. But on the other hand, he constructed and refined the eastern autocratic political system with the divine power, the monarchical power, the husband power, and the clan power as the main body, and with the characteristics of disdaining people and alienating people. The humanistic dream of idealism conceals or embellishes the power arrogance of despotism. Both are the connotation and function of Confucianism. The two systems intertwined with each other and develop into a complex whole.

Altogether, the people-centered politics in Confucianism does not equal to democratic politics. The benevolent ruling remains classical politics filled with moral idealism rather than modern politics of constitutional democratism. The two are separated by a time and space gap of modernization of capitalism.

For the contemporary Chinese, there is no question of the ethical relationship between the emperor and his subjects today. We are modern citizens with independent personality and free spirit, who abide by contracts and act according to law. But even as citizens, we still need to practice certain political ethics. For example, we need to be loyal to our country, we need to strengthen patriotic education, carry forward the spirit of patriotism, and work hard for the rejuvenation of our country. Modern patriots should have a world vision and a sense of the community of human destiny, which is also the world consciousness and universal feelings of Confucianism.

Politicians in modern civil society certainly have a lot of new modern knowledge and skills that the ancients did not have. However, they still need to modestly learn the beneficial experience and negative lessons from the traditional wisdom of Confucianism in order to train and enhance their modern political ability to serve the country and the people. Many thoughts in Confucius' Confucianism are related to the so-called "leadership" cultivation today. How should politicians strengthen their self-cultivation, what kind of skills should the leaders have in controlling people, how should governance be orderly and progressive, and what is the good governance pursued today? How can this be achieved? And so on.

The ancients can still give us valuable reference and enlightenment.

6.5 Trust between Friends
—Ancient Chinese Way of Treating Friends

According to *The Book of Poetry*: "Cut the trees with sound ding dong, and the birds in the forest sing their songs. The birds come out of the deep vale and fly in the tall trees. They do not stop their songs to call their company. " The poem is praised for speaking out the sincere hope of people longing for friendship. Friends are very common interpersonal relationships in social life. The existence of friends makes us not so lonely and cold, and our life can be comforted and self-sufficient. It is said that you are lucky enough to have a bosom friend in your life and you should treat him or her as a sibling. Then, how did ancient Chinese get along with friends?

To begin with, one has to make it clear whether his friend does good or harm. There are three kinds of friends that do good and three that do harm. Friendship with the upright, the sincere, and the one who has seen and heard much will do good.

Faithful and intelligent friends will benefit each other, make progress and cultivate their mind. It should be our best luck to meet them. Therefore, when friends come from afar, it is definitely a great joy. What about friends that do harm to you? Friendship with the flatterer, the one who fawns in face and speaks ill behind one's back, and the glib-tongued will do harm. For they are dishonest and filled with honey words without sincere mind. Faced with harmful friends like this, we should pay special attention to discern them and stay away from them.

The second point represents being loyal to each other and ready to offer help. As the saying goes, "a friend in need is a friend indeed". If there is anyone who "go to and from work in a friendly way, aid one another by keeping watch and ward, and sustain one another in sickness", there should be barely anything more blessing in our life. Generally, when meeting someone who treat others frankly, has a strong sense of honor towards his friends, and boasts generosity and kindness, isn't it reasonable for him or her to become a popular guy? As friends who share common ground and get on well with each other, they should also share rightcous goals to fight for justice, and there remain duties for each of them to take on.

The third way of good friendship is "never forget old friends". It is said that "Clothes are not as attractive as the old whereas old friends are better than the new." One of Confucius childhood friend, Yuan Rang, did not work hard and failed to gain any achievements when he grew up. Even at an old age, he still could not be seated properly. When Yuan's mother died, Confucius helped him to prepare the coffin inner and outer, whereas Yuan jumped onto his mother's coffin and started dancing. Seeing that, his students all persuaded him that "Teacher, you are a saint, don't bother yourself to help this kind of person." Then what is the answer of Confucius? "As far as I know he is my kinsman. I should never lose our kinship. He is my old friend. I should never lose our friendly relation." In his opinion, kinship is forever, so is the old friend. Therefore, he never forgets the old friend and old relationships.

The fourth point of getting along with friends represents being loyal and frankly. In order to do so, friends should be honest to each other and tell their suggestions sincerely. When having disagreement, one chooses not to speak it out but pretends to be as friendly as ever, then it can be regarded as a shameful behavior. However, although a friend deserves to be frank and honest, he still needs to pay attention to the way and method of giving suggestions while aiming to get expected results. And if the friend chooses not to listen to your suggestion, just let it go. Therefore, Confucius expressed his idea that "Admonish your friends with a faithful mind and enlighten them in a good way. If this proves vain, stop, and do not disgrace yourself." If you provide too many suggestions and end up in vain, your friends may feel disappointed and thus it may disgrace yourself.

The fifth way of treating friend is to keep your word. As is said that "Contact one's friends with sincere words." The ideas all stress the importance of being faithful. There are three wishes of Confucius, and we can see "make my friends trust one another" in it: "I am willing to make the old peaceful, to make my friends trust on another, and to make the young cared for." Therefore, it is necessary for friends to be "faithful" to each other and keep their word wholeheartedly.

The sixth way of treating friends is that those who are moral are destined to have friends. It means that everyone has to be sure that he or she will find a good friend. Yet there remains one premise-as Confucius said, "virtuous man never lacks neighborhood". "He who is virtuous is not isolated; he will have neighbors to aid him." The good man never feels lonely. Why? It is because people with virtue is like a magnet that attracts people to surround him. Therefore, one only needs to become a man of virtue: "All are good brothers under heaven." Mencius further promotes the distinguished under heaven to make friends with all other distinguished under heaven. And if it is not enough to satisfy him, then he would "discuss and commend on those in the ancient time—to make friends with ancient people. Thus, we often read books, including books of ancient people and study their thoughts and the way of conducting themselves. And therefore, making soul mates with them. For Neo-Confucianists: "Birds on the tree can be my friend of studying, and even flowers falling on the river can be my spark of writing." The one who unites with the Heaven can become friends of all under heaven and be regarded as "the one boasting friend everywhere". It reminds me of a paragraph written by Thoreau in *The Walden*: "In the very pattering of the drops, and in every sound and sight around my house, an infinite and unaccountable friendliness all at once like an atmosphere sustaining me."

It can be said that the Chinese ethical system formed under the influence of Confucianism focuses on the study of human ethics, humanity and human nature. It puts the Five Ethics first and also advocates "Four Principles and Eight Virtues" to cultivate one's way of treating others in the moral category. This has led to an invention of the goodness of man's nature that highlights the original aspiration and intuitive knowledge. A normal system with benevolence and ethics as its center is thus taken shape, featuring emotions, mutual values and benefits remain all in harmony. Chinese people will cherish their nation's traditional ethics forever, critically inherit and innovatively develop the classical moral spirits, and showcase the world morality of Chinese nation in the new era.

第七讲

尊祖重族
——中国村落宗族文化的要素

本讲中，我们要给同学们介绍一下中国村落宗族文化的基本情况。中华宗族文化源远流长、内涵丰富，它能串联起诸如祖先崇拜、血缘伦理、风俗礼仪、村落建筑、风水堪舆、典章制度、乡土文学等中国文化的一系列内容。它是中国传统文化中最悠久、最重要的社会文化现象之一，曾经影响和规范了无数中国人的日常生活和精神世界。

7.1　宗族与宗法

我们知道，世界人类基本上都是以血缘家庭为基础生活在一起的亲缘性的社会动物，但古代中国汉族社会的家庭是一个更特殊的、宗法制家族大群落。

提到宗族文化，就必须历史地提到儒家的宗法文化。宗法文化的来龙去脉简略地说，所谓"宗法"即宗族之法，是指中国汉民族按照"尊祖重族"的思想来管理和建设血缘家族生活共同体的一套原则和制度。溯其渊源，它最初也同氏族时代的祖先崇拜、灵魂崇拜、父系家长制有莫大的联系。但其奠基却始自西周时期周公旦"制礼作乐"的建制工作。周公旦设计了诸如嫡长子继承制①、分封制、大小宗、宗庙昭穆制和祭祀制等具体伦理制度。而后来孔子更进一步地基于这套礼乐制度阐发了他的"仁德"学说。周公和孔子两位圣哲前后相继，"摄巫归礼—释礼归仁""把这种血缘关系和历史传统提取、转化为意识形态上的社会礼教和仁学的自觉主张，即整个的宗法礼教文化。让这种基于生物种属性质、起着社会结构作用的血缘亲属关系和等级制度作超越生物和血缘

---

① 西周宗法制下的嫡长子（又称宗子）是土地、财产和权利的主要继承者，有主祭祖先的特权，地位最尊贵。在宗法制度下，由嫡长子传宗继统，这个系统成为大宗。嫡长子的同母弟和庶母兄弟为小宗。

的、明朗的政治学的解释和重构，使之摆脱特定氏族社会的历史限制"①。这对中华文化的发展而言，具有长远和重要的社会影响力。

儒家宗法制度先后经历了先秦阶段的王族宗法制、汉唐阶段的门阀宗法制和宋元明清阶段的平民宗法制这样三个大的历史阶段。而这个变迁过程，也是早期宗法文化政治功能减弱而社会功能转强，走出特权上层、走向民间社会的历史过程。相较于以"家国一体"为特征的王族宗法制和"大家世族"为特征的门阀宗法制阶段，明清阶段的平民宗法文化准确地说，应该叫宗族文化或家族文化。它以尊祖、敬宗、睦族为宗旨，"尊祖"必叙谱牒，"敬宗"当建祠堂，"睦族"须有族产助济。有谱、有祠、有田成为这种新的家族制度的根本特征。

我们这里的讲述，主要是对平民宗法制（明清）时代、民间村落所展示的宗族文化的基本要素的介绍。分为四个部分：宗祠与祭祖、族谱与家风、族权与乡绅、义门与和家园。需要说明的是，不仅是汉民族，我国各少数民族中至今还广泛保持着以祖灵崇拜和祖先祭祀为核心的原始宗教习俗，中华民族内部的祖先崇拜和祭祖文化是多元一体的复杂整体，既有内在联系，又有丰富区别。我们这里主要集中于汉民族的村落宗族文化要素的介绍。

7.2　宗祠与祭祖

我们先看一下"宗"字的小篆写法🈲，其中的"宀"就是房屋，"示"就是祖先牌位。这个"宗"字表示的，就是对祖先进行祭祀的房屋，即宗祠。

7.2.1　宗　祠

宗祠，也就是祖宗庙，是中国传统社会中家族供奉祖先的神主牌位、举行祭祖活动的场所，又是从事家族教育、执行族规家法和议事宴饮的家族聚会的地方。有时人们会把祠堂、宗祠两个概念等同使用，严格说是不对的。祠堂可能祭祀各种神灵人物，但宗祠专用于祭祀家族的祖宗神灵（祖灵）。但宽泛地用用也没有什么不可。

---

① 李泽厚. 中国思想史论［M］. 合肥：安徽文艺出版社，1999：23.

（1）宗祠的来历：从贵族特权到平民社会的变迁

最初，宗祠只是贵族特权阶层才有资格兴建的礼制建筑。按照周制：天子可建七庙，供奉七世的祖宗。诸侯建五庙，大夫建三庙，士建一庙，而庶民无权建独立的祠庙，只能在民居里进行祭祀。到汉代开始允许民间建墓下祠，就是挨着祖先的坟墓旁建立一个小小的祭祀设施（墓祠）。到南宋，理学家朱熹提倡建立"寝祠相连"的家祠，即香火堂，专祭高、曾、祖、祢（父）四世之祖。直到明代嘉靖十五年（1536）《大礼仪》颁布后，国家才正式允许民间联宗建宗祠，向平民开放了建宗祠祭祖的这种权利。民间遂大兴建祠之风，可谓凡有村落人家，便有宗族祠堂。在中国江南各省至今仍留有各类明清古祠堂，虽在偏远的山区和乡村，数量之多令人难以想象。

（2）古村落和祠堂建筑的风水讲究

谈起祠堂营建，首先要谈民间村落布局，那是农耕时代中国社会的构造主体。中国古村落大都是一个姓氏的族人聚族而居。人们新迁一地，村落建设的头等大事往往会是先建宗祠，而后再考虑营造民居。宗祠的选址大都是村落中的最佳地段，一般首选"坐下龙脉，有形势，有堂局，有上砂，有结构，有明堂，有水口"（《宅谱指要》）等诸要素的风水吉地，可谓占尽好山好水。宗祠建好后，村民再围绕宗祠以规划民居、街巷、牌坊等建筑，便形成了宗祠为中心的团块式、拓展式村落布局①。

这里也要略说几句村落风水学。所谓"风水"，风也，水也，研究一方山形水势、气运良劣之人居生态学也。古人认为只有好的风水才能福泽后人，这个风水原理简单说就是所谓左青龙、右白虎、南朱雀、北玄武。左青龙，即村落左边应有水流；右白虎，是指村落之右要邻近大路；北玄武，即北方应有靠山；南朱雀，因南方属火，故需设水塘，以水济火。大的原则上，村落选址需要遵循这种风水学原则②。说风水决定家族兴衰、子孙前程，当然是迷信的说法，但它所考虑山形水势对人居生产生活的生态影响是很有道理的。临近水道便利汲饮灌溉，临近通衢则进出不至于阻碍，若干山势环抱则前屏后靠，能阻挡风寒湿热侵扰。当然，鉴于各地的自然环境迥异，左青龙右白虎云云，实际中也难

① 在广东潮汕地区就有很多这类以祠堂为中心的"四点金"民居村落，如汕头市潮安区彩塘镇以丛熙公祠为中心的"三壁连"布局，浙江省建德市大慈岩镇新叶村也是以"有序堂"为中心组织的村落布局。

② 徽州地区流传有一首风水民谣云：阳宅须教择地形，背山面水称人心。山有来龙昂秀发，水须围抱作环形。明堂宽大斯为福，水口收藏积万金。关煞二方无障碍，光明正大旺门庭。

于严格拘泥。但山水环抱是人们择居的先决条件。天然符合之，最善，若不足，则需在风水先生指导下群策群力加以弥补和改善。

例如安徽歙县呈坎村，坐西朝东、背山面水，体现了"负阴抱阳"的形势。整个村子按《易经》"阴（坎）""阳（呈）""二气统一"和"天人合一"的八卦风水理论选址布局，四周有葛山、鲤王山、龙山、长春山、观音山等八座山岭恰如八卦对应，一条众川河由北向南穿村而过。村中三街、九十九巷，宛如迷宫。河东地势平坦，是数千亩的田园。又如龙岩培田村，它坐西面东，背靠卧虎山，左有河源溪绕村而过，右临大道，祠堂和民居前多有半月形泮池，以水济火，而村口建有文武庙和水车锁钥水口气势，村落前方正对笔架三山，宛如天然屏障。

图7-1　培田村风貌

我们可以得出结论，这些古村庄的营建都非常讲究并努力去吻合风水原则的。可以说，经过屡世苦心经营发展而来的古村落不仅有经典的历史建筑群，而且包含着儒家思想、风水堪舆等人文地理信息，是我们进行传统中华文化学习研究必须充分利用的宝贵资料。

（3）宗祠建筑结构

就实际所见，各地村落祠堂多为两进或三进式，少数也有四进，以中轴对称，围合成庭院。分为：1. 大门。2. 前堂，即享堂，是祭祖仪式中上供和跪拜之所。3. 正堂，即寝堂或龛堂，是供奉祖宗牌位之所。4. 夹室，与寝堂相连，可为存放族谱或祭具的地方。5. 两庑，或连廊，可用来设置家族私塾，供子弟学习之所。6. 有些地方的宗祠大门内外设戏台、半圆形池塘（泮池）、照壁，以及彰显家族荣耀的石龙旗杆，祠堂后或靠风水林。

因为祠堂是祖灵所归，是家族的集体象征和村落的荣耀之地，所以家族无论大小都会倾资建设，各种设计宏丽庄严，用材考究，雕刻装饰也尽显中国传统工艺的细节之美。更有各种寓意深刻、书法高超的楹联，悬挂着各类家规祖训、旌表族人功名与贞孝美德的牌匾，让人宛如置身一座民间艺术博物馆。如黄山市歙县棠樾村鲍氏家族的古祠堂"敦本堂"，坐北朝南，三进五开间，五凤楼门厅。祠内大厅的左右墙壁上拓印着朱熹书法作品"忠孝廉节"。整体结构简洁明了，银杏为柱，樟木作梁，砖、木、石雕洗练不繁，处处透露出儒家人生哲理和文化内涵，显示着不偏不倚的"中和之美"。

（4）宗祠的等级

宗祠作为祖宗庙，它是根据祭祀对象划分为不同的等级。一般有：总祠、支祠和家祠这样三个等级。

总祠是族裔为祭祀一世祖及其下若干代子孙所建的总祠堂。总祠在祠堂类型中地位等级为最高。如广州市内的陈家祠是广东省 72 县的陈姓的总祠，龙岩连城县的培田村吴氏总祠衍庆堂（供奉培田吴氏 1~9 世祖)①。这里讲的一世祖或始祖，都是本族确有传承线索可查可据的第一代祖先（或开基祖），一般不会早于宋代。

支祠，也叫房祠。姓氏家族繁衍绵延、开枝散叶，到若干代后遂分房立派，他们为各自房派的祖先所建的祠堂就叫支祠。如培田村吴氏家族以元末明初吴八四公为宣和乡吴氏开基祖，第三代吴文贵公迁至今培田村，传至第十代分为四大房：敬公房、崇公房、中公房、宏公房。而四房中又以敬公房后裔为兴发最盛。培田村现存祠堂中多数是属于敬公房的房祠，如容庵公祠、久公祠等。

家祠，也叫香火堂，是祠寝相连的位于民居之中的祭祀室，即"飨堂"。一般设在厅堂，或家中置有祖龛的房间。依朱熹制定的祠堂礼制，家祠只能供奉自高祖以下的四世祖的神主牌位。五服以外的先祖、始祖是享受不到家祠祭祀的香火的。因为农村之中土地资源紧张，若没有土地或者也没有财力，来为祖宗兴建祠堂的话，就只能设置在民居之中开辟一处作为香火堂。香火堂是宗祠类型中最普遍也是等级最低的祠堂形式，曾广泛地建于中国南北各地的传统民居之中。今天，在东南亚老派华人家中，这类供奉四世祖的香火堂也很常见。四世之祖灵与子孙"一本至亲。先灵依乎后嗣"，朝夕鉴临庇佑，也算是一种特殊的天人合一的生活方式了。

除此之外，还有一些专门类型的祠堂。如长房享堂是在宗祠旁边独立供奉历代

---

① 祠中年代最早者为"祖祠"（众祠之祖），祖祠未必是总祠。

长房长孙的享堂，特祭祠是供奉那些香火不续的先辈成员的。另外有两种更为特殊。

女祠就是女性祠堂。如安徽歙县棠樾村的鲍氏姝祠，建于清嘉庆十年（1805），又名"清懿堂"。女性祠堂非常独特，因为祠堂是男性的圣地，一般只有男性祖先的名字才被写上牌位摆在祠堂里接受供奉（香火堂神主除外），族中女性以及未成年人无特殊理由都不被允许进入祠堂。所以棠樾村鲍氏家族能为女子建祠堂的做法，可以说难能可贵。鲍氏姝祠的建筑面积甚至比对面的男祠"敦本堂"还要大50平方米，其正大门外墙的雕刻也更为精美。由此可见古徽州人对女子的贞节精神和坚毅品德的高度肯定和由衷赞美。

双姓祠，就是一个祠堂供奉两个姓氏的祖宗。原因需要具体考察。如陕西省韩城市徐村的冯氏家族和同氏家族每年的清明、春节进同一祠堂祭祖，两千多年从未间断。原因是冯同两家其实都是司马迁的后裔。司马迁因事入狱，怕皇帝株连家人，就改"司马"为"同""冯"，让后代改姓之。歌谣说：韩城汉后无司马，冯同两姓撑门庭；花开两枝根相同，清明同祭一祖宗。又如黄山市绩溪县的龙川胡氏大宗祠里面也有一座两进三开间的丁姓家族小祠堂，胡氏和丁氏合祠一处则是一个听起来颇有趣的风水故事。当地村落地势像条船，胡姓谐音是浮（萍），而丁姓的谐音是钉（子），所以需要用钉子钉住船只，以保浮萍免受风浪的灾难。

（5）祠堂堂号的命名

传统祠堂都会有个堂号，其命名方面一般会特别体现出某种家族伦理观念。比如表明勿忘祖先根本的观念，像敦本堂、务本堂、叙伦堂。什么是本？祖先就是本。水木的源头和根本，那就是祖先，家族生命的源头。还有表明宗族的郡望，就是家族的来源地，比如说中山堂、江夏堂、渤海堂、三槐堂，就是地名了。另外表明某些赞美或祈愿的寓意，比如说清懿堂、衍庆堂、敬承堂、双善堂、万寿堂等。祠堂也有悬挂一些代表祖上获取何种功名以及入仕官职的牌匾，如将军府、尚书第、大夫第、翰林第等。这些堂号取好后都会请书法高手书写并做成宽大的堂匾悬挂起来，成为族人仰望之所止。

7.2.2　宗祠祭祖及其规范

宗祠传统上有许多功能，它是祭祖的圣地、行使族权的法庭、日常要务的礼堂、教育子弟的学校等，而祭祀祖宗是毋庸置疑的第一位。按照儒家思想——祭祀活动是国家的大事之一。宗祠的祭祖活动也是家族最重要的集体活动，是宗族成员的神圣义务。祭祖的目的与意义在于寄托追慕思远、尊祖敬宗之情，借以达到凝聚人心、团结族人、维系宗族组织的发展。当然，祭祖有一套明确而固定的仪典，在族谱中都会对本家族的祭祀种类、时间、执事、程序、祭物、纪律等做出详细的说明。

（1）民间祭祖的日期

民间祭祖的日期虽然不能如贵族（如皇家和孔府祭祖）动辄一年数十次那么频繁，但一般也有如下数种：1. 四时祭，春、夏、秋、冬四季的首月十五日祭祖叫四时祭，其中冬祭（烝祭）因在夏耕秋获后，在四时祭中最为隆重。2. 年节祭，即逢年节祭祖。像除夕、清明节、重阳节、中元节，是汉族年节祭祖的四大节日。3. 特祭，祖先的忌日做祭祀，这叫特祭。4. 遇到特殊事由需要祭祖，这叫"告祭"。5. 香火堂中需每日早晚给祖先上香上供，所谓"晨昏须荐祖宗香"，这叫"常祭"。

如我们上面提到的龙岩市连城县培田村吴氏家族的祭祖习俗。在每年的正月初二，吴姓男丁都要集中到吴氏宗族的总祠"衍庆堂"里共拜"祖图"，拜他们从一世到九世的祖宗。初三到初五，各房族人又在本房支祠，或老宅祭拜本房派的祖先。先共祭总祠，再到支祠。三月、八月他们又祭拜各方历代的祖墓。清明节只特别地祭祀培田吴氏始祖吴八四。因为宗堂众多，为了祭拜有序，宗族还为各房祭拜统一安排了时间表，以免冲突。在浙江建德市的新叶村，他们祭祖的日期是每年的农历三月初三，这是一个特别的日子，外地子孙都要返乡参加祭祖活动，场面非常的热闹，规模远胜春节等节日。

（2）祭祖的一般仪式

举办祭祖仪式的主体一般是宗亲会主持，具体由各房派按年份轮流负责。像新叶村叶氏宗族有崇仁、崇智等五个房派，他们按照天干地支的顺序，轮流举办每年的祭祖活动。但无论哪房举办，都以族长来做主祭，由年辈和"文化地位"较高的人来担任陪祭（有些家族是长房长孙为主祭，而由族长任陪祭）。另外从各房中安排头面人物任通赞、引赞、司祝、司尊、司帛、司爵、司馔、司盥等执事人员（助祭），负责赞礼以及奉献各种祭品供物。如果家族条件可以的话，可能还会有钟鼓生、歌诗生、舞生。其他族人就各依辈分次序和身份尊卑列队肃立。

传统祭祖仪式按照鼓乐、迎神、揖拜、上供、唱祭、祭宴、送神、焚帛等一应既定仪式，井然进行，但各地也会自有特色。据培田村吴氏族人介绍，吴氏家族的祭祖仪式大概如下[1]。

---

[1]　培田祭祖习俗亦可参看郑振满、张侃著《乡土中国：培田》，生活·新知·读书三联书店 2005 年版相关记述。

1. 祭祀日一早，随着十番鼓乐奏响，全族裔亲，按辈序大小排班，齐聚祠堂，执事、司祭职责分明。由族中辈分最高的人，郑重请出祖先画像，将画轴按辈分悬挂起来，然后将族谱开箱展示，供族人祭拜。同时杀猪宰羊，准备鸡、鱼、猪三牲祭品，待一切齐备后，点烛焚香，更衣赞拜。2. 祭祀开始，发初鼓、二鼓、三鼓，奏乐（祠堂的戏台就是"十番"乐队的乐池）。3. 瘗毛血迎神，即将鸡、猪的毛血洒于天井内求神荫佑。接着行三叩九拜大礼，三次献牲、汤、果品，三次赞唱叩拜。4. 族人在族长率领下，先由族长和长辈开始，然后众裔嗣一一向祖像和族谱一跪四叩首，举爵三酬后，所有人员礼毕，便开始"饮福受胙"，这是全族人规模盛大的祭宴。5. 祭宴尽兴后，又开始新的画谱仪式，即将历代祖先的名字重新誊录在纸上，抄毕后撤馔，送神，行二跪三叩礼。6. 之后便是捧祝进帛，望燎焚祭，礼毕。更衣收图，鼓乐奏响，将图卷起行送图仪式。

香烟袅袅中念祭声声，这是一个子孙和祖灵心心相通的对话，整个过程庄严肃穆。参加祭祀的人员一个个虔诚而恭敬，且衣冠端正，如祖考临之在上，不可以戏谑谈笑。凡"行礼不恭，离席自便，与夫跛倚、欠伸、哕噎、嚏咳、一切失容之事"，都要议罚（《浦江郑氏世范》）。祭祖当然是肃穆庄重的事。但到了祭毕的"饮福受胙"环节，气氛就开始变得轻松而欢快。"饮福"就是饮用祭酒，"享胙"就是食用祭肉。祖先用过的祭品，按照民众的理解，饮食之可以获得祖先的福泽。在宗族文化里头，有一种对犯有过失的族人的重要的惩罚，就是"革胙"，或者叫作"停胙"，就是不允许他们参加祭祀活动，不给他们分发祭祀的祭肉，是一种比较严重的处罚的方法。除了欢快的聚宴，有些宗族在祭祖后还会举行地方戏剧的表演，或者会有鼓乐仪仗绕村（祠）一周，以追念祖上恩泽，颂扬其贤德，并祈求宗族旺盛。这都是家族民众的喜乐时刻和娱乐时间，欢声笑语一扫之前的肃穆之气。

（3）祭祖的经济条件

祭祖活动所费不菲，那么经费从哪来呢？一般来讲有两种，一是募资制，即向家族成员定期地筹募，以备特定的祭祀活动所用；二是祭田制，就是祖先早有远见，早就备下了田产，指定这个田产不能被分割，只能作为家族祭祖的基金。当然，后来的子孙们自己兴家发业可以追加捐献，如徽商和晋商有钱有势，他们非常热心家族公益，也会慷慨捐献（其他如兴建祠堂、牌坊与族学等家族公共事业上，也有此类情况）。所以祖先留一部分、子孙不断地捐献，这就会形成一个比较庞大的家族祭田。祭田的管理也非常严格。因为它是属于家族共有的资产，一般是由族长或者宗亲会来给予管理，或者是由轮值年祭活动的房派来管理，严禁变相侵吞，甚至是变卖。

祭祖之礼，固然力求隆重，但更重要的是子孙的一份诚意。毕竟每个家族、每个人的经济能力是有差别的。儒家并不主张不顾条件的奢祭，孔子就说"礼，与其奢也，宁俭。丧，与其易也，宁戚"（《论语·八佾》）。如果一定要用贵族或富人的标准来定义尽孝和祭祖的方式，那穷人家又该怎么办呢？孔子云"虽疏食菜羹，瓜祭，必齐如也"（《论语·乡党》）。也就是说，对普通人家而言，就是奉献刚刚采摘的菜蔬、洁净的瓜果做的菜羹作为祭品，也是最好的奉献了。比如贵州的侗族同胞在尝新节的时候，就用新结的稻穗泡自酿的白酒，外加一点鱼肉和蔬菜来祭祖。这种形式简洁朴素而不奢侈浪费，很符合儒家讲的中庸尽孝的要求。有念亲、敬祖之心，就是极好的孝道。

（4）宗祠的其他功能与日常管理

除了作为祭祖场所之外，宗祠还有其他一些功能。

我们已经说过，它是祭祖的圣地、行使族权的法庭、举办日常要务的礼堂、教育子弟的学校等。比如家族的长老们可以在祠堂开会议事，凡族人违反族规，则在这里被教育和受到处理，直至剥夺族籍。在封建时代，它是一个族内法庭和议会场所。宗祠还是本族子弟接受蒙学教育的义学或私塾的开设地，也就是教育机构。族人的成人礼、婚礼、寿宴活动，也会放到祠堂里头来进行，这当然是利用祠堂的空间场地比较敞阔便于聚众活动之故。如娶妻、嫁女要进入祠堂行"告庙"之礼，而后婚姻才有其合法性。族人亡故之后，也会在祠堂停灵收敛做法事，或者是举办周年祭。有的宗族还定期到祠堂来进行看谱、读谱的活动。吉安市泰和梅岗王氏宗祠每年暑假都会为金榜题名的家族学子举办赠送贺喜对联、发放奖学金的活动，这都是祠堂作为事务礼堂的功能的表现。祠堂通常也是举办节庆活动的娱乐场所。像韶山毛氏宗祠里就有一个戏台，在祭祖活动之后进行地方戏的表演，既是供祖灵观赏，更是农村民众难得的文化娱乐时间。祠堂周边一般还包括水塘、广场等外围空间，可供村妇们洗衣淘米、孩童们玩耍、小商贩们兜售物品、定期集市等。

宗祠如此之重要，每个家族都会重视对祠堂的日常维护和管理。平时宗祠是锁闭的，如果说家族经济条件允许，就会出资请专人来看管，以保证祠堂安全和内部的整洁。这个看祠人一般是家族里人品端正，或者是家庭生活有困难的鳏夫、无嗣者。当然会从家族的公产里头给予一定的经济报酬，这也表示了家族对他们的体恤与照顾。看祠人需要每日上香，打扫厅堂、严防火烛。在家族有祭祀活动的时候，看祠人也要负责维护秩序，帮助准备各种祭品、香烛、仪式、明器等。

7.2.3　宗祠和祭祖文化的影响

数千年来，"孝亲"情感一直在中华民族的社会观念中占据着至高无上的地位。祭祖则是由传承孝道衍生出来的一种形式。人们认为其他神灵都不如祖先神尊贵，因而各地都建有祠堂、家庙，各家都奉祀祖先牌位，定期举行祭祖仪式则是中国民间最重要的信仰活动。孔子云："践其位，行其礼，奏其乐，敬其所尊，爱其所亲。事死如事生，事亡如事存，孝之至也。"（《中庸》）祭祖活动中，人们站立在先前排定的位置上，行使祭祀的礼节，奏起祭祀的音乐，尊敬那些理应尊敬的人，爱护那些理应亲近的人，侍奉死去的人就像侍奉活着的人一样，这才是孝的最高标准。曾子云："慎终追远，民德归厚矣。"（《论语·学而》）即是说通过培养对祖先的尊重、回忆遥远的过去，人的性情就会醇厚、美德就会提升。

祭祖文化作为一套行为仪式，体现了人们对特殊生活意义的崇尚和追求。正如格尔茨所说，仪式是"当地人讲给他们自己听的关于他们自己的故事"。《人类简史》的作者尤尔瓦·赫拉利认为：一个会讲故事的种族，事实上就更有生存下去的活力和动力。中国民间村落一代接一代、每年重复做的一件大事（或者说集体讲述的故事）就是对去世先祖的隆重祭奠和顶礼膜拜，以此祈求祖先保佑后人人丁兴旺、家族昌盛。正是通过不绝如缕的孝亲敬祖和相应的祭祖文化的熏陶教养，中华民族才养成了今天这种慎终追远、孝道至上、温和敦厚的民族文化性格。正如《人民日报》曾有一段刊文如此说道：

"祠堂是存放我们乡愁的陈列馆，是安放我们灵魂的栖息地。……祠堂祭祖，已然成为血脉汇聚、增进感情、精神认同的家族功课和不忘根系、感恩思孝、端修品德的人生功课。"[1]

7.3　族谱与家风

下面我们来看一下族谱这种非常有特色的华夏民间文献。

它有很多种名称，如族谱、宗谱、家谱、世谱，也可以单独称作谱。族谱是以记录宗族世系源流为主，收集登载其他宗族文件为辅的一种文献。家谱记载的方式，曾有结绳记述，有口头代代相传，还有碑文记述和图书记述等。我

---

① 可参看《人民日报》（2016 年 09 月 05 日 24 版）《进得祠堂》一文。

国在汉唐宋时期便有谱，但撰谱主要是帝王和贵族、官家的特权。直到明嘉靖、万历时期，一种有别于唐宋家谱，记载一个家族的源流、世系、血缘关系、人丁、先世功绩、氏族居住地、莹墓、族产、族规和家族文献等各种情况的新型家谱开始出现。自明清以来，民间修谱成风，至今存谱何虞上万种。族谱与正史、方志构成了中华民族历史学大厦的三根支柱，在记录家族历史的同时，也为历史学、社会学、人口学、民族学的研究提供了丰富的信息。

7.3.1 族谱的体例和格式

（1）传统族谱的格式和体例

以《醴东仙石汤氏族谱》为例，可见其包括如下的内容。

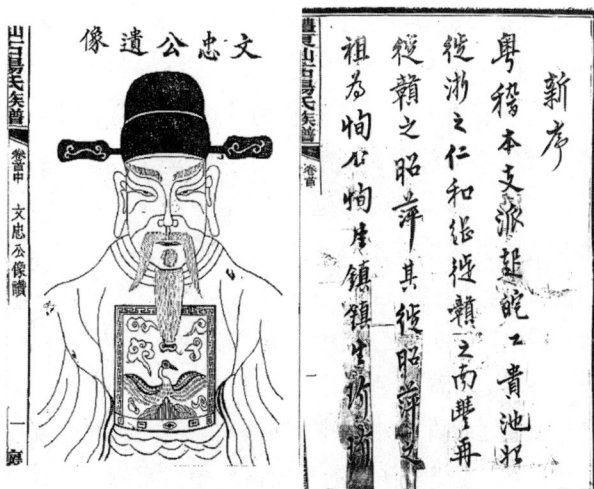

图 7-2 醴东仙石汤氏族谱新序与东分始祖文忠公像

第一，序言：一篇以书法形式刊印的、（某次）编修族谱的序言。

第二，族谱目录：全谱各卷篇目。

第三，祖先遗像及像赞。

第四，敕命与旌表文件：朝廷或官府对族人的表彰文件和风评勘语。这部分也被视作家族所获的恩荣。如《汤氏族谱》中收录了如宣和七年北宋皇家颁给的"敕命提点两广宣抚史都御史汤梦观父母诰命一道""奖励宣抚使御史汤梦观敕命一道"等朝廷旌表文件。另外还有"雪峰公祀乡贤县府勘语""瞿孺人节孝部文"等公文，则是各级官府对该族中人物的风评申报的正式批复。能得到国家和地方政府的褒奖与肯定，对一个家族而言，这当然是一件值得荣耀的事件，也令后世子孙望而生敬。

第五，原序、原跋：包括各代、各次重修族谱的序言与跋文。

《醴东仙石汤氏族谱》自明清以来，已迭经十一次编修续修，其间各次修谱所撰之序言、跋文凡二十四篇，一并存谱传诸后世，可见古今同心、一脉相承。这些序言和跋文，对后人回顾和了解历史上各次修谱的原因和具体过程，非常有帮助。

第六，凡例：关于编修本族谱所遵守的体例和编辑原则的说明。

该谱"凡例十六则"中对编辑族谱过程中涉及的诸多情况确定了统一的处理原则，并做了说明。如编订家世的"信实原则"的说明，所用谱式体例（欧苏谱牒法式）及其特点的说明，关于"元亨利贞四大房派"的说明，采用"纪年方式"的说明，本族所用"字派"的说明，族人"取名命字"的说明，各类人员（如夫妻、过继者、姻亲、外迁者等）"入谱书写术语"的说明，以及"保存和补录文献"的说明等。其中，关于入谱资格的问题，传统家族文化都看得很重要，对何人可有资格入谱，以及特别处理的方式，都详加了规定。目的就是严防紊乱，追求父系血缘的纯粹性。如离婚带回家的夫家之子，收养的义子都不可以入谱，过继子嗣首选同房近支等。

另外就是确定家族世系次序的"字派"。"字派"也叫"字辈"，或者"行辈"，是中国人命名时用以表明代次（辈分）的用字。一般会有 20 个或 30 个字，形制似诗，又称"派语"，可供二三十代子孙取名使用，并借此确定个人的辈分次序。族人中谁是哪一辈，一看名字即了然于胸，自然不会紊乱了长幼先后的伦理。一代人用一个字，用完之后再另外续补。过去时代都是严格沿用字辈语的次序取名，不遵者不允许入谱。《醴东仙石汤氏族谱》中规定的"字辈语"有 20 个字，供第 20 代到第 39 代子孙取名之用。这 20 个字是：象添光大清，如有正其中。道学从先守，修培继述隆。如我的祖父汤正梅先生是二十七代"正"字辈，家父汤其连先生是二十八代"其"字辈，到我是二十九代"中"字辈。

我国彝族民众在历史上有过一种"父子连名系谱"的习俗。在彝语中把父子连名系谱叫"茨"，这是他们口口相传以存家族史的方式。比如彝族命名均是儿子以父亲的名字中后一个或两个字音为姓。"细奴逻、逻盛皮、逻盛、盛逻皮、皮逻阁、阁罗凤、凤牟异、异牟寻……"儿时熟记，成年后熟诵无误，否则会被歧视为"外人"。我看这个命名之法，与汉族以"字派语"为基础命名，并借以确定世系传承次序的传统相似，可以算作广义的中华命名文化的相近形态。当然，随着时代的变化，今天的人们都不知族谱为何物，也就不再用族谱中的"派语"来命名。如我儿翊钧，就没有再用族谱中第三十代的"道"字辈的那个"道"字。这种普遍存在的情况，可以说是中国人"字辈取名制"传统模式的彻底"断裂"。

第七，家训、家法、族规。

就是祖辈留下的各种人生训诫和约束性的道德规范。像我们《汤氏族谱》就载有家训十六条、族约三十二条、祠规十三条。可谓谆谆教诲、殷切寄望。

第八，世系传承的图、表。

世系是直观呈现从始祖（或始迁祖、开基祖）以来，传承至今、确有实据的每一代家族成员的基本信息。其呈现的格式有两种：一种是欧式谱式，一种是苏氏谱式。这两种谱式据说是北宋时的欧阳修和苏洵所创制的。

欧式谱也叫瓜蔓谱式，它的特点就是父子相继、兄弟平列，五代一提，只列其名，简明直观，而且女子不列入。如图所示，我族的东分始祖第一代是文忠公汤梦观，其有六子，为第二代，各人名下或有子若干，为第三代，如是延续，至第五代之后，则另外开列第六代到第十代，仍循如上原则。应该讲，非常直观，非常清楚。

苏式谱也叫齿录谱式，就像今天的表格式人口信息登记表。比较于欧式谱，苏式谱更为详细，记录了各代之人的生卒、婚配及子嗣的情况，若有功名者则更予概述。如图所见，表格中载述文忠公汤梦观的字号、生卒年月、科举功名和任职之事，他的德配黄氏夫人的生卒年月及其子嗣的情况。第二代亦复如是。比较而言，苏式谱更为详细，容量更大、反映情况更全面立体。

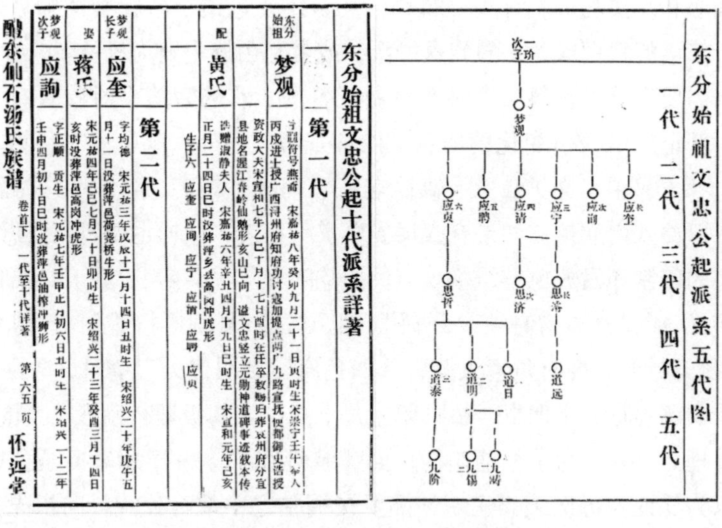

图7-3　欧式谱与苏式谱的特点

世系图（表）是一套族谱里最核心的信息，所占分量也最大，家族中一代代的人口传承资料全保存在这一页页的记录之中。我们按图索骥，可以溯流而上，准确找到自己直系和旁系的祖宗的信息。貌似很单调的一个个名字，一段段生配卒葬的信息，却写尽了"人生代代无穷已"的丰富多彩与世事如烟的唏嘘感慨。中华民族是个文字性的民族，也是个历史性的民族。他那厚重的历史理性意识，就在这由世系图表纵横编织而成的生命长河中熠熠生辉。

第九，传记：一些家族成员的生平传记，有些是夫妻合传。

第十，文学作品：历代族人文艺作品如诗词歌赋的选录。

第十一，各种贺寿文章、墓志铭的选录。

第十二，家族祠堂图、墓地图及其说明。

第十三，祭祀的陈设图、仪式的注说。

第十四个内容，就是族谱领取分发的记录。

以上就是一般族谱的基本格式和体例所包含的主要内容。

（2）关于修谱的时间和程序

族谱一般而言是要求 20 年一修，或 30 年一修。山东曲阜孔氏家族则特别规定一甲子（60 年）修谱一次。如果长期不续修家谱，任其荒废中绝，会被认为是一种不孝的行为。那么编修家谱，谁来组织这项工作？作为家族中的一件大事，一般是由宗亲会来发动和组织，由族中的头面人物如族长、房头或者有文化修养的族亲和热心者，由这些人来具体主持族谱的修订。这当然需要付出极大的细心和扎实功夫。有些大的家族甚至还要邀请一些社会的知名学者来充任此职。修谱的费用或者是向族众摊派，或者是由族中财力雄厚者来承担。

修谱需要充分的资料，平时要早做准备的。有的宗族平时就置有一本添丁簿，随时登记族中人口变化的信息，以备查考。另外，族中或有科第显宦、道德硕儒、孝子悌弟、义士仁人、高隐名流、词林艺苑者，各户头应一律撰写事迹上报，以便入谱立传。如果有假报或事实不符者，同样也要以家法惩罚。

族谱的印制和发放也有严格规定。如乾隆九年（1744），孔府订出修谱"条规"就多达 34 条。修谱时须"开馆"、祀祖先，颁发"格册"，严防"诡名冒认"。印刷开始时，要有负责人监督，如孔府印制明代天启谱时，"县主同至卑庭，面看刷印卷首一十四页，每页印完九十八张，其板即行刮毁"。康、乾诸谱亦效此办理。另外，为了杜绝诈伪，谱牒装订完毕，一律加盖衍圣公府和世职县印，以为凭证。每次续修完毕，都要在祠堂之中举行仪式，向祖先禀告，然后分发给各房派各持若干套（孔府族规领谱须将旧谱上交，立行焚毁）。

7.3.2 家训、族规和家风

家训也叫祖训，是一套家谱里重要的组成部分。它是祖先们对子孙后代为人处世的训诫和教诲。而家法和族规是家族中具有惩戒性质的道德约束的规章。家训和族规是国家的伦理教化和国家法律的重要配合与补充，对一家之门风的形成发挥着建设性的作用。我国各姓氏家族自古以来就非常重视家训族规问题，其族谱文献中一般都会专列家训族规等条目。开卷有益，这些丰富而各有特色的家训文献，至今仍很有参考价值。

（1）以培田村《吴氏族谱》之家训、族规为例

该村的族谱有乾隆、同治、光绪三个版本，先后载入了《家训十六则》《家法十条》和《族规十则》。

他们的《家训十六则》，是这样的："敬祖宗、孝父母、和兄弟、序长幼、别男女、睦宗亲、谨婚姻、慎丧葬、勉读书、勤生业、崇节俭、戒淫行、戒匪僻、戒刻薄、戒贪饕、戒争讼。"这十六条家训侧重对孝、悌、仁、爱、勤、俭等传统道德的倡导，鼓励族人遵守。每则还备注 32 字释文，指向清晰。

光绪本《吴氏族谱》增录了《家法十条》："孝弟宜敦、勤俭宜崇、廉耻宜励、伦常宜肃、忠厚宜尚、品行宜端、礼义宜明、争竞宜平、刑罚宜公、身家宜清。"虽然家法是带有惩戒性质的道德约束，但本意是为了警醒后代，"顾立训使人遵，立法使人畏"。因此，家法是对家训的一个延续扩展，与家训相辅相成。

《族规十则》："祖堂——妥先灵而庇后裔；图谱——考世系而知始终；图银——权子母而资修刻；冠婚——荣宗族而继宗祧；丧制——尽子道而报亲恩；后龙水口——蓄树木而卫风水；前朝屏山——拱祖堂而壮观瞻；路内水圳——护祖堂而便汲饮；田禾蔬菜——备饥荒而佐餐飨；松杉竹木——生财源而资利用。"从中可以看出，族规所规定的大部分是一些需要整个宗族重视、配合和参与的集体性的公共事务，尤其是对村落的生态环境、风水的保护、家族的成员的冠婚丧祭等活动做出了统一规定。比较于家训，它侧重的是全族人必须共同遵守的约束性的行为规范。培田吴氏家族把个体的道德修养和家族的集体行为统一起来。族谱的编修者们希望整个家族能同心遵行，以期实现"风纯俗美，可称仁里"的目的，归根到底还是为整个家族的每个人创造一个宜居的美好家园。

除了家族内部的家法族规的各种要求，《吴氏族谱》还有收录了一些家族范围之外、关注乡里公共社会事务的乡规民约。如光绪二十三年（1897）培田吴

氏制定的《公益社章程》里就提倡乡里各村各坊共遵共行如下乡规条款："警察盗匪、严禁赌博、劝戒鸦片、改良地约、平息争讼、振兴实业、修蓄竹木、崇尚节俭、敦崇伦纪、修明礼法。"这些条款关注社会治安、社会习俗以及当地实业发展。其治理范围从家族进一步往外扩展，有着比较强的乡规民约的意味。培田人在晚清时期就发起组织过一些公益组织，如"朱子惜字社""拯婴社"等。"拯婴社"的宗旨就是阻止农村存在的重男轻女溺杀女婴的行为。

（2）从家训到门风

应该说祖训家规在中国人的文化史上一直有着特殊的色彩。中国传统社会历来高度重视家训、家教和家风问题。"孟母三迁""岳母刺字""画荻教子"的故事广为流传，《诫子书》《颜氏家训》《朱子家训》《温公家训》《袁氏世范》等备受推崇。可以说，中华家训文化，代表的是一代代家族先辈对后裔的殷切嘱托和深切厚望，对一个个家族的人心建设和代代相传良好家风的形成与传承发挥过积极的作用。

像江苏无锡的钱氏家族，是令人仰望的、以门风注重教育而知名天下的名门望族，涌现了像近代文化名人钱学森、钱基博、钱穆、钱钟书、钱伟长等一大批杰出人才。据统计，无锡籍的两院院士共有 67 人，而钱氏家族的成员就占了其中的 8 人，这自然是与钱武肃王钱镠留下的"为国尊贤、崇教重学"的精神训教有直接的关系。

在田野调查之中，我们也注意到，培田村民风淳朴，人才辈出。不仅有吴拔祯这样的文举人、武进士，也有吴昌同这样的商业奇才、"乐善好施"的义士。到民国后，培田就有 4 名学子赴日本和法国求学，其中的吴迺青与我们的周恩来总理还是同学。有 5 人于黄埔军校学习。新中国成立以后共培养了博士、硕士、工程师以及大中专毕业生数百人。这正是得益于培田吴氏不断完善家训族规，兴养立教、耕读传家，范导了吴氏家族的精神血脉，使得善行忠义之风薪火相传，代代不息。

这种崇文重教、力行道德的家风，大概也是闽西客家人共有的一种文化性格和精神。像我们走进土楼人家，就可以看到那些土楼的大门上的门联，都是他们的客家先人为子孙后代留下的一条条的祖训。像漳州南靖怀远楼的门联：怀以德，敦以仁，藉此修齐遵祖训。远而山，近而水，凭兹灵秀育人文。龙岩永定的振远楼的门联是：振纲立纪，成德达材。

习近平主席非常重视家教家风建设问题。《习近平关于注重家庭家教家风建设论述摘编》一书就集中表现了习近平主席在这一方面的重要思想。比如习主席指出：家训是家庭的核心价值观，家规是家庭的"基本法"，家风是家族子孙代代恪守家训、家规而长期形成的具有鲜明家族特征的家庭文化，是一个家庭最宝贵的财产，是每个家庭成员自豪感的源泉。他强调家教要注重崇德向善与做的人气节，这是家教的核心内容。要注意发挥母亲的独特作用，要在新时代把兴家和强国相统一，要运用多种方法开展家教活动等。

总之，族谱文献的主体内容是世系传承的人口信息，但其他如家训与族规，重要先辈的人物传记，文学作品和家族祠堂墓地等材料也具有非常重要的史料价值，所以它被叫作是家族的《史记》。每一代的子孙可以靠阅读家谱来了解家族的来龙去脉，从而兴起一种强烈的血缘共同体的历史意识。对于加强家族的认同感和荣誉感，进而形成良好的家风，激发子孙后代继往开来、光前裕后的奋发之心，对于促进家族的持续发展和整个社会的文明进步，可以起到巨大的、不可替代的作用。

7.4 族权与义门

我们知道，一个村落的宗族涉及一众族人，一年中大小事务还是不少的。如祭祀祖先、共有祖产的经营及使用、村落环境的保护、宗谱的撰修和各种护卫乡里的敬神游神活动等，而这些重要的宗族活动都是在族长为核心的宗亲会领导下进行的。

7.4.1 族长和族权

作为家族的核心人物——族长，是宗族事务的主管人，是家族的对外代理人。他所掌握和运用的宗族权力具有复杂的特性。这方面，有几点信息值得我们注意。

第一，族长来自乡土中国的乡绅（缙绅）阶层。

民间村落的族长并不遵守古典宗法制下的嫡长子继承原则，而是选举所出。其候选人的条件一般而言，或"尚齿"即论辈分年龄，或"尚德"即看个人是否德高望重，为人所推重钦佩。但这两个条件是比较虚的，起决定作用的还是候选人个人和家庭的财富和社会权势。如其本人（或其家人）是在职或退休的官员，受过一定的儒学教育，或经商而富，见多识广，广有人脉和社会资源可借用。这些宗族中的能人，也正是居乡的实力阶层，他们构成乡村社会的缙绅阶层，即"乡绅"。

以山东曲阜孔子世家为例，衍圣公作为大宗主，"统摄宗族"是其主要职责之一。孔氏宗族人数众多，仅聚居在曲阜的族人就分为六十宗户。在整个家族范围内，设"孔庭族长"作为除衍圣公外的最高管理人员，又设"林庙举事"辅佐族长。各宗户内则仿设户首、户举，管理本户内事宜。外地孔氏族人的组织与曲阜孔氏大致相同，接受衍圣公的管理。此外，立行辈、订族规、修族谱也是进行宗族管理的有效方式。又以培田村为例，约在清朝康乾时期，培田村就形成了有规模、有权威的宗族组织，组织的领导成员由各房派中的房头组成。另外，再从族内经济实力强的豪绅、卸职官吏、德高望重的老者中选出族长。最后组成一个七至九人的吴氏宗族董事会。董事会管理事项很多，而所有的议事活动都在宗祠中进行，当然是根据内容和性质，在不同等级的宗祠、房祠或香火堂中举行。

第二，中国乡土社会的宗族权力系统具有特别的复杂性。

（1）从宗族社会的管理方式上看具有亲族伦理性的特点。宗亲会管理宗族社会，主要是用非法制的血亲伦理方式（家训家法族规乡约）来教育约束族人，一般并不"擅兴词讼"，而是靠亲情和伦理的方式来协调宗族社会的矛盾与冲突，表现了亲情+道德的柔性力量的灵活性和弹性空间。正如黄山市歙县唐模村许氏家族的《许氏家规》（乾隆六年订）中所说：

凡因小过，情有可宥者，而欲尽抵于法，亦非所以爱之也。莫若执于祠，祖宗临之，族长正、副斥其过而正之，棰楚以加之，庶其能改，而不为官府之累，其明刑弼教之行于家者乎？

（2）族长及其族权是宗族社会和政府权力系统的联结中心和辅佐力量。族长对内主持祭祀典礼之权（充当主祭）、主管族产（如祭田、书院、祠堂等家族共产）之权、教化惩教族人之权、纠纷调停之权。对外，则与地方各姓氏家族的族长们协调乡村事务，与地方政府接洽处理上传下达的必要事务如纳粮、徭役、缉盗、送凶等工作。所以，他是宗族的内政官与外交官。族长为代表的乡绅阶层掌握族权，负责上传下达，主管乡土社会，布满农村各个角落，成为仅次于政权的地方权力体系。

宋明以后，民间社会的宗族制得到统治阶级的广泛支持。官方看重的既是宗族系统重视儒家宗法思想，其发展有助于封建统治所需要的伦理教化与人心约束。同时，还有借重宗亲会来维持地方社会政治经济秩序的工具性考虑。因此官方对地方权力有一定的下放，授权给乡绅阶层代行管制之权。所谓"皇权不下乡"即是此意。费孝通先生在《乡土中国》将其概括为中国传统社会的"双轨政治理论"：自上而下的皇权 + 自下而上的绅权和族权，两者平行运作，互相作用。乡绅管理乡土中国的事实，就表现了族权和政权的融合性。族权与政权互补、官员与乡绅互用，是中国封建社会得以长期延续的重要原因。

应该说，实际的大量例子也证明，亲族网络中同样交织着君权对民权、礼教对人权、有产对无产、男权对女权的压制和侵害。正如我们看到的有些宗族的族规就明确规定族人所涉"轻罪"和"重罪"及其相应的惩罚的方式。对所谓"轻罪"如父母奉养不周，不敬长上，不听教训，口舌有过，惰怠游荡等的处罚方式是训斥、罚跪、罚钱米、杖责、革胙（即暂停祭祖权）。而对所谓"重罪"，如殴打父母、祖父母，偷盗祖坟树木，以及交结非人，奸宄不法，伤风败俗，邪教惑众，造反抗命等的处罚方式则非常之严厉。族长们可能私设刑堂，滥施私刑，如吊打等，甚至处死。但这其中很多过错就算有错，也罪不至死，但族长们却可以不经官府审判而自行决定处死。由此观之，所谓宗亲，何见其亲？族人，又何族谊之有？其残毒冷酷或有甚于官府。

封建时代的族权，必须说，就是封建专制力量在家族范围内的延伸和运用，曾对底层族众（尤其是对女性）的人权和自由造成过沉重的压迫。因此，必须看到乡土社会的管理系统、管理方式与权力性质中，确实杂糅了血亲集团的"亲情性""道德性"与封建社会的"政治性""阶级性"的综合因素。正如那一座座月夜下的棠樾村贞节牌坊，既很静美，又透着一种阴森。封建家族体制统治下的传统乡村，既有族亲之情、家园之美，又有封建专制体系下的人性扭曲和恐怖的暗影。

7.4.2　义门和典范宗族

在长期的村落宗族文化的实践历史上，各地家族中曾涌现出一大批优秀的堪称典范的"义门"，它们是儒家宗族文化的忠实信仰者和积极的践行者。

所谓"义门"，一般有几个标准：

第一，同居：多代同堂、同居共爨，也就是不分家，同吃同住同劳动的家族。

第二，共财：家族（一定范围内）共享资产如祖屋、祖祠、祖山、族田、义庄、义学 。

比如祠堂和义田的价值相辅相成："祠堂者，敬宗者也；义田者，收族者也。祖宗之神依于主，主则依于祠堂，无祠则无以妥亡者。子姓之生依于食，食则给予田，无田则无以保生者。故祠堂与义田并重而不可偏废者也"（清：张永铨《先祠记》）歙县棠樾村鲍氏宗祠古代有义田（祠田）1200 亩，所收租谷主要用于赡养族内鳏、寡、孤、独四种穷人及残疾之人。这当然是一种对族内弱势者的关爱之举。又如义学的意义被自觉肯定：宗族常在祠堂中设有家学，学中塾师由族中"品学兼优"的士人担任，办学经费由族产收入开支，"凡族中子弟入学，不另具修金供膳等费，外姓不得与入"（《郴阳陈氏族谱·创立义学记》）。

第三，敦伦：家族内部人心凝聚、宗族团结、家风淳厚。

我们可以看几个"义门"的实例。（1）唐代山东张公艺家族的"百忍义门"：张公艺家族自北朝传至唐代，全家有900多人口同居同爨。土地及一切财产完全归集体所有，男女服装统一制作，每到吃饭时间便以击鼓为令，群坐餐厅，区分内外，男女分别入席，老人在上，晚辈在下，儿童另设桌凳。族人们彼此"谦恭礼让，上下仁和，雍睦熏蒸"。唐高宗与皇后武则天泰山封禅后，曾亲自访问张公艺家族。问及张家同居睦族之秘。张氏族人书写一百个"忍"字，意即相忍相让才能相安无事。高宗闻之亦为之感动落泪，亲书"百忍义门"四个大字赞颂之。（2）南宋金溪县陆氏义门：南宋理宗淳祐二年（1242），朝廷敕旌陆氏义门，圣旨中表彰说，"江西金溪青田陆氏，代有名儒，载诸典籍，聚食逾千指，合灶二百年，一门翕然，十世仁让。特加褒奖，光于闾里，以励风化"。中国哲学史上著名的陆象山就是这个义门的子弟。我曾实地考察过金溪陆氏义门，现存的陆氏大儒家庙也让我印象深刻。陆氏义门的家规也洋溢着典型的儒家伦理之道：读书明理、孝亲和睦、仁义为本、量入为出、助困扶弱、清心俭素。另外像浙江浦江郑氏、"范氏义庄"，我们也多次提到这两个典范家族的家族规范，这里就不再介绍了。

义门，可以说都称得上是践行儒家宗族文化的典范的血缘大家庭，具有家族集体主义和家族公益慈善性质。但其优点和缺点都很明显，如价值认同上的儒教宗族伦理的绝对性、生活方式上的强制单一性和生活消费上的平均主义，另外，义门多代同堂，规模实在太大而难于有效管理，还让政府隐忧其尾大不掉控制地方等。这些综合因素都造成了义门的内在限制性，使得义门终究难以普遍推广和长久地维持。比如宋仁宗嘉祐七年（1062），朝廷下令江州义门陈氏分家，由三千余口聚居的家族，变为约300个小家庭、小"义门"。

7.5　总结：生生不息的中华宗族文化

简单总结一下本讲，我们认为中华宗族文化蕴含了深厚的历史、伦理、建筑、艺术、民俗方面的信息，是值得中华民族永久珍视和接续发展的宝贵文化财富。但对宗族文化中包含的复杂因素与影响要做历史的分析，重点是要着眼于发展的可能性，思考未来它向何处去。

第一，宗族文化历久流传，表现出了积极的社会功能与伦理表现。

（1）在政治上：宗族文化起着巨大的凝聚作用，使中国人对宗族和家乡，乃至对民族和祖国形成了文化心理上的真挚亲和感和认同感。（2）在伦理上：宗族文化以儒家"亲亲、尊尊"的思想教育和约束族人，陶冶了整个中华民族在生活世界中道德本位的价值取向与人生境界。（3）在文化上：通过宗谱与地方志、地方戏曲、方言与田园文学形成了具有地方特色的学术流派。（4）在地缘上：以家族为本位，形成遍布国内外、港澳台的宗亲联谊会，宗族文化成为华人世界的连接纽带。

第二，受到历史复杂因素的局限，中国的宗族文化也表现了一定的消极面需要引起注意。

如历来被批评最多的，无非是说传统的宗族文化中族权与封建政权、神权、夫权一起成为捆绑普通家族民众尤其是妇女的绳索。英国哲学家罗素就说宗族思想中的孝道与族权有碍中国现代公共精神的发展：

"孝道，以及家族力量，可能是儒家伦理道德中最弱的一环。只有这一环是儒家思想体系与常识大相径庭的地方。家庭私情掺杂进来，公益精神弱化，老者坐上权位，古制旧风横行。今天，我们应该用完全崭新的视角看待中国遇到的问题。而儒家思想体系所具有的这些特征是重建必要体制的一道障碍。"①

孝道和族权是不是孔子伦理中最大的弱点，这里不去辩论。但注意和思考这个"罗素问题"总是没错的。不可否认的是，宗族是一个亲族势力集团。他们聚族而居控制一方的话，是容易引起各种问题的。因为宗族集团一般都有强烈的封闭性，表现出比较保守的特点。倾向于产生排斥外族、外乡人的思想与行为，甚至为彼此的宗族利益引起怨怼与械斗。古代有地方豪强的门阀主义令国家深深忌惮，今天在个别地区也发生过地方宗族势力实际控制乡里和村落的情况，同样值得关注。

对复杂的宗族文化，我们的基本立场还是要批判继承、扬弃封建性，追求新时代良性发展。那种无条件赞美和放任村落宗族力量"还原式发展"的论点和做法是欠妥的。

第三，关于宗族文化的未来发展的问题。

中国的宗族文化流传了几千年，中国人那种重视家庭、推崇孝道和重视血脉根源的宗族文化性格可以说早已经沉淀在基因里头。那么，它未来的发展方向在哪里呢？窃以为，在大的方面我们还是希望未来的宗族应该成为敦亲联谊性的宗族、文明平权性的宗族、公益文化性的宗族。

---

① ［英］伯特兰·罗素. 中国问题 [M]. 田瑞雪，译. 北京：中国画报出版社，2019：37.

（1）当代新宗族文化的发展应与现代农村振兴和农村社区建设的工作相结合，尤其是探索传统宗族村落与现代旅游业相结合的方式与路径。

改革开放后，随着人们观念的改变和寻根热的兴起，宗族文化复兴势头在不断加强，这对建设和谐团结的乡村文化有着不可替代的作用。中国南北各地尤其是南方，保留了许多古香古色的古村落。那一片片山环水抱、坐北朝阳的梦里老家，一座座古朴的小桥，潺潺的流水，鳞次栉比的古民居，庄严肃穆的祠堂，巍巍耸立的宝塔，飘逸的凉亭，生命力极其旺盛的古树，闲散安逸的村民，古村落确以其历史的魅力深深地吸引着我们无所归依的"后现代的心灵"。随着旅游业的勃兴，很多有幸保存下来的明清祠庙，被当作名胜古迹开发使用。同时，各地在规划城乡发展计划时，很多地区都将祠堂为代表的传统历史文化作为政府发展规划的一部分。比如福建晋江市的梧林传统村落保护发展项目，其重点规划区域为村庄文化遗产比较集中的村落核心区域，占地约 21 公顷，规划建设的目的旨在形成以文创、休闲、民宿为新兴主导产业的宜居、宜业、宜游的特色文化，造就华侨博物馆和闽南文化后花园，带动闽南特色乡村经济的发展。

（2）应加强对当代新祠堂、新祭礼、新族谱的建设与实践探索。

祠堂作为家族祭祖的传统圣地，历来被人们所重视。以著者所见，当今南方各地的农村祠堂大都得到了维修或新建，祠堂内外也改造新增了诸如家史展馆、农家书屋、曲艺社、地方民俗专题展览室、老人活动中心和健身娱乐区等多种新功能，这也为地方经济文化的传承与发展提供了一个很好的契机。古代那些庄严肃穆、外人与女子不可入内的家族神秘之地，如今也与时俱进地成为助力乡村振兴、传播中华传统优秀文化的平台与媒介。我想，日新月异的新时代的祠堂文化，也会让那些祖灵们不至于太寂寞而深感了一份欣慰吧。另外，20 世纪 80 年代以来的修谱热至今还方兴未艾，在沿海、江南、华南地区开始流行。但今天的族谱的内容和旧式的宗谱已不尽相同，增添了很多新的内容，更多地体现了在自由平等和法治文明的新社会里，人们对村社和谐生活的美好要求。进入 21 世纪，数字族谱这种基于互联网的族谱编撰方式开始出现，善于运用互联网的青年人群将逐渐成为中华民族族谱建设的主力军，学术界也出版了各类宗族文化研究的丛书或文献集成①。这都值得我们充分利用，以提高对宗族

---

① 如上海图书馆编纂、上海古籍出版社（2013 年出版）的《中国家谱资料选编》、冯尔康编（2014 年出版）《清代宗族史料选辑》都是从事宗族文化研究必须拥有和充分运用的学术文献资源。

文化的现代学术研究的水平，让宗族文化之花更加璀璨盛放。

（3）我们还要特别注意海峡两岸、大中华文化区宗族文化的和谐互动、联动发展。

宗族文化是华人世界重要的共有文化符号和精神联结的纽带。华人世界的宗族文化情意结浓厚，传统观念重的华侨华人身在海外心系家园，追慕祖宗牵念祠堂，常以能回乡寻根谒祖为渴望，也以能替祖宗和家园长增光添彩为骄傲。台湾是中国不可分割的神圣领土，海峡两岸的人民地缘相近、血缘相亲、文缘相承、商缘相连、法缘相循。80%以上的台湾民众祖籍是福建，其中泉州籍占44.8%，漳州籍占35%，福建的台胞出生地、祖居、祖祠、祖堂、祖墓等涉台文物众多。台湾人口数量居前三十位的姓氏绝大多数直接源于福建，台湾的福建同乡会、宗亲会遍布台湾25个县市，台湾不少政要和工商界重量级人士的祖籍就在福建。如漳州市南靖长教村渡台简氏后裔总计23万，常回来寻根谒祖重温乡情。台湾政坛知名人物王金平于2019年5月7日回到他的祖籍地福建漳州白礁村寻根谒祖。马英九携家人于2023年4月1日回到祖籍地湖南湘潭县茶恩寺镇双阳村寻根祭祖，泪洒故园。同文同种、一脉相通，我们和台湾人民永远是不可分割的一家人。

移民海外的华侨华人就算走到天涯海角都仍然记挂家园，怀念祖先。除了在海外兴建祠堂，组织各种同乡会、宗亲会，并推动建立跨地区、跨国别的世界性宗亲团体与组织，并开展联谊活动，他们还经常回到祖国大陆，回到家乡，寻根谒祖，表现了浓浓的赤子情怀和故园乡愁。如菲律宾前总统阿基诺夫人和阿基诺三世分别于1989年4月和2011年9月回到福建漳州角美镇鸿渐村寻根谒祖。泰国前总理他信、英拉兄妹2019年1月7日回到广东梅州丰顺塔下村探亲祭祖。

请注意我这里用的是"回到"，而不是"前往"，因为他们本来就是故园出去的孩子，他们都是炎黄的后裔，这里就是他们的家乡。我们不拿他们当外人，这叫"中华一家亲"。我想，我们福建省是海外侨胞重要的祖籍地。我们在大陆、在福建生活工作的人们，要多做工作，做好工作，为海内外华侨华人回国寻根谒祖服务，以实现他们找到故乡、畅叙亲情族谊的梦想，并以此推动中华一家亲的大统战工作上一个新台阶。

在2022年3月5日召开的十三届全国人大五次会议上，福建省代表团以全团名义向大会提出议案：第一，支持福建创办"华侨论坛"暨"世界华侨华人大会"。第二，支持福建建设华侨历史博物馆。第三，持建设全国性"寻根"平台。建议把泉州市南洋华裔族群寻根谒祖综合服务平台①升级为全国性平台，设立专门机构，逐步加大经费投入、扩大建设范围、增加平台容量、提升服务和承载能力。第四，支持建设"寻根"文化家园。第五，支持打造一批"寻根"活动品牌。

　　总之，中国传统文化的基本特征之一就是悠久的宗族社会生活。以"首人伦—孝父母—敬祖宗—重宗族—慎祭祀—编族谱—传家风—念故乡—爱中华"为特点的宗族文化精神，是中国人根深蒂固的民族性和集体意识，是中国传统文化千年不绝的鲜明而重要的线索。而本质上，数千年的中华宗族文化反映了中国人民对生命的热爱，对生活的珍惜，以及对给予我们生命的本源的礼敬，也是对未来更美好的恒久的祈愿。

---

① 泉州市南洋华裔族群寻根谒祖综合服务平台（http：//www.nanyangxg.com/#slide1）通过族谱数据导入，运用云计算和人工智能技术，实现海量数据分析、查询、定位，一键即为海外侨胞迅速查找到自己祖籍根脉，深受广大海外侨胞的关注和支持，也是全国第一个官方综合性寻根服务平台。自2021年4月23日建成上线以来，已发挥了多方面的社会服务作用。

The Seventh Chapter:

Respecting Ancestors and Valuing Relatives
—The Brief Introduction of Patriarchal Clan System in Ancient Chinese Villages

In this chapter, we are going to give a brief introduction of patriarchal clan system in ancient Chinese villages of the Han nationality. Patriarchal clan system dates back to ancient times and is rich in connotations. It can be related to many aspects of Chinese culture, such as ancestor worship, consanguinity and ethics, folklore and rituals, village architectures, Feng Shui (geomantic theory), ancient laws and regulations, local complex and so on. In traditional Chinese culture, it is one of the oldest and most important social and cultural phenomena. It has affected countless Chinese people, and has standardized and influenced their daily life and spiritual world. Not only the Han nationality, but also the ethnic minorities in China have widely maintained the cultural customs with ancestor worship and ancestor sacrifice as the core, although there are many differences between them. So, it's safe to say that if one does not understand the patriarchal clan system, it is impossible for him/her to understand Chinese culture, or to understand Chinese people.

7.1 Patriarchal Clan and Clan System

As we know, human beings basically live together on the basis of consanguineous family, they are kin social animals. But the family of Chinese Han Nationality is different. It is like a large special patriarchal community.

When we talk about family culture, we must mention the patriarchal culture of Confucianism. As we mention here, the patriarchal clan system has rich connotations. It would take too long to tell that in full. So here I only give a brief introduction of it. The so-called "Patriarchal Clan System" (宗法) means regulating the family by the law of clan. It means to follow the principle of "Respecting Ancestors and Valuing

Relatives". By doing so, people build and manage their consanguineous families. And the law of clan is a set of principles and a system for people to build and manage their families.

At first, patriarchal culture also originated from the ancestor worship, soul worship and paternalism in the period of clan society. As far as the Han nationality is concerned, however, its foundation was laid by previous Confucian philosophers Ji Dan and, the Duke of Zhou, when he was building the system of rites and music. He designed such concrete ethics systems including the linear primogeniture system, the system of enfeoffment, the system of the great clansman and the small clansman, the ritual system of ancestral temple, and so on. Later, Confucius further elaborated the theory of benevolence and virtue based on this system of rites and music. Duke Zhou and Confucius successively extracted and transformed this blood relationship and historical tradition into the conscious proposition of social ethics and benevolence in ideology, that is, the whole patriarchal ritual culture. Let this kind of kinship and hierarchy, which is based on the nature of biological species and plays the role of social structure, be explained and reconstructed in a clear political science beyond biology and blood, so as to get rid of the historical limitations of a specific clan society. It had a long-term and important social impact on the development of Chinese culture. The system of regulating the family by the law of clan, formed the basis of patriarchal thought and patriarchal clan system. And this patriarchal clan system experienced three major historical stages: the patriarchal clan system of royalty in the pre-Qin period, the patriarchal clan system of aristocracy in the Han and Tang Dynasties, and the patriarchal clan system of populace in the Song, Yuan, Ming and Qing Dynasties. And it kept evolving through these three major historical stages. In China's medieval times, that is, after the Song Dynasty, it finally took shape and had these characteristics: building ancestral halls, holding sacrifice rituals for ancestors, compiling genealogies, establishing clan rules, electing clan elder as the head, reclaiming the land for clan, building free schools and so on.

And these are the main elements of the society of patriarchal clan system. During the evolution of patriarchal clan system its political function gradually weakened with its social function strengthened. Its evolution is also a historical process of moving from the privileged class to the civil society. What we are talking about here is mainly the introduction of the basic elements of patriarchal culture displayed by folk villages in the

Ming and Qing Dynasties. Our introduction will be divided into four parts below: the Ancestral Hall and the Ancestor Worship; Genealogy and Family Traditions; Clan Power and Gentry Class; Yi Men and Homelands. And we will introduce them in order.

It should be noted that not only the Han nationality, but also the ethnic minorities in China have still widely maintained the primitive religious customs with ancestor worship and ancestor sacrifice as the core. Of course, the ancestor worship culture within the Chinese civilization has the characteristics of unity in diversity. It has both internal relations and rich differences. Our discussion here mainly focuses on the introduction of the cultural elements of the patriarchal clan system in the villages of the Han nationality.

7.2   The Ancestral Hall and the Ancestor Worship

Let's talk about the ancestral hall first.

If we look at the Chinese character "宗" in small seal script 宗 , we can see that there is a character component "宀" on the top of it, which symbolizes people's house. And below that component there is a character "示", which symbolizes the memorial tablets of ancestors. Therefore, the character "宗" symbolizes the house where people worship their ancestors. Namely, it refers to the ancestral hall.

7.2.1   Ancestral Hall

The ancestral hall is the same as the ancestral temple. It is the place where people shrine the memorial tablets of their ancestors, and hold sacrifice rituals. It is also the place for educating family members, carrying out clan regulations and family laws, discussing family affairs and holding banquets.

Sometimes, people regard the "memorial hall" and the "ancestral hall" as identical. Strictly speaking, it is not correct. The memorial hall may be used for worshiping various gods, spirits or great people. But the ancestral hall is mainly used for worshiping ancestors. But in broad sense, it's acceptable if we use both of these two expressions.

（1）The Origin of the Ancestral Hall

At first, only the privileged aristocracies were qualified to build ancestral halls. According to the etiquette of sacrifice in the Zhou Dynasty: the king should establish seven ancestral temples to offer oblations to ancestors of seven generations. The prince of a state builds five ancestral temples. A minister builds three and a officer builds only one. The common people have no right to build ancestral temple. And they sacrifice their ancestors in their own houses. In the Han Dynasty, common people were allowed to build ancestral halls next to the tombs of ancestors, people could build a small ancestral temple for worship（墓祠）. In the Southern Song Dynasty, Zhu Xi, a philosopher and a Confucian scholar advocated building family temples where people offer oblations to ancestors of four generations. It was not until the promulgation of *The Great Rites* in the 15th year of Jiajing in the Ming Dynasty that the state officially allowed the people to jointly build ancestral temples. Therefore, more and more ancestral halls were built. Nowadays, in China's southern provinces, there are so many ancient halls of the Ming and Qing Dynasty. Although they are located in remote mountainous areas and villages, they are so exquisite and magnificent, which are beyond people's imagination. They are the collective symbol of families and the place of honor of villages. So they are generally very grand and solemn. Now we are going to see some pictures of the ancestral halls in different places. ①is the ancestral hall of the Hu Family in Jixi County, Anhui Province. Its wooden decorations are very exquisite. ②is the ancestral hall of Mao Family, which is the ancestral hall of Chairman Mao Zedong's family in Xiangtan, Hunan Province. ③is the ancestral hall of Zhang Family in Taxia Village, Nanjin County, Zhangzhou, Fujian Province, which is also called "De Yuan Hall". ④is the ancestral hall of Chen Jia-geng's Family in Dashe, Jimei of Xiamen City. ⑤was built in 1897, the ancestral hall of Chen Family in Kuala Lumpur, Malaysia, also called "Chen Academy". And ⑥is the ancestral hall of my family, which is located in Xianshi Village, Liling County, Hunan Province.

7-4 The Ancestral Halls in Southeast China villages

(2) The Principles of Feng Shui of Ancient Villages and Ancestral Halls

When we talk about ancestral halls, we must first talk about villages. That was the main structure of Chinese society in the agricultural era. As we known, most of the ancient villages in China are inhabited by a small number of people with one surname. Traditionally, when people move to a new place to live, they usually build their ancestral halls first. And when people build their ancestral halls, they will also take the principles of Feng Shui into consideration. Their first choice must be those places which have excellent geological and ecological conditions. These places which accord with the principle of Feng Shui can be regarded as ideal ones. After the ancestral hall had been built, then those descendants build their own dwellings around the ancestral halls. Gradually a lump-type layout will formed. This is in sharp contrast with the mosque as the core of the Hui living area[1].

I would like to say a few words about the so-called Feng Shui. Feng（风）means wind and Shui（水）means water, both of them are the main components of the geographical surroundings. It studies the shape of a mountain and the direction of water around the village, and then speculates on the ecology of good or bad luck. The ancients believed that only good Feng Shui could benefit future generations. In the light of the principle of Feng Shui, villages should meet several requirements.

---

[1] Xinye Village, in Yuhua County, Jiande, Zhejiang Province, is a village layout centered on "YuHua ancestral hall".

Left represents azure dragon, so there should be water on the left side of people's villages. Right represents white tiger, so there should be road on the right side of people's villages. North represents black tortoise, so there should be a mountain in the north of people's villages. south represents vermilion bird. South also refers to fire, so ponds should be built for putting out fires.

It is of course superstitious to believe that Feng Shui is related to the prosperity of one's descendants, but it takes the geological conditions into consideration, as well as their ecological effect for people's production and life, which are quite reasonable. If the village is close to waterways, it can facilitate daily water collection and irrigation. If it is close to thoroughfares, it will not hinder access. If it is surrounded by several mountains, there are barriers around it to prevent wind, cold, moisture and heat. But in fact, people should consider the specific geographical factors of their villages. So it is hard for them to abide by this principle strictly. Therefore, people can only build their ancestral halls in the light of local conditions. But surrounded by mountains and rivers is a prerequisite for people to choose their homes. If they do not meet the requirements, they will strive to make up and improve under the guidance of geomancer.

Take Chengkan Bagua Village as s example, which originally founded during the Three Kingdoms period in the Eastern Han Dynasty and has a history of more than 1800 years. The whole village is arranged according to the theory of "the unification of Yin (Kan) and Yang (Cheng) achieves harmony between man and nature" from "the Eight Diagrams" in *the Classic of Changes*. There are eight mountains around, such as Ge Mountain, Liwang Mountain, Long Mountain, Changchun Mountain and Guanyin Mountain, which correspond to the Eight Diagrams. The Zhongchuan River passes through the village from north to south. Chengkan Village turns out to be a "maze" in a bird view: three main streets and ninety-nine lanes crisscrossing the village with hills and rivers surrounding it. The terrain in the east of the river is flat and it is a garden of thousands of mu. Take Peitian Village as an example. It is backed by Wohu Mountain. Heyuan River curves round it. On its right side there is a thoroughfare. In the front of the ancestral halls of these villages, large ponds are dug.

So we can draw a conclusion that these villages accord with the principles of Feng Shui. The ancient villages not only have classic historical buildings, but also contain Confucian thoughts, geomantic omens, and other cultural and geographical information.

They are valuable materials that we must make full use of in studying and studying traditional Chinese culture.

(3) Layout of Ancestral Hall Buildings

Let's firstly talk about the inner structure and layout of the ancestral halls. Generally speaking, the traditional ancestral hall usually shows a compound of two, or three rows of houses. In terms of its inner structure can be classified into different parts below: 1. The main gate, the front hall, the main hall, the left and right wing rooms. They are symmetrical in the middle axis and surround the courtyard. 2. The front hall is also called "Xiang Hall". It is the place for people to kneel down for ancestor worship. 3. The main hall is also called "Kan Hall" or "Qin Hall". It is the place for people to shrine the memorial tablets of their ancestors. 4. Chambers are attached to it on both sides. They are the places for storing genealogies, and sacrificial vessels. 5. As for the left and right wing rooms, they can be used as a private school for members of the family. 6. In some places, there are small theatres, semi-circular ponds, screen walls, stone dragon flagpoles that show family glory, and accessories such as Fengshui forest behind the ancestral hall.

Because the ancestral hall is the home of the soul of the ancestors, all clans will attach great importance to and invest in the construction of it. Various designs are magnificent and solemn, the materials are exquisite, and the carving decoration also shows the beauty of the details of Chinese traditional crafts. There are many couplets written with superb calligraphy and profound meanings as well as plaques of family disciplines and rules, as well as plaques of honoring people with academic honor and official rank, all this makes modern visitors feel like they are in a folk-art museum. For example, Dunben Hall of Tangyue Villagel, dignified and imposing, faces the south. It is a compound of three rows of houses, each of which is about 16.5 meters long. The arch of the gateway is decorated with five phoenixes. On the left and right walls of the hall are rubbings of Zhu Xi's calligraphy works "loyalty, filial piety, honesty and integrity". The whole hall is of simple and direct style with the ginkgo pillars and camphor girder frames. The engraving in the bricks wood and stones is of simple and mediocre style which is consistent with the spirit of Confucian philosophy and cultural tradition.

(4) About the Rank of Ancestral Hall

Ancestral halls can be divided into different types according to the identity of the ancestors who are sacrificed: General Ancestral Hall, Branch Ancestral Hall, and Family Ancestral Hall.

1. General Ancestral Hall is the highest rank. It is the place for worshiping the ancestors of the first generations, and their lineal descendants. For instance, the ancestral hall of Chen Family in Guangzhou City shown is the general ancestral hall for members of Chen family in 72 counties of Guangdong Province. The general ancestral hall of the Wu Family in Peitian Village: "Yanqing Hall of the Wu Family". Built in Chenghua period of the Ming Dynasty, it is the place for worshiping their ancestors from the first to the ninth generations. The first ancestors mentioned here are the one whose inheritance clues can be traced. Generally, they are not earlier than the Song Dynasty. It depends on the available information available to each family.

2. The second one is the branch ancestral hall. The later generations multiplied and lived apart. Therefore, people build ancestral halls for the ancestors of their own branches. By doing so, they could worship and make sacrifice to their early ancestors. Take Peitian Village as an example. The Wu family in Peitian Village took Wu Basi in the late Yuan Dynasty and the early Ming Dynasty as the founder of the Wu family in Xuanhe township. The third generation of Wu Wengui moved to Peitian Village. It was not until the tenth generation that the Wu family was divided into four four branches: the branch of Jinggong, Chonggong, Zhonggong and Honggong. And each branch built their own ancestral halls. Among the four branches, the descendants of the branch of Jinggong (Wu Daoqin) are the most prosperous. Most of the existing ancestral halls in Peitian Village, just like, the Rong'an Ancestral Hall and the Jiu Ancestral Hall, are both belong to the branch of Jinggong.

3. The third one is the family ancestral hall, which is also called "the Hall of Incense" （香火堂）. It is a sacrificial room in a residential house connected. It is generally located in the hall or the place where the shrines set. But in this kind of the Incense hall can only be used for enshrining the ancestral tablets below the great-great-grandfather (within four generations). Ancestors beyond five generations, cannot enjoy the incense offered in the family ancestral hall. Because the land resource is very limited in the villages. If there is no land, or enough financial resources to build the ancestral halls, people have to set up a place in their houses as the "Hall of Incense". So, it is the most common, most basic and lowest kind of ancestral hall, and widely built in the families throughout the country. The souls of the four generations of

ancestors and their descendants live together day and night.

Of course, there are also some special types of the ancestral halls. You should also pay attention to them. 1. Xiang Hall: it is an ancestral hall where people worship the eldest son of the eldest branch of all generations. 2. As to the Ancestral Hall of Special Purpose, it is built for worshiping those ancestors without descendants. 3. Ancestral Halls for Women: they are ancestral halls especially for Chaste martyr. For example, the ancestral hall for women in Bao Family in Tangyue Village (鲍氏妣祠), She County, Anhui Province, also called the "Qingyi Hall". In the past, only the male tablets could be placed in the ancestral hall for worship. Women, including minors, were not even allowed to enter the ancestral hall. Qingyi Hall even covers an area of 50 square meters larger than the male ancestral hall "Dunben Hall" opposite, and the carving spirit of the outer wall is far better than that. Therefore, the practice of building ancestral halls for women in Tangyue Village is very valuable. It shows the sincere praise of the local people for the chastity spirit and perseverance of the women. 4. The Ancestral Hall with Double Family Names. Why does this happen? Maybe, there was a close relationship between these two families. For example, the Feng family and the Tong family in Xucun Village, Hancheng City, Shaanxi Province go to the same ancestral hall and worship the same ancestor during the Qingming Festival and the Spring Festival every year. Because the two families actually originated from a common ancestor: Sima Qian, a historian in the Western Han Dynasty. Sima Qian committed crimes and was jailed. For fear that the emperor might implicate his family, he changed "Sima" to "Tong" and "Feng" and asked his descendants to change their surnames accordingly. In addition, there is also a small ancestral hall of the Ding family in the Hu family ancestral hall in Jixi County, Huangshan City, that is because of a somewhat ridiculous Feng Shui consideration. The terrain of the local village is like a boat. Hu's homonym is duckweed, while Ding's homonym is nail. Therefore, it is necessary to nail boat to avoid the disaster of wind and waves to duckweed.

(5) Naming of the Ancestral Halls

The traditional ancestral hall usually has a hall name, and it's naming generally reflects a certain family ethics concept. For example, if people want to express the idea of remembering ancestors, they can name their ancestral hall as "Dunben Hall", "Wuben Hall" and "Xulun Hall". What is "本" (root)? Ancestors are our roots.

They are like the origin and root of waters and woods. They are the source of our lives. What else? Sometimes people want to show the prefecture location of their families （郡 望）. What is prefecture location? It refers to the origin of the pedigree, and the place where their ancestors came from, such as Zhongshan Hall, Bohai Hall, Sanhuai hall. Yes, "Zhongshan" and "Bohai" are the names of places. In other cases people want to show other moral implications, they name their ancestral halls as Yanqing Hall, Jingcheng Hall, Shuangshan Hall and Wanshou Hall. These names can reflect some special moral or blessing significance.

7.2.2　Ancestor Sacrifice and Rituals

The ancestral hall has many functions traditionally. It is a holy place for ancestor worship, a tribunal for patriarchal ethics, a place for holding daily important affairs, a school for educating the people. Of course, ancestor worship is undoubtedly the first place. According to Confucianism, sacrificial activities are important events for people and the state. The sacrifice rituals for worshiping ancestors held in the ancestral halls are even more significant. They are the sacred obligation of the family members, and the most important activities for families. Ancestor worship refers to offering oblations to ancestors. By doing so, people can carefully attend to the funeral rites of parents and worship remote ancestors devoutly; they can think of and be grateful to their ancestors; they can show admiration and respect for their ancestors. The purpose of ancestral rituals are: promoting the relationship between family members, and maintaining the patriarchal clan system within families.

Generally speaking, sacrifice rituals are definite and fixed. In the genealogies of families, there are detailed records and explanations about sacrifice rituals.

(1) Date of Ancestor Worship in Folk Ancestral Hall

Although the dates of ancestor worship in folk ancestral halls cannot be as frequent as those of nobles (such as the royal family and the Confucius family), they are generally as follows: 1. The four sacrifices for four seasons. Namely, the spring sacrifice, the summer sacrifice, the autumn sacrifice and the winter sacrifice. That's all on the 15th of the first lunar month of these four seasons. Among them, the winter solstice ancestor worship is the most ceremonious because it is after the autumn harvest. 2. Festival sacrifice. I. e. offering sacrifices to ancestors during the new year and other important festivals. For example, New Year's Eve., Qingming Festival,

Chongyang Festival and Zhongyuan Festival are the four major festivals for the Han people to worship their ancestors. And on the anniversary of death of ancestors, there is a special sacrifice. 3. In addition, when a family needs to sacrifice its ancestors for special reasons, it is called "the sacrifice of reporting". 4. Of course, the family incense hall needs to offer incense and offerings to the ancestors every morning and evening, which is called "daily sacrifice".

Take Peitian Village we have mentioned above as an example. On the second day of the first lunar month every year, all the male members of the Wu Family should go to their ancestral hall, "Yanqing Hall", and worship their ancestors from the first to the ninth generations. This is the sacrifice ritual on the second day of the first lunar month. From the third day to the fifth day, they worship the ancestors of their own branches in their ancestral halls or old houses. First to the general ancestral hall, then to the branch ancestral hall. Therefore, we can see that people worship their ancestors in a certain order. In March and August, they worship the tombs of the ancestors of their own branches of all generations. In the Tomb-sweeping Festival they only worship their earliest ancestor: Wu Basi. Take Xinye Village, Jiande City, Zhejiang Province, as an example. They worship their ancestors on the third day of the third lunar month; This is a special day for them. All descendants from other places have to return home to participate in ancestor worship activities. It is very lively and solemn, and the sacrifice ritual is even larger and grander than that in other festivals including the Spring Festival.

(2) General Rituals for Ancestor Sacrifice

The main body of the ancestor worship ceremony is generally presided over by the clan association, and held by the branch of the clan family in turn. Just as we can see, the sacrifice rituals in Ye Family of Xinye Village, are generally held by the members of five branches in turn according to the order of heavenly stem and earthly branch. However, no matter which branch of the clan is arranged to hold the ancestor worship ceremony, the head of the family will be the officiant (主祭) in sacrifice rituals. The senior and people who have high-ranking cultural posts will be the assistants (陪祭). What's more, there are other people like "Tongzan" "Yinzan" "Sizhu" "Sizun" "Sibo" "Sijue" "Sizhuan" "Siguan" and so on. These people are responsible for the tribute and offering various oblations. If the family is prosperous and wealthy, there will be people who perform bells and drums and chant poems. As for other members of the family, they will worship ancestors according to their seniority and precedence in the family. And they will kneel down in an orderly manner along with the officiant and his assistants.

According to the introduction of the Wu family in Peitian Village, the process of ancestor worship activities of the Wu family on the second day of the first lunar month is as follows: playing drum music, welcoming ancestors' spirits, bowing to worship, offering sacrifices, singing sacrifices, sacrificial feasts, giving ancestors' spirits away, burning silk, etc. But different families in different regions have their own characteristics. Obviously, the attitude for sacrifice rituals is also important. Every people participating in the sacrifice rituals should be devout, serious, and respectful. They should dress properly, as if their ancestors linger all around above them. They cannot chat or jest, because the sacrifice ritual is a solemn and sacred family affair.

The part of "sacrificial feasts" of the sacrifice rituals mentioned above, also called "Yinfu" and "Xiangzuo". "Yinfu" refers to drinking the sacrificial wine. "Xiangzuo" refers to eating the sacrificial meat. This is a happy part for all. According to people's understanding, if they eat the sacrificial offerings for ancestors, they will receive the blessing from their ancestors. In addition to the joyful banquets, some village clans will also hold local drama performances after ancestor worship after worshipping their ancestors, or some village clans will follow the drum music and ceremonial and march around the village (ancestral hall) to commemorate the blessings of their ancestors, praise their virtues, and pray for the prosperity of their clans.

(3) Economic and Material Preparation For Sacrifice Rituals

People should make economic and material preparations for sacrifice rituals. But where does the money come from? Generally speaking, there are two ways of collecting money. The first one is fundraising. It means to raise money from family members regularly. And the money will be used for specific sacrificial activities. The second one is to use the income from the land property for sacrificial activities. Ancestors of some families had the foresight. They purchased the land for descendants long ago, and demanded the land could not be divided. It could only be used as the funds for families' sacrificial activities. Of course, the descendants may make a fortune and prosper their families. Then they may donate money for purchasing more sacrificial land if they are rich and powerful. Therefore, if ancestors have already left some land property and descendants keep donating money continuously, there will be a large amount of sacrificial land. The management of the sacrificial land is also very strict. Because it is the common assets of the family. It is generally managed by the head of the family, or the relatives of the same family, or the members of the family branch who are in charge of the sacrificial activities. They cannot embezzle or even sell the sacrificial land off in disguise.

Although we strive to give a grand sacrifice ritual, the economic capacity of each family is different, Confucius said: "In ritual, it is better to be frugal than extravagant; in funerals deep sorrow is better than ease. " What is more important is the sincerity of descendants. For ordinary people, it is also very good to offer fresh vegetables, clean melons and fruits according to Confucius. Actually, it's similar to the Dong people, living in Guizhou Province, habitually prepare some offerings, which are mainly newly ripe grains or cooked rice as well as fish, meat and wine, to sacrifice their ancestors and to congratulate a harvest beforehand in Chixinjie (festival of eating newly ripe grains). This is some kind of simple and not extravagant form of ancestor worship, and also a manifestation of rational filial piety according to the principle of the golden mean.

(4) Other Functions and Management of Ancestral Halls

As we have said, ancestral halls are sacred places for ancestor worship, courts for exercising clan power, auditoriums for daily important affairs, schools for educating children, and so on. Ancestral halls have additional functions. Besides serving as a place of worship, for example, the elders of the family may hold meetings in ancestral halls and discuss major family affairs. That is to say, ancestral halls can serve as an organ of authority within the family. It is also a place for educating adult members of the family, and punishing those who have done something wrong. The ancestral hall is also the site of family schools or private schools for educating the children of the clan, that is, educational institutions. Sometimes, people's weddings and funeral ceremonies are carried out in ancestral halls. This is also because the space of the ancestral hall is relatively wide and convenient for gathering people. For example, People should held sacrifice rituals in the ancestral hall when getting married or marrying off their daughters. So as to prove the legitimacy of marriages. Isn't it? If you want to marry a girl who comes from another family, you need to worship her ancestors in her family's ancestral hall. It is the same for the new daughter-in-law. She also needs to worship her husband's ancestors, to tell the ancestors that their family has a new member. Then after the death of a family member, his or her coffin will be temporarily kept in the ancestral hall before burial. And people may held anniversary sacrificial rituals for the death in ancestral halls. They will read or chant genealogies in ancestral halls regularly. In the ancestral hall of the Wang Family in Meigang Village, Taihe County, people often send congratulatory couplets for those who have succeeded in the National College Entrance Examination. Sometimes, people held entertaining activities in their ancestral halls. There is a stage in the ancestral hall of Mao's family in Xiangtan, Hunan Province, which is the place for people to perform local operas after sacrificial activities. The surrounding areas of the ancestral hall generally include ponds, squares and other peripheral spaces for village women to wash clothes and wash rice, children to play, peddlers to sell goods, and regular fairs.

The ancestral hall is so important that every family attaches great importance to the daily maintenance and management of the ancestral hall. By doing so, they can ensure the halls safety, and keep them tidy and clean. Usually, ancestral halls are locked. But if the family enjoys favorable economic conditions a caretaker will be hired to watch the ancestral hall. Generally, the people with good moral character can be the caretaker, or those people who have financial difficulties, such as the widower, or people who have no children. It also shows the family's sympathy and care for them. Of course, they will receive economic reward from the family's public property. So, these caretakers need to burn incense regularly every day. They should clean the hall and prevent fires. During the sacrificial activities, they are also responsible for maintaining order, helping to prepare various oblations, incense, ceremonies, sacrificial vessels, and so on.

7.2.3　Cultural Influence of Ancestral Hall and Ancestor Worship

For thousands of years, "filial piety" has always occupied the supreme position in the social concept of the Chinese nation. Ancestor worship is a form derived from the inheritance of filial piety. People believe that other gods are not as noble as their ancestors. Therefore, ancestral halls and family temples are built in various places. Each family worships its ancestors, and the regular ancestor worship ceremony is the most important religious activity among the people. Confucius says: "To gather in the same place where our fathers before us have gathered; to perform the same ceremonies which they before us have performed; to play the same music which they before us have played; to pay respect to those whom they honored; to love those who were dear to them; in fact, to serve them now dead as if they were living, and now departed, as if they were still with us, that is the highest achievement of Filial Piety. "

That is how Confucianism, awakens and kindles in men, the inspiration or living emotion necessary to enable and make them obey the rules of moral conduct. Thus, Confucianism also mellowed the people's moral personality. Zeng zi, a disciple of Confucius, further says: "By cultivating respect for the dead, and carrying the memory back to the distant past, the good in the people will grow deep. " By cultivating respect for ancestors and recalling the distant past, people's virtue will be deepened.

Cultural research focuses on explaining the pursuit of meaning in people's lives. As a kind of behavior and ceremony, ancestor worship culture, as Gertz said, is the story that the local people "tell themselves about themselves". Yuval Harari, the author of *A Brief History of Humankind*, believes that a nation that can tell stories has more vitality and motivation to survive. From generation to generation, a major event that Chinese folk villages have repeatedly done is to solemnly pay tribute to and worship the deceased ancestors, to pray for the prosperity of everyone and the prosperity of the family. It is through the continuous cultivation of filial piety, ancestor worship that the Chinese nation has developed today's national cultural character of ethics based, filial piety supreme, grand historical view, and mild and honest. Just like *People's Daily* once said:

"*The ancestral hall is an exhibition hall for our homesickness, and it is the rest place for our souls. Worshiping ancestors in ancestral halls has become a family lesson of enhancing people's mutual affection and building people's spiritual identity. It is also a life lesson of being grateful to our ancestors, and cultivating filial piety and morality.* "

7.3　Genealogy and Family Traditions

Genealogy: it is a very special folk literature in China. It has many names. Chinese people call it "Zu Pu" "Zong Pu" "Jia Pu" and "Shi Pu", or just "Pu". Genealogy is a kind of literature which mainly records the origin of one clan, and collects documents of other clans. The methods of genealogical records include tying rope, oral transmission from generation to generation, inscriptions and books. In China, there were genealogies in the Han, Tang and Song Dynasties. It's mainly the privilege of emperors and noble officials, and the genealogies at this time only had lineages and achievements of previous generations. Until the Jiajing and Wanli periods of the Ming Dynasty, a new type of family tree, which is different from the Tang and Song Dynasties, records the origin, descent, blood relationship, population, previous achievements, clan residence, ancestral hall, tomb, family property, family rules and family documents of a clan began to appear. They not only record the history of families, but also provide rich information for the study of history, sociology, demography and ethnology. So far, there are more than 20000 genealogies of various surnames in China. Genealogy, authorized historical books and local chronicles constitute the three pillars of the historical building of the Chinese nation.

7.3.1　What is the Format and Style of a Genealogy

(1) The Format and Style of the Genealogy

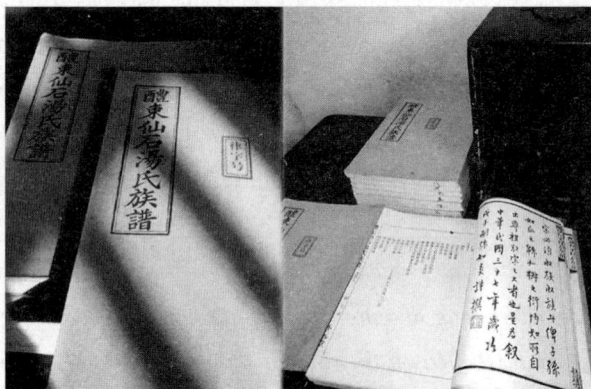

7-5　Genealogy of the Tang Family in Xianshi Village

The Tang family in Xianshi Village, Lidong County started from Guichi, Anhui Province in the Song Dynasty, and later moved to Xianshi, Lidong, Hunan Province through Pingxiang, Jiangxi Province. Tang Mengguan (1063—1125) in the Northern Song Dynasty was the founder of the Tang family in Xianshi. Since then, the descendants have flourished to this day. Fortunately, the genealogy of our family has been meticulously compiled by our ancestors for more than ten times. Although a thousand years have passed, thanks to this set of genealogy, we can still clearly understand the family history. Looking through *the Genealogy of Tang Family*, we can see that it includes the following contents.

The first part of a genealogy is the preface written in calligraphy style, which may give the reasons or the process of genealogy revisions.

The second part is the genealogy directory: refers to the items of contents contained in each volume of the whole genealogy.

The third part is the portray of ancestors and panegyrics of their portrays.

The fourth part is about the honors of the family.

Namely, it is about the rescripts from the imperial court or other authorities. As we see in the genealogy, this is an imperial mandate for the parents of Tang Mengguang, which was bestowed by the imperial court of the Song Dynasty in 1125. It is like a national certificate of honor. And this is in accordance with the idea of Confucianism: "The ultimate goal of filial piety is to bring glory to the parents by making them famous in later generations." For example, in another edict on rewarding Tang Mengguan, as an imperial censor. Others, such as official comments on Xuefeng Gong's admission to the county sage temple and official comments on old lady Qu's virtue of chastity and filial piety, are the official replies of the governments at all levels to give moral recognition to the well-known figures in the family. It is certainly a matter of honor for a family to be praised by the state and local governments, and it will make future generations look forward to and respect it.

The fifth part is the preface which includes the former prefaces and explanations of the revised genealogies of each generation.

Since the Ming and Qing Dynasties, the pedigree of Tang's family in *Lidong Xianshi* has been revised for 11 times. Sixteen preface and postscript written for each revision have been preserved. It is very useful to help future generations understand the reason and process of each revision of the genealogy.

The sixth part is the explanation of the editing format of the genealogy.

The "*Sixteen General rulers*" of the genealogy involves many explanations, such as the explanation of the "principle of faithfulness" in compiling the family history, the explanation of the genealogy of Ouyang style and Su style and its characteristics, the explanation of the "four branches of the family", the explanation of the "chronological method", the explanation of the "verses of generations" (字辈语) used by the ethnic group, the explanation of the ethnic group's "naming", the explanation of the "written terms for entering the spectrum" （such as husband and wife, remarriage, adopters, in laws, emigrants, etc.）and the explanation of "preservation and supplement of documents". Especially the explanation of the qualification of being recorded in the genealogy and the naming characters for descendants. Clan Families usually attach great importance to the qualifications of being written in the genealogy. They aim to prevent the disorder of genealogy and maintain the purity of patrilineal blood relationship. For example, if you bring home your son after divorce, he will be not allowed to enter your family's genealogy. The same rule applies to one's adopted son. It is preferred to choose someone who is from the same branch of your family when adopting a child. Moreover, clearly defines whom will be deprived of the right of entering the genealogy. This is a severe punishment for those who have violated the family regulations.

What's more, in order to determine the order of generations, "Verses of Generations" will be given in this part. Generally, there are 20 or 30 characters, which could be used for naming the descendants of 20 or 30 generations, to determine a person's generation. By doing so, people can fully understand others' generation from their names. Naturally, the ethics of elder and younger generations will not be disturbed. The names of the descendants of one generation start with the same character, people will add new characters after using up all of them. In the past people's name were strictly determined according to the "Verses of Generations". People who do not comply with it are not allowed to enter genealogy.

There are 20 characters in the Verse of Generations of *the Genealogy of Tang Family*, which are used for naming the descendants from the 20th generation to the 39th generation. They are: *Xiang Tian Guang Da Qing*, （象添光大清）*Ru You Zheng Qi Zhong.* （如有正其中）*Dao Xue Cong Xian Shou*, （道学从先守）*Xiu Pei Ji Shu Long.* （修培继述隆）For example, my grandfather, Mr. Tang Zhengmei, is a member of the 27th generation of "Zheng", and I am a member of the 29th generation of "Zhong".

Yi people practiced a joint name system of father and son, called Ci （茨）. Such as names like Xi Nuluo, Luo Shengpi, Luo Sheng, Sheng Luopi, Pi Luoge, Ge Luofeng, Feng Mouyi, Yi Mouxun... The last one or two syllables of the father's name should be put in front of the son's name. They can pass the family traditions through this naming system. They should recite the names of their ancestors, or will be regarded as "outsiders". In my opinion, this naming method is similar to that of the Han nationality, which is based on the "verses of generations" and uses it to determine the order of inheritance. It can be regarded as the same form of Chinese naming culture in a broad sense. Of course, with the change of times, today's people do not know what the genealogy is. And they no longer use the characters from the verse of generations in their genealogy. Take my son Tang Yijun as an example. He did not use the character "Dao" as his name, which is the character for members of the 30th generations.

The seventh part is about family discipline, family law, clan regulations.

This is all kinds of life admonitions and binding moral norms left by our ancestors. For example, in *the Genealogy of Tang Family* there are 16 rules of family disciplines, 32 rules of family laws and 13 rules of clan regulations.

The eighth part is about the diagram of lineage.

It visually presents the lineage information of all generations from the earliest ancestor. Each member of each generation are clearly recorded. The genealogy can be classified into two types: the Genealogy of Ouyang Xiu Style and the Genealogy of Su Xun Style (Both of them are cultural masters of the Northern Song Dynasty).

1. The Genealogy of Ouyang Style is also called the Genealogy of Melon Vine Style. It has these characteristics: the son closely follows after his father; brothers are parallel with each other in the same row; five generations are written in the same diagrams; one will be recorded in detail only in his generation; female members are excluded from the lineage diagram. As we see in the genealogy of Tang family, Tang Mengguang is the ancestor of first generation in my family. His six sons are the second generation of our family. And each of them have a number of children. So their children are the third generation of our family. And so it went on until the fifth generation. The diagram recording the ancestors from the sixth to the tenth generation still follows the above pattern. It's safe to say the genealogy written in this style is very clear and direct.

2. The Genealogy of Su Style is like today's table form. It is more detailed than the Genealogy of Ouyang Style, recording the birth and death, marriage, and children of each generation. People who have scholarly honor or official rank will be recorded with more details. As we see in the Genealogy of Tang's clan, the diagram contains the name, date of birth and death of my first ancestor, Mr. Tang Mengguan, as well as his

scholarly honor and official rank, the date of his wife's birth and death, and some information about her sons and daughters. It should be said that the diagram of lineage is the most core information in a set of genealogy and occupies the largest proportion. For thousands of years, the population information of the whole family from generation to generation has been kept in this page by page record. By following the diagram of lineage, everyone can find the information of those ancient ancestors he has never met.

The ninth part is about the biographies of some important family members of all generations. Some biographies record both the husbands and the wives.

The tenth part is the collection of literary works of important family members of all generations, such as verses, ditties, odes and songs and so on.

The eleventh part is the birthday articles of some important family members of all generations, as well as the excerption of their epitaphs.

The twelfth part is the portraits of the important ancestors of the family, including the panegyrics for their portraits, the map of family's ancestral hall and the cemetery as well as their description.

The thirteenth part is about the layout and displays of the ancestral hall, and the annotations about the sacrifice rituals.

The fourteenth part is the record of genealogy distribution.

So these fourteen parts constitute the basic format and content of the genealogy that we mentioned.

(2) The Time and the Source of Funds for Genealogy Revisions

It is usually required that the genealogy should be revised every ten years, or every twenty years, or thirty years. The Kongs family in Qufu, Shandong, specially stipulates that the genealogy should be revised once every sixty years. If people do not revise the genealogy for a long time, they will be considered as unfilial descendants. Then who can be in charge of the work of compiling the genealogy? Compiling the genealogy is an important event in the clan family, it is usually initiated and organized by the clan association. There are leading figures in the family or cultural relatives and enthusiasts, who are responsible for the revision of the genealogy. Some big families even invite some well-known scholars who are capable of and suitable to take charge of the revision of their genealogies. The cost of revising the genealogy is either apportioned to the members of the family, or borne by the members who are financially powerful. The work of revising the genealogy needs the materials which have been already sorted out. So people should make preparations early. For example, some families keep a book to record the babies (especially boys) when they are born. By doing so, people can record the population changes in their families at any time for reference, and be better prepared for revising their genealogies. There will be a work of distribution after revising the genealogy. In addition, if there are high-ranking officials, knowledgeable scholars, filial piety, benevolent people, hermits, and literati in the clan, each household needs to report their deeds in order to enter them into the genealogy and write a biography for them. However, if there is a false report or a discrepancy with the facts, it is also punishable by family law.

There are also strict rules for the printing and distribution of genealogies. In the 9th year of Qianlong (1744), the Confucius House formulated as many as 34 "rules and regulations" for the revision of genealogy. It is necessary to set up a printing office, worship the ancestors, and issue a "code of practice" to strictly prevent "false name and false recognition". At the beginning of the printing, there must be a person in charge to supervise. In addition, in order to put an end to fraud, the genealogy was bound and stamped with the seal of Duke Yansheng Mansion and local government as a certificate. After each revision, a ceremony will be held in the ancestral hall. People will report to their ancestors about the revision of the genealogy. And then the copy of the genealogy will be distributed to all branches.

7.3.2 About Family Disciplines, Family Laws and Clan Regulations

Family disciplines refer to ancestors' instructions. They are the precepts and teachings for later generations. As for the family laws and the clan regulations, they are the disciplinary moral constraints for family members. Family disciplines and clan regulations are lifelong lessons for family members, which help them to school their behaviors. Inseparably interconnected with the national ethical education and national laws, they have become an important supplement to the national ethical education and national law.

(1) Take *the Genealogy of Wu Family* of Peitian Village as an Example

Peitian Village's genealogy has three versions, because it was revised three times under the reign of the Emperor Qianlong, the Emperor Tongzhi, and the Emperor Guangxu. This genealogy has successively included *Sixteen Rules of Family Disciplines*, *Ten Rules of Family Laws* and *Ten Rules of Clan Regulations*.

1. Their *Sixteen Rules of Family Disciplines* are as follows.

"Respecting ancestors; being filial toward parents; getting along well with brothers; respecting the senior and loving the younger; paying attention to the prudent reserve between men and women; living with relatives in harmony; handling matrimonial affairs cautiously and prudently; attending to the funeral rites of parents carefully; studying with assiduity; working with diligence; practicing frugality; abstaining from immoral behaviors; abstaining from doing wrong and evil; abstaining from speaking with acerbity; abstaining from unlimited desires; abstaining from quarrels."

These *Sixteen Rules of Family Disciplines* emphasize the promotion of traditional ethics such as filial piety, fraternal submission, benevolence, love, diligence and thrift, and encourage people to abide by them. Each article is also annotated with 32 words of explanation, pointing clearly.

2. *Ten Rules of Family Laws* formulated under the reign of the Emperor Guangxu are as below.

"Filial piety and fraternal duty should be promoted, and diligence and thrift should be advocated; honesty and shame sense of shame should be encouraged, and ethics should be strictly implemented; loyalty and kindness should be respected, and integrity should be respected; propriety and righteousness should be clearly understood, and disputes should be settled; the punishment should be fair, and the family should be pure and unsullied."

Although the family law is a moral constraint with the nature of punishment, it is intended to alert future generations. "The purpose of formulating family law is to make people abide by it and make people have a sense of awe." Therefore, family law is a continuation and expansion of family precepts, which complement each other.

3. *Ten Rules of Clan Regulations* as below.

"Ancestral House-to house the souls of the ancestors so that they may protect their descendants. Genealogy-to know the history of a family by examining its lineage. Accounts and Funds-to balance principal and interest to support family building. Capping and wedding ceremony-to glorify and inherit the blood of the clan. The system of mourning—to fulfill filial piety and repay the kindness of parents. Mountain range and water gap—to store up trees and protect Feng Shui. Mountain in front of the village-to surround the ancestral hall and make the view spectacular. Water channel in the village-to guard the ancestral hall and facilitates the people to drink. Rice and vegetables-to prepare for famine and assist daily meal. Pine, fir, bamboo and wood-to provide profitable resources for us to use. "

Ten Rules of Clan Regulations regulated the public affairs of the family. Such as the arrangement of the ancestral hall and the compilation of the genealogy, the management of the public assets, people's Cap Wearing Ceremony, wedding ceremony and funeral rite and so on. It may also contain the regulations about the locations of mountains and rivers, water systems for irrigating the farmland, vegetables in the fields, all kinds of trees and plants and so on. Therefore, we can draw a conclusion. Most part of the clan regulations are about public affairs of the family. It is the code of conduct observed by the whole clan. It can be seen from this that the Wu family in Peitian unifies the individual moral cultivation and the collective behavior of the family. The compilers of the genealogy hope that the whole family can follow it with one heart and ultimately create a beautiful and livable home for everyone.

4. In addition, the Wu family tree also contains some township rules and regulations that span the family scope and concern the public and social affairs of the whole township. For example, in *the Articles of Association for Public Welfare* formulated by the Wu family of Peitian in the 23rd year of Guangxu in the Qing Dynasty (1907), the following clauses are advocated for all villages in the township: "Prevent bandits; prohibit gambling; discourage opium; improve land contracts; settle disputes; revitalize industry; store up bamboo and wood; advocate thrift; respect ethics; cultivate etiquette and laws. " These articles focus on social security, social customs and local industrial development. It can be said that the scope of these articles is further expanded from the family to the outside, which has a strong meaning of township rules and regulations. Besides, Wu clan family in Peitian Village also set up some public welfare organizations, such as the "Life Saving Society" (拯婴社), whose purpose is to call for the prevention of the drowning of female babies in rural areas.

(2) From Family Disciplines to Family Tradition

It's safe to say in the history of Chinese nation, family regulations and family disciplines play a special role. Like *An Admonition to My Son* by Zhuge Liang, and *Dictum about Keeping Order in a Family* by Zhu Bolu, all kinds of family disciplines and education of family rules are significant. They represent the earnest entrusts and great expectations from ancestors to their descendants, which have played a positive role in cultivating people's mind, and promoted the formation and inheritance of excellent family traditions.

For example, the Qian Family in Wuxi City, Jiangsu Province is a distinguished family, which is famous for its fine family traditions and emphasis on family education. It has cultivated many outstanding talents in contemporary China, such as Qian Xuesen, Qian Jibo, Qian Mu, Qian Zhongshu, Qian Weichang and so on. The amount of talents in all fields from Qian Family is beyond counting. According to statistics, there are 67 academicians of the Chinese Academy of Sciences and the Chinese Academy of Engineering come from Wuxi, and 8 of them are from Qian Family. This is naturally related to the spiritual precepts of Qian Liu, the founder of the Wuyue Kingdom. He advocated that people should respect the virtuous and attached great importance to education.

In the field investigation, we also noticed that the people from Peitian Village are simple and honest, and talented people are produced by each generation. In modern times, the Wu family in Peitian not only had people like Wu Bazhen, who was a martial Jinshi of Qing Dynasty, but also commercial wizards and philanthropists like Wu Changtong. According to statistics, during the period of the Republic of China, four students from Peitian Village went to study in Japan and France. Among them, Wu Naiqing was a classmate of our Premier Zhou Enlai; five people studied at the Huangpu Military Academy. Since the founding of the People's Republic of China, this village has fostered hundreds of graduates with a doctor's, a master's, or a bachelor's degree, engineers, college students and technical school students.

This should be attributed to the family disciplines and clan rules of Wu Family. What's more, the Wu Family continuously perfect its family disciplines and regulations continuously. "Promoting production for improving people's living standards and strengthening cultural, ideological, and moral education." "The tradition of farming and studying hands down from generation to generation." These ideas sink deep into the hearts of the people of the Wu Family. Therefore, people of each generation can cultivate the heart of kindness and loyalty.

This is probably a cultural spirit shared by Hakka people in Western Fujian. When we walk into the Earthen Buildings, we can see couplets on their doors left by their Hakka ancestors. These couplets are ancestral instructions for later generations. Like the couplet of Huaiyuan Building in Nanjing County, Zhangzhou: "Cultivating morality and treating others with kindness, people who abiding by ancestral instructions improve and cultivate themselves. " "Living in the place with faraway mountains and nearby waters, well-endowed region has produced men of talent. " The couplet of Zhenchen Building in Yongding County, Longyan is: "People should abide by the ethics and disciplines, so as to be the one with attainments and virtues. "

President Xi Jinping also pays great attention to Chinese traditional family education. *A compilation of President Xi Jinping's words and thoughts on the importance of family education and virtues* has been published. This book is a good example. It contains the important discourses of President Xi Jinping on family education and virtues. For example, President Xi Jinping emphasizes the importance of family education, he believes that family disciplines are the core values of the family. Family laws are the "basic law" of the family. Family customs are the family culture with distinctive family characteristics that has been formed for generations by the family to abide by family disciplines and rules. They are the most precious property of a family and the source of pride of every family member. And family education should pay attention to the cultivation of virtues and integrity. He also emphasizes that we should pay attention to the unique role of mothers in family education; we should achieve the unity of prospering families and enhancing national strength in the new era; and carry out activities of family education in a variety of ways and so on.

The genealogy is regarded as *the Records of the Grand Historian* of families. Descendants of every generation can read their family genealogies. So that they can understand the origin and developments of their families. And they can raise a strong historical awareness of consanguineous community. The genealogy plays an important role in strengthening people's sense of identity and honor, promoting the formation of fine family traditions, inspiring the descendants to carry forward the tradition and forge ahead into the future, bolstering them to bring honors to their ancestors and prosperity to their own descendants. It has promoted the sustainable development of families, as well as the civilization progress of the whole society.

7.4 Clan Power and Yi Men

As we know, clans in a village involve clansman, and there are many affairs in a year. Such as ancestor worship, the management and use of public ancestral property, the protection of the village environment, the compilation and revision of the genealogy, the mediation of internal contradictions, and rural festivals and celebrations. All the discussions and important activities are conducted under the leadership of the patriarchal clan association.

7. 4. 1　The Patriarch and Clan Power

When it comes to the Clan Association, its core figure, the patriarch, must be mentioned. As we know, the patriarch is the head of clan who is in charge of the affairs within the clan, and the agent of the affairs outside the clan. The clan powers wielded by the patriarch is very complicated. And there are some points worthy of our students' attention.

First, the patriarch does not implement the system of primogeniture, but is elected. The patriarch usually comes from the gentry class in Chinese society, or the peerage class. The candidate of patriarch should meet the requirements of seniority. What really counts is the wealth and social power of the candidate and his clan, for example, if he or his family members are officials in service or retired ones, who have received certain Confucian education, and have known a lot of important influential people. Therefore, patriarchs and retired officials formed the gentry class of the local society.

Yan Shenggong, the great patriarch of the Confucius family in Qufu, Shandong Province, "dominating the clan" is one of his main duties. The number of Kongs' clans is large, and the clans living in Qufu alone are divided into 60 clans. In the whole family, the patriarch of kongting (孔庭族长) was set up as the top manager except for Yan Shenggong, and the Lin Temple was set up to assist the patriarch. Each branch has its own management personnel, such as Hushou (户首) and Huju (户举), to manage its own affairs. The organization of the Kongs in other places is roughly the same as that in Qufu, and they are under the management of Yan Shenggong. In addition, the establishment of generations, the formulation of family rules, and the revision of family tree are also effective ways of clan management.

Take Peitian Village as an example. Around the Kangxi and Qianlong periods, Peitian Village had formed a large-scale and authoritative clan organization. The leading members of the organization were composed of the heads of the various branches. In addition, the patriarch was elected from the gentry with powerful economic strength, retired officials and respected elders in the clan. Finally, the patriarchal clan association of seven to nine members was formed. The patriarchal clan association has many management matters, and all the deliberations and important activities are held in the ancestral hall. Of course, according to the content and nature, they are held in different levels of ancestral hall, room ancestral hall or incense and fire hall.

Secondly, the authority system of clan has a special kind of complexity.

(1) In terms of the management mode of the clan, it is advocate to govern the clan by using a non-legal way of kinship ethics.

For example, the Clan Association can make use of family disciplines, family laws, clan regulations and local rules. By doing so, they can educate and guide their family members. And people should not engage themselves in lawsuits. That is to say, the Clan Association does not rely on rigid national laws. Instead, it rely on the family affection and ethics norms, by which they coordinate the contradictions and conflicts of the clan society, showing the power of family affection and morality, as well as their flexibility. As stated in *the Xu Family Rules* (the 6th year of Qianlong) of the Xu family in Tangmo Village, She County, Huangshan City:

For those who have only made small mistakes that can be forgiven, you insist that they should be sent to the court, this is not the right way for lovers. It's better to take them to the ancestral hall, and in the presence of the ancestors' soul, the patriarchs point out their mistakes and correct them, and whip them as punishment. Perhaps they will make a fresh start without adding troubles and burdens to the government. Isn't this the behavior of a person who knows how to practice enlightenment within the family?

(2) The patriarch and his clan power are the connecting center and auxiliary force of the clan society and the local government power system.

Within the clan, the patriarch has the right to preside over sacrificial rituals, and be in charge of the management of sacrificial lands, clan academies, ancestral halls and so on. That is to say, the patriarch has the power to manage the public property of the clan. Besides, he also has the power to educate and punish clan members and mediate disputes. Outside the clan, he works with other patriarchs from different families to coordinate rural affairs. He communicates with the local government to handle necessary matters. He provides assistance in paying taxes, enlisting corvee labourors, capturing thieves, escorting criminals and so on. Therefore, he is an official and a diplomat of the clan. Patriarchs have the clan power on behalf of the gentry class. Serving as the connecting link between the local government and their clans, They wield clan power everywhere in the country. And they can be regarded as the local authority system second only to the government.

After the Song and Ming Dynasty, the clan system of civil society was widely supported by the ruling class. The fact that the clan system attached importance to the Confucian patriarchal ideology accorded with the need of the ruling class. And its development might contribute to the ethical enlightenment of the state. And at the same time, the ruling class also made use of the power of the Clan Administration. By doing so, it could better maintain the political and economic order of the local society. So the ruling class delegated its power to the gentry class, and the gentry class acted on behalf of the ruling state. That is what we called "the imperial power does not have direct control over the countryside". Fei Xiaotong, a Chinese anthropologist and sociologist wrote a book called *Earthbound China*. In this book, he gave an explanation about the clan system. The "Dual-Track Political Theory" of the traditional Chinese society has the following characteristic. "The top-down imperial power and the bottom-up gentry power and clan power, are parallel and interwork with each other." The fact that the gentry class rule China's local society, shows the integration of clan power and political power. And these two kinds of power contemplate with each other, so do the officials and gentries. The actual historical examples prove the following fact. Within the network of kinship, there is also the suppression and infringement of proprietary classes against the proletariat, the patriarchal power against the females, the feudal ethical code against human rights, the monarchical power against civil rights. we must notice the dark side of the clan power, its feudal political nature and class nature.

For example, we can see that the clans will prescribe the "misdemeanors" and "felonies" involved by the clansmen and the corresponding punishment methods. For the so-called "minor crimes", such as not being filial to parents, disrespecting parents, not listening to instruction, quarrelling, laziness and wandering. The punishment methods for misdemeanors include reprimands, kneeling, money and rice fines, and suspending the right to worship ancestors. The punishment for the so-called felonies, such as beating parents and grandparents, stealing trees from ancestral graves, and associating with bad people, committing crimes against lawlessness, immorality, cults, and rebellious disobedience, is very severe. The patriarchs may set up a private execution hall and commit lynchings indiscriminately. Such as hanging them, drowning in a pond, and so on. Even after the execution, the corpse will be burned. Where can we see any family affection and tolerance? Its cruelty and indifference are even worse than that of the feudal government.

Therefore, we can draw a conclusion: the management system, management mode and the nature of managing power of the local society involve many complicated factors. They are mixed with the "family affection" and "morality" of the kinship group as well as the "political nature" and "class nature" of the feudal society. So we can see that they are very complicated. Therefore, just like the chastity archways in Tangyue Village under the moonlight, the traditional villages under the patriarchal clan system have not only the affection of families and the beauty of their homeland, but also the distortion of human nature and the shadow of terror under the feudal autocratic system.

7.4.2 Yi Men (Families with Chivalrous Spirits) and Homelands

(1) Yi Men's Characteristics

In the long history of village patriarchal culture, in various places, a large number of excellent and exemplary "Yi Men" have emerged. And they are the faithful and active practitioners of the patriarchal culture. The so-called "Yi Men" generally has the following characteristics.

The first characteristic is cohabitation. Cohabitation refers that many generations live together and have meals together. It means that people do not break up the family and live apart. They live under the same roof and eat at the same table and work together happily.

The second one is property sharing. Within a certain limit, family members can share some property, such as ancestral house, ancestral hall, ancestral mountains, family lands, farmstead for helping the poor of family, free schools and so on. The values of ancestral halls and ancestral fields complement each othe. For example, in ancient times, the Bao family in Tangyue Village of Shexian county had ancestral fields of up to 1200 mu, and the rent valley was mainly used to support the widows, orphans, the disabled and ancestral school. "If the children of family members are admitted to the family academy for studying, there is no need to pay intuition and extra fees. "

The third characteristic is respecting and abiding by the social ethics and morality.

People unite with each other as one and stick together. And they are simple and honest.

（2）Examples of Yi Men

We can give you some examples of Yi Men.

①The first example is Zhang Gongyi's family in the Tang Dynasty. Their family carried on from the Northern Dynasty to the Tang Dynasty. Nine generations lived together and there were more than 900 people in the family. The land and all property belonged to every member of the family. Men's and women's clothes were made together. People beat the drum when it was the time for having meals. They had meals in the dinning hall together. There were different tables for family members, visitors and guests. Men and women did not sit together. The elder sat in the seat of honour while the younger sat according to their ages. There were proper formalities between the elder and the younger. Children sat separately in other tables. People were very polite and considerate to each other. After offering sacrifices to Heaven, Emperor Gaozong of the Tang Dynasty and his empress, Wu Zetian, visited Zhang Gongyi's family in person, and asked them about the secret of nine generations living together. Zhang Gongyi ordered his clansmen to write one hundred characters of "忍" （endurance）. Emperor Gaozong was moved to tears and bestowed his handwriting to it.

②Another example of "Yi Men" is the Lu Family in the Southern Song Dynasty, which is in Jinxi County, Fuzhou, Jiangxi Province today. In the 2nd year under the reign of Emperor Lizong, the Imperial Court commended Lu Family, and the Imperial Decree said："Your family in Qingtian Village, Jinxi County have cultivated famous scholars in every generation. and they have been written into the annals of history. It is said that your family have been living together for more than 200 years, and there are more than one hundred people in your family. You are very polite to each other and live in harmony. And you have fostered excellent family traditions. Therefore, we confer an honor upon your family. So that you can play a better role in promoting morality and excellent family traditions. " The family rules of Lu Family involves many aspects. For example：people should study and know the rules of propriety, and fulfill their filial duty to their parents and live with other family members in peace and harmony. People should adhere to the principle of benevolence and loyalty and plan their expenditures in the light of their income. People should help and support the poor and the weak and practice frugality. Lu Family has also cultivated many famous people, such as Lu

Xiangshan, a famous philosopher and writer. As we know, he can be equated with Wang Yangming, another great philosopher. He is a famous scholar from this family.

We can safely draw a conclusion that "Yi Men" refers to the big kinship family which plays a model role in practicing the Confucian patriarchal culture. The big kinship family has the characteristics of collectivism. What's more, it is like a charitable organization and acts for the public good. However, the shortcomings are obvious, such as the absoluteness of Confucian patriarchal ethics in value identification, the compulsion of unilateralism in life style and the equalitarianism in life consumption, and the scale is too large to manage. These comprehensive factors have caused the inherent limitations of "Yi Men", which makes it difficult for them to popularize and maintain for a long time. For example, in the 7th year of Jiayou of Renzong of the Song Dynasty (1062), the court ordered the Chen family of Yimen in Jiangzhou to be separated. From a family of more than 3000 people, it became about 300 small families and small "Yi Men".

7.5   Summary: The Endless Chinese Patriarchal Clan Culture

To sum up this chapter, we believe that the Chinese patriarchal clan culture contains profound information in history, ethics, architecture, art, folk customs and other aspects, and is a valuable cultural wealth worthy of the Chinese nation's permanent treasure and continuous development. There are several points I would like to talk about.

(1) The Chinese clan culture has been handed down from generation to generation for a long time. It has shown positive social functions and ethical effects.

First, in terms of politics, the patriarchal clan system plays a cohesive role. It connects Chinese people to their clans, their hometowns their nation and their motherland. And people gradually developed a sincere sense of affinity and identity to them. Second, in terms of ethics, the clan culture advocates the Confucian thought of "loving relatives and respecting worthy persons". And it educates and restrains its clansmen with this thought. By doing so, it has exerted great influence on the Chinese people's life, as it has cultivated the value orientation on morality and personality of the whole Chinese nation. Third, in terms of geography, with families as the bases, many clan associations are built all over the world, which have become the links of the Chinese community. The Chinese community thinks highly of the clan culture. Fourth, in terms of culture, through the genealogy, local chronicles, local operas, dialects and pastoral literature, the clan culture has formed a distinctive academic school.

(2) Of course, influenced by historical limitations Chinese clan culture and patriarchal clan culture also have their dark side.

The clan power has also been criticized by people a lot. For example, it was a rope that binds ordinary family members, especially women together with the feudal regime, theocracy and authority of the husband. Bertrand Russell, a British philosopher once made a comment in his *The Problem of China* that the patriarchal clan concept is hindering the development of modern public consciousness, and people's civic spirit. "In the present day, when China is confronted with problems requiring a radically new outlook, these features of the Confucian system have made it a barrier to necessary reconstruction. " Actually, the clan family is a group of local power, which can easily be extended into various local cliques, such as the families of hereditary power and groups of localism. Even today, the folk clan is still a closed group with a feature of conservative, it usually tends to have the thoughts and behaviors that exclude strangers. Therefore, they used to arouse resentments and provoke large-scale fights with weapons. So when we look into the future development of patriarchal clan culture, we should take the following aspects into consideration.

(3) In terms of the direction of clan culture's development in the future.

China's patriarchal culture has been spread for thousands of years. The Chinese cultural character of attaching importance to the family and advocating filial piety can be said to have been deposited in the gene. I believed that we should turn it into a clan of fraternization, and a clan of civilization equality and public welfare culture.

Firstly, we should combine the development of the patriarchal culture and construction of the new countryside in the new era, especially to explore the way and path of combining traditional patriarchal villages with modern tourism.

After the reform and opening-up, with the change of people's ideas and the rise of the national learning craze, the revival of clan culture has been constantly strengthened, which plays an irreplaceable role in building a harmonious rural culture. With the booming of tourism, many ancient temples in Ming and Qing Dynasties were developed and used as scenic spots. At the same time, when planning urban and rural development plans, many regions take the traditional history and culture represented by ancestral halls as part of the government's development plans. For example, the Wulin traditional village protection and development project in Jinjiang City, Fujian Province, the Key Planning Area is the core area of the village where the cultural heritage of the village is relatively concentrated. It covers an area of about 21 hectares and aims to form a characteristic cultural settlement of livable, suitable and tour-able for the emerging leading industries with cultural creation, leisure and home stay. The Huaqiao Museum and the Minnan Cultural Back Garden are created to promote the development of rural tourism in southern Fujian.

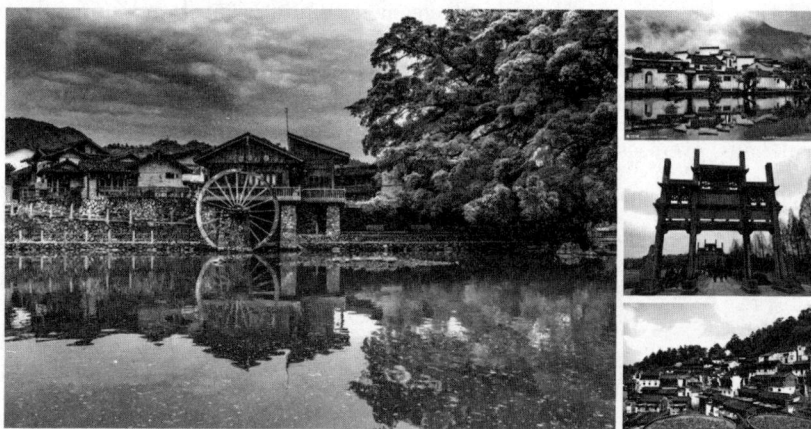

7-6 Patriarchal Villages with Modern Tourism

Secondly, we should consider the modes of building a new ancestral hall, new patterns of compiling genealogy, and new ways of organizing sacrifice rituals.

In my observation, most of the ancestral halls in southern rural areas have been repaired or newly built, and many new functions such as village history exhibition hall, farmer's bookshop, drama club, special exhibition room, elderly activity center and fitness and entertainment area have been added. This also provides a good opportunity for the development of the local economy. In ancient times, those solemn and mysterious places where outsiders and women were not allowed to enter have also become platforms and media to promote rural revitalization and spread Chinese traditional excellent culture. In addition, the content of today's genealogy is different from the old one, adding many new contents, which is more reflected the people's beautiful requirements for a harmonious life in the new society of freedom, equality and the rule of law. In the 21st century, the way of compiling digital genealogy based on the internet has begun to appear. Young people who are good at using the internet will gradually become the main force of the construction of the genealogy. The academic community has also published various books or material collections on patriarchal culture research. We should make full use of them to improve the level of modern academic research on patriarchal culture.

Thirdly, we should also pay special attention to the harmonious interaction and linkage development of the clan culture in the three regions of the mainland, Taiwan and Hong Kong, and the Greater China Cultural Area.

Patriarchal culture is an important common cultural symbol and spiritual link in the Chinese world. Overseas Chinese who have emigrated overseas still remember their homes and ancestors when they go to the ends of the earth. In addition to building ancestral halls overseas, it has organized various hometown associations and clan associations, and promoted the establishment and networking activities of cross regional and transnational world-wide clan groups and organizations. They also often return to the mainland of China, return to their hometown, seek their roots and pay homage to their ancestors.

Taiwan is China's inalienable sacred territory. People on both sides of the Taiwan Strait are geographically close, related by blood, cultural, commercial and legal ties. More than 80% of the Taiwan people's ancestral home is Fujian, of which Quanzhou nationality accounts for 44.8%, Zhangzhou nationality accounts for 35%, Fujian Taiwan compatriot's birthplace, ancestral residence, ancestral hall, ancestral tomb and other Taiwan-related cultural relics are numerous. The vast majority of the surnames in the top 30 of Taiwan's population are directly derived from Fujian, and Taiwan's Fujian hometown associations and clan associations are spread across 25 counties and cities in Taiwan. As we know, the Jian Family in Changjiao Village in Nanjing County, Zhangzhou, has moved to Taiwan since the Ming Dynasty, and up to now there are 230000 descendants of Jian Family in Taiwan. The descendant of Jian family often returned to Changjiao Village to find root and worship ancestors. In addition, Wang Jingping, famous political figure in Taiwan, returned to his home place to worship ancestors in 2019.

For overseas Chinese who believe in traditional ideas, they long for returning to their hometowns and worshiping their ancestors. They hope to bring honors to their ancestors and family, if they successfully do so, they will be very proud of themselves. Maria Corazon Sumulong Cojuanco, the 11th president of Philippines, and her son Benigno Simeon Cojuangco Aquino Ⅲ, the 15th President of Philippines returned to Hongjian Village, Jiaomei County, Zhangzhou, Fujian Province in 1989 and 2011 respectively. Thaksin Shinawatra, the 23rd Prime Minister of Thailand and Yingluck Shinawatra, the former Prime Minister of Thailand returned to Taxia Village, Fengshun County, Meizhou, Guangdong Province to visit their ancestral family and relatives and worship their ancestors.

I think Fujian Province is an important ancestral place for overseas Chinese. We people living and working in the mainland and Fujian should play the card of patriarchal culture well, do a good job for our overseas relatives, and strive to realize their dream of finding their hometown and expressing their family feelings and friendship, so as to promote the United Front Work of the Chinese family to a new stage.

At the fifth session of the 13th National People's Congress this year, the delegation of Fujian Province put forward a proposal to the Congress in the name of the whole delegation: first, support Fujian to establish the "overseas Chinese Forum" and the "World Conference of overseas Chinese". Second, support the construction of overseas Chinese History Museum in Fujian. Third, support the construction of a national "root seeking" platform. It is suggested to upgrade Quanzhou Nanyang Chinese ethnic group's comprehensive service platform for seeking roots and paying homage to ancestors to a national platform, set up special institutions, gradually increase investment, expand construction scope, increase platform capacity, and improve service and carrying capacity. Fourth, support the construction of a "root seeking" cultural home. Fifth, support the creation of a number of "root seeking" activity brands.

In short, one of the basic characteristics of Chinese traditional culture is the patriarchal social life of long history. Attaching great importance to moral relations between people, fulfilling the filial duties to parents, respecting ancestors, thinking highly of their family, organizing and attending sacrificial rituals carefully, compiling family genealogies, handing down excellent family traditions, loving hometown and China. These are the characteristics of Chinese people's consciousness of consanguineous community. This consciousness of consanguineous community is a deep-rooted national and collective consciousness of the Chinese people. And it is a distinct and important clue of the Chinese traditional culture for thousands of years. In essence, it reflects the Chinese people's cherish and love of life, as well as their respect for the origin of life, and also their sincere wish to live forever.

第八讲

和而不同
—— 中国的多元宗教及其特质

在讨论中国文化特征的时候，我们介绍了梁漱溟先生的一个观点，与罗素相同，他也认为：中国文化特征之一是"几乎没有宗教的人生"。那么，中国文化和中国人生活中真的几乎没有宗教吗？

8.1 宗教和中国宗教

一般而言，中国人对宗教的态度，似乎是若有若无之间。尤其是汉族地区的人民，貌似确实没有什么严肃和常态的宗教生活习惯。2015 年底，美国皮尤研究中心（Pew Research Center）发布过一项关于"宗教信仰在个人生活中是否非常重要"的主题调查报告[①]，研究结果显示，在参与调查的全球 40 个主要国家中，中国人对主题问卷做肯定选择的人口比例处于最低水平，仅 3% 的中国人认为宗教重要，远远低于全球 55% 的平均水平。此外，还有民调机构盖洛普国际 2015 年就信仰状况搜集数据，有来自 65 个国家的 63898 人接受了调查，其中中国大陆地区的信教比例为 7%，而无神论者竟高达 61%。那么，通过上面的调查数据能看出中国的信教人数确实是非常少的。那么，为什么会出现这种现象呢？是因为中国文化里真的没有宗教信仰吗？答案当然是否定的。但这里必须先澄清一个概念：何谓宗教。我们需要了解宗教是什么？以及它所具备的定义要素是什么？

一般来看，宗教是指有一定教义、教规，有一定仪式和组织系统的信神的社会"实体"。它至少包括五大要素：（1）对超人间力量的信仰，如上帝、真主、宇宙精神；（2）有规范的宗教仪式，如祈祷、念经、受洗、剃度；（3）有

---

① "The Importance of Religion in People's Life" Pew Research Center［EB/OL］. https://wmich. edu/globalstudies/pew-research-center. 2015.

专门的宗教组织和神职人员，如丛林、教团、教会、神父、僧侣；（4）有特殊的情感体验，如天启、顿悟、入定、超自然体验；（5）有专门的道德规范，如摩西十诫、佛门五戒等。而在宗教的本义上看，它确实更强调一种人与神的特别的关系。如果一种所谓的宗教的核心位置上没有神，或不是指向对神的崇拜和皈依，或是指向多神的杂乱的实用主义的膜拜，则往往不被认为是成熟而严格的、正信的宗教。

如果按照这个理解模式来审查中国的传统宗教，其特征的确有些不同，其本质指向与其说是人和神的关系，毋宁说，它们更指向人和天道（或人与真理）这样一种本体论的信仰。"敬鬼神而远之"，这在儒释道三教或精英知识分子中是普遍的常识。而民间对传统宗教的信仰确实具有多神论和实用主义的特点，这些我们在第二节中将会专门讲解。我想说是，按严格的一神论为核心的基督教标准，中国古代的主要宗教和民间信仰都与之不契合，无宗教的结论因此也似乎是可以成立的。

当然，如果把宗教的定义放到世界宗教史的大视野中，放到人类思想史的多元信仰的大范畴看，放到人类生命对绝对真理和终极价值的追问和信仰（即"终极关怀"）① 这一点原初精神上来说，则我们可以认为每一个民族都可能有他们各自形态的宗教。宗教形态应该是多元和多样的。宗教的标准应该是开放而包容的，它的基础应该是超越的信仰，它的对象是最高的宇宙精神，即真理。

应该说，古代中国文化里蕴含着丰富的宗教和民间信仰形式。我们可以看几幅图片。第一幅图片展示的是山东曲阜的孔庙，始建于鲁哀公十七年（公元前478年），孔庙是儒教的圣地。第二幅图片是道教的三清殿，道教有三清上人，分别是上清灵宝天尊、玉清元始天尊、太清道德天尊。第三幅图片是龙门石窟，它是佛教的建筑。第四幅图片是济南洪家楼教堂，它是中国三大著名天主教堂之一。第五幅图片是关于泉州的元代伊斯兰教寺庙"清净寺"。第六幅泉州晋江摩尼草庵的摩尼光佛，它是全世界仅存的摩尼教遗迹。通过这几幅图片，我想给大家一个基本的印象：中国传统的宗教文化丰富多样，作为中国多元宗教类型的儒教、道教、佛教是一个主体，它们和基督教、伊斯兰教、摩尼教等宗教一起，在长期历史上发挥了巨大的文化影响力。

---

① 德国神学家保尔·田立克（Paul Tillich，又译"蒂利希"）提出的将宗教信仰当作是"终极的关怀"的思想颇有代表性。在他看来，每个人都有以自我生命之最终意义与价值为中心的关于"终极"问题的思考即终极关怀，正是这样一种对于人之生命意义如何从有限达于无限、从短暂进于永恒的追寻构成了人之自我的"宗教信仰"。

图8-1 中国的多元宗教

其实，我国自古就有以"万物有灵"观念为核心的各种原始宗教，多类型的民间信仰文化在中国民众的日常生活之中也有丰富多彩的表现。这种原始宗教的信息在各类史前文明遗址和考古发掘中都有大量的文物证据。我们可以将其大概分为：（1）自然崇拜，崇拜天地日月山水石风雨雷等自然对象。如苗族民众以天为父、以地为母；藏族同胞虔诚绕行冈仁波齐、大理白族崇拜玉龙雪山为保护神；西藏当雍措湖地区的人民崇拜圣湖；闽南和台湾地区广泛崇拜风狮爷和石敢当。（2）动植物图腾崇拜，即崇拜各种植物和龙、犬、象等动物为始祖的图腾崇拜。如苗族崇拜竹和枫树，畲族崇拜神犬盘瓠为始祖，土家族崇拜白虎始祖，蒙古族崇拜白鹿和苍狼为始祖。（3）鬼魂和祖先崇拜，各民族中广泛存在，并普遍地表现出各自的祖先崇拜和祭祖文化；如彝族的"尼木措毕"送祖归灵祭祀，高山族的祖灵（彩虹）桥信仰，汉族的祠堂和祭祖传统等。（4）另外还有生殖崇拜、天神崇拜等。

应该说，中国传统宗教和民间信仰丰富多彩，是中国文化的重要组成部分，对中国古代哲学、政治、经济、伦理、文学、绘画、雕塑、建筑以及名山大川在内的整个生活世界的各个方面都有巨大而深刻的影响。我们这里不打算分别地对这些宗教的产生和发展做历史的回顾，有关原始宗教和民间信仰形式也暂时略过。在下面，我将直接谈对中国传统宗教的整体特质，分作四点略做考察。（1）儒教：道德宗教的主导地位；（2）伦理本位的人文宗教气质；（3）多元宗教之间和而不同的融合性；（4）实用主义的入世性。

8.2 儒教："道德宗教"的主体地位

儒学是否为一种宗教，这是一个有争议的学术问题。

近代大学者康有为和章太炎在此问题上就针锋对立。与康氏沿承汉儒以孔子为素王，奉其为儒教教主之说不同，章太炎反对儒学为宗教之说，他认为孔子的意义在对古籍的整理。现代新儒家的第一代学者如梁漱溟也反对以宗教来定位儒学，他强调人文性与哲学性（而不是宗教性），才是儒学和儒家的精神。但新儒家的第二、第三代学者们则不以为然。如牟宗三和唐君毅等人联合发表的《为中国文化敬告世界人士宣言》中，就从"儒学的第三期发展"和"复兴儒学"的需要出发，从"人文的道德宗教"或"人文宗教"的角度给予儒学以性质定位，不断强调儒家的人文精神的普遍性意义和超越的性质，进而确定儒家的宗教性质。华裔学者、现代新儒家第三代杜维明甚至认为："儒家思想既不只是一种政治意识形态，也不只是一种社会经济的伦理，而主要是宗教性神学的传统。"①

这里必须提到一套由大陆学者任继愈顾问、李申主编的《儒教资料类编》。这套书从十五个主题方面采掇了大量原始材料，核心宗旨就是揭示儒教历史存在。这套丛书分为15辑，在儒学研究界颇具开创性，非常值得参考。如第1辑，儒教、孔教、圣教、三教称名说；第2辑，儒经"圣经"说；第3辑，儒教敬天说；第4辑，儒教报应论等。

以我们的研究来说呢，我们也倾向认为儒学是一种特殊类型的"人文宗教"，因为从形式上看，它完全符合我们前面提到关于宗教的一般定义要素。1. 儒教的信仰对象：天地（之道）为核心，包括圣贤、祖宗在内的超越实体。2. 儒教的教主：孔子。3. 儒教的教团：儒生集团（文官、士绅）。4. 儒教的教义：四书五经（十三经）。5. 儒教的教规：经礼三百，曲礼三千。在长期的中国历史上，儒学确实也被叫作"儒教"，而且并不简单的是人文教化的学术派别的意思，它更有一层宗教的指向。

第一，以儒教的信仰对象而言，儒教历来主张：敬天、法祖、尊孔。在儒家看来，"敬天"是因为天地（之道）代表了超越的宇宙本体，是万物和生命

---

① 杜维明. 儒家自我意识的反思 ［J］. 船山学刊. 2017,（03）.

的本源，所谓"天地之大德曰生"，所以要把天放在第一位来信仰和崇拜，要敬之畏之，不可欺，不可怨。"法祖"是因为祖宗代表了一个家族生命的现世来源，是血缘生命的超越性共同体的本质精神。"法祖"就是感恩和崇拜生生不息的生命本身。"尊孔"是因为孔子被认为代表了儒家开辟和传承的宇宙人生的真理（道统和文脉），这套文化系统化成天下，让中国人成为"文明以止"的族类。所谓"天不生仲尼，万古长如夜"。

第二，从祭祀系统来看，儒家尤其重视"三祭"，以为国家和人民的大事。儒家的前身本来就是主管部落祭祀的祭祀阶层。儒家历来重视对天地、祖宗、对圣贤的祭祀，认为"国之大事，唯祀与戎"（《左传》），并重视通过祭祀礼仪和虔诚感格以求得感应于他们的信仰对象，达到特定的诉求与精神目的。

（1）祭天：中国古代帝王以天子自居，认为执政得自天命，所以敬畏天命，实行祭天的目的就是要与天意相契合。在儒家的推动下，古代王朝无不重视祭天大典，如秦始皇、汉武帝、汉光武帝、唐高宗、武则天、唐玄宗、宋真宗等都曾到泰山举行封禅大典，就是"报天之功"。明清朝冬至日在天坛祭天，典礼仪式也非常的庄重肃穆。当然，中国民间也重祭天，所谓"天地君亲师"的牌位普遍地挂在民居正厅之上；闽南人至今有春节初九"拜天公"的传统，以求一年国家风调雨顺，百姓万事顺心。（2）祭祖：这方面已经在第六讲村落宗族文化中专题讲解过，这里不再赘述。但祭祖的香烟袅袅中，寄托了中国人对祖先的崇拜和生命本源的超越性信仰，是中国人最传统的一种生活内容，甚至是义务，这也醇厚美化了民族的德性生命，所谓慎终追远，民德归厚。（3）祭圣贤：孔子作为儒家的教主，是儒教文化的核心人物，也是儒教圣贤祭祀的主要对象。另外，也有一些配享孔庙的先哲、先贤和先儒，也是接受祭祀的。先哲是指在孔庙中从祀的颜回、曾子、子思、孟子等"四配"，子贡、子路、冉有等"孔门十二哲"。先贤主要是指其他孔门弟子及再传弟子。先儒是指在历史上对儒学有杰出贡献的学者如董仲舒、朱熹、王阳明等。

第三，孔庙或文庙是儒家祭祀圣贤的主要场所。

因儒学的广泛的影响，遍布南北乃至海外的孔庙数量庞大，据统计至今仍有两千多座，可谓壮观。以曲阜孔庙为例。曲阜孔庙南北长约1300多米，东西宽150多米，占地140000平方米，三路布局，九进院落，贯穿于一条中轴线上，左右对称排列，与故宫、承德避暑山庄并称为中国三大古建筑群。庙内存有汉以来历代石刻1000余块，尤以汉魏六朝碑刻、汉画像石和明清雕龙石柱驰名中外，是研究政治、历史、文化艺术的宝库。孔庙面积之大，历史之久，气魄之雄伟，保存之完好，被中国古建筑学家称为世界建筑史之奇迹"唯一的孤例"，不仅是儒家文化载体，更是一座屹立于世界东方的文化艺术殿堂。

为表达对孔子的尊崇和对儒学的推重，历史上曾有 12 位皇帝亲临曲阜致祭，并将孔门弟子和历代国学大师 172 人配祀孔庙。孔庙始建于春秋，历经两千多年历朝各代近百次增修扩建，至明清时形成现在的规模。衍圣公府承担了祭孔的主要任务，设置了相应的组织架构和工作人员，每年投入巨资进行各类大小不等的祭祀活动多达八十多次。各地的孔庙一般都按照"左学右庙"的格式与各级官学教育机构（如国子监或地方的府学、县学）设置在一起。儒生们按时如礼祭祀，以表达对圣贤的仰望和崇拜之情。

第四，儒教的本质信仰具有非人格神的本体论特点。

比较地看，与世界其他传统宗教不同，儒教的核心信仰是非人格神的超越本体，即天道或道。我们知道，儒教讲的"天道"不是一个神灵形象。孔子所谈的"天之三义"中，有意志的神灵之天的意义只是其一。另外也有物质之天和义理之天，尤其是义理之天更是人们的道德理性的根本源头，孔子和儒学对其的强调和重视明显高于另外两层天。如孔子一方面说敬畏天命，天不可欺，但另外一面他又说"务民之义，敬鬼神而远之""未能事人焉能事鬼"。孔子对学生追问死后有没有鬼的问题是采取悬置的态度①，因为他关心的是让生命活出意义。他重视下学而上达，重视在人间的伦理生活中敦伦尽分、克己复礼，以实现天下归仁的目的，从而弘扬了人的生命主体性、达到天人合一的美好境界。这个天人合一终极境界，也不是神的王国，而是万物一体的本真心境和生活世界。

道教虽然有诸多的神灵谱系，但其最高的信仰对象也是道。道在"象帝之先"，是万化的根源，是神灵们都要尊崇和服从的本体。天道高于神灵，神要服从于道。所谓"一气化三清"，三清尊神也要服从这个非人格的天道。佛教也一样，九法界无非缘起性空，天神饿鬼乃至佛菩萨，本质上都是同一的空空如也。所谓佛，也不是宇宙创世主和命运主宰者，他不是上帝。佛者觉也，是宇宙精神的领悟者和践行圆满者而已。佛法之法，宇宙的根本真理之谓也。儒释道三教的核心信仰：天、道、空，都属于非人格化的超越的宇宙本体，比较地看，倒是非常相似于西方近代哲学史上的自然神论（理神论）及其所讲的宇宙精神。牛顿、莱布尼茨和爱因斯坦都鄙视传统的有情绪意志的人格神，而其所使用的

---

① 子贡问孔子："死人有知无知也？"孔子："我欲言死后有知，恐孝子顺孙妨生以送死也；我欲言无知也，恐不孝子孙弃而不葬也。赐，欲知死人有知无知，死徐自知之，犹未晚也。"（《说苑·辨物》）

"神"或"上帝"的概念，只是自然实体，是宇宙的规律。数学就是神的语言，到达天堂的手段不是祷告而是掌握物理学①。中国儒释道三教的信徒本质上看，即使不是无神论者，但也不是神本论者，他们以心性的本真融合天道的本体，而是心物一元论者，或天人合一的超神论者。

儒释道等人文宗教，以东方的方式定义和阐发了宗教的道德内涵。宗教被看成是人的生命和基本价值的拓展，而宗教之为"教"，强调了人文的生命之在于人自身而不是人格神，重在发挥德性主体的明心见性的自我修养的力量，以道德理性的"内在超越"而非向彼岸的外在超越来实现自我的完美。并始终联系并强化其社会向度的精神功能，强化其对现实世界的伦理指导和社会生活的道德干预作用。梁漱溟先生因此把儒学叫"伦理教"，并认为它完全取代了宗教的情感安慰功能。应该说，这种以自力求人格完美的道德宗教对疗治外在超越（如基督宗教）导致的人文精神的式微，进而追求人的生命的主体性自觉和人类社会的文明圆满，无疑具有重要的价值意义。当然，这大概也是他们不被西方宗教承认为是宗教，而自诩为即宗教并超宗教的独特原因。

8.3　伦理本位的人间宗教

我们常说，中国文化的重要特点是人伦本位，注重人间伦理生活的修养和践行，有一种远神近人的特点。这是不错的，反映在中国宗教中这个特点也很明显。可以说，儒释道三教乃至中国化的伊斯兰教都注重人间伦理建设，实践儒家的宗族思想与人格修养，它们本身都是人间宗教——伦理教。

儒教自然不用说，五伦本位的文化本来就是儒教的贡献。儒教安于生活世界，中国民众的传统信仰是敬天法祖。比较于敬天背后对天的自然神论式的虚化，以宗祠祭祖和族谱编修所维系起来的祖宗信仰，反而更实在和有力。光宗耀祖、光前裕后的宗族共同体信念，亦最普遍于中国人的现实生活。中国人以享受天伦之乐为最大快乐，以哀哀无告为人生最大悲剧，以承前启后、子孙恒昌为最大追求。"拜神不如敬祖"和家族生命共同体的优先位阶，乃是宗族时代民众的宗教观念的基本特色。宗族文化的修养和价值追求，让中国人既避免了

---

① 自然神论认为1. 宇宙存在一种超越的精神（上帝），创造万物，但却不干预世界的进程，也无人格，不会惩恶扬善。2. 自然神论者认为世界提供了一系列有待破解的符号，这些符号包含着永恒、神圣、超验的真理。而破解的手段只能是理性和实验。

放任欲望的庸俗和追逐功利的肤浅，又避免了坠入宗教的空疏与狂热，同时还获得了历史心境的精神安顿和意义安慰。

　　道教虽然追求羽化登仙，但不迷信"长生久视"。"以道观之"让他们获得了潇洒的相对论智慧。道教也强调伦理道德，老子所谓"万物尊道而贵德"，《道德经》其实就是一本教导中国人为人处世和治国平天下的宝典。道教的《太平经》融合儒家的伦理道德，表示对明君清官的拥护和对太平盛世的向往。它以神道的权威，劝诫和警告昏君和贪官污吏，谴责他们的贪婪，不劳而获和残暴。要求众生平等，反对过度剥削，提出一种以人人劳动、周济贫穷的平等社会为目标的太平思想。"医圣"、道士孙思邈在他的著作《千金要方·养性序》中提出："德行不克，纵服玉液金丹，未能延寿；道德日全，不祈善而有福，不求寿而自延，此养生之大旨也。"①

　　中国化的佛教顺应中国伦理本位的传统氛围，实行"佛法在世间，不离世间觉"的宗旨，强调"报四恩"，其中父母恩、国土恩与众生恩，都是典型的人间取向。佛教徒提倡尽孝道和尽臣民之责（"庄严国土，利乐有情"），奉行"一日不作，一日不食"的农禅并重的修行，到近代太虚法师更提出：人间佛教，所谓"仰止唯佛陀，完成在人格。人成即佛成，是名真现实"。印顺导师和星云法师等佛门大德将其发展为"人生佛教"。

　　中国回族地区的伊斯兰教重两世、积商德。所谓"两世"，是伊斯兰教关于现世生活与死后归宿的理论观点。伊斯兰教正统学者依据《古兰经》和圣训，将今世的现实生活视为人的旅途，将后世视为人的归宿。倡导两世并重，善良行事，做个好人，功在当代、利在千秋。以福建泉州市惠安百崎回族乡的郭氏家族为例：该回民家族数百年来深受儒家宗族伦理影响，也建有自己的家庙和族谱，清明节也祭祀祖宗，也会焚香叩拜，表现了浓浓的人间烟火气，他们甚至认为关帝爷是穆罕默德的化身，这些都与世界各地的伊斯兰文化有了很大的不同吧。

　　我们可以说：祭天地、祭祖宗、祭圣贤为核心内容的儒教影响了佛教、道教和伊斯兰教的发展与传播，如梁漱溟先生说的，它们本质上都可以说是一种伦理教，中国人皆伦理教教徒。而基督教虽然早在唐代即有传入中国，但明末清初则戛然中断。原因之一就是罗马教廷与在华传教士之间围绕如何处理拜上帝与敬祖宗、敬圣贤、敬王者的中国传统信仰文化之间的矛盾无法达成一致。适用和尊重中国文化习俗的调和派的"利玛窦规矩"无法得到教皇的支持，顽

---

　　① 孙思邈. 千金要方·养性序 [M]. 北京：华夏出版社，1993：1.

固坚持不许中国教民的"三祭"风俗，因而最终被康熙所禁止和驱逐。信耶稣，就不能信天地祖宗和圣贤，这是基督教无法被中国化的原因。他们根本忽视了一点：中国有深厚的伦理本位的文化土壤，传入中国的宗教必须适度地人间化、人伦化、人文化，否则就难以在中国人的生活世界里真正扎根并长远发展。

8.4　多元宗教之间和而不同的融洽性

宗教冲突甚至宗教战争，是人类历史上屡见不鲜的现象，但在中国传统宗教史上并无此类情况。它们在和而不同的基础上和平相处，融洽一体。这方面我们可以有许多证明可说。以被誉为"世界宗教博物馆"的泉州为例。在泉州，中国传统文化与古代波斯、阿拉伯、印度和东南亚诸种文化曾交融汇合，留下了佛教、伊斯兰教、天主教、景教、印度教、摩尼教、犹太教等外来宗教的历史遗存，它们在泉州的土地上共同服务于这里的人民，彼此相安无事和睦融洽，而且彼此吸收和借用，生动活泼地共同发展。

（1）开元寺里的多宗教元素

泉州开元寺是一座始建于唐代的佛教寺庙，同时也是一座多元宗教融合的寺庙，尤其是印度教的痕迹非常显眼[1]。比如在开元寺大雄宝殿前，有两座南宋绍兴十五年泉州柳三娘捐建的印度萃堵波格式的方形石塔，塔上刻有萨锤太子舍身饲虎的故事。在大雄宝殿的月台须弥座束腰处，有 72 幅辉绿岩狮身人面像和狮子浮雕。大雄宝殿殿后廊檐间那对 16 角形辉绿岩石柱，雕刻着古代印度和锡兰流传的古印度教大神克里希那的故事和花卉图案 24 幅。这些遗存，都是（南）宋代以来印度教在泉州传播并有其影响的写照与证明。开元寺的大雄宝殿也被叫作百柱殿，在殿内木柱的顶端都装饰着手捧南音乐器、飘逸着裙带的飞天塑像（"妙音鸟"），而这些飞翔的天使，洋溢着鲜明的基督教色彩与风格。

（2）又如中外闻名的"刺桐十字架"

"刺桐十字架"是泉州多元宗教融合的重要石刻证据。如果大家去泉州海外交通史博物馆参观，就能看到这些古代的石刻遗物。在其中你会发现既有典型的基督教的天使形象、十字架，也有属于中国佛教与道教的文化符号，如华盖、

---

[1] 我国各地多有如此"混搭"的多元宗教和谐共处的名胜古迹。如恒山悬空寺也是一座多元宗教融合的寺庙。悬空寺始建于北魏，到金代，悬空寺变成了一个儒释道三教融合的独特寺庙。雷音殿中供奉着佛教的释迦牟尼，纯阳宫中供奉着道教的吕洞宾，三教殿同时供奉老子、孔子、佛祖。

瑞云、海水、火焰、莲花座。而石刻上的十字架造型也类型多样，有希腊风格、拉丁风格、波斯风格、凯尔特风格、马耳他风格；从石刻的文字看，既有汉文，也有拉丁文、八思巴文、突厥文、波斯文。如此"混搭"，世界罕见。

图8-2　泉州开元寺里的多元宗教元素

　　其实不仅在宋元时代的基督教文化中国传播中有这种融合现象，在近代也有这种倾向。比如山东济南洪家楼天主教堂，虽然主体上它属于西方哥特式建筑，但细节上也有不少中国元素，如屋顶的中国小黑瓦，尤其是教堂中门上方左右两侧各雕刻有一个怒目张口的"中国龙头"，造型生动夸张。因为"龙"在西方文化中历来是邪恶撒旦的化身，能在教堂这一神圣之地使用龙造型，恰恰说明在逐步了解到中国"龙文化"的独特内涵后，西方宗教界已经能够折中彼此的文化意象的冲突，能入乡随俗地做一些文化元素的融合运用。在澳门的天主教建筑"大三巴"牌坊中也可以看到许多中国建筑元素的化用，这既是西方基督教文化在适应中国文化环境的过程中逐步中国化的证据，也是对中国文化的理解和尊重的态度表现。

　　（2）"三一教"

　　如果说上面的例子是不同宗教元素的混搭使用，在泉州的隔壁莆田市，曾在明代诞生过一个多元宗教融合而出的新教——"三一教"，又名"三教""夏教"，是明代嘉靖三十年（1551）由兴化府布衣林兆恩所创立。三一教主张儒释道三合一，以"道释归儒，儒归孔子"为教旨，盛行于明末清初，至今仍在福建、台湾地区和东南亚一些国家流行。

而这似乎有点类似于我国白族群众的"本主崇拜"。本主崇拜是我国白族同胞全民信奉的宗教。本主白语叫"武增",是"本境福主"的简称,意即"我的主人"。他们是白族村社的保护神,有的一村供奉一个本主,也有几村供奉同一本主的情况。只要和白族村社有密切联系的人和事物都可以成为本主,所以在本主神祇中既有原始宗教色彩浓厚的山川树木、虫鱼鸟兽之神,也有佛道之神、儒家典范人物及民间传说中的人物;既有王室、贵族,也有英雄、平民;既有白族人物,也有汉族和其他民族的人物。这充分体现了本主崇拜兼容并蓄的特点。我想以狭隘的一神论宗教的标准来看,本主崇拜也好,"三一教"也罢,大概都没有资格叫宗教吧。但这就是当地人民虔诚信仰的和而不同的宗教。

谈到传统的多元宗教宽容融合的原因,我想简单地看无非是:1. 世界各国家和地区人民的密切联系交往是宗教多元交融的外在条件。2. 中国人民对异域文化持有的开放、实用的精神是多元交融内在条件。3. 儒家文化并育不害、和而不同的中庸之道是多元融合的思想保障。4. 中国历代政权和社会各界文化人士的积极推动是多元融合的积极力量。5. 历史的自然演绎和风云涤荡是多元交融的全息场域。

8.5 实用主义的入世性

从入世性的角度看,宗教都具有为现实生活服务的功能。神为人服务,从而得到人们的热爱和崇信,这个大众的功利主义的实用心理并不难理解。在过往的年代,频繁的天灾人祸让生产力低下的人类感到无助和恐惧,往往以为灾祸是鬼神之怒,认为平息了鬼神的怒气就可以度过天灾,而平日里多多叩拜神灵、奉献祭品,就能消灾免祸。要金榜题名就拜拜孔子和文昌帝君,要海上航行一帆风顺就拜拜妈祖娘娘①,其实祷告上帝与崇拜真主,不也是希望获得神的庇护与保佑吗?新冠疫情暴发后,美国白宫和国会还组织牧师进行祈祷法会以驱逐病魔,这不也一样是宗教的实用主义的表现吗?

趋利避害的实用主义本来就是古今中外所有宗教的共同品质,并不因此而

---

① 泉州的民间信仰中最为古老的当属海神崇拜,是独具地方特色的信仰,也是泉州海洋贸易繁荣的产物。为了保佑海上一帆风顺,泉州人多方祈求各路神灵,也把当地神灵都打上了庇佑海路安全的海神功能。如真武大帝在泉州地界增加了海事管理职能(九日山上有真武庙)。泉州也有"通远王"这样由山神转岗而来的海神。此外,观音、龙王、王爷、阴公、好兄弟等,在泉州沿海都在自己的本职外兼具了海上保护功能。

有损信仰的严肃，或因此就不那么神圣。宗教的实用主义特性，在我们看来，恰恰是中国宗教追求伦理本位，强调要仁者爱人、为人服务的文化特性的表现。

中国的神灵系统非常复杂，但其大部分是来自现实社会中真实存在过的历史人物。这些神仙人物大多是"聪明正直、死而为神"——因他们生前关爱世人，为社会做了大的贡献，人民深深怀念他们，并希望他们成为神，继续在天国保佑世人去灾免祸逢凶化吉。

例如每年的元宵节，厦门市集美区大社村民开展的"刈香游神"的民俗活动。游的何方神圣呢？就是"开闽王"——王审知。王审知和他的兄弟王潮、王审邽合称"开闽三王"，他们在五代乱世时期入主福建，施政有方，恩泽八闽，深为福建人民所崇敬，他们去世后，便被闽人尊奉为神了。又如在闽台地区广有信众的厦门海沧青礁慈济宫保生大帝，本是南宋时的大名医吴夲，他悬壶济世救护人民，民间俗称其为"大道公"。以泉州这座"诸神之城"再看几个例子。

泉州的文庙奉祀的圣贤，都是儒家历史上的重要文化人物。涂门街的关岳庙，供奉的是关羽和岳飞这两位真实的英雄人物。老君岩供奉的是道教的太上老君是西周时道家思想家老聃。泉州也是众所周知的海神妈祖信仰最重要的传播中心，而妈祖就是莆田仙游人林默娘。

中国的神灵大都如此，比如"八仙过海"里的八仙，基本上都是民间人物形象。如蝗神，或认为来自宋代的抗金将军刘锜，或认为来自元代灭蝗将军刘承忠。各行各业都把自己的祖师爷当作神灵来祭拜。由此可见中国的神灵跟世俗世界的联系紧密（至于家族祖灵那自然也是如此，朝夕与子孙相依），人们把关爱人民的伟大正直的历史人物都视作神灵，这与其说是迷信崇拜，不如说是一种崇敬，是为了抒发纪念和缅怀之情。

当然，关于中国宗教的特质，还可以有其他一些概括方式。

比如有人提出政教分离也是中国宗教的基本特色。但如果按照我们这里的讲法，把儒教当作宗教，则无法使用政教分离这个提法了。毕竟如果把儒学当成宗教，则儒家是深度介入了政权和整个社会的治理和权力运作的。儒家是力图建立王道政治和大同社会的，各级官员都是儒生出身，读的是儒教的经书，奉行的是儒教的"三祭"。按这个视角，则也可以说，中国是儒教和政权深度融合的政教合一国家。但鉴于儒家本质上是"即宗教超宗教"的特殊的"道德宗教"和"伦理教"，我们可以选择保留这个看法。你承认儒教是宗教，则中国传统上就是个是政教合一的国家。如果你不认为儒家是宗教，认为它只是一个负责教化的学派和思想流派，则会支持中国文化属于政教分离的类型。依据这个判断，即狭义地把中国宗教仅仅指向于佛教、道教或伊斯兰教、基督教，则在中国历史上（个别地区如旧西藏农奴制时代除外）确实没有出现过宗教与政权合为一体甚至高于并控制政权的这种西方中世纪现象①。

虽然中国历史上不少帝王贵族信佛信道，支持它们的传播与发展，如南朝的梁武帝舍身佛门，明代嘉靖皇帝被称为"神仙皇帝"；龙门石窟得到了从拓跋宏到武则天在内的各代君主的支持才得以开凿完成；十堰武当山作为"治世玄岳"，是明代的"皇室家庙"所在。但从政治上看，并没有因此而出现佛道宗教一教独大的局面，都没有动摇"独尊儒术"即儒教的优势地位。有些时代，甚至因为佛道宗教势力过大，在经济上妨碍国家的财政税收，影响了国政的稳定，而出现过"三武一宗"的灭佛事件②。所以，佛道宗教力量都很有自知之明的顺从统治集团，显得非常的温和。从这个意义上看，中国的传统宗教总体上是真正遵守了"恺撒的归恺撒，上帝的归上帝"的原则啊。

总之，中国的传统文化中宗教和民间信仰是个重要的客观存在的领域。

儒教作为道德宗教奠定了伦理本位、人间宗教的大气场，各种本土或外来的宗教都必须遵守这个规律和规定才能生存和发展，这是主干文化系统的作用力所致，无可避免。而多元宗教之间又深受和而不同的中庸之道的影响，彼此交流探讨，互相取法借鉴，从而促进了中国多元宗教（以及哲学和文化）内部及整体的新生长和繁荣。它们的繁荣与和传播，普济众生，也给民众提供了安顿自我的法门，让他们在无奈或者无望的生存中获得精神力量的慰藉和超拔。因此中国民众对各种类型的宗教都有着由衷的欢迎。他们敬天、祭祖、祭圣贤，也祭佛道各家的各种神灵。而我国各少数民族中更广泛保留着各种原始宗教的万物有灵信仰和图腾崇拜的痕迹。中国民众的信仰生活兼容并包，并不极端排他。他们需要神灵世界和人间世界融合一体，让生活过得更有滋有味、有情有义。

在21世纪的新时代，中国人民享受着他们的思想自由和信仰自由的文明之光，信教与不信教都自由。中国政府尊重并保障人民的这种信仰与选择的基本权利，并采取很多积极恰当的政策和措施，来促进中国宗教事业的健康发展。

---

① 西藏从13世纪到1959年废除农奴制之前，长期实行政教合一的社会政治制度。

② 中国历史上曾掀起灭佛事件的"三武一宗"是指北魏太武帝拓跋焘，北周武帝宇文邕，唐武宗李炎和后周世宗柴荣。

The Eighth Chapter:

Unity in Diversity
—Multiple Religions and its characteristics

When talking about Chinese cultural characters, we introduced to you a point mentioned by Mr. Liang Shuming. In his opinion, he regards Chinese culture, like Russell, as the one featuring almost no religion. Therefore, when it comes to Chinese culture and people's daily lives, is religion really absent from both of them?

8.1　Religions and Chinese Religions

Generally, China seems to indeed lack religious belief. For people living in Han areas, especially, there seems to be no serious or prevalent habits of religion. A report issued by the end of 2015 by Pew Research Center— "The Importance of Religion in People's Life". The result of this research shows that, among the 40 main countries in the world, China stays at the bottom among countries with a positive answer, with only 3% of its population regarding it as important, far lower than the global average—55%. Besides, according to the data collected by the opinion pool institution, Gallop International in 2015, among 63898 people in 65 countries, the rate of those with a religious belief accounts for only 7% in the Chinese mainland, while the atheists of which accounts for nearly 61%. Therefore, we can see it clearly from the data above that there remain very few people who believe in religion in China. What accounts for this phenomenon? Is it because there has never been religious belief in Chinese culture?

Of course not. Yet it is necessary for us to first understand what exactly religion represents. To begin with, what does religion mean? What are its main factors? Religion means an "entity" in the society, boasting certain doctrine, rule, ceremony and organization systems that worships God. Edward Teller once noticed that "Religion

represents the faith in sacred existence. " Generally, religion comprises five factors:
1. The belief in superhuman power—including God, Allah, or universal spirit, etc.
2. Standard religious ceremonies—praying, chanting scriptures, baptism, and tonsure.
3. Special religious organization and clergy—tempo, religious body, church, priest, monk. 4. Special emotional experience—Apocalypse, Satori, meditation, and supernatural experience. 5. Special moral regulations—The Ten Commandments, The Eight Commandments, etc.

In terms of the essence of religion, a relationship between man and God is truly stressed. If a so-called religion contains no god as its core, or it shows no worshipping towards God or taking the vow, or it aims to accept pragmatism with complex polytheism, it often fails to be taken seriously as a mature religion. If we see traditional Chinese religion according to the explanation mentioned above, the most central essence of which is indeed not the relationship between man and God. Rather, it focuses more on the relationship between man and the "Tao", or the seek for truth itself, featuring the impersonal, supra-divine, ontological belief. In three major religions in China—Confucianism, Buddhism and Taoism, or among social elites, this idea is widely accepted as common sense. When it comes to the belief in traditional religions among common people, there remains indeed many a character of polytheism and pragmatism, which will be further interpreted in the second lecture.

What I mean to say is that according to the strict Christian standard of monotheism in the West, major religious and folk beliefs in ancient China can neither match their requirements. The conclusion of atheism or no religion in China can thus be justified. If we put the definition of religion into a bigger picture of the history of global religions, if we see it in a wider range of the plural beliefs in the history of human thought, and if we take it in terms of human's exploration of and belief in the absolute truth as well as the ultimate value of the original spirit, we may come to the conclusion that every nation may boast its religion respectively in various shape. Therefore, the standard of religions should be both open and inclusive. Its basis should be the transcendental faith, while its goal should be the highest universal spirit. It is worth mentioning that in ancient Chinese culture, there boast abundant forms of religious and folk beliefs.

Let's have a look at several pictures as follows: the Confucian Temple in Qufu City of Shandong Province, built as early as the 17th year of Aigong, the King of Lu (499 BCE). The Hall of Three Purities in Taoism. The three highest gods in the Hall represent the Universal Lord of "the Way and Virtue" in Supreme Clarity Realm, the Universal Lord of Primordial Beginning in Jade Clarity Realm, and the Universal Lord of the Numinous Treasure in Higher Clarity Realm respectively. The Longmen Grottoes, a typical architecture in Buddhism. The Hongjialou Cathedral in Jinan City, one of the three most well-known Catholic churches in China, reflecting the spread of Christianity. Quanzhou's Islamic temple, the "Qingjing Temple", which can be traced back to the Yuan Dynasty. The statue of Mani in the temple in Jinjiang of Quanzhou City, which represents the only historical remains of Manichaeism in the world. I would like to leave you a basic impression of the rich and colorful religious culture in traditional China. And as a representation of China's plural religions, its main body, comprised by Confucianism, Taoism and Buddhism, exerts a magnificent cultural influence in the long-lasting history. While Christianity, Islam, Manichaeism, and other religions also play an important role.

In addition, primitive religions, which represent the core of animism, also matter in traditional Chinese society. And they can be divided into: (1) Worship of nature, natural force such as the sun, moon, mountains, water, stones, wind, rain and thunder. For example, the Miao people regard heaven as their father and earth as their mother; the Tibetan compatriots devoutly detoured the Gangrenboqi and Dali Bai ethnic groups to worship Yulong Snow Mountain as the protective god; the people of Dang Yongcuo Lake region in Tibet worship the holy lake; southern Fujian worships the wind lion God and shigandang (石敢当). (2) Worship of animals and plants, animal totem worship such as trees and various dragons, dogs, elephants, etc. The Miao people worship bamboo and maple trees, the She people worship the god dog Panhu, the Tujia people worship the white tiger, and the Mongolian people worship the white deer and the wolf as the ancestors. (3) Worship of ghosts and ancestors, such as the culture of ancestor sacrifice. The belief that the soul is immortal widely exists in all ethnic groups, and their respective ancestor worship and ancestor worship culture are widely displayed; for example, the soul sending ritual "Nimu Cuobi" of Yi people in Liangshan, and the ancestor spirit (Rainbow) bridge belief of Gaoshan people, Ancestral halls and ancestor worship tradition of Han nationality. (4) Worship of fertility, celestial, etc.

The splendid Chinese traditional religions and folk beliefs boast important parts of Chinese culture and have influenced its ancient philosophy, politics, economics, literature, calligraphy, painting, sculpture, architecture as well as famous mountains and rivers hugely and deeply in all respects. We will not review respectively of the history and development of these religions. Nor will we talk about primitive religious forms right now. Next, we will talk directly about the holistic characters of traditional Chinese religions in four aspects as follows: To begin with, Confucianism that represents the dominant role of moral religions. Second, the human religious character of ethical standards. Third, the integration of pluralistic religions featuring harmony in diversity. Forth, this-worldliness of pragmatism.

8. 2　Confucianism: the Dominance of a Moral Religion

Is Confucianism a religion? It's a controversial academic question, in which Kang Youwei and Zhang Taiyan were diametrically opposed to each other. Unlike Kang, who inherited the idea of Confucianism in Han Dynasty and regarded Confucius as the uncrowned king as well as the master of Confucianism, Zhang Taiyan disagreed with the idea of seeing Confucianism as a religion and believed that the significance of Confucius only lay in his arrangement of ancient records. The first generation of the modern Neo-Confucianism, such as Liang Shuming, was also against positioning Confucianism as a religion. He put emphasis on the humanism and philosophy, rather than religion, that represents Confucianism. Yet the second and third generations of Neo-Confucianism did not think so. As can be seen in what co-issued by Mou Zongsan and Tang Junyi—A Manifesto on the Reappraisal of Chinese Culture, from the need of "the development of the third phase of Confucianism" and "revitalizing Confucianism", they saw Confucianism in perspectives of "humanistic moral religion" or "humanistic religion" to define the nature of Confucianism. Through constant emphasis on the humanistic spirit of Confucianism and its universality and transcend identity, they therefore ensured the religious nature of Confucianism. Du Weiming, an ethnic Chinese scholar and the third generation of Neo-Confucians, even believed that Confucianism is not merely a political ideology, nor is it a socio-economic ethic. Rather, it is primarily a tradition of religious theology. It is obliged to mention a series of book consulted by mainland scholar, Ren Jiyu and edited by Li Shen—a Compilation of Confucianism Records, in which 15 volumes are included. The book focuses on 15 main themes and collects a large sum of relevant original materials. The core purpose of which is to disclose that the existence of Confucianism. It is quite groundbreaking in the study of Confucianism and is well worth referring to. Such as The First Volume—*The Names of Confucianism and the Three Religions.* The Second Volume— *taking the Confucian Scripture as the "Saint Scripture".* The Third Volume— *Respecting the Heaven by Confucianism.* From the above 15 volumes of studies on Confucianism, we may conclude that Confucianism can indeed be considered as a special type of religion, which, as we mentioned earlier, fully applies to the general definition of religion. What Confucianism believe are objectives far beyond entity, including saints and ancestors with the (way of) Heaven and Earth as its core. The hierarch of Confucianism: Confucius. The group of Confucianism: Confucians. The doctrine of Confucianism: The Four Books and Five Classics. The rules of Confucianism: 300 articles of rites and 3000 elements of propriety. The long-lasting Chinese history witnessed the study of Confucianism being regarded as a "religion". It does not simply mean an academic school of culture and education. Rather, it contains an implication of religion.

What are the Characteristics of Confucianism

(1) In Terms of the Faith of Confucianism

Worshipping the Heaven, ancestors and Confucius is always advocated. 1. For Confucianism, the respect for heaven can be explained as the (the Way of) Heaven and Earth representing the essence above the universe. It can be regarded as the origin of all beings and lives. "The great attribute of heaven and earth is the giving and maintaining of life. " Therefore, one should put the Heaven first for believing and worshipping and should be in awe of it without cheating or complaining. 2. Ancestors represent the this-worldly source of human's family life. They also represent the essential spirit of the transcendental community of blood relationship. Whereas worshipping ancestors aims to show gratitude and admiration to the ever-lasting life itself. Which naturally relates to the long history of ancestral worship. 3. The respect for Confucius represents the admiration of the nature gifted by Heaven with Confucian orthodoxy as well as the unity and coherence of its theory. This cultural system nourishes all under Heaven and makes Chinese people the ethnic group of "elegance and intelligence". As is said that "Had Confucius not come to this world, humans would have been like living in the long and dark night. "

(2) In Terms of the Sacrificial System

Confucianism puts much emphasis on the "Three Sacrifices" as major events for countries and people. It has always attached importance to the sacrifice of heaven and earth, the ancestors, and the sages, believing that the only main events of the state are sacrificing and military activities. Confucianism always values the ritual ceremonies and devout praying to be answered by their faith and achieve certain demands and spiritual comfort.

First, take the sacrifice of Heaven as example. Ancient Chinese emperors regarded themselves as the sons of Heaven and regarded themselves as ruling the country by the order of Heaven. Thus, they are in awe of the way of Heaven. The purpose of practicing heavenly rituals was to remain in harmony with the will of heaven. Under the promotion of Confucianism, ancient dynasties all attach importance to the ceremony of worshipping the Heaven. Emperors such as the First Emperor of Qin, Emperor Wu of Han, Emperor Guangwu of Han, Emperor Gaozong of Tang, Empress Wu of Tang, Emperor Xuanzong of Tangand Emperor Zhenzong of Song, all held grand ceremony offering sacrifices to Heaven report their performance to the Heaven. The Winter Solstice of Ming and Qing Dynasties saw the worship of Heaven held in the Temple of Heaven with solemn and dignified ritual ceremonies. There were also worships of Heaven among the people. The "Heaven, Earth, lords, forefathers and ancestors, teachers" tablet were commonly hung in the main hall of residential houses.

Second, Ancestor Worship. The incense of worship, there remains people's shared transcendental belief in and worship of their ancestors and life. There is no doubt about it. It indicates a most traditional living condition, or even duties of Chinese people—be cautious to deal with the death of one's parents and remember to mourn one's ancestors frequently. If so, one can certainly make people honest.

Third, worship of sages. Confucius, the patriarch of Confucianism, represents the core figure of Confucian culture as well as the main object of the sacrifice of Confucian sages. There are other wise men, former scholars and ancient Confucians who should be offered sacrifice. The wise men mainly refer to the four major developers of Confucianism being elevated to sainthood, such as Yanhui, Zengshen, Zisi and Mencius, as well as the twelve other statues of philosophers such as Zigong, Zilu and Ranyou, etc. Former scholars mainly mean the disciples of Confucius and their later disciples. Ancient Confucians are scholars who made great contributions to

Confucianism in history, such as Dong Zhongshu, Zhuxi and Wang Yangming, etc.

(3) Major Places for Worshipping

Confucian temples, or "Wen Temple"（文庙）, are major places for worshipping the sages of Confucianism. Thanks to the wide influence of Confucianism, there are a huge number of Confucian temples all over China and even the world. According to statistics, two thousands of them are well-preserved nowadays. To show respect for Confucius and attach importance to Confucianism. 12 Emperors have come to Qufu to make sacrifices to Confucius in history. The Temple of Confucius in Qufu was built in the Spring and Autumn Period, over the past 2000 years. The Temple of Confucius has undergone hundreds of expansions and renovations. Its "Yan Sheng Gong" Mansion took charge of the main duty of sacrificing Confucius and arranges corresponding framework and working stuff as well as heavy investment in various rituals of different scales for more than eighty times a year. The Confucius temples all over China are generally arranged by the style of "school on the left and temple on the right", which means that along with the temple, there often exists an official such as the Imperial College or local official institutions. The institution would offer sacrifice according to rules on time to express its respect and admiration of the sages.

(4) The Essential Belief of Confucianism

But what needs to be mentioned is that the essential belief of Confucianism is also characterized by ontology of impersonal god. Different from other traditional religions in the world, the essential belief of Confucianism is not impersonal god but the transcendental ontology of impersonal god instead.

When speaking of the Way of Heaven, Confucianism does not regard it as a divine figure. Among the three meanings of Heaven that Confucius talked about, the implication of deity represents only one of them, and there remains the Heaven of materials and the Heaven of reason and sense, and the latter one is even the root source of transcendentalism, to which Confucius paid more attention than other two "Heavens" distinctively. On the one hand, Confucius said that one should be in awe of Heaven and that Heaven should not be deceived. Yet on the other hand, he commented that "One must submit to the public will. One should respect religion but keep oneself away from it." "Haven't one even well attended people, then how can he well attend ghosts?" Confucius took a suspensive attitude towards the question of whether there was a ghost after death, because he was concerned about making life meaningful. Confucianism attached great importance to the way that signifies a nobler power of the soul which apprehends God in his own naked being as well as what of moral ethics among humans— "Set strict demands on oneself so as to make his action conform to standards of proprieties. Then, our society will be put on tract of humanity." In this way, the inner nature of one's life is advocated and a perfect situation of combining man and nature is achieved. This ultimate state of unity means not the kingdom of God, but the true state of mind in which all things are one.

Although there are many deities in Taoism, its highest faith remains "The Way" (Tao), which was formed before "the Ancestor" (the Yellow Ancestor of China) and represents the source of every being. The Way is followed and admired by all pieties. Therefore, Tao is superior to the gods, and the gods must obey the Tao. And the so-called "Three Universal Lords created by 'Qi'" should also observe the impersonal "Way of Heaven". The same goes with Buddhism. The nine Dharma Realms all originate from "svabhāva" (Emptiness of nature), gods, ghosts or even Buddha and Bodhisattva. are all essentially empty inside. The Buddha represents neither the Genesis of the universe nor the master of destiny. He is not the God, the "enlightened", the one who realizes the spirit of universe and practices his understanding in a perfect way. The way of Buddhism means the fundamental truth of the universe.

The core beliefs of Confucianism, Buddhism, and Taoism: the Heaven, the Way as well as the Emptiness all belong to the impersonal on to log Comparatively, is quite similar to the Deism in the West and the universal spirit that it talks about. Newton, Leibniz, and Einstein all looked down upon the traditional theory of personal god and promoted that god means natural entity as well as the law of universe. The language of God is mathematics, and the means to reach heaven is not prayer but physics.

The followers of Chinese Confucianism, Buddhism, and Taoism are, in essence, neither atheists nor theists. Rather, what they follow is the Deism that abides by the truth of the universe, or the Way of Heaven. The humanistic religious meaning of Confucianism also influenced other religions such as Buddhism, Taoism and Islam. Therefore, the moral connotation of religions is defined and indicated by the unique Eastern thoughts. Religion is therefore regarded as an expansion of man's life and basic values. And religion can become a "doctrine" for its emphasis on life of humanism being within the human being himself but not the personal god. It also values the "inner transcendence" of the virtuous subject rather than the outer transcendence to the Kingdom of Heaven. This is undoubtedly what religion means in value building and represents the unique reason for their not being recognized as religions by the Western world, or for their boasting themselves as religions, or even what beyond religions.

8.3 Ethics—Based Earthly Religion

It is well-known that ethical orientation represents an important character of Chinese culture, which values the cultivation and practice of ethical lives. It boasts an admirable feature of approaching humans rather than gods, which is also shown clearly in the Chinese religions. We can say that the Three Major Religions-Confucianism, Buddhism, and Taoism, and even the Sinicized Muslim all focus on the construction of human ethics as well as the practice of patriarchal clan system and character cultivation. All of them are religions among humans-religion of ethics.

Undoubtedly, Confucianism puts its contribution— "the Five Ethical Relationships" first. Confucianism settles in the living world, while the traditional belief of the Chinese people means to honor the Heaven and ancestors. Compared with worshipping the Heaven, a virtual form of Pandeism, the family tree and ceremonies of Ancestral Hall that sustains the ancestral worship is rather more pragmatic and powerful. The clan faith of glorifying the ancestors and creating a promising future for the family are also most popular in the real life of Chinese people. Family union as their greatest joy, and no listener for sadness the greatest tragedy. Therefore, the thriving fertility and prosperous descendants become the greatest pursuit of Chinese. "Worshipping ancestors is more important than worshipping gods" and the priority of faith in the community of life are basic characters of religious concept of common people in the era of patriarchal clan system. With the cultivation and value pursuit of the clan system, Chinese people can overcome the vulgar and shallow desire and material gain. And obtain peaceful settlement and comfort above the state of mind.

Although Taoism seeks for becoming immortals, it also stresses ethical virtues. As is mentioned by Lao Tsu: "All things honor the Tao and exalt its out flowing operation." *Dao De Jing* is a treasure book that teaches Chinese people to deal with the world and govern the country. *Tai Ping Jing* of Taoism incorporates ethical morality of Confucianism to indicate the support and admiration of a benevolent lord and transparent courtiers. In the name of god, Taoism persuades and warns the fatuous monarch and corrupt officials to condemn their greed, seek for unearned income, and cruelty and urges for equality. It also opposes excessive burden on people and refers to an ideal of national peace in an equal society that people from all walks of life can fulfill their duty and help the poor. In *The Invaluable Prescriptions for Emergencies*, the volume of Self-cultivation: "For those who lacks virtue, even if they take precious medicines, their life may not be prolonged. Whereas for those with good morality, even if they do not pray, their life can be blessed and their life span can be extended. This is the great goal of health-nurturing practices. "

The Sinicized Buddhism follows the traditional atmosphere of putting ethics first, and implements the aim of "always practice the Dharma you have learned to your life, for life is the real path of self-cultivating". The Buddhism stresses "Gratitude for four kindnesses" —including kindness of parents, kindness of motherland, and kindness of all beings, which are all in terms of human world. Followers of Buddhism advocates filial piety and the duties of courtiers. They obeyed the cultivation of "one day without work means one day without food" that emphasizes both on agriculture and Zen. In modern times, Master Taixu further promoted the idea of "Living Buddhism". That is: "The Buddha represents the saint in virtue for people to look upon. And People must complete their own character to attain the Buddha's conduct. To become a sage or a saint as a human is the best reflection of reality. " Masters with great virtue, such as Master Yinshun and Xingyun developed this idea into "Life Buddhism".

Islam in Hui Autonomous Region of China values "two lifetimes" and the accumulation of commercial virtues. The so-called idea of "two lifetimes" represents the theory of the present life and the destination after one's death. Orthodox scholars of Islam, according to the *Koran* and its Holy Teachings, the real life of this world is regarded as the trip of a man, and his destination is the afterlife. Thus, both two lifetimes are of equal value, and being benevolent and doing good deeds will not only benefit one's current life, but the afterlife as well. In the Hui Village in the Quanzhou City, as the Guo family, Taiwanese Merchants settling in Bai Qi, Quanzhou Taiwanese investment zones, families are deeply influenced by the patriarchal clan system and boast their own ancestral temple and family tree. On the Tomb-sweeping Day, they would also offer sacrifice to ancestors and pray with incense. Among the devout villagers, Emperor Guan Yu is seen as the incarnation of Muhammad. Compared with Islam in other regions of the world, this belief is quite different.

We may say that Confucianism, with worshipping the Earth and Heaven, sages and ancestors as its core, affected the development and spread of Buddhism, Taoism an Islam. According to Professor Liang Shuming, they are essentially a "religion of ethics", and the followers of which are all the Chinese.

Although history has seen Christianity being spread in ancient China, development halted during the late Ming and early Qing Dynasty (1600—1644). One of the reasons was that between the Vatican and the missionaries in China, there were disputes over the solution of the worship of God as well as the traditional Chinese faith and culture of honoring the ancestors, sages and kings. An agreement failed to be made at last. Those who applied to and respect traditional Chinese culture—the "Riccian Rule" of the mediators could not gain support from the Pope; whereas those who insisted on forbidding Chinese followers sacrificing the ancestors, sages and kings turned out to be banned and expelled by Emperor Kangxi. Believing in Jesus means not believing in the Heaven and Earth, sages and ancestors. This idea represents why the Christianity could not be embraced by China. Fundamentally, they missed the point that China boasts a deep soil of culture for ethical norms. Therefore, religions in China are obliged to be localized, ethicized and humanized.

8. 4　Harmony of Diverse Religions

Religious conflicts and even wars of the mare quite common in human history. But there is no such case in the history of traditional Chinese religions. Religions, instead, live in peace and keep harmony in diversity here. Which can be proved by abundant evidence. Take Quanzhou, entitled as "the religious museum in the world. " for example here, traditional Chinese Culture integrate with ancient Persian, Arab, Indian and Southeast Asian cultures and left Buddhism, Islam, Catholicism, Nestorianism, Hinduism, Manichaeism and other foreign religions as historical remains here in Quanzhou City. They all serve the people here, in a peaceful and harmonious way, and learn and absorb good parts from each other to thrive together energetically and happily.

(1) Multi Religious Elements in Kaiyuan Temple in Quanzhou

Kaiyuan Temple in Quanzhou represents a Buddhist temple under the influence of multiple religions, especially distinct marks of Hinduism. For example, before the Great Buddha Hall, there are two square stone pagodas donated by Liu Sanniang of Quanzhou in the 15th year of Shaoxing during the Southern Song Dynasty. The two pagodas are in the form of Indian Stupa, on which the story of Prince-Maha Sattva sacrificing himself to feed the tiger and save the cubs is carved. At the waist of the Sumeru throne in the Great Buddha Hall, there are 72 reliefs of men with lion's body and lions made of diabase. Between the eaves of the corridor at the back of the Great Buddha Hall, there stands a pair of 16-angle diabase pillars carved with stories of Krishna, the Hindu god prevalent in ancient India and Ceylon, as well as 24 pictures of flowers. These heritages all witness the spread of Hinduism in Quanzhou City and its local influence ever since the Song Dynasty. The Great Buddha Hall is also called the Hall of 100 Pillars, and the top of these stone pillars are decorated with wooden sculptures with musical instruments playing Nanyin (music sung in Minnan dialect) and dress waving in the sky. And those flying angels also contains certain colors and features of Christianity.

(2) Another Example is the "Cross of Zaitun"

Being well-known at home and abroad and represents a significant inscription evidence of the intergrated multi-religions in Quanzhou City. When you come to Quanzhou Overseas Transportation History Museum, you will see the inscriptions: there are typical signatures of angels and crosses with typical Christian characters as well as those of Chinese Buddhism and Taoism, like Baldachin, Propitious Clouds, wave of sea water, Flame and Lotus Throne, etc. The crosses on the Christian stone carvings in Quanzhou have a variety of shapes, including styles of Greece, Latin, Persia, Celtic and Malta, etc. In terms of the characters of the stone carvings, there are Chinese, Latin, Bathsheba, Turkic, and Persian, leaving the "mixture" rare all over the world.

8-3　"Cross of Zaitun" of Quanzhou

In fact, this kind of integration not only occurred in the spread of Christian culture in China in the song and Yuan Dynasties, but also in modern times. For example, the Hongjialou Catholic Church in Jinan, Shandong Province, although it belongs to the Western Gothic architecture in the main body, there are also many Chinese elements in the details, such as the Chinese small black tiles on the roof, especially the "Chinese dragon head" carved on the left and right sides of the door in the church, which is very vivid and exaggerated. Because "dragon" has always been the embodiment of evil Satan in western culture, it is possible to use the dragon shape in the holy place of church, which shows that after gradually understanding China's "dragon culture", Western religious circles have been able to compromise the conflict of cultural images of each other, reconcile differences, or even do as the Romans do with some cultural elements.

(3) "Trinity Denomination" and the Worship of Ben Zhu

Here, during the Ming Dynasty, a new religion that integrates pluralistic religions came into being— "Trinity Denomination", also known as the "Three Religions" and "Xia Religion". Founded by a commoner—Lin Zhaoen in Xinghua Mansion of Xinhai during the 30th year of Emperor Jiajing of Ming Dynasty (1551), it advocates an integration of Confucianism, Buddhism and Taoism. Its doctrine is to "put Confucianism above Taoism and Buddhism, and put Confucius above Confucianism".

Being a folk religion that took shape in the middle and end of the Ming Dynasty and thrived between the end of Ming and the beginning of Qing Dynasty, it is still popular among several regions of Fujian and Taiwan provinces as well as some Southeast Asian countries nowadays.

According to the standard of monotheism, neither the worship of Ben Zhu, nor the "Trinity Denomination" are qualified for being seen as a true religion. But this is the religion of harmony but difference that the local people sincerely believe in.

When it comes to the reasons for tolerance and integration of these traditional pluralistic religions, to put it in a simple way, it can be explained as: Firstly, the close contact and exchanges of people from all countries and regions represent the external condition of the pluralistic integration of religions. Secondly, the open and practical spirit of the Chinese people toward foreign cultures is an internal reason for the pluralistic integration. Thirdly, the Doctrine of Mean by Confucianism, featuring an embracing mind and the seek for harmony in diversity, sets the ideological foundation of pluralistic integration. Fourthly, the active promotion by successive Chinese governments as well as wise men from all walks of life remains the positive force of pluralistic integration. Fifthly, the development and twists and turns of history are regarded as the whole background of pluralistic integration.

8.5   Worldliness of Pragmatism

In terms of this-worldliness, religion boasts the function of serving the reality. Gods help humans, so that they gain admiration and worship from humans. This pragmatic mentality of utilitarianism among the masses is not a problem to understand. In the past, frequent natural and man-made disasters left human beings with weak vitality being lost and fearful. They often resort to disasters as the rage of gods and believe that calming their anger is the way to overcome the disasters. Normally, regular worship of gods can help achieve their dreams and eliminate disasters. Worshipping Confucius helps one succeed in examinations, and worshipping Matsu ensures one a smooth and safe trip. As for praying to God or worshipping Allah, doesn't it mean the hope for protection and blessing of gods? During the epidemic, the White House and U. S. Congress also organized priests to conduct praying ceremonies. Weren't they out of pragmatical purpose as well? Pragmatism, featuring drawing on the advantages and avoiding disadvantages remains a character shared by all religions, past and present, from home and abroad, and it does not hence harm the seriousness of faith or make it less sacred.

When it comes to the widely criticized pragmatic feature of Chinese religions, it is, in our opinion, the very manifestation of the priority of ethical norms, stressing cultural characters such as men being benevolent and serving their people. As for most of the Chinese gods, they are often real people in history. Most of them became immortals for "being wise and upright, and died as gods". They used to be benevolent and made great contributions to the society. People missed them deeply after their death and wished them to become gods, who, in heaven, would continue to bless the living from disasters.

8-4　Folk Beliefs in Fujian

For example, there is a local activity of pageant on immortals during the Lantern Festival in Dashe of Jimei District in Xiamen. And the immortal they show is the statue of "King of Min" —Wang Shenzhi. He, together with his brothers Wang Chao and Wang Shengui, were called "Three Kings that Create Min". During chaos of the Five Dynasties, they three migrated into Fujian Province. The good governance of them and the benefits they brought were deeply respected by Fujian people. After their death, they were revered as gods by local Fujianese. Another example is the Baosheng God (Guardian of health and well-being) of Qing jiao Ci Ji Palace in Haicang of Xiamen City, widely worshipped by people in Fujian and Taiwan provinces. The Baosheng God is originated from a well-known doctor— Wu Xuan, being commonly called as "Da

Dao Gong".

Such as the Guan Yue Temple in Quanzhou City, which enshrines the two heroes, Guan Yu and Yue Fei.

We may easily come to the conclusion that Chinese gods are closely related to the reality. And people tend to see the great and upright historical figures who have cared for them as gods. It is more for commemoration and remembrance than for superstitious worship.

Certainly, there are also other conclusions. For example, it has been suggested that "the separation of religion and state" is also a fundamental feature of Chinese religion. But if, according to the above waying, we see Confucianism as a religion, then we won't be able to use the idea of "the separation of religion and state". If we see Confucianism as a religion, then it is deeply involved in the governance and power operations of the regime and the whole society. Confucianism aims to build a benevolent governance and a society in great harmony, with all officials being Confucians, reading the classics of Confucianism and following the "Three Sacrifices" of Confucianism. China can therefore be said as the state where Confucianism and the regime were united.

But since Confucianism represents a religion or even what beyond religions—the special "humanistic moral religion" and "ethical religion", the answer is then changeable. If you see Confucianism as a religion, China can be regarded as a country that unites politics and religion. Yet if you don't see it as a religion, but a school of thought responsible for educating people instead, then you would support the idea that China is of separation between religion and state. Based on this judgment, if Chinese religions narrowly mean Buddhism, Taoism, Islam, or Christianity, then, in the history, there indeed wasn't any story of their integration with the regime or even supremacy and control over it, like what happened in the Medieval Western world. Although history has seen many emperors and nobles believing in Buddhism and Taoism and supporting their development, such as Emperor Wu of Liang in the Southern Dynasty who tried to become a monk for several times, as well as Emperor Jiajing of Ming Dynasty, being called as "Emperor of God"; what's more, the building of Longmen Grottoes received support from various generations of monarchs, from Tuoba Hong to Wu Zetian. And the Wudang Mountain in Shiyan, being well-known as "Xuan Yue Rules the World", represents the "Ancestral Hall of the Imperial Family" during the Ming Dynasty. However, in terms of politics, there never emerges the situation of religions like Buddhism and Taoism becoming dominant exclusively in politics and affecting the " Confucianism as the Top Ideology" situation or the dominance of Confucianism. There were times in history that, due to the extreme power of these religions that hindered the financial income of the nation economically and the stability of national governance. Emperor Taiwu of Northern Wei, Emperor Wu of Northern Zhou, Emperor Wuzong of Tang, as well as Emperor Shizong of Zhou all resorted to the ban of Buddhism. Therefore, the Buddhism and Taoism groups were well aware of the submissiveness of the ruling regime and behaved themselves mildly. In this sense, traditional Chinese religions truly obeyed the principle of "give back to Ceasar what is Ceasar's, and to God what is God's".

In all, religions and folk beliefs in traditional Chinese culture is an important existence in traditional Chinese culture. Confucianism, as a moral religion, lays the foundation of putting ethics as its center and positioning itself as a " living religion". Since then, all religions are necessary to obey this regulation and rule for survival and further development. This can be seen as the unavoidable force from the main cultural system. And among the pluralistic religions, they, under the influence of the Doctrine of Mean that seeks for harmony in diversity, communicated and learnt from each other to thrive the inner and outer parts of multiple religions in China. The faith of the Chinese people remains inclusive and not extremely rejective to other religions. They need the world of gods and spirits to be integrated with the living world and to make life colorful and humane.

Chinese people nowadays are enlightened with civilization to enjoy freedom of thoughts and beliefs, as well as the freedom to choose whether to believe in a religion. Chinese government respects and guarantees people's basic rights of believing and choosing their beliefs. Many active and appropriate policies and measures are applied to promote the healthy development of Chinese religious career.

第九讲

崇文重教
——中国传统教育风貌掠影

我们常说中国有悠久的文明，但这个悠久不绝的原因，一半在于一代代中国人重视教育，用教育来传承文明，用创新来促进这文明。也就是说，正是因为有了光辉灿烂的古代教育，才使得传统文明得以"历千万祀而不朽"，才使得中华民族养成了崇德好礼、温和敦厚的文明性格，才使得中华文明能在人类发展史上大放异彩。

9.1 中国——一个崇文重教的文明国度

"教育"这个词，就其古典的运用而言是对人的教化，令人具有文明的人格，如《周易》中指出的：观乎人文，以化成天下。这就是说，教之以人文即人道，使得天下人民皆蒙教化，去恶从善也好，启蒙去蔽也罢，总之，要让人成为人，真正的人。如孟子就指出："人之有道也，饱食暖衣逸居而无教，则近于禽兽。"（《孟子·滕文公上》）在中国尽人皆知的《三字经》中也用清朗上口的语句诉说了关于教化的道理："人之初，性本善。性相近，习相远。苟不教，性乃迁。教之道，贵以专。……养不教，父之过。教不严，师之惰。子不学，非所宜。幼不学，老何为。玉不琢，不成器。人不学，不知义。"这里的字字句句只有一个关键词——教化成人。

教育即教化，这跟我们提到的文化即是人化、文明化，是同一内涵指向。应该说，中国古代有一段悠久的重视教育、发展教育的历史，自古也流传下来无数脍炙人口的求道向学、重教尊师的动人故事。我们华侨大学厦门校区面对着海天一色、风光旖旎的厦门市园林博览苑，里面有一座中华教育岛。在这个岛上就树立着许多的中华教育人物群像。对这些人物故事，中国人可谓是家喻户晓童叟皆知的。我这里给大家举几个例子。

图9-1　厦门园博苑中华教育岛

（1）孟母三迁：这个故事说的是孟子的母亲为了让孩子能有一个良好的读书向学的生活环境，三次搬迁住所。因为家近坟墓区，孩子就玩丧葬的游戏，家近市场，孩子就玩吆喝做买卖的游戏，家近屠场就玩杀猪宰羊的游戏。孩子的天性是最易于模仿的，而这些生活环境都不符合孟母的理想。最后呢，孟母把家搬到了学宫也就是文教区附近（就如今天的学区房），孟子就开始模仿学习礼仪和学习做人的道理，孟母这才放了心。可见孟母是个用心良苦的有智慧的母亲，她看到了生活环境对孩子的成长就有潜移默化的作用，所以她不惜数次搬迁，目的只有一个——让孩子受到积极向上的氛围熏陶以促进其人格修养。而孟子，我们知道，后来成了在儒家历史上几乎与孔子齐名的大师。（2）悬梁刺股：汉代的孙文宝勤奋好学，晨夕不休，以至于困顿瞌睡，他就以绳系头，悬诸屋梁，以防止自己陷入睡眠。这个故事和另外一个讲战国苏秦"锥刺股"的故事并称"头悬梁、锥刺股"，宣扬的都是中国古人珍惜光阴、刻苦治学的感人精神。（3）铁杵成针：唐代诗人李白年少时心浮气躁，读书时用心不恒，求学不能持久。有一次他经过一个路口，见到一位老奶奶拿一根铁杵在磨，李白就好奇地问她磨铁杵作甚，老奶奶就说是磨绣花针。李白就笑，铁杵如何能磨成绣花针呢？老人就说出了一句中华教育史上的至理名言"只要功夫深，铁杵磨成针"。李白顿感了惭愧和启发，遂反身回去专力向学，后来终成一代"诗仙"。（4）如坐春风：讲的是宋代的朱光庭师从理学大师程颢，他在汝州听程颢讲学一个月，如痴如狂。回家后逢人便夸老师讲学的精妙，他说，"光庭在春风中坐了一月"。于是，后人就用"如坐春风"来形容幸遇良师、身心受益的欣喜之状。教的善于教，学的善于学，春风化物，自然乐不可言。（5）程门立雪：这个故事来自《宋史·杨时传》，讲的是福建人杨时和同学游酢去拜访老师程颐。那时老师正在午睡瞑坐，杨时与游酢便在屋外静候不去。当时正下着漫天飞雪，他们就这样等啊等，直到老师醒过来，这时"门外雪深一尺矣"。这个故事表现的就是中国古人对自己老师的由衷尊敬和爱戴，表达了尊师重道、矢志向学的坚决精神。在佛教中甚至还有僧人神光断臂求法的故事，则更加令人可望不可及了。

园博苑教育岛上这样的教育成语故事还有很多，诸如伯乐相马、曾子杀猪、囊萤映雪、凿壁借光、负薪挂角、管宁割席、闻鸡起舞、以荻画地、岳麓会讲、东林议政、倾家兴学等，都是令人印象美好而深刻的古典之光。

这些故事之所以能流传千古，深入人心，就在于它们谈及了教育的一些最核心的品质，如家庭与教育、教育与成才、读书与成人、勤学与成学、教师与学生的关系、治学与经世的关系等。其中也透露出一些具有超越历史的恒久价值的教育学规律，如读书进学、勤能补拙、温故知新、尊师爱生、言传身教，等等。可以说，中国人，无论是从国家或官方系统，还是思想家知识分子，乃至普通的人民群众，无不具有一种崇文重教的文化意识和自觉行动。他们高度重视教育的价值意义和社会功能，不断探索完善教育制度，深化教育思想，阐发教育的价值追求。作为崇文重教的文明国度，中国给世界提供了一套独创性的教育文化，至今仍然具有不衰的魅力。

9.2 从太学到国子监：中国古代的官学

学术界一般把中国的传统教育史分为先秦的形成奠基期，秦汉宋明发展辉煌期，清代到近代为衰微期和转型期这样三期。我们这里当然不能一一去详细讲说，只拟沿着官学和私学两个方面，给大家梳理一个概貌。

坐落于北京东城区的国子监（Imperial College），它毗邻着北京孔庙（古制"左庙右学"），是我国元明清三朝的最高学府，也是最高教育主管机关的所在地。走进国子监，依次穿过集贤门、太学门、琉璃牌坊，我们就能看到一处四角重檐攒顶、四面辟门、四周环水、白玉护栏的建筑，它叫"辟雍"，它是国子监最早的前身。

（1）辟雍与西周官办教育

西周时天子于京都的东西南北中各设置一所国家学校，分别取名叫东序、成均、瞽宗、上庠和辟雍。五所学府中又以辟雍为最尊贵。周天子每年"临雍视学"也就是到辟雍来视察学校的发展建设成就，听取学者讲座。所以，辟雍就是三代时期国家最高学府的代名词，虽然到汉代，辟雍已被"太学"取代，但它是最早的原型，在文化人士心中的地位仍是温情不去，以至于在明清国子监里还要用"辟雍"来为一处建筑命名。我们在民间书院里也常能见到悬挂着"学著雍宫""直著雍宫"字样的匾额，这也是寄望学子奋发直上、身列雍宫的美好寓意。当然，西周时代不仅中央有供成年贵族求学的五所最高级学校，还有供贵族少年上学的"小学"。各诸侯国所在都邑也创办"泮宫"——地方最高官方学校。后来，在科举考试得中秀才者，都可获得入府学习的资格，就叫"入泮""游泮"。在今天泉州府文庙里面也有一座泮桥和泮池，其渊源现在大家就清楚了。而在其他各级地方行政区划如闾、党、州、乡，国家也分别设立各级教育机构分别称为"塾、庠、序、校"（汉代地方区划为郡、县、乡、聚，相应设立学、校、庠、序），作为地方学校，培养地方各类人才。应该说，从夏商周三代以降，中国的教育就有相当的积累，后世各代王朝政府无不兴办从中央的太学到地方各种庠序学校。

（2）汉代的太学教育

汉武帝首创太学，罢黜百家独尊儒术，立《诗》《书》《礼》《易》《春秋》五经博士。博士的职责除议政、制礼、藏书之外，还具有国家教授的职能。博士领袖叫"仆射"，学生叫"博士弟子"。太学初建时为 50 人，汉昭帝时增至100 人，王莽时增至 10000 人。太学的教学内容除了进行"礼乐射御书数"的六艺之学的教育，更精专于五经的教学和研究（《白虎通义》就是博士们讲论五经同异，统一今文经义的一部重要著作）。士子们读太学之后以"射策"即随机选题作申论的方式进行学业考核，合格者可以授官①。应该说，这时的官立教育已不是贵族教育，而是平民教育。西汉教育制度的重要性，在于育才与选贤双轨并进。换言之，就是教育制度与选举制度配合实行。所以，汉代政府成员都是太学出身。与以前相比，显示了巨大进步。

（3）隋唐时代的教育

从教育制度和教学内容、教育队伍的选配运用、考试选拔制度等一整套的体系而言，隋唐时代的教育都继往开来更加完备而独到。值得注意的有三点：一是始设国子监取代太学，内设祭酒一人，总管教育事业，它标志着中国古代教育事业成为独立部门。二是教育部门及其专业性更加发展，既有国子学、太学、四门学，属普通高等教育系统；又有律学、书学、算学、医药学、兽医学、天文学、音乐学等专业学校；更有为专门人士量身定制的特殊教育系统，如弘

---

① "及汉武帝时，开设学校，立《五经》博士，置弟子员，射策设科，劝以官禄，传业者故益众矣。"（《南史·儒林传序》）

文馆、崇文馆、崇贤馆，是皇家子弟学校和外国留学生学校。还有职业教育系统，如太医署、太卜署、司天台、太仆寺、校书郎。以太医署为例，里面又细分医学、针灸、按摩、咒禁等五个具体专业，并规定了具体的学习年限。三是科举制度的创立和推行。与汉代的人才选拔制度如察举、征辟、任子，或魏晋时代的"九品中正制"不同，隋炀帝大业二年（606）设置进士科，标志着科举制度的诞生。科举制度可谓是封建时代所能采取的最公平的人才选拔形式。只要你肯用心读书，学业优卓，就可能"朝为田舍郎，暮登天子堂"。科举考试通常分为地方上的乡试、中央的省试与殿试。乡试、省试、殿试的第一名分别为"解元""会元"和"状元"。唐朝科举考试相应其多元的教育专业而设有秀才、明经、俊士、进士、明法（法律）、明字、明算（数学）等多种科目，考试内容有时务策、帖经、杂文等。

（4）宋朝的教育变革

宋朝的科举考试中官府设置的科目比唐朝时的少，但考"进士"依然很流行，并且身居高位的大臣都必须通过相关科目的考试，考试体制在形式和内容上都有很大变革。变革第一是招生规模扩大。唐朝每年的"进士"不过二三十人，但在宋朝每年却有数百人通过考试。甚至对于那些多次考试但屡考不中的人，皇帝也会给他们提供一些次要的岗位。第二个变革是考试的频率确定为每3年一次。地方考试定在秋季，通过地方考试的人次年春天到都城参加考试。第三个变革是考试内容。以前的考试强调经书，改革家王安石（1021—1086）强调考试要切合实际。他把填诗、默诗变成作诗、作文。但这种主张受到了贵族阶层的批评，没有持续多久。最后，为了体现公平竞争，应试者的姓名被封住，试卷在不同地区交换阅卷，减少了舞弊现象。

应该说，中国的科举制度扩展了封建国家引进人才的社会层面，吸收了大量出身中下层社会的人士进入统治阶级。特别是唐宋时期，科举制度之初，显示出生气勃勃的进步性，形成了中国古代文化发展的一个黄金时代。中国古代教育成语中有一个"雁塔题名"，专指考中进士者到唐长安的大雁塔题名入册，代指考中进士金榜题名之意。在北京国子监里至今藏有元明清三代的"进士题名碑"198块，它们是国家教育成就的象征，当然也是进士和他们家族的荣耀记录。

（5）"国子监"与明清教育的衰退

第一，到了明清两代，国家教育事业的发展表现在制度和措施上也有继续的推进与发展。从中央官学的国子监教育看，内设祭酒、司业、监丞、博士和典簿等七种教官，入监的生员数量空前增多。1. 它的生源主要分为四类。贡监：

地方府、州、县学生生员被选贡入监。举监：会试下第举人入监。荫监：品官之子特权入监。例监：通过纳粟纳马等捐资入监。另外，也有一种特殊的夷生：即来自领邦高丽、日本等国的留学生，可以入读国子监。2. 从监生们学习的主要课程上看，主要是程朱学派注释的《四书》《五经》以及《资治通鉴》等；八股文到明朝成为必修课程。3. 监生按年级分为三种层次。初级班：通《四书》而未通经者。中级班：初级班一年半以后经过考试，文理通顺者。高级班：中级班一年半后，经史兼通、文理俱优者。再一年结业。4. 监生历事制：监生的去向。历事即"历练政事"，是实习官吏的制度。凡在监十余年者，派到六部诸司实习吏事，历练 3 个月，并考察其勤惰。

第二，从地方官办教育上看，明清时代也在持续延续发展。到清代，凡州府县学总计就达 1700 余所，学生 27000 余人。以泉州府学为例，它冠胜东南七省，是泉州府教育教学事业的历史见证。从公元 9 世纪到 20 世纪初，泉州考中进士者多达 2454 人，本籍或原籍泉州的文武状元就有 19 位，有二十多人位列宰相之职，可见泉州文风鼎盛人才辈出，不愧于"海滨邹鲁"的美誉。

第三，从科举考试上看，明朝的科举考试达到了巅峰。考试程序、过程更加严格。明朝政府建立学校，加强学校的功能，让其成为考生参加科举考试的必由之路。考试内容是八股文——固定的文体，固定的字数，固定的八个部分。这种方法忽视了别的形式和内容，限制了人们的创造性和想象力，是十分有害的。清朝是满族统治，汉族人地位低。满族人参加科举考试无需考试只要做些翻译，参加科举考试大部分是汉族人。旧的教育制度日渐衰朽，亟须注入新的思想和观念。买官卖官的倾向日益蔓延，也破坏了考试的公平竞争。吴敬梓的小说《儒林外史》里所描写到的范进屡考不中，考到五十多岁才得到回报。当他得知自己中举的消息后，欣喜若狂，立即精神错乱发了疯癫。这个闹剧也预示着中国古代教育确已活力不再。

风流总被雨打风吹去，传统官方教育随着历史的发展，尤其是近代西学东渐之后，日渐衰微凋落。无论教育机构和专业设置、人才考核与选拔方式，都逐渐变得暮气沉沉不能适应时代的进步，因此也在内外危机中悄然发生历史的重大变革——古代的太学（国子监）变成了京师大学堂，经学衰退而实学思潮兴起，洋务学堂（外语、武备、实业）、教会学堂，及其西式的近代学制被逐渐引进推广。1905 年科举制度的废除则意味着充满了辉煌的历史的一页终被掀去，也象征着故国新纪元的到来。

9.3 从书院到义学——中国古代的私学发展

中国的私学系统也发轫甚早。可以说春秋战国时代"礼崩乐坏"使得官方知识分子纷纷流向民间，开始了设账授业的民间私家教育的历史。唐宋以降，私学蓬勃发展，其形式从知识分子创办的各种民间文人书院，到乡土社会举办的各种家族书院，可以说体系完备。尤其是怀抱理想主义心境的思想家或者士大夫们满腔热忱，非常看重教育的"化人"功能。他们把传道授业解惑，上升到道义的层次，事关"为天地立心，为生民立命，为往圣继绝学，为万世开太平"的高度上来常抓不懈。他们一方面努力探究真理，另外一方面努力地记载心得，并将其传授给学生们，留下了许多的教育专著和宝贵的教育思想。如大家知道，孔子就是开创私学的伟大教育家之一，孔子首先提出"有教无类"的大众教育方针。他的教育学思想也非常丰富，涉及教育的必要性、内容、性质，学习的态度、对象以及方法。在教育过程中，孔子作为教育的主导，和作为学习主体的学生结合得非常融洽，孔门师生之间的关系可谓严肃认真又和乐融融。限于篇幅，关于民间私学的问题这里直接从宋代书院教育谈起。

9.3.1 宋代民间书院：私学发展的主要形式

书院的发展源自唐代，最早是修书、藏书、校书之所。五代时名流学者常择名胜之地，聚徒讲学，书院遂成教育机构。到宋代，民间书院兴盛，遍布天下，其中又以"四大书院"最为知名：白鹿洞书院、应天府书院、岳麓书院、嵩阳书院。这些书院管理严格、规制完备，名儒硕德往复研讨学术蔚然成风。到元代，官方指派山长的措施使得书院很大程度被官办化。虽在明代有所恢复，阳明心学随着书院流布南北各地，但遗憾的是到明中后期先后遭四次禁毁，及至清朝康熙时代才得以开禁重启，官方的资助和监管同时存在，这层管理限制使得它不能重现宋代的自由活泼之风①。

比较于国家官学，民间书院具有如下特点：一是自由风气浓重，教学上实

---

① 可参考阅读《中国书院制度研究》：由湖南大学岳麓书院文化研究所的陈谷嘉、邓洪波主编，2017 年由浙江教育出版社出版。全书分为十章，凡 54 万字，对于书院的起源、发展、书院类型和级别、书院的管理制度、职事人员、经费来源、教育方法、刻书印书，以及书院对外国的影响等都做了系统的较全面的研究。

行自由讲学、思想辩论，以个人钻研为主，不以科举考试为主要目标。二是教学条件（场所、设备）逐渐规模化。三是教育管理的规范化，如延聘管理人员（以名儒出任山长）、严格管理制度（学规）、筹措各类经费用度等。四是师生之间有着极强的和谐友爱，展示了良好的精神风貌。

第一，书院的制度管理。

如南宋朱熹为庐山白鹿洞书院制定的教规五原则是：

五教之目——父子有亲、君臣有义、夫妇有别、长幼有序、朋友有信。为学之序——博学之，审问之，谨思之，明辨之，笃行之。修身之要——言忠信，行笃敬，惩忿窒欲，迁善改过。处事之要——正其义不谋其利，明其道不计其功。接物之要——己所不欲，勿施于人，行有不得，反求诸己。

而吕祖谦在乾道四年（1168）为丽泽书院制订的学规多达十数则，非常详明切实，包括如：克尽伦理而不可违反；师友间相劝以善、平等相处；严肃听讲、举止得当不可轻慢；尊师重教不可违礼；以及不得论人是非长短、浮夸自大；不可结交败类，以及从事鄙俗请托戏谑等低级趣味和事务等内容规定。从这些民间书院的学规可见，古代书院对制定规范性管理制度非常重视，其制定的学规一般分为两部分：一部分是道德修养的要求，另一部分是学习态度和方法的要求。前者规范的是德育，后者规范的是智育。二者之中，传统书院都更侧重突出了德育，即使在讲学习方法的条文中也贯穿融合了德育的内容。既以传统伦理美德作为书院教育的宗旨，又突出以儒家道德规范来塑造生徒的品格，立德树人是最大的特点，贴近生活，至今仍有参考价值。

第二，书院的学术研讨活动。

书院内部或书院之间，常有如今天的学术会议之事，学者们彼此聚会，自由畅谈，往返辩论儒家经典义理。如岳麓书院的"中和之辩"：南宋乾道三年（1167）八月，应湖湘学派张栻的邀请，闽学学派的朱熹带着门人弟子亲赴岳麓书院，围绕"中和"问题，双方往复辩论了三天三夜，盛况热烈。又如鹅湖书院的"朱陆之辩"：南宋淳熙二年（1175）六月，朱熹与陆九渊兄弟相约来到江西上饶的铅山县鹅湖寺，双方围绕尊德性与道问学孰先孰后的问题展开了激烈的辩论，史称"鹅湖之会"。

第三，书院师生的精神风貌写照。

《陆九渊集》中记载了心学大师陆九渊的象山精舍中师友讲习的日常精神风貌。象山先生常住方丈，清晨精舍鸣鼓，则乘山茓（轿）至。师生如礼作揖问候，象山升讲座，"容色粹然，精神炯然"。听讲的学者以一小牌书写姓名年甲，按序入座，人数不下数十百，学斋内静肃无哗。象山先生清音徐吐，开头即要求学者们"收敛精神,涵养德性,虚心听讲"。诸生皆俯首恭听。象山先生不仅讲儒家经典,更重在启发人之本心,"听者无不感动兴起"。师友们平时或观书,或抚琴,佳妙天气之时则徐步观瀑,登高处则朗诵经训,歌《楚辞》及古诗文,风度雍容自适。就算天热盛暑,象山先生也衣冠整肃,望之如神。

第四,书院的平民主义和爱国主义取向。

如明代泰州学派王艮创立的安定书院以平民化路线而特有个性。王艮不作应试的科举教学研习,而发扬阳明心学的特色,深入发明人心,主张"百姓日用即是道"。与一般的知识分子为主的书院不同,王艮的安定书院的门徒以平民百姓居多,计有农夫、樵夫、陶匠、盐丁等487人。王艮非经院出身,一生文词著述很少,着重口传心授,使"愚夫愚妇"明白易懂,这成了泰州学派的特色之一。所谓"入山林求会隐逸,过市井启发愚蒙",因而也独树一帜特色鲜明。

另外,以东林书院为代表的清流议政型书院充盈着饱满的爱国情怀。东林书院创建于北宋,知名学者杨时长期讲学于此,后废。明朝万历三十二年(1604),由东林学者顾宪成等人修复并在此聚众讲学。他们倡导"风声雨声读书声声声入耳,家事国事天下事事事关心",把"读书、讲学、爱国"的精神相结合,大胆议论朝政,抨击朝廷腐败,引起全国学者普遍响应、声名大振。东林书院成为江南地区人文荟萃、议论国事的舆论中心。

总体而言,因为相对自由的办学政策支持和书院师生们严谨求真的治学精神激荡,书院比较官学,更能闪耀真理之光,既积淀和传承了中华文化和学术思想,也培养了许多优秀人才,形成了我国教育史上最浓墨重彩的一笔。正如岳麓书院山门的楹联就自信地宣称"惟楚有才,于斯为盛",而白鹿洞书院里也有一副楹联如此说道:"十步之内有芳草,广厦所育皆英才。"习近平主席2020年9月17日在湖南大学岳麓书院视察时候指出:"于斯为盛"的"斯",既指这个地方,也指这个时代。我们非常有必要弘扬传统文人书院的这种求真务实、修己报国的精髓,推动中国当代教育体系的创新进步,以更好地为国家培养天下英才。

9.3.2 遍布乡土社会的家族书院

我们已经在第七讲提到,中国的家族文化非常发达。各地家族建设中非常注重对子弟的教养,希望他们成才成人,将来好继往开来荣耀门楣。所以他们的祖训族规中都反复强调要重视教育,特别是立德树人的伦理教育。一般来说,家族的教育机构往往设立在宗族的祠堂中,学中塾师由族中"品学兼优"的士人担任，或选聘社会学者来担任，办学经费则由族产如祖田收入开支。因为对宗族内部成员具有免费和公益性质，所以又称义学。家族书院承担的往往是基础教育，或称蒙学（当然也有一些是为科举考试服务的馆学，层次就更高了）。蒙学教材有《三字经》《百家姓》《千字文》《幼学琼林》《唐诗三百首》等，多融知识性、伦理性和趣味性于一体。

我们可以略举几个民间村落的家族书院的例子。

比如我多次提到的黄山市黟县宏村。明清时期，徽州私塾遍布城乡，"十户之村，不废诵读"，"远山深谷，居民之处莫不有学有师。"在明末，宏村人就在南湖北畔修建了六所私塾（依湖六院）。清嘉庆十九年（1814），此六院被合并，取名"以文家塾"，又称"南湖书院"。南湖书院是座具有传统徽派风格的古书院，占地约6000平方米。书院由志道堂、文昌阁、会文阁、启蒙阁、望湖楼及祇园六部分组成。一湖碧水位于书院之前，连栋楼舍接着书院，书院黛瓦粉墙，与碧水蓝天交相辉映。书院里的志道堂是讲学的地方；文昌阁供奉孔子牌位，学生在这里对孔子瞻仰膜拜；会文阁是学生读四书五经的场所；启蒙阁是启蒙读书之处；望湖楼是闲时观景休息之地；祇园是内苑。曾任清政府内阁中书，民国时驻英、日公使，代总理大臣的汪大燮，以及当代著名的科学家（澳星发射研制专家之一）的李小鹍等学者，都是在这里启蒙的。作为徽州地区代表性的古书院建筑群，南湖书院现为省级重点保护单位。

我再给大家介绍一些我们在培田古村看到的家族书院的情况。培田村吴氏家族注重教育有悠久传统，从明初创建第一所石头丘草堂以降，先后兴办二十多所家族书院，至今保存完好的明清书院还有如南山书院、紫阳书院、锄经别墅、修竹楼等五所，其中有专门的女子培训学校"容膝居"和农艺技术学校"锄经别墅"①。如该村的南山书院，前身是"石头丘草堂"，始建于明成化年间（1465—1487），乾隆三十年（1765）改建，面积有8000多平方米。整个南山书院傍山而建立，圆石铺阶，院门秀雅，透出浓浓的书卷气，曾在这里潜修执教的清代名士曾瑞春将南山书院与朱熹讲学的鹅湖、鹿洞相提并论，由此可见这里的环境是真的很清幽了。

客家人特有的重视教育的传统、明代理学的兴盛与传播、闽商的财富积累和持续的资金支持，使得培田村的家族教育事业兴旺发达，有所谓"距汀城廓

---

① 培田人的"锄经别墅"门前对联就标明了该"别墅"的农艺性质，"半亩砚田余菽粟，数椽瓦屋课桑麻。"而始建于康熙年间的"修竹楼"的门口也有楹联写道："非关避暑才修竹，岂为藏书始筑楼。"修竹楼以交流手工艺为主，培田祖先精湛的泥、木、雕、塑、剪、编织等民间技艺大都源于此。

数百里，入孔门墙第一家"和"渤海飞暎"的美誉。明清时期培田书院培养了大批的人才。从明弘治元年（1488）到清光绪三十一年（1905）的四百余年里，培田村累计取得功名者达 311 人，仅培田吴氏第十五世就有 40 人登科入庠，父子连科、兄弟同榜的美谈比比皆是。近现代各种留学生和高才生与专家学者人才辈出，至今不衰。

当你走进漳州南靖怀远楼，会发现中间是他们的祖堂兼家族学堂叫"斯是室"，顾名思义是取自"斯是陋室，惟吾德馨"之意，室外的一副对联写道："斯堂讵为游观，祈计敦书开耳目。是室何嫌隘陋，惟思尚德课儿孙。"祖德拳拳、寄望子孙之心，可谓溢于字面。

中国的民间书院制度也对周边国家及东南亚也广有影响。据统计，历史上朝鲜的书院有六百几十所。朝鲜书院受朱子学影响很大，一般均供奉朱子。2019 年 7 月，在第 43 届联合国教科文组织世界遗产委员会会议上，韩国 9 所保存了朝鲜王朝时代儒学私塾原貌的书院，以"韩国新儒学书院"之名（Seowon, Korean Neo-Confucian Academies），成功入选世界文化遗产。当然，在海外的华人社会也把母国的崇文重教的传统带到了异国他乡，如在新加坡有萃英书院、养正书院等。关于海外华人创办华文学校方面的资料也很多，如华侨领袖陈嘉庚先生就是华侨崇文重教精神的杰出代表。他认为"教育为立国之本，兴学乃国民天职"。

9.4 中国传统教育文化的基本特色

我们在上面简单梳理了中国古代教育的发展概貌，如它在教育制度、教育方式与教育追求等方面的基本线索和内容，也可以从中总结出几点关于中国传统教育的重要特性和特征来。在这方面，不少学者做过许多有价值的探讨，如从教育哲学的角度概括为天人合一、政教统一、文道结合、师道尊严；或从中西对比的角度概括为重世俗、轻神性，重道德、轻功利，重政务、轻自然，重和谐、轻竞争，以及重整体、轻个体等。我们认为从教育整体方法论和价值追求上看，可以把中国古代教育的基本特征概括为以下几点①：

（1）综合观，即大教育观，突出教育在整个社会大系统中的重要性。在古代，教育家们早就认识到教育的重要性，发现许多教育问题实质上反映的便是

---

① 此处论述多据郭齐家. 中国教育史［M］. 北京：人民教育出版社，2015.

社会问题，所以认为必须重视教育，将其放在整个社会中去解决教育问题，而教育问题的解决，又会促进整个社会的发展进步。孔子十分重视教育，把人口、财富、教育当作立国的基本要素。他认为，在发展生产使人民富裕之后，唯一的大事是"教之"，即发展教育事业。从他之后，历代教育家都从不同方向认识到了教育发展的重要性。例如《礼记·学记》①中提出"建国君民，教学为先""化民成俗，其必由学"，即认为教育的社会功能是培养国家需要的人才，形成社会的道德风尚，形成良风美俗。这种经典论述，应该说具有恒久的借鉴意义。

（2）辩证观，即对立统一观。就像孔子一方面主张"君子怀德"，同时又说"好仁不好学，其蔽也愚""仁者安仁，知者利仁"，这都表现了孔子懂得用中庸之道的辩证法理性看待教育所涉及的道德与知识之间的统一关系，道德教育和知识教育互济其美、互相渗透、互相促进、互相统一。又如孔子辩证地看待学习过程中学与思的关系，"学而不思则罔，思而不学则殆"，两者对立统一、相辅相成。民间有谚语说"鸳鸯绣出从君看，不把金针度与人"，说的是秘诀和技术要领不能教给人，明代的徐光启则反其道而说"金针度去从君用，未把鸳鸯绣与人"。他强调的是培养人的才能和实际本领，就如"临渊羡鱼，不如起而结网"，点出了教育给人实际的能力，而不是包办代替、给人现成的知识的正确道理。还有如古人强调的教学相长、师生相须，也是辩证观的表现。丰富的教育学辩证观，是中国教育文化的一大特色，在世界教育史中看也不多见。

（3）内在观，即强调心的内在道德功能或内在自觉性。中国传统教育思想的另一个显著特点是启发人的内心自觉，注重自我修养。就像我们今天常说的"自立志、自努力、自责备、自鼓励、自得、自叹……一切都是在'自'之中"。强调人心中具有一种判断价值的自觉能力，即悟性、领悟力，只有悟性才能使一个人真正成长起来，在自己内心之中寻找美丑善恶的标准，追求道德自律，而不是他律。如孔子说的"仁者人也，我欲仁斯仁至矣"，主张"克己复礼天下归仁"，这个己，就是自己，就是张扬了人的道德主体性。仁德就是人的主体性之德，强调内在超越而非外在的模仿或强迫，从而以心性之光普照天下，达到"天人合一"境界。中国古代教育思想以天人合一为最高境界，而这个境界全在仁德内在的敞开才有可能。重视人内在的力量，重内过于重外，启发内心，相信主体内在力量，这是一个值得深思的教育特色。

（4）除此三点外，我们也要注意另外一些特点，如注重学校教育、家庭教

---

① 《学记》是中国古代一篇教育论文，也是世界历史上最早专门论述教育和教学问题的文献。

育、社会教育三者并重和有机结合；注重教育方式的灵活性，采用灵活的因人因事而异的教育方式；注重德智结合，突出德育、美育重要性；强调教育与实践相结合；重视人文教育文史哲不分家。限于时间，我这里就不一一展开了。

总之，中国传统教育文化源远流长，博大精深，是长时间思想和实践的积淀，具有强大磁场，散发着迷人的魅力，是一个无限丰富的知识宝藏，是中华传统文化的重要组成部分。它既是一种资料，也是一种资源。我们需要进一步研究发扬传统教育其中蕴含的方法论价值，让它们在现代化社会绽放属于他们的色彩，发挥属于它们的作用。

The Ninth Chapter:

Advocating Literacy and Emphasizing Education
—Traditional Chinese Education Culture

We often say that China is a time-honored civilization. Half of the reason for that lies in the fact that generations of Chinese people attach great importance to education. Chinese people inherit their civilization by means of education, and promote the development of their civilization by means of innovation. In other words, it is because of the glorious ancient education that the traditional civilization can last for thousands of years, that the Chinese nation has become a gentle and honest civilization with respect to morality and courtesy, and that the Chinese civilization can shine brilliantly in the history of human development.

9. 1　China—a Civilized Nation Advocating Literacy and Emphasizing Education

Let's look at the word "education". In Chinese classic thoughts, it refers to civilizing people, and endowing them with civilized personality. Just like the saying in *The Book of Changes*: "We look at the ornamental observances of society, and understand how the process of transformation is accomplished all under heaven." That is to say, education refers to teaching people the general knowledge of human culture and nature, so as to enlighten them and civilize them. The purpose of education is to make people exterminate the evil and follow the good, or to enlighten them and help them discard backward and ignorant ideas. In short, the aim of education is to make people real people. As Mencius pointed out: "Men have their own principles for their beings. If provided with sufficient food, warm clothing and comfortable dwelling but no civilization, they would be about the same as beast." In the earliest pedagogical document in China, *The Book of Rites* · *The Book of Learning*, it is proposed that a gentleman must attach importance to education and learning if he wants to build a country and rule the people, and if he wants to educate the people and form good customs. *The Three-Character Classic*, which is well-known to all Chinese people, also tells the truth about education in clear and catchy sentences: "Man on earth, good at birth. The same nature, varies on nurture. With no education, there'd be aberration. To teach well, you deeply dwell." Each sentence here has only one key idea: to make people civilized through education. Education refers to teaching people, which is the same as the idea of civilizing people with culture mentioned by us. These two ideas have the same connotation.

It's safe to say that China has attached great importance to education as well as the development of education for a long time. Since ancient times, numerous stories of respecting teachers and pursuing truth have been handed down from generation to generation. Across from the Xiamen campus of Huaqiao University, Xiamen Horticulture Expo Garden enjoys a charming sight of beautiful seascape. There is a "Chinese Education Island". In this island, there are many figure sculptures of Chinese educators. Their stories are very famous. Almost everyone in China knows about their stories. Now I will give you some examples.

(1) "Mencius' mother moving house for three times" (孟母三迁). Mencius's mother, in order to give Mencius a good learning environment, moved their home for three times. Because children who lived next to a cemetery liked to play a game of holding funerals; children who lived next to a market liked to play a game of trading with other people; children who lived next to a slaughterhouse liked to play a game of butchering animals. Children are good at imitating other people's behaviors, so Mencius's mother believed that these places were not good for her son's upbringing. Finally, they moved to a place which was near a school. (Just like living in today's school district houses.) And then Mencius began to learn etiquette and the rules to conduct himself. Mencius's mother was relieved and satisfied. From this story we can see that Mencius's mother is really a wise mother who has given much thought to her son's education. She knows well that the living environment can influence children's behaviors. It can exert an imperceptible influence on children's growth. So she moved for several times without hesitation. She had only one aim: to let her son receive positive education of personality. And Mencius, of course, as we know, became almost as great a master as Confucius in the history of Confucianism.

(2) "Tying one's hair on the house beam and jabbing one's side with an awl to keep oneself awake" （悬梁刺股）. That is a story of Sun Jing in the Han Dynasty, who studied day and night without rest. So, he was very sleepy and kept dozing off. Therefore, he tied his head to a beam. By doing so, he prevented himself from falling into sleep. This story, usually called together with the story of Su Qin, who took an awl and stabbed it into his own legs when studying. These stories advocate the learning spirit of ancient Chinese people, the spirit of cherishing time and studying hard.

(3) "An iron pestle be grounded into an embroidery needle" （铁杵成针）. Li Bai, a great poet of the Tang Dynasty, he was flighty and impetuous when he was young. Once, he saw an old woman who was grinding an iron pestle, Li Bai asked her what she was doing. The old woman answered that she was grinding an embroidery needle. Li Bai laughed and asked: "How can an iron pestle be grounded into an embroidery needle?" The old woman gave her answer, which later became a golden saying in the history of Chinese education: "If you work hard enough, you can grind an iron rod into a needle." Li Bai felt ashamed and inspired. He returned home and devoted his heart and soul to study, and eventually became the "Poetic Genius".

(4) "Just like being in the warm and soft wind in spring" （如坐春风）. It tells a story of Zhu Guangting of the Song Dynasty, who learned from Cheng Hao, a great philosopher and the founder of the Cheng Zhu school of Neo-Confucianism. Once he listened to Cheng Hao's lecture in Ruzhou, he was so addicted to Cheng Hao's lecture, and he attended his lectures for more than a month before going home. After returning home, he praised his teacher to everyone he met. He said: "I sit in the warm and soft wind in spring for a month." Later, the idiom is used to describe the joy of receiving education, and deriving the benefits both physically and mentally.

(5) "Standing in the snow in front of Cheng Yi's gate" （程门立雪）. And this story is from *History of song Dynasty*: *Biography of Yang Shi*. Yang Shi who came from Fujian Province visited his teacher Cheng Yi with his friend You Zuo. At that time, Cheng Yi was sitting quietly in meditation. Yang Shi and You Zuo stood outside quietly and didn't disturb their teacher. It was snowing heavily outside. But they waited and waited until their teacher woke up. And when their teacher woke up the snow was one chi deep (about 0.3 meter) outside the door. This story reflects the spirit of respecting teachers and studying with determination.

There are a lot of idiom stories of famous educators like these in Xiamen

Horticulture Expo Garden. Their stories are so impressive and these great people are beacons lighting up our advance. Because they talk about some of the core qualities of education, such as the relationship between education and family, the relationship between education and becoming a useful person, the relationship between teaching people and growing to manhood, the relationship between studying with diligence and academic success, the relationship between teachers and students, the relationship between pursuing study and managing state affairs, and so on. What's more, these stories also reveal some laws of pedagogy with lasting value beyond history: studying with diligence and assiduity for making academic progress; diligence being the means by which one makes up for one's dullness; reviewing what you have learned to perceive what is new; the students respecting their teachers and the teachers loving their students; setting up examples for others with both precept and practice and so on.

It's safe to say that Chinese people, whether they are officials of the state, the intellectuals and thinkers, or even ordinary people, they all advocate literacy and put emphasis on education. They all have a kind of cultural awareness and conscious action of advocating literacy and emphasizing education. They attach great importance to the significance and social function of education, constantly explore and perfect the educational system, deepen the educational thought, and elucidate the value pursuit of education. As a civilized nation of advocating literacy and emphasizing education, China has provided the world with a set of unique educational culture, which still has an unfailing charm that continues to this day.

9.2 From National University to Imperial Academy: Official Schools in Ancient China

The academia generally divide the history of traditional Chinese education into three periods: the foundation period in the Pre-Qin Dynasties, the golden period in the Qin, Han, Song and Ming Dynasties, and the period of decline and transformation from the Qing Dynasty to contemporary times. Of course, we can not give a detailed description of all these three periods. We will only give you a brief introduction about official and private schools. And we hope you can gain a general understanding about traditional Chinese education.

Let's talk about the official schools first.

(1) "Bi Yong": Official Education in the Western Zhou Dynasty

In the Western Zhou Dynasty, the King of the Zhou Dynasty set up national schools in the east, west, south, north and center of Haojing, the capital of the Zhou Dynasty. They were named "Dong Xu", "Cheng Jun", "Gu Zong", "Shang Xiang" and "Bi Yong" respectively. Among these five schools, "Bi Yong" was the most respectable. Every year, the king of the Zhou Dynasty came to "Bi Yong" and tested students. In other words, he came to "Bi Yong" to see its development and construction, and listened to lectures given by scholars. Therefore, "Bi Yong" was the top learning institution in China in the Xia, Shang and Zhou Dynasties. Although "Bi Yong" was replaced by "Tai Xue", National University in the Han Dynasty, it was the earliest prototype. So literati had a special feeling for "Bi Yong". Therefore, in the Imperial Academy of the Ming and Qing Dynasties, the word "Bi Yong" was used to name one of the buildings. Of course, in the Western Zhou Dynasty, there were not only five highest level schools for the children from aristocratic families to study, but also "primary schools" for the young. "Pan Gong" was built in the capital city of all kingdoms, which was the highest seat of learning of kingdom. Later, "Xiu Cai", who passed the Imperial Examination at the county level in the Ming and Qing Dynasties, could be admitted to the "Pan Gong" to study, which was called "Ru Pan" or "You Pan". In other local administrative divisions at different levels, such as the local administrative divisions of "Lv", "Dang", "Zhou" and "Xiang", the state also set up educational institutions at different levels, and they were called "Shu", "Xiang", "Xu" and "Xiao" (In the Han Dynasty, the local administration divisions were "Jun", "Xian", "Xiang" and "Ju". Correspondingly, there were schools of different levels such as "Xue", "Xiao", "Xiang" and "Xu"). These local schools were established for cultivating all kinds of talents in local areas.

(2) The National University (太学) of Han Dynasty

The Emperor Wu of the Han Dynasty established the National University. He carried out a policy of proscribing all non-Confucian schools of thought and espousing Confucianism as the orthodox state ideology. There are five Confucian classics: *Book of Songs*, *Book of History*, *Book of Rites*, *Book of Change*, and *Spring and Autumn Annals*. So he set up the official position of court academician of these five Confucian classics. In addition to discussing state affairs, establishing the rite system, being in charge of books, these court academicians also served as the professors of the state. The head of the court academician of five Confucian classics was called "Pu Ye", while students were called the "the disciples of the court academician of Confucian classics". When the National University was established, there were only 50 students; during the reign of the Emperor Zhao of the Han Dynasty, there were 100 students; during the Reign of the Emperor Wang Mang of the Xin Dynasty there were 10000 students. In addition to teaching students rites, music, archery, riding, writing, arithmetic, which were six classical arts advocated by Confucianism, court academicians of Confucian classics were more specialized in the teaching and research of the Five Classics. (*Bai Hu Tong Yi* was an important classic which recorded the similarities and differences of the Five Classics given by the court academicians, and it integrated the Confucian thoughts of contemporary classic school and traditional classic school.) After studying in the National University, scholars randomly chose their topics and made essays according to their topics. By doing so, they could be tested for what they had learned. And those who passed the academic examination could be honored with official positions. The subsidized education was no longer just of the aristocratic realm, but also intended for commoners. The emphasis on the system of education during the Western Han Dynasty aligned in combining the cultivation of talent with a selection of worthy individuals.

(3) The Education in the Sui, Tang Dynasties

The whole set of education system, including the education scheme, teaching contents, construction and placement of teaching staff, the mechanism of examination selection, was more complete and detailed than former ones. Three points are worth noting.

First, the Imperial Academy was established to replace the National University, with an official position called "Ji Jiu", the head of court academicians of Confucian classics, who was in charge of the course of education. The founding of the Imperial Academy marked that there was an independent department of education in ancient China. Second, there were more professional and developed educational departments of different levels. There were educational departments like "Guo Zi Xue" "Tai Xue" "Si Men Xue" respectively for the children of aristocracy, high-ranking officials, or ordinary people. There were also other professional schools of law, calligraphy, arithmetic, medicine, veterinary science, astronomy, musicology and so on. There were also some special schools for some special people, such as "Hong Wen

Academy", "Chong Wen Academy" and "Chong Xian Academy", which were schools for children who came from the royal family and foreign countries. There were also vocational education departments, such as the education department of medicine, divination, astronomy, carriage and horses, and classics. Third, the Imperial Examination System was established. During the 2nd year under the reign of the Emperor Yang of the Sui Dynasty, he examination for "Jin Shi" was established, which marked the birth of the Imperial Examination System. The Imperial Examination System was the fairest form of talent selection that could be adopted in feudal times. As long as you studied hard with diligence and assiduity, and made achievements, it was possible for you to become the ministers of the imperial court. The Imperial Examination could be divided into three types: examination held by a country government, examination held by the central government, and final imperial examination which was presided over by the emperor. The one who came first in the three examination above respectively was called "Xie Yuan", "Hui Yuan" and "Zhuang Yuan". Because there were multiple education subjects in the Tang Dynasty, many specific examinations were established, such as the examination of writing essays about state policies and the examination about Confucian classics. These specific examinations met the need of the multi-culture education of the Tang Dynasty. And the content of these examinations included writing essays about current policy, filing the blanks in classics, writing poem and odes and so on.

(4) The Innovation of Education System in Song Dynasty

In the Song Dynasty subjects raised by government had been much less than that in the Tang Dynasty, but the examination for "Jin Shi" was still fashionable. Meanwhile, regardless of form and content, the system underwent great innovation. Firstly, the extension of matriculation was broadened. In the former dynasties like the Tang Dynasty, each year the "Jin Shi" were no more than twenty to thirty in number but in the Song Dynasty, there were as many as hundreds of people passing the exams and even those who failed the exams many times could apply for tolerance of the emperor and so serve as officials with less important positions. Secondly, the frequency of exams was limited to a fixed once every three years. The local tests came first in autumn and in the following spring the qualifying candidates would trudge to the capital for the higher imperial examination. Thirdly, so far as content was concerned, while the earlier examinations laid much stress on the ancient classical texts, the great reformer Wang Anshi (1021—1086) advocated an innovation which was much more practical. He changed the blank-filling of verses into composition about the verse, giving free reign to the ability of the candidates. However, this was opposed by other grandees and did not last for long. Finally, to prevent the practice of favoritism, examinees' names were closely covered on their papers which were then exchanged among different local examiners. This did indeed greatly reduce the incidence of cheating.

China's imperial examination system provided opportunities for talented people to become government officials in the feudal country, and enabled large number of people from the middle and lower classes to enter the ruling class. Especially in the Tang and Song Dynasties, the imperial examination system showed its vitality, and it is the golden age of the development of ancient Chinese culture. In the Imperial Academy of Beijing, up to now, there are 198 stone tablets for honoring "Jin Shi" of the Yuan, Ming and Qing Dynasties. They are symbols of the country's educational achievements, as well as the glorious records of "Jin Shi" and their families.

(5) The Imperial Academy: the National Education in the Ming and Qing Dynasties

Firstly, in the Ming and Qing Dynasties, the national education cause also enjoyed development and progress. Education system and measures were further improved. In terms of the Imperial Academy, there were seven kinds of instructors including "Ji Jiu" "Si Ye" "Jian Cheng" "Bo Shi" "Dian Bu" and so on. Students from different places could have the opportunities of being admitted to the Imperial Academy, which resulted in an unprecedented increase in the number of students.

① The students could be divided into four types. The first type was "Gong Jian" which meant that the students were recommended to the Imperial Academy by prefectural and subprefecture schools. The second type was "Ju Jian" which meant scholars who have passed examination held by the central government could be admitted to the Imperial Academy. The third type was "Yin Jian" which meant that children of officials could have to the privilege of entering the Imperial Academy. The fourth type was "Li Jian" which meant that students could be admitted to the Imperial Academy by donating grains or money. In addition, there was a special kind of students who came from neighboring countries such as Korea and Japan. ② In terms of the main courses for students of the Imperial Academy, they mainly studied *the Four Books*, *the*

Five Classics, and *General Mirror for the Aid of Government* with the annotations of Cheng-Zhu School. Writing the Eight-part Essay became a compulsory course in the Ming Dynasty. ③Students could be divided into three different grades. The first grade students were in the junior class and thoroughly understood *the Four Books*. The second grade students were in the middle-level class, which was the class for those who had passed the examination after one and a half years' study in the junior class, and excelled in writing essays of literary grace and clear logic. The third grade students were in the senior class, which was the class for those who had passed the examination after one and a half years study in the middle-level class, and had a good command of classics and history, and excelled in writing essays of literary grace and clear logic. And these students would graduate from the Imperial Academy after one-year's study in the senior class. ④The Internship Program in the Imperial Academy. Under this program, the Students who had been in the Imperial Academy for more than 10 years were sent to the six ministries to learn how to handle government affairs. They usually studied at these six ministries for 3 months, and their work attendance were recorded.

Secondly, in terms of the local official education, it also enjoyed continuous development. Up to the Qing Dynasty, there were more than 1700 prefectural and subprefecture schools, with more than 27000 students. This is the prefectural school of Quanzhou was once the most magnificent in seven provinces of the southeast China. according to the statistics, it was the historical witness of education and teaching of Quanzhou. From the 9th century to the beginning of the 20th century, as many as 2454 people who came from Quanzhou had passed the highest imperial examinations. 19 civil or military Number One Scholars once lived or were born in Quanzhou; and more than 20 scholars were honored as prime ministers. Therefore, we can say that Quanzhou has cultivated many talents. And Quanzhou is worthy of the reputation of "Kingdom of Lu in the seashore" (海滨邹鲁).

Thirdly, the establishment of Ming Dynasty brought the Peak of the Imperial Examination System, which entered a period of great prosperity. The methods of selection were much stricter than that of any other past generation. During the Ming Dynasty, one had to directly enter the Imperial Examination System. And the main contents of the imperial examination included a specific eight-part essay. The examinees were to answer the questions in the style of ancient writing, within a particular format. Furthermore, the number of words was strictly limited and the syntax required an antithesis. The eight-part essay brought forth great harm and seriously fettered the thoughts of people. Fan Jin, one of the characters depicted in the novel of *The Scholars* by Wu Jingzi, is quite a typical victim of the declining system.

The glorious achievements of the past will eventually disappear with the passing of time. Traditional official education has declined with the development of history. Especially after the introduction of western learning to the east in contemporary China, it kept declining day by day. From the education institutions and specialty setting, to the talent examination and selection system, they all became stagnant and could not keep abreast of the times. Therefore, significant historical changes had been made unconsciously during crises. For example, the Imperial Academy of ancient China turned into the Imperial University of Peking of contemporary China. There was a new trend of advocating real learning and practice in administering the world affairs. Westernization Schools and Church Schools were built. And the modern western school system was gradually introduced and established. The Imperial Examination System was abolished in 1905, which meant that the glorious old China's education system finally came to an end. but it also symbolized the arrival of a new era of education for our country.

9.3 From Folk Academy to "Free Private Schools"
—Non-governmental Education

China's private school system also dates back to ancient times. The rites collapsed and the elegant music disappeared during the Spring and Autumn and Warring States Periods, which made the official intellectuals go to populace one after another, and started the history of private education for populace. Private schools flourished since the Tang and Song Dynasties, various literati academies were established by intellectuals, and various family academies were organized by local communities. We may say that the private education system for populace was very complete. In particular, idealistic thinkers and scholar-officials had their hearts filled with great enthusiasm and joy. They attached great importance to the function of education, "Civilizing people". They believed the action of propagating the doctrine, imparting professional knowledge, and resolving doubts was in accordance to morality and justice. And it was in accordance to the saying: "To ordain conscience for Heaven and Earth, to secure life and fortune for the people, to continue the lost teachings of past sages, and to establish peace for all future generations." On one hand, they tried to explore the truths, on the other hand, they tried to record what they had gained from studying, and imparted them to students. They have left a large number of educational monographs and educational thoughts. As we known, Confucius was one of the earliest educators who set up private schools, he first put forward the policy of "providing education for all people without discrimination", Confucius had rich pedagogical thoughts in terms of the necessity of education, teaching content, the nature of education, the attitude of learning, the role models for our learning and the method of learning. Both Confucius and his students were very scrupulous and earnest to each other.

Limited to space, about the Non-governmental Education, I will start with the folk academies in the Song Dynasty.

9.3.1　The Flourishing Folk Academies of the Song Dynasty

After the Song Dynasty, the development of the private schooling was mainly reflected in the flourishing folk academies. The folk academy was originated from the Tang Dynasty. At first, it was the place for book compilation, collection and proofing. During the Five Dynasties Period, distinguished scholars chose places of interest and gave lectures together, and gradually academies were built in these places. Academies of the Song Dynasty were the grandest, and they were established in every place. Among them, four great academies were the most famous. They were the Bailudong Academy, Yingtian Academy, Songyang Academy, and Yuelu Academy. These academies had strict and complete management regulations. Many great scholars came to these academies for academic discussions, which became the order of the day. In the Yuan Dynasty, the central government assigned chief lecturers to academies, so to some extent the academies were actually operated by the central government. Even though after the Ming Dynasty, the central government didn't assigned chief lecturers to academies, and Wang Yangming's Philosophy of Mind was prevalent throughout the north and south as academies were established everywhere. But unfortunately, the academies have been banned and destroyed for four times in the middle and late Ming Dynasty. And it was not until the reign of Emperor Kangxi of the Qing Dynasty that these academies were reopened. However, official subsidies and supervision still existed, and such administrative restrictions made them impossible to reproduce the free and lively spirits of the Song Dynasty.

Compared with national official schools, folk academies had the following characteristics.

First, teachers and students enjoyed academic freedom in folk academies. Teachers could give lectures on academic subjects freely, and students could have free debates with each other. People studied here for gaining and digging into truths instead of participating in the Imperial Examination. There were good teaching conditions in these academies. Standardized education management systems were established in academies, such as the system of employing and managing teachers and administrative staffs, the system of academy management, the system of raising all kinds of funds and so on. There was a harmonious relationship between teachers and students, which reflected the good spiritual characteristics of the folk academy.

(1) The Institution Construction of the Folk Academies

For example, these are the five cardinal principles of Bailudong Academy founded by Zhu Xi in the Southern Song Dynasty. ①As regard to the essence of the five ethical issues, there should be affection between father and son; righteousness between sovereign and subject; different emotion expressions between husband and wife on different occasions; proper priority between the young and the elder; trust between friends. ② As regard to knowledge, one must learn it extensively, inquire into it prudently, think about it cautiously, apprehend it clearly, and practice it earnestly. ③ As regard to cultivating one's moral character, one should say faithful words, take earnest actions, abstain from resentment and rapacity, correct evil doings and become good. ④As regard to conducting oneself in daily life, one should uphold justice without seeking personal gains, and expound truths without taking credit for his own. ⑤As regard to the manner of dealing with people, you should never impose on others what you would not choose for yourself. When your conduct brings forth no desired results, reflect and find fault in yourself.

These are the academy rules of the Lize Academy established by Lv Zuqian, a famous scholar of Neo-Confucianism of the Southern Song Dynasty. Including one should comply with moral ethics and fulfill one's moral duties. Teachers, students and friends should treat each other equally with kindness and respect. One should listen to the lectures carefully with proper behaviors. One should respect teachers and their teaching, and shouldn't act against the etiquette. One should neither gossip about others nor be supercilious and self-conceited. One should not associate with bad companion or engage in vulgar activities of unrefined taste, and so on.

It can be seen from the cases of these folk academies that the ancient academies attached great importance to the formulation of normative management systems. However, the academic rules formulated by them are generally divided into two parts: one is the requirements of moral cultivation, and the other is the requirements of learning attitude and methods. The former regulates moral education, while the latter regulates intellectual education. Among the two, the traditional academies have more emphasis on moral education. Even in the articles on learning methods, the contents of moral education are integrated. It not only takes traditional virtue as the purpose of academy education, but also requires the Confucian moral standards to shape the character of students and conduct moral cultivation, which is the biggest characteristic. For example, the provisions on learning attitude and methods in the school rules set by Wang Wenqing are also very distinctive, not only specific, but also close to life.

9-2　Academic Activities of the Academy

Second, in terms of the daily academic activities of the academy.

People gathered in the academy to held academic meetings, just like today's academic conferences. Scholars gathered, freely talked about and debated the Confucian classics with each other. For example, the debate of "Moderation and Consonance" in Yuelu Academy. In August of the 5th year of the emperor Xiaozong, invited by of Zhang Shi, a Confucian scholar of Huxiang School, Zhu Xi, a Confucian scholar of Min School went to the Yuelu Academy with his disciples. They debated the issue of "Moderation and Consonance". They had heated debates which lasted three days and nights. Another example is "the Debate of Zhu Xi and Lu Jiuyuan" in Ehu Academy. In June of the 13th year of Emperor Xiaozong, Zhu Xi, Lu Jiuyuan and his brothers made an appointment. They gathered in the Ehu Temple of Qianshan County, Shangrao, Jiangxi Province to discussed one question: which should be given priority to, honoring virtuous nature, or following to the path of inquiry and study? They had heated debates on their respective views, which was known as "the Meeting of Ehu Temple" in history.

Third, in terms of the spiritual outlooks of teachers and students of academies.

According to *Complete Works of Lu Jiuyuan*, we can get a glimpse of the daily spiritual outlook of teachers and students of the Xiangshan Academy. Lu Jiuyuan, or Master Xiangshan, lived in the Xiangshan Academy and acted like an abbot. He arrived at the academy at the sound of drum every morning. He greeted with others by making bows with hands folded in front. When Master Xiangshan gave lectures, he always impressed others with pleasant appearance and good spirit. The students who listened to his lecture wrote their names and ages on small cards, and took their seats in order. There were dozens of students, but a perfect silence prevailed in the study room. Master Xiangshan gave his lecture with clear and accurate enunciation. In the beginning of the class, he required that students should be concentrated, cultivate their morality and listen attentively. The students all obeyed him with servility. Master Xiangshan not only talked about the Confucian classics, but also paid attention to enlightening people's conscience. Master Xiangshan's lectures struck deep into the minds of the people. In normal times, teachers and students either read books, or played the guqin, a seven-stringed plucked instrument. When the weather was fine, they walked slowly and enjoyed the wonderful sight of waterfall. When they climbed high, they recited the explications of classics and doctrines, and ancient poems and proses including *Chu Ci* with much elegance and gentility. Even in the heat of the summer, Mr. Xiangshan was properly dressed and looked dignified.

Forth, the populism and patriotism orientation of the academy are also two highlights worthy of attention.

Wang Gen, a Confucian scholar of Taizhou School and a disciple of Wang

Yangming established Anding Academy, a unique academy for populace. Unlike those academies which were orientated towards elite intellectuals. The students of Wang Gen's Anding Academy were mainly common people, including 487 farmers, woodcutters, potters, and labourors of salt corvee. Wang Gen did not receive Confucian education in classic academies, and he left a few scholarly works. He emphasized that oral teaching can inspire true understanding. He aimed at making foolish men and women understand Confucian thoughts, which became one of the characteristics of Taizhou School. His saying "go into the mountains to meet ordinary people and go to the town to enlighten the ignorant", fully showed his unique pursuit.

In addition, the style of academies (such as Donglin Academy) characterized by scholars discussing national politics is full of patriotic feelings. In the 32nd year of Wanli in the Ming Dynasty (1604), Gu Xiancheng, a scholar from Donglin, and others revived Donglin Academy and gathered here to give lectures. They advocated "close to the ears are the sounds of wind, rain and reading; deep in the heart are the affairs of home, state and world". they combined the spirit of "reading, lecturing and patriotism", boldly discussed the government and criticized the corruption of the imperial court, which caused widespread response from scholars throughout the country. Donglin Academy has become a gathering place of talents in Jiangnan area and a major public opinion Center for discussing state affairs.

It should be said that since the Song Dynasty, the literati academies in China have been able to shine the light of truth more than the official academies because of the relatively free school running policy support and the rigorous and truth-seeking spirit of teachers and students. They have not only accumulated and inherited Chinese culture and thought, but also trained many outstanding talents, forming the most colorful painting in the history of education in China. Just as the couplets on the Mountain Gate of Yuelu Academy confidently proclaim that "genius is all in Chu, especially in the Yuelu Academy", there is also a couplet in Bailudong Academy that says: "There are fragrant grasses within ten spaces, and there are outstanding talents in every room."

9.3.2　Clan Academies in the Rural Society

As the grass-rooted academies, clan academies or family academies were established everywhere in the rural society. As we mentioned in the seventh chapter, the patriarchal clan culture played a significant role in Chinese people's life. In families of various places, great attention is paid to the upbringing of children, hoping that they can become useful people so as to bring honor to their families by carrying forward the tradition and forging ahead into the future. Therefore, they had repeatedly emphasized the importance of education. Family academies were often set up in the ancestral halls, those who were excellent in characters and academic performance usually served as the teachers of family academies, or families would employ social scholars to serve as teachers in their academies. In terms of the operating expense of the academy, it was derived from the family property, such as the earning of the ancestral land. Because the family academies were free for family members, they were also called "Free Private Schools".

The family academies provided the most basic education. So, it was like today's primary schools. There were many teaching materials such as *the Three-Character Classic*, *the Hundred Family Names*, *the Thousand Character Text*, *Enlightening Stories for Children*, *Three Hundred Poems of the Tang Dynasty* and so on. And these delighting and interesting books are rich in knowledge and moral ethics.

We can give you a few examples of family academies in folk villages.

For example, during the Ming and Qing Dynasties, Huizhou family academies were all over the urban and rural areas. "Even in the remote mountains and valleys, if there were people living, there were private schools and teachers." Hongcun, Yi County, Huangshan City, in later Ming Dynasty, the villagers set up six private schools by the north of the lake, called "six Schools by the Lake", for the education of the clan's youngsters. In 1814, the six schools merged into one and named as "Yiwen Family School", also referred to as South Lake School. Nanhu Academy is an ancient academy with traditional Hui style, covering an area of about 6000 square meters. The academy consists of six parts: Zhidao hall, Wenchang Pavilion, Huiwen Pavilion, enlightenment Pavilion, Wanghu tower and Qi garden. Wang Daxie, who once served as the Secretary of the cabinet of the Qing government, and a famous contemporary scientist Li Xiaojuan, one of the experts in the development of the Australian satellite launch, were all enlightened here.

The Wu family in Peitian Village has a time-honored tradition of attaching importance to education. Since the establishment of the first academy, "Stone Hill Thatched Cottage" in the early Ming Dynasty, more than twenty family academies had been set up successively. Up to now, there are five well-preserved academies of the

Ming and Qing Dynasties, including Nanshan Academy, Ziyang Academy, Chujing villa and Xiuzhu Building. There were even the special skill training school for women named "Rongxi School" and for farmers named "Chujing villa". Nanshan Academy of Peitian Village was built in the Chenghua Period of the Ming Dynasty and rebuilt in the 30th year of Emperor Qianlong of the Qing Dynasty, covering an area of more than 8000 square meters. Situated at the foot of a mountain, this academy, with boulder-paving and delicate door, looks very refined and elegant. Zeng Ruichun, a famous scholar of the Qing Dynasty who gave lectures and studied in the Nanshan Academy, equated the Nanshan Academy with the Ehu Academy and Bailudong Academy where Zhu Xi lectured. Thus, the Nanshan Academy did enjoy the quiet and beautiful environment. With the prosperity and spread of the Agency study in Ming Dynasty, the family's special attention to education, continuous investment and abundant financial support, the education cause of Peitian Village kept prospering. Therefore, it enjoys the reputation of "second to none in terms of talent cultivation in Tingzhou" and the "village of advocating literacy and putting emphasis on education". Talented people are produced by each generation, including hundreds of scholars who succeeded in the Imperial Examination. Even today, Peitian Village is still cultivating many talents for our country. We have already given a brief introduction about the education of Peitian Village. So, it is unnecessary to go into details again.

9-3 The Nanshan Academy of Peitian Village

When you walk into the ancestral hall and the family academy of Huaiyuan

Building in Nanjing County, Zhangzhou, you will also find that their ancestral hall and family academy is called "A Humble Hut", which is derived from the poem of Liu Yuxi, a famous poet of the Tang Dynasty. "Humble is the hut where I dwell, yet all shames my virtues dispel." Outside the doors there are two pairs of couplets: "This place is not only for visiting, but mainly for educating children." "You should not disgust this humble and simple hut, but to educate and cultivate children with morality and virtues." From the couplets we can feel ancestors' sincere hearts and ardent expectations for descendants.

Of course, China's folk academy system also exerted a wide influence on neighboring countries as well as the countries in Southeast Asia. There were more academies in Korea According to statistics, more than 600 academies were established in Korea. The academies in Korea were greatly influenced by Confucianism. So generally, the statue of Zhu Xi was enshrined in Korea's academies. In addition, some Chinese people who live abroad have brought the tradition of advocating literacy and putting emphasis on education to other countries. In Singapore, there were Cuiying Academy, Yangzheng Academy and so on. There are plenty of materials about overseas Chinese people establishing Chinese schools. For example, overseas Chinese leader Mr. Tan Kah Kee was an outstanding representative in this field. He once said: "Education is the foundation of a strong country, and it is every citizen's responsibility to ensure that good schools are established and that all children are well educated."

9.4 Features of China's Traditional Education

We have already given a brief introduction about the development of ancient China's education cause, such as the education systems, education methods, education pursuits and values and so on. We can draw some conclusions, and sum up some important characteristics of China's traditional education.

(1) A Holistic View of Education

Ancient Chinese held a holistic view of education, emphasizing life-long education, and they thought highly of the value of education in the whole social system. They found that many educational problems were essentially social problems. So, they believed that people should lay stress on education, and solve educational problems under the context of the whole society system. Once the problems of education had been solved, it would promote the development and progress of the whole society. Confucius regarded population, wealth, and education as three basic elements of governing a country. He believed that after making people rich by advancing production, the only important thing that should be done is to educate people. After Confucius, educators of every generation all realized the importance of educational development in different ways. There is a saying in *Record about Education* in *Book of Rites*: "The ancient kings who established the country and governed the people put building schools first." "If the sovereign wishes to enlighten people by education and form perfect customs, he should start to establish the education system." These classical expressions on education have permanent reference significance.

(2) A Dialectic View of Education

A Dialectic View of Education refers to view education based on the law of unity of opposites. as an example. On the one hand, Confucius said: "A superior man holds to morality." On the other hand, he said: "Loving to show benevolence without loving to learn may lead to random actions." "The virtuous devote their minds to benevolent conducts; the wise make the most of their benevolent conducts." They all show the fact that Confucius viewed education according to the Doctrine of the Mean. Moral education and knowledge education supplement each other, interpenetrate each other, promote each other and achieve unity with each other. Confucius held a dialectic view upon the relationship between learning and thinking. Confucius said: "He who learns without thinking will be bewildered; he who thinks without learning will be in danger." Supplementary to each other, learning and thinking form a unity of opposites. Just as the saying goes: "It is better to start weaving your fishing nets than merely coveting fish at the water." It pointed out the truth that education can cultivate people practical abilities rather than granting people ready-made knowledge. What's more, ancient Chinese people also emphasized that teaching benefits both teacher and pupil alike, which also shows a dialectic view of education. A dialectic view of education is rich in connotations, which is a characteristic of Chinese education culture, and it is rarely seen in the history of education in the world.

(3) Self-consciousness Emphasized

Another distinctive feature of Chinese traditional education is encouraging people to improve and cultivate themselves self-consciously. As we often say today, people should make up their minds, strive to make progress by themselves; people should be critical about themselves and motivate themselves; people should be pleased with what they are and what they have yet often acknowledge the superiority of others. Which show that everything is related to "self". It emphasized that people have the ability of developing value consciousness. Namely, the ability of understanding and comprehending. Only with the ability of understanding can a person really grow up. Confucius said: "I wish to be benevolent, and then benevolence is here in mind. " He advocates that once everybody has become self-restrained and observed the rules of propriety, benevolence will prevail in the whole kingdom, which emphasizes one core concept— "self", and shows the moral noumenon of people. Benevolence is a subjective virtue of human beings, which emphasizes advancing people's subjectivity and making them transcend themselves rather than forcing them to imitate others. The benevolent can be the models for us and illuminate everything on earth, and they can achieve the spiritual state of "unity of man and nature". Ancient China's educational thought regarded the "unity of man and nature" as the supreme spiritual state, and only the benevolent could achieve this spiritual state.

(4) In addition to these three points, we should also pay attention to other characteristics, such as paying equal attention to school education, family education and social education; pay attention to the flexibility of educational methods and adopt flexible educational methods that vary according to people and things; pay attention to the combination of morality and wisdom, and highlight the importance of moral education and aesthetic education; emphasizing the combination of education and practice; we should attach importance to the humanities education, and we should not separate literature, history and philosophy. Limited by time, I will not expand them here.

In short, time-honored Chinese traditional educational thoughts are very extensive and profound. They are the result of a longstanding accumulation of thoughts and practice, which has a strong historical enchantment. Chinese traditional education is like a treasure house of rich knowledge, and is an important part of traditional Chinese culture. We can continuously get valuable ideas from Chinese traditional educational thoughts. Further studies and researches need to be carried out. We should further study and promote the methodological value contained in traditional education. By doing so, traditional education can realize its value in the modern society, and give full play to its role.

第十讲

美美与共
——中外文明的交流与互鉴

"文明因多样而交流，因交流而互鉴，因互鉴而发展。"（习近平）中国文化史，就是一部中华民族同异域文明在交流互鉴中发展的漫长历史。悠悠五千年，中国文化不仅同一衣带水、山水相连的东（南）亚近邻相交往，更与中亚游牧文化、西亚波斯和阿拉伯文化、南亚的印度文化、欧洲文化逐步接触，展开各种交往和交流。中国传统文化在与不同文明的交流互鉴的过程中成长，并对人类文明的发展进步做出了重要贡献。

10.1　中外文化交流史回眸

抚今追昔，我们仿佛还能看到古代商人的驼队和航船、政府的使团、虔诚的僧侣和传教士、热衷探险的旅行家和文人学者，他们沿着陆路或海陆，穿越千里戈壁、万里波涛，从东南西北各个方向，走进中国或离开中国，或带来琳琅满目的异域风情，或带走异彩纷呈的中华特色，描绘了中外文明交流的一幕幕故事和一幅幅画面。

第一，从文化输入的视角。

西域的馕（胡饼）变成了汉朝人食用的烧饼；爪哇（印度尼西亚）传入的刺桐树让南唐的泉州城既多了一份艳丽的风景，又多了一个以树得名的别称Zayton；吕宋的"朱薯"（番薯）变成了清朝遍种南北、抗击饥馑的宝物，也让中国人口在道光朝直接倍增到三亿之众；天竺（古印度）的蔗糖提炼法，被唐人改进为"糖霜法"，糖粒结晶白净细腻，古印度人遂以 Chini（糖）指称大唐国；来自阿富汗的青金石制成的颜料，装饰在魏晋时新绘的敦煌壁画之上，千年不褪，让蓝色的洞窟更显幽远神秘；而中东矿产"苏麻离青"的使用，让元明时代的中国青花瓷更透出一份清新淡雅、青翠欲滴。波斯的竖箜篌，西方的胡琴等乐器，以及柔术、耍剑和吐火等杂技与魔术表演艺术也被中国人学习、掌握，并被彩绘在山东、四川等地汉墓的画像砖石上。玄奘法师历时十九年取回来的非止佛经，更以《大唐西域记》推进了中国人对西域和南亚地理风物的观察与了解。自中亚而来的祆教、摩尼教、景教、伊斯兰教等宗教纷传大唐，掀起了外域宗教输华的第一个高潮。而与唐代传教士不同的是，明末清初的利玛窦、南怀仁、汤若望等人在华数十年，传播的除了基督教义，更有全新的地图和空间观念、天文历算和时间观念、几何和逻辑思维……

第二，从文化输出的视角。

（1）东向：是东亚文化圈的日本、朝鲜半岛。它们和中国山水相连、风月同天。欣赏日本京都的古城风貌、《万叶集》中的汉字，让人恍在中华；韩国首尔的成均馆（高丽国时代的开城国子监）里，宣讲着孔子伦理和朱子哲学的高深奥义。

（2）南向：越南人至今崇拜炎帝，过中国的端午和中秋，科举制度历行近900年，其体例几乎与中国无异。缅甸人用"胞波"（一母所生的同胞）或"瑞苗"（亲戚）称呼中国人；泰国人则不仅用心记住了昔日郑和下西洋途径暹罗的故事，更把他供奉在当地的"三宝公庙"享受历代的香火。菲律宾达雅克族每年过新年、拜偶像、贴对联、穿新衣、贺新禧，展示了满满的中国风；如印尼巴厘岛从明初就引种了来自中国的白葱和荔枝，岛上至今流行一种造型和舞姿都酷似中国舞狮的民间舞蹈。

（3）西向："中国"在英文中叫China，那是因为欧洲人欣赏产自中国的瓷器；希腊雅典的帕特农神庙的"命运三女神"雕像和意大利那不勒斯博物馆收藏的酒神巴克科斯的女祭司像，都身着丝质服饰，轻柔细薄，说明至少在公元前五世纪，欧洲贵族就在热捧中国的丝绸；而中国丝贩运到波斯，就被加工成极富民族特色的波斯丝毯（波斯锦）；客居撒马尔罕的唐代士兵分享了遥远中土家乡的造纸术，自此结束了欧洲使用羊皮纸的历史；宋代泉州出发的古船队把中国茶叶和西方人渴望的肉桂、甘松、花椒和丁香等香料运往欧洲。而蒙古西征大军所到之处，也顺便把中国的传统中医药学、网格坐标制图法和绘画艺术传入西亚和欧洲；古老的活塞式木风箱启迪了瓦特的蒸汽机；《周易》阴阳二爻则让莱布尼茨顿悟了二进制原理；而蹴鞠也被公认为当代足球的来源。中国的指南针、印刷术和火药则被认为是点燃欧洲人走进了近代资产阶级时代的引线。

图 10-1　输入—输出：文化的交流互鉴

诸如此类、不胜枚举，这里当然不可能一一为大家做详细的介绍工作。推荐大家阅读《中西交通史料汇编系列》，这是一部非常厚实的、为中外关系史研究者普遍重视的名著。此书由张星烺先生（1881—1951）编著。他从中外文 42 种著名史籍中辑录了大量有关中外关系史的资料，并以地区和国家分类，按时间顺序先后排列，并对其中某些地名和史事详加考释。全书 6 册，共分 8 个部分，依次叙述古代中国与欧洲、非洲、阿拉伯、亚美尼亚、犹太、伊斯兰、中亚、印度半岛之交通史。各章节中的附录为作者的专题研究论著和考证注释。

10.2　丝绸之路与中外文化交流的渠道

谈到中外文化"引进来""走出去"，进行文化传播和文化吸纳的历史交流，人们谈最多的自然是古代的"一带一路"，即陆上丝绸之路和海上丝绸之路。丝绸之路的概念不见于中国古籍，而是分别由德国地质地理学家李希霍芬于 1877 年和法国汉学家沙畹于 1913 年在各自的著作中提出来的。丝路文化的研究，其内涵不仅仅是研究古代丝绸贸易与道路走向的问题，本质上是试图解析整个古代东西方世界之间的全方位的文化交流活动的问题。而其外延，也不仅止于陆路、海路两个维度，学者们按丝路穿越的地理空间，也可以将其细化为绿洲之路、草原之路、南海之路、沙漠之路、吐蕃之路、西南丝路；按运载的货物又可分为：丝绸之路、玉器之路、黄金之路、瓷器之路、香料之路、青金石之路、茶马古道等。而牛津大学历史教授彼得·弗兰科潘（Peter Frankopan）在他的《丝绸之路》一书中就以"多线程"的方式，综合性地把丝绸之路梳理为具有不同功能和意义的 28 种路：从 4000 年前的"丝绸之路"到"宗教之路"乃至探讨到当代"美国的丝绸之路"和跨世纪的"悲剧之路"。有兴趣的同学可以去看看这位教授的论述。

我们这里略说说陆上丝路、海上丝路的开发和运行问题。

（1）陆上丝绸之路

说起陆上丝绸之路，必须说到张骞出使西域。公元前 138 年，任皇宫中的郎官的张骞奉汉武帝之命，到西域（今甘肃玉门关和阳关以西的地区）寻找大月氏等国建立联盟，以共同夹击匈奴。张骞初次出使西域历时长达 13 年时间，虽未达成这一战略任务，但却打通了西域和汉朝交往的通道，开辟了中国和欧洲、非洲大陆的通道。班超是另一位汉朝派遣出使西域的使者，他带领的使团 36 人，不仅到达了西域，而且远至波斯湾的大秦（古罗马）。从此，驼铃声声，商旅不绝，虔诚的僧侣不避风沙，军士的队伍也策马扬鞭。通过这条通道，中国不断地向西方输出丝绸、茶叶、瓷器、漆器和汉族地区的农耕、工艺技术；西方则通过此通道向中国传入胡麻、胡桃、胡椒、葡萄、番石榴等物产，箜篌、胡琴等乐器和歌舞、杂技等艺术形式。我们知道，带有"胡"字的植物和器具大都是来自异域的（因为"胡"是古代汉族对北方和西方少数民族的代称，后来泛指来自国外的东西）。

需要说明的是，丝绸之路虽起于长安，但并非只有一条线路，而是有很多分支。通常有南线、北线之分。北线通过玉门关，沿戈壁沙漠至哈密。南线从敦煌分出，穿越阳关，沿南部沙漠至和田，莎车，最后往北，与其他线路交会于喀什。

由于地缘的关系，河西走廊地区的各民族，最早感受到这种多类型文化的冲击与交融的空气，并悄然间发生生产生活方式和习惯的变化。2021 年 5 月 21 日在中国国家博物馆举办的"图画众生——河西画像砖上的古人生活"专题展览，首次大规模集萃展出了河西走廊地区 258 件（套）彩绘画像砖及相关文物。由于河西地处丝绸之路的廊道，是商贸往来、文化交流和民族融合最集中的区域，这些画像砖恰恰典型地表现了河西各族人民在中原汉地文化的影响下，实行农牧并重的生产生活的具体风貌。这些画砖中，他们进行各种农耕劳作诸如犁地、播种、耙地、耱地；有的进行蚕桑采摘、庖厨切肉、酿造酒醋、品茗清谈；男女人物所用服饰也大都有汉族式特征；有些画砖则表现游牧民族式的驰马引弓、鹰犬围猎、扬鞭放牧、牲畜觅食场面。可以说，这些画砖生动直观地再现了魏晋时期河西走廊和丝绸之路上农耕民族和游牧民族两种文化交流融合的社会生活百态。

在物质文化交流的同时，通过丝绸之路开展的精神文化交流也在不断地进行。有人说，丝绸之路上来往最重要的商品不是丝绸，而是宗教。作为世界三大宗教之一的佛教，就是通过丝绸之路上的使者、僧侣、香客和商人的共同努力，慢慢地向东传入中国的。沿着丝绸之路留存下来的佛教石窟，著名的如龟兹的克孜尔、吐鲁番、柏孜克里克、敦煌莫高窟、安西榆林窟、武威天梯山石窟、永靖炳灵寺、天水麦积山、大同云冈石窟、洛阳龙门石窟等，大多融会了东西方的艺术风格，是丝绸之路上中西文化交流的鲜明见证。

（2）海上丝绸之路

一般认为，海上丝绸之路形成于秦汉时期，发展于三国至隋朝时期，繁荣于唐宋时期，转变于明清时期，是已知的最为古老的海上航线。从广州、泉州、杭州等地出发的海上航船，东北可抵达日本、朝鲜等国，向南可抵达东南亚和南亚等地。海上丝绸之路因其主要是以南海为中心，故又称为南海丝绸之路。海上丝路是宋明时代中国与西方国家贸易交通和文化交往的最主要的通道。陆地丝绸之路衰落的原因，一方面是水上交通比陆地交通更加容易，更加安全可靠。另一方面，水上航线经过南亚诸国，这里充满商机，市场潜力很大。再者，陆地部落间的冲突不断，双边贸易并非总是畅通无阻。

我们华侨大学所在的古城泉州，就是一座因海而兴的丝路城市。泉州，古称温陵、刺桐，与杭州、扬州、广州同为我国海上丝路的重要节点城市。泉州港兴于唐、盛于宋，是宋元时代的"东方亚历山大港"。繁盛之时的泉州港，"有蕃舶之饶，杂货山积"（《宋史》），刺桐港贸易互通的国家增至近百个，"船到市井十洲人，涨海声中万国商"。运载了中国陶瓷、丝绸、日用品，装载国外香料、珠宝的中外商船也由刺桐港穿梭进出。向北可航行至高丽、日本等东北亚地区。反向则抵达东南亚、南亚、西亚和东非海岸。宋明时期，政府为了有效管理海运贸易事务，特将管理海运事务的福建市舶司设置在泉州①。外国

---

① 北宋元祐二年（1087），朝廷设立福建市舶司于泉州。直到明朝成化八年（1472），市舶司才迁往福州。福建市舶司在此的四百年间，管理着泉州诸港的海外贸易及有关事务，福建市舶司的税收占当时全国财政支出的1/5。

商客每年五六月乘南风而来中国，十二月份又乘北风而去。泉州九日山上留下的大量祈风摩崖石刻，记录的就是官员们对离开泉州的商队海上航行一帆风顺的祝福与祈愿。

发达的海洋贸易曾给泉州带来了经济富庶，也带来了丰富的海外文化信息，为泉州这座城市平添了一抹格外靓丽的色彩。泉州这座"世界宗教博物馆"见证了海上丝绸之路的兴衰沉浮。2021年7月25日，在中国福建福州举办的第44届世界遗产大会上，"泉州：宋元中国的世界海洋商贸中心"被批准作为文化遗产列入《世界遗产名录》。世界遗产委员会会议决议认为，"泉州：宋元中国的世界海洋商贸中心"反映了特定历史时期独特而杰出的港口城市空间结构，其所包含的二十二个遗产点，涵盖了社会结构、行政制度、交通、生产和商贸诸多文化元素，共同促成泉州在公元十到十四世纪逐渐崛起并蓬勃发展，成为东亚和东南亚贸易网络的海上枢纽。

可惜的是，明代嘉靖年后明政府实行海禁政策，民间"片板不许下海"，只准官方朝贡贸易的政策，世界最大的港口泉州刺桐港从此一落千丈。直到清末的长时期，海上丝路不复昨日繁华。但其中仍有小段和局部的对外通商的回光返照，如隆庆开海①，官民再合作，创造了明代漳州月港的闪烁余晖。厦门大学林仁川教授就评价说：月港是"大航海时代国际海上贸易的新型商港；美洲大航船贸易的重要起始港；大规模华商华侨闯荡世界的出发港；中国封建海关的诞生港"，对中国、世界社会经济都产生相当的影响。明代的漳州月港和厦门密切相连，厦门扼守着月港的出海口，因而月港的兴盛也推动了厦门港逐步崛起。厦门港是闽台对渡的唯一口岸，又是闽南人过台湾、下南洋的出发地和归来港口。月港—厦门港，以及20世纪中期崛起的台湾高雄港，都可以历史地看成中国传统海上丝路的近现代串联，也为闽南文化写入了丰厚的海洋文化的历史信息。

总之，丝绸之路是古代东西方商贸往来极其重要的联系通道。丝绸之路的历史漫长而久远。它传播了友谊，也饱受了战争铁蹄的践踏。近年来，联合国教科文组织发起了"丝绸之路研究计划"，把丝绸之路称作"对话之路"，这将为东西方的交流与合作起到积极的推动作用。了解丝绸之路上不同国家与地区之间的文明交流的历史，对于我们今天"一带一路"的共建及当下不同文明之间的交流与互鉴具有重要启示和促进的作用。

---

① 1567年，福建巡抚都御史涂泽民利用隆庆改元而政治布新之机，奏请在漳州月港开放海禁，准许中国商民出海贸易。月港乃至所在的漳州一跃成为明王朝试点改革的新区。

10.3　中外文化交流的推动机制

必须指出，中外文化交流的推动机制，历史地看，主要是得益于历代以来官方和民间的多主体的共同参与和建设性工作。比如丝绸之路，就是一条集民间力量推动、政府指导与监管作用于一体、丝路沿线各国的通力配合，即国际合作而发展起来的交流之路，而不是哪个人哪个方面单独可以支撑的大厦。

（1）从官方或制度性接触来看

对中外文化交流，政府采取什么国策至关重要。中国文化历来实行"天下一家、协和万邦"的开放、和平的态度，一直主张用"以文怀远"的方式来处理好中外关系。开辟对外交流的多渠道，既有经济收益，也能传播中华文化与大国声威，一般情况下，也具有部分军事的积极意义，所以历代王朝政府还是乐见中外之间搭建和谐友好、互通有无的交流网络的，也愿意为此采取积极的建制性工作以玉成其事。

比如陆上丝绸之路这条道路的开辟，就与西汉张骞和东汉班超这两位国家公使的外访工作有直接的联系；比如唐代万国来朝，长安成为国际化都市，西市居住着粟特人、波斯人等各国商人多达三万，外国人甚至可以参加国家公务员考试，任职朝廷等，这自然跟唐政府的开放、优容和鼓励的国策有关；郑和七下西洋这一欧洲航海时代之前世界上规模最大、船只和船员最多、时间最久的国家航海工程，也与明成祖朱棣的决策和支持密不可分。大食阿拉伯政府派出遣唐使多达四十多次，比日本国派遣唐使更频繁。丝路沿线国家为了维护丝路的畅通，一般都会建立口岸、设立驿站、建设贸易场馆、修筑道路和完善基础设施，或为之提供观察所、巡查站、治安亭等各种安全措施，并配套制定各种交流规则、化解纠纷矛盾等机制。如汉唐王朝都曾设置西域都护府，用于维护丝路交通安全；宋元明政府为协调管理对外海贸事务而设置市舶司。这些都是从政府层面，为中外文化更好的交流提供有力的保障体系。而相反的，若一国政府夜郎自大、盲目排外，则可能阻碍对外交流事业；或因地区冲突加剧、民族战争持续，或地区强权想独占商贸利益，都会根本破坏这种双方和多边的交流合作关系的开展。

可见为国政者是否有良好的国际视野和积极的配套政策的鼓励支持，地区和相关国家之间是否有齐心聚力、协调配合，都对文化交流的开展有着关键性的影响作用，不可不慎。

（2）非制度性接触即民间交往

比较于官方，非体制的民间交往则更具有多元、柔性的特殊地位。文化交流说到底还是要靠民间各阶层人士的积极参与。历史地看，国家间政治层面的友好或许有时而断，但只要民间的联系不断，保持接触，秉持彼此交流的信念，通过共同的坚持与努力，就能克服战乱带来的各种破坏、困难与不便，重现交流队伍的络绎不绝，实现文化交流之路的持续畅通与繁荣。这里的民间交流，大概可以分成这么几类。

一是各国的商队。"苍官影里三洲路，涨海声中万国商"，说的就是商人航海梯山、无远弗届。与安土重迁的农人不同，商人为了利润，哪怕天涯海角、刀山火海呢？这是商人精神的表现。可以说，商人和商贸是民间交往的主要力量。

二是各种宗教的僧侣和传教士。如7世纪，大唐高僧玄奘通过丝绸之路前往印度取经。他取道北线到达印度；又从南线返回。他对沿线各地的风俗、文化作了详细的记录，翻译佛教经典，带回600多册印度文献，对佛教在中国的传播做出了不可磨灭的贡献。明末清初的西方传教士是向西方翻译、传播中国经典最早的一批文化使者。据统计，1552—1773年间，传教士撰写的有关介绍和研究中国的著作共有422部，内容涉及中国历史、地理、宗教、哲学、政治制度以及中国古籍的翻译等方面。同时，正是由于传教士的活动，西方先进的天文、历法知识得以输入中国。传教士不仅更新了中国的天文仪器，而且还与中国的天文学家编译了一系列天文历法书籍，培养了一批应用西法的天文人才，初步改变了中国天文、历法方面的落后状况。必须指出，宗教作为文化的重要内容，教徒为其内在极大的宗教虔诚和信念所驱动，为求取真经或为普度众生，不避风霜雪雨万里航程，为"中学西渐"和"西学中渐"，为创造、繁荣人类文化和促进文明交流，是作出了不朽贡献的。

三是热衷探险的博物学家和旅行家。遥远的中国及其独特的魅力吸引了世界各地的旅行家们的向往，他们跋山涉水来到中国，仔细观察和记录了游历各地的见闻，反映了当时中国的城乡景物和风土人情，并介绍给他们各自的国家。马可·波罗（1254—1324）是一位意大利商人、探险家。他属于第一批经过丝绸之路来到中国的西方人。马可·波罗一行于1271年离开威尼斯，在中国度过了17年，1292年回到意大利。回到意大利后，他完成了著名的《马可·波罗游记》，记录了他对沿途各地的风俗、习惯、服装、语言、礼仪，到它们如何受东方帝国的影响等都作了详细的记录。这本书至今还是研究中国历史尤其是元代历史的权威文献之一。意大利商人兼学者雅各·德安科纳的《光明之城》。他在

1271年即南宋度宗咸淳七年到达泉州，他把泉州形容为"光明之城"，是欧洲比《马可波罗游记》更早访华游记。"阿拉伯的徐霞客"——伊本·白图泰（1304—1377）是著名的阿拉伯旅行家。他花了30年时间游历了非、亚、欧三大洲44个国家，其中不少位于丝绸之路沿线。他到过元朝中国南部的主要港口泉州，游览了广州、鄱阳、杭州等地，还对当时中国的穆斯林生活做了详细的考察。伊本·白图泰对元代中国社会的繁荣、进步和稳定非常赞赏。

四是学者和汉学家的学术研究。传教士们翻译和传播的中国文化经典在欧洲的流传，不仅增进了西方对中国文化的认识和了解，也直接推动了西方人研究中国文化的热潮。16世纪的欧洲因此产生了专门研究中国文化的汉学。欧洲学者们用他们的视角和方法对中国文化进行宽广领域的研究和介绍，尤其在翻译和研究儒家经典上发挥了积极的作用。18世纪对中国文化西传影响最大的是法籍传教士和学者在巴黎编辑出版的介绍和研究中国的三部大型丛书，即号称欧洲18世纪关于中国的三大名著：《耶稣会士书简集》《中华帝国全志》《北京传教士关于中国人的历史、学术、艺术和风俗习惯札记丛刊》（简称《中国丛刊》）。这三部丛书成为欧洲人了解和研究中国的必读书籍，特别是《中华帝国全志》在欧洲学术界影响之大，甚至有"西洋中国学之金字塔"的称号。

被誉为"欧洲的孔子"的伏尔泰（1694—1778）非常崇拜孔子，欣赏中华文化，甚至早晚在自己的书房膜拜孔子像，在《风俗论》中他甚至说："当你以哲学家的身份去了解这个世界时，你首先把目光朝向东方，东方是一切艺术的摇篮，东方给了西方一切。"又如"美国的孔子"爱默生（1803—1882）编辑《日晷》刊物在美国传播儒家的思想。他的弟子梭罗（1817—1862）在其名著《瓦尔登湖》里对儒家和孔子的思想反复称引、非常熟稔。

近现代以来当然涌现了更多的、从各领域研究中国文化问题的汉学家，我们也要记住并感谢他们的贡献。像德国汉学家李希霍芬（1833—1905）、法国汉学家沙畹（1865—1918）、英国汉学家李约瑟（1900—1995）、美国汉学家费正清（1907—1991）。又比如日本爱知大学的汉学家加加美光行教授和澳大利亚拉筹伯大学的汉学家梅约翰教授，这两位我所敬仰的前辈和师长一手创建了各自所在大学的中国学研究中心，取得了许多优秀的学术成果，培养了许多中国问题研究人才。我曾有幸分别于2004年和2017年到这两位先生的研究中心访学过一年，他们对中国文化的深入研究，对中国文明的深入洞察和了解，以及对中国人民的友好态度，都给我留下了难忘的记忆。

图 10-2　天下华人是一家

五是中国移民（华侨华人）的贡献。

中国在历朝历代都有外域移民，他们漂洋过海，遍布世界各地，而近代向东南亚移民尤其多。华侨华人是中外文化融合的历史践行者。他们把中国社会制度、语言文字和礼仪文化、成熟的耕作和养殖技术、中国传统民俗文化向海外扩布。多民族通婚和人口繁衍造就了包含中华文化要素的新土著文化（峇峇娘惹），并对侨居国文化的发展产生了不可低估的力量，对多元化的世界文化的形成作出了贡献。从渴望"落叶归根"到最终"落地生根"，他们逐步融合不同国家、不同地区之间的差异，不同阶层、城乡之间的差异，适应国际环境的变化冲击（如多元文化、种族冲突、经济全球化、中国的发展），并取得了各自人生和事业的新成就。海外 6700 万华人都是中华民族的骨肉同胞，他们是中华文化的传播者、中外交往的友好使者、"一带一路"建设的参与者、和平统一的促进者。我们永远情系于他们并祝愿他们生活和事业的成就与幸福。

几千年来的中外文化交流之路，总体上看是一条众多国家参与、政府指导监管、民间各阶层积极参与下发展起来的交流互鉴之路、开放合作之路、和平友好之路。用中国伟人毛泽东的话来说就是：人民，只有人民，才是创造历史的动力。

10.4　中外文化交流的理念启示

简单梳理了中外文化交流发展的若干问题，我们可以从中窥见到人类多元文化和文明交流发展的一般规律和重要经验，这就是：交融互鉴、美美与共。

第一，交流融合是人类文化发展的王道。

中国文化之所以具有悠久不绝的生命力，很大程度上得益于它自始至终保持了一种文化交流的自觉意识和开放的胸襟。五千年中大部分时间（战乱期除外），中国都没有关闭对外交流的大门，而是保持了迎进来、走出去，广交天下之友，接四海宾朋的热忱态度。中国人这种开放而不保守、交流而不封闭、融合而不蔽固的态度使得中国文化形成了"输入——吸收——输出"的模式。既善于在文化的交流中吸收广博的营养，可谓"人耕我获""坐集千古之智"，又能根据自身的民族特色和国情条件，对外来文化选择取舍，加工改制，发扬了高度的主体性和内核稳定性，表现了对自己的文化极高的自信心，才逐渐形成了多元一体、美美与共、气象万千、博大精深的中华文化。这给我们的启示是：无论到什么时候都必须拥有开放交流的胸怀，而不能封闭于夜郎自大盲目排外，只要我们能继续五千年来中外文化交流、融合、互鉴的有益经验，发扬开放合作、互利双赢的丝路精神，新时代的中国文化的长河就会生机勃勃，继续一往无前地奔涌。

第二，天下文明观而非文化中心主义，是文化交流融合中根本的方法论保障。

中国是一个"文明型国家"，中国文化是一种超国家的、典型的"天下文明"。所谓天下，既包括民族国家，又高于民族国家。天下文明，追求天下太平、天下大同，提倡人类是个命运共同体，主张创造一个开放、包容、流动、变通和发展的人类生活世界。天下文明观与文化的中心主义不同，它主张任何一种类型的文明都有其历史形态和社会价值，而没有绝对唯一的价值标准，更没有高低贵贱之分。正如习近平主席2014年3月27日在联合国教科文组织总部演讲时提到："各种人类文明都各有千秋，没有高低、优劣之分。要了解各种文明的真谛，必须秉持平等、谦虚的态度。傲慢和偏见是文明交流互鉴的最大障碍……只要秉持包容精神，就不存在什么'文明冲突'，就可以实现文明和谐。"

从方法论上看，文化的"中心主义"和"一元主义"就是文明冲突的毒根，都可能导致一种文化对另外一种文化的霸权和践踏。与此不同，天下文明观本质上是文化的多元主义和文明和谐论，它追求保持富有弹性的多元文化、多元宗教和多元治理体制的和谐一体，实现"一个世界，不同文明""一种文明，不同制度""一种制度，不同模式"以及"一个国家，不同文化"。只有在这个基础上，才能谈得上平等、和谐、深入的文明交融互鉴，才能推动人类文化的整体进步和发展。

第三，和平互惠、创新发展，人类文化才能日新又新、不断进步。

和平与发展是相辅相成的，没有和平就无法发展。中国历朝历代坚持实行"以和为贵""万国咸宁"的邦交原则，使得中国与周边乃至远方国家能够长期保持亲仁善邻的邦交关系。没有和平则谈不上交流合作，谋利益求发展，实现各方互利共赢，实现共同繁荣。比如安史之乱就中断了陆上丝路，近代的殖民战争则让各个非欧国家陷入灾难深渊，都是历史的教训。在新的时代，要坚持共商、共建、共享原则，各国共同努力，建构共同、综合、合作、可持续的国际安全观。

世界上从来不存在什么绝对完美的文化，只有永远追求"人文化成、文明以止"的初心。各民族的文明体系要自觉重塑、不断超越，文明交流方式与体制路径，也要不断更新、与时俱进，才能永葆昌盛生生不息。21世纪是日新月异的时代，不日新者必日退。各个民族只有正确看清自己的文化体系的内外特征及其优点与缺点，优秀的传统文化，继续发扬；糟粕的亚文化，果断扬弃。改革图强、日新又新，才能在文明竞争和文明发展的大潮流中勇立潮头。当然，我们相信，中华文化的"天下文明""四海一家""持中守正""和而不同""礼尚往来""义重于利""平等共治""顾全大局"等优秀传统文化的养素，都将在新时代中外文明的交流交往中发挥积极作用。

文明的交流融合是当代中国的最强音！这是一个拥有5000年历史的文明国度对发展文明的经验之谈，也是一个最大的发展中国家的切实行动。正如习近平主席所指出的："世界已经成为你中有我、我中有你的地球村，各国经济社会发展日益相互联系、相互影响，推进互联互通、加快融合发展成为促进共同繁荣发展的必然选择。"有鉴于此，中国倡议的"一带一路"建设，旨在传承丝绸之路精神。自2013年建设启动以来，逐步取得积极进展。各方努力推进政策沟通、设施联通、贸易畅通、资金融通、民心相通，启动了大批务实合作、造福民众的项目，构建起全方位、复合型的互联互通伙伴关系，开创了共商共建共享的合作局面，也获得了世界上大多数国家的关注和好评，许多政要、学者等各方有识之士都给予了高度评价与积极肯定。

以文明交流超越文明隔阂，以文明互鉴超越文明冲突，以文明共存超越文明优越，这是中国智慧的结果，也是中国贡献全球治理观的实践经验。作为古代丝绸之路的倡导者和开创者，在新时代文明交流互鉴的进程中，中国也将继续以大国的担当和责任意识，秉持天下一家的文明观，扮演积极的建设者角色。当然，"一带一路"背景下，推动中华文化海外传播既需要宏观层面的深层思考，还需要实践和操作层面的合理运作和科学安排。我们将更多地依靠文化软实力，创新传播方式途径，讲好中国故事，传播好中国声音，展示真实、立体、全面的中国，着力打造人心相通、人情相亲、和谐亲睦的国际环境、积极提升中华文化国际影响力。

10.5　"会通中外"的华侨大学正携梦前行

我们华侨大学是国内唯一用"华侨"命名的大学，肩负着独特的使命。这就是对外传播中华文化，促进文明交流互鉴，为实现中华民族伟大复兴，构建人类命运共同体而凝聚人心和力量。自建校以来，华侨大学始终坚持"面向海外、面向港澳台"的办学方针，秉承"为侨服务，传播中华文化"的办学宗旨，贯彻"会通中外、并育德才"的办学理念。已为海内外培养了各类优秀人才20余万名，其中近6万名校友分布在海外，主要集中在港澳台及海上丝绸之路沿线国家和地区，成为促进中外交流合作的友好使者。

图 10-3　多元多彩的华大校园风情

华侨大学现有全日制在校学生3万余人，其中有来自50多个国家和地区的华侨华人。华侨大学有港澳台和外国学生5000余人，是全国拥有境外学生最多的大学之一。不同语言、不同文化背景的学生汇集在华侨大学这一方沃土，充满异域风情的文化节、泼水节、水灯节、美食节等世界各地的文化活动如绚丽的鲜花常年盛放，形成了"一元主导、多元融合、和而不同"的特色校园文化，每个国家和地区的学生都能在华园里找到家的温暖。学校连续两年获全国高校校园文化建设优秀成果一等奖。

华侨大学拥有泉州、厦门两个校区。泉州是中国历史文化名城，也是古代海上丝绸之路的起点，21世纪海上丝绸之路战略支点和先行区。厦门是最早实行对外开放政策的四个经济特区之一和21世纪海上丝绸之路的战略支点城市。

传承海纳百川、互通共享的"海丝精神"，学校积极开展国际交流合作，国际化特色鲜明，已与五大洲50多个国家和地区的200多所高校签署了校际合作协议。华侨大学是中国政府奖学金来华留学招生院校，在全球设立了84个办事或招生机构，设有全英语授课的国际学院。作为国家华文教育基地，国家"支持周边国家汉语教育重点院校"，华侨大学创办了"一带一路"沿线国家政府官员中文学习班和"安哥拉政府科技人才班"等一系列华文教育品牌项目。一年一度的由华侨大学与泰国国家研究院、泰中文化经济协会联合主办的"中泰战略研讨会"成为中泰两国专家学者的学术盛事，引人瞩目。华侨大学大力推广华文教育，为全球55个国家570多所华校培养师资、编写教材、开展中华传统文化体验，助力国家华文教育标准化、正规化、专业化建设。

服务于国家"一带一路"建设是华侨大学新时代的使命担当。作为华侨华人研究和"一带一路"研究的重要智库，学校通过与境外研究机构合作，开展境外驻地调查研究，为国家决策提供咨询报告和智力支持。在2018年，国家发改委发布的"一带一路"国内高校智库影响力排名中列第二位。

当中国梦铺陈出中华的未来，站在新的起点，华侨大学不忘初心、牢记使命，坚持"侨校+名校"的发展战略，以"双一流"建设为契机，坚定不移地走内涵发展之路、特色兴校之路、人才强校之路，全面提升人才培养质量和整体办学水平。广泛凝聚侨心、侨力、侨智，加快建设特色鲜明、海内外著名的高水平大学。

包括我们为境外生讲述多年的本门《中国文化概论》课程，其创设目的，也与华侨大学"为侨服务，传播中华文化"的办学方针相一致。我们很注意创新教学思路、改革实践模式，以不断加强港澳台侨及外国留学生对中华优秀传统文化的学习热忱与心理认同。应该说，已经产生了积极的育人效果。我们还将继续努力工作，以提高我们的工作水平，以更好地服务于广大海外学子。我们只有一个心愿：愿来华大、来中国的各国（各地区）青年才俊能了解传统中国，认识当代中国，热爱中国文化，热爱中国人民，正如华侨大学校长吴剑平先生在华侨大学2022届毕业典礼上对留学生们所寄望的那样：

希望同学们做中华文化的坚定信仰者、中华文化的模范实践者、中华文化的积极发展者！……将来积极推动中外文化交流和友好合作，为你们的国家经济社会发展、为建设人类命运共同体发出一份光和热。

本书到此就全部结束了，谢谢大家。

The Tenth Chapter:

Shared Prosperity of Different Cultures
—Mutural Learning between Chinese and Foreign Cultures

"Diversity spurs interaction among civilizations, which in turn promotes mutual learning and further development. " The history of Chinese civilization is a long history of its development through mutual learning and exchanges with foreign civilizations. For 5000 years, China has not only interacted with its neighbors in East and South Asia, which have been backing each other by mountains and rivers, but also with nomadic pastoral cultures in Central Asia, Arabian cultures in Persia, Indian cultures in South Asia, and European cultures, which have gradually come into contact with each other and started various exchanges. Chinese traditional culture has also made important contributions to the development and progress of human civilization in the process of blending and mutual learning with different civilizations.

10. 1 Retrospect on the History of Sino-foreign Cultural Exchanges

First, from the perspective of cultural input.

Nang (Uyghur flatbread) originally from the west has become Shaobing (Chinese Sesame Flatbread). The coral tree (Erythrina variegata) which was originally from Java gave the City of Quanzhou in the Southern Tang Dynasty both a beautiful landscape and an alias (Zayton 刺桐) named after the tree. In Qing Dynasty, the sweet potato, originally from Philippine, was planted in the whole China to fight against famine, and let Chinese population in the rein of Daoguang Emperor directly multiply to 300 million. Pigment made from Lapis Lazuli from Afghanistan which adorned the newly painted Dunhuang murals in the Wei and Jin Dynasties, has remained intact for millennia, adding to the mystery of the blue caves. Method of refining sugar of Tianzhu (the ancient Chinese name for India) was improved by Chinese people in the Tang Dynasty as the "icing method" in which the sugar crystal produced were white and delicate. Therefore, the Indians at that time used Chini to refer to China. The use of the Middle Eastern mineral "Sumaliqing" (cobalt oxide) made Chinese Blue and White Porcelain in Ming and Qing Dynasties fresher and more elegant. Musical instruments like Persian Konghou, western Huqin, and acrobatic performing arts such as contortion acts, sword playing and fire spitting were popular among the Chinese, which were painted on the portrait masonry of Han tombs excavated in places like Shandong and Sichuan. Master Xuanzang spent 19 years bringing not only Buddhism east, but advanced observation and understanding of the geography and customs of Western Regions and South Asia with *Great Tang Records on the Western Regions*. Religions from Central Asia such as Zoroastrianism, Manichaeism, Nestorianism, and Islamism spread to the Tang Dynasty, setting off the first climax of foreign religions to China. Different from the missionaries of the Tang Dynasty, those of the late Ming and Qing Dynasties like Matteo Ricci and Nan Huairen who were in China for decades, spread not only Christian doctrine, but also a new perspective of map and geographic space, astronomical calendars and time thinking of Geometry and logic.

Second, from the perspective of cultural output.

(1) In the east, Japan and Korean Peninsular in the East Asian cultural circle are connected to China geographically. The ancient City of Kyoto in Japan Chinese characters contained in *Man'yōshū*, the Sungkyunkwan in Seoul of Korea, the imperial college of Kaesong in the Koryo Dynasty all make you remind of China.

(2) In the south, people in Vietnam still have customs of worshiping Emperor Yandi, and celebrating the Chinese Dragon Boat Festival as well as Mid-Autumn Festival. The Imperial Examination System has gone through about 900 years in Vietnam, and it is almost the same as that of China. Burmese used "Baobo" which literally means "blood brother", or "Ruimiao", which means "relative", to refer to the Chinese people. The Thais not only keep in mind the voyage of Zheng He in which he passed through Siam, but also enshrine him in the local "Wat Phanan Choeng" to be worshiped by generations. The Dayaks in the Philippines celebrate New Year every year. They worship statues of gods, put up couplets, wear new clothes and greet each other. All these are full of Chinese style. People of Bali Island in Indonesia since the early Ming Dynasty has introduced scallion and lychee from China. In addition, on the

island to this day, there is a folk dance that resembles the Chinese lion dance in dressing and posture.

(3) In the west, China got its English name. Why "China"? Europeans appreciate the porcelain made in China. Figures of three goddesses of the Parthenon in Athens, Greece and on the Druidess of Bacchus in the Naples Museum in Italy, are dressed in costumes made of silk, soft, light and thin. It indicated that at least in the fifth century, European aristocrats were in favor of silk from China. Chinese silk which was trafficked to Persia was processed into the Persian silk carpet with a rich national characteristics. That is, the Persian Brocade. Soldiers in the Tang Dynasty visiting Samarkand shared the paper-making skills of their homeland. After that, the history of parchment used by Europeans came to an end. The ancient fleet of ships from Quanzhou in the Song Dynasty Carrie Chinese tea and the spices such as cinnamon, Nardostachydis Radix Et Rhizoma, Zanthoxylum, Syringa, curry to Europe. Wherever the Mongol army facing west went, they incidentally introduced traditional Chinese medicine, cartographic grid and the art of painting to Western Asia and Europe. Ancient piston wooden bellows of ancient China inspired Watt's steam engine. The yin-yang symbol of *The Book of Changes* gave Leibniz an inspiration of the binary number. Chinese Cuju is recognized as the source of contemporary soccer. While the Chinese compasses, printing and gunpowder are considered to lead the Europe to the modern bourgeois era.

The list goes on and on. It is of course impossible for us to talk about everything. We recommend you to read the *Compendium of Historical Documents on Sino-foreign Communications*. This is a very substantial and famous book which is highly thought of by researchers of the history of Sino-foreign communication. It is edited by Mr. Zhang Xinglang. From 42 famous historical books in Chinese and foreign languages, he found and recorded a large amount of information about history of Sino-foreign relations, classified them by regions and countries, arranged them in chronological order, and examined some of the names and historical facts in detail. The six volumes, divided int eight parts, describe in turn the communication history between ancient China and Europe, Africa, Arabia, Armenia, Judea, Islam, Central Asia, and the Indian Peninsula, with appendices in each chapter containing the author's topical research papers and testimonial notes.

10. 2　The Silk Road and Means of
Sino-foreign Cultural Exchanges

When it comes to the exchanges and mutual learning of Chinese culture and foreign cultures, the most talked about is the ancient "Belt and Road", namely the Silk Road Economic Belt and the 21st Century Maritime Silk Road. However, the notion of Silk Road cannot be found in Chinese ancient books. It was proposed by the German geographer Ferdinand von Richthofen in 1877 and the French sinologist Émmanuel-Édouard Chavannes in 1913 in their respective works. The study of Silk Road culture is not only a matter of studying the ancient silk trade and changes of the route, but essentially a matter of trying to analyze the whole range of cultural communication activities between the East and West world in ancient times. And its outreach does not limit to just land and sea routes. According to the geographical space that the Silk Road traversed, scholars can classify it into the Oasis Road, the Grassland Road, the South Sea Road, the Desert Road, Tibetan Road and Southwest Silk Road. According to the goods carried, the Silk Road can be divided into the Jade Road, the Gold Road, the Silk Road, the Porcelain Road, the Lapis Lazuli Road, and the Tea Horse Road. Peter Frankopan, the Professor of Global History at Oxford University, in his book *The Silk Roads* takes a "multi-threaded process" and comprehensively classifies the Silk Road into 28 roads with different functions and meanings: from "the Silk Road" and "the Road of Faiths" of 4000 years ago to the contemporary "the American Silk Road" and the cross-century "the Road to Tragedy".

Now let's discuss the development and operation of the Silk Road and the Maritime Silk Road.

(1) In Terms of the Silk Road

In terms of the Silk Road, we must mention Zhang Qian's expedition to the west. In 138 BCE, Zhang Qian, an imperial envoy, was dispatched on a mission by Emperor Han Wudi to seek a military alliance with peoples in the west of China such as the Yuezhi tribe to fight against the northern tribes. Zhang Qian's first mission to the west lasted 13 years. Although he failed to accomplish this strategic task, he opened up a channel of communication between people of the West Regions and Han and a channel for China to reach Europe and Africa. Ban Chao and his assistant Gan Ying are other two diplomats sent to the Western Regions by the Han government. They led a diplomatic mission of 36 people and arrived at the Western Regions and Daqin (ancient Rome) on the Persian Gulf. From then on, camels bell echoed along the silk road; endless merchants came and went; pious monks were not afraid of winds and sands; and soldiers of the army rode their horses with whips. Through this channel, China continued to export silk, tea, porcelain, lacquer ware, farming technology and crafts to the west. While the West introduced to China such products as sesame, walnut, grapes, guava and art forms such as konghou, huqin, song and dance, and acrobatics through this channel. These things in China begin with the word "胡", which refers to something coming from the north and the west minority groups. Later on, it is widely used to represent something brought in from abroad.

Although the route started from the capital in Chang'an, there are many branches. The northern route then passed through Yumen Guan (Jade Gate Pass) and crossed the neck of the Gobi desert to Hami. The southern route branched off at Dunhuang, passing through the Yang Guan and skirting the southern edges of the desert, via Miran, Hetian and Shache, finally turning north again to meet the other route at Kashgar.

Because of the geographical location, people in the Hexi Corridor were the first to feel the impact of this multi-type culture. And they gradually changed their ways of production, lifestyle and habits accordingly. Hosted by the National Museum of China, "Picturing all Beings: Life of the Ancients on the Brick Reliefs from Hexi" which was an exhibition inaugurated on May 21, 2021, is the first large-scale centralized display of 258 pieces of the finest painted brick reliefs and related cultural relics from the Hexi Corridor region. Since Hexi was located on the Silk Road, it was the most concentrated area for trade, cultural exchanges and ethnic integration. These bricks typically reflect that people of Hexi who were under the influence of the Han culture, practiced both agriculture and husbandry. From these bricks, we can see them performing various farming tasks such as plowing, sowing and harrowing; see them picking mulberry, cutting meat in the kitchen, brewing wine and vinegar, and sipping tea and chatting; see the clothing and vehicles used by males and females featuring Han Chinese style. Some of the bricks demonstrate nomadic scenes of hunting with hawks and dogs, herding with whips and livestock foraging. It can be said that these bricks are a vivid and intuitive reproduction of the cultural exchanges and integration of farming and nomadic peoples along the Hexi Corridor and the Silk Road during the Wei and Jin Dynasties.

With the exchange of material culture, the diffusion of spiritual culture continued along the Sik Road. In a way, the most significant commodity carried along this route was not silk, but religion. One of the world's three major religions, Buddhism, entered China as early as the final years of the Western Han Dynasty through the joint efforts of messengers, missionaries, pilgrims, and merchants on the silk road. Along the Silk Road lie many Buddhist grottos such as the Mogao Caves in Dunhuang county, the Anxi Yulin Caves, Cloud Ridge in the Datong prefecture, and Luoyang's Longmen, etc. These sites reveal an integration of eastern and western art styles, the Silk Road being a witness to the cultural exchange. With its long history, the Silk Road has helped foster friendly relations, but the iron hoof of warfare has also trampled it.

(2) In Terms of the Maritime Silk Road

Generally, we believe that the Maritime Silk Road was formed in the Qin and Han Dynasties, developed from the Three Kingdoms Period to the Sui Dynasty, boomed in the Tang and Song Dynasties, and transformed in the Ming and Qing Dynasties. It is the oldest maritime route. The Maritime Silk Road was mainly centered on the South China Sea, so it was also known as the South China Sea Silk Route. The Maritime Silk Road became one of the most important channels of transportation, trade and cultural exchanges between China and the West in the Song, Yuan Dynasties. The decline of the Silk Road in the Tang and Song Dynasties owes much to the development of the silk route by sea. It was becoming rather easier and safer to transport goods by water rather than overland. Ships had become stronger and more reliable, and the route passed promising new markets in Southern Asia.

The ancient City of Quanzhou, where Huaqiao University is located, is a city on the Silk Road, which has flourished because of the sea. Quanzhou, with the ancient name as Wenling or Zayton. Together with Hangzhou, Yangzhou and Guangzhou is an important city of China's Maritime Silk Road. The port of Quanzhou flourished in Tang and Song Dynasties, and was described to be "the Alexandria of the East" in the Song and Yuan Dynasties. During the prosperous period, the number of countries that trade with Citong port has increased to nearly 100: "When ships arrive, the city is embraced with foreign merchants." Those merchants carried Chinese ceramics, silk and daily necessities abroad. Chinese and foreign merchant ships which carried foreign spices and jewelry also shuttled in and out from the port of Citong. To the north, ships can be sailed to Koryo, Japan and other Northeast Asian regions. To the south, ships went to Southeast Asia, South Asia, West Asia and even the coast of East Africa during the Song, Yuan and Ming Dynasties, in order to effectively manage maritime trade affairs, the government specially established Bureau for Foreign Shipping in Quanzhou.

Foreign merchants came to China from the north in May and June and left in December every year. Wind-Praying Inscriptions left in the Jiuri Mountain in the City of Quanzhou record the ritual ceremonies held by local officials to pray for favorable winds to aid voyages. As shown in the figure is the inscription of the Prayer for Lucky Wind in Jiuri Mountain. This stone inscription recorded the two prayers for lucky wind in April (summer) and October (winter) in the reign of the 15th year of Xiaozong Chunxi in the Southern Song Dynasty. Among the ten stone inscriptions, this is the only once recording the two prayers for lucky wind both in summer and winter. The Arabian merchants from Central Asia and the Middle East lived here, and their descendants gradually evolved into the Hui community in Quanzhou today.

10-4　Wind-Praying Inscriptions in the Jiuri Mountain

The developed Marine trade brought economic affluence to Quanzhou, as well as colorful foreign culture for which Quanzhou was dubbed "a museum of the world's religions". The diverse culture, connection to the overseas as well as open and inclusive attitudes have added the charm of the City of Quanzhou. It witnessed the rise and fall of the Maritime Silk Road. As per a decision passed by the UNESCO World Heritage Committee, Quanzhou: Emporium of the World in Song-Yuan China showcases a unique, spectacular spatial structure of the port city established during a specific historical period. The 22 historical sites there encompasses social structure, administrative system, traffic, production, business and other cultural elements. These combined contributed to, from the 10th to 14th centuries, the rise and prosperity of Quanzhou, and later made the city a maritime hub for the East and Southeast Asia trade network.

After the Jiajing year of the Ming Dynasty, the state implemented the policy of sea ban and only allowed official tribute trade. The world's largest port: Citong port in Quanzhou has plummeted since then. Until the late Qing Dynasty, the maritime silk road was no longer prosperous. However, there are still some reflections on foreign trade. For example, during the Longqing period, the government of the Ming Dynasty reopened small-scale marine trade, and the government and the people cooperated again, which created the short-term glory of Yue port in Zhangzhou. Xiamen University Professor Lin inchuan commented that Yue port is "a new commercial port for international maritime trade in the era of great navigation; an important starting port for large-scale ship trade in the Americas; a departure port for large-scale Chinese businessmen and overseas Chinese to roam the world; and a birth port for China's feudal customs", which has a great impact on China and the world's social economy.

In the Ming Dynasty, Yue port in Zhangzhou was closely connected with Xiamen, and Xiamen held the outlet of Yue port. Therefore, the prosperity of Yue port also promoted the gradual rise of Xiamen port. Xiamen port is the only port between Fujian and Taiwan. It is also the starting point and return port for people from southern Fujian to cross Taiwan and go to Southeast Asia. Yue port, Xiamen port, and Taiwan's Kaohsiung port, which rose in the middle of the 20th century, can all be linked in history to form a modern and contemporary connection of China's traditional maritime Silk Road, and write rich historical information of marine culture for Southern Fujian culture.

In short, the Silk Road was an extremely important channel for business exchanges between the East and the West in ancient times. With its long history, the Silk Road has helped foster friendly relations, but the iron hoof of warfare has also trampled it. For the past few years, UNESCO has initiated a Silk Road research project, claiming the Silk Road is the path to dialogue. This project aims to positively promote the exchange and cooperation between the East and West. Understanding the history of cultural exchanges and mutual learning between different countries and regions on the Silk Road has a positive reference value for our joint construction of the "Belt and Road Initiative" today and the exchanges and mutual learning between different civilizations.

10.3   Driving Forces of Sino-foreign Cultural Exchanges

It must be pointed out that the promotion of cultural exchanges between China and foreign countries, historically, is mainly due to the joint participation of the government and people.

Firstly, from the perspective of official or institutional contacts.

For cultural exchanges between China and foreign countries, what national policy the government adopts is of great importance. The Chinese people have always adopted an open and peaceful attitude of "we are in the same world and we live together peacefully". And they have advocated to use culture to attract people in the distance. Moreover, opening up diversified channels of communication will not only bring economic benefits, but also spread Chinese culture and the prestige of the great powers. As is often the case, there are also part of the military's positive significance. Therefore, the successive dynasties are still happy to see the establishment of a harmonious and friendly exchange network between China and foreign countries, and they are also willing to take active institutional work for this, and make things successful. For example, the creation of the Silk Road is directly linked to the foreign visits of two state ministers, Zhang Qian and Ban Chao in the Western and Eastern Han Dynasty respectively. In addition, many affiliated countries paid tribute to China during the Tang Dynasty, and the City of Chang'an became an international city. There were almost 30000 merchants from various countries, such as the Sogdians and Persians, living in the Xishi District. Foreigners were even allowed to take the Imperial examinations, and serve in the imperial court after passing the exam. Of course, this was closely related to the state policy of openness, inclusiveness and encouragement in the Tang Dynasty. Before the Age of Great Voyage, Zheng He's voyages to the west seas boasted the world's largest scale with the largest number of ships and crews and the longest duration. It's closely related to the decisions and support of Zhu Di, the emperor of Ming Dynasty. Arabia sent envoys to China more than 40 times, even more frequently than Japan.

To maintain the smooth flow of the Silk Road, most countries along the Silk Road established commercial ports, set up courier stations, built trading venues, roads and improved infrastructure or provided various security measures such as observations posts, patrol stations, security booths, etc., and made various rules for trading, dispute resolution and other mechanisms. Emperors of Han and Tang Dynasties set up the protectorate of the Western Regions for maintaining the traffic safety of the Silk Road. Governments of the Song, Yuan and Ming Dynasties set up the Maritime Trade Bureau for coordinating the management of foreign maritime trade affairs. These can be seen as the powerful guarantee system of governments for better cultural exchanges between China and foreign countries. On the contrary, if a country is arrogant and sticks to blind exclusion, its cause of foreign exchanges may be hindered. Because the intensification of regional conflicts and wars, or the desire of regional powers to monopolize the benefits of trade and commerce, will fundamentally destroy the development of such bilateral and multilateral exchanges and cooperation. So whether the rulers of a country have a good international vision, whether there are active policies to encourage and support the cultural exchanges, and whether there is unity of effort and coordination, between the regions and countries, all play a key influence on the development of cultural exchanges.

Secondly, from the perspective of non-official contacts, or people-to-people exchanges.

Compared with the official contacts, they have more pluralistic and flexible place and functions. Cultural exchanges anyway depend on the active participation of people from all walks of life.

(1) The Merchants from Foreign Countries

"When ships arrive, the city is embraced with foreign merchants. " This poem refers to merchants' arduous journey. Unlike the peasants who are attached to their native land, merchants can pursue profits no matter how far they would rove and no matter what difficulties they would meet. This is the merchants' spirit. Therefore, merchants are the main forces for people-to-people exchanges.

(2) Monks, Priests and Missionaries from Various Religions

For example, In the 7th century, the Chinese traveller Xuan Zang crossed the region on his way to obtain Buddhist scriptures from India. He followed the northern branch on his outward journey, and the southern route on his return; he carefully recorded the cultures and styles of Buddhism along the way and brought back 600 scriptures from India. The western missionaries in the late Ming and early Qing Dynasties like Matteo Ricci, Adam Schall and Ferdinand Verbiest, stayed in China for decades and made a lot of contributions with perseverance. According to statistics, westerners wrote, between 1552 and 1773, 422 books about China, dealing with its history, geography, religion, philosophy and political system. Apart from that, they also put many Chinese classics into foreign languages. At the same time, it was precisely because of the missionary activities that western advanced astronomy and calendar knowledge was imported into China. This has initially changed China's backward situation in astronomy and calendar. We should notice that religion is an important element of culture, and religious people who were driven by great religious devotion and faith, made a great contribution to the introduction of Western civilization to China and the introduction of Chinese civilization to the West.

(3) The Avid Explorers and Travelers

The remote China and its unique charm attracted travelers from all over the world. They made an arduous journey to China, observed and recorded their travels here. Their records showed the urban and rural scenes and customs of China at that time, and helped to introduced China to their own countries and peoples.

① Marco Polo (1254—1324) was an Italian trader and explorer who gained fame for his worldwide travels. Polo was one of the first Westerners to travel the Silk Road to China (which he called Cathay). They spent 17 years in China and left China in late 1290 or early 1291 and were back in Venice in 1292. After returning to Europe, he wrote *The Travels of Marco Polo*, describing his traveling experiences. In his book, Marco Polo recorded in detail what he saw in the Western Region and Persia, from custom and habit, dressing, languages, etiquette, character and script to how they were influenced by the eastern empire. The book had been an authoritative book for those who studied the history of China, especially the history of Yuan Dynasty. ② Jacob D'Ancona, the Italian merchant and scholar, wrote the book *The City of Light* which is also an important book. He arrived in the City of Quanzhou in 1271, and described Quanzhou as "the City of light" for the first time. His book was the travel notes of China even earlier than *The Travels of Marco Polo*. ③ Ibn Battuta was a famous Arab traveler, also known as the Arabian Xu Xiake (a well-known Chinese traveler). He spent 30 years traveling to Africa, Asia and Europe, 44 countries in total. Many of these countries were located along the Silk Road. He also visited some major port cities in South China in the Yuan Dynasty, including the City of Quanzhou. He started his travel in China from Quanzhou to Guangzhou, Boyang, Hangzhou and other places. Ibn Battuta greatly appreciated the prosperity, progress and stability of Chinese society during the Yuan Dynasty. He also made a detailed observation of the Muslim life in China at that time.

(4) The Research of Scholars and Sinologists

The circulation of Chinese Classics translated by missionaries in Europe not only enhanced westerners' awareness and understanding of traditional Chinese culture, but also ushered in a great upsurge in the study of Chinese culture. The 16th century saw the emergence of Sinology in Europe specializing in the study of Chinese culture. European scholars, based on their perspectives and methods, studied and introduced a broad range of Chinese culture. They took an active role in the translation and research of Confucian classics in particular. The 3 masterpieces of the 18th century included *Letters from Christian Missionaries*, *The Chinese Empire and China Series* or *Chinese History*, *Learning*, *Art*, *and Customs in the Eyes of Western Missionaries in Beijing*. These series of books became a must for Europeans who wanted to get a general idea or make a close study of China. It was otherwise known as the Pyramid of Chinese Studies in the West.

Voltaire (1694—1778), known as "Confucius of France", worshipped Confucius very much and appreciated Chinese culture. In "on custom", he even said: when you understand the world as a philosopher, you should first look to the East. The East is the cradle of all art, and the East gives everything to the West. In America, the journal *Dial* edited by "American Confucius" Ralph Waldo Emerson disseminated Confucianism in the United States. His student Thoreau kept quoting Confucianism and Confucius' ideas in his famous book *Walden*.

Since modern times, more and more Sinologists studied Chinese culture from more specific fields. We should remember and appreciate their contributions. Such Sinologists include Ferdinand von Richthofen from Germany, Emmanuel Édouard Chavannes from France, Joseph Needham from Britain and John King Fairbank from the United States. Japanese Sinologist Pro. Kagami Mitsuyuki from Aichi University and Autrailn Sinologist Pro. Makeham from La Trobe University established the Institute of Chinese Studies in their universities respectively, achieved many excellent academic achievements, and cultivated many foreign experts on China. I once had an opportunity to visit the two professors' research centers in 2004 and 2017 respectively, and studied there for a year. Their in-depth study of the Chinese culture, their insight and understanding of the Chinese civilization, and friendly attitude to the Chinese people. have left me with unforgettable memories.

(5) The Contribution of Chinese Emigrants and Chinatown

There were emigrants throughout the Chinese history. Emigrants traveled a long way across the sea to settle down in foreign countries, they are all over the world, especially in Southeast Asia. Overseas Chinese are the practitioners of cultural integration. They disseminated and introduced Chinese social systems, language and characters, rites, mature farming and breeding techniques, and traditional Chinese customs to people of foreign countries. Multi-ethnic intermarriage and population reproduction inspired a new local culture with elements of Chinese culture. It exerted significant impact on the cultural development of the countries where they lived in.

From longing for "falling leaves and returning to their roots" to finally "taking root", they have gradually integrated the differences between different countries and regions, between different classes and between urban and rural areas, adapted to the changes and shocks of the international environment (such as multiculturalism, ethnic conflicts, economic globalization and China's Development), and made new achievements in their lives and careers. The 67 million overseas Chinese are all compatriots of the Chinese nation. They are Chinese culture disseminator, envoy of friendship between China and other countries, promoter of One Bell One Road, and supporter of peaceful reunification. We will always care about them and wish them success and happiness in their lives and careers.

The way of Cultural exchanges between China and foreign countries for thousands of years, generally speaking, is a way of exchanges and mutual learning where many countries join and guide to supervise, people from all walks of life actively participate and make joint effort to develop; it's a way for openness and cooperation, peace and friendship. In the words of the Chinese people: Only people of all nations together are the driving force of history. (Chairman Mao)

10. 4　Enlightenment from Sino-foreign Cultural Exchanges

After reviewing some issues in the development of cultural exchanges between China and foreign countries, we can get a glimpse of the general rules and important experiences about the development of exchanges between different human cultures and civilizations.

First, exchanges and integration are key to human cultural development.

Why the Chinese culture features long-lasting vitality is largely benefiting from the consciousness and openness in cultural communication that China has maintained all the time. For most of the 5000 years, except for the period of war China didn't close the door to foreign exchanges. Instead, China has maintained an enthusiastic attitude of bringing in, going out, making and greeting friends from all over the world. The attitude of the Chinese people, namely openness, communication, and integration rather than conservation, closure and segregation, has led to the formation of the "Input-Absorption-Output" model of Chinese culture. Thus, it is adept at benefiting from exchanges and mutual learning, which can be described as "learning widely from others' strong points". And according to their own national characteristics, the Chinese people can take the essence of foreign cultures, and process them to suit their own culture. These behaviors reflect a high degree of subjectivity, core stability and self-confidence in their own culture, gradually forming a pluralistic integration of Chinese culture which is beautiful, diverse and profound. This gives us the inspiration that we must have an open mind to exchanges at all times instead of being confined to arrogance and blind exclusion.

Second, the concept of world civilization rather than cultural centrism is the fundamental methodological guarantee of cultural exchanges and integration.

China is indeed a "civilizational state". Chinese culture is a supranational and typical civilization of the world, which is advocating that mankind is a community with a shared future. The world civilization pursues peace and harmony and promotes to create an open, inclusive, mobile, flexible and developing world for human life. As President Xi Jinping mentioned in his speech at UNESCO headquarters. "All human civilizations have their respective strengths, and no one civilization can be judged superior to another. An attitude of equality and modesty is required if one wants to truly understand the various civilizations. Pride and prejudice are two biggest obstacles to exchanges and mutual learning among civilizations... If all civilizations can uphold inclusiveness, the so-called 'clash of civilizations' will be out of the question and the harmony of civilizations will become reality. " From the methodological point of view, cultural "centrism" and "monism" are the poisonous roots of the clash of civilizations which may lead to the hegemony and trample of one culture over another. In contrast, the concept of world civilization is essentially cultural pluralism as well as a theory of civilization and harmony. It pursues the harmonious integration of multiple cultures, religions and governance systems with flexibility and realizes the goals of "one world, different civilizations" "one civilization, different systems" "one system, different models" and "one country, different cultures". Only on this basis can we advance the equal, harmonious, and deep inter-civilization exchanges, and promote the overall progress of human culture.

Third, with peace, reciprocity and innovation human culture can be updated and advanced.

Peace and development go hand in hand. There will be no development without peace. Throughout the history, China adhered to the principles of "harmony is invaluable" and "all's well with the world", which enabled China to maintain friendly relations with neighboring countries and even distant countries for a long time. Without peace, there is no exchange or cooperation; it is impossible to seek benefits and development, let alone achieving mutual benefit, win-win situation, and common prosperity. In the new era, we should adhere to the principle of extensive consultation, joint contribution and shared benefits. All countries should make joint efforts to build a common, integrated, cooperative and sustainable concept on international security.

Certainly, there is no a absolutely perfect culture in the world, but only the original purpose of "pursuing ideal society by education". The civilization system has to reinvent and surpass itself continuously. The ways, institutions, and methods of civilization exchanges also need to be constantly explored. Only by keeping pace with the times can the culture remain prosperous. The 21st century is a time of rapid changes and those who does not move forward will go backwards. We should carry forward the excellent traditional culture and discard the dregs of subculture. With reform and innovation, we can ride the tide of development of civilization.

Of course, we believe that the excellent traditional culture concepts of China, such as View of World Civilization "we are the world" "The Doctrine of the Mean" "Harmony in diversity" "Courtesy demands reciprocity" "Righteousness is superior to benefit" "Equality and co-governance" "Taking the interests of the whole into account", etc., will play an active role in the exchanges between the Chinese and foreign civilizations in the new era.

The inter-civilization exchanges are one of the main trends in contemporary China. It is the experience of a civilization with 5000 years on how to develop civilization, and the practical action of the largest developing country. In view of this, the Chinese government initiated the construction of "Belt and Road", aiming to inherit the spirit of the Silk Road. Since the launch of the construction in 2013, positive progress has been made gradually. All countries have actively promoted policy coordination, connectivity of infrastructure and facilities, unimpeded trade, financial integration and people-to-people bonds, launched many practical cooperation projects that benefit the people, established a comprehensive and compound connectivity partnership, created a new prospect featuring extensive consultation, joint development and shared benefits, and gained many interests and praises from most countries in the world.

We should transcend the estrangement of civilizations with the exchange of civilizations, transcend the conflict of civilizations with the mutual learning of civilizations, and transcend the superiority of civilizations with the coexistence of civilizations. This is the result of Chinese wisdom and the practical experience of China's contribution to the idea of global governance. In the new era, China will continue to shoulder its responsibility as a major country uphold the concept of civilization as an integration, and play an active role as a builder. In the context of "The Belt and Road Initiatives", to promote Chinese culture across the world requires not only in-depth thinking at the macro level, but also reasonable operation, and sound design and arrangement at the practical level. We should rely more on the soft power of culture, create new ways of communication, tell stories about China well, and spread China's voice to present a true, multi-dimensional and panoramic image of China.

10. 5   Huaqiao University is Forging Ahead with Dreams of Connecting China and Foreign Countries

HQU is the only one named after "overseas Chinese" and has a unique mission. This is to spread Chinese culture to the outside world, promote exchanges and mutual learning among civilizations, and rally people's hearts and strength for the great rejuvenation of the Chinese nation and the construction of a community with a shared future for mankind.

For more than 62 years, by adhering to the policy of "tracing overseas, tracing Hong Kong, Macao and Taiwan" and the mission of "serving overseas Chinese and promoting Chinese culture and implementing the school principle "Integration of Chinese Wisdom and Foreign Expertise. Unification of Moral Character and Professional Excellence". Huaqiao University has cultivated over 200000 outstanding talents at home and abroad, of which about 60000 alumni are distributed outside Chinese mainland, mainly in the countries along the Maritime Silk Road and the regions of Hong Kong, Macao and Taiwan, playing important roles in promoting exchange and cooperation between China and foreign countries.

Huaqiao University has more than 30000 full-lime students. Including more than 5000 overseas Chinese students, students from Hong Kong, Macao, Taiwan and international students from more than 50 countries and regions. It is one of China's universities with largest number of overseas students. Students with different languages and cultural backgrounds gather in the fertile field of Huaqiao University. Cultural events such as the exotic cultural festivals, Songkran Festival, Water Lantern Festival and Gourmet Festival flourish on the campus. With the unique campus culture of "the Leading Culture Blended with Multi-Cultures. Seeking Harmony in Diversities", students from every country and region can feel the warmth of home here. As a result, the university has won the first prize of outstanding Culture achievements for two consecutive years in the National Campus Culture Construction of Colleges and Universities.

Huaqiao University has campuses in Quanzhou and Xiamen. Quanzhou is a famous historical and cultural city in China, the starting point of the ancient Maritime Silk

Road, and the strategic fulcrum and pioneer area of the 21st Century Maritime Silk Road. And Xiamen is one of the four Special Economic Zones that first implemented the policy of opening to the outside world. And the strategic fulcrum city of the 21st Century Maritime Silk Road.

By carrying forward the Maritime Silk Road spirit of "Inclusiveness interconnection and Sharing", the university actively promotes international exchanges and cooperation and has established collaborations with more than 200 universities from over 50 countries and regions in the world. As the university to recruit international students under Chinese Government Scholarship Program. Huaqiao University has set up 84 offices or admission agencies around the world, and the International School with English-medium curricula. As the Chinese Language and Culture Education Base of the Overseas Chinese Affairs Office of the State Council, and one of "the key universities to support neighboring countries' Chinese education" approved by the Ministry of Education, Huaqiao University has launched a series of brand-name projects Chinese language and culture education, such as "Chinese Language Class for Foreign Government Officials" and "Science and Technology Talents Training Program for Angolan Government". The annual "China-Thailand Strategic Seminar" co-sponsored by Huaqiao University, the National Research Academy of Thailand and the That-Chinese Cultural and Economic Association has become an important and eye-catching academic event for experts and scholars from both countries. Huaqiao University vigorously promotes Chinese education, cultivates teachers, compiles teaching materials, and carries out traditional Chinese culture experience for more than 570 Chinese schools in 55 countries around the world, so as to help the standardization, normalization and specialization of national Chinese education.

In the new era, it is Huaqiao University's mission and responsibility to serve the country's "Belt and Road" construction. As an important think-tank for overseas Chinese studies and the "Belt and Road" studies, the university has conducted overseas field researches in collaboration with overseas research institutions to provide advisory reports and intelligence support for national decision-making. In 2018, Huaqiao University ranked the 2nd in the Influence Rankings of Domestic University "Belt and Road" Think Tanks published by the National Development and Reform Commission.

When the Chinese Dream unfolds the future of China, standing at the new starting point, Huaqiao University remains true to its original aspiration and keep its mission in mind. By adhering to its developmental strategy of "Overseas Chinese University + Prestigious School", taking the "Double First-class" university construction as an opportunity, the university is unswervingly taking the road of connotative development, characteristic-based revitalization, and talent-centered self-improvement, and improve the overall quality of talent cultivation and educational level. By extensively uniting overseas Chinese and their strength and wisdom, Huaqiao University is speeding up to construct itself into a high-level university with distinctive characteristics and high prestige at home and abroad. Let's stride ahead with the brilliance and dreams of Huaqiao University.

The purpose of creating this course "Introduction to Chinese Culture" for overseas graduate students at Huaqiao University is consistent with Huaqiao University's school-running policy of "serving overseas Chinese and spreading Chinese culture" by facing overseas, facing Hong Kong, Macao and Taiwan. We have paid great attention to innovative teaching and practice models to constantly strengthen the enthusiasm and psychological recognition of Hong Kong, Macao, Taiwan, overseas Chinese and foreign students for learning Chinese excellent traditional culture. Around the theme of "Roots in China", we actively implement various cultural training activities such as "Chinese Culture Tour", culture study and practice for overseas Chinese, and overseas culture communication practice. Besides, we also pay great attention to the combination of "knowledge, emotion, intention and action", and have produced positive educational effects. We will continue to work hard to improve our work level and better serve the vast number of overseas students.

We only have one wish: May the young talents who come to HQU and China could learn about the ancient China, know the contemporary China, love Chinese culture and the Chinese people, as Mr. Wu Jianping, the President of HQU said to overseas students at the 2022 graduation ceremony of HQU:

We hope that students will be firm believers in Chinese culture, model practitioners of Chinese culture and positive developers of Chinese culture!... In the future, you will actively develop cultural exchanges and friendly cooperation between China and the rest of the world, so as to give light and warmth to your country's economic and social development and the construction of a community with a shared future for mankind.

That's all for the book. Thank you.

参考书目（Bibliography）

［1］梁漱溟.中国文化要义［M］.上海：学林出版社，1987.

［2］钱穆.中华文化十二讲［M］.北京：九州出版社，2012.

［3］张岱年，方克立.中国文化概论［M］.北京：北京师范大学出版社，2004.

［4］杨敏，王克奇，王恒展.中国传统文化通览（英汉版）.青岛：中国海洋大学出版社，2003.

［5］国务院侨务办公室，国家汉语国际推广领导小组办公室小中国文化常识［M］北京：高等教育出版社，2007.

［6］俞晓群.中国地域文化丛书（全24册）.大连：辽宁教育出版社，1998.

［7］白寿彝.中国通史纲要［M］.北京：外文出版社，2002

［8］［英］伯特兰·罗素.中国问题［M］.田瑞雪，译.北京：中国画报出版社，2019

［9］辜鸿铭.中国人的精神［M］.李晨曦，译.上海：上海三联书店，2010.

［10］张维为.文明型国家［M］.上海：上海人民出版社，2017

［11］［英］马丁·雅克.大国雄心［M］.张豫宁，张莉，刘曲，译.北京：中信出版社，2016.

［12］［德］马克斯·韦伯.儒教与道教［M］.洪天富，译.南京：江苏人民出版社，2008.

［13］李泽厚.中国思想史论（三卷）［M］.合肥：安徽文艺出版社，1999.

［14］徐万邦，祁庆富.中国少数民族通论［M］.北京：中央民族大学出版社，2018.

［15］费孝通.中华民族多元一体格局［M］.北京：中央民族大学出版社，2018.

［16］赵杰.中华民族共有精神家园论［M］.北京：人民出版社，2012.

［17］庄国土.华侨华人分布状况和发展趋势［M］.国务院侨务办公室政策法规司编，2011.

［18］林语堂.孔子的智慧［M］.长沙：湖南出版社，2016.

［19］陈东原.中国妇女生活史［M］.北京：商务印书馆，2015.

［20］王沪宁.中国村落家族文化［M］.上海：上海人民出版社，1991.

［21］冯尔康.中国宗族制度与谱牒编纂［M］.天津：天津古籍出版社，2001.

［22］江巧珍，孙承平.徽州盐商文化研究——以棠樾为例［M］.合肥：合肥工业大学出版社，2017.

［23］阮仪三.遗珠拾粹——中国古城古镇古村踏察［M］.上海：东方出版中心，2021.

［24］郑振满，张侃.培田［M］.北京：生活·读书·新知三联书店，2005.

［25］牟钟鉴，张践.中国宗教通史［M］.北京：中国社会科学出版社，2007.

［26］郭齐家.中国教育史［M］.北京：人民教育出版社，2015.

［27］陈谷嘉，邓洪波.中国书院制度研究［M］.杭州：浙江教育出版社，1997.

［28］张国刚.中西文化关系通史［M］.北京：北京大学出版社，2019.

［29］［英］彼得·弗兰科潘.丝绸之路［M］.邵旭东，孙芳，译.杭州：浙江大学出版社，2016.

［30］张星烺.中西交通史料汇编［M］.北京：华文出版社，2018.

［31］［英］理雅各英译，杨伯峻今译.四书［M］.长沙：湖南出版社，1992.

［32］许渊冲译.诗经［M］.长沙：湖南出版社，1992.